AF576726

Las Vegas

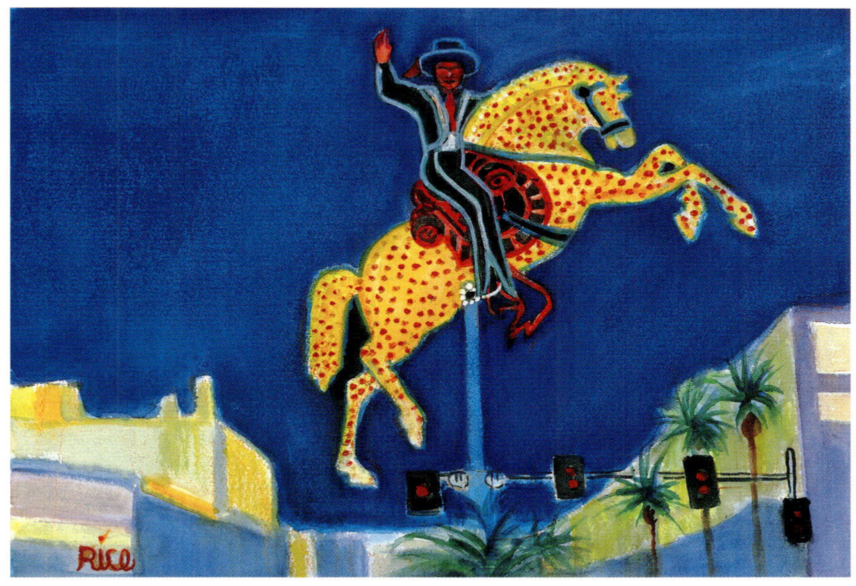

with Love

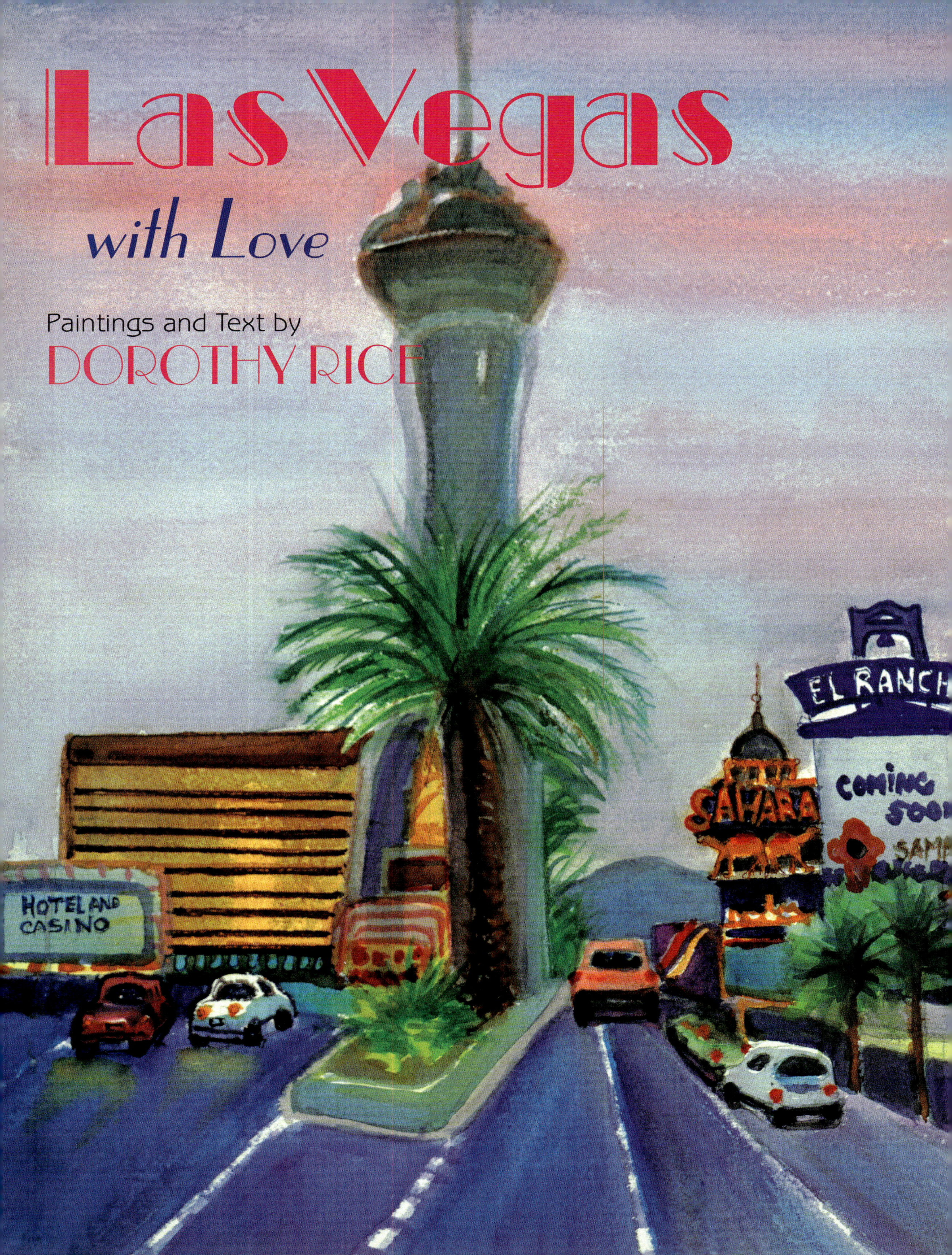
Las Vegas
with Love
Paintings and Text by
DOROTHY RICE
HOTEL AND
CASINO
SAHARA
EL RANCH
COMING

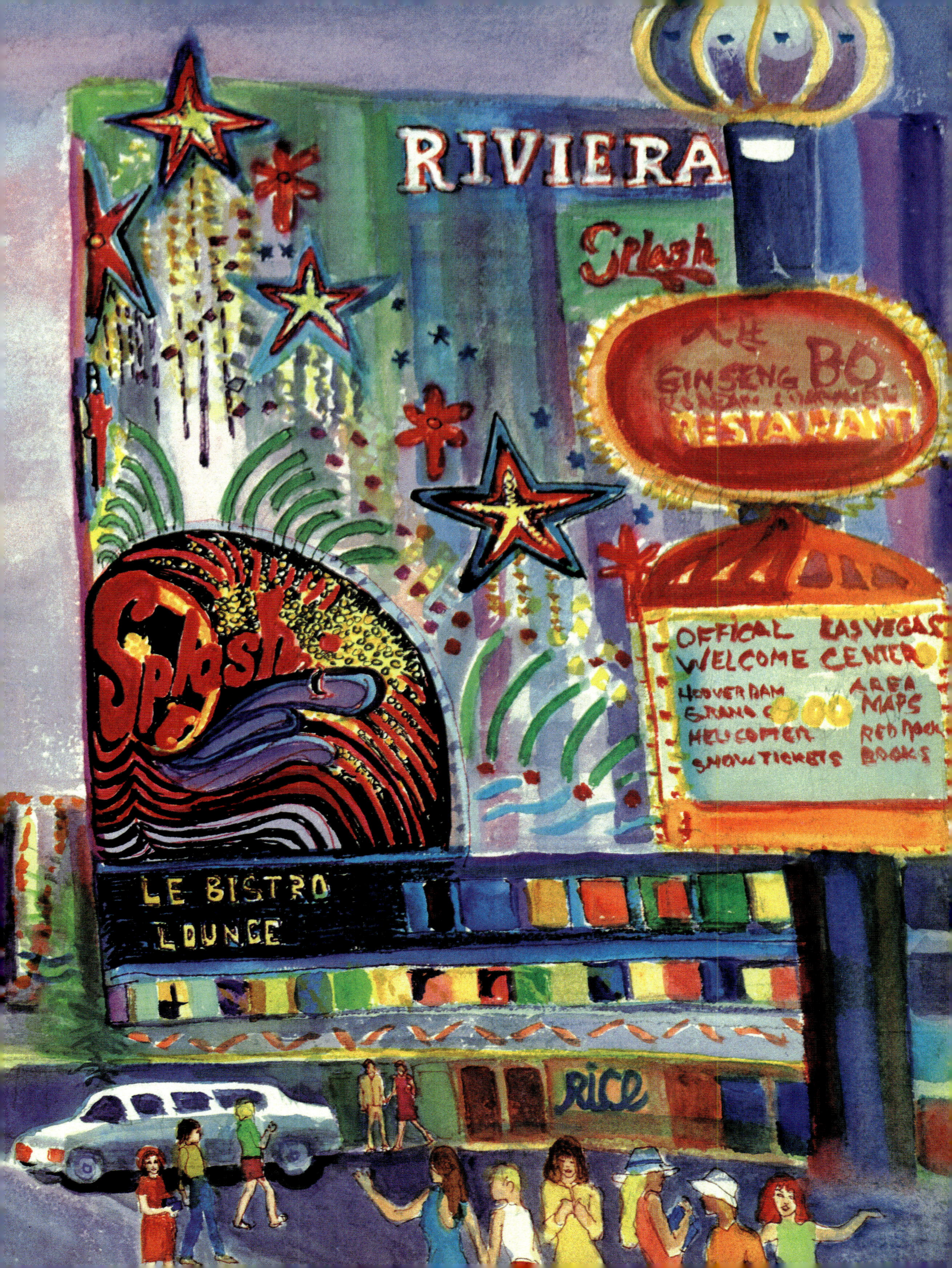
RIVIERA
Splash
GINSENG BO
RESTAURANT
Splash
OFFICAL LAS VEGAS
WELCOME CENTER
HOOVER DAM
AREA MAPS
RED ROCK
SHOW TICKETS
BOOKS
LE BISTRO
LOUNGE
Rice

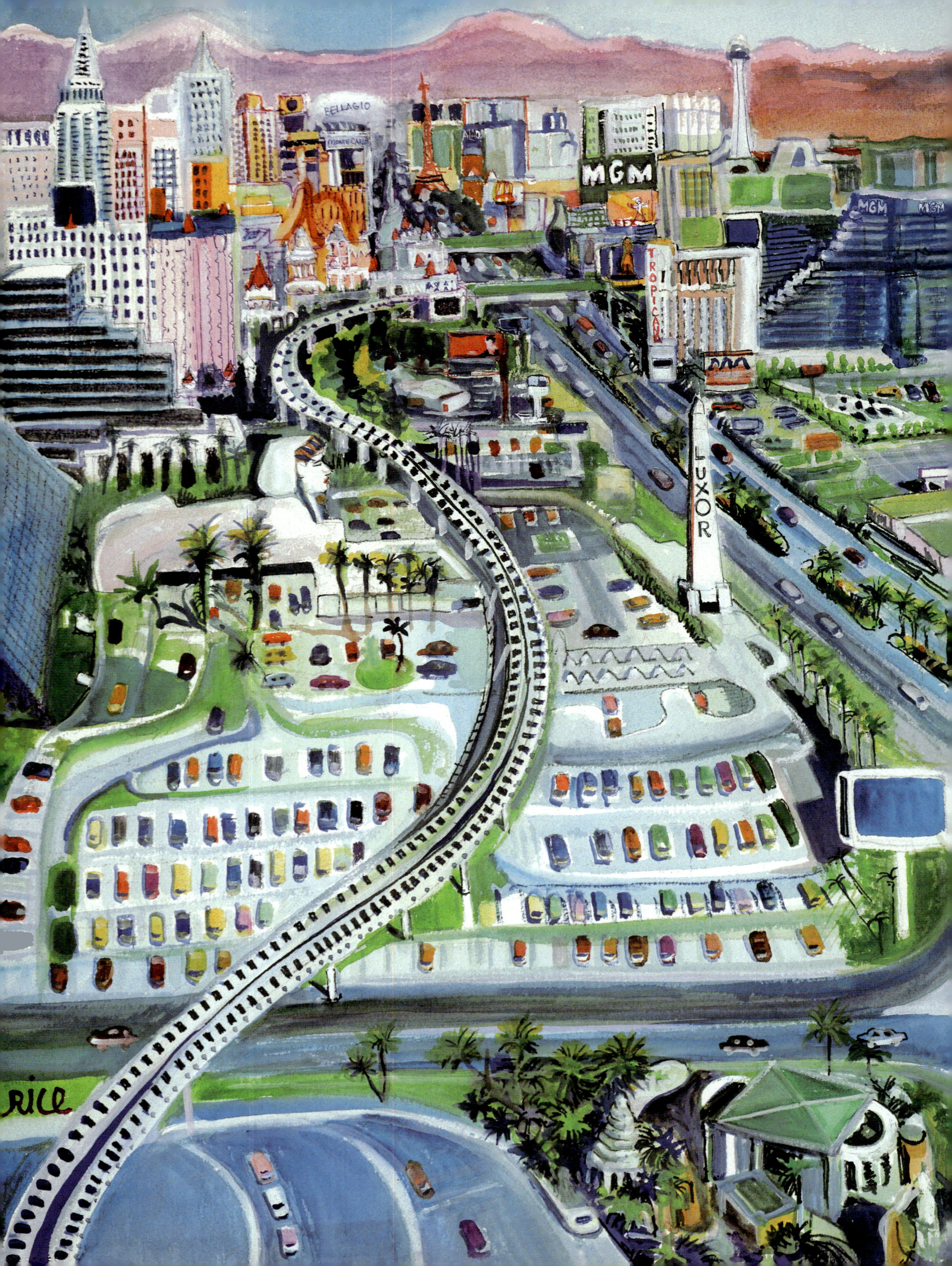
BELLAGIO
MGM
TROPICANA
MGM
MGM
LUXOR
RICE

CONTENTS

Timeline: The Sky's the Limit 6

Introduction: An Open Letter 9

The Strip 11

Off the Strip 91

- Chinatown 105
- UNLV 106
- Latino Las Vegas 108

Downtown 111

- The Westside 126

Tying the Knot 129

A Touch of Old Las Vegas 135

Las Vegas Lifestyles 143

- Green Valley 154
- Henderson 156
- Summerlin 160
- Red Rock 166
- Hoover Dam & Lake Mead 170
- Boulder City 176
- Lake Las Vegas 178
- Mount Charleston 179

Sports and Games 181

Acknowledgments 189

About Dorothy Rice 191

Page 1

THE NEON CABALLERO

Stretching across Las Vegas Boulevard, this flashy Latin horseman was originally part of the marquee for the Hacienda Hotel, which opened in 1956 and was demolished in 1997.

Pages 2–3

THE RIVIERA

The Riviera made a big splash when it opened in 1955, paying the famed pianist Liberace a then astronomical $50,000-per-week salary to headline there. Such financial flamboyance has caused the Riviera to close more than once, only to rise again like a phoenix from the ashes. Today its world-famous shows include the female impersonator extravaganza "An Evening at La Cage," the aquacade "Splash" and "Crazy Girls."

< **TOP OF THE MORNING**

How can you *not* be excited to be in Las Vegas when you wake up to this breathtaking view of the sprawling Strip, which I painted from my room on the 36th floor of the Four Seasons Hotel?

The Sky Is the Limit!

The History of Las Vegas

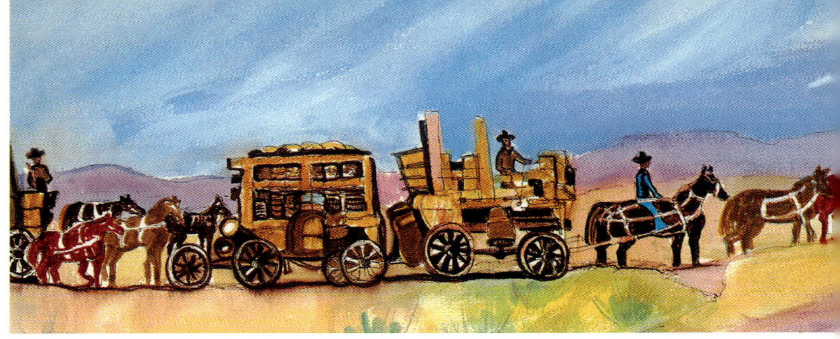

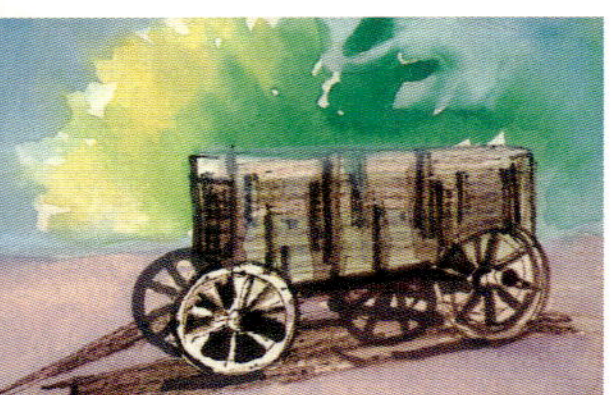

pre-1800s Native Americans from the Paiute tribe thrive off the land of the valley, the most livable area in the desert, thanks to its springs. In their leisure time they sometimes enjoy simple games of chance.

1829 Spanish scout Rafael Rivera is the first Caucasian to discover the desert oasis soon called Las Vegas ("The Meadows").

1844 An expedition led by John C. Fremont makes camp and maps the region before moving on with the difficult journey further West, losing many on the trek.

1850 A mail road is established, marking Las Vegas as the midway point between San Diego and Salt Lake City. Many Mormon missionaries follow this route—called "The Mormon Trail"—and settle in Las Vegas, hoping to convert the local Paiutes.

1855 The Mormons establish a missionary outpost, but abandon it after three years of hardship and struggle.

1862 The U.S. Army establishes Las Vegas' Fort Baker, a nearly non-existent military outpost designed to confuse enemy troops during the Civil War.

1864 Nevada becomes the 36th U.S. state.

1865 Octavius D. Gass establishes the Las Vegas Ranch, the region's most enduring early settlement.

1902 The Oregon Short Line and San Pedro-Los Angles & Salt Lake Railroad bring railways into Las Vegas, purchasing land owned by Helen Stewart, whose late husband had foreclosed on O.D. Gass' Las Vegas Ranch.

1905 The town of Las Vegas is established after an auction of 40 blocks of land owned by the San Pedro-Los Angeles & Salt Lake Railroad. One year later, on a plot of land that sold for $1,750, the Hotel Nevada—later the Sal Sagev and now the Golden Gate—opens on Fremont Street, the first such establishment in town.

1906 Las Vegas Age, the city's first newspaper and a precursor to the Review-Journal, begins publishing.

1909 Gambling is made illegal in Las Vegas, with Prohibition and crackdowns on brothels soon to follow; Las Vegas residents and visitors alike generally ignore such attempts to eliminate these "social evils."

1911 Las Vegas becomes an incorporated city, with about 1,500 residents. The Las Vegas Chamber of Commerce is founded.

1920 Thomas Young establishes the sign company that would become YESCO, provider of almost every major neon sign in Las Vegas; pilot Bob Hausler lands the first airplane in Las Vegas at Anderson Field.

1926 Western Air Express begins passenger flights to and from Las Vegas.

1930 Las Vegas' population exceeds 5,000.

1931 Gambling is permanently legalized in Las Vegas. The Northern Club casino is granted the first gambling license. The Meadows Club opens. Construction begins on Boulder Dam at the nearby Colorado River, bringing an influx of workers—including many African-American laborers—to the area.

1934 The Boulder Club opens, the first gambling den with neon signs, prompting the city's nickname "Glitter Gulch." Downtown emerges as the city's hub of activity.

1935 Boulder Dam—later renamed Hoover Dam—is completed, bringing a tremendous amount of electrical power to the region. Five thousand Shriners from Southern California attend the first convention held in Las Vegas.

1941 El Rancho Vegas opens as the city's first highway resort hotel and the first major establishment on The Strip. The half-block El Cortez Hotel opens. The Las Vegas Army Air Field, later Nellis Air Force Base, is established. The opening of Basic Magnesium, Inc.'s, magnesium plant in neighboring Henderson and the advent of World War II combine to draw the military and throngs of new settlers into Las Vegas, bringing the population to over 8,500. Sam Boyd opens his first bingo parlor. "Las Vegas Nights," the first major motion picture set in the city, premieres, featuring an appearance by the Tommy Dorsey Orchestra and a boy singer named Frank Sinatra.

1944 The Will Mastin Trio, featuring Sammy Davis, Jr., makes its Las Vegas debut at the Last Fontier, as does pianist Liberace.

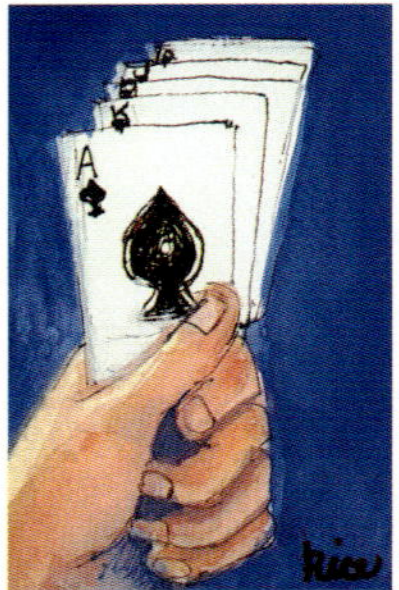

1945 Gangster Benjamin "Bugsy" Siegel makes a car trip to Vegas from Los Angeles to check on minor mob interests and envisions an elegant gambling palace in the desert; he muscles in on the Flamingo, the brainchild of Hollywood Reporter founder and publisher, Billy Wilkerson.

1946 The Strip comes into its own when Bugsy Siegel opens the Flamingo Hotel and Casino on New Year's Eve, bringing chic glamour, top-name entertainers and a luxury resort atmosphere to town. Downtown, the Golden Nugget opens; mob interest in the city booms.

1947 Bugsy Siegel is assassinated gangland-style in Beverly Hills for skimming from the Flamingo's funds; his murder is never officially solved. Three local newspapers merge to form the Las Vegas Review-Journal.

1948 Clark County purchases Alamo Airport, renaming it McCarran Field after Nevada Senator Pat McCarran, whose legislation greatly influenced the development of commercial aviation in the U.S.

1949 Dean Martin and Jerry Lewis make their Las Vegas debut at the Flamingo. Benny Binion hosts the first high-stakes poker marathon, pitting Nick "The Greek" Dandolos against Johnny Moss.

1950 The Desert Inn opens, funded and controlled by racketeer Moe Dalitz, who becomes the most effective and influential mob boss in town. Hank Greenspun, who had worked as a publicist for the Flamingo and founded KLAS-TV (Channel 8), launches the scrappy Las Vegas Sun, a crusading daily newspaper.

1951 Frank Sinatra makes his Las Vegas debut at the Desert Inn. "Vegas Vic" is installed above the Pioneer Club. Atomic testing begins 70 miles northwest of town. Benny Binion—the colorful, controversial character who raises the stakes of Las Vegas gambling to high art—opens Binion's Horseshoe.

1952 "The Las Vegas Story," a mob melodrama starring Jane Russell and Victor Mature, plays in theaters.

1953 The Sands debuts with its massive, splashy neon sign, sparking a huge neon rivalry. The Sahara pioneers themes borrowed from other countries.

1954 The mismatched husband-and-wife team Louis Prima and Keely Smith open their wild-and-wooly routine with Sam Butera & the Witnesses in the Sahara's Casbah Lounge, defining the Vegas lounge act.

1955 Liberace headlines at the opening of The Riviera. The Dunes opens. The Golden Gate begins the tradition of buffet food at bargain prices. The population reaches 40,000. The Moulin Rouge opens on the Westside, the only venue where black entertainers and patrons could play and stay; the hippest place in town, it mysteriously closes six months later. The Gaming Board is established to regulate and control gambling operations.

1956 Elvis Presley makes a disastrous Las Vegas debut at the Frontier; his contract is torn up. The Hacienda debuts. The 15-story Fremont opens as the tallest hotel in the city, featuring teenage headliner Wayne Newton.

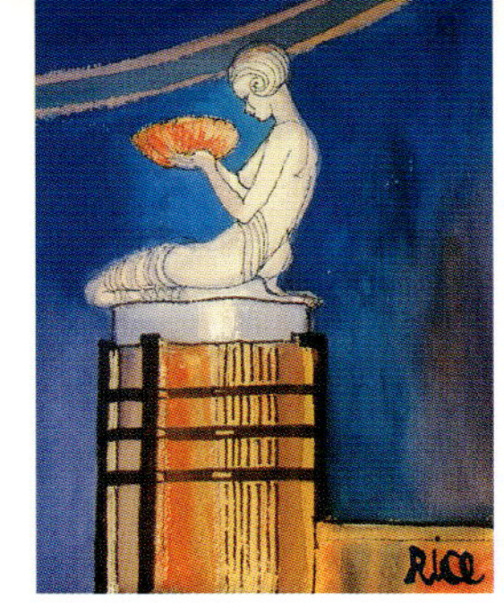

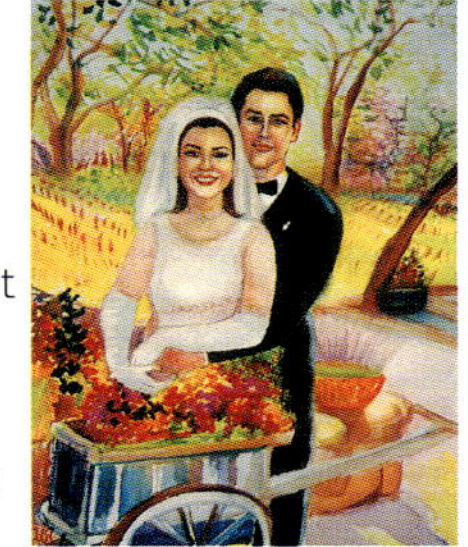

1957 The Tropicana opens, soon becoming the most profitable hotel and casino in town. Nevada Southern University—later the University of Nevada, Las Vegas (UNLV)—is established.

1958 The Stardust Resort & Casino—the largest hotel of the era, with the biggest neon sign in the world—opens, the dream of the notorious Tony Cornero, who died three years earlier while shooting craps at the Desert Inn.

1959 The Las Vegas Convention Center opens. San Souci debuts. Some 30,000 weddings (and 10,000 divorces) are performed annually.

1960 "Ocean's Eleven"—starring Frank Sinatra, Dean Martin, Sammy Davis, Jr., Joey Bishop, Peter Lawford and pals—films while the Rat Pack performs at the Sands. Welterweights Benny Parcet and Don Jordan compete in Las Vegas' first championship boxing match. Over 60,000 people call Las Vegas home.

1962 Kirk Kerkorian buys 80 acres of Strip property at a low price, one of the most profitable land speculation deals in the city's history, making him a fortune which allows him to later purchase MGM Studios.

1964 Elvis Presley and Ann-Margret star in "Viva Las Vegas," directed by George Sidney.

1966 Caesars Palace arrives, foregoing neon and setting the standard for promoting a unique theme to the *nth* degree. The Aladdin and the Four Queens open. Howard Hughes moves to Las Vegas, buys seven hotels and begins to clean up the city's image. Underworld interests in the city begin to wane as big corporations take over. Frank Sinatra and Mia Farrow marry at the Sands.

1967 Siegfried & Roy make their first magical performance in Las Vegas at the Tropicana. Steve Wynn moves to town. Elvis Presley and Priscilla Beaulieu marry at the Aladdin. The Las Vegas Country Club opens.

1968 Circus Circus opens, bringing family-style entertainment to Sin City.

1969 Elvis Presley, now sporting capes and rhinestone jumpsuits, makes a triumphant return to Las Vegas at the International Hotel.

1970 Howard Hughes mysteriously leaves Las Vegas for the last time; he dies five years later. The Las Vegas Hilton opens. Johnny Moss wins the World Series of Poker at Binion's Horseshoe.

1971 The Hilton Corporation takes over the Flamingo. State legislators ban prostitution in Las Vegas and Clark County. "Fear and Loathing in Las Vegas", a psychedelic account of journalist Dr. Hunter S. Thompson's road trip to Sin City, is published.

1973 The original MGM Grand opens and oddsmaking becomes big business. Jerry Tarkanian becomes the head basketball coach at UNLV.

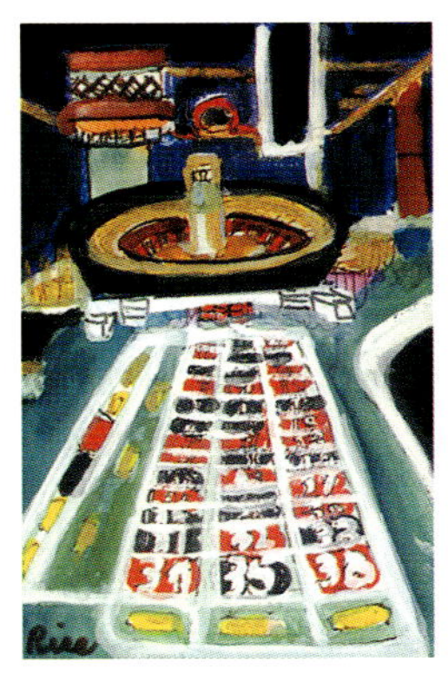

1977 The Golden Nugget becomes a hotel. The East Coast crime syndicate pulls out of Las Vegas. Elvis Presley dies; thousands of Elvis impersonators live on in his image. County gambling revenues top $1 billion.

1978 The popular TV series "Vega$," starring Robert Urich as private eye Dan Tana, premieres. Louis Prima dies.

1979 Barbary Coast, Sam's Town, the Imperial Palace and the Liberace Museum debut.

1986 Bally's takes over the MGM Grand. Gold Coast opens with its popular slot club. Moe Dalitz is forced out of the casino business for good by the Gaming Commission.

1987 Liberace dies.

1989 The Mirage opens, pioneering the free show on the Strip with its regularly erupting volcano. "Rain Man," starring Dustin Hoffman and Tom Cruise and filmed in Las Vegas, wins the Best Picture Oscar. Moe Dalitz dies. Hank Greenspun dies.

1990 The Excalibur ushers in the era of the mega-theme resort. Siegfried & Roy begin performing at the Mirage. The UNLV Runnin' Rebels win their first NCAA basketball championship under coach Jerry Tarkanian. Sammy Davis, Jr., dies.

1992 The arrival of the Forum Shops at Caesars Palace signals a new era of luxury in Las Vegas. "Bugsy," starring Warren Beatty as Bugsy Siegel and Annette Bening as Virginia Hill, is released and later nominated for 12 Oscars. After a long dispute with the NCAA over alleged improprieties in its basketball program, coach Jerry Tarkanian leaves UNLV.

1993 Treasure Island, the Boardwalk Holiday Inn and the Luxor hotels open, continuing theme-mania; and the new MGM Grand becomes a premiere sporting venue. Debbie Reynolds opens her own hotel-casino. McCarran International Airport becomes the eighth busiest airport in the U.S. and the 14th busiest worldwide. Sheryl Crowe releases her hit song "Leaving Las Vegas."

1995 The dazzling Fremont Street Experience debuts. The Hard Rock Hotel and Casino opens, providing a major venue for cutting-edge rock acts. Martin Scorcese's film "Casino," starring Robert De Niro and Sharon Stone, premieres, as does Paul Verhoeven's "Showgirls." Clark County's population exceeds 1 million. Dean Martin dies.

1996 The Stratosphere, the tallest structure in the city at 1,149 feet, opens, as does the Monte Carlo. Nicolas Cage—who previously starred in "Honeymoon in Vegas" and returned to town again for "Con Air"—wins an Oscar for his role opposite Elizabeth Shue in the film "Leaving Las Vegas."

1997 New York-New York brings the Manhattan skyline to the desert.

1998 Steve Wynn's Mirage Resorts opens the Bellagio, launching the new era of massive, opulent, super-luxurious resorts. Coach John Robinson joins UNLV's football program. Benny Binion's son Ted dies of a heroin overdose, later revealed to be a murder engineered by his girlfriend and her lover. Frank Sinatra dies and Las Vegas mourns by dimming lights on the Strip.

1999 The Venetian, Paris Las Vegas and Mandalay Bay open, bringing even more deluxe accommodations and theme attractions to the Strip. At the MGM Grand, Barbra Streisand performs her last live show in Las Vegas on New Year's Eve.

2000 Kirk Kerkorian's MGM Grand buys Steve Wynn's Mirage Resorts in a multibillion dollar deal. The Desert Inn closes after Wynn buys it with big plans for the new incarnation. The Aladdin reopens. "CSI," a realistic TV detective series set in Las Vegas, debuts on CBS.

2001 A remake of "Ocean's Eleven"—another all-star production starring George Clooney, Julia Roberts, Brad Pitt and Mark Wahlberg—films in Las Vegas.

Today Las Vegas boasts more hotel rooms than any other city (more than 100,000), has nine of the largest hotels in the world, draws more than 35 million visitors each year, is home to 1.4 million residents, brings in almost $15 billion annually and delivers endless action and excitement twenty four hours a day, seven days a week, 365 days a year.

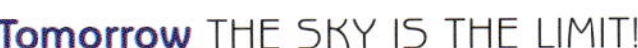

Tomorrow THE SKY IS THE LIMIT!

THE POOL AT THE FLAMINGO HOTEL

Nowhere is the image of the bright pink namesake of the Flamingo more prominent than at its luxurious pool. The flamingo became a good luck talisman for Ben Siegel and boyhood pal Myer Lansky in the 1930s while visiting Florida's Hialeah Race Track, where the indigenous birds flew overhead during a lucky streak. Later he nicknamed his girlfriend Virginia Hill—who had reddish hair, strutted on long legs and turned pink when she drank (which was often)—"Flamingo." Either for luck or to impress his girl, Bugsy used the name once more in 1944 when he, Lansky and their mob cronies bought into the planned Monte Carlo-style luxury hotel on the Strip—thus the legend of the Flamingo took flight.

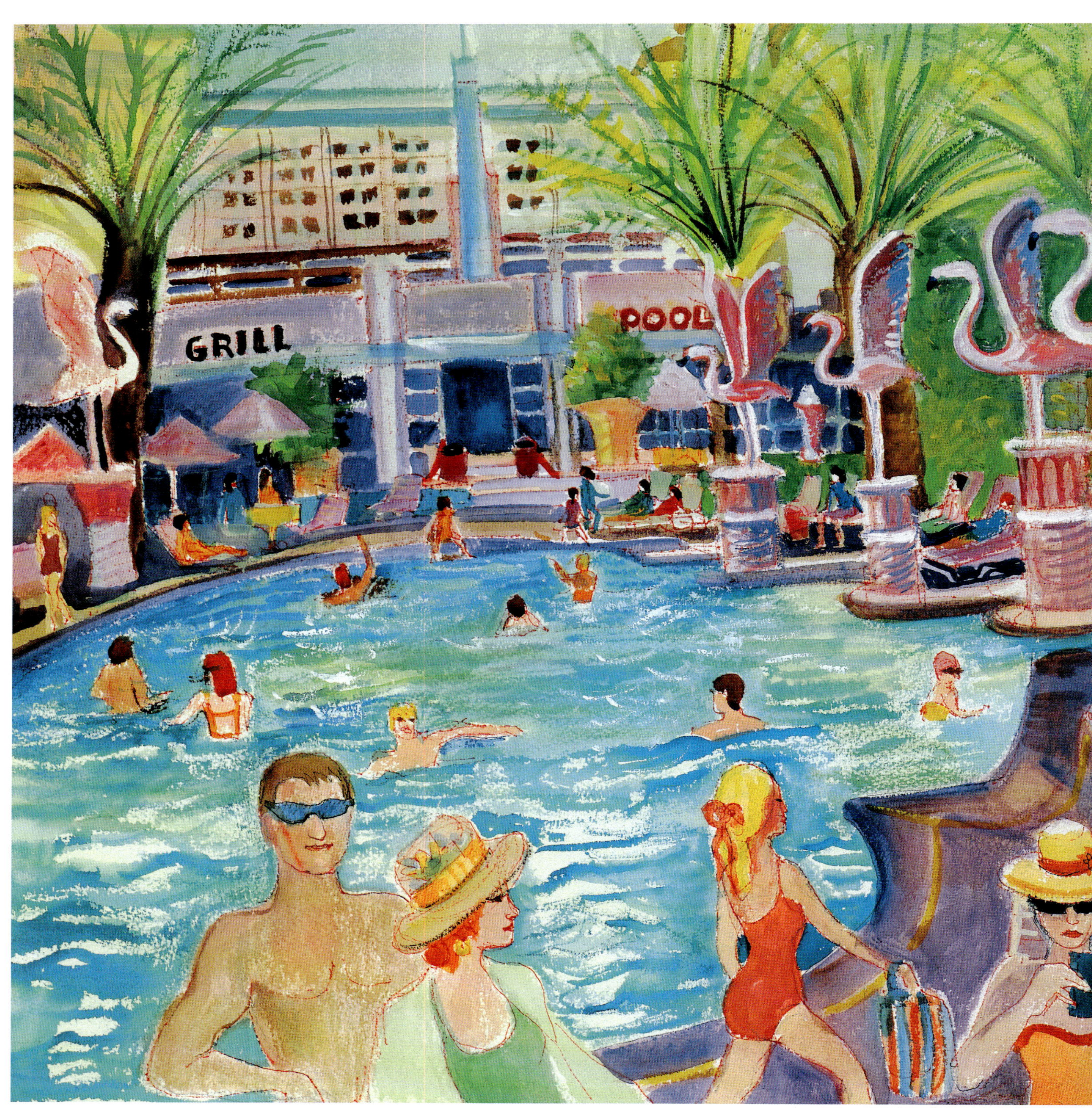

An Open Letter to Benjamin Siegel
(1906-1947)

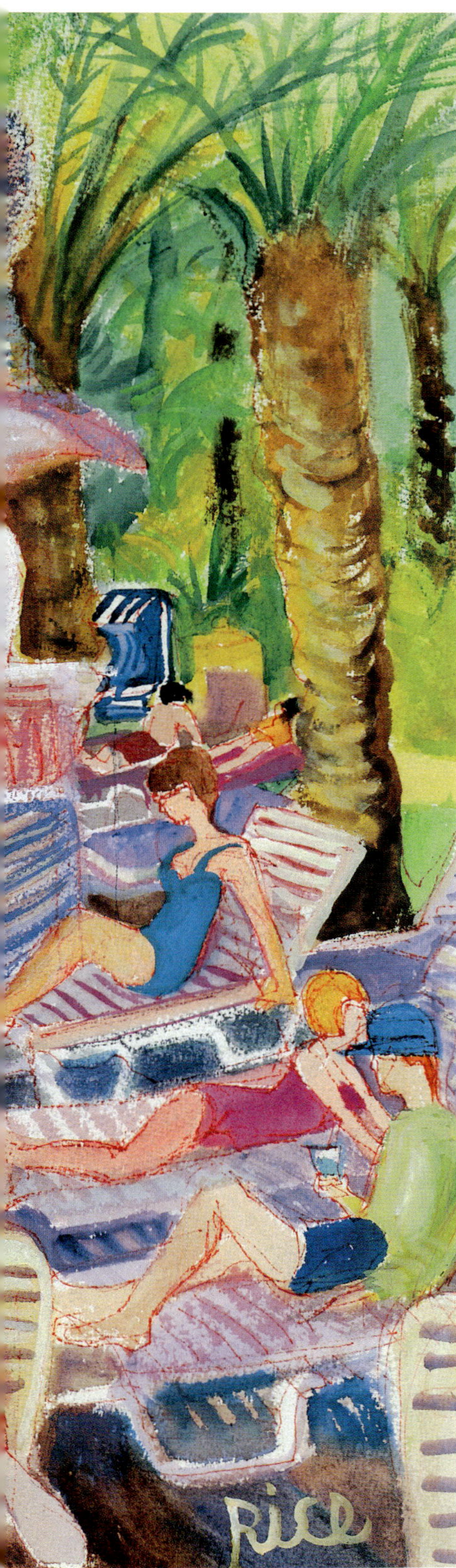

DEAR MR. SIEGEL,
(I wouldn't dare call you "Bugsy"—I heard how it upset you.)

Remember that fateful day in 1945 when you first drove from Los Angeles into the dry, dusty little desert town called Las Vegas, Nevada, to scout out opportunities for the Mob's gambling operations? How different it must have been back then. The streets were quiet. Just a few rustic poker parlors and ramshackle gas stations—nothing more than a railroad stop on the way to more interesting places.

But you saw a dream in the desert. An oasis where people could come to spice up their lives at the blackjack table, roulette wheel or whatever other diversion Nevada law would allow. You made the transition from gangland enforcer to "gentleman sportsman." Rubbing elbows with the Hollywood elite, you ran with that dream and made it a reality.

Rain poured on Christmas Day, 1946, when you opened your beloved hotel and casino The Flamingo, but did you care? You brought the top names in entertainment like Jimmy Durante and Xavier Cugat to perform and you set a new standard for promotion and publicity. You made black tie and evening gowns the name of the game. You knew early on that Las Vegas was about taking risks and having faith.

STANLEY CHASE

Dorothy Rice posing with Bugsy Siegel's image at Madame Tussaud's Museum.

Your dream in the desert was just the beginning. Las Vegas is now the most successful entertainment playground in the world, a place for everyone to enjoy. Glamour, glitz, fun, fabulous attractions and A-list entertainment. Could you have envisioned today's Las Vegas? Aladdin, Bally's, Barbary Coast, Bellagio, Caesars Palace, Circus Circus, Excalibur, Hard Rock, Harrah's, Hilton, Imperial Palace, Luxor, Mandalay Bay, MGM Grand, the Mirage, New York-New York, Orleans, Paris, Rio, Riviera, Sam's Town, Stardust, Stratosphere, Treasure Island, Tropicana, Venetian and even your beloved Flamingo has risen again. All miracles of creativity and excitement for more than 35 million visitors annually from all over the world. All followers in your footsteps.

Have you seen what else has come to town? The resorts and the sports venues and the spas and the chic boutiques and the amazing restaurants? And best of all, the growing communities full of families and new homes, schools and playgrounds for children, museums and universities as people continue to put down roots. In fact, more than 1.4 million people now call Las Vegas home.

Weren't you clever to follow your dream? You deserve credit for your early vision, which has inspired others to make Las Vegas into the "Dream Capital" of the world. Wish you were here to enjoy the fun!

Sincerely,

Dorothy Rice

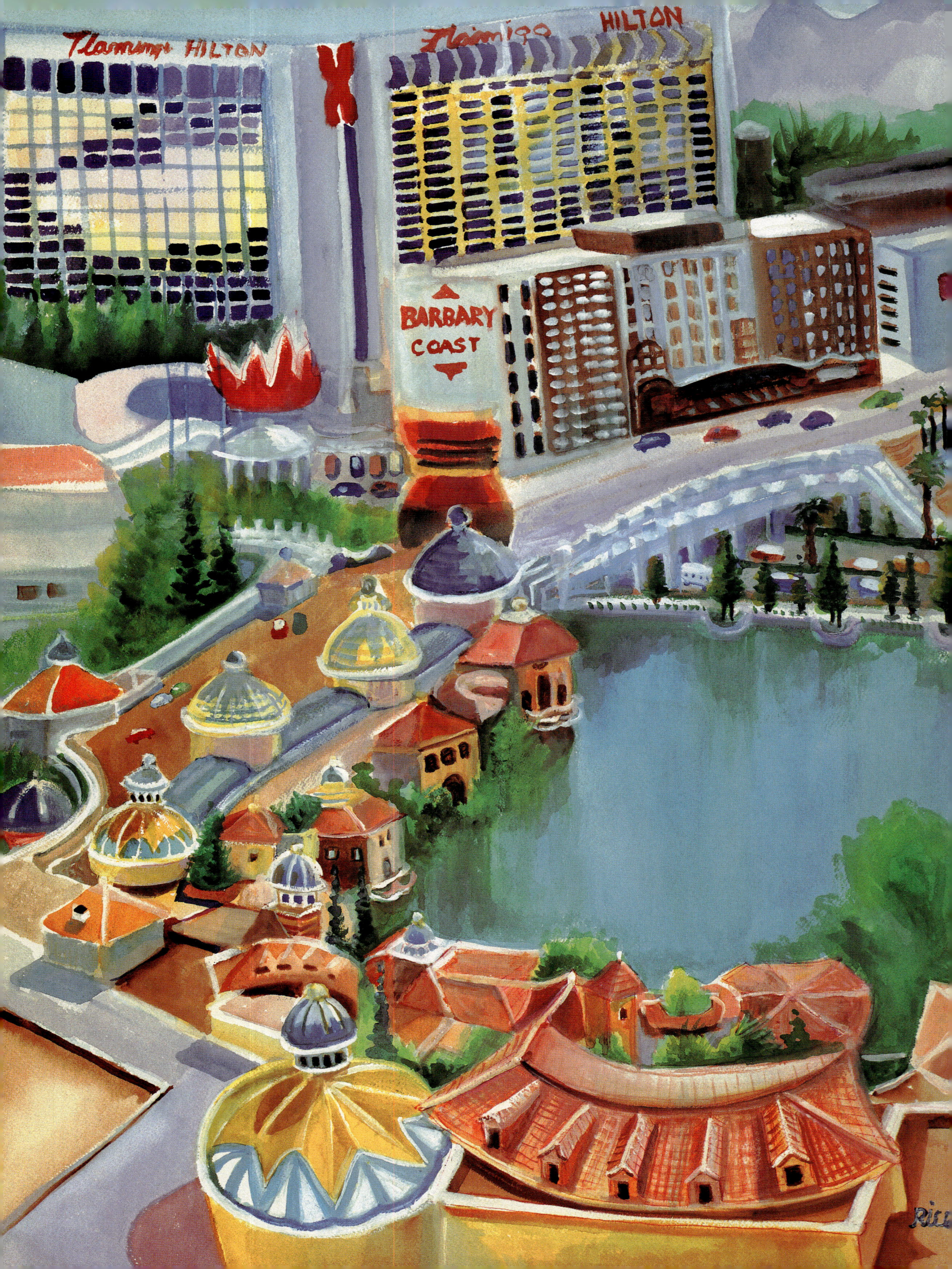
HILTON
HILTON
BARBARY
COAST

THE STRIP

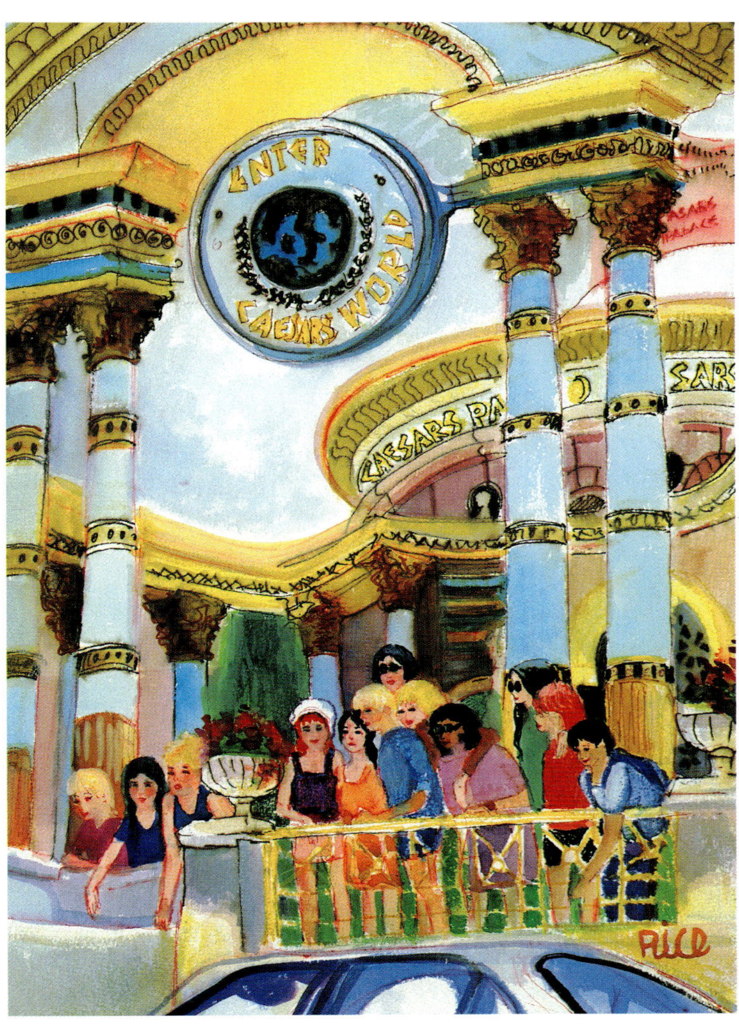

HAIL UNTO CAESARS

Caesars Palace has reclaimed much of the glory of its historical namesake by establishing itself as one of the premiere destinations on the Las Vegas Strip. Debuting in 1966, Caesars has expanded at a dramatic rate that rivals the Roman Empire's. Its famous features include the Centurion, Roman and Olympic Towers, Cleo's Barge, the Ah'so restaurant, the Forum Shops, and a super-deluxe, high-tech race & sports book. By the way, the name features an apostrophe-less, plural Caesars, not the possessive Caesar's—founder Jay Sarno believed the Palace belonged to its guests, so each one would feel like an Emperor.

< THE VIEW OF THE STRIP FROM MY ROOM AT THE BELLAGIO

COULD ANYONE HAVE EVER FORESEEN the amazing evolution of the Las Vegas Strip from a dusty stretch of desert road into one of the most celebrated thoroughfares on the face of the earth? The Strip had humble beginnings as home to a ragtag assembly of gas stations, poker joints and dude ranches like El Rancho Vegas. World War II brought an infusion of G.I.s and defense workers, re-invigorating the town. When America's crime syndicate realized the amount of money that could be made in a state with legalized gambling, they grabbed a stake in casinos all over Las Vegas, but it was gangster Bugsy Siegel who ran with Hollywood Reporter founder Billy Wilkerson's concept to marry Vegas-style gaming with Monte Carlo-style elegance. He brought flashy showmanship to town via the Flamingo Hotel and Casino, which opened in 1946. The Flamingo's grand, "top-this" style would catch on and set the Strip tradition which still endures.

Neon became the norm in the 1950s and 1960s, which introduced the Sands, the Sahara, the Stardust, the Desert Inn, the Dunes, Caesars Palace, the Golden Nugget and dozens more to Las Vegas, and the Strip became the place to catch Frank Sinatra, Dean Martin, Sammy Davis , Jr., and all of the A-list nightclub entertainers of the day. The 1970s, when Elvis Presley reigned as King, saw the arrival of even grander (and gaudier) pleasure palaces. By the 1980s and 1990s, many of the venerable hotels and casinos were replaced by sprawling, corporate-owned mega-complexes built around outlandish themes, amazing attractions and outsized luxury, luring such top-name entertainers as Barbra Streisand, Jay Leno, Cher, the Rolling Stones, and enduring mainstays like Wayne Newton, Tom Jones and Englebert Humperdinck.

Today the glittering, gleaming Strip is a crazy-quilt of towering icons from practically every era in history, temporarily populated by a throng of tourists making pilgrimage from every corner of the globe. Truly, the former cowtown has become a cosmopolitan metropolis like no other.

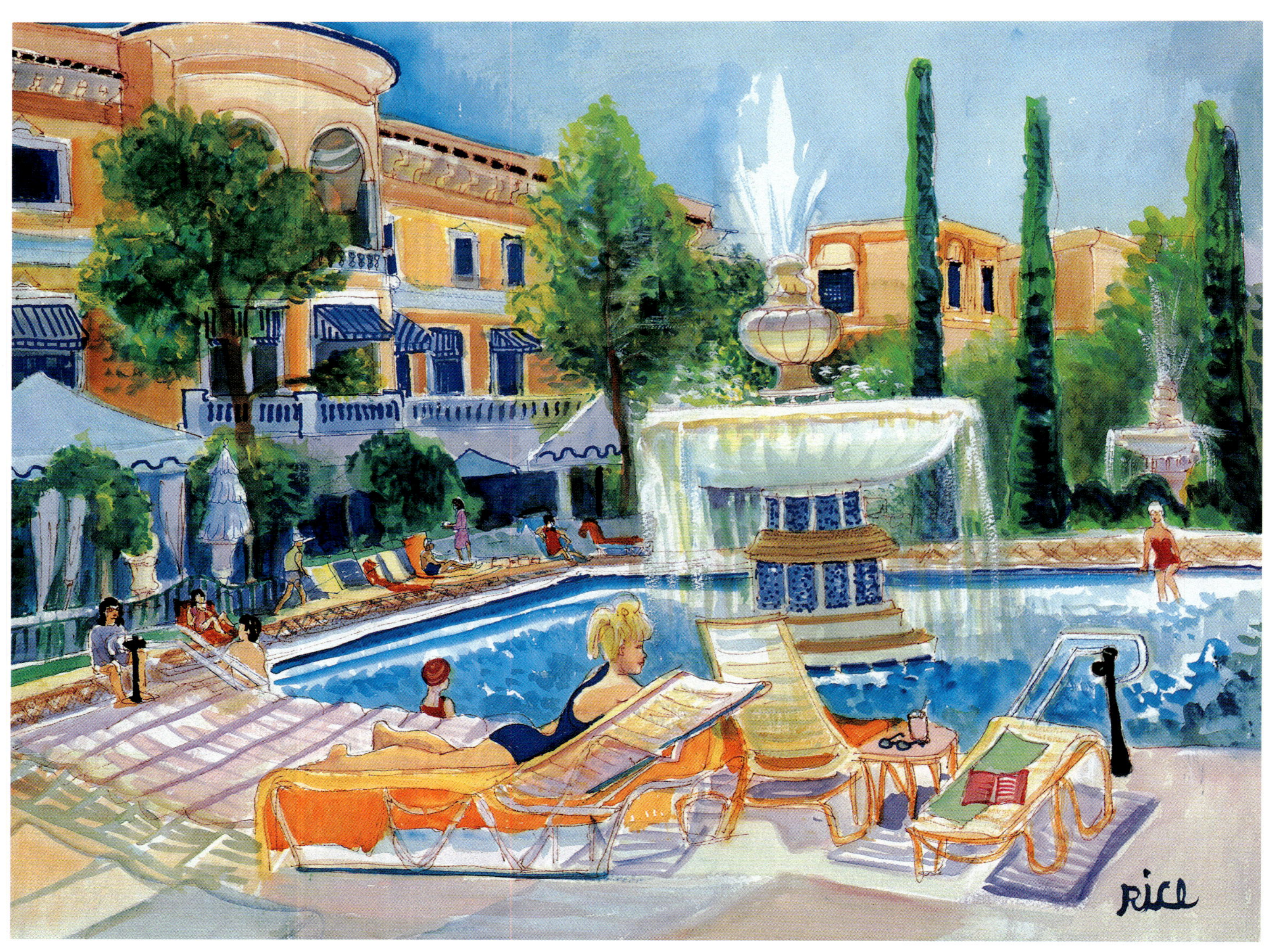

RELAXING AT THE BELLAGIO POOL

Two seemingly disparate themes become apparent when you spend time at the Bellagio. With its dancing fountains, fantastic lake and hydro-themed shows, water is abundant. Art is equally ever-present, with the Bellagio's elaborate Italianate architecture and the amazing masterpieces loaned by world class museums on rotating display in the Gallery of Fine Art.

THE CONSERVATORY AT THE BELLAGIO HOTEL >

Countless exotic orchids, lilies, hyacinths and other flowers and plants populate the Bellagio's lush gardens, surrounding statues made of flowers. The hotel changes and refreshes the floral displays with each change of season. Bring your camera—it's a wonderful photo op.

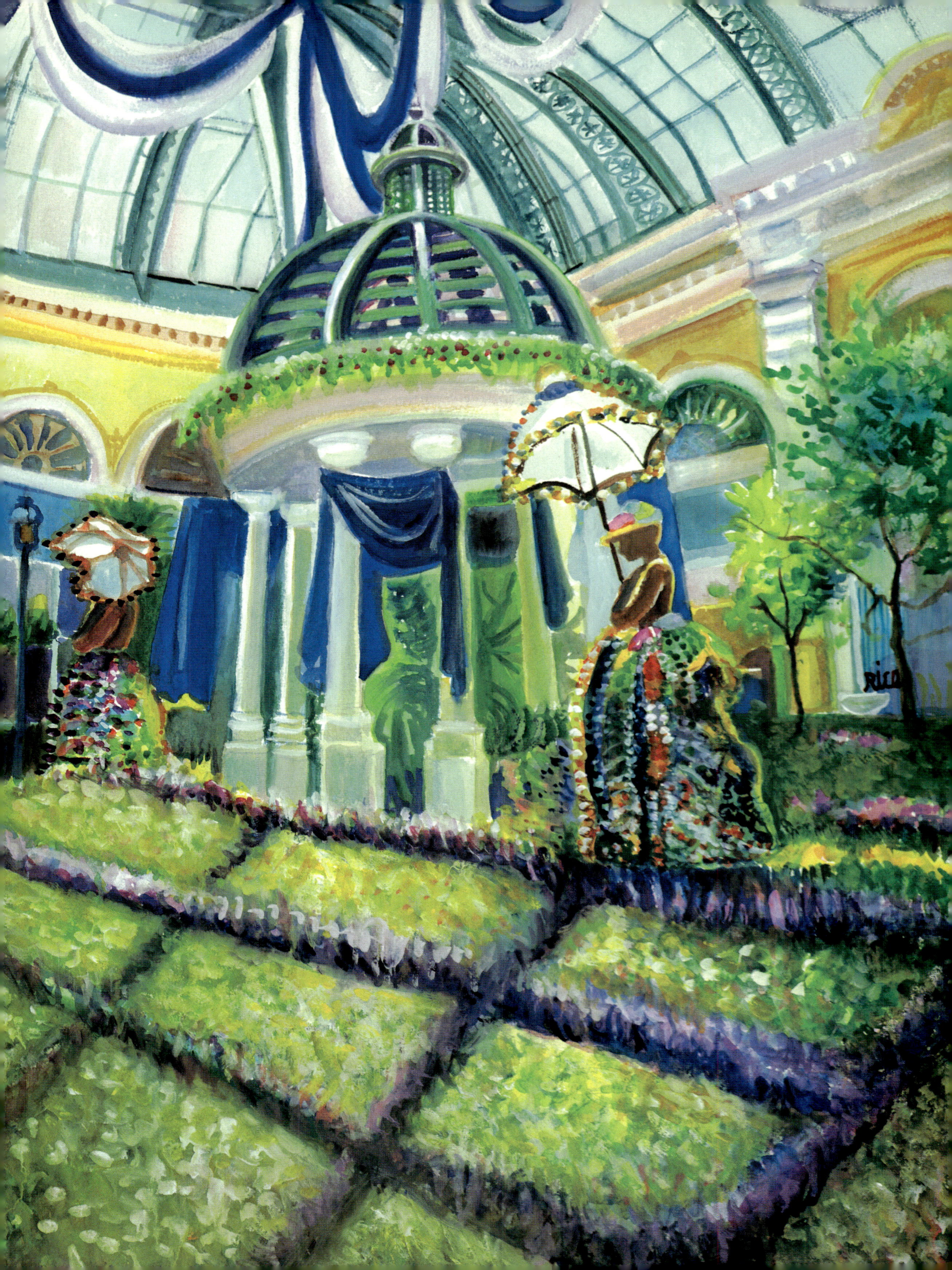
Rico

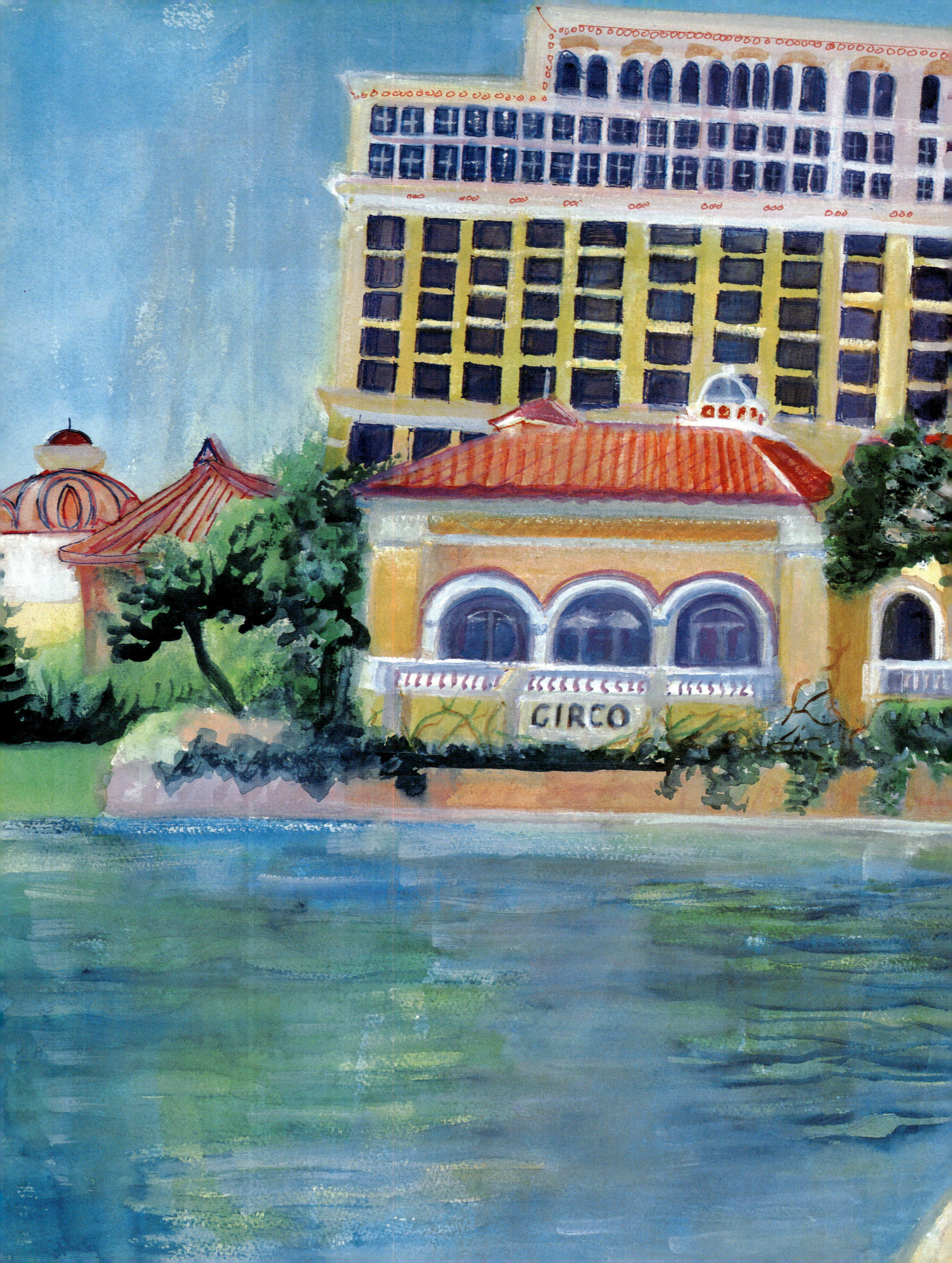
CIRCO

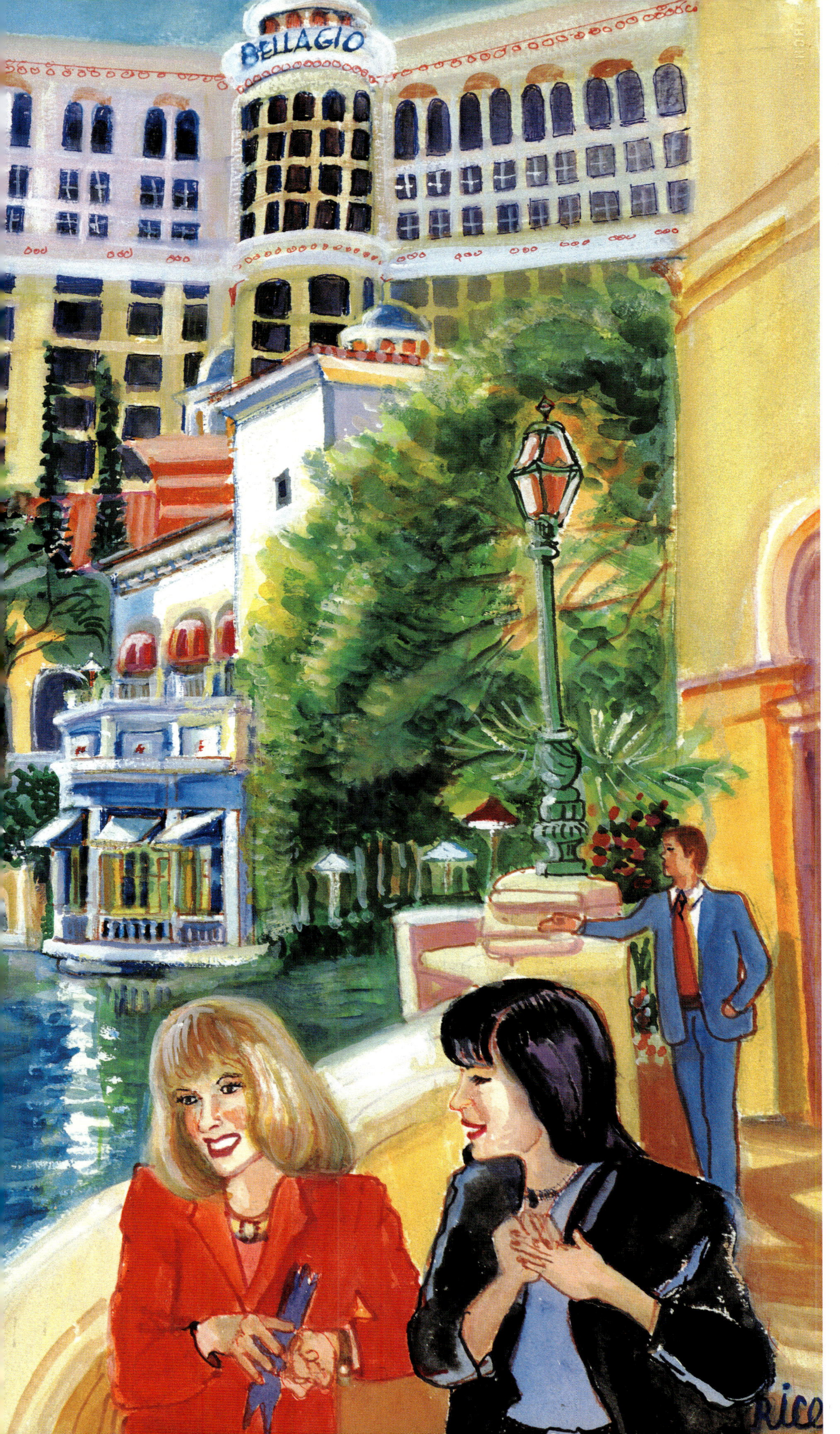

AWAITING THE SPLASHY SPECTACULAR

Joan Stevens and Kara Lee Fox enjoy the view from the balcony of the Picasso Restaurant as they await the Bellagio Hotel's amazing water show, which can also be enjoyed from the Strip. Mark Fuller of WET Design has created an imaginative form of art and entertainment in which fanciful jets and sprays of H_2O from more than a thousand fountains magically dance to a variety of music—from whimsical to grand, classic to pop, Sinatra to Bocelli—as colorful lights reflect off the aquatic streams, some of which soar 240 feet into the air.

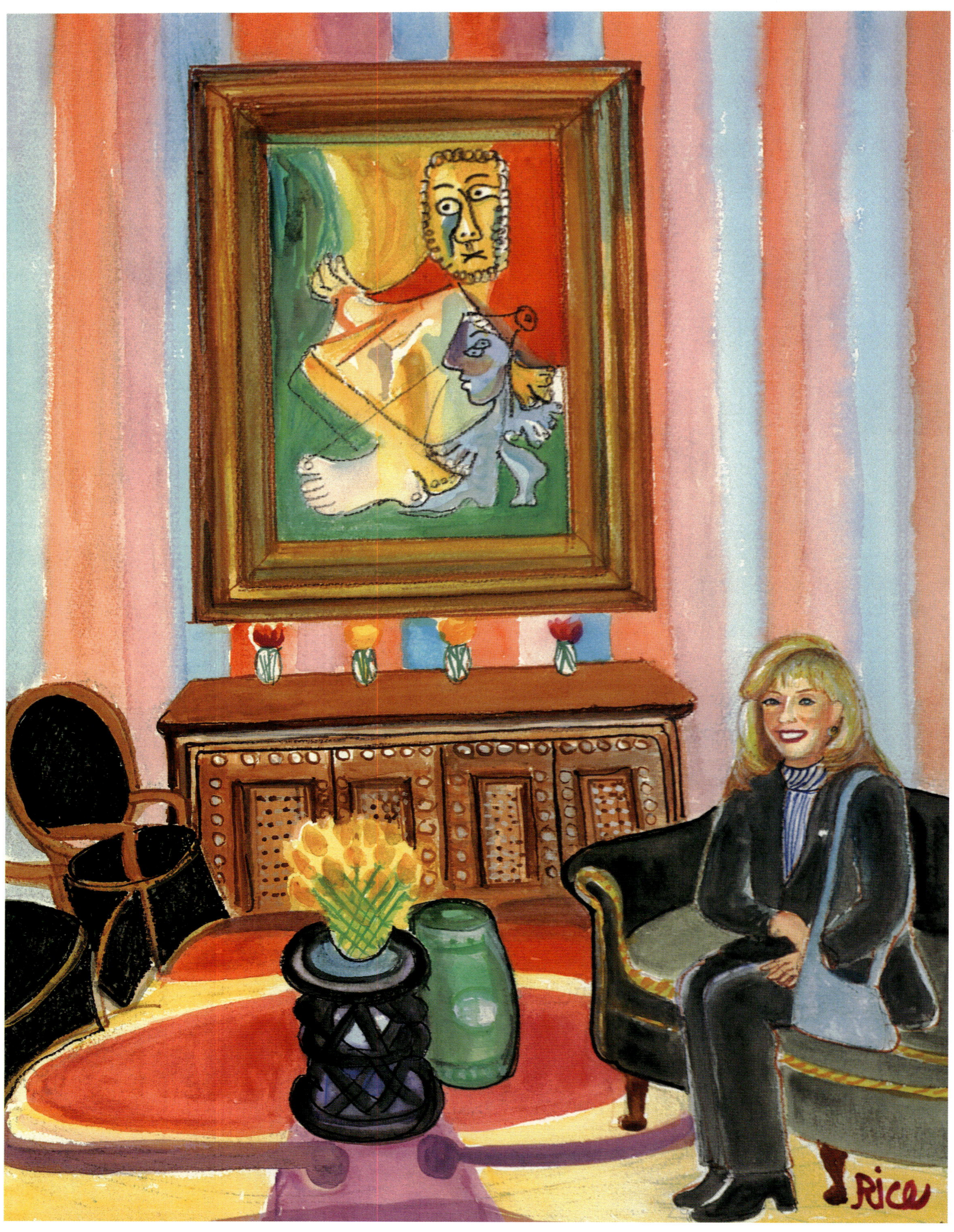
Rice

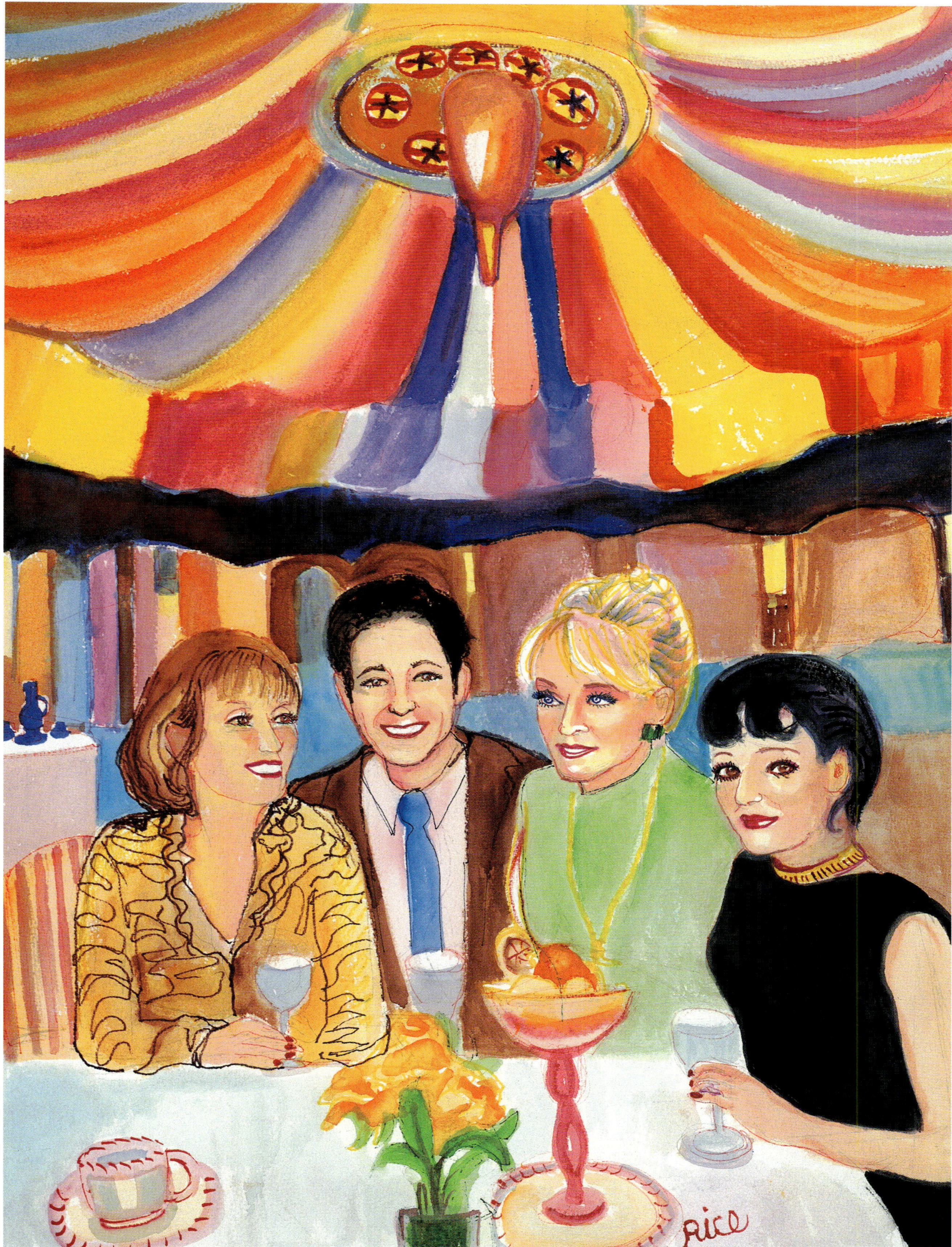

< PICASSO RESTAURANT

Jan McClain anticipates a great dinner in one of the finest restaurants in Las Vegas, Picasso at the Bellagio Hotel. Adorned with original paintings and ceramic works by Pablo Picasso, the master of Cubism, the interior is color-coordinated to best display his paintings. The excellent service, grand style and gourmet cuisine of chef Julian Serrano are perfect—a terrific convergence of fine food and fine art. Picasso—the artist—was known to frequently exchange a sketch for a meal. Just imagine how many dinners one of those sketches could buy today!

LOOKING CHIC AT LE CIRQUE

How could I resist a party thrown by my good friend, Broadway and television actress Paula Stewart (the elegant blonde on the right), at the Bellagio's Le Cirque? Paula was fêting her son, entrepreneur Michael Carter, and we were joined by Gigi Forest and entertainer Irina Maleeva. The Las Vegas Le Cirque is, of course, a desert spin-off of the famed New York restaurant. As a native Gothamite, I've dined there many times and painted it for my book "Manhattan With Love". Now I've done them both.

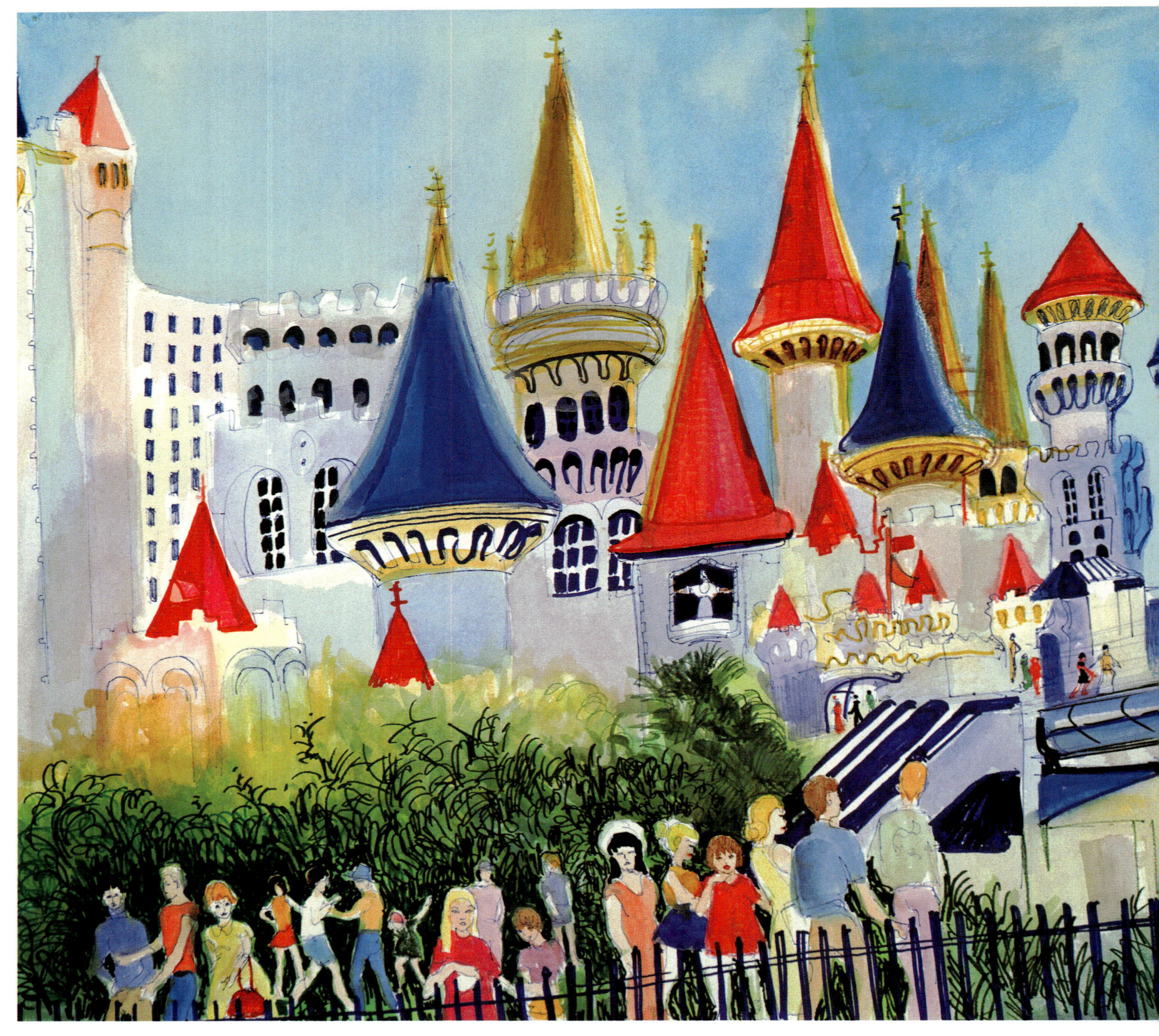

ARRIVING AT THE EXCALIBUR

Rising from the south end of the Strip as if out of the mists of Avalon are the candy-colored castle spires of the Excalibur Hotel and Casino. One of the largest establishments in town and the first of the mega-theme resorts, the Excalibur plays up a medieval ambiance with attractions like the Renaissance Village (featuring, at 1,450 seats, the largest buffet in town) and entertainment including minstrels, acrobats, jugglers, magicians, fire-eaters and the Magic Motion Machine, where Merlin the Magician battles a fire-breathing dragon.

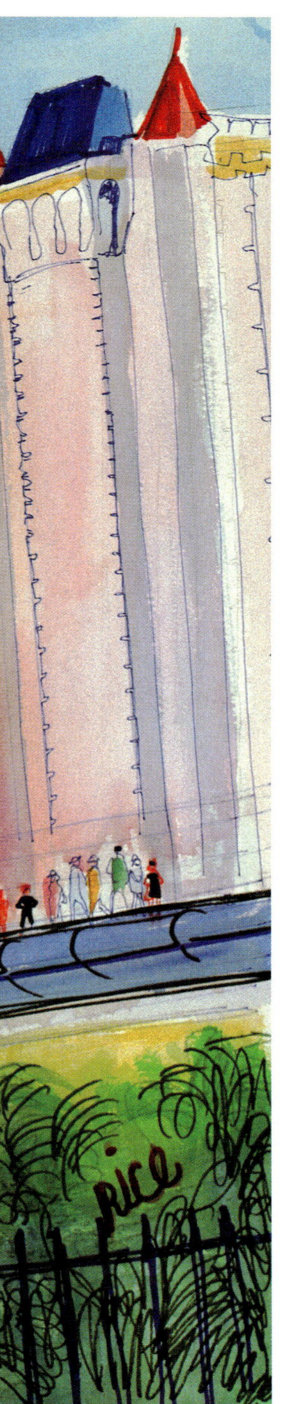

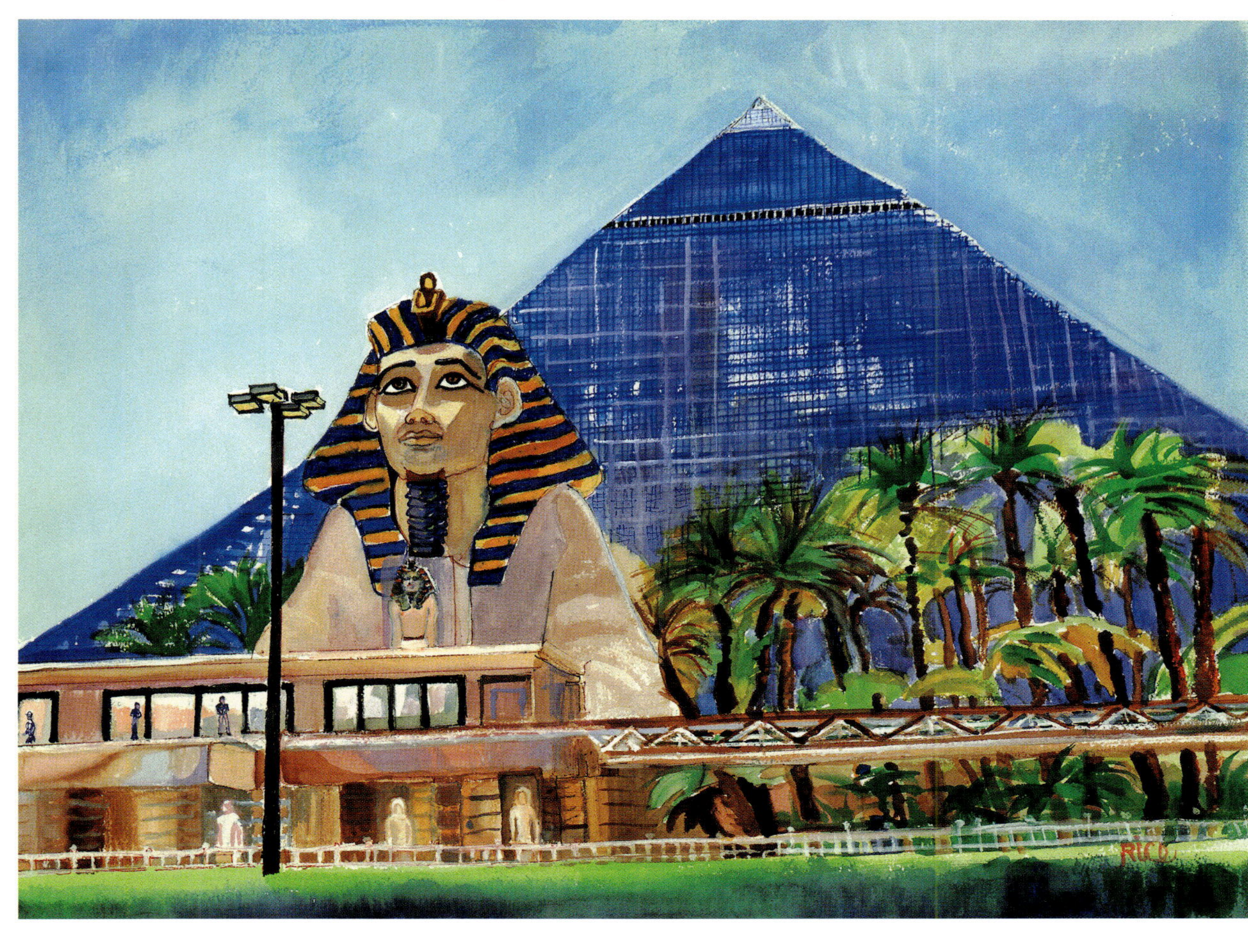

THE SPHINX AT THE LUXOR

As impassive and cryptic as his Egyptian counterpart, this colossal Sphinx stands watch outside the sleek black pyramid of the Luxor, transplanting the majesty of the pharaohs to the Nevada desert. Built during the early 1990s boom, the Luxor features a 29-million-square-foot atrium (the largest in the world), elevators (called "inclinators") that rise at a 39-degree angle, and 13 acres of exterior glass in the form of 39,000 windows. The Attraction Level features an IMAX theater and a people mover to whisk you from faux-Gaza to faux-Camelot at the Excalibur. But the literal pinnacle is the spotlight at the pyramid's apex: at 40 billion candlepower, it's the brightest in the world and can even be seen from space—a new high in Vegas' ever-increasing competition to attract new customers with bigger, brighter lights.

EGYPTIAN MAJESTY AT THE LUXOR

The Luxor is filled with grand Egyptian motifs and is a great mix of the everyday and the extraordinary, such as the scene here in which people plot out their next Las Vegas experience, dwarfed by an immense statue in classic Egyptian style.

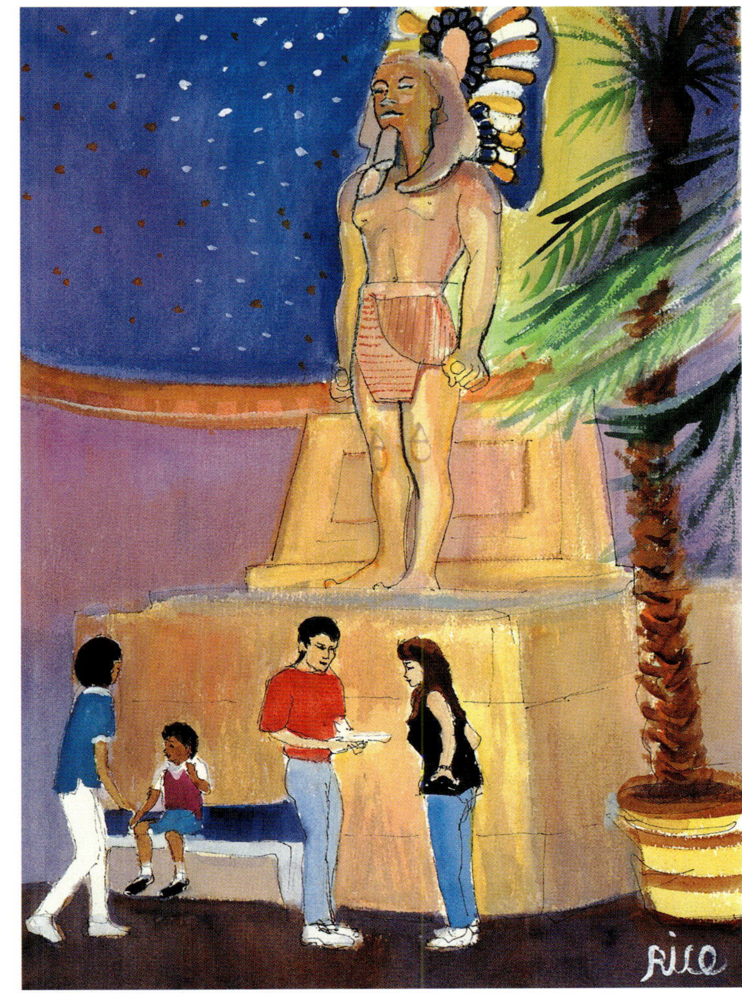

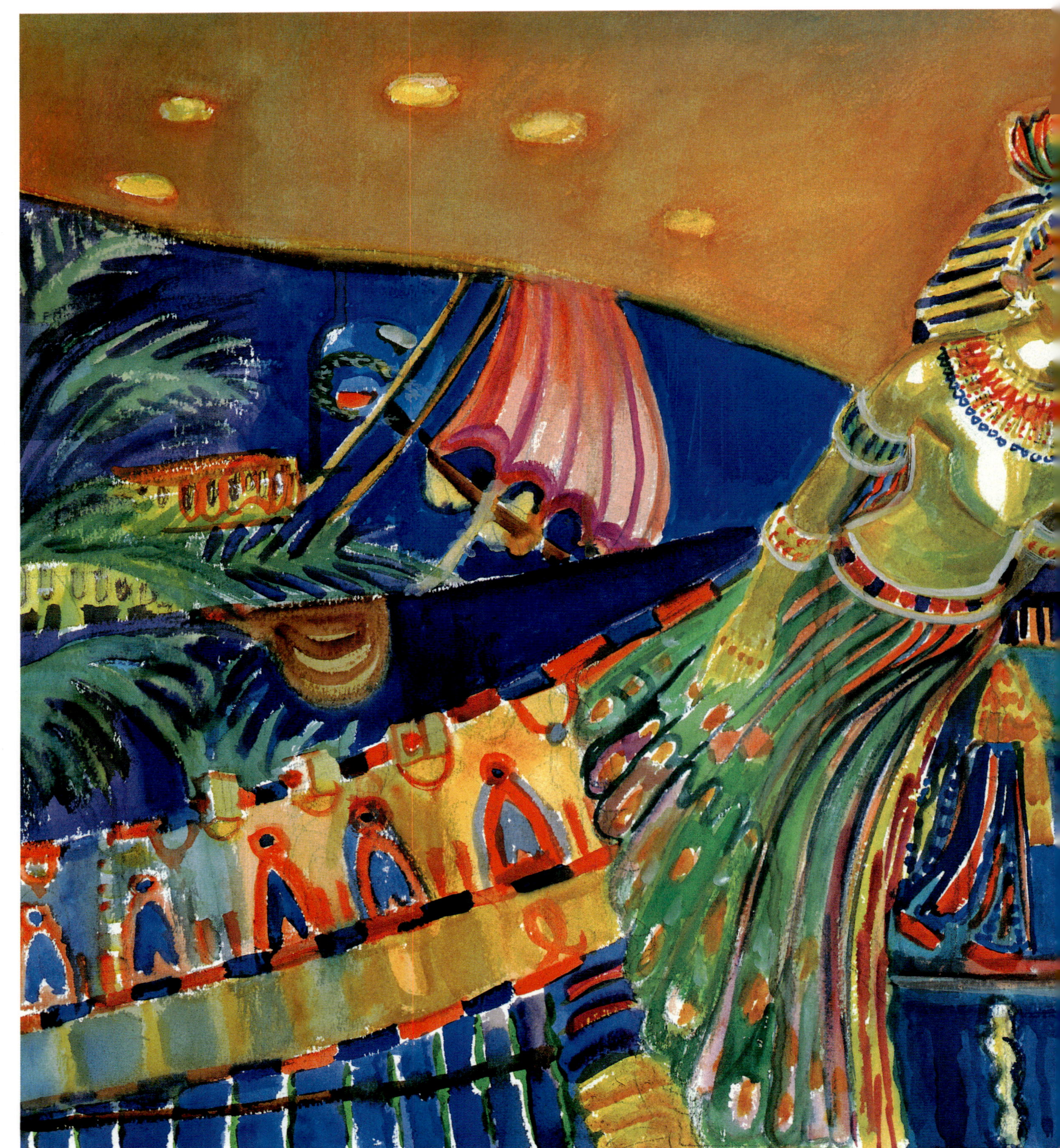

CLEOPATRA'S BARGE

Climb aboard this replica of an Egyptian barge with an ancient version of a hood ornament. I think the golden girl looks a little like Liz Taylor, the most famous big-screen Queen of the Nile, don't you?

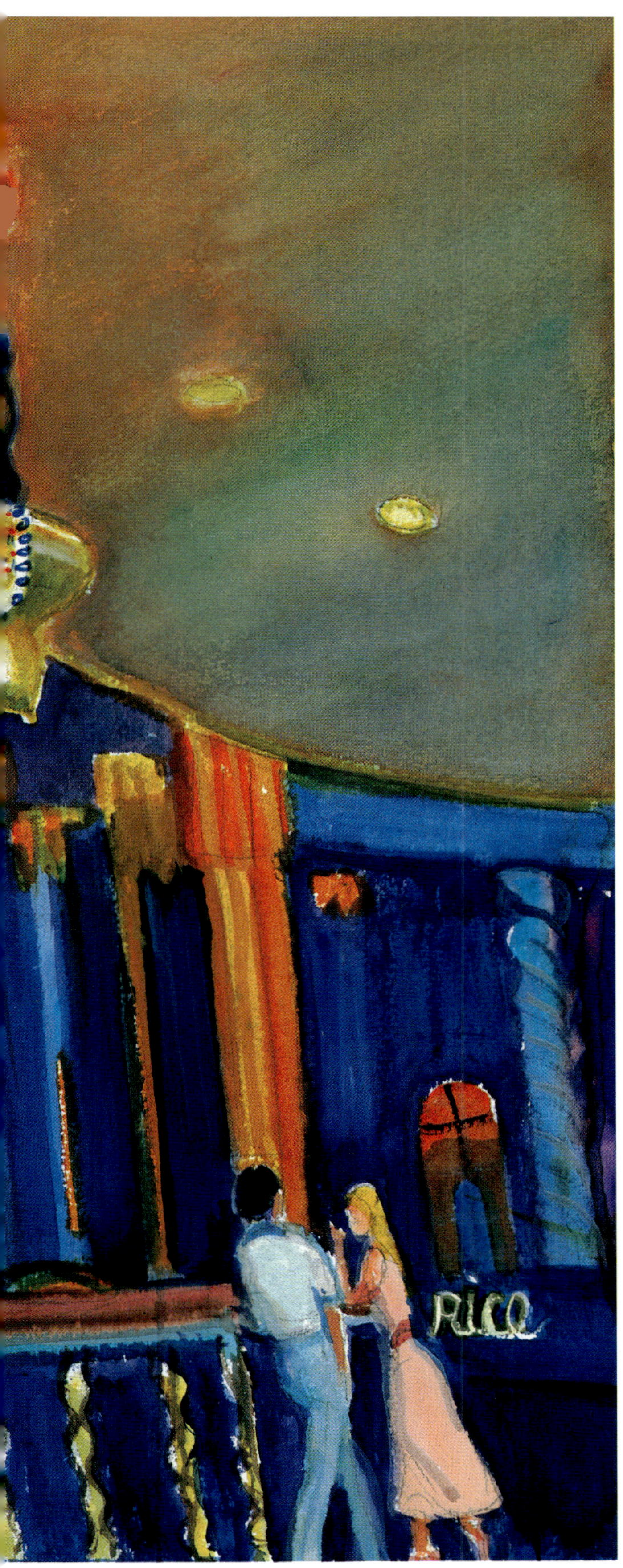

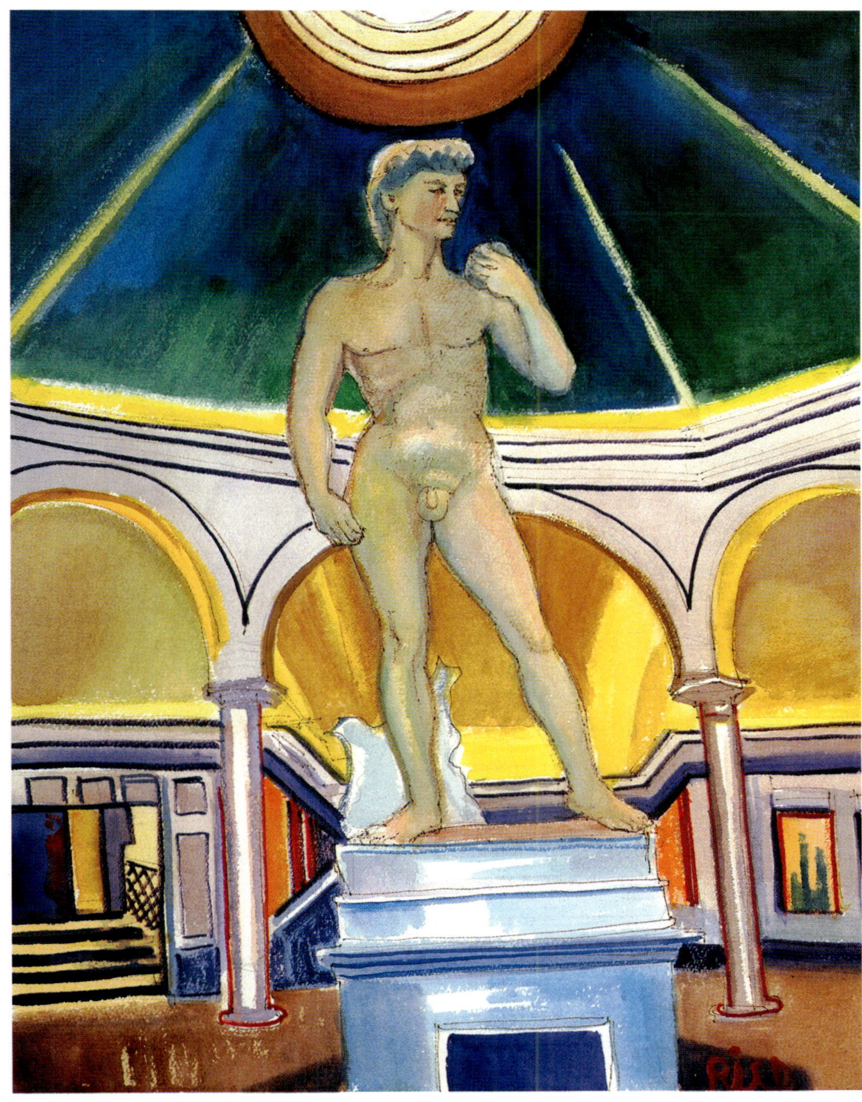

DAVID COMES TO VEGAS

Set in a beautifully-designed alcove within the Forum at Caesars Palace, I discovered a familiar face and form—Michaelangelo's David. Not the original which I've admired in Florence, Italy, of course, but a spectacular reproduction that is nearly as stunning as the real thing, one of the finest sculptures in the world. The legendary Biblical warrior who slew the giant Goliath with a well-slung stone and later became king, David is more of a natural fit for Las Vegas than you might think at first: he's the quintessential longshot, an emblem of fantastic success against almost unbeatable odds.

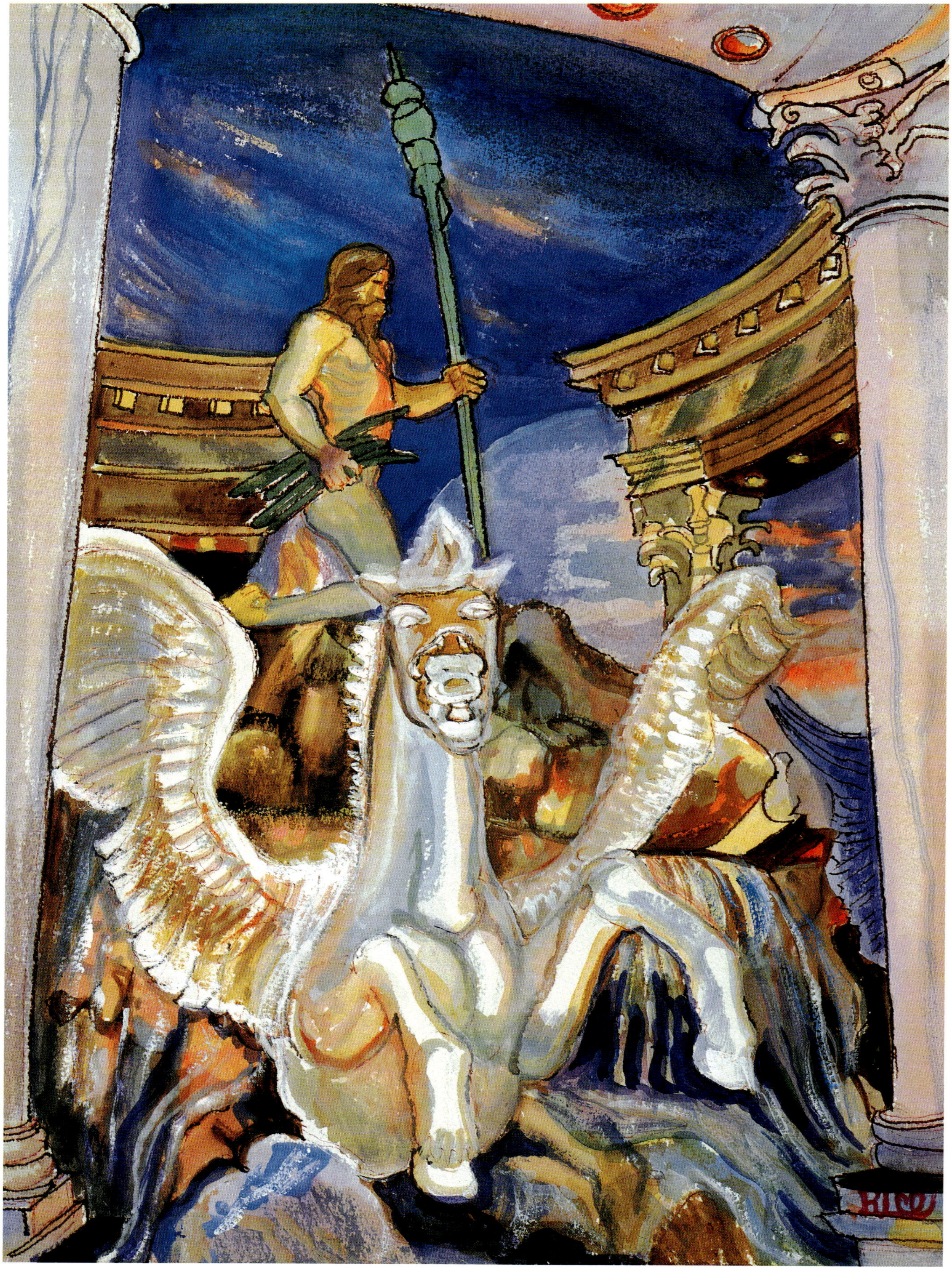

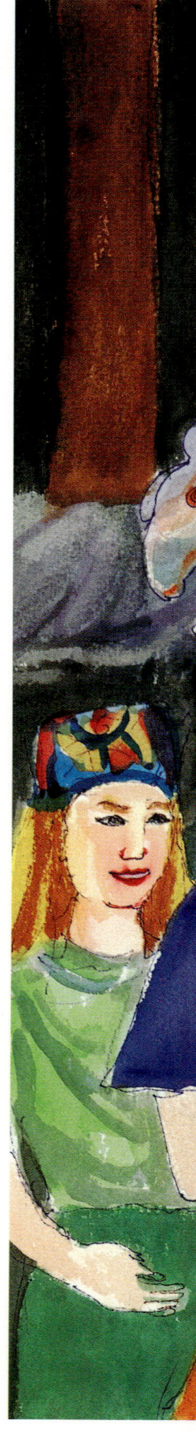

THE FORUM SHOPS AND THE FOUNTAIN OF THE GODS

Caesars Palace's ultimate triumph is the $100 million Forum Shops, featuring a fantastic array of more than 100 luxury retailers (Gucci, Dior, Versace, Vuitton and more), famous-name eateries (Chinois, The Palm, etc.) and attractions like the Festival Fountain with animatronic statues of ancient Olympian deities. The wonders of the Forum are all housed under a gigantic dome designed to resemble a clear sky (changing from day to night at regular intervals).

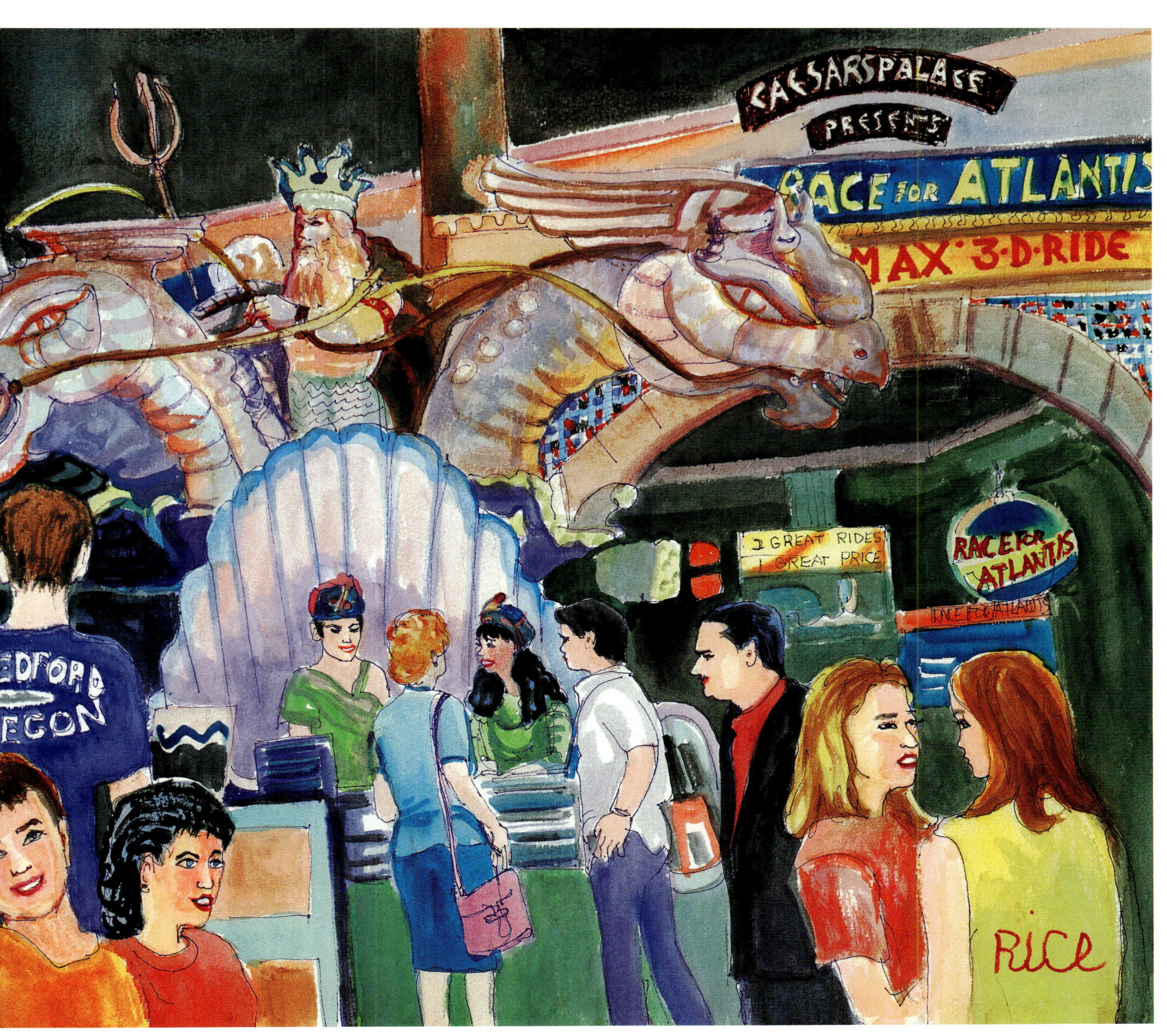

RACE FOR ATLANTIS

In the thrilling "Atlantis" show, Neptune, Roman God of the Sea, comes to life in a 50,000 gallon aquarium.

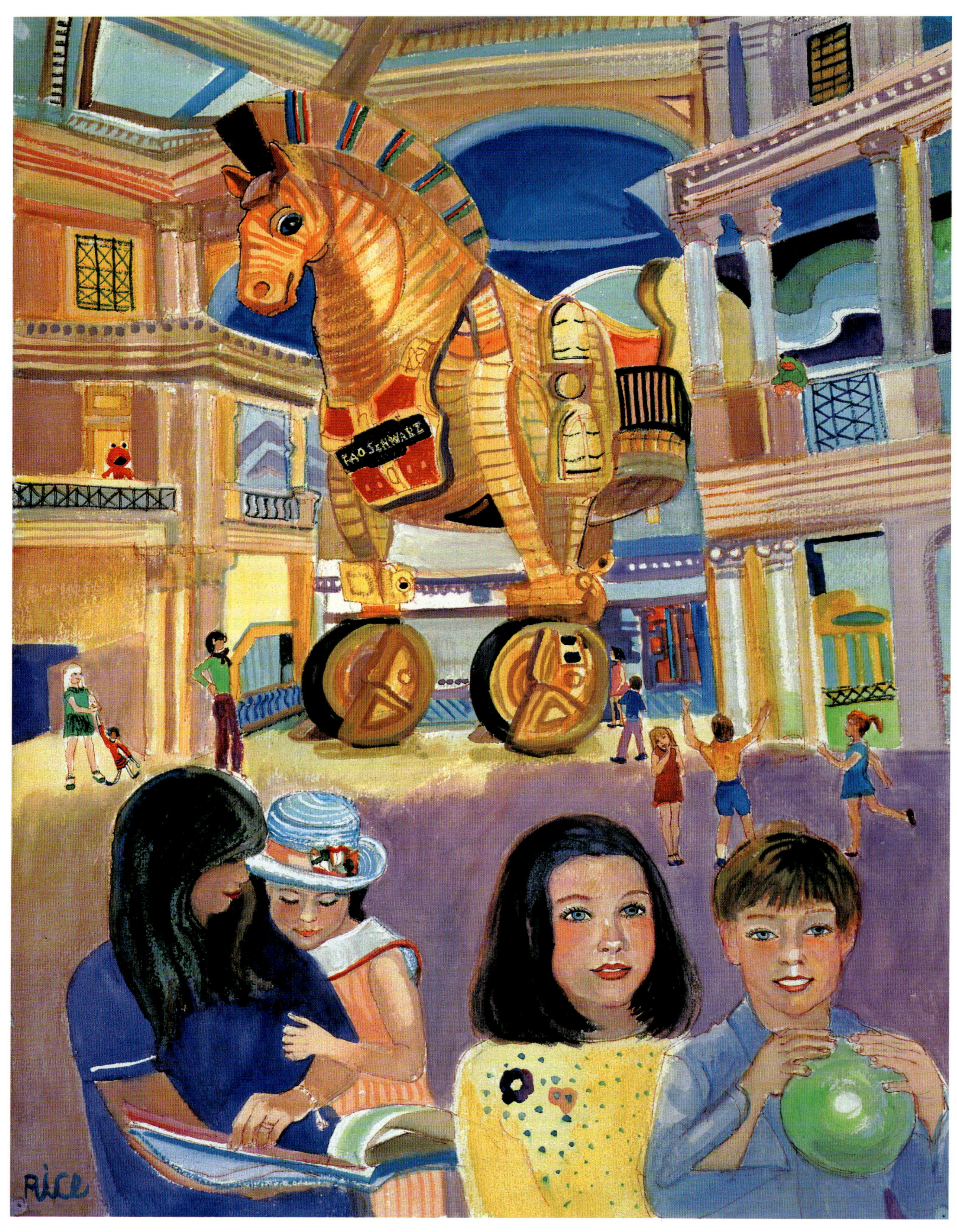

HORSING AROUND AT F.A.O. SCHWARTZ AT THE FORUM

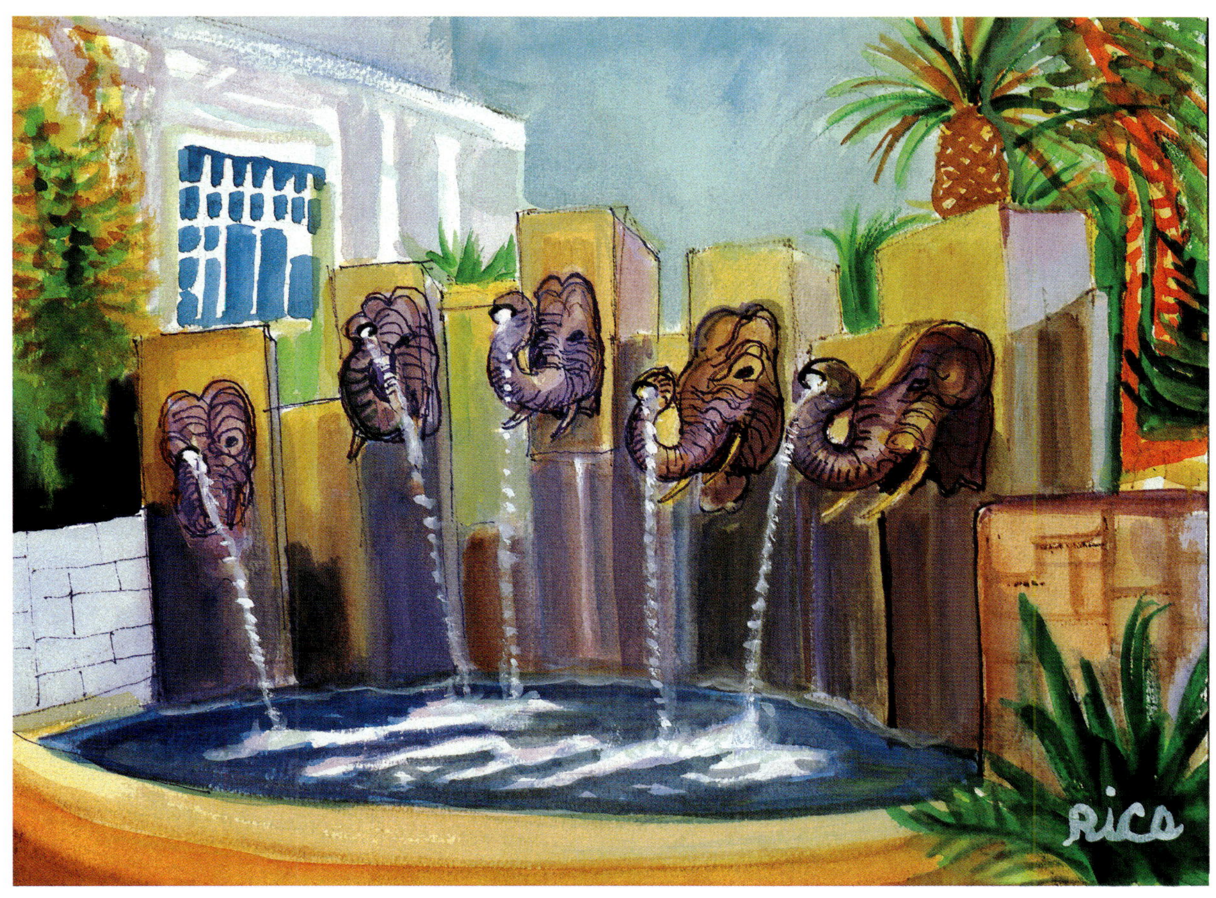

A REAL TRUNK SHOW

Mandalay Bay has a number of playful yet elegant design elements, like the adorable Elephant Pool where five pachyderms gently spray water for the delight of passers-by.

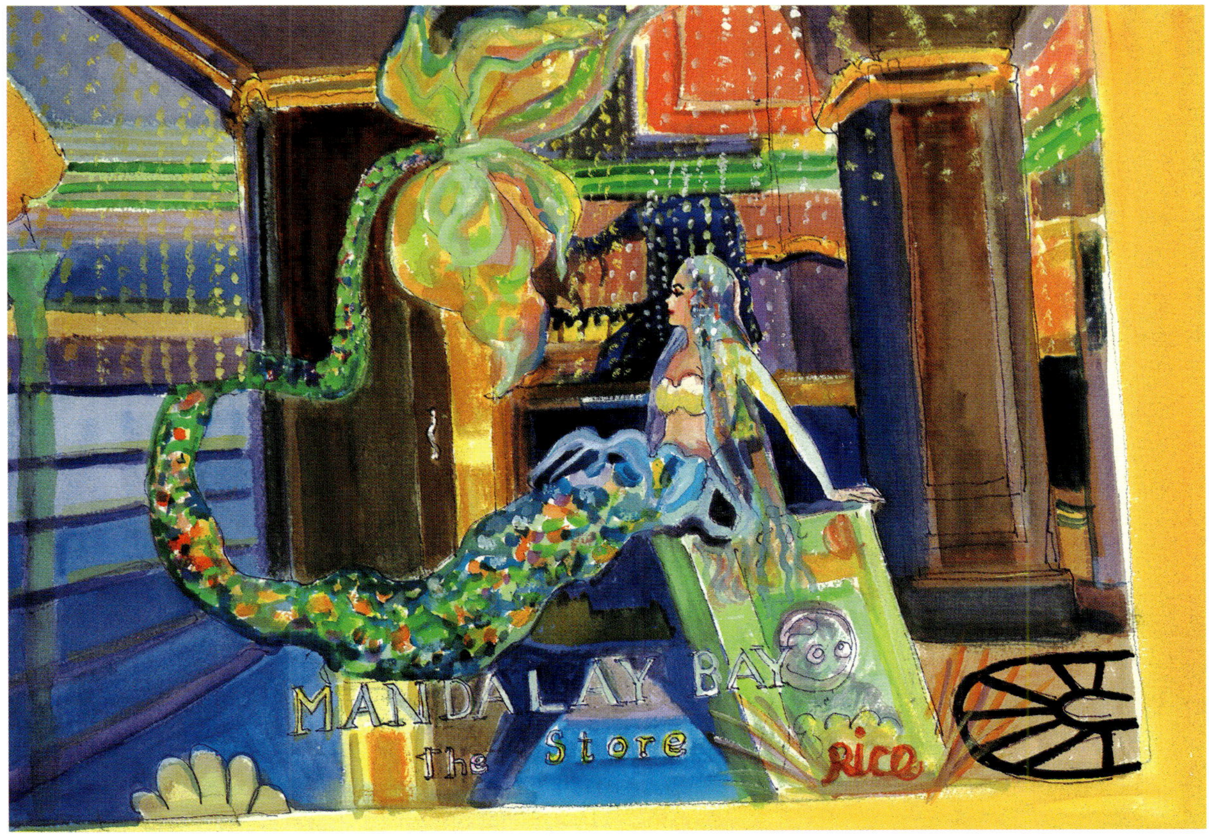

THE MERMAID AT MANDALAY BAY

This very colorful and tastefully designed window display caught my eye as I strolled past the storefronts within the Mandalay Bay Hotel. Whoever designed it has my kudos.

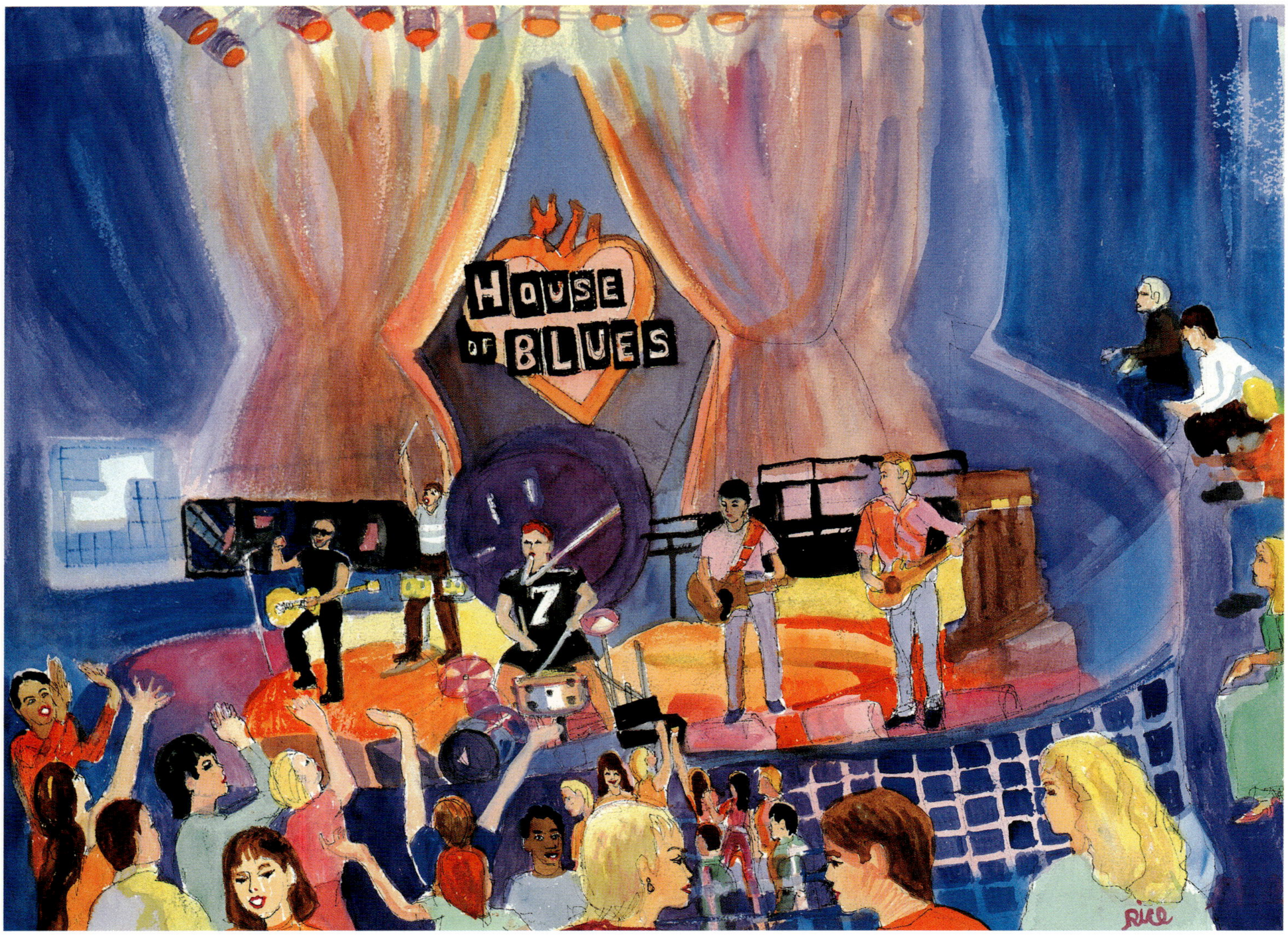

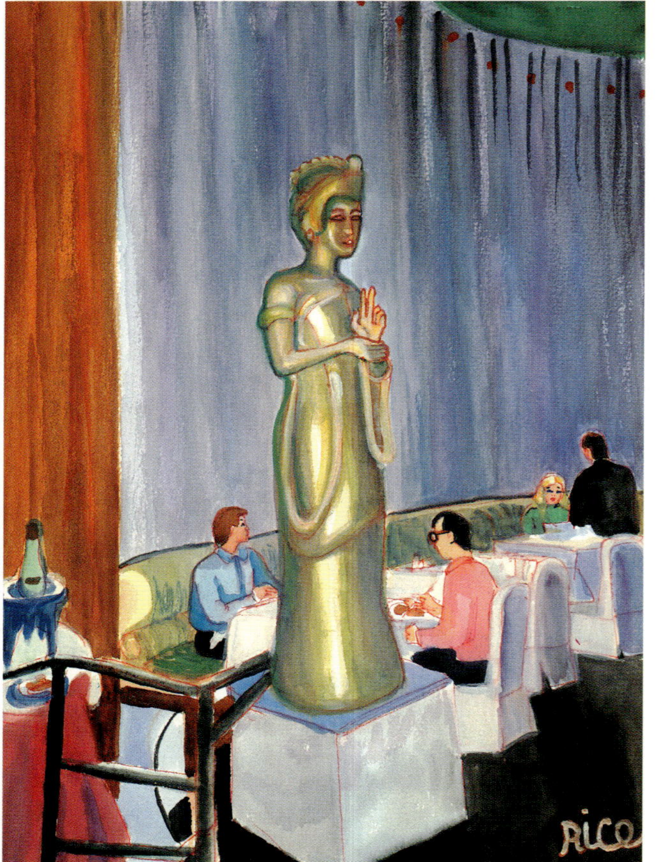

THE HOUSE OF BLUES AT MANDALAY BAY

Cinematic "Blues Brother" Dan Aykroyd opened another of his renowned House of Blues Clubs within the Mandalay Bay and quickly established the 1,900-seat hot spot as one of the city's cutting-edge venues for live music, including blues, rock, reggae, swing, ska, Latin, country, hip-hop, progressive, alternative and, of course, the legendary all-you-can-eat Gospel Brunch.

SHANGHAI LILLY AT MANDALAY BAY

I don't know if this statue's hand sign translates as "peace" in the Far East, but the atmosphere was certainly tranquil and serene. In cuisine, service and decor, Shanghai Lilly equals any Chinese restaurant in Shanghai or Beijing for top quality.

INSIDE THE MANDALAY BAY CASINO >

One of the newer entries in Las Vegas' trend toward ultra-luxurious digs, the Mandalay Bay Resort & Casino ups the ante for amazing amenities. The 43-story resort (which includes the separately-managed Four Seasons Hotel—sans gambling—on Floors 35-39) features a lush lobby complete with a huge aquarium and tropical birds in 12-foot tall bamboo cages, a 30,000-square-foot spa, a 1,200-seat arena, a massive theater that hosts top Broadway productions and an 11-acre water park with sand-and-surf beach.

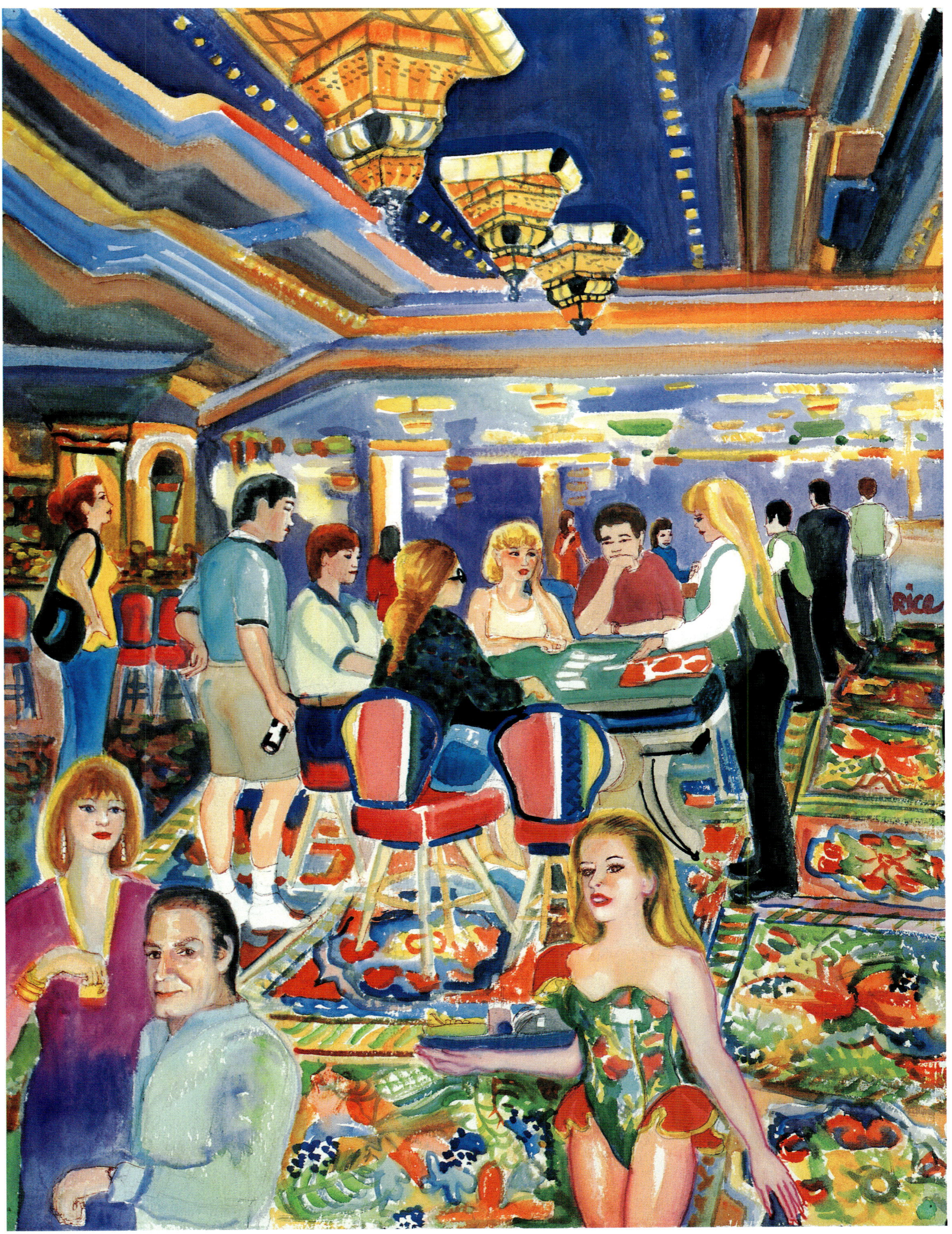

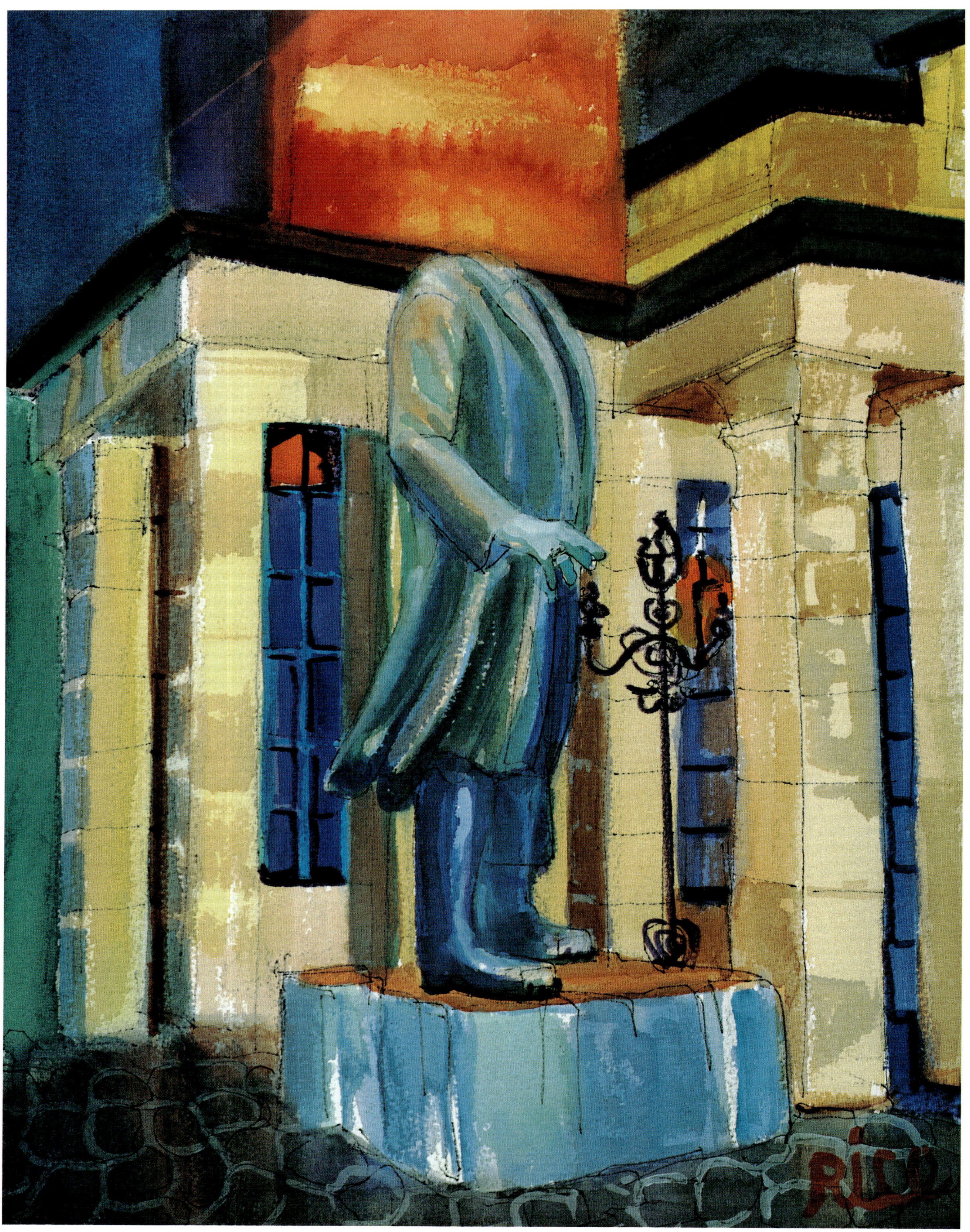

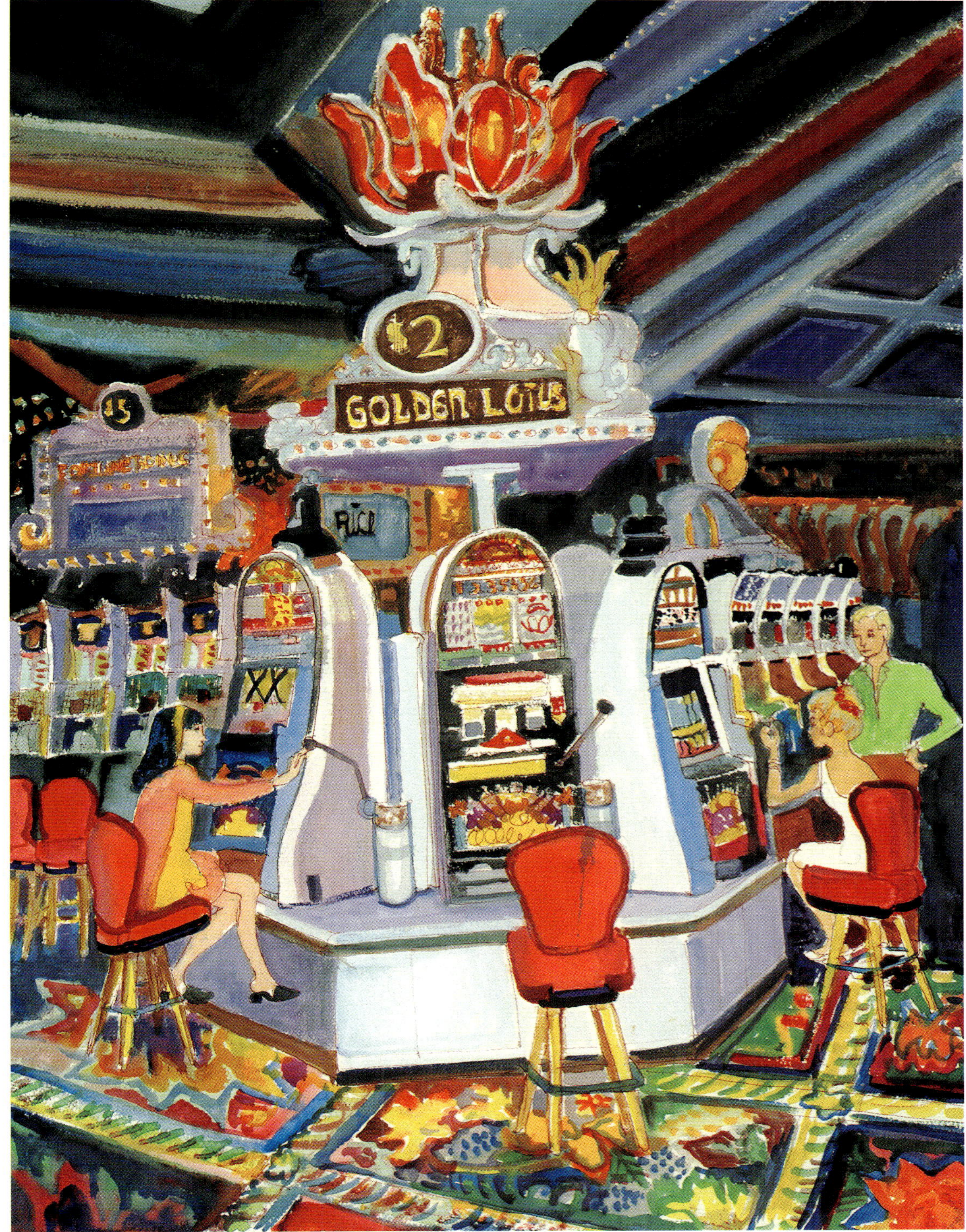

THE GOLDEN LOTUS AT MANDALAY BAY

Try your luck at the Golden Lotus, an intriguingly-designed bank of $2 slots at Mandalay Bay and a standout among its 2,400 gaming machines. The Circus Circus Enterprises-owned resort has spared no detail in creating a luxuriant casino environment complete with flowing water, tropical foliage and hybrid-Polynesian architecture.

< RED LOSES HIS HEAD

Las Vegas may be the world's leading example of conspicuous Capitalism, but Communism is also remembered at Mandalay Bay with this 16-foot statue of Vladimir Lenin, the Russian revolutionary who founded the Soviet Union. A duplicate of the famed bronze sculpture in Moscow's Red Square, this one stands outside Mandalay Bay's own Red Square—a vodka bar designed in a retro-Bolshevik proletarian style. The statue was originally installed in one piece, but letters objecting to the statue's Communist theme inspired the management to lop off Lenin's noggin, mirroring the many headless Lenins that dot the post-Soviet landscape. Faux pigeon droppings were added for authenticity. Then came a bizarre twist, even by Vegas standards: somebody stole the 250 lb., two-foot-tall plaster head from a wall on its first day on display! The hotel, which hoped to encase the head in ice and use it as the centerpiece of Red Square's Siberia-cold vodka locker, offered a $5,000 reward, no questions asked. When I visited, the call was still going out: "Bring me Lenin's head!"

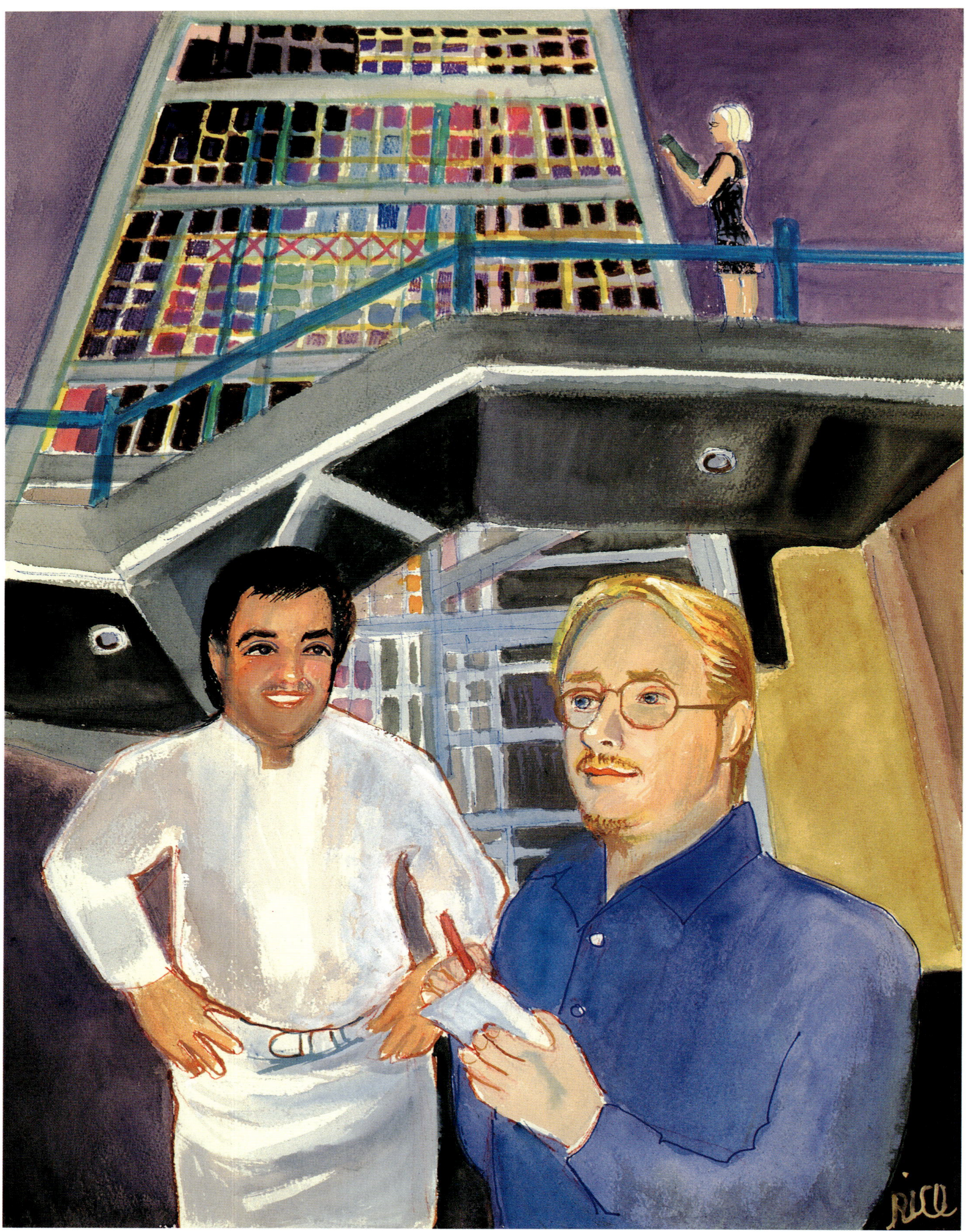

SCOTT HUVER AT AUREOLE

A Las Vegas getaway is just a one-hour plane trip for Scott Huver, a Los Angeles-based screenwriter and journalist who mixed business and pleasure by doing research at chef Charlie Palmer's posh and popular Aureole restaurant at Mandalay Bay. Scott chatted with chef Joe Romano to learn all the inside dish on Aureole's ingenious, incredibly well-stocked four-story wine tower and the graceful "wine angels" who are hoisted into the air on cables to retrieve a select vintage for diners. Charlie Palmer's particular style of cooking is based on *culinary tradition* with strong infusion of classical French cuisine.

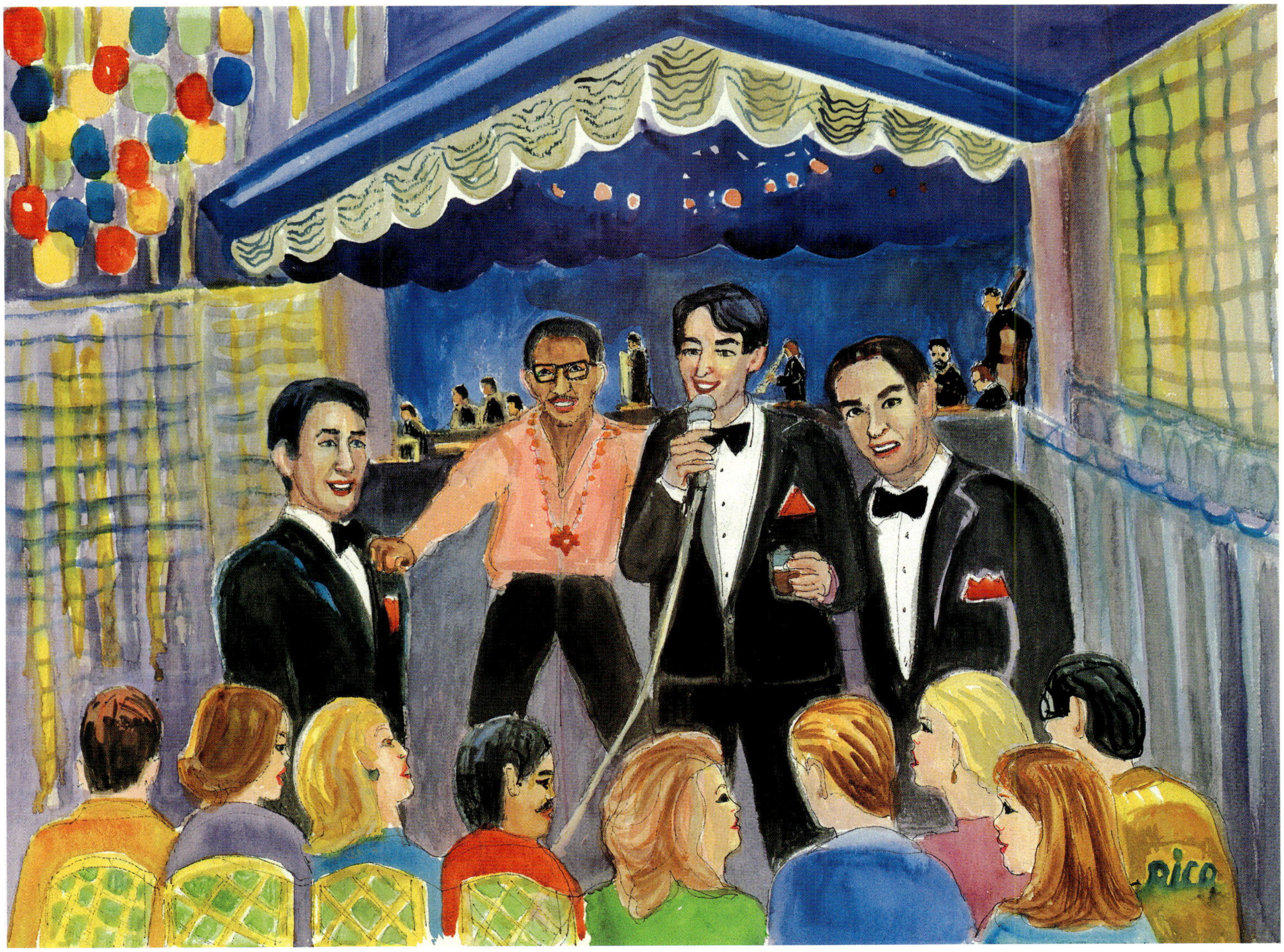

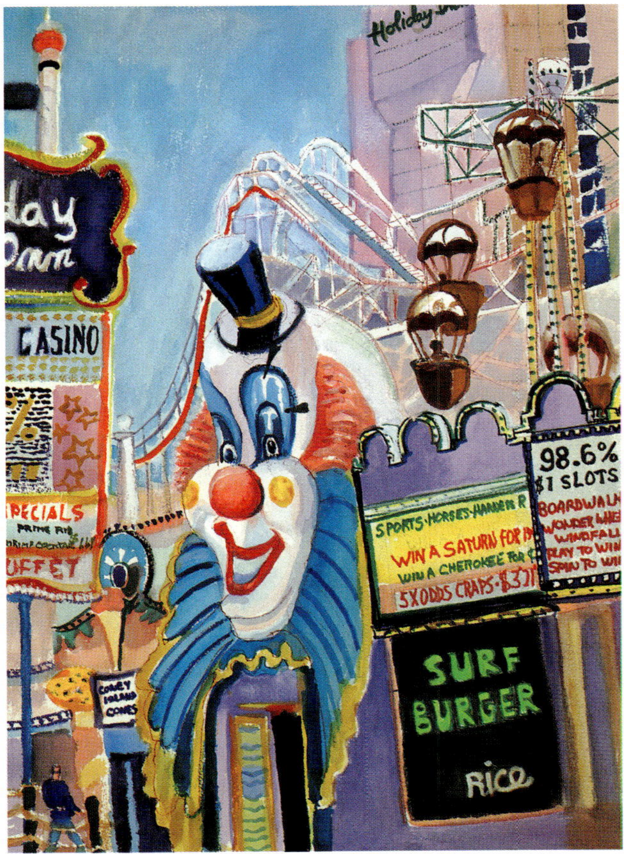

THE RAT PACK—THEN AND NOW

The very mention of the "Rat Pack"—or The Summit, as they preferred (as in The Summit of talent)—conjures up images of the original Sin City party animals: Frank Sinatra, Dean Martin and Sammy Davis, Jr., along with Peter Lawford and Joey Bishop. Martin played there first with Jerry Lewis at the Flamingo beginning in 1949; Sinatra made his Vegas debut performance in 1951 at the Desert Inn (where he also played his final Vegas concert); and Sammy Davis, Jr., broke the color barrier in 1954 when he and the Will Mastin Trio were the first black performers to play and stay at the Frontier.

But it was in 1960, when the celebrated cronies assembled in Las Vegas to film "Ocean's Eleven" and decided to take their off-stage friendship on stage at the Sands—including their love for booze, broads, and politically incorrect jokes—that the Rat Pack mystique was born. In the 1990s, when the entertainers at last cashed in their chips, the entire Strip dimmed each and every neon light in tribute.

Their spirit is recaptured in "The Rat Pack Is Back," a terrific show at the Sahara Hotel's Congo Theater. Doug Voet, a former Broadway performer, introduced me to the cast: Bobby Caldwell (Frank), Steve Apple (Dean), Tony Tillman (Sammy) and Hiram Kasten (Joey). The show was conceived by David Cassidy—the former "Partridge Family" star who sometimes joins the faux Pack on stage singing "Mack the Knife" as Bobby Darin—and his partner, TV producer Don Reo ("Blossom").

THE BOARDWALK CLOWN

This happy-faced harlequin grinned invitingly at me from the entrance to the Holiday Inn's Coney Island-style Boardwalk. I just had to paint him.

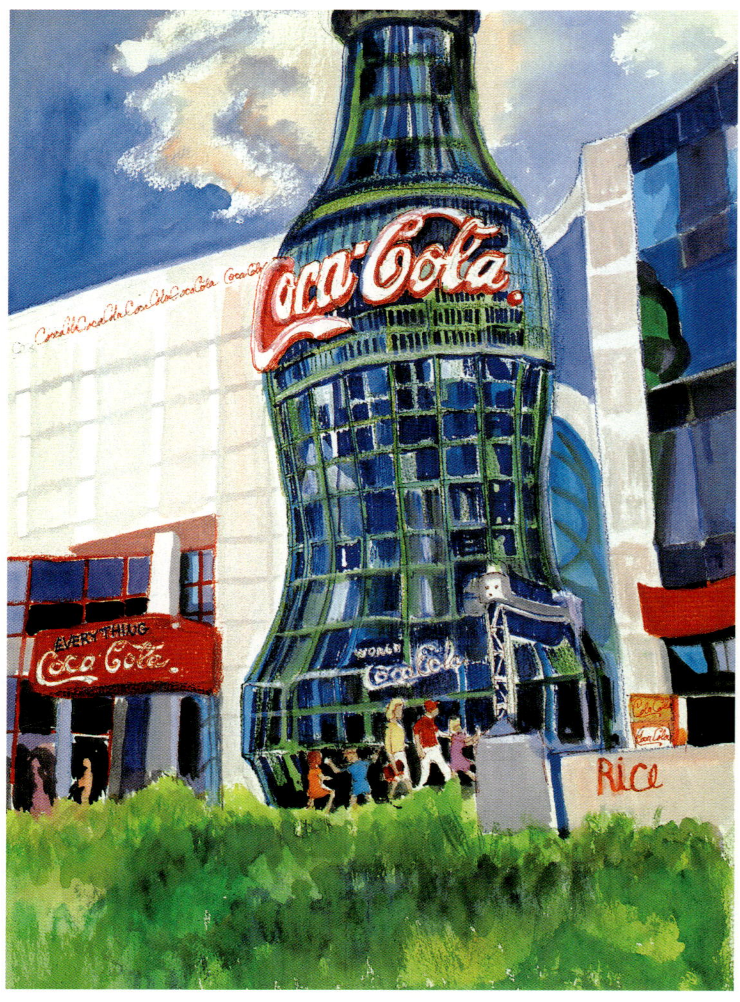

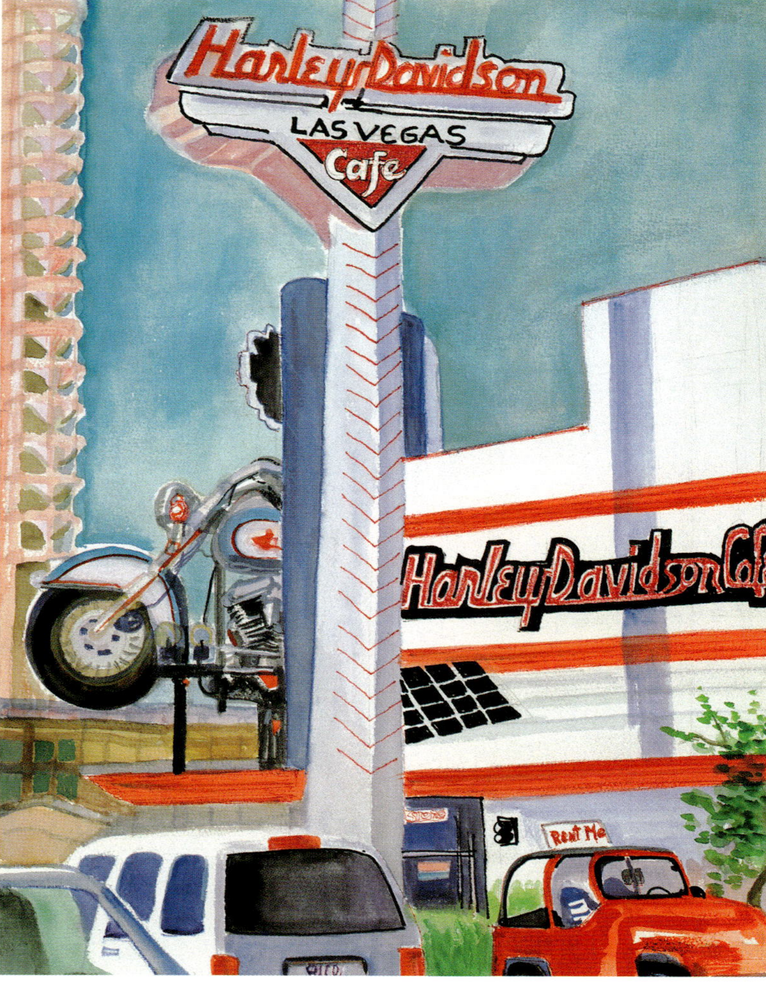

ABOVE LEFT

WORLD OF COCA-COLA

Remember the old jingle, "I'd like to buy the world a Coke?" At World of Coca Cola you can sip Coke products from all over the globe, including places as far away as Thailand and Mozambique. When you're done, you can use all that extra energy to scale the world's tallest Coke bottle.

ABOVE RIGHT

THE HARLEY-DAVIDSON CAFE

Motorcycle lovers will be revved up to visit the Harley-Davidson Cafe, a veritable "Hawg Heaven" devoted completely to one of the world's most popular cycle brands.

M&M'S WORLD

It's the candy that melts in your mouth, not in the Nevada sun. Ethel M Chocolates hosts M&M's World, a four-story mecca for the sweet-toothed which includes M&M's Academy—everything you always wanted to know about chocolatey goodness wrapped up in a candy shell. Vegas always offers more, more, more, so here you can sample 21 different colors of M&M's—15 more than in the standard bag!

SPEED >

Speed at the Sahara is one of the newest rollercoasters in town. It combines electromagnetic slingshot technology, a 225-foot climb/drop and a 360-degree loop to create a hair-raising experience with such fierce acceleration, it's over in just 48 seconds. As if the ups and downs of the casinos aren't enough for visiting thrillseekers, such daring loop-de-loops have become almost as integral a part of the Las Vegas landscape as gambling and showrooms.

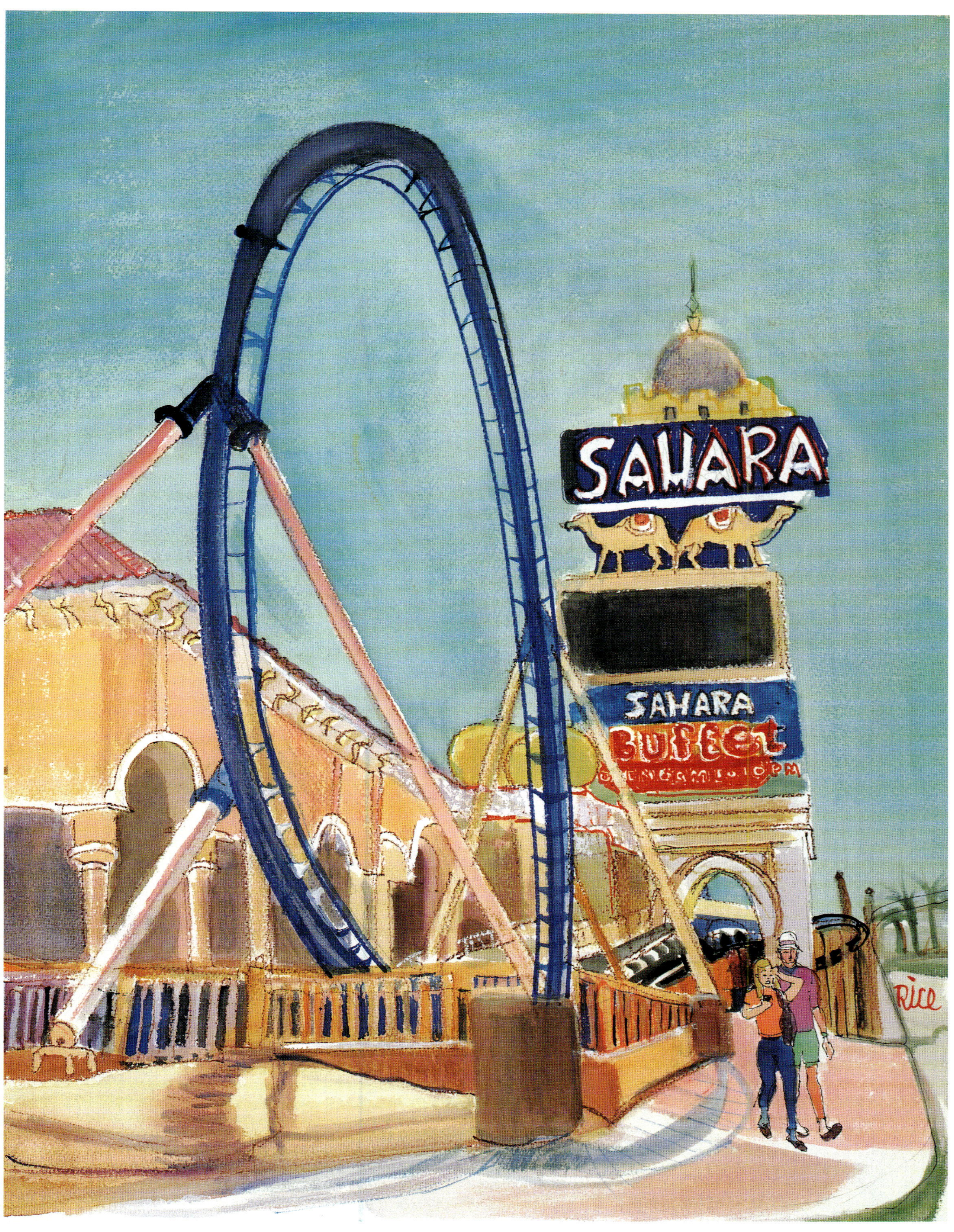
SAHARA
SAHARA
Buffet
Rice

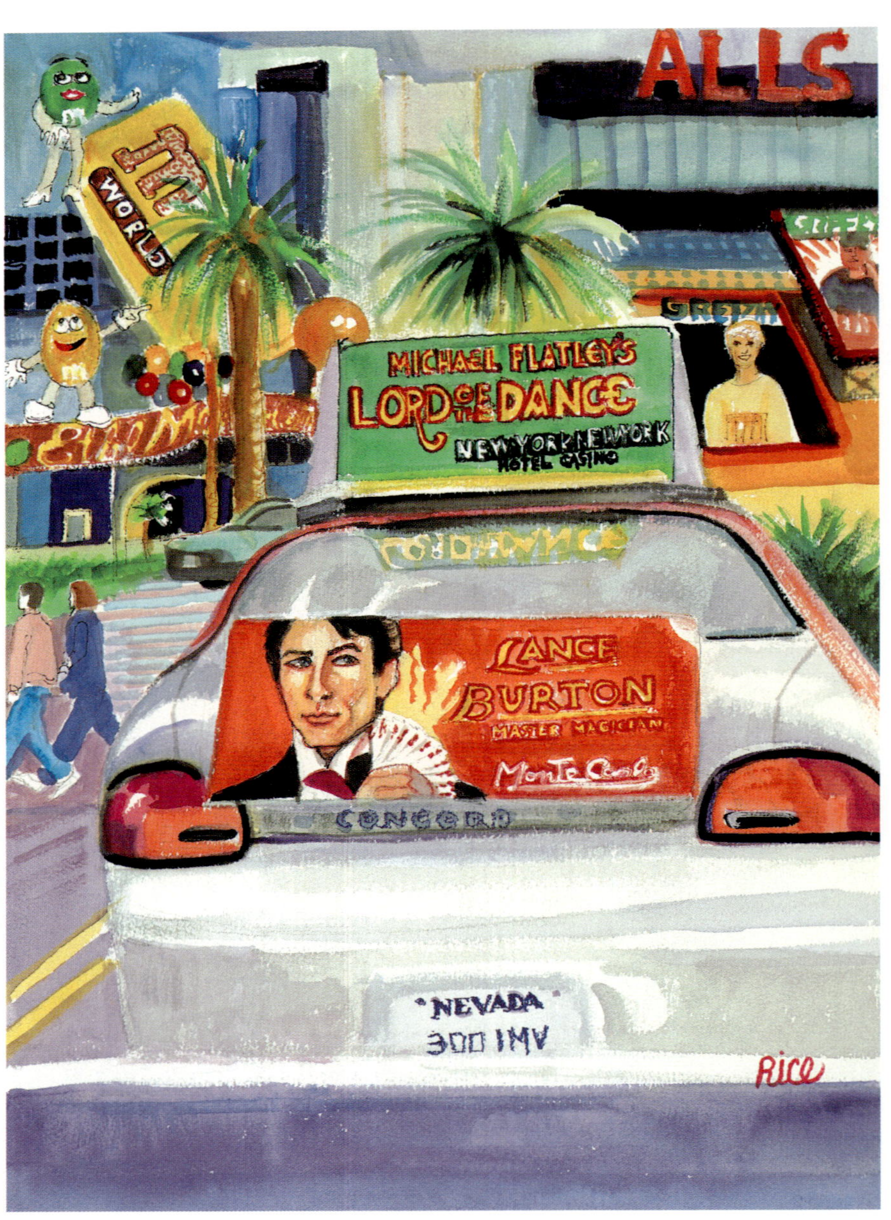

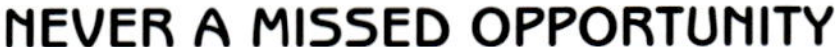

NEVER A MISSED OPPORTUNITY

Las Vegas is filled with many innovative promoters who don't miss a trick when it comes to marketing, like this taxi cab that simultaneously hypes both Michael Flatley's "Lord of the Dance" extravaganza at New York-New York and handsome Lance Burton's magic show at the Monte Carlo. Even caught in a bumper-to-bumper back-up, there's never a dull moment here!

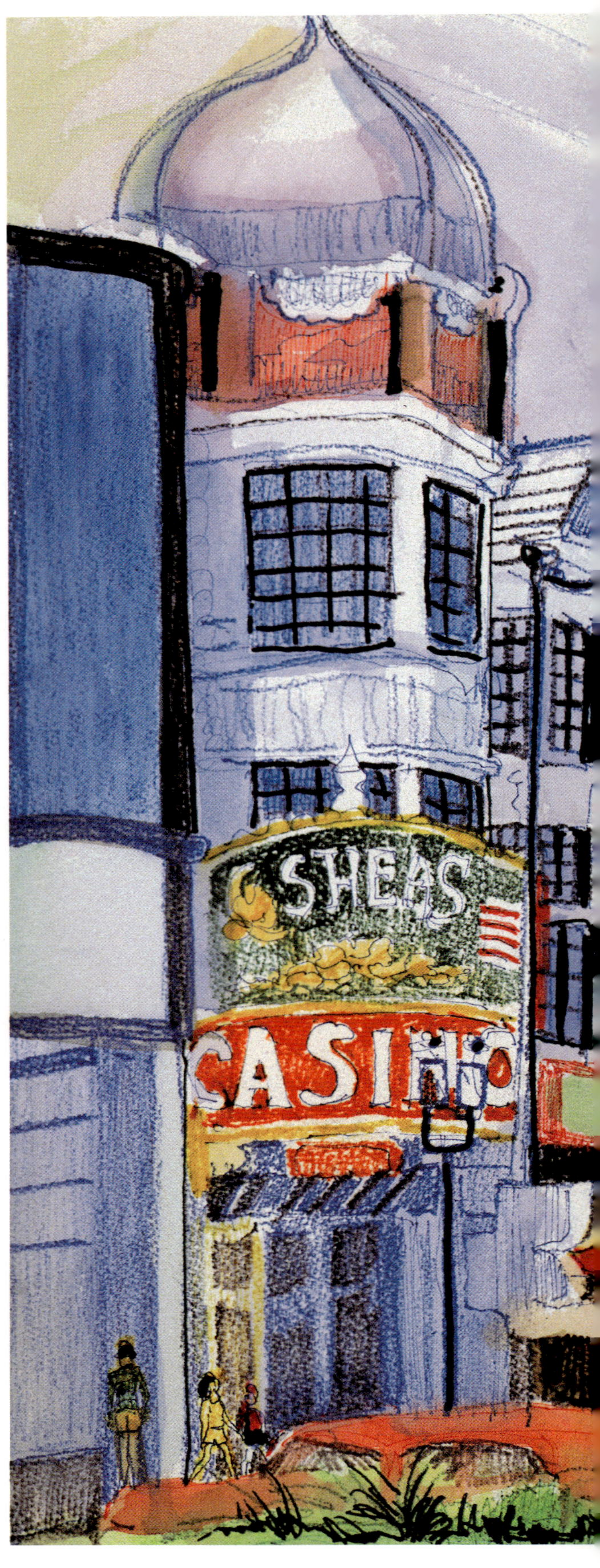

ALONG THE STRIP

Tucked in among the super-sized theme attractions and hotels are slightly more intimate casinos like O'Sheas, where one can get down to the business at hand. In addition to gaming, O'Shea's houses a Magic and Movie Hall of Fame upstairs, featuring all sorts of arcane memorabilia.

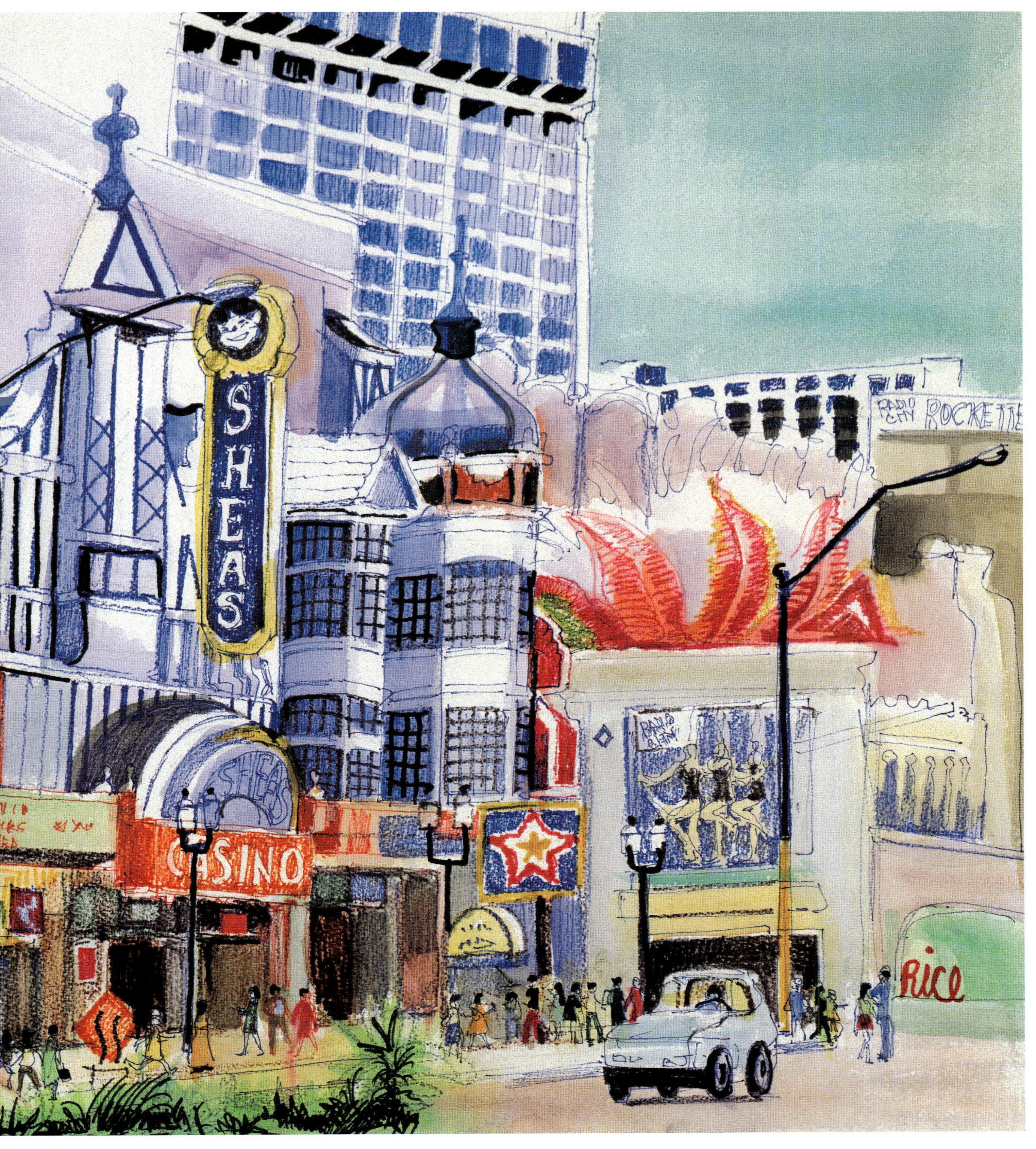
SHEAS
CASINO
RADIO CITY ROCKETTE
Rice

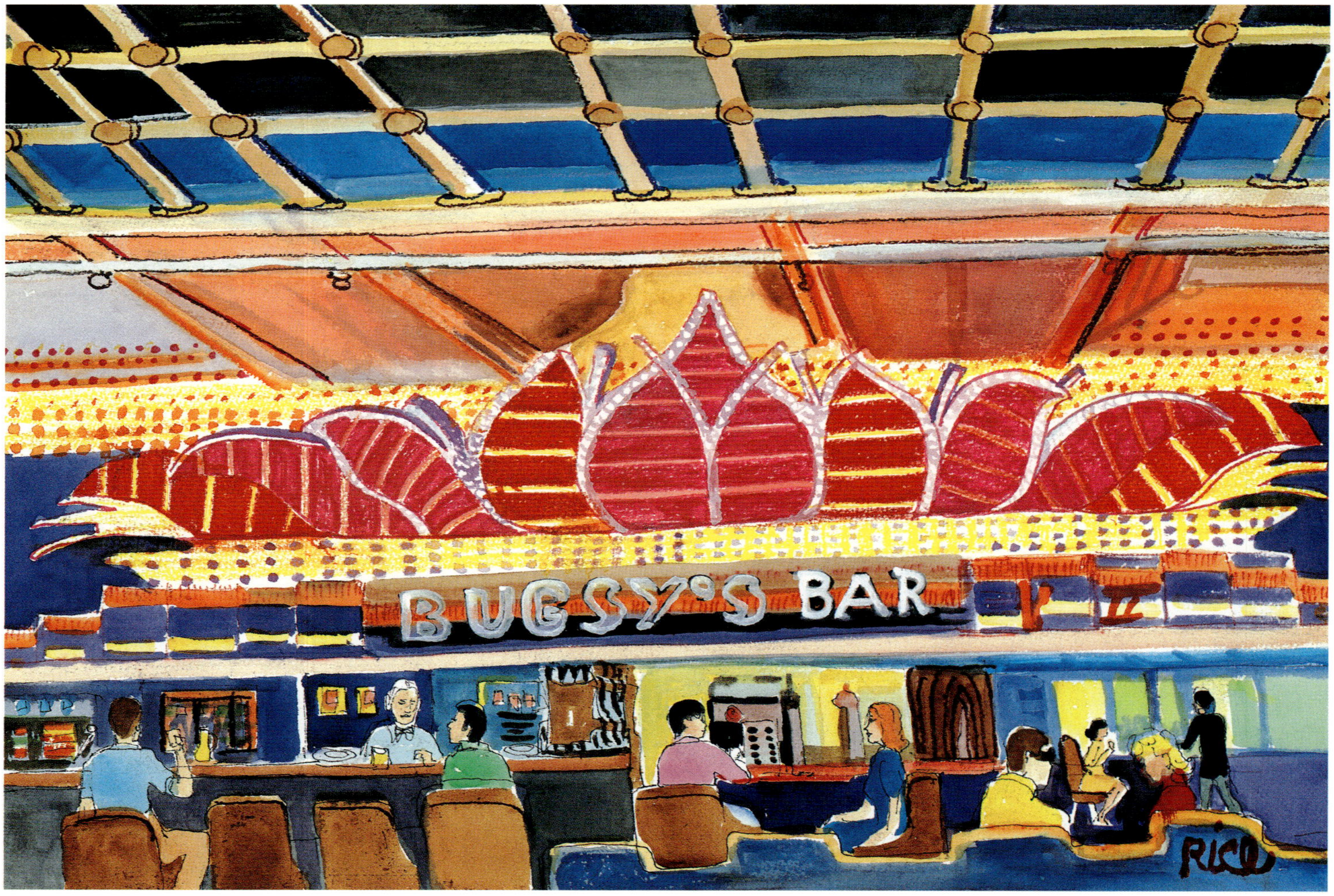

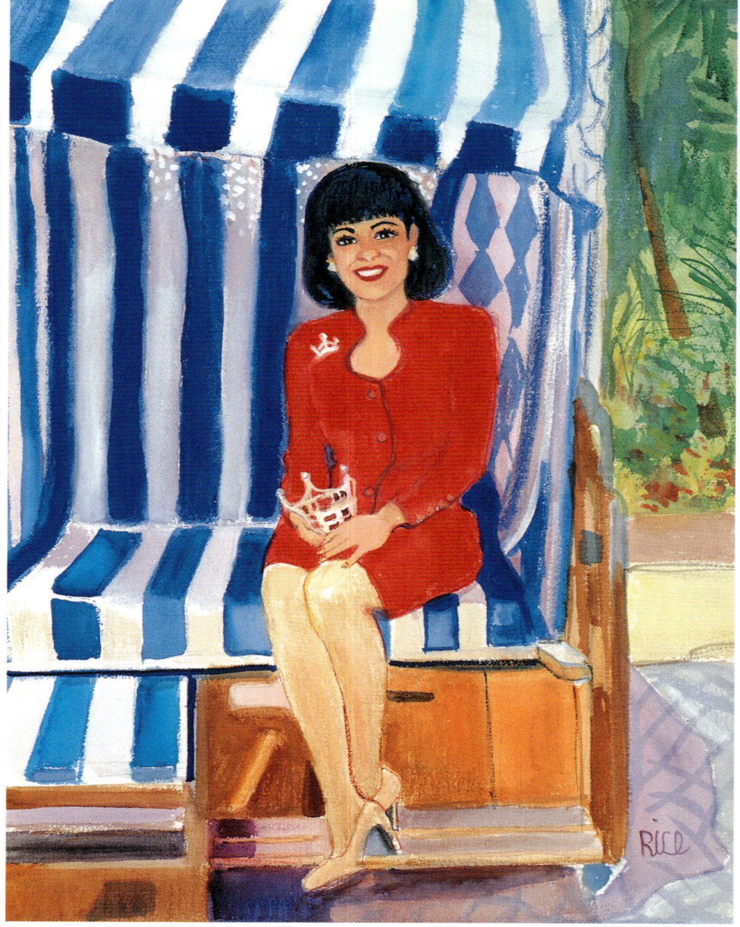

BUGSY'S BAR

The Flamingo Hilton has embraced the legend of its notorious founder Ben Siegel. The mention of his nickname "Bugsy" reportedly drove him instantly into a rage that only proved its appropriateness. He is remembered all around the Flamingo at places like Bugsy's Celebrity Theater, Bugsy's Deli, Bugsy's Bar, Bugsy's Video Poker and a street called Bugsy Siegel Circle.

MISS NEVADA'S CROWNING GLORY

Miss Nevada, 1999, Gina Giacinto looked appropriately regal when she met me poolside at the Flamingo Hilton—although the crown precluded her from taking a dip. Gina is as multifaceted as the jewels on her headgear: she's a full-time student at UNLV majoring in speech pathology and a high-kicking Rockette in the Flamingo's "Great Radio City Spectacular" show. She's also aiming for more crowns—Gina hopes to become the first Miss U.S.A. from the state of Nevada.

BUGSY'S GARDEN >

Within a lovely garden at the Flamingo Hilton that includes transplanted rose bushes lovingly planted by Benjamin Siegel himself, you can find a bronze bas-relief of Siegel and an equally affectionate plaque dedicated to the gangster-visionary.

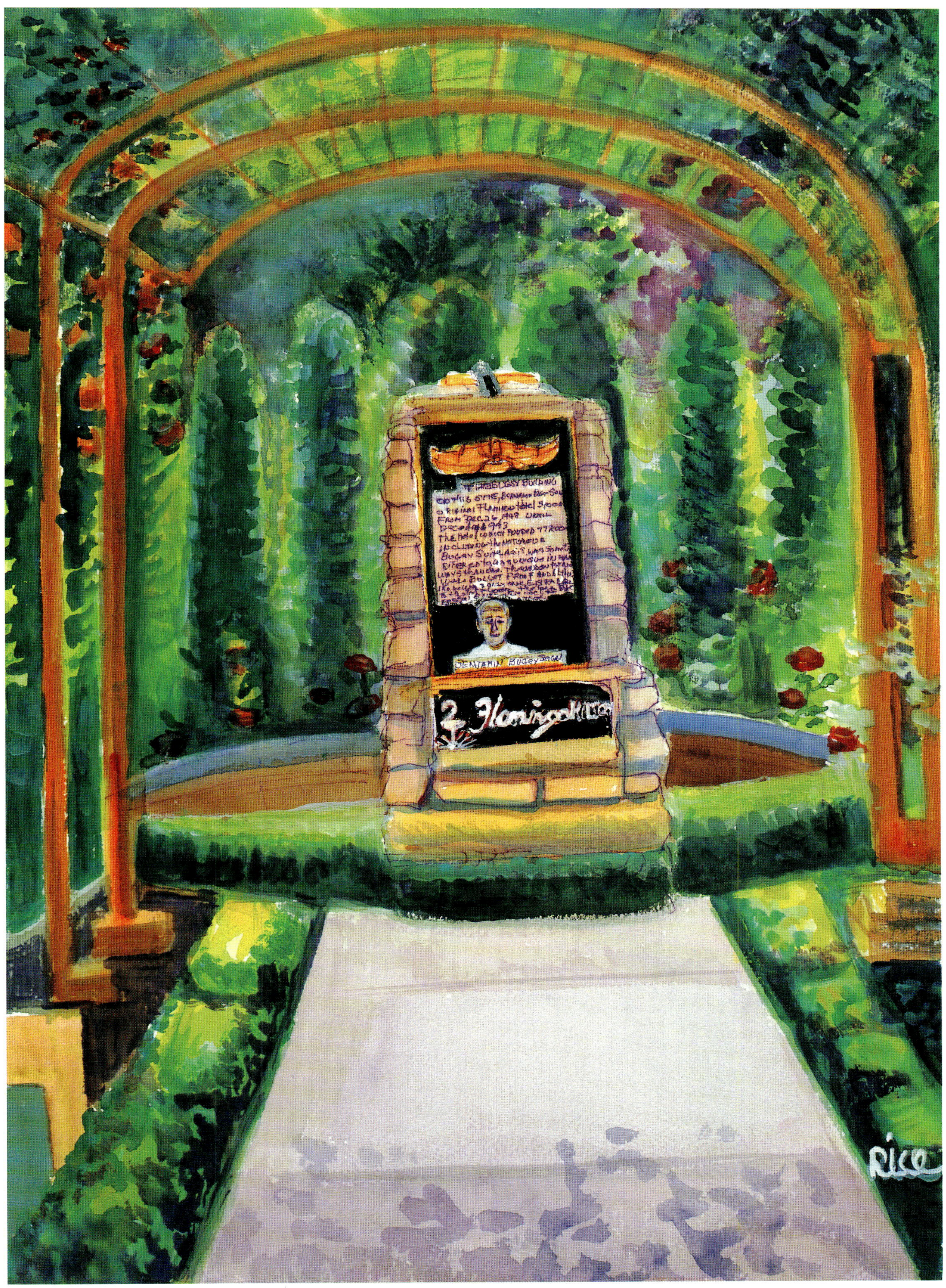
BENJAMIN BUGSY
Rice

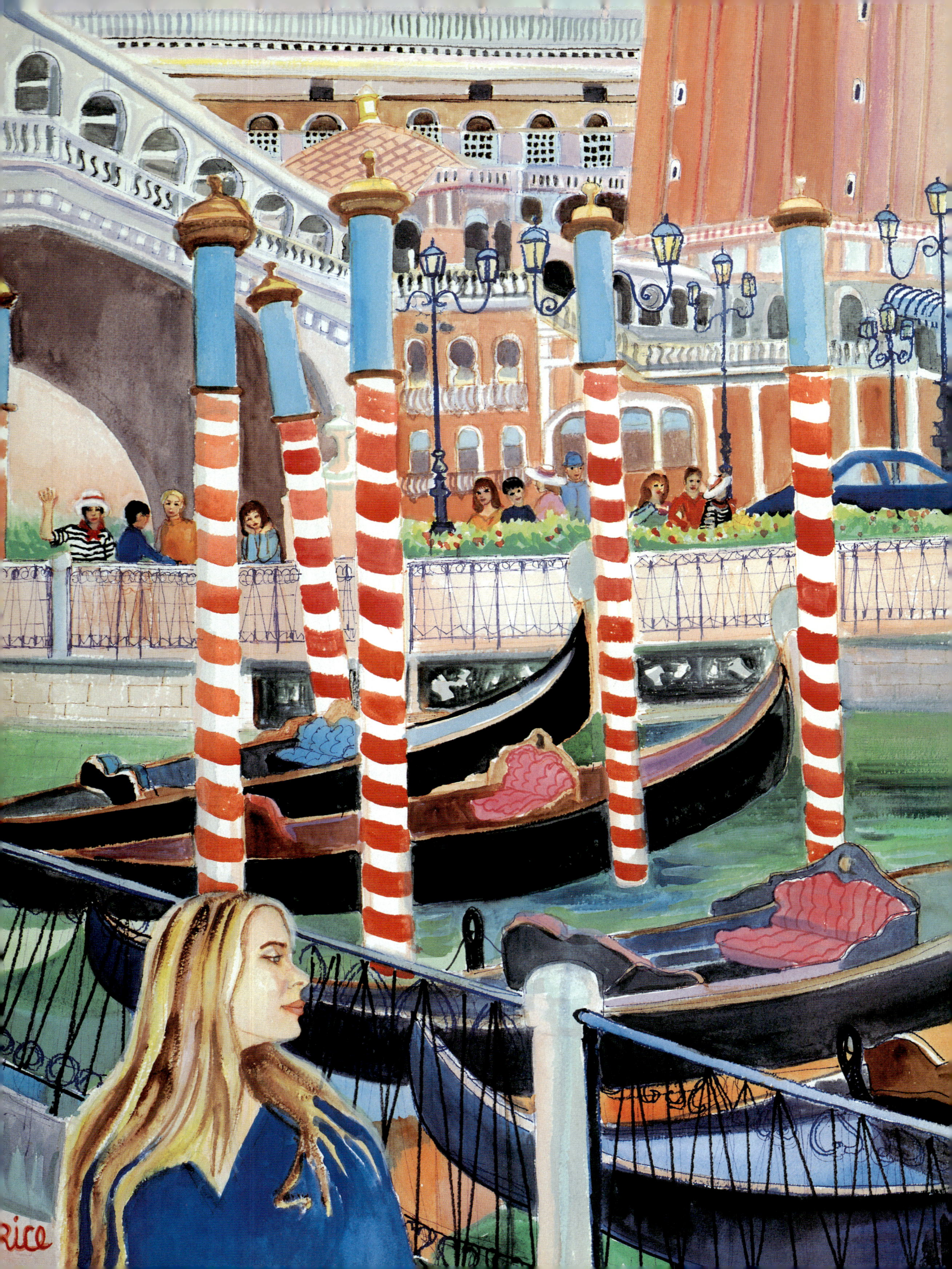

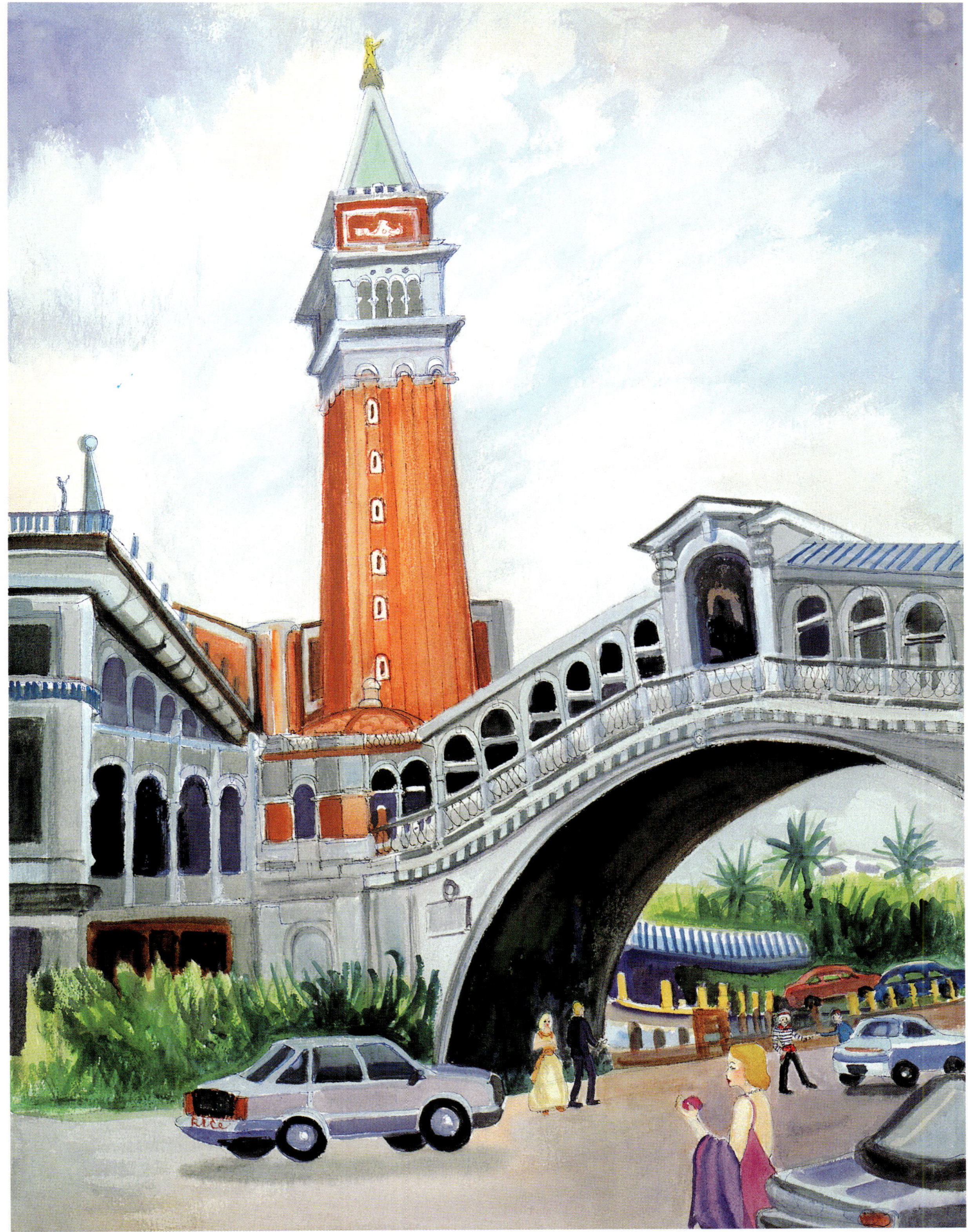

THE VENETIAN

Crafted to mirror Venice of the Renaissance Era, The Venetian has gone to extraordinary lengths to create an idyllic environment filled with elaborate Italianate opulence. Reproductions of the works of inspiring artists like Titian, Tintoretto, Veronese, Tiepolo and others adorn the walls. Venice landmarks such as the Campanile Tower, St. Mark's Clock Tower, Doge's Palace, the Bridge of Sighs, the Rialto Bridge and the famed canals are reconstructed faithfully. Incidentally, Venice was the first European city to open a public gaming house.

< THE VENETIAN CANALS

With the help of an able gondolier (who's also a well-tuned singer), you can navigate the Grand Canals of the Venetian. The Grand Canal Shoppes that line the waterway vie with Rodeo Drive for world-class upscale appeal, with storefronts including the likes of Jimmy Choo, Mikimoto, Movado, Brookstone, Ann Taylor, BCBG Max Azria, Bebe, Kenneth Cole, Lladro, Davidoff, Sephora and more.

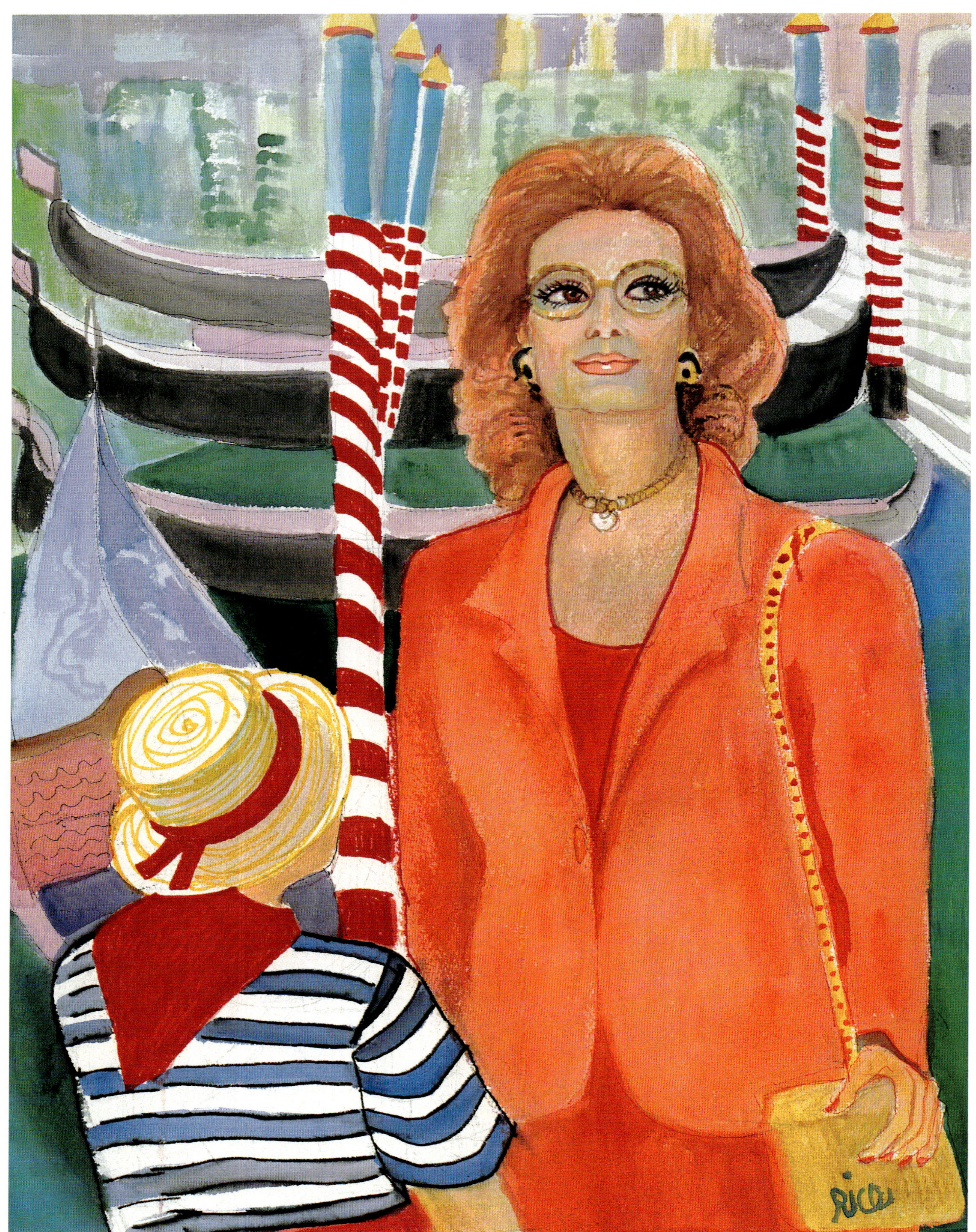

A VENUS AT THE VENETIAN

Appearing at the grand opening celebration of the Venetian, legendary screen icon Sophia Loren rises like a modern-day goddess. The hotel promised to deliver many of Italy's most splendiferous sights, and Miss Loren certainly fills that category.

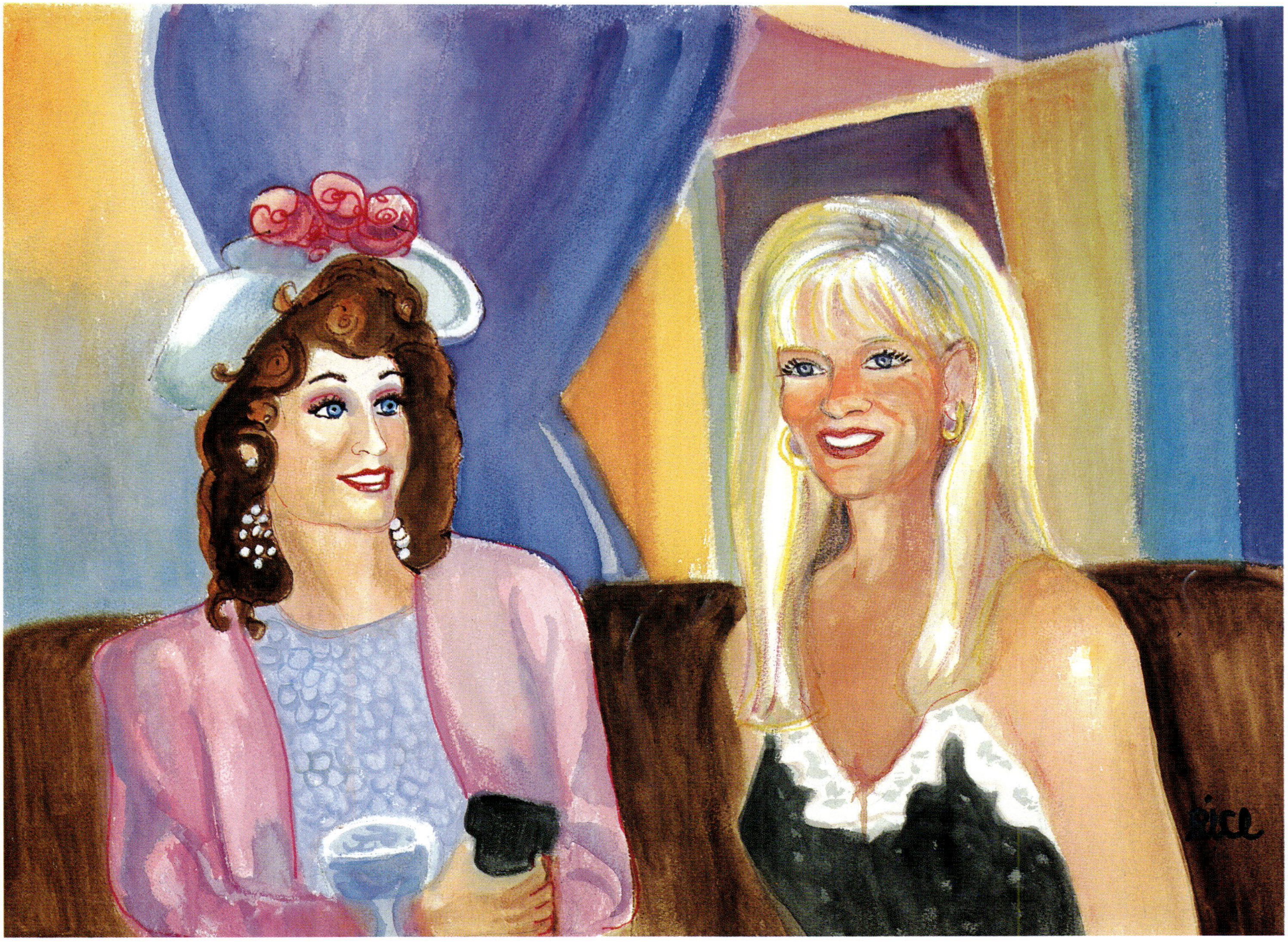

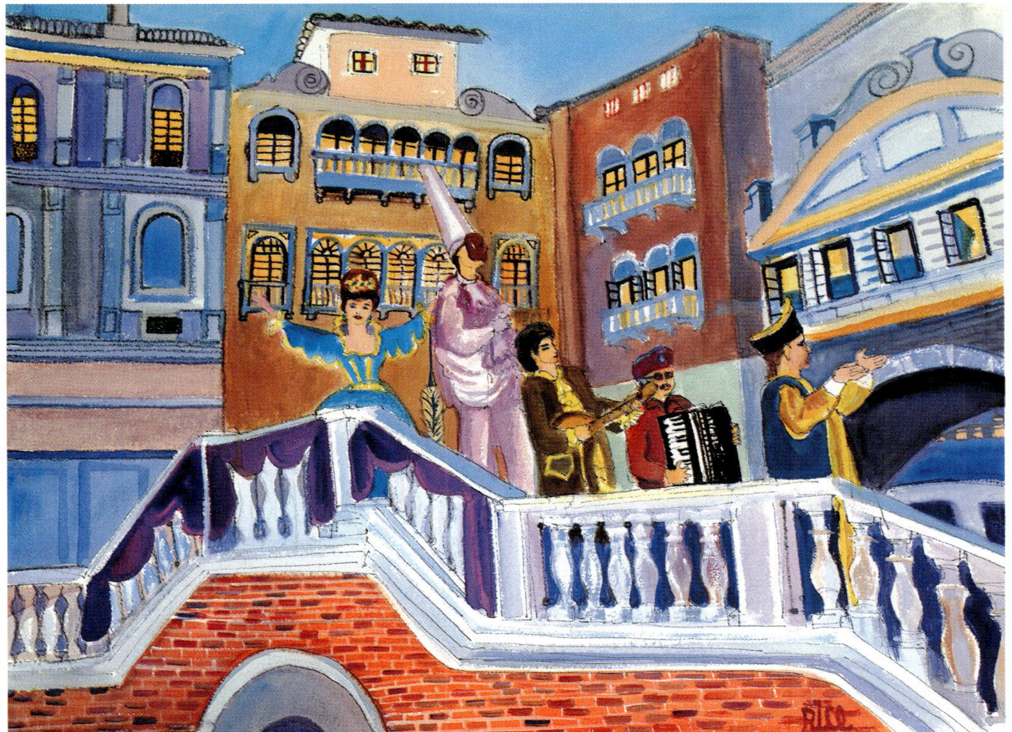

INTERVIEWING THE INTERVIEWER AT PINOT BRASSERIE

We enjoyed a delicious dinner in an elegant private enclave at the Pinot Brasserie restaurant in the Venetian when local lifestyle columnist, film reviewer and television personality Polly Peluso (left) interviewed health and fitness guru Greer Childers. Possessing a perfect smile and a Barbie Doll shape, Greer has become fantastically successful with her fitness and weight-loss book "Be a Loser," which sells like crazy on the Home Shopping Network. While Polly interviewed Greer, I interviewed Polly, and I picked up a few tips from both of these highly accomplished women.

THE VENETIAN MINSTRELS

Sometimes the Venetian seems more like the real thing than Venice itself, with special touches like the roaming minstrels in masquerade garb who fill the air with the romantic music of Italy.

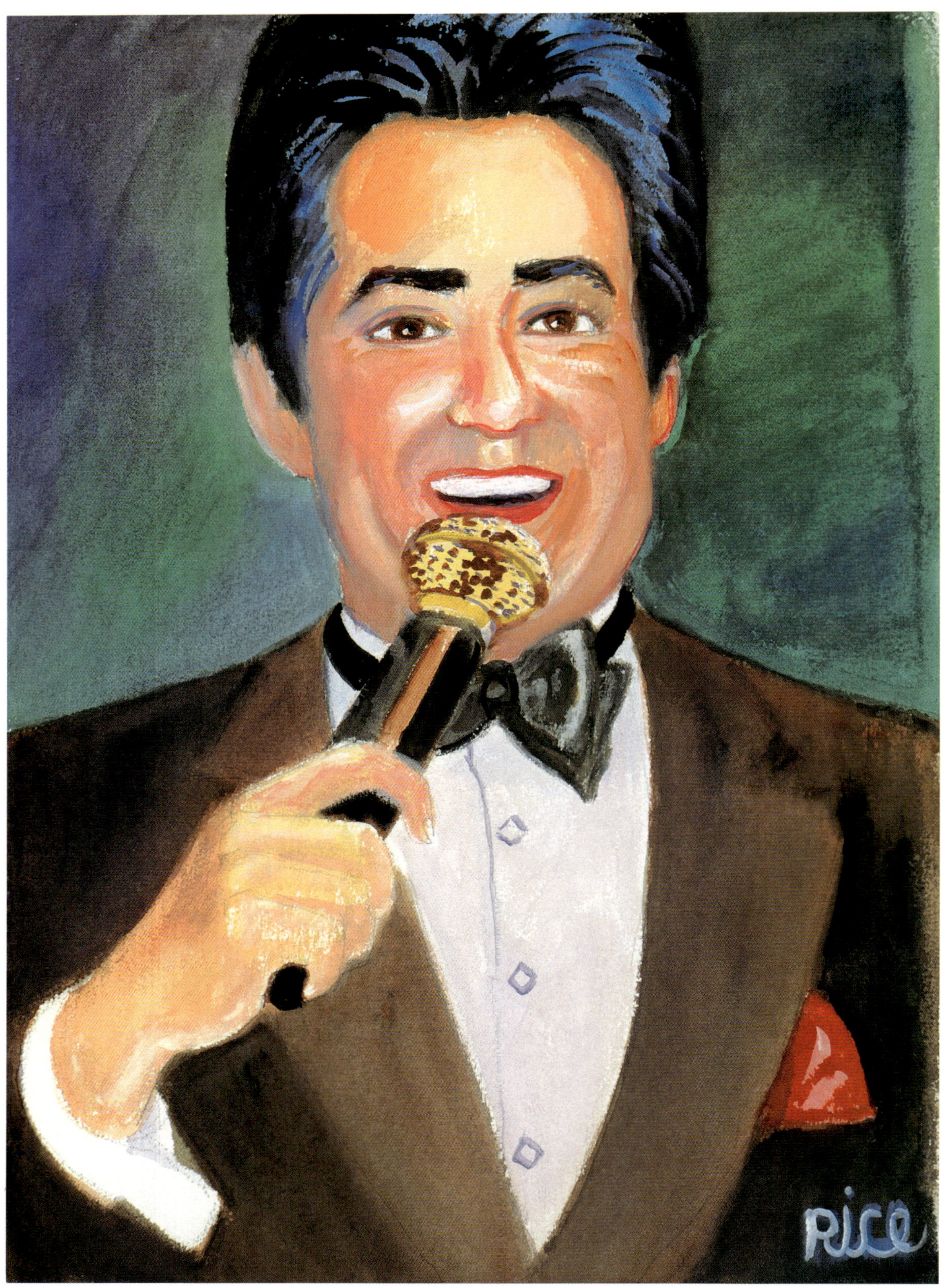

DANKE SHOEN, WAYNE

Singer Wayne Newton has become an icon as indelibly identified with Las Vegas as Liberace, the Rat Pack and Elvis—and he's the only one still perfoming. A part-Native American musical prodigy, Newton was working at the Fremont Hotel as a teenager in 1956. The cherubic lad became a national sensation when pop star Bobby Darin handed him "Danke Shoen," a too-much-like-"Mack-the-Knife" tune Darin passed on and which became Newton's breakthrough hit.

Chided for his boyish image, Newton remade himself as "the Midnight Idol" in the '70s by taking up karate and adding a Presley-esque wardrobe (Elvis was a close buddy). He assembled a legion of devoted fans known as "Wayne-iacs." As Merv Griffin once put it, "Las Vegas without Wayne Newton is like Disneyland without Mickey Mouse."

Today, he holds all Las Vegas records for number of weeks played and number of hours on stage. Wayne made a triumphant comeback in 1999 by signing an exclusive 10-year, $250 million deal to play 40 weeks a year at his own 920-seat theater at the Stardust. Wayne is so busy the only way I could catch up with him for a portrait was to visit his likeness at Madame Tussaud's Celebrity Encounter at the Venetian!

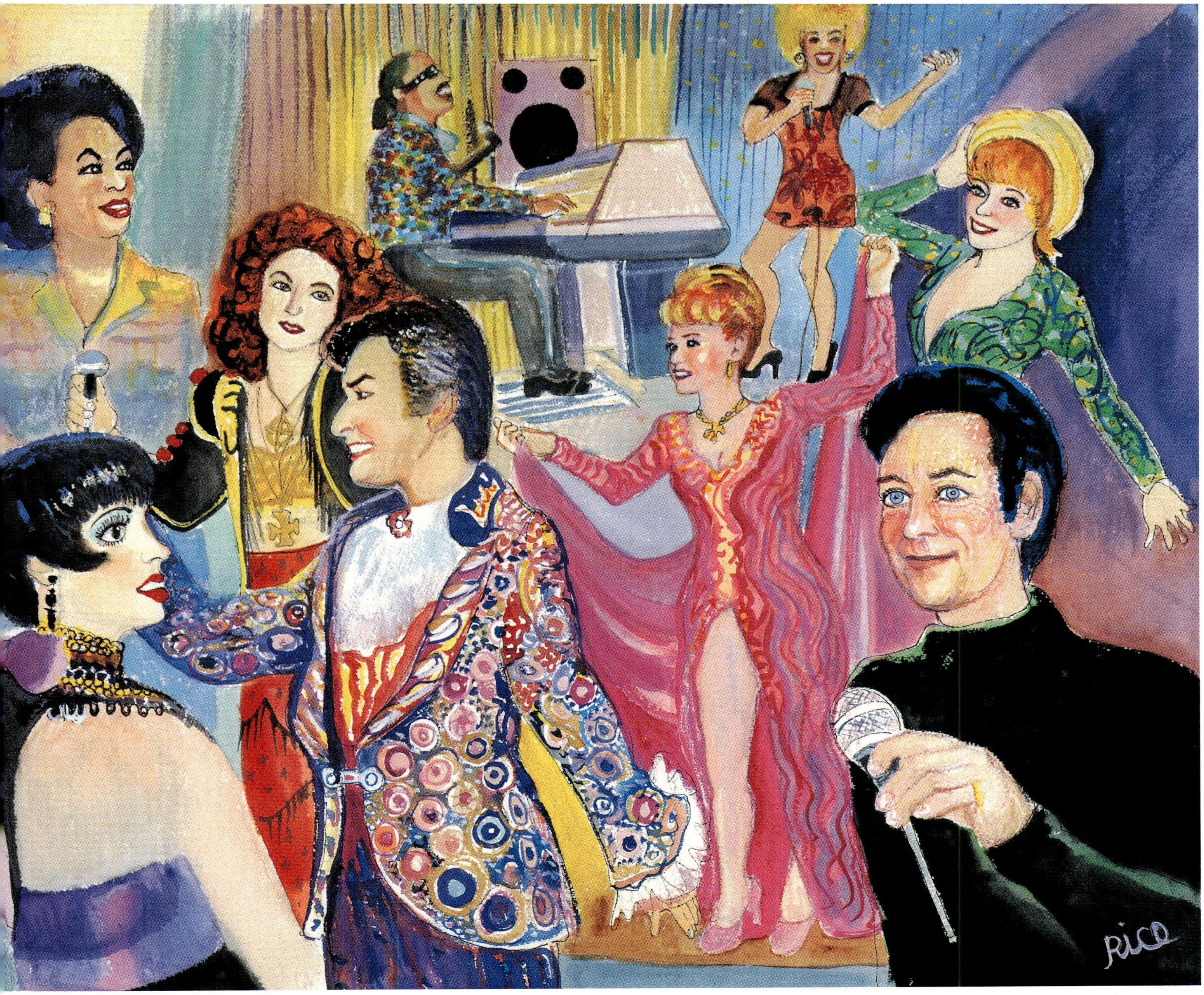

A STAR-STUDDED LINE-UP AT MADAME TUSSAUD'S

Want to see Oprah Winfrey, Shania Twain and Liza Minnelli? And how about Shirley MacLaine, Stevie Wonder and Tina Turner? And then there's Tom Jones, Debbie Reynolds and Liberace—hey, isn't that last one a little hard to pull off? Not at Madame Tussaud's Celebrity Encounter at the Venetian, where legends live forever—immortalized in an uncannily accurate wax likeness. The original London museum has been capturing famous personalities for more than 200 years, and the Las Vegas outpost (the first in the U.S.) features 100 stars of movies, music, TV and sports, from Muhammed Ali to Marilyn Monroe to Brad Pitt. Can't get tickets to Siegfried & Roy? Born too late to see the Rat Pack? Convinced that Elvis lives? At Madame Tussaud's, you can visit the best of the Las Vegas entertainers whenever you want.

HOUDINI'S MAGIC SHOP

A purveyor of magic tricks, gags and novelties, Houdini's Magic Shop at the Venetian is also a showplace where free magic shows entertain customers throughout the day. And if you purchase a magic trick, the Houdini Magicians will give you private lessons in a secret room—to protect the illusion, of course! Houdini's Magic Shop (one of eleven across the city) is the brainchild of Geno Munari, a prominent and respected professional in the magic community who also knows a thing or two about another tricky subject: gaming. He has provided technical assistance for popular Vegas-based motion pictures like "Rain Man" and "Indecent Proposal."

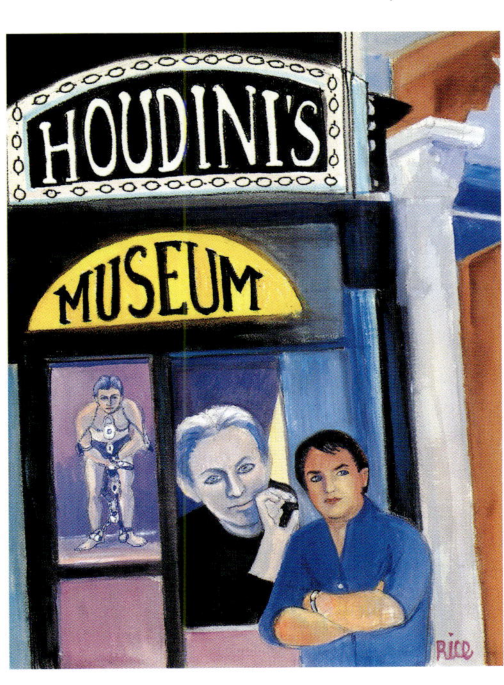

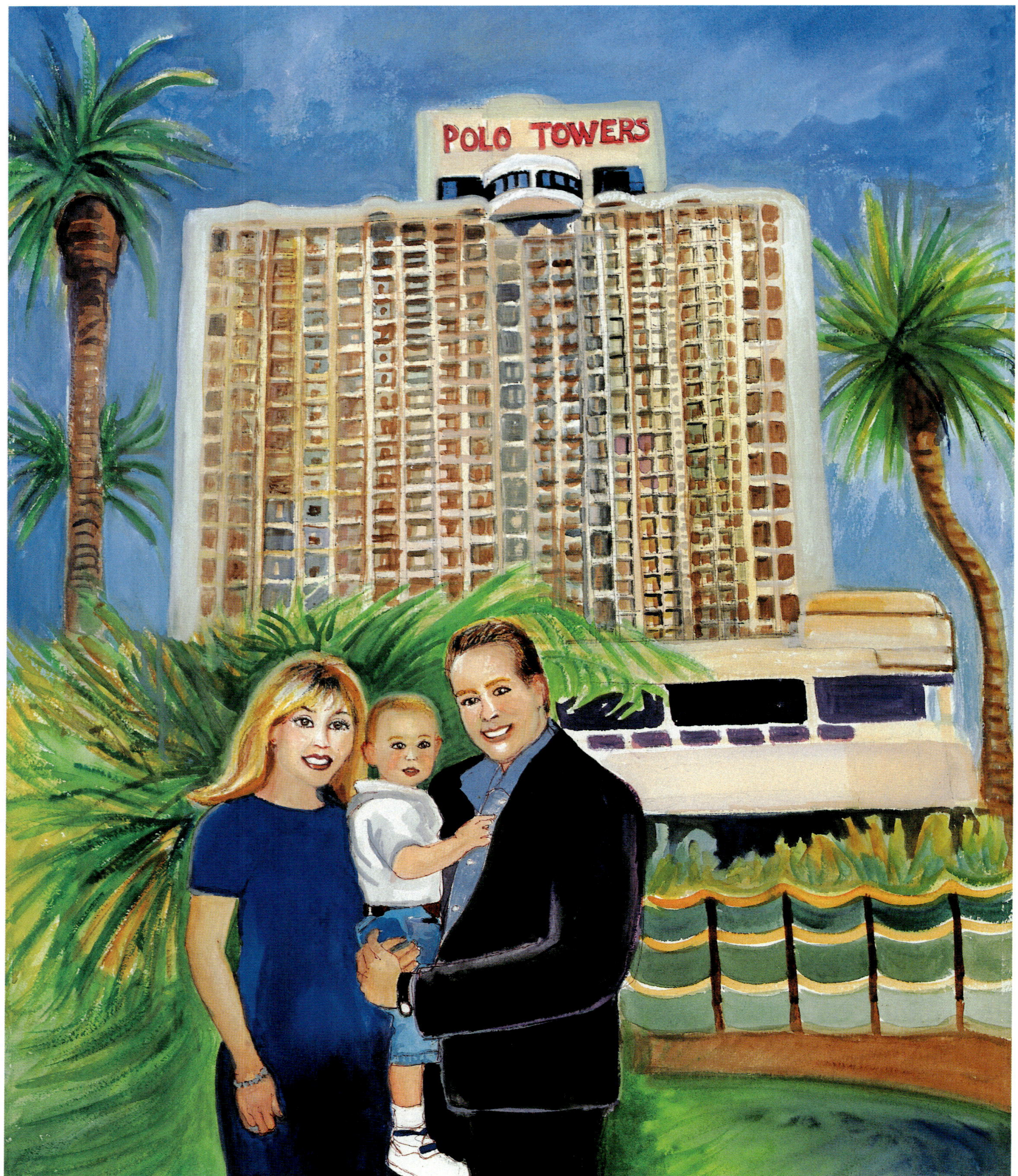

THE CLOOBECK FAMILY AT THE POLO TOWERS

It's all about family for second generation hotelier Stephen J. Cloobeck—with his wife Chantal, a former top print model and "Star Search" winner, and son Jacob (baby number two, Jaden, was on the way when I met them). In addition to maintaining the Polo Towers' enviable reputation as a world-class luxury time-share resort *sans* gaming, Stephen is also responsible for the beautification of the vibrant center median which runs the entire length of the Strip. Lavishly appointed with a variety of spectacular palms and lush foliage, this splendid divide is anything but "middle of the road."

SMITH & WOLLENSKY >

Artist-designer JoAnne Ruzzi enjoys lunch under a patio umbrella at Smith & Wollensky, yet another New York landmark adding Big Apple ambiance to the Strip. I was a sometime visitor to the original Manhattan steak house and enjoyed this one as well during my stays in Las Vegas.

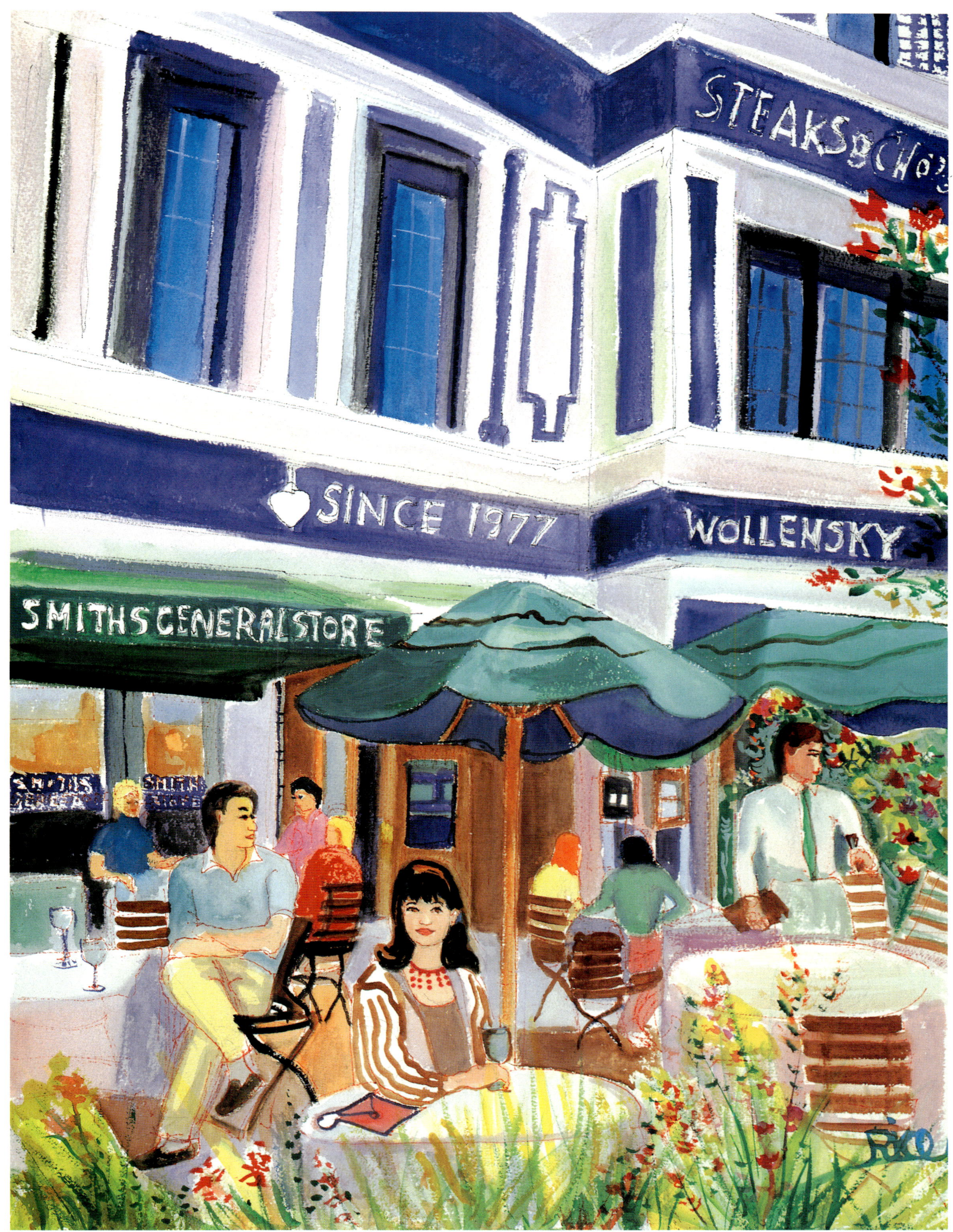
STEAKS
SINCE 1977
WOLLENSKY
SMITHS GENERAL STORE
Rico

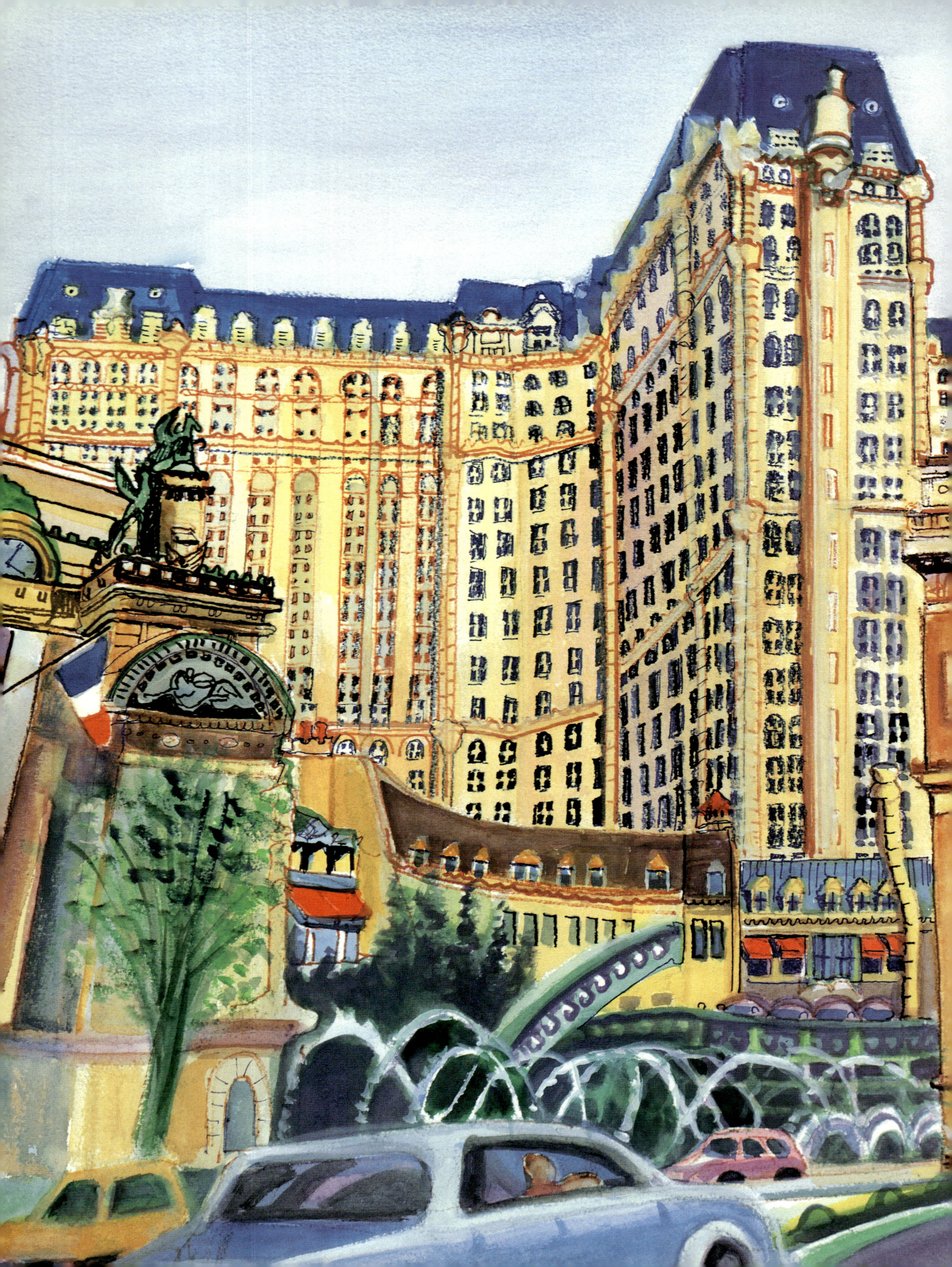

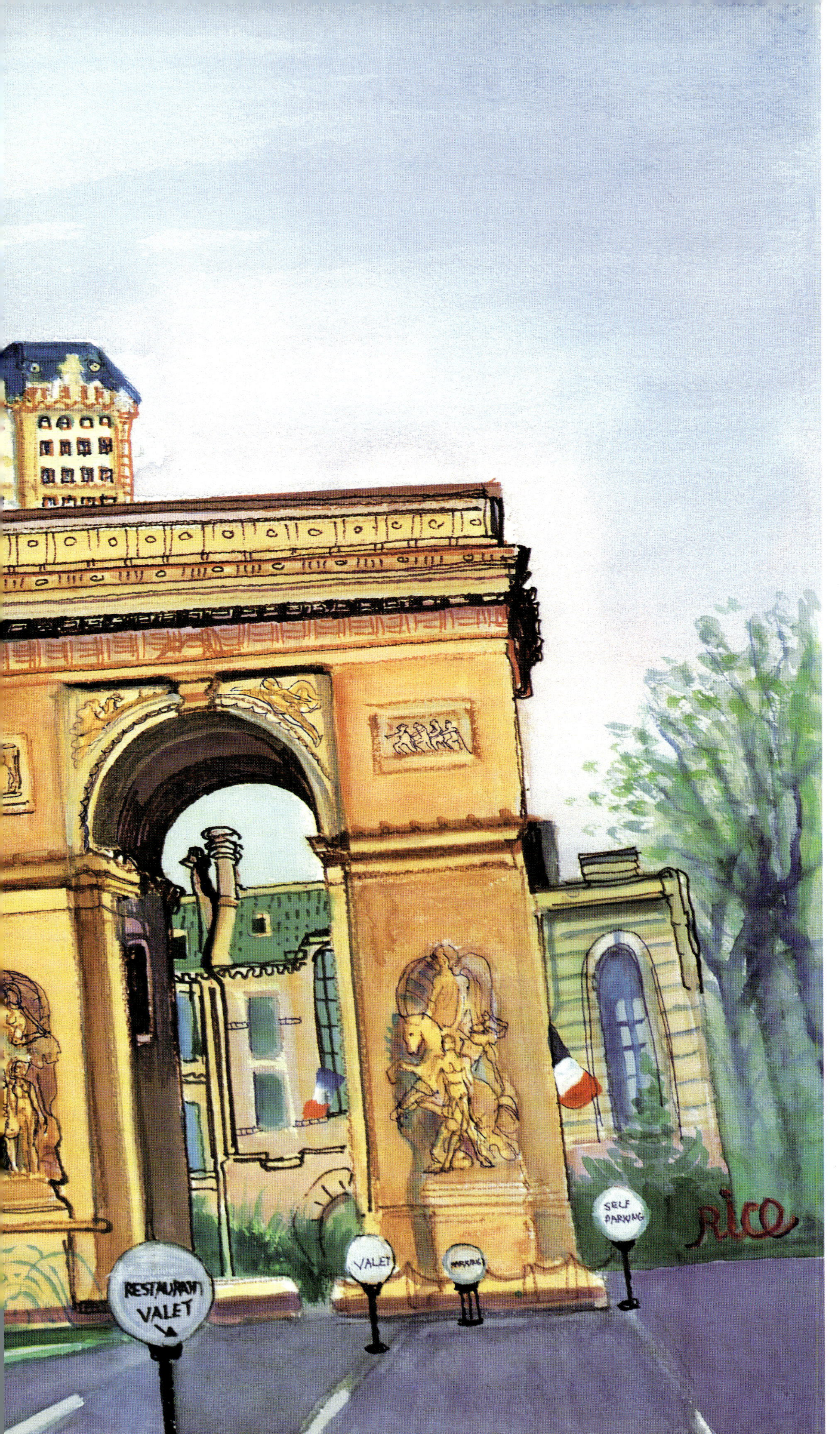

ENTERING L'ARC DE TRIOMPHE AT PARIS LAS VEGAS

Sacre bleu! The Park Place Entertainment Co.'s Paris Las Vegas, a 2,916-room showplace, brings Parisian ambiance to the Strip with a 34-story hotel in the style of the famous Hotel de Ville. It boasts impressive facsimiles of L'Arc de Triomphe and the Paris Opéra House, and also features replicas of the Louvre and the Eiffel Tower, and an assortment of gaming machines with French names like "Le Jacques Pot." Shop along the cobblestone streets of Le Boulevard District and then dine á la French style at La Rotisseirre des Artistes, Le Bar de Sport, Le Village Buffett, Le Cafe du Parc, Cafe Ille St. Louis or the Mon Ami Gabi, where you can people watch on the Strip as you eat.

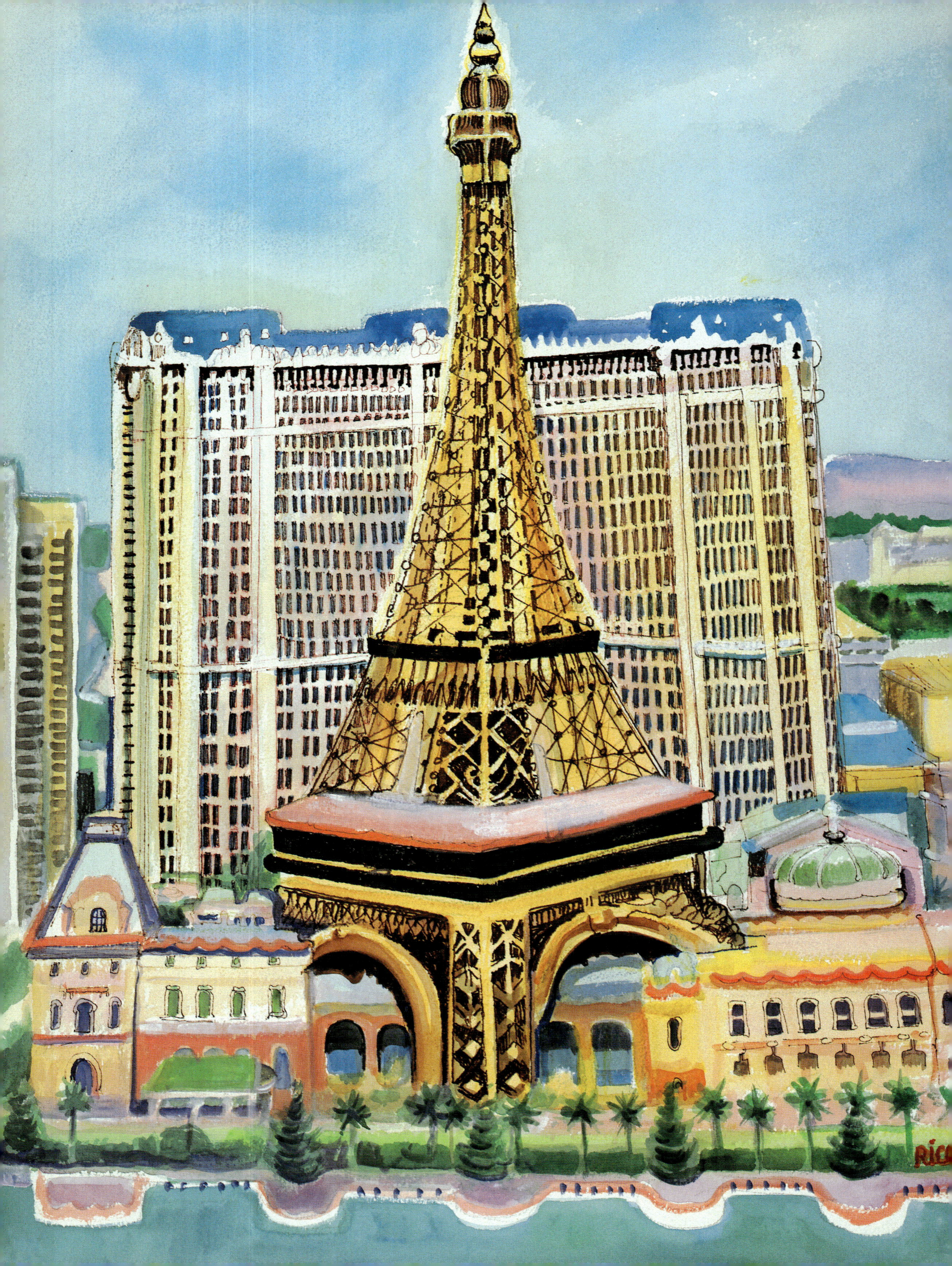

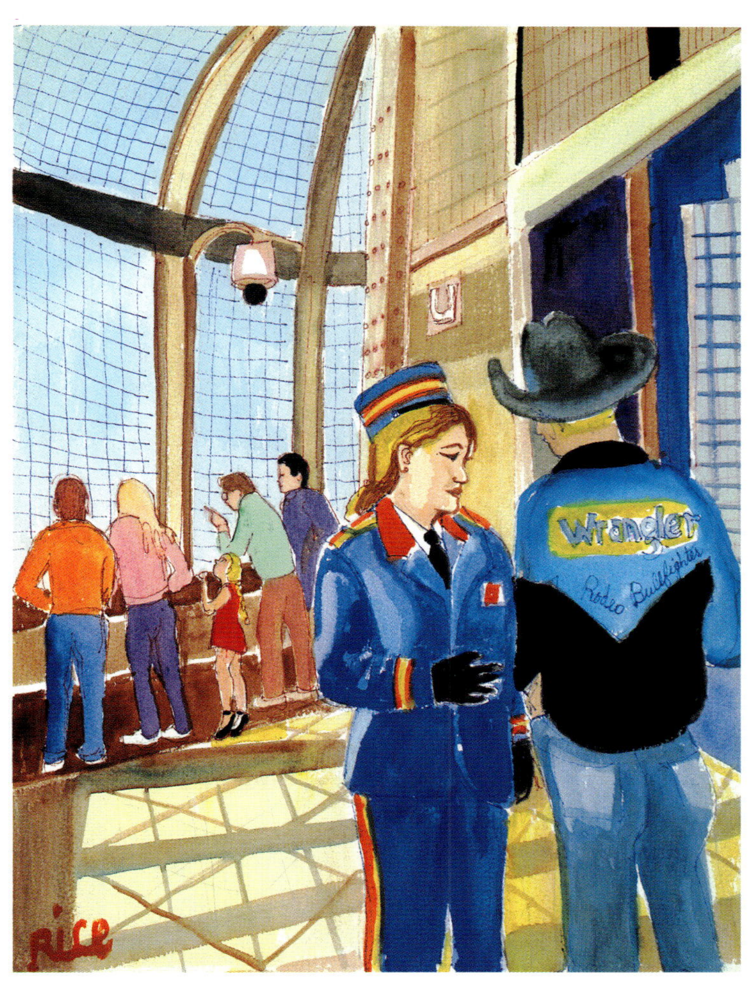

THE VIEW FROM THE EIFFEL TOWER OBSERVATORY

For me, it was an exhilarating but white-knuckled ascent—at 350 feet per minute—in the glass-walled elevator to the top of Paris Las Vegas' Eiffel Tower, and I didn't dare look down. The butterflies in my stomach fluttered away when we arrived at the observation deck, which offered telescopes and unobscured views for taking photographs. The spectacular panoramic view of the entire Strip was definitely worth the trip.

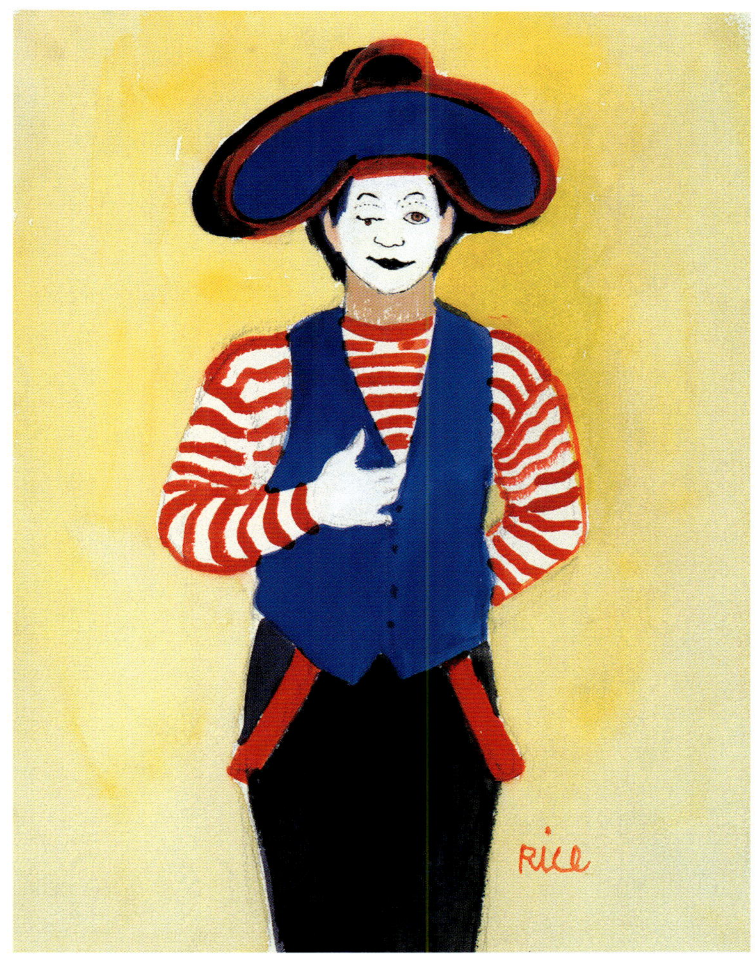

SPEECHLESS

I met a French mime with a lopsided smile in the lobby of Paris Las Vegas. Every employee has completed a two-day French class, but this fellow didn't need any words to communicate.

< THE EIFFEL TOWER AT PARIS LAS VEGAS

This half-scale replica of France's landmark Eiffel Tower is the centerpiece of Paris Las Vegas. The Tower has glass-enclosed elevators that rise 45 stories above street level and an 11th floor Nouveau French restaurant.

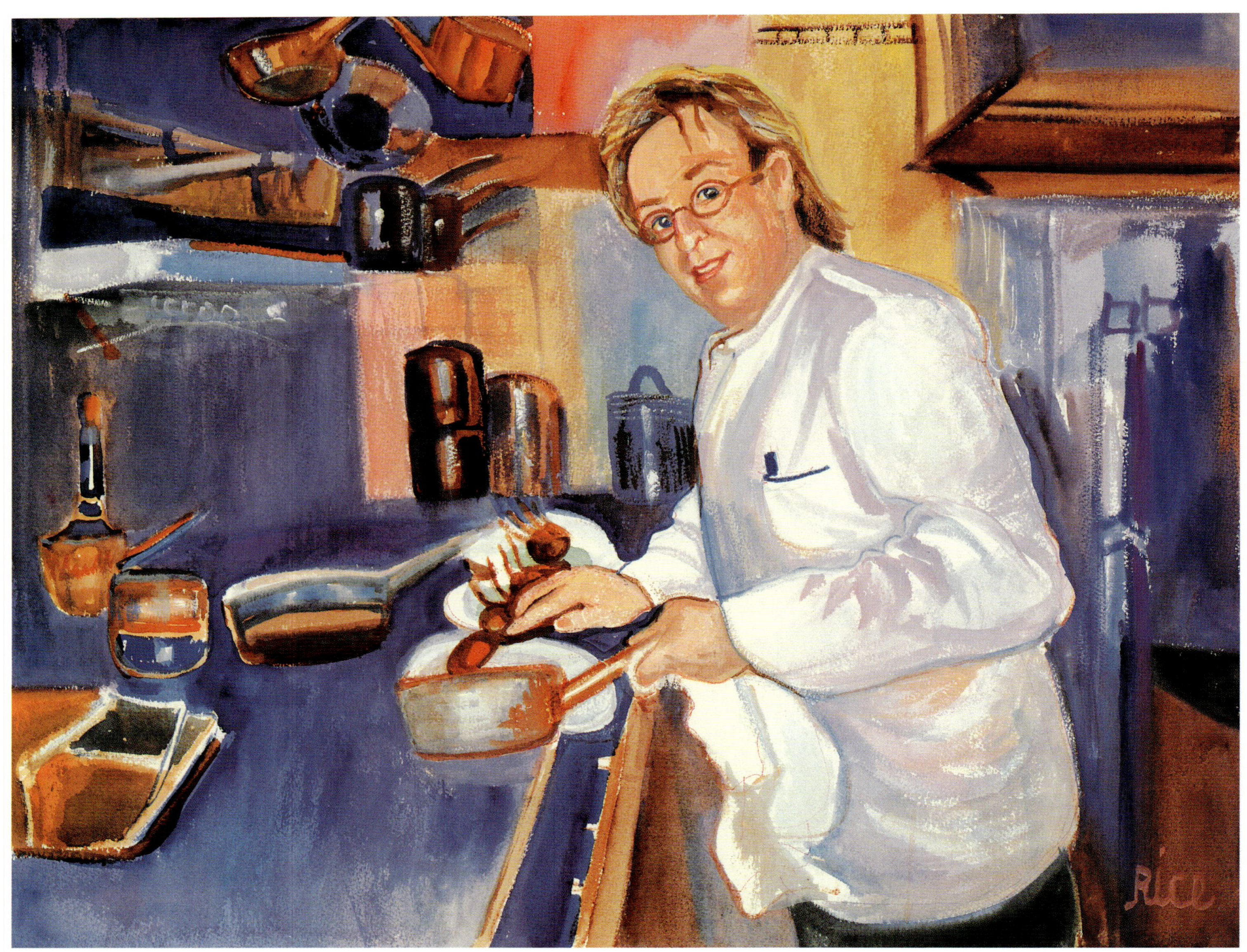

MASTER CHEF J. JOHO

Chef Joho presides in the kitchen of the Eiffel Tower Restaurant at the Paris Las Vegas, where he works his culinary magic some 11 stories above the Strip. His smiling face is one of the first to greet you because the elevator deposits you near the kitchen before you are led to your seat. The Eiffel Tower Restaurant is one of Las Vegas' emerging gourmet centers, known for an incredible menu of the finest French fare that's as remarkable as the view.

LE CAFE ILE ST. LOUIS >

You can sip espresso and munch on homemade French bread sandwiches any time of day at Paris Las Vegas' 24-hour Le Café Ile St. Louis, where the architecture—inspired by the Notre Dame Cathedral on France's original Ile St. Louis—is as engaging as the menu.

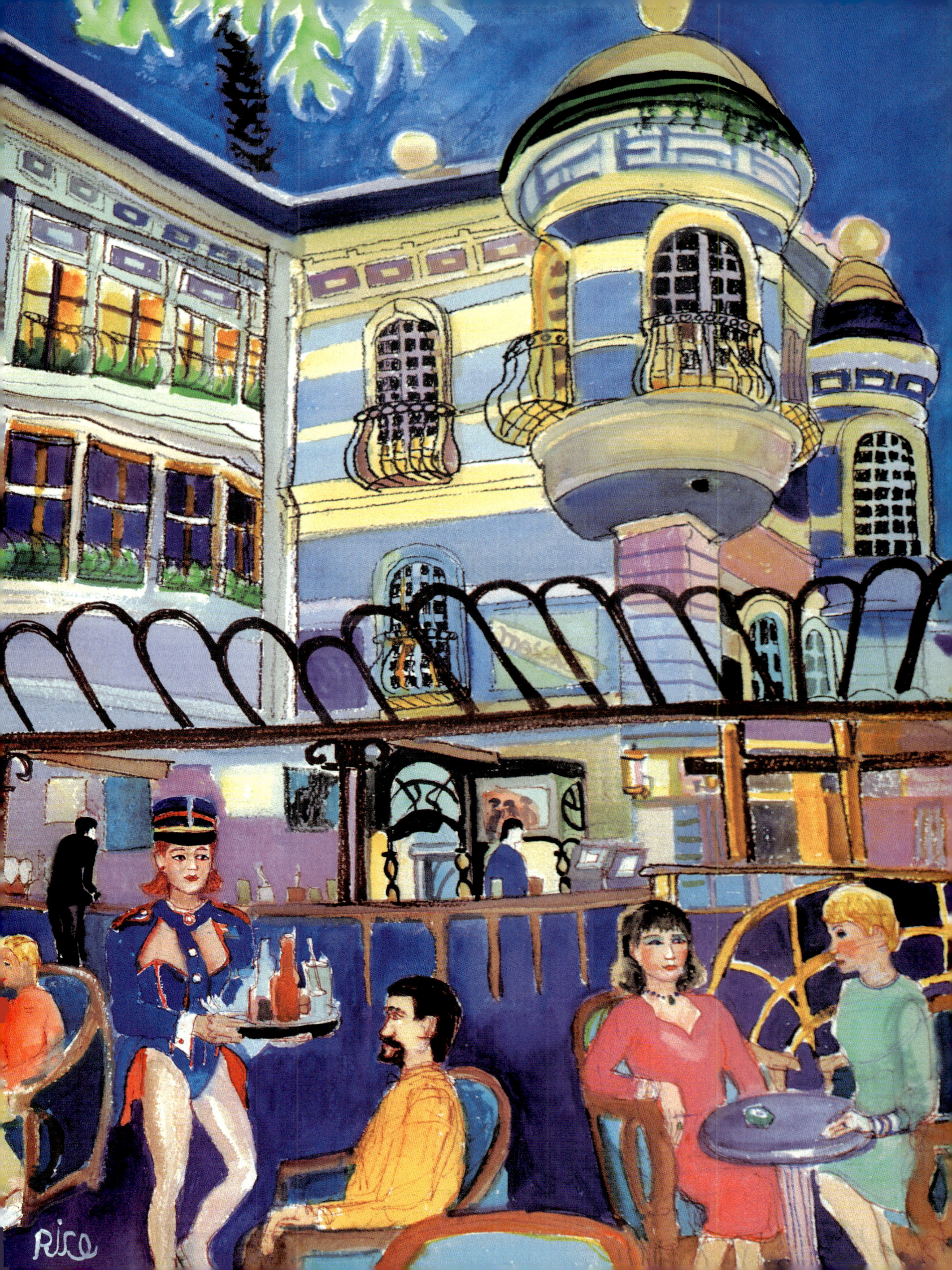
Rice

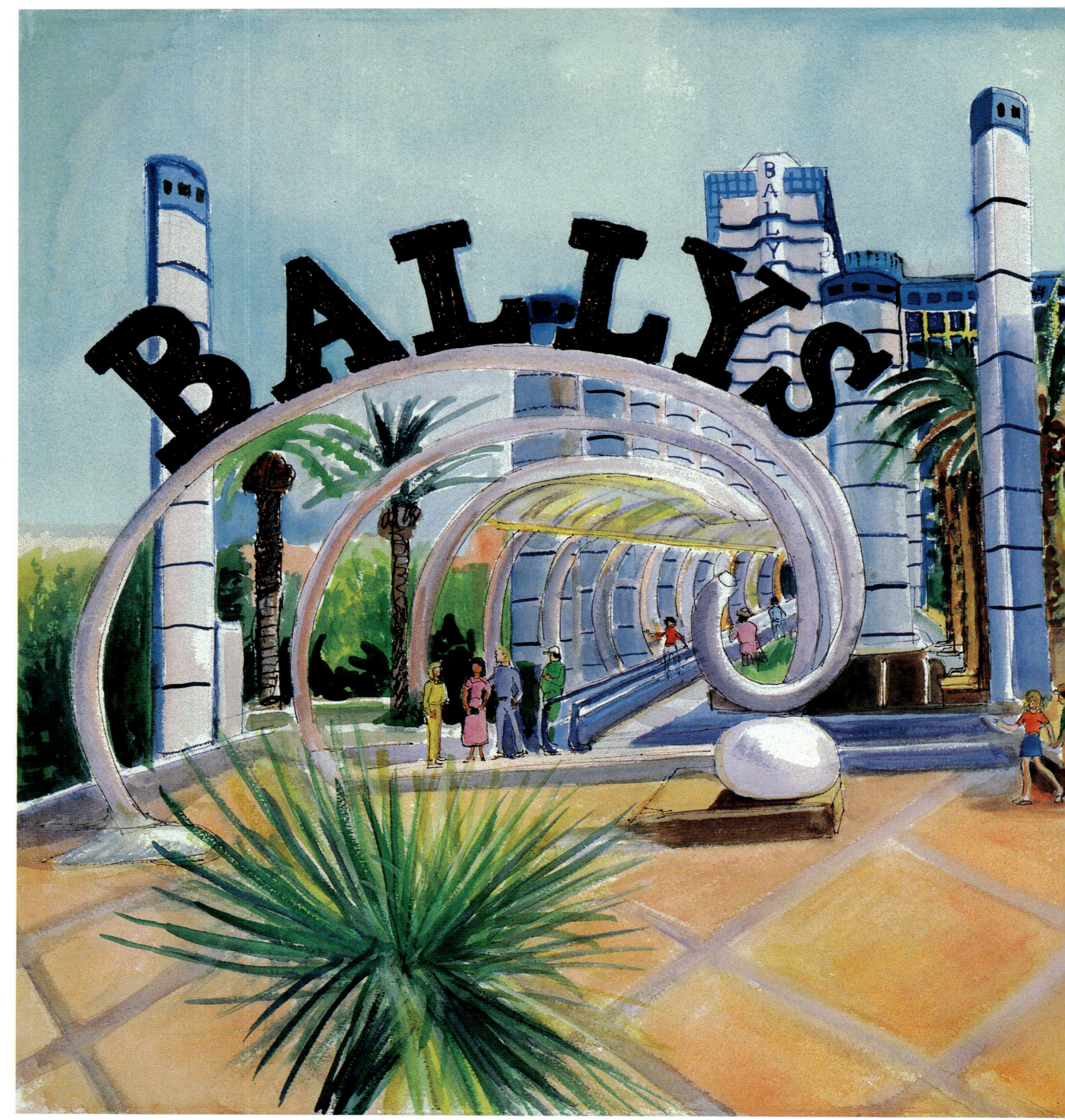

BALLY'S LAS VEGAS

I enjoyed the distinctive stylings of Bally's Plaza, the grand entryway into the hotel/casino which features four 200-foot-long people movers and dramatic light and sound displays. Bally's Las Vegas began as the original MGM Grand Hotel, the world's largest casino when it debuted in 1973. It is now operated by Park Place Entertainment, the biggest gaming corporation in the world. Filled with an array of posh amenities, restaurants, showrooms and gaming options, Bally's is perhaps best known for oddsmaking and is often consulted by the media before top championship matches like the Superbowl, the World Series and even the Academy Awards®.

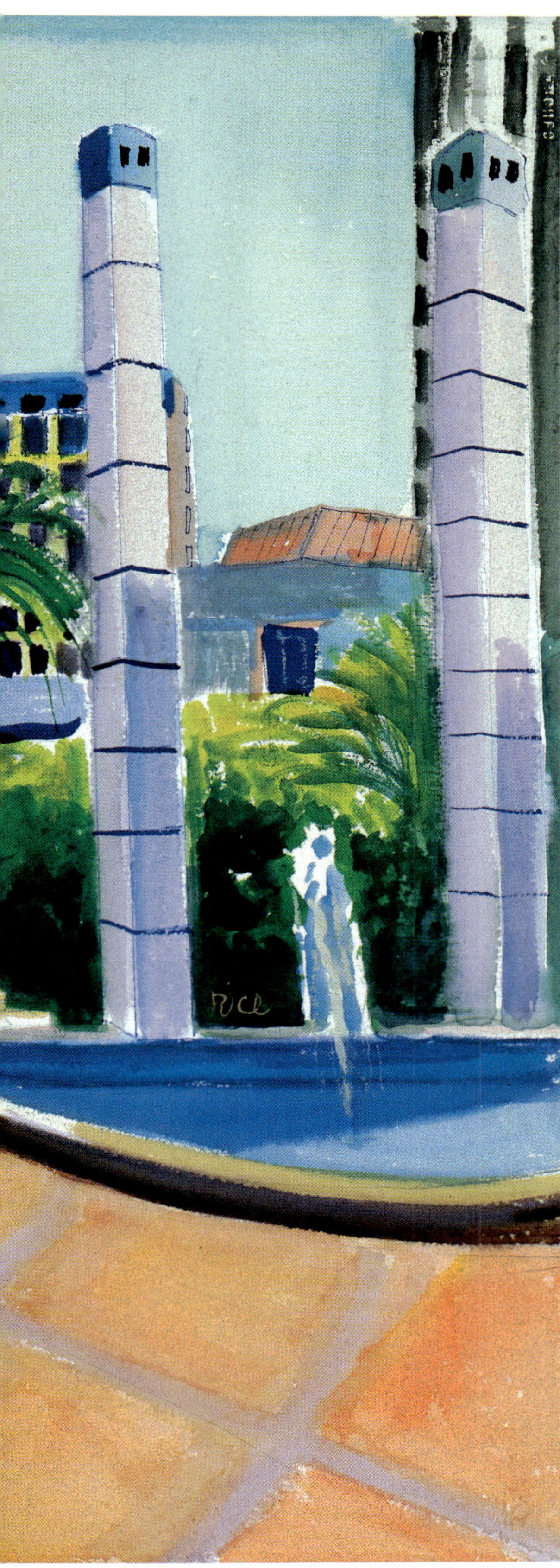

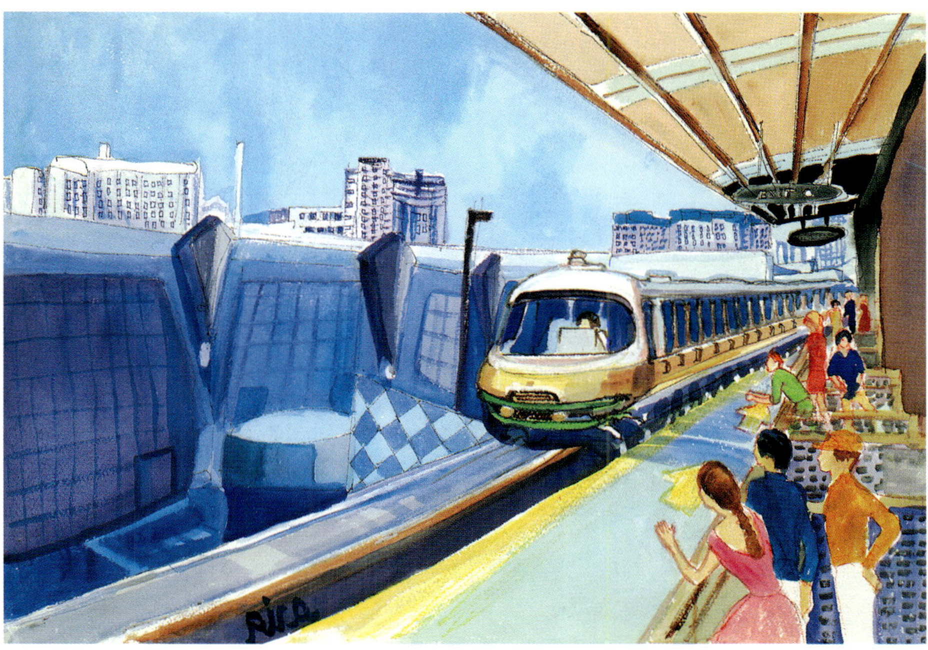

THE MONORAIL

Futuristic people-movers like this sleek tram on the Strip have made it easier to take in all of the Vegas sights between Bally's and the MGM Grand—easier on the feet and, thanks to some scenic views, easier on the eyes.

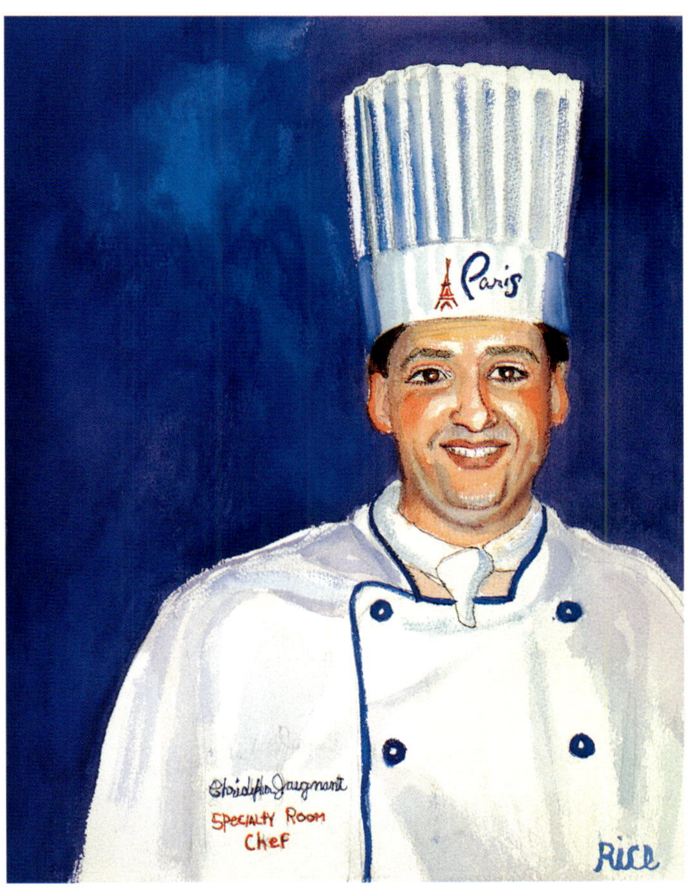

SERVICE WITH A SMILE

With a sparkling personality and a smile to match, Christopher Jaignant, the talented Specialty Room Chef at Paris Las Vegas, has obviously found a calling that keeps him happy.

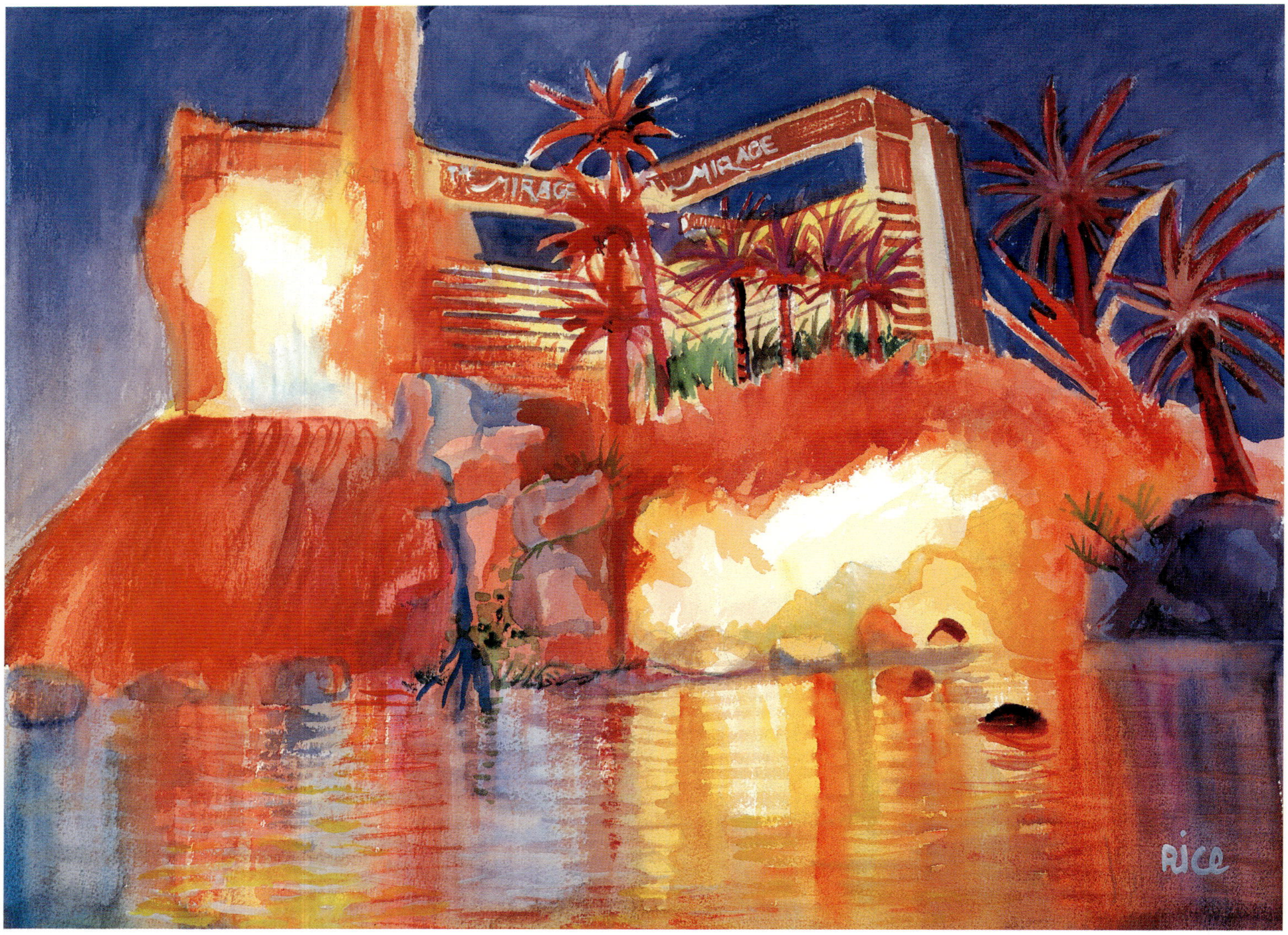

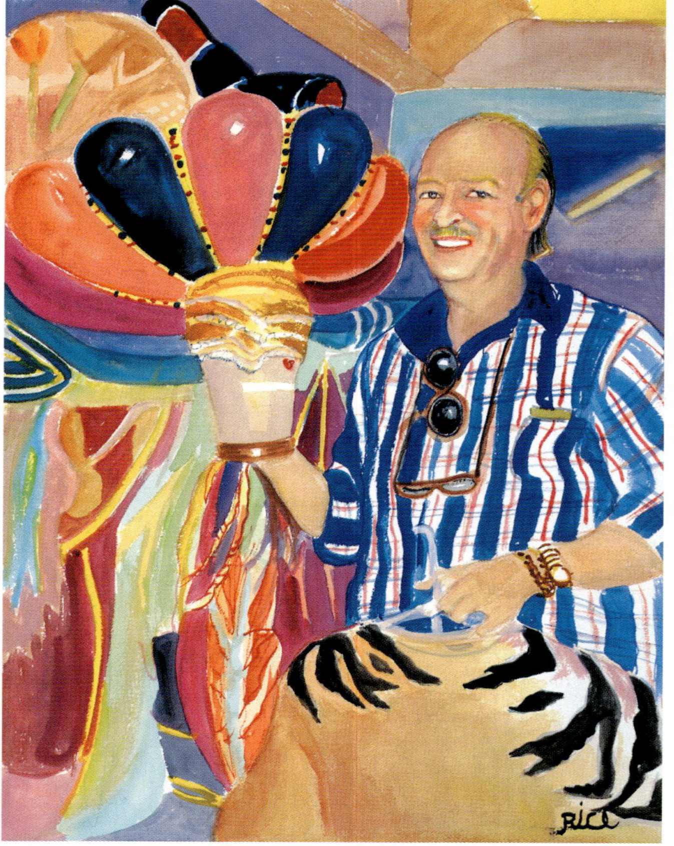

HAVING A BLAST AT THE MIRAGE VOLCANO

Jimmy Buffett famously sang about not knowing where he "was gonna go when the volcano blows," but in Las Vegas, the answer is simple: to the Strip in front of the Mirage Hotel and Casino. Here the famous 54-foot-tall volcano erupts for three minutes every half-hour, just feet away from the many sidewalk spectators who flock to watch the spectacle. Steam shoots upward, flames lick the air, water bubbles and lava oozes forth from the man-made summit. The Mirage volcano pioneered the first free "public show" on the Strip and set the stage for more attractions to follow.

MAX HAGER

You can't buy the fashions designed by Max Hager off the rack, but he's the costumer to go to whenever you need a truly show-stopping ensemble for your latest stage extravaganza. Max has been the wardrobe supervisor and costume designer for the supreme showmen Siegfried and Roy since 1991. He's also been responsible for costume design, construction and/or supervision on a host of acclaimed Broadway and touring stage productions, including "La Cage Aux Folles," "Cats," "Phantom of the Opera," Disneyworld's "Beauty and the Beast" show and the Ringling Bros. Barnum & Bailey Circus.

LOOKING REGAL AT THE MIRAGE >

This beautiful snow-white big cat posed gracefully at one of The Mirage's most popular attractions, Siegfried & Roy's Royal White Tiger Habitat, where visitors can safely observe the magical duo's rare Siberian tigers—now extinct in the wild—from behind slanted glass walls.

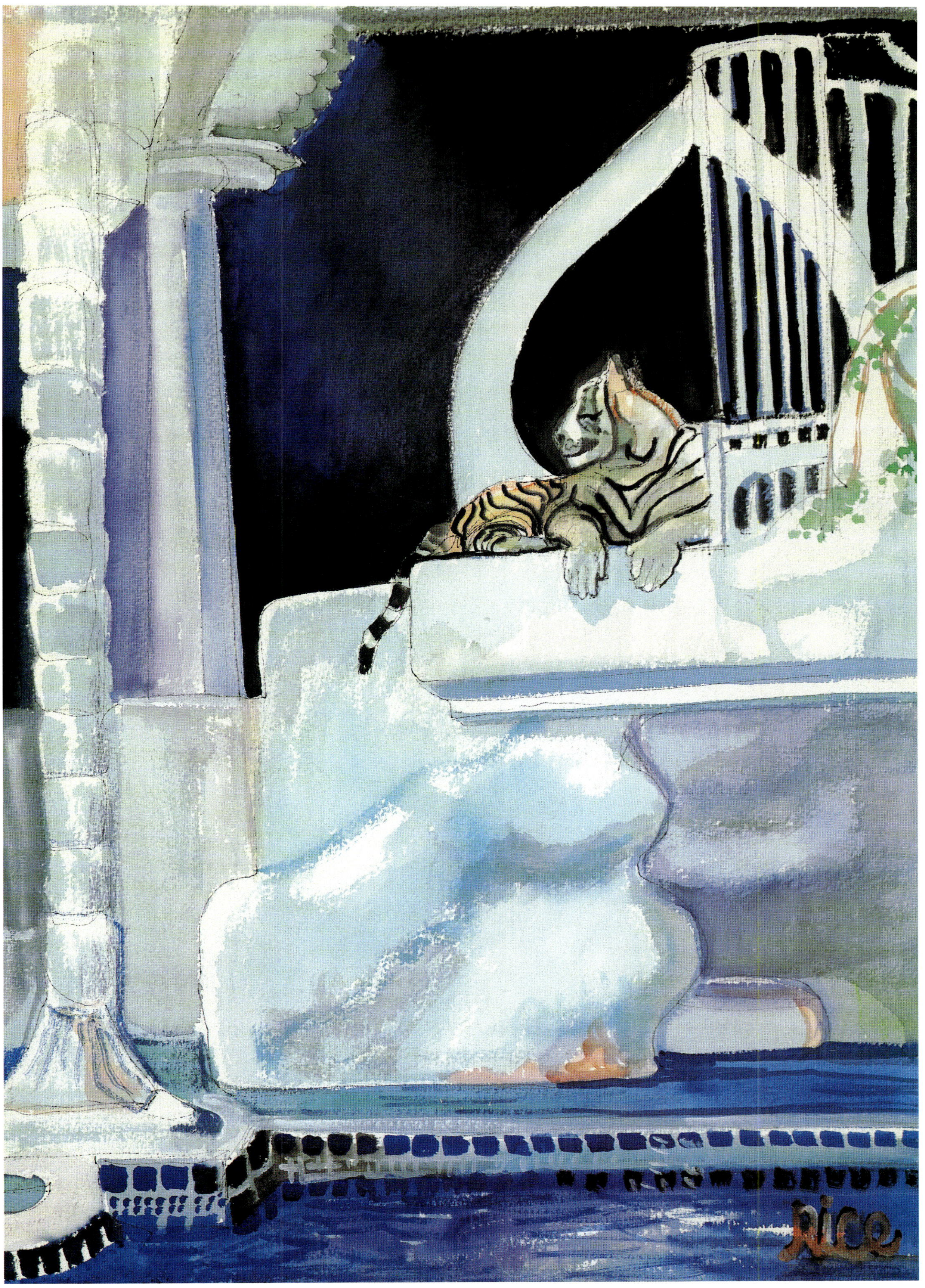
Rice

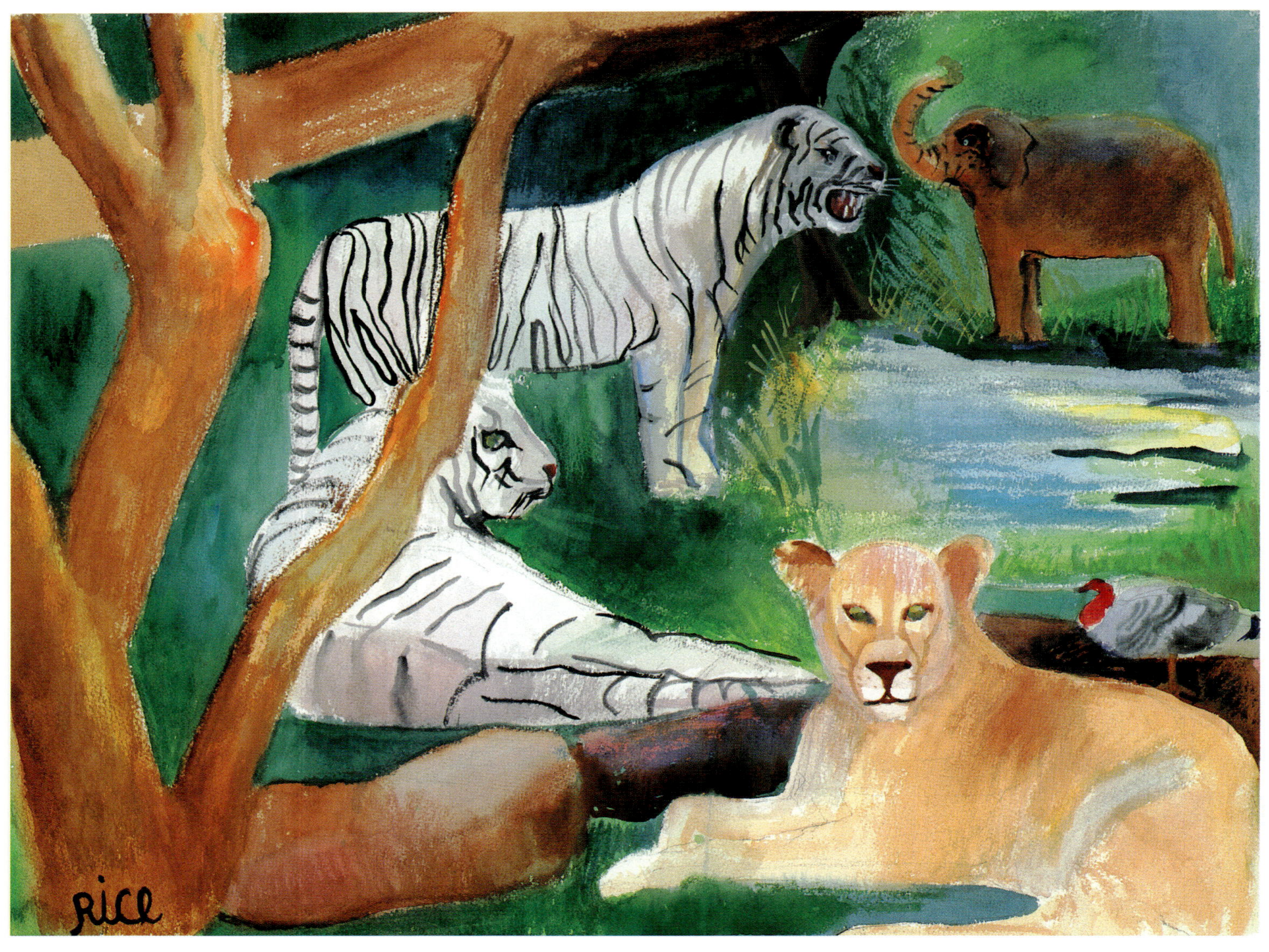

THE SECRET GARDEN

Siegfried & Roy's glorious big cats have disappeared on stage from time to time, but the magical duo is working on a more difficult feat: keeping the endangered animals from disappearing from the planet. Striving to promote conservation and preservation, they created the Secret Garden at the Mirage as a lush sanctuary for their rare feline friends—snow white tigers and striped white tigers, snow leopards, and white lions.

SIEGFRIED & ROY, KINGS OF THE JUNGLE >

The reigning kings of the increasingly crowded jungle of the Las Vegas entertainment scene are the phenomenally popular magical duo, Siegfried Fishbacker and Roy Uwe Ludwig Horn—better known as Siegfried & Roy. For more than a decade the partners have headlined at the Mirage, packing in crowds—about 18,000 people per week—into their own theater to view their breathtaking, fast-paced show. The German-born magicians met and formed their act as teenagers on a cruise ship in 1957 and got their big break performing for Monaco's Prince Rainier and Princess Grace. After wowing audiences at the Lido in Paris, Siegfried & Roy embarked for the Tropicana in Las Vegas in 1967, the beginning of a fateful pairing of nonpareil performers and locale. Over the years they have become a bona fide Las Vegas institution, bringing large-scale theatricality, dramatic flourish, feline grace and an inimitable Sin City grandeur to the world of illusion. It was while watching these two handsome performers and their incredible feats of magic that I was first inspired to paint the colorful city of Las Vegas. Today Siegfried & Roy—who are dedicated to the preservation of the exotic big cats that have become their signature—can proudly take their place in the amazing pantheon of entertainers who have contributed to the success, mystique and evolution of the Las Vegas entertainment scene. They have signed a lifetime contract to perform only at the Mirage for the remainder of their career.

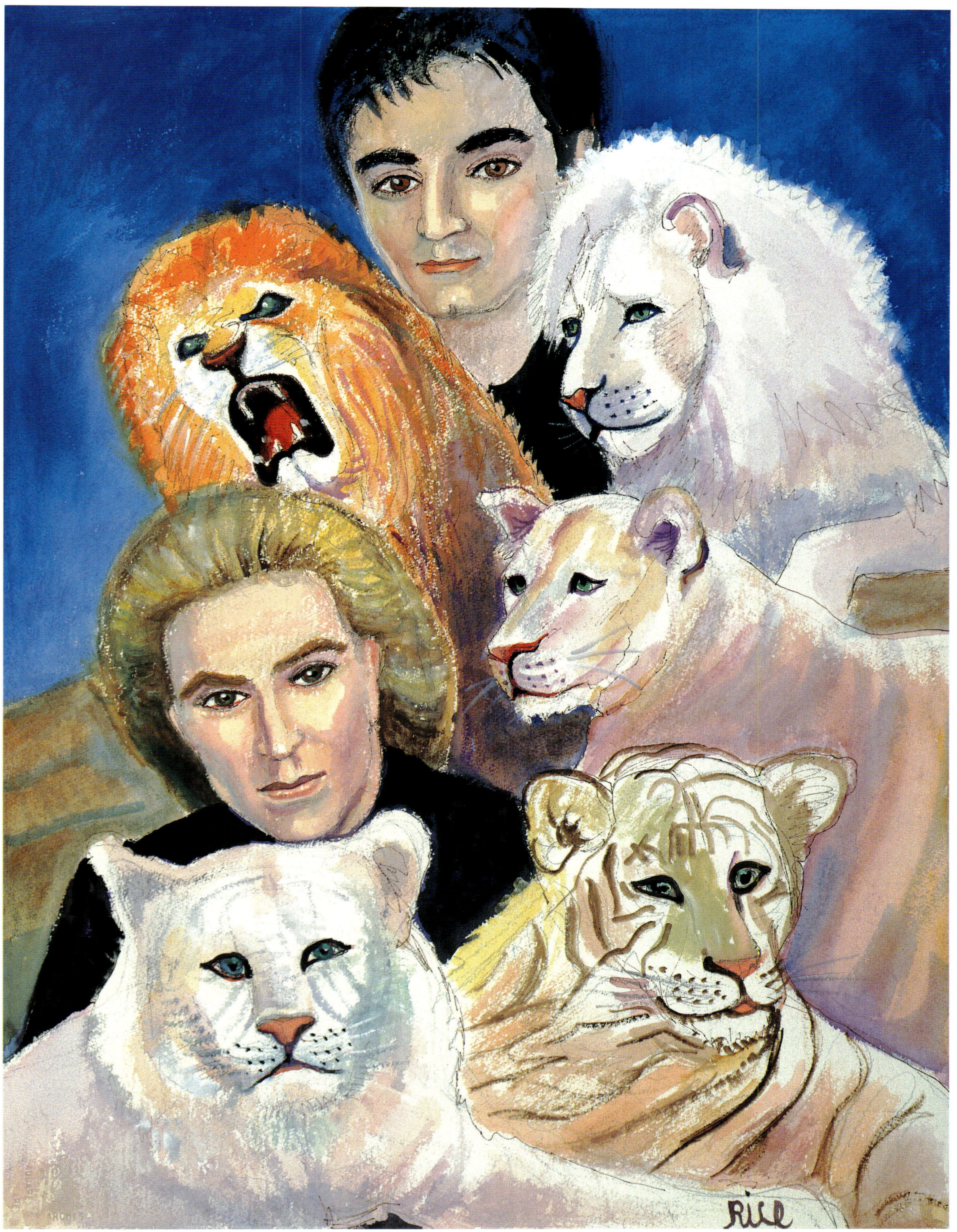
Rice

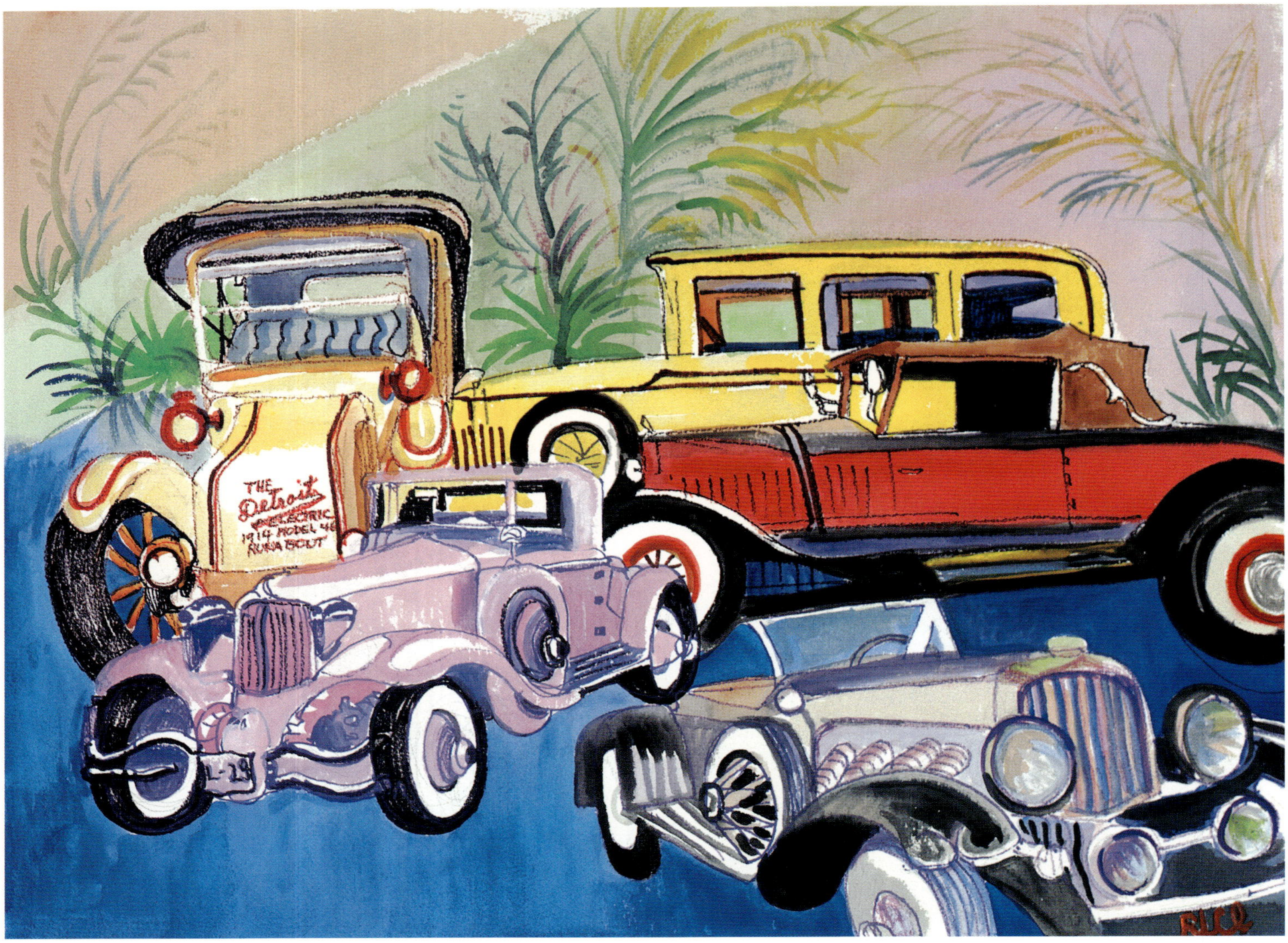

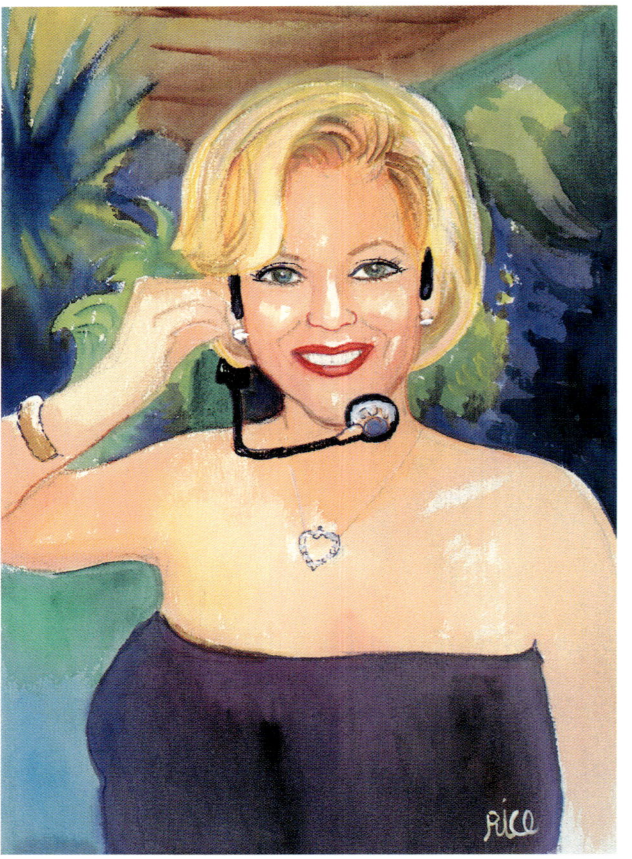

IMPRESSIVE AUTOS AT THE IMPERIAL PALACE

Some of the most rare and exotic automobiles in history are on display in the Imperial Palace Auto Collection. The exhibit features 200 vehicles out of a rotating collection of about 750, including the largest Deusenberg collection in the world. Among the more infamous cars in the collection are Adolph Hitler's armored, mine-proofed 1932 Mercedes and a 1962 Lincoln with bulletproof bubbletop used by President John F. Kennedy. Other autos in the collection include vehicles previously owned by Howard Hughes, Liberace, Elvis Presley, Al Capone and W.C. Fields.

CONNIE ROSS GOES "BACKSTAGE LIVE"

The lovely Connie Ross readies herself for another two-hour broadcast of the popular and award-winning "Backstage Live" series at the Imperial Palace, which she co-hosts with former newsman Gary Campbell. Connie moved to Las Vegas in 1992 as the advertising and public relations director for the Imperial Palace. The show is a Vegas-based entertainment-themed talk show that reaches 20 million cable subscribers and radio listeners nationwide. They broadcast the show live in front of a studio audience at the Imperial Palace, interviewing a roster of guests ranging from local live bands to showroom staples to well-known celebrities like Charlton Heston, Debbie Reynolds and Louie Anderson.

THE MAN OF MANY VOICES: DANNY GANS >

Danny Gans posed for me outside his dressing room one night before his performance. Everybody loves Danny and I know why. His voice can range an octave up or down in a split second and on stage he can be Neil Diamond—no, wait—Rodney Dangerfield—that is—Michael Bolton—Garth Brooks—John Travolta—wow, Nat "King" Cole and Natalie Cole dueting, and even more stars ranging from George Burns to Eric Clapton to Sarah Vaughn to Harry Connick, Jr. to entire pop muscial acts. It's showmanship at its best! A versatile actor, singer, dancer and comedian, it's no wonder he was voted Best Las Vegas Performer and has his own theater at the Mirage. The "real" Danny Gans is most of all a very warm, humorous person. Of all the stars in his repertoire, Danny Gans was my favorite.

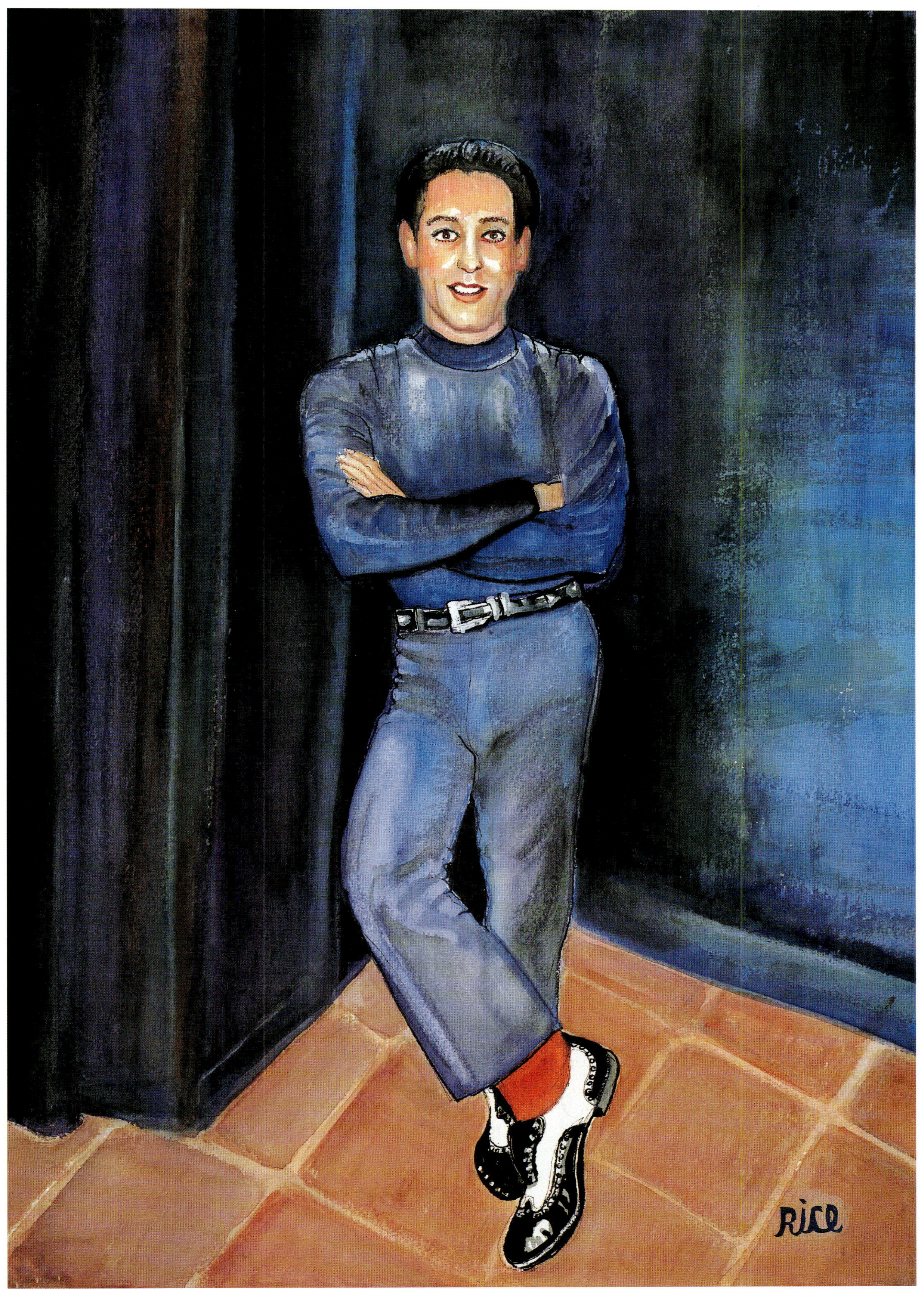
Rice

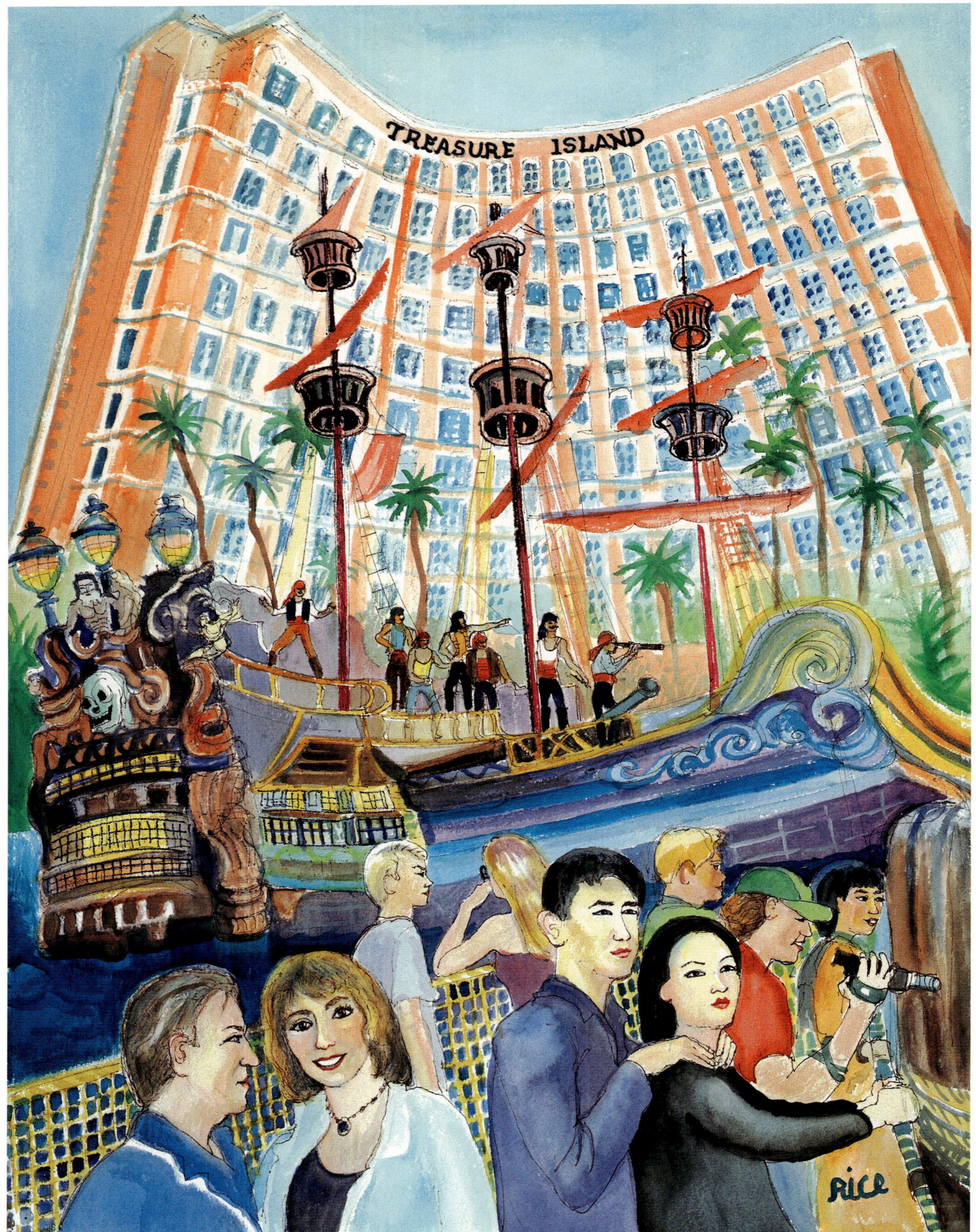

THE BATTLE LINES ARE DRAWN

Anticipation builds outside Buccaneer Bay at the Treasure Island Hotel and Casino, where a crowd gathers to watch the exciting battle between the marauding pirates of the Hispañola and the British Navy of the HMS Britannia. Cannons fire, smoke billows and splashy pyrotechnics dazzle the onlookers as all sorts of swashbuckling derring-do ensues.

It's an old-fashioned Errol Flynn movie come to life on the Strip, with modern "Die Hard"-style explosions that culminate with the total sinking of the Britannia—and best of all, the free show happens all over again every 90 minutes.

ROUNDING THE BEND FOR THE BATTLE >

Treasure Island's hidden treasure is its collection of terrific restaurants, including the Buccaneer Bay Club, the Plank, Madame Ching's, the Black Spot Grill and especially Francesco's, where I enjoyed some of the best seafood I've ever tasted.

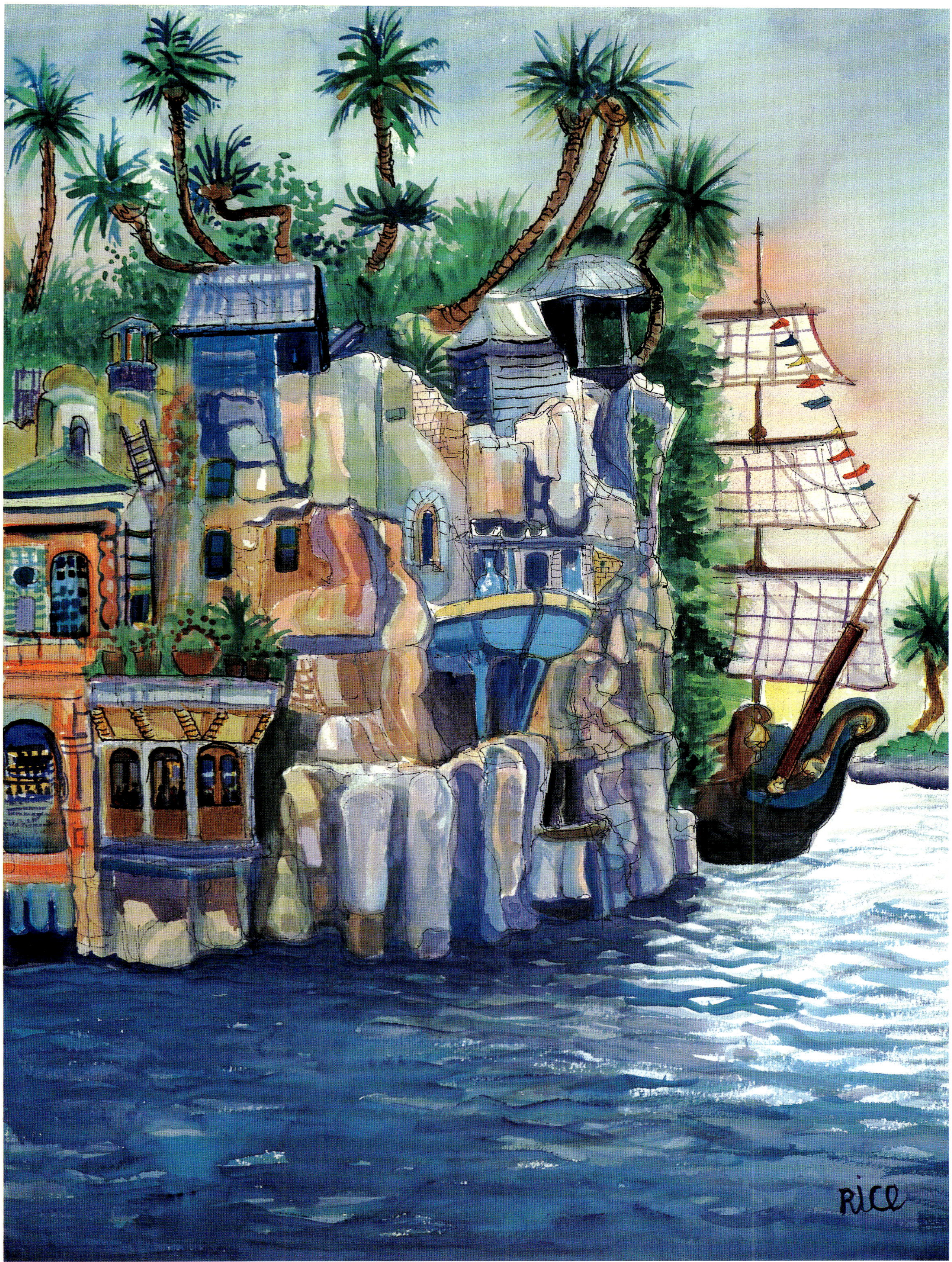
RICE

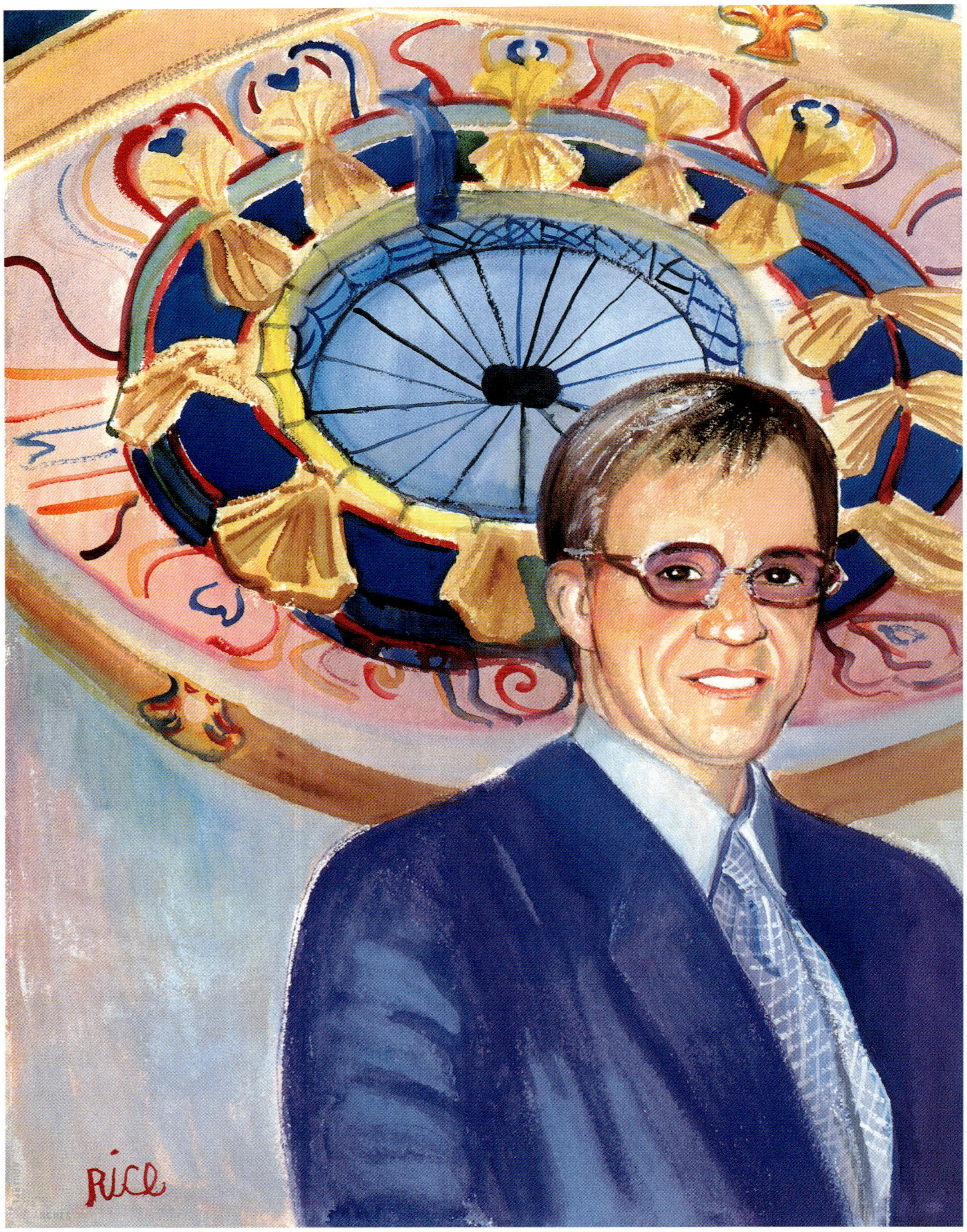

JAY BERNSTEIN AT THE TROPICANA

One of the most successful manager-producers in Hollywood, Jay Bernstein is known as a genuine "Starmaker" who helped build the careers of icons like Farrah Fawcett, Suzanne Somers, Drew Barrymore, Sharon Stone, Pamela Anderson, Linda Evans and Mary Hart—and those are just the blondes! He also managed several superstars in their Las Vegas gigs—including Sammy Davis, Jr., Aretha Franklin, Tom Jones, Diana Ross and Dionne Warwick—and he claims he left most of his commissions at the blackjack tables. I usually run into Jay in Beverly Hills, but this time he was at the Tropicana to serve as a judge in the famed Miss Hawaiian Tropic competition. If anyone can be the judge of beauty and talent, it would have to be Jay.

OOH LA LA

These curvaceous cuties hail from the Folies Bergère, the longest-running show in all of Las Vegas. I've seen the original show in Paris and this impressive production at the Tropicana's Tiffany Theater captures the extravaganza's magic, with tireless and talented dancers, wacky comics and nubile, semi-nude showgirls.

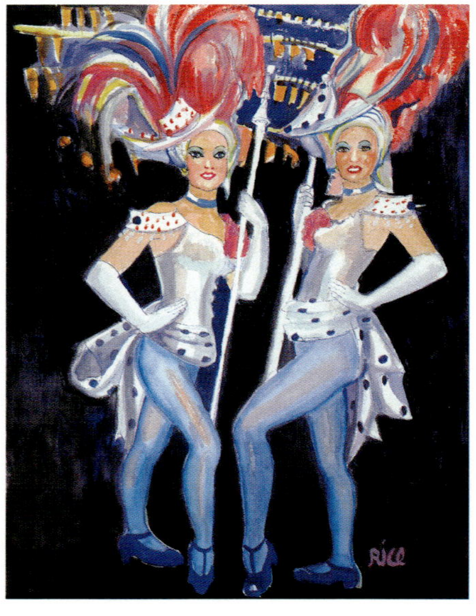

VIVA LAS VEGAS! >

It probably goes without saying, but Elvis lives! Especially here, the karate-chopping, scarf-tossing, cape-wearing King's favorite kingdom, from his late-era comeback at the International hotel through his "death" in 1977. At the top of the heap of the myriad Elvis impersonators that inhabit modern Vegas is my friend Jesse Garon (named after Elvis Aron Presley's stillborn twin brother), who struck a pose for me in front of the Tropicana Hotel's appropriately themed slot machines. Jesse, who hails from Texas rather than Memphis and assumes the sleeker, sexier style of Presley in the 50s and 60s, is a popular performer—especially at weddings where King-wannabes finally slip the ring on the finger of their aspiring Priscillas.

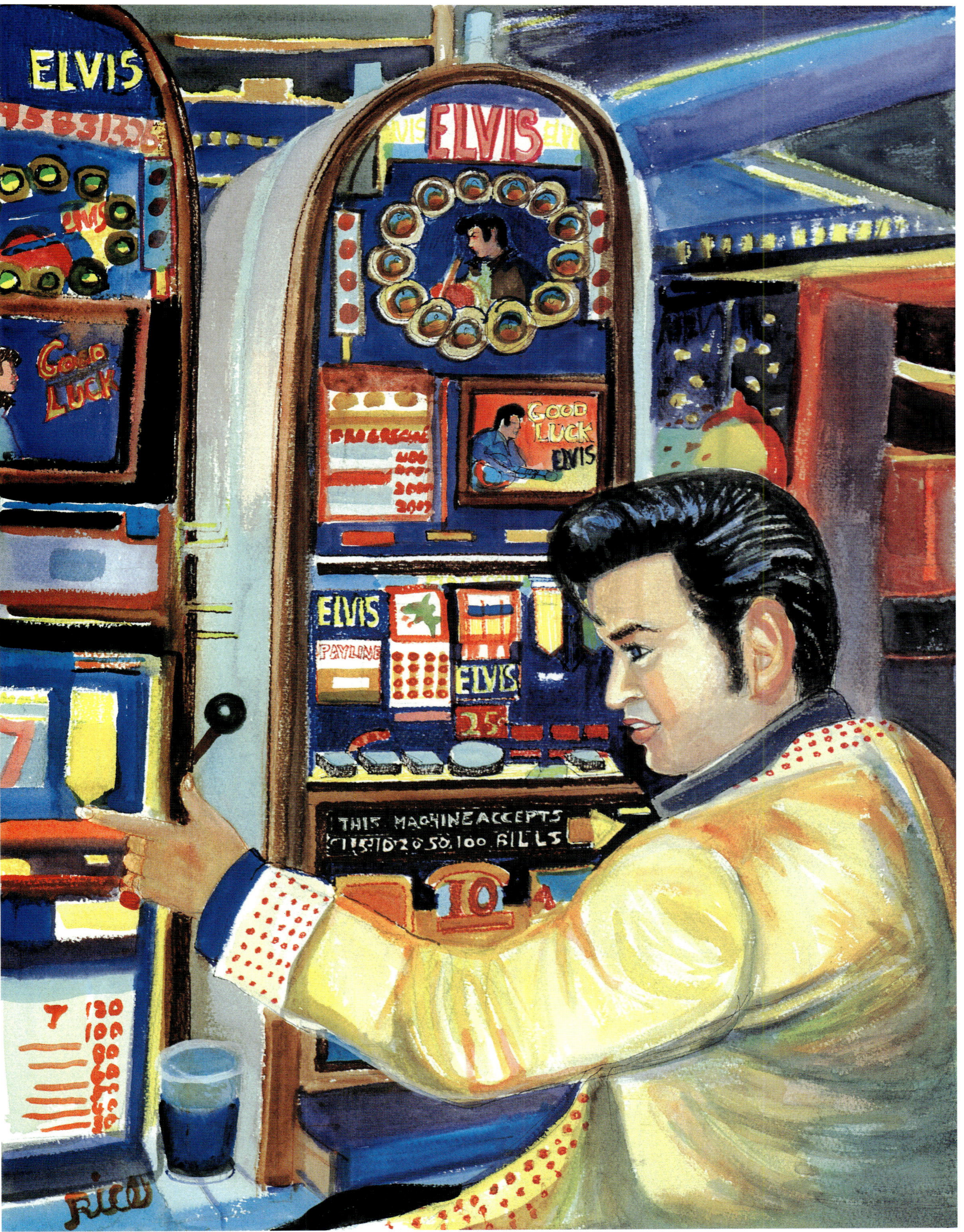

ELVIS
ELVIS
GOOD LUCK
GOOD LUCK
ELVIS
ELVIS
PAYLINE
ELVIS
THIS MACHINE ACCEPTS
BILLS
10

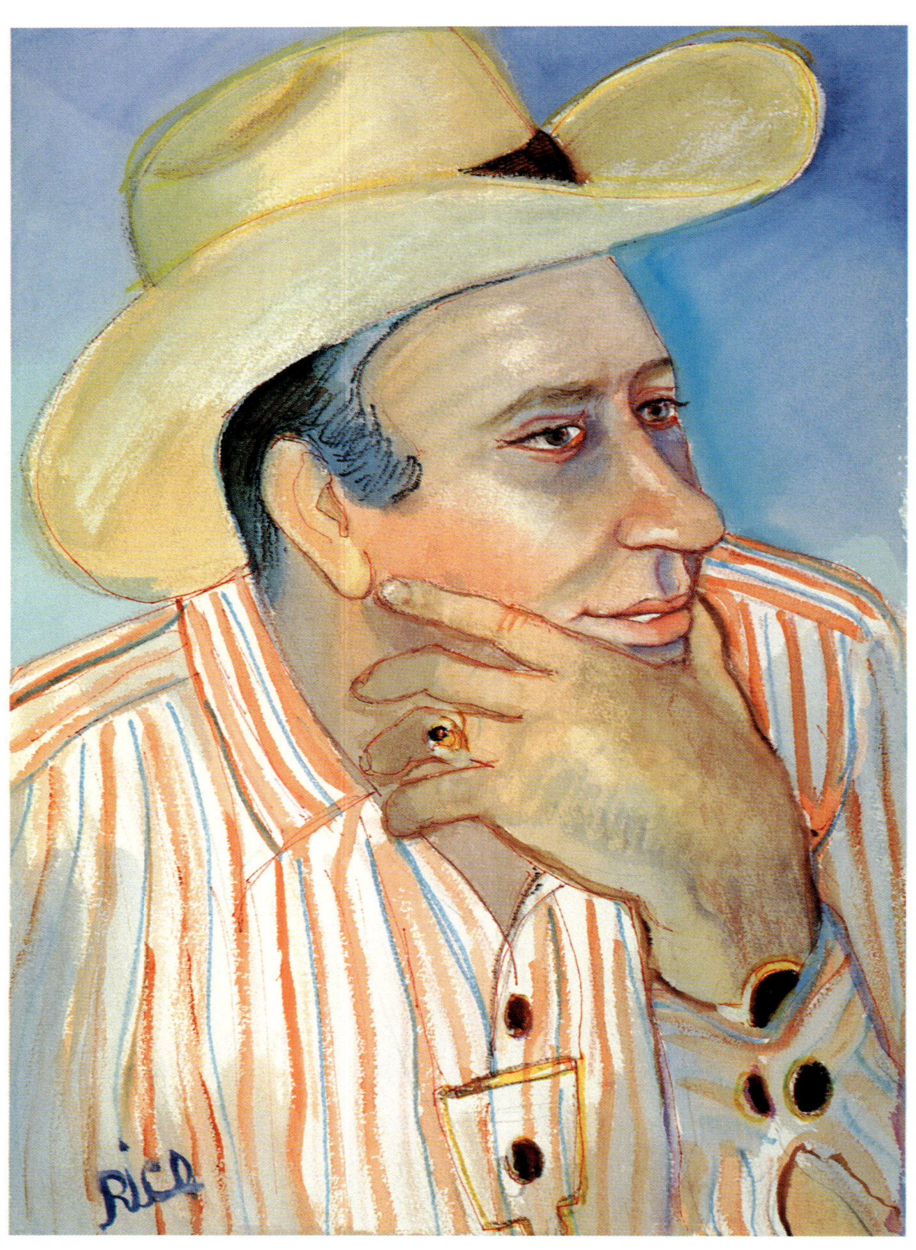

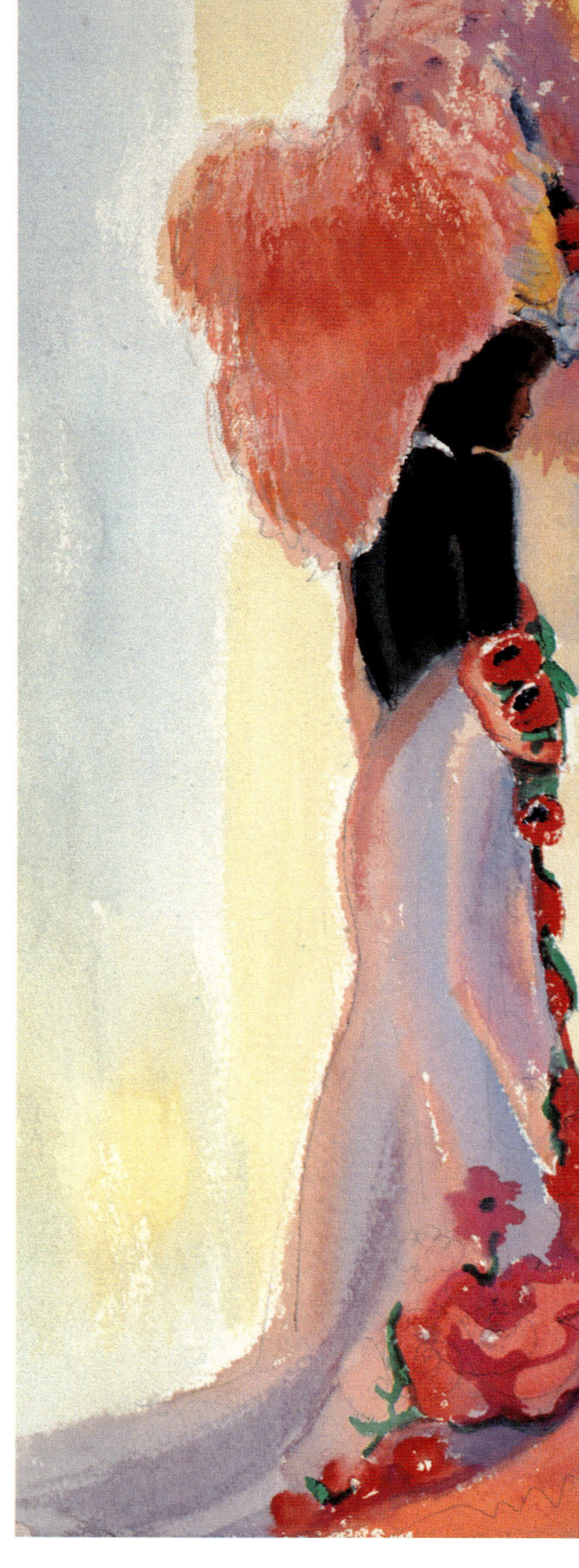

A CONVERSATION WITH AMARILLO SLIM

When the legendary gambler Amarillo Slim enters a high-stakes tournament, a hush typically falls over the room as opponents and onlookers await his first move—and as a Texan who prides himself on his ability to intimidate, that suits him just fine. I caught up with Amarillo Slim—a poker-playing Hall of Famer—just as he was about to depart for the Isle of Man for a $1.6 million tournament. Talking to him was like a trip around the world as he recounted his poker exploits all over the map, including twice-annual treks to Africa in search of big game—card games, not the animal kind. When he's not on the road, Slim continues to call his home—where else?—Amarillo.

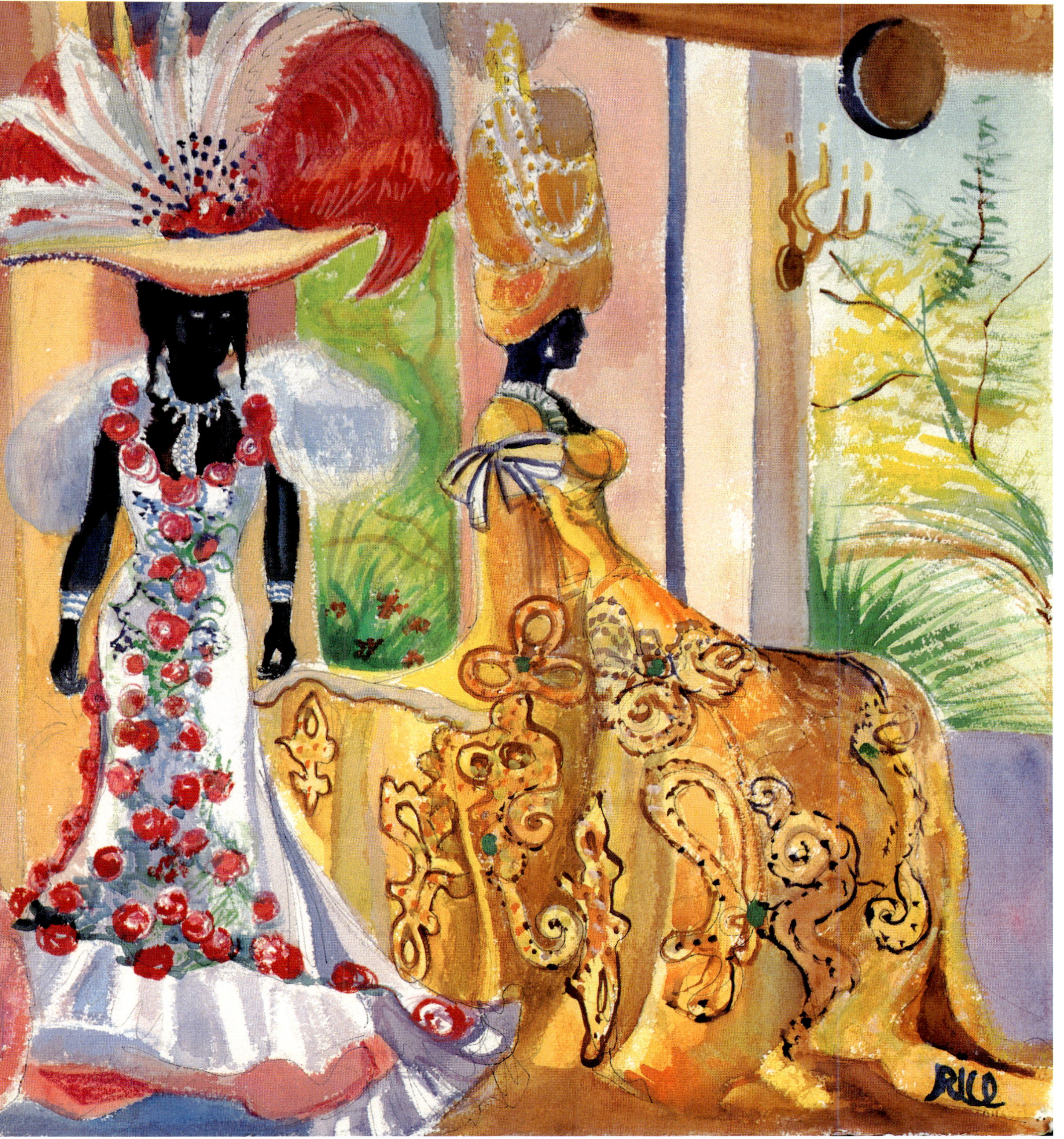

THE CASINO LEGENDS HALL OF FAME

Las Vegas' brief, colorful history is celebrated at the Tropicana's Casino Legends Hall of Fame. You can find treasures such as these sumptuous costumes and ornate head pieces from an early production of the long-running Folies Bergère; a showgirl costume designed by Nolan Miller for a 1975 Toulouse-Lautrec number; Mademoiselle De Paris, designed by Jerry Jackson, is a 1983 costume featuring red rose highlights and was worn by a lead singer; and a golden showgirl costume also designed by Jackson for the Versailles number. Charming Steve Cutler has organized more than 15,000 exhibits from every Vegas era—vintage items and video presentations relating to casinos, hotels, visionaries, builders, mobsters, gamblers, showgirls, headliners, movies, murders, accidents, fires, demolitions, even chips and tokens. It's the largest collection of Nevada casino memorabilia in the world.

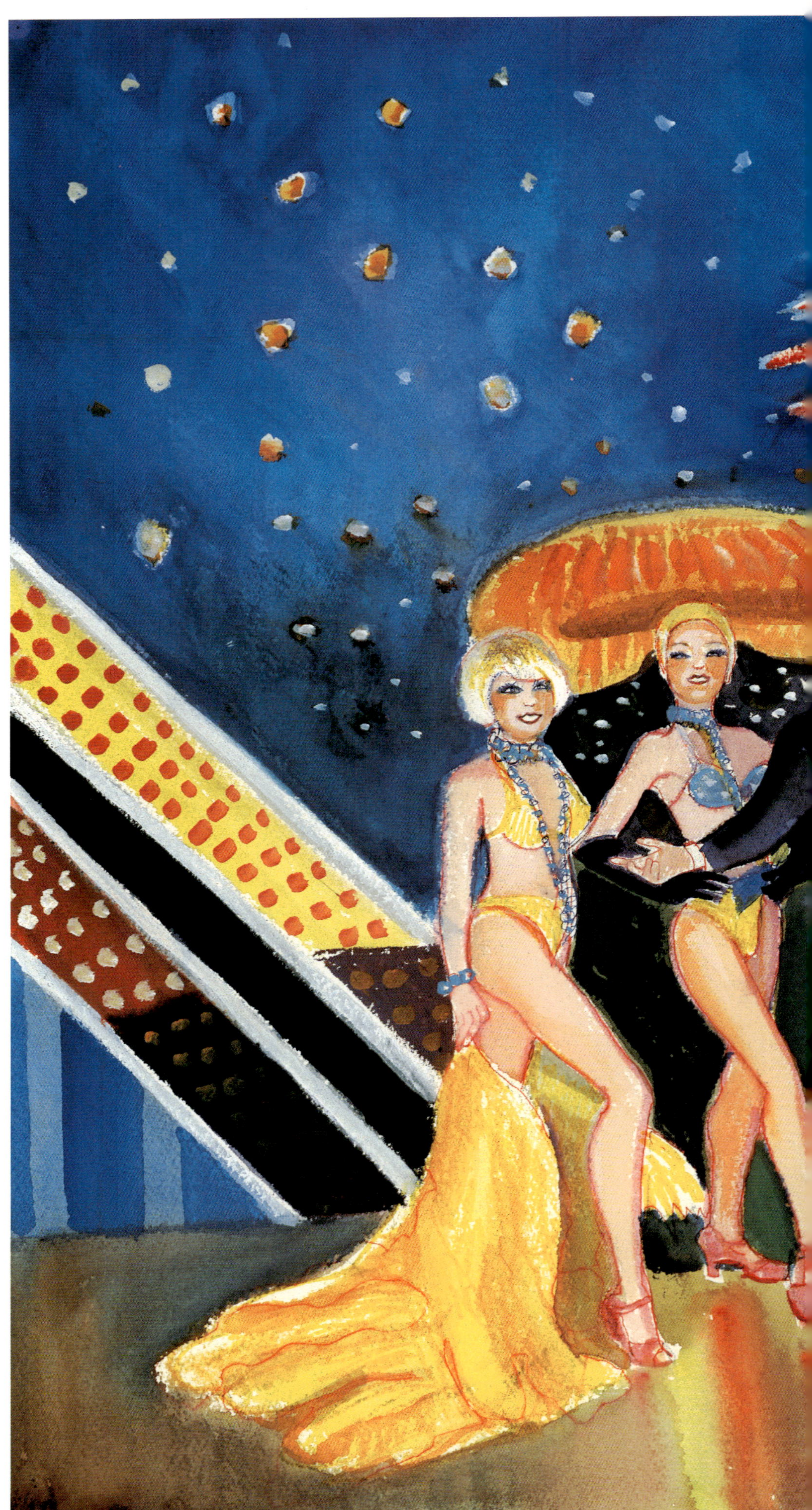

JERRY JACKSON AND THE FOLIES BERGÈRE

As the creative force behind the Tropicana's prestigious Folies Bergère since 1997, Jerry Jackson is one of those amazing multiple hyphenates: a producer-director-choreographer-writer-designer-composer. Early in his career, he was a dancer for Danny Kaye's TV series and an assistant to the legendary Hermes Pan. He first became involved with the Folies Bergère in 1966 when he choreographed the show's 100th anniversary in Paris. His masterful touch has been seen in TV series ("The Tony Orlando and Dawn Show"), motion pictures ("The Godfather Part II"), stage ("Seven Brides For Seven Brothers"), star acts (Goldie Hawn, Juliet Prowse) and international resort shows.

Jerry's dancers, the leggy Folies showgirls, have been recruited from near and far: Trish Willes (in the yellow feathered cape) is from Richmond, Virginia; Kristine Perchette (in the red and blue sequined cape) is a native Nevadan; Janu Tornell (in the big yellow hat) is from Las Vegas; and Kristin Wolner (in the red and white striped bow) is from San Jose, California.

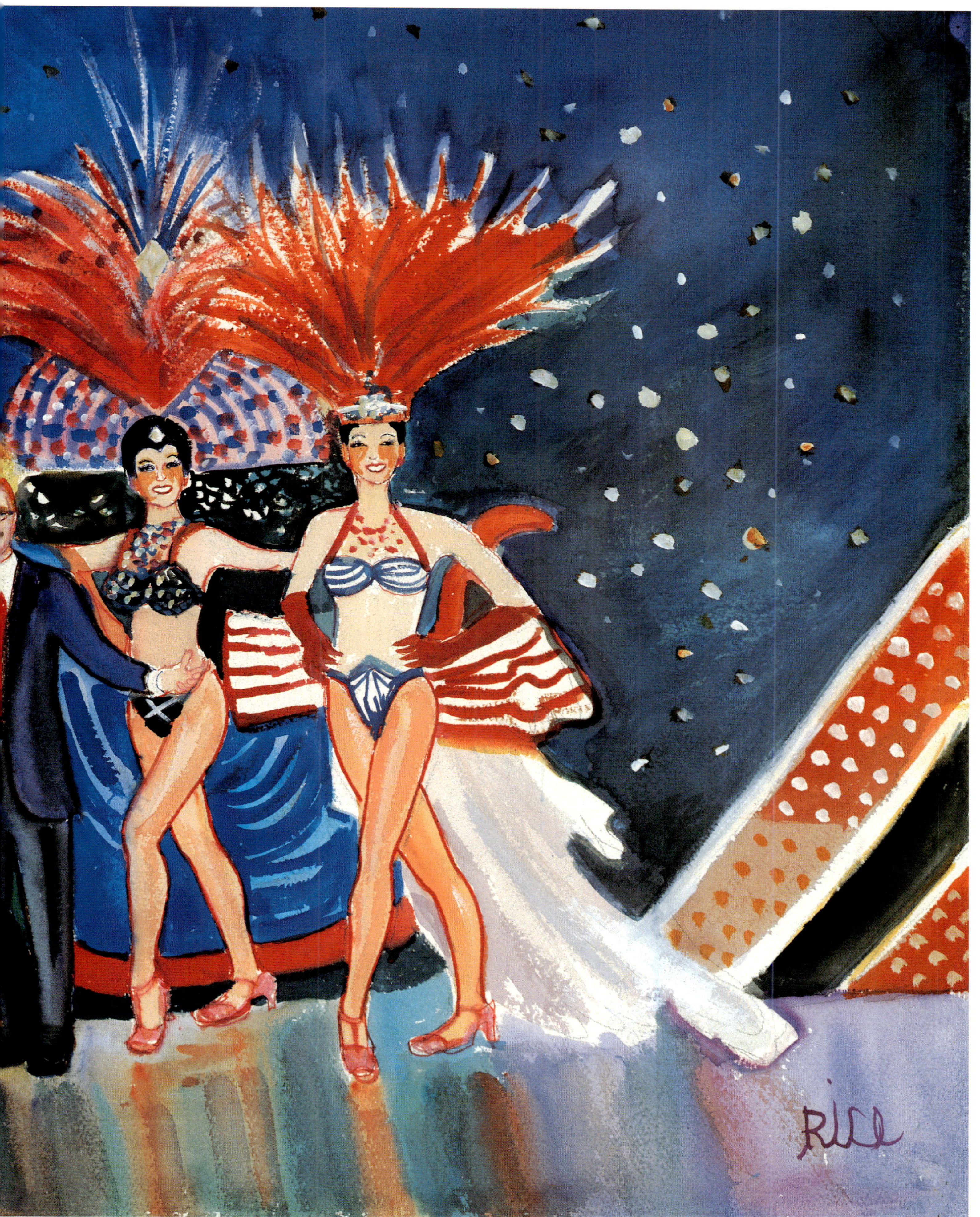
Rice

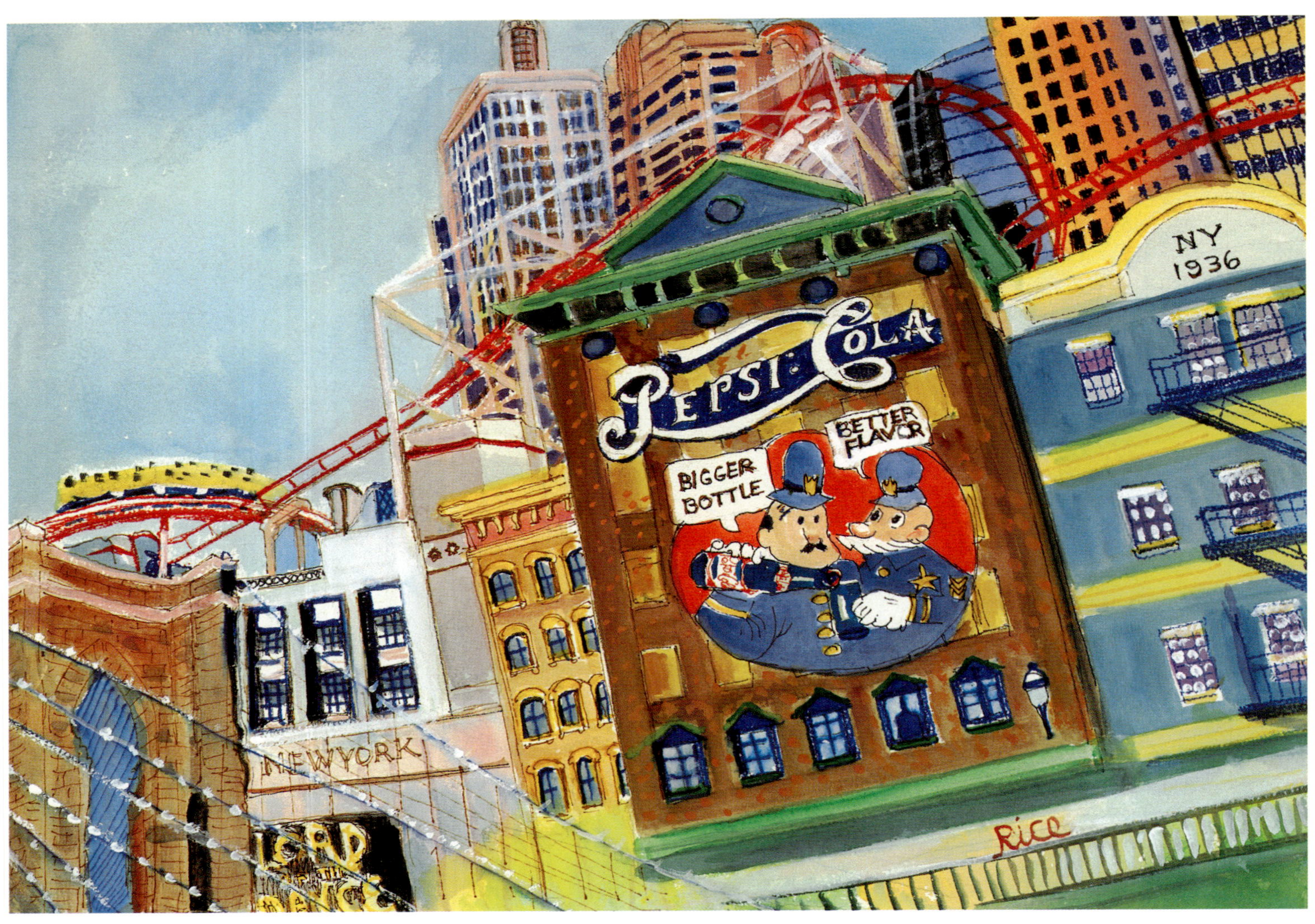

PRODUCT PLACEMENT

This Pepsi-Cola sign on the facade of New York, New York is clever product placement, designed to match the old-fashioned style of the "neighborhood" in which it appears.

THE STATUE OF LIBERTY AT NEW YORK-NEW YORK >

"Give me your tired, your hungry, your poor," proclaims this 150-foot-tall replica of the original Statue. Well, you might get tired taking in all that New York-New York has to offer, including uncanny reproductions of highlights like the famed Manhattan skyline, Central Park, Park Avenue, a Coney Island-style rollercoaster and the Brooklyn Bridge. But you'll never go hungry with its vast array of Big Apple eateries, including a Little Italy food court and Nathan's Hot Dogs. As for poor, I guess that depends more on Lady Luck than Miss Liberty.

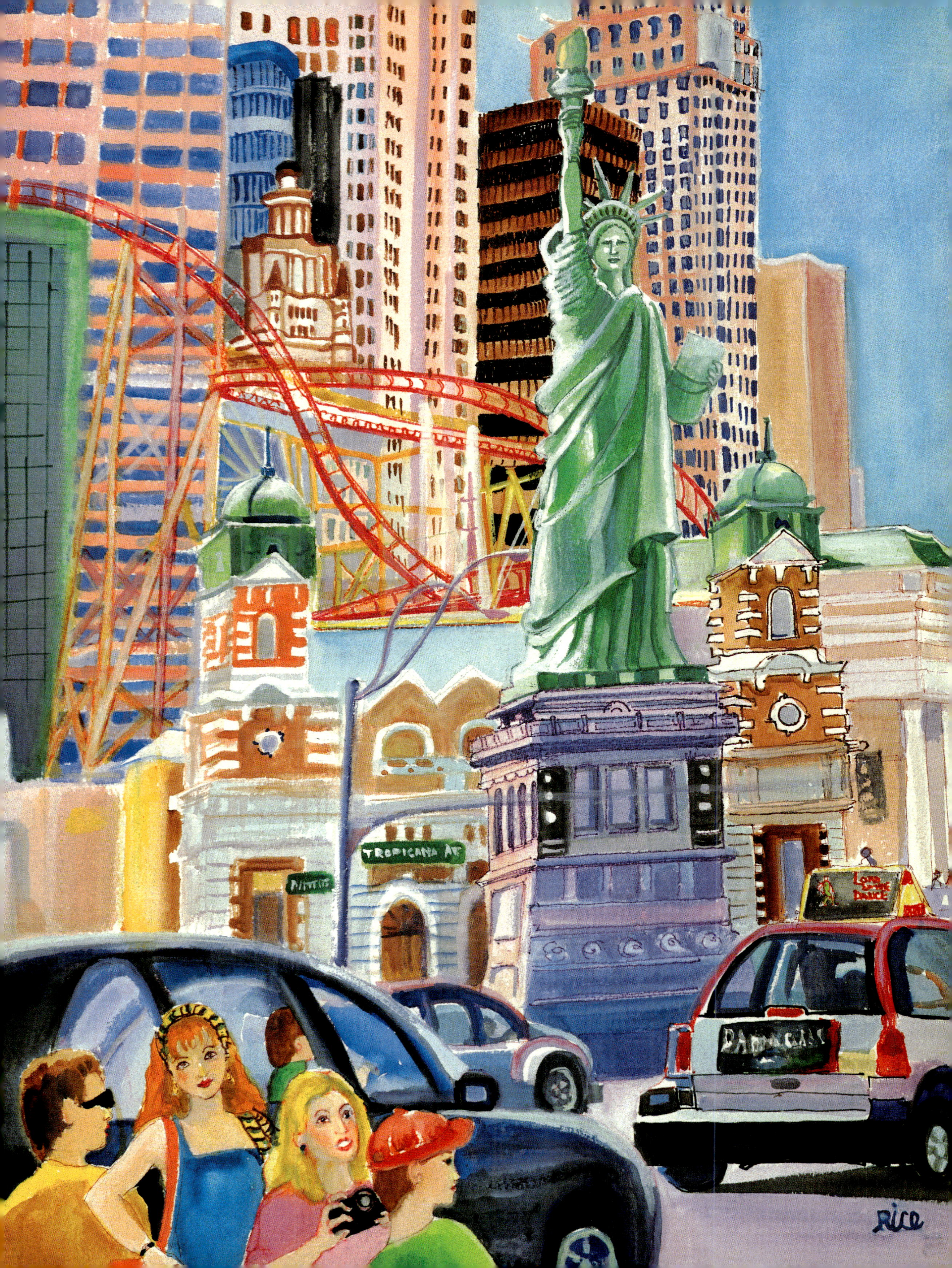
TROPICANA AV
Rice

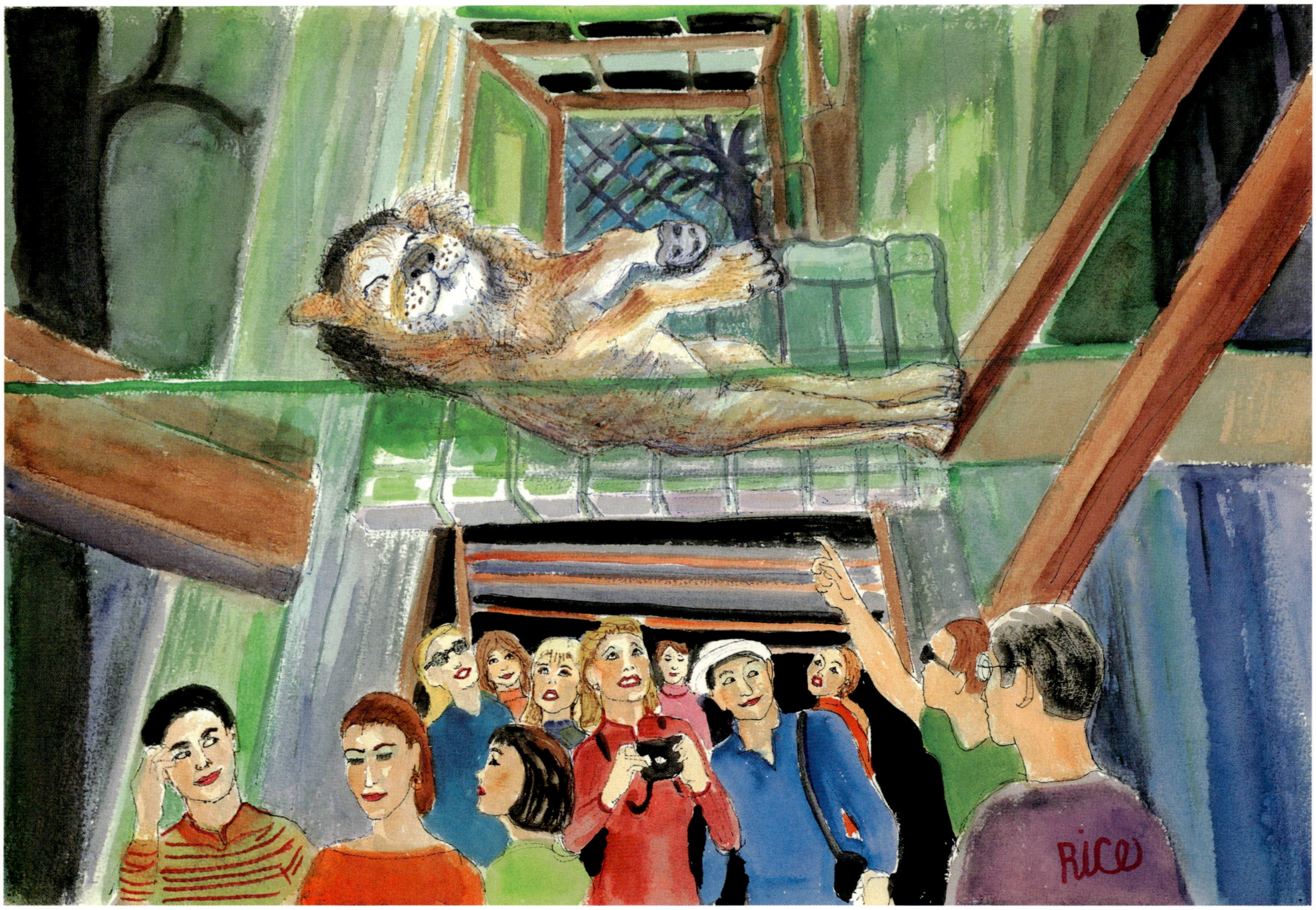

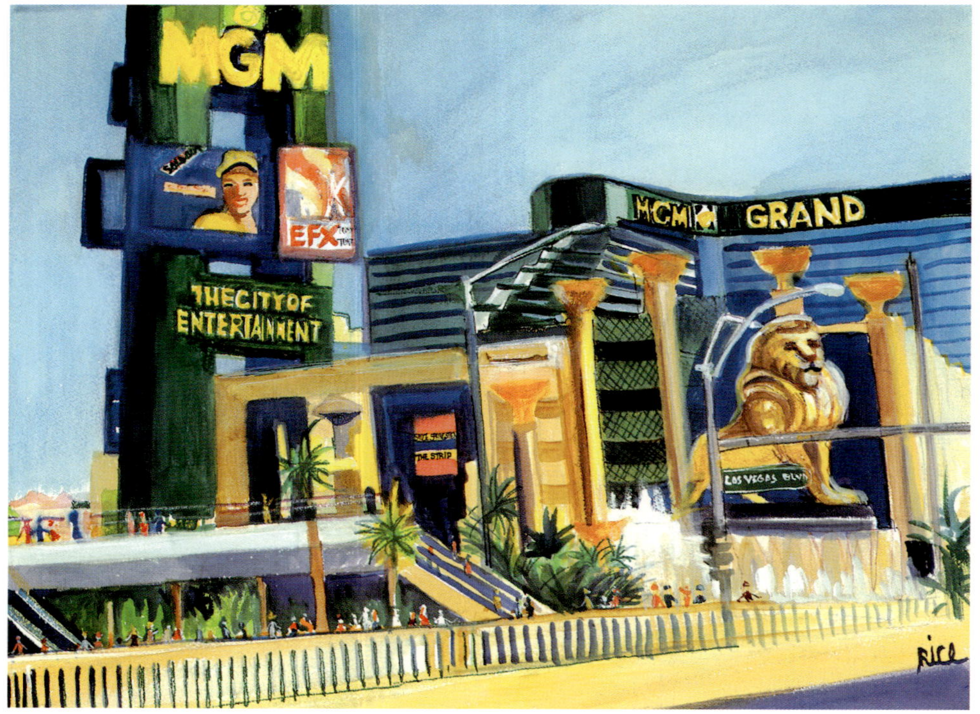

KING OF THE JUNGLE?

If "ferocious" ol' Leo here is the king of the beasts, then (to quote Mel Brooks) "It's good to be the king." The live version of the venerable logo of MGM Studios lives with family and friends in the jungle-like Lion Habitat at the MGM Grand. Above the see-through glass tunnel, I found the lion king sleeping with a snore, rather than his trademark roar.

MOVING ALONG AT THE MGM GRAND

Hundreds of pedestrians are hustled along on the people-movers outside the towering emerald expanse of the MGM Grand (it's larger than Yankee Stadium). The motorized tracks whisk people safely to and from other nearby destinations and attractions. You can get all the way from one end of the Strip to the other without ever walking on a Las Vegas sidewalk. With people-movers, monorails, hotel shuttles and public transportation, there's always a way to get around the entire town quickly.

CHER AT THE MGM GRAND >

You can certainly "Believe" that the ever-glamorous, always-interesting Cher blew away the audience that gathered at the MGM Grand to watch her tape a tour-de-force concert special for HBO. The singer and Oscar-winning actress is riding a crest of renewed popularity, re-inventing herself yet again for old and new fans alike.

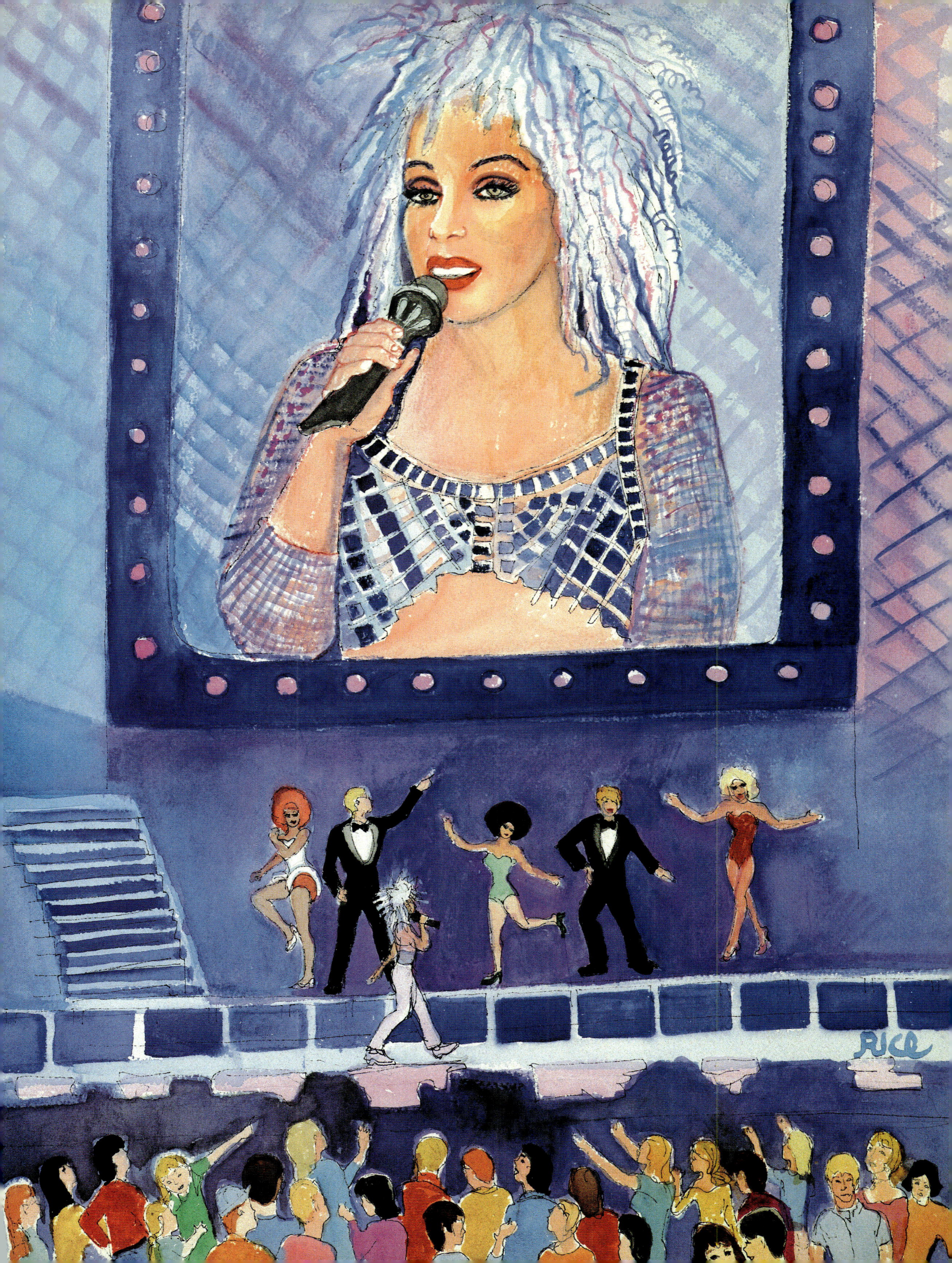
RICE

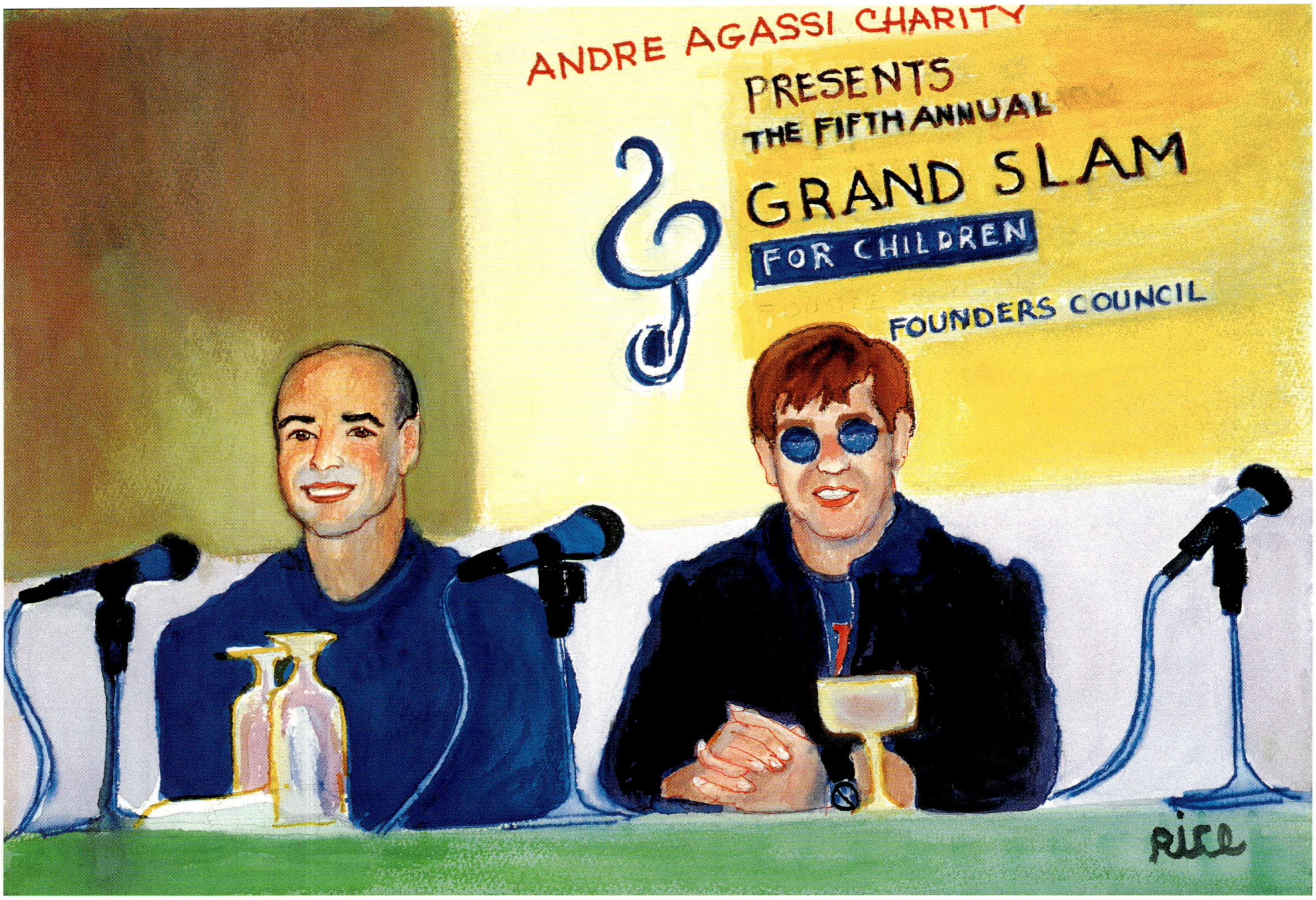

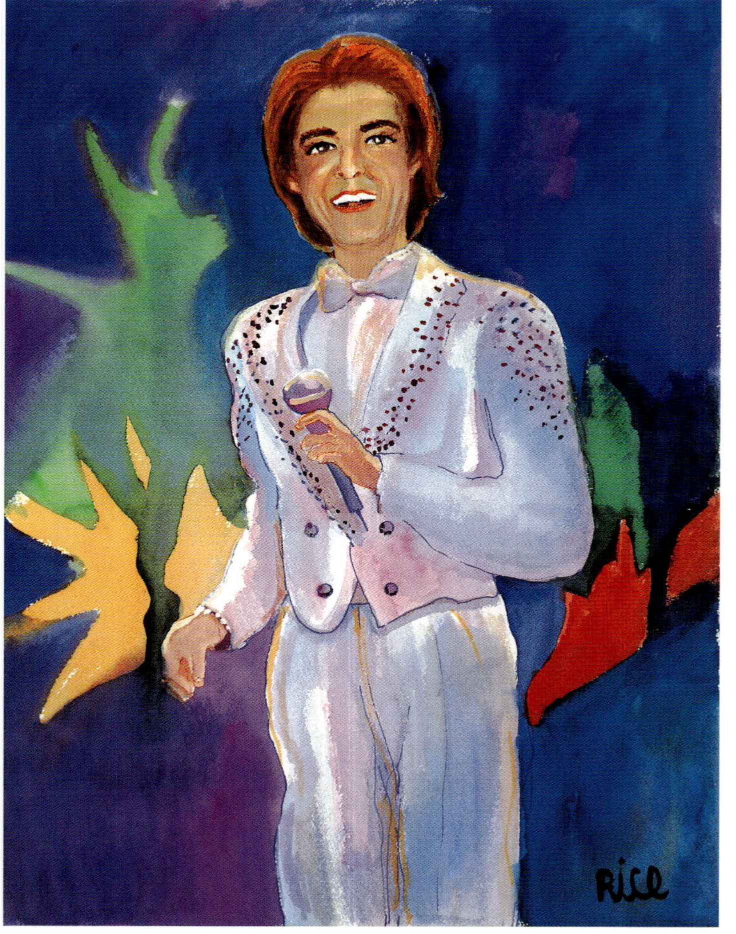

ANDRE AND ELTON

The king of the tennis court joined the musician behind "The Lion King" when Las Vegas hometown boy Andre Agassi and singer Elton John teamed up at the Andre Agassi Charitable Foundation's annual Grand Slam for Children Concert at the MGM Grand. The $1,000-a-plate gala always draws sell-out crowds and has raised millions for abused and neglected children. Sir Elton performed, as did Gloria Estefan, Robin Williams, Stevie Wonder, Luther Vandross and LeAnn Rimes. Andre underwrote the event out of his own pocket, and all of his endorsement contracts contain provisions to help benefit his charitable efforts.

TOMMY TUNE

What does a legend do after he's conquered Broadway? Why, conquer Las Vegas, of course! Tommy Tune, the lanky, seemingly ageless 6-foot-6-inch hoofer (Andy Warhol called him a "human exclamation point"), was the toast of the Great White Way for four decades, appearing in shows like "The Best Little Whorehouse in Texas," "Grand Hotel" and "The Will Rogers Follies" and garnering an unprecedented nine Tony Awards. Tune starred in the amazing $45 million stage extravaganza "EFX" at the MGM Grand. An incredible 90-minute production, each night features 70 supporting cast members, 250 special effects, 450 elaborate costumes, 6,000 lights, 10 pounds of explosives, and dozens of 3-D effects .

BOOGIE AT STUDIO 54 >

Visit the MGM Grand for a flashback to the disco scene of the 1970s with a glittery recreation of New York's famous Studio 54, one of Las Vegas' latest hot spots where clubhoppers make the scene to shake their booty. The three-story club's dance floor pumps out the Bee Gees and Donna Summer (as well as today's top dance hits) with a state-of-the-art sound, video and lighting system, while dancers in superfly 70s threads add to the retro ambiance. When you take a break from the Hustle, check out the gallery of celebrity-filled black-and-white photos from the original club's heyday.

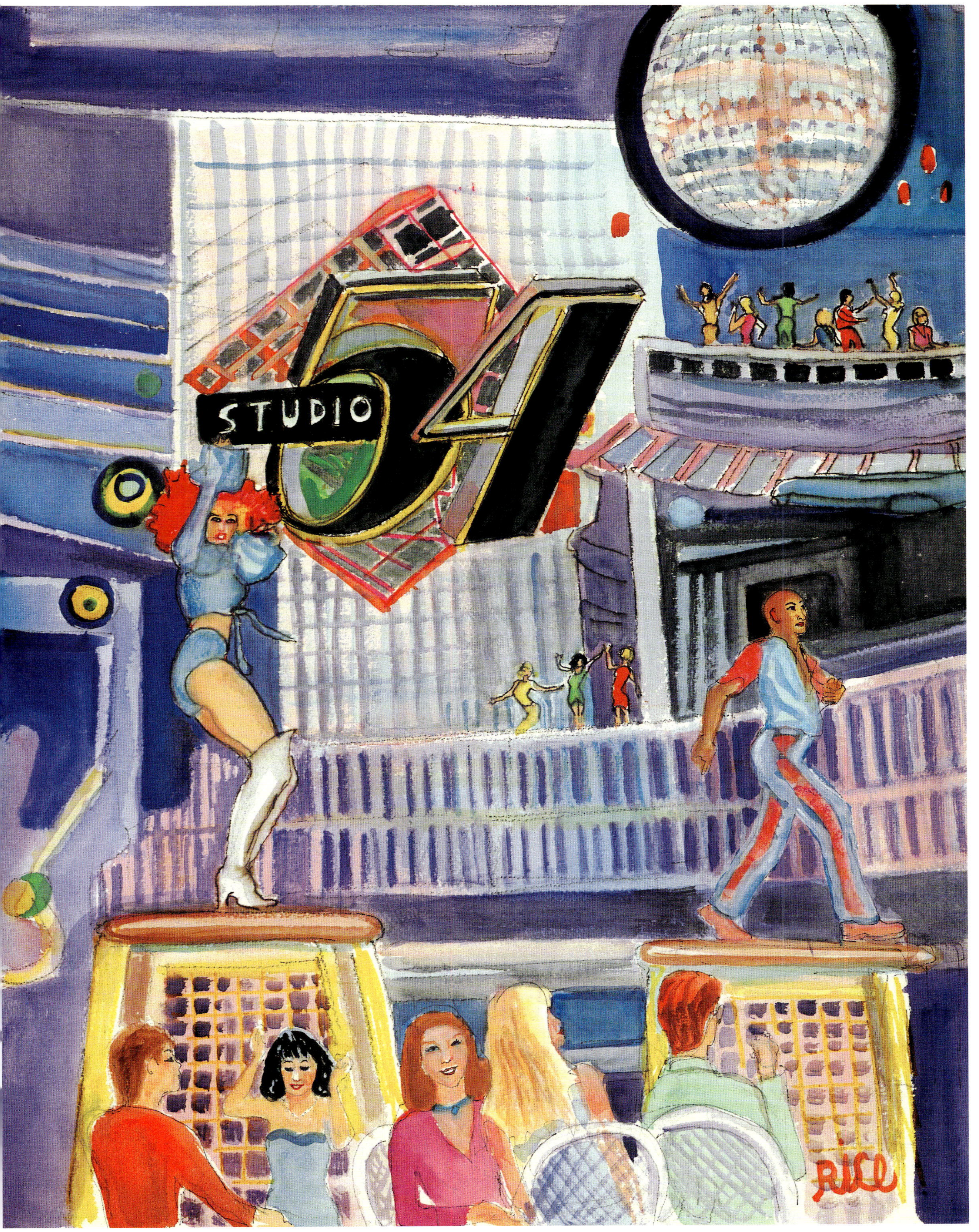
STUDIO
54
RICE

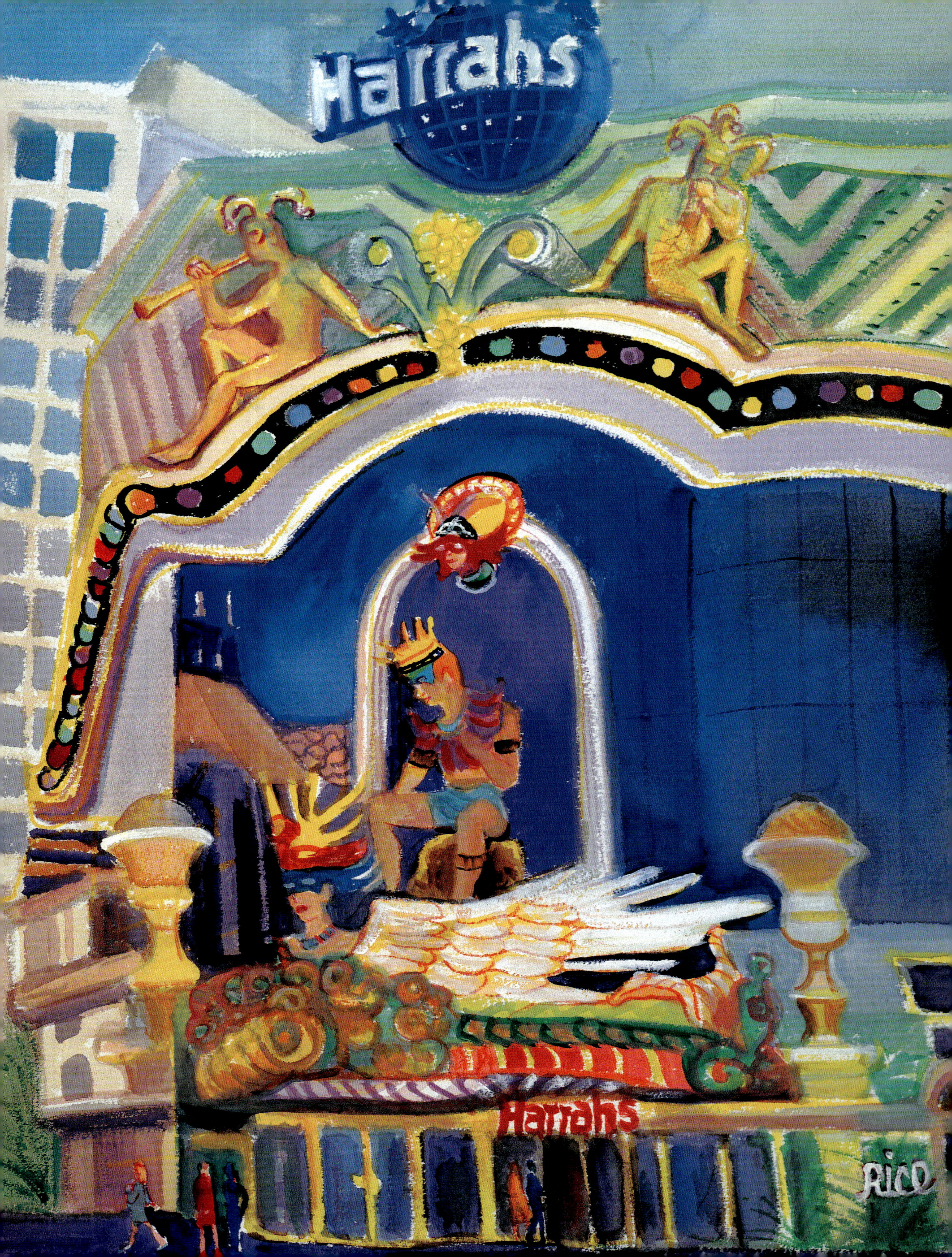
Harrahs
Harrahs
Rico

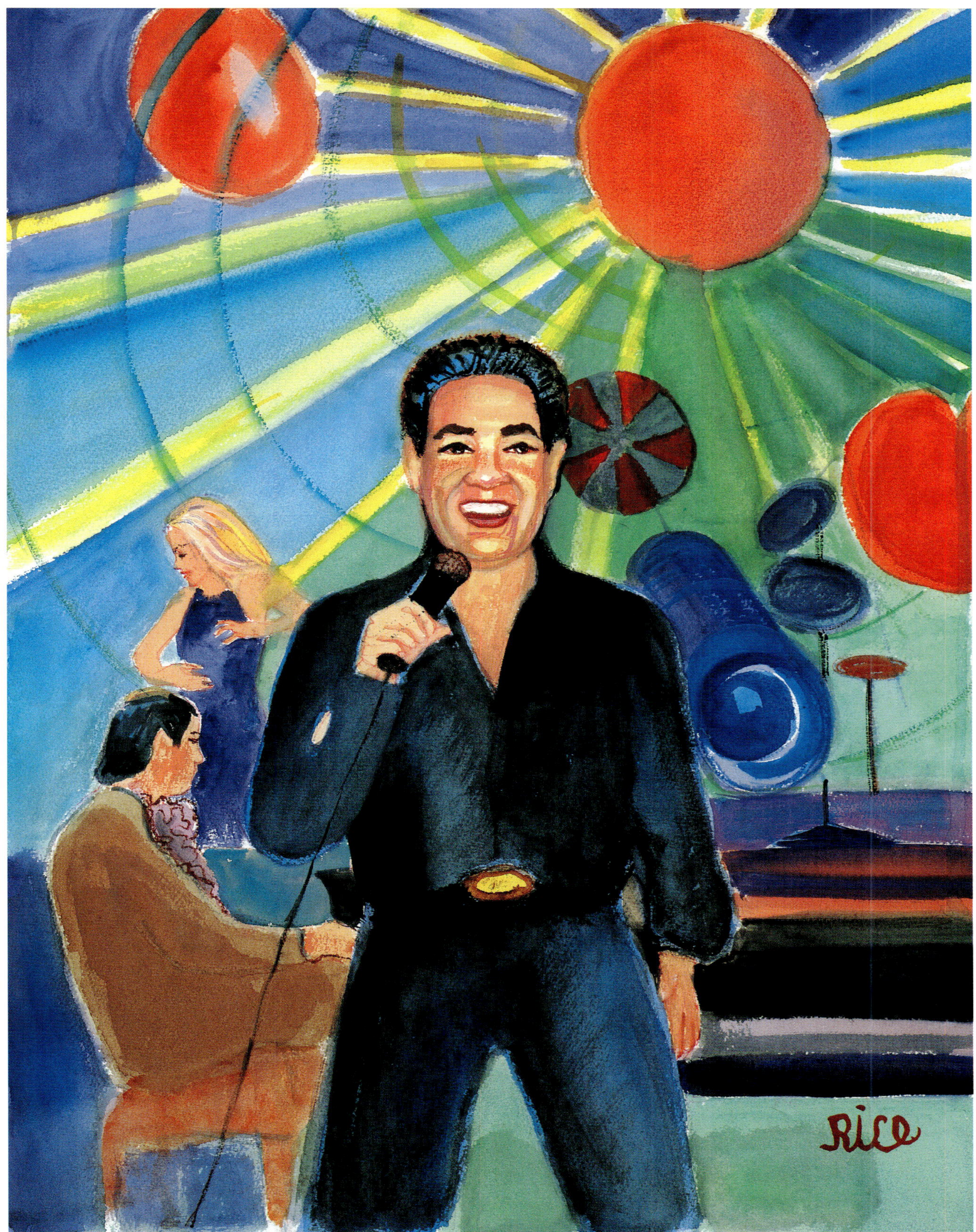

< HARRAH'S LAS VEGAS

A recurring motif of colorful harlequins reveling Carnaval-style is the hallmark of Harrah's Las Vegas, a fanciful 2,600-room hotel and casino which features fine restaurants like The Range Steakhouse and Cafe Andreotti, unique shopping outlets like the Ghiradelli Chocolate Company and Carnaval Corner, and state-of the-art spa facilities. Harrah's is known for having one of the most bustling casinos in town, as well as the Carnaval Court Live outdoor entertainment experience and the popular Las Vegas outpost of the Improv comedy club, where the nation's top stand-ups leave 'em laughing like one of Harrah's harlequins.

CLINT HOLMES AT HARRAH'S

Harrah's is the place where I caught entertainer Clint Holmes' popular show "Takin' It Uptown," where he lends his smooth and silky baritone to a diverse collection of contemporary hits, old standards and almost-forgotten gems—from jazz to samba to ballads. Backed by a 12-piece band, Clint—who was once Joan Rivers' late night sidekick and hosted his own Emmy-winning TV talk show—also adds an engaging storytelling element to his show. Crediting Bill Cosby and Don Rickles (both of whom he formerly opened for) as influences, Clint proves night after night he's as deft with comedic anecdotes as he is with a song.

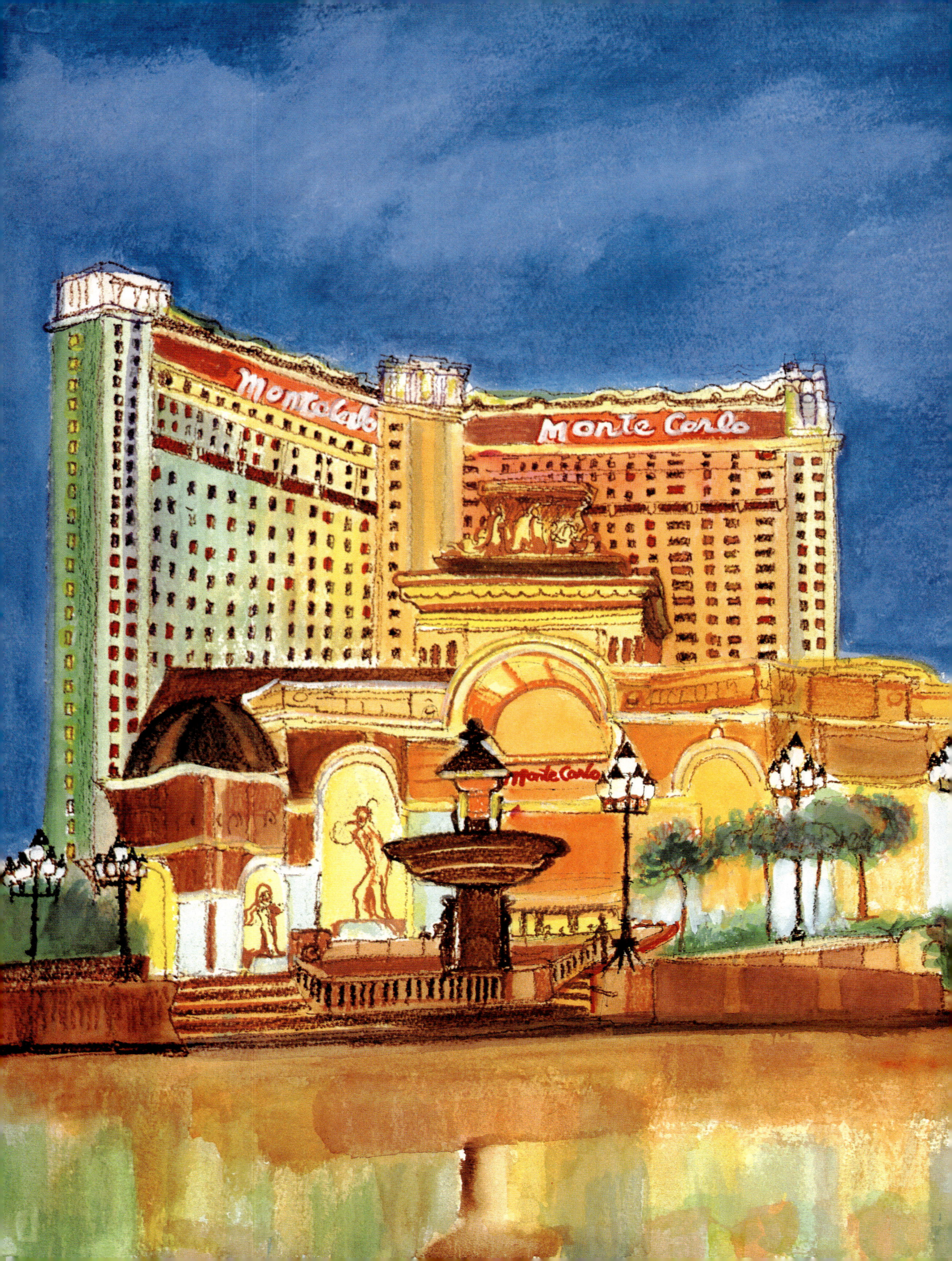
Monte Carlo
Monte Carlo

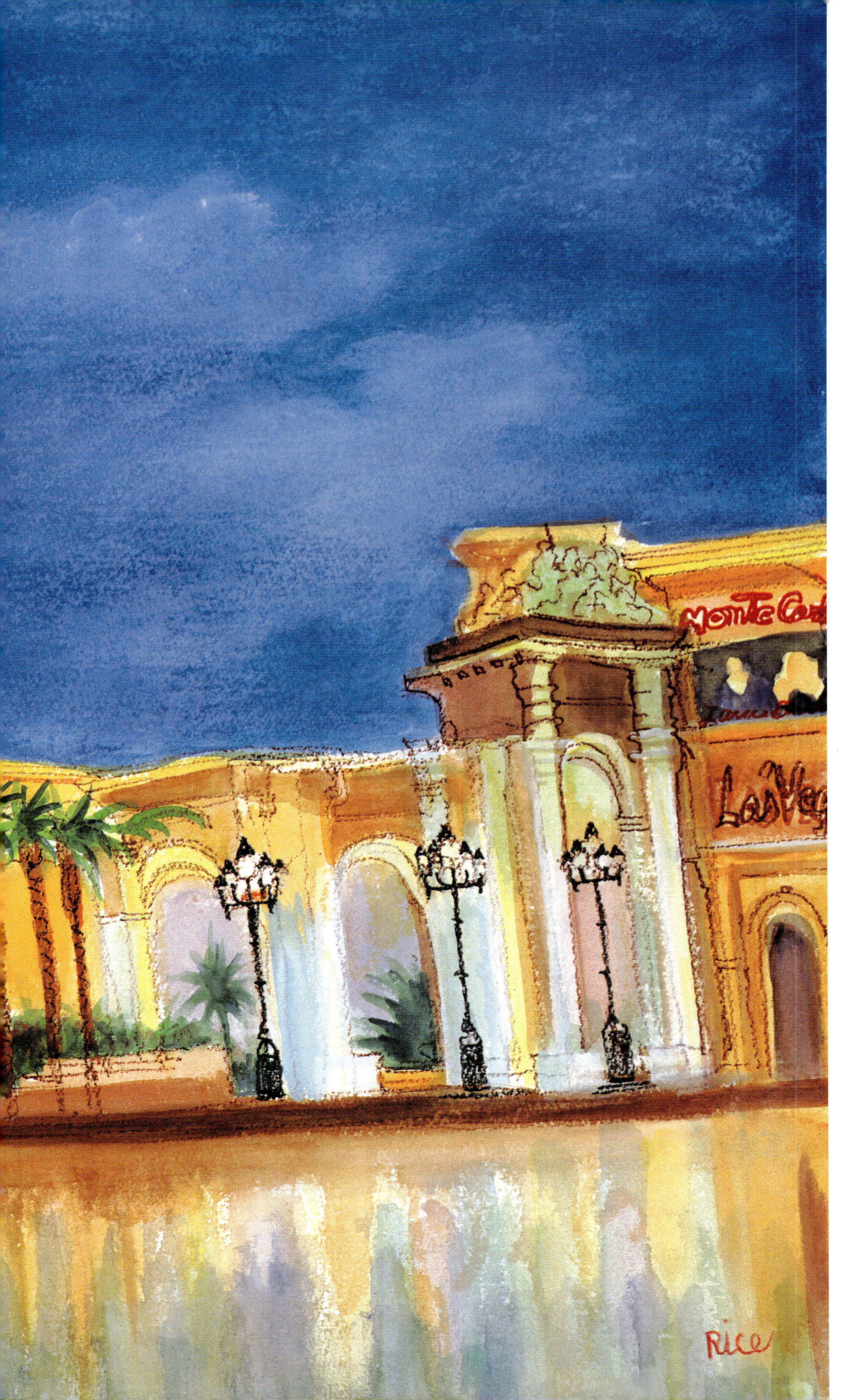

THE MONTE CARLO AGLOW

The Monte Carlo Resort & Casino looks almost like a magical kingdom amid the glow of a glittery Las Vegas night—which is only appropriate, since it is the home of the $27 million, custom-built Lance Burton Theater, performing home of the reigning Master Magician. Part of the Mandalay Resort Group, the Monte Carlo opened in 1996 and features a vast array of attractions, including the Street of Dreams shopping boulevard, restaurants, a unique pub and brewery, spa facilities and several swimming pools and tennis courts.

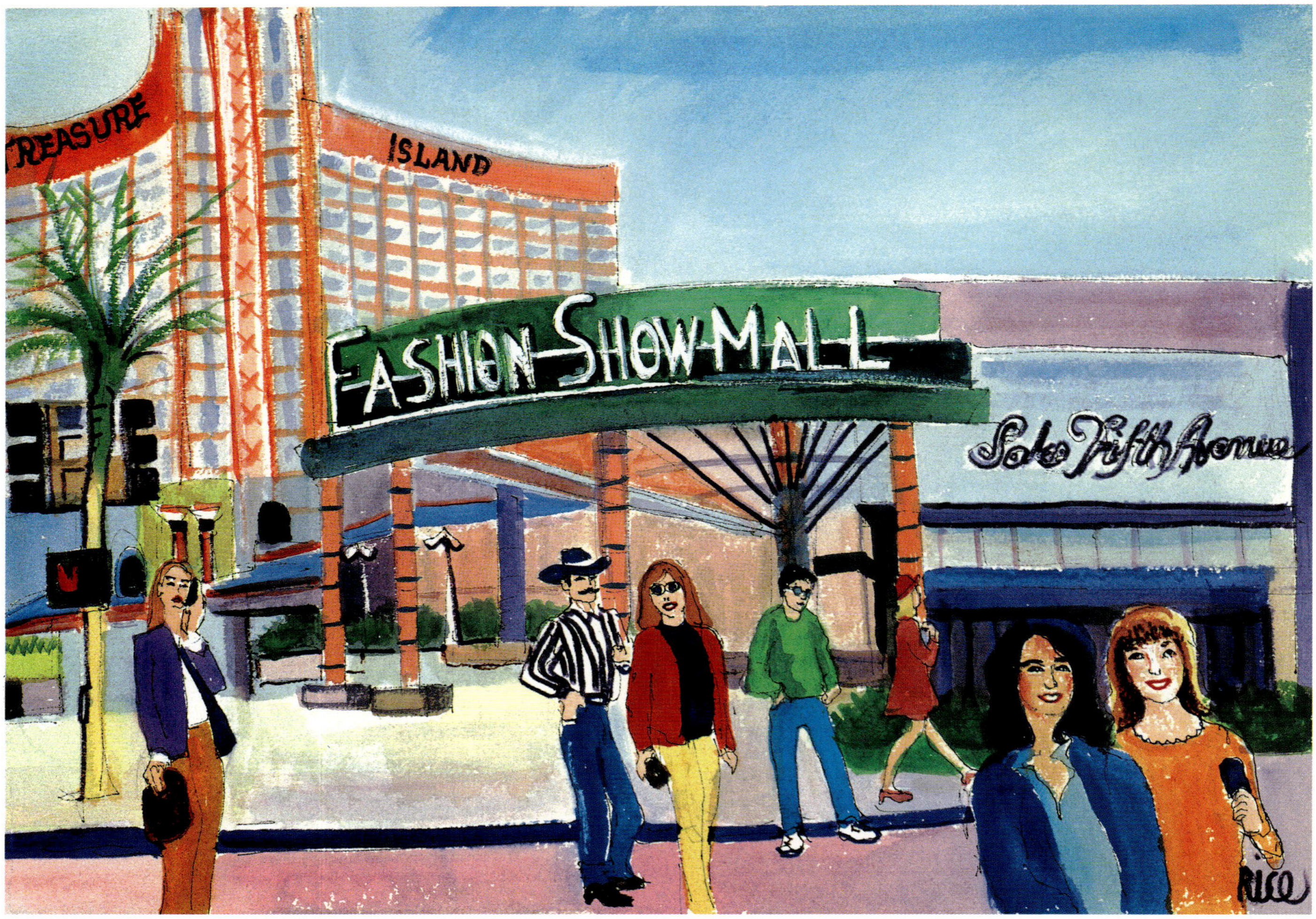
TREASURE
ISLAND
FASHION SHOW MALL
Saks Fifth Avenue
RICE

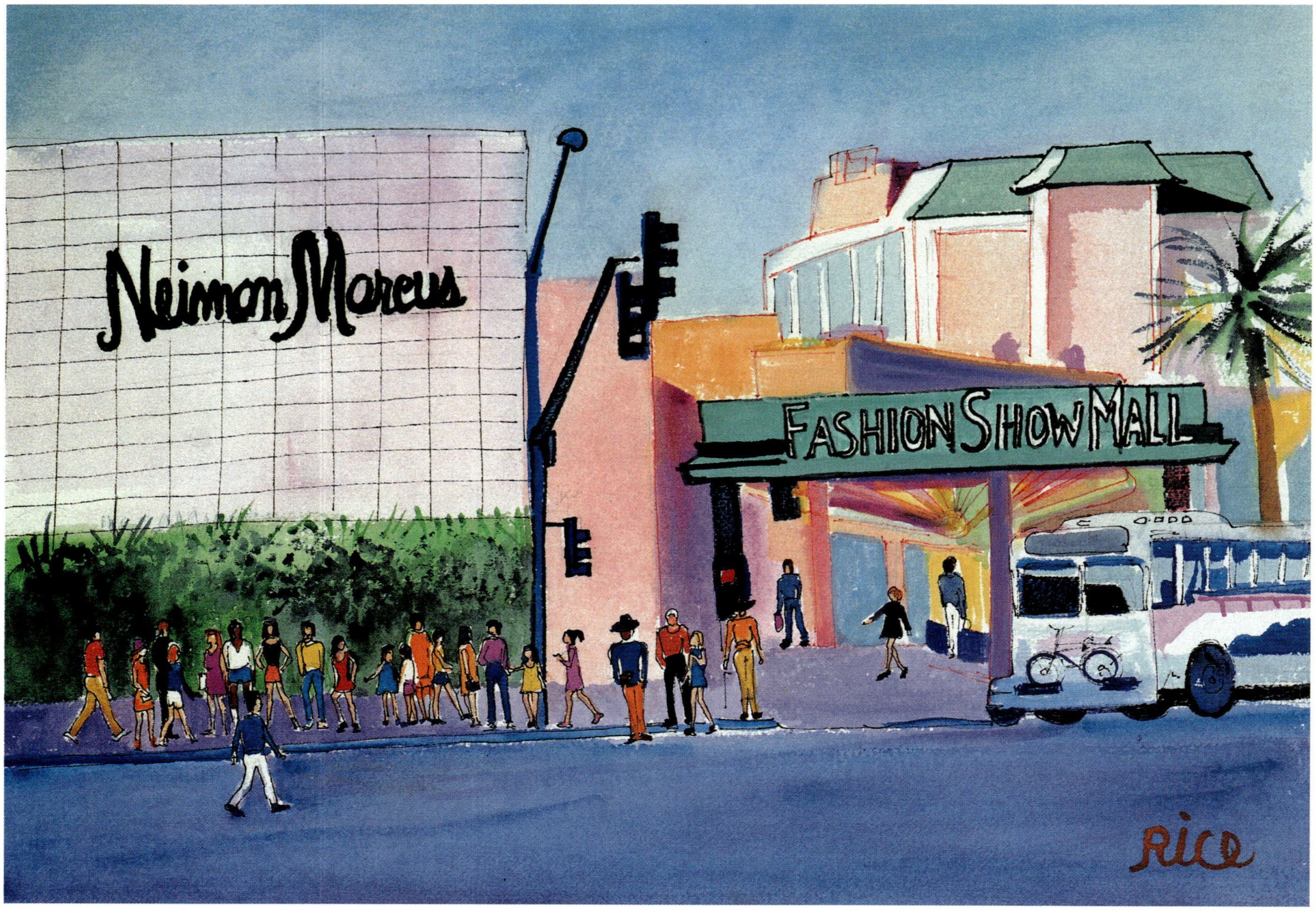
Neiman Marcus
FASHION SHOW MALL
RICE

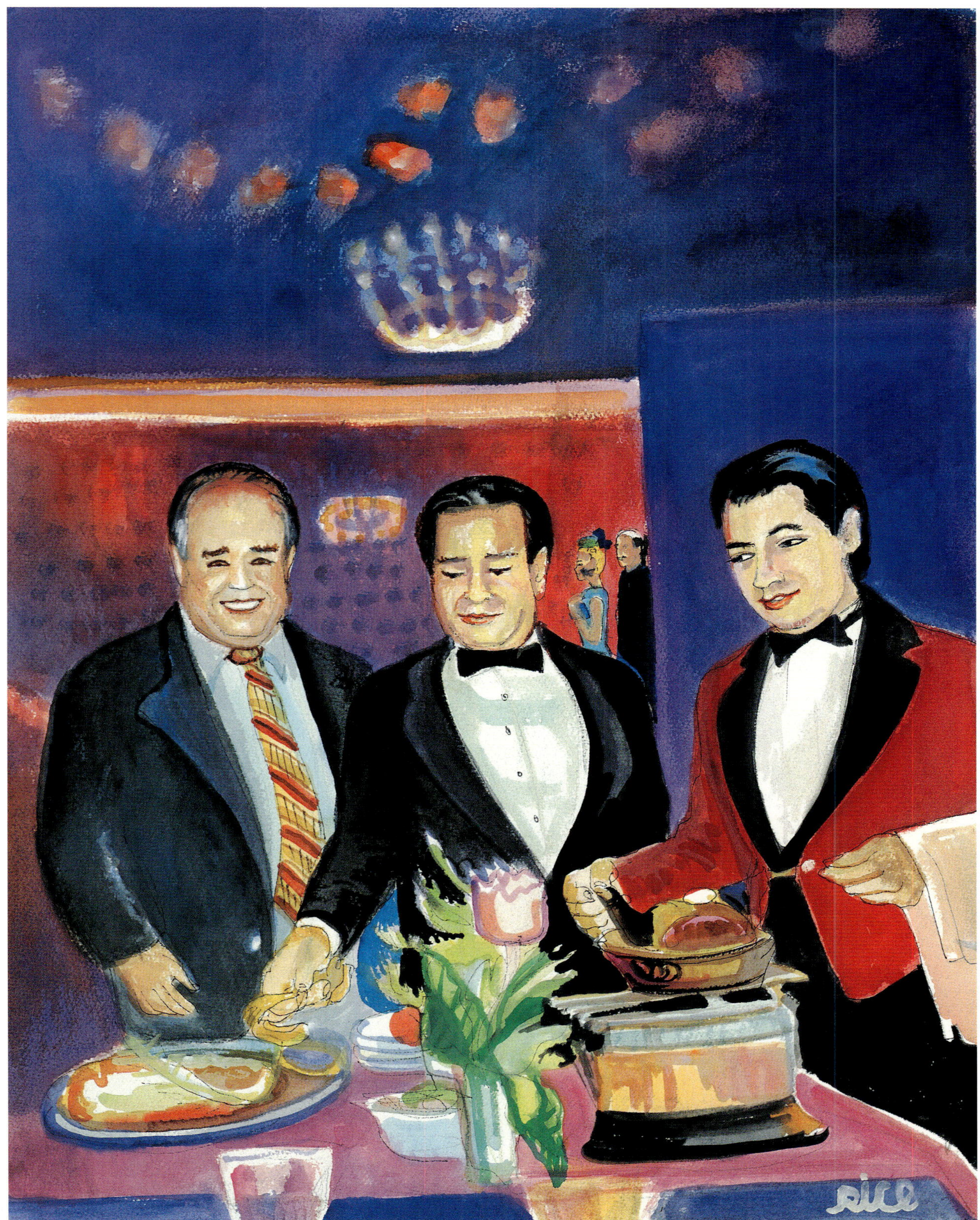

< THE FASHION SHOW

Luxury shopping in Las Vegas has taken a quantum leap forward in recent years, and The Fashion Show on the Strip remains the epicenter of conspicuous consumerism. Currently undergoing an expansion that will double the mall's size to 2 million square feet. The Fashion Show will be anchored by Macy's, Bloomingdale's Home Store, Lord & Taylor, Saks Fifth Avenue, Robinsons-May, Dillard's and Nordstrom when the renovation is complete. The Fashion Show—where fashion is the show.

< SHOPPING AT THE FASHION SHOW MALL

You can find everything from Louis Vuitton to Liz Claiborne at the Fashion Show. Even Picassos and Ertes are available in some of its fine art galleries. Letters and autographs from notables ranging from Abraham Lincoln to Marilyn Monroe in various collectible stores can also be purchased there.

MICHAEL'S RESTAURANT AT THE BARBARY COAST

Did you just score a major slot jackpot or make a killing at the tables? Then I suggest you take your winnings over to Michael's at the Barbary Coast Hotel & Casino, a Victorian-style gourmet restaurant where the superb continental cuisine and intimate, high-style environs (check out the plush velvet and rich furnishings) make for a wonderful celebration dinner. Host Michael Gaughan and his staff are simply impeccable—even if you didn't walk in a big winner (at the casinos, at least), you'll feel like one coming out.

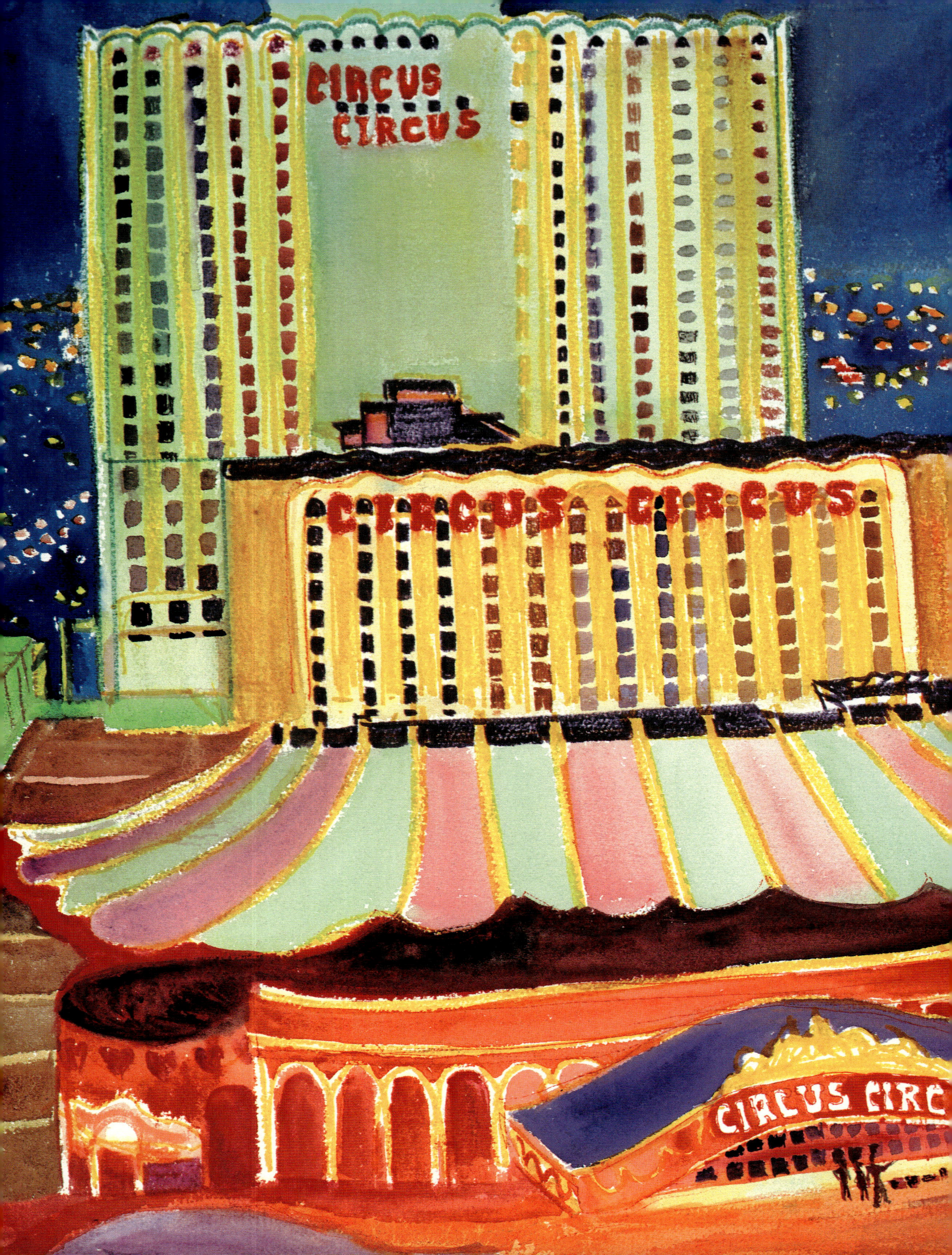
CIRCUS
CIRCUS
CIRCUS CIRCUS
CIRCUS CIRC

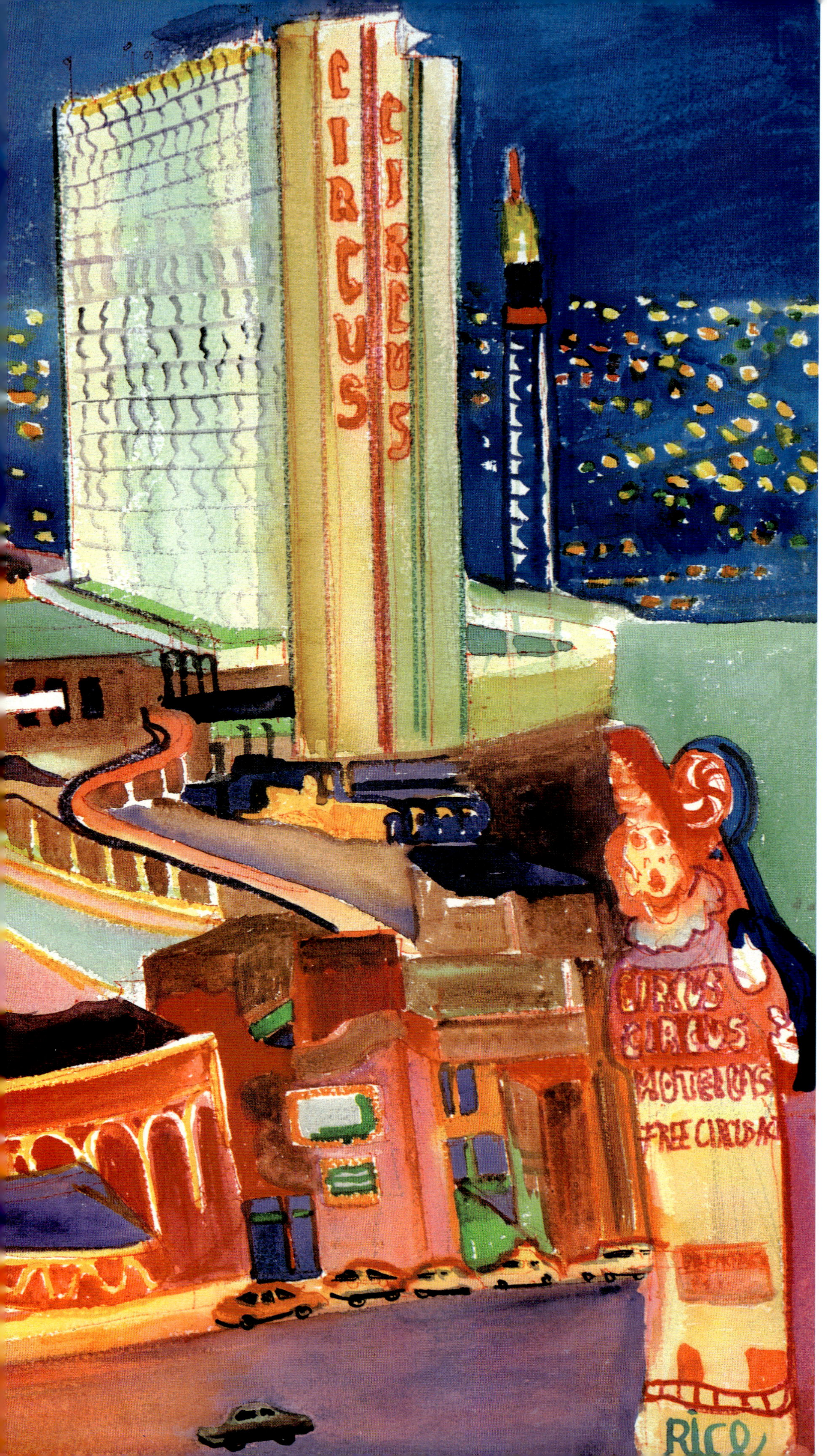

CIRCUS CIRCUS

The candy-colored, clown-filled world of Circus Circus was the brainchild of Jay Sarno, who previously struck Roman gold with Caesars Palace. Launched in 1968, Circus Circus originally had no hotel rooms; it featured live trapeze artists, elephants and other circus performers and—gasp!—charged admission to the high-rolling casino—a tough sell back then. Circus Circus didn't really take off until William Bennett took over in 1974, but it eventually shot to the top like a human cannonball by adding accommodations (it's now one of the largest hotels in the world, so big I literally got lost in it) and a family-fun flavor with the Grand Slam Canyon amusement park. A three-ring attraction, Circus Circus set the tone for the family-friendly theme resorts that dominate the Strip.

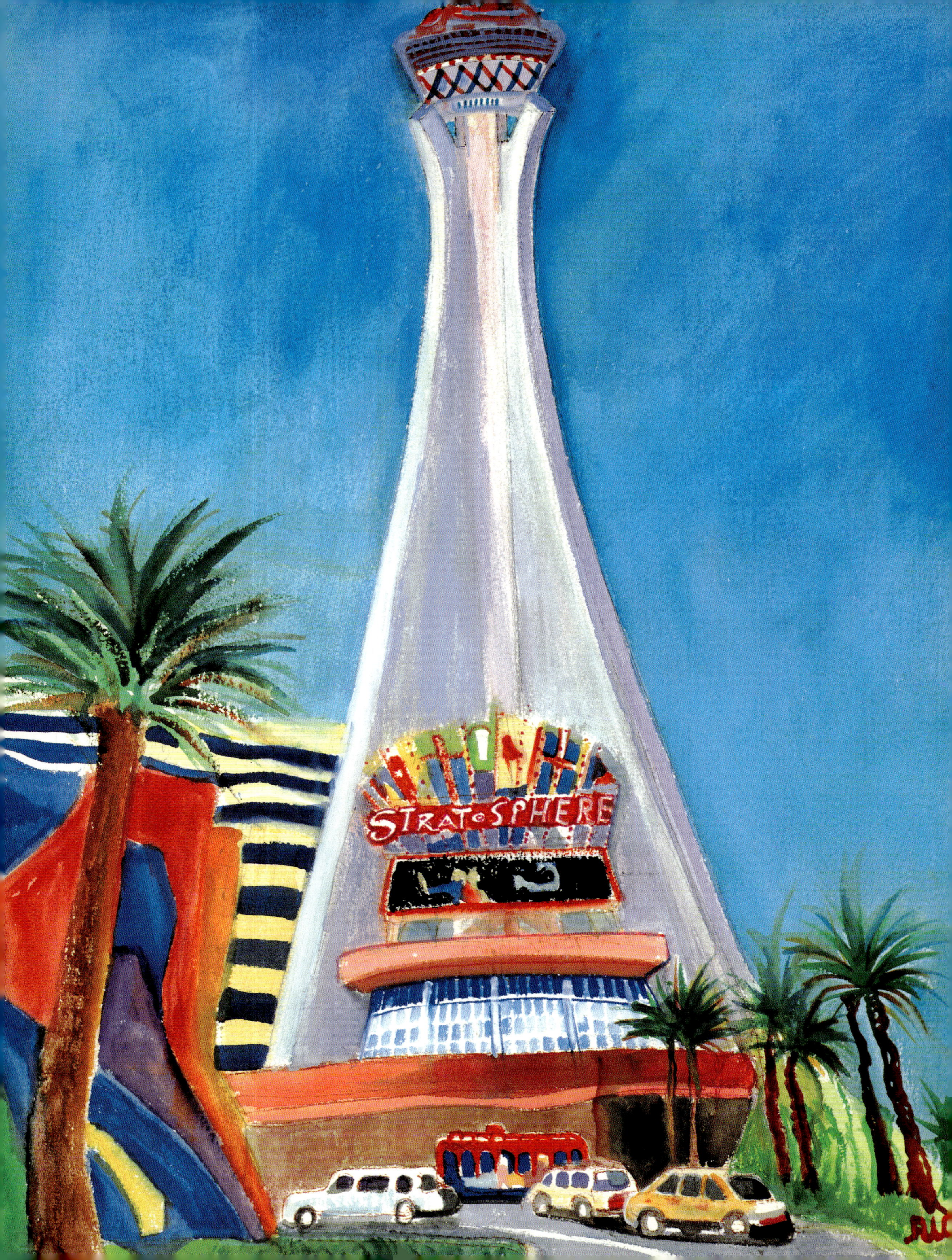
STRATOSPHERE

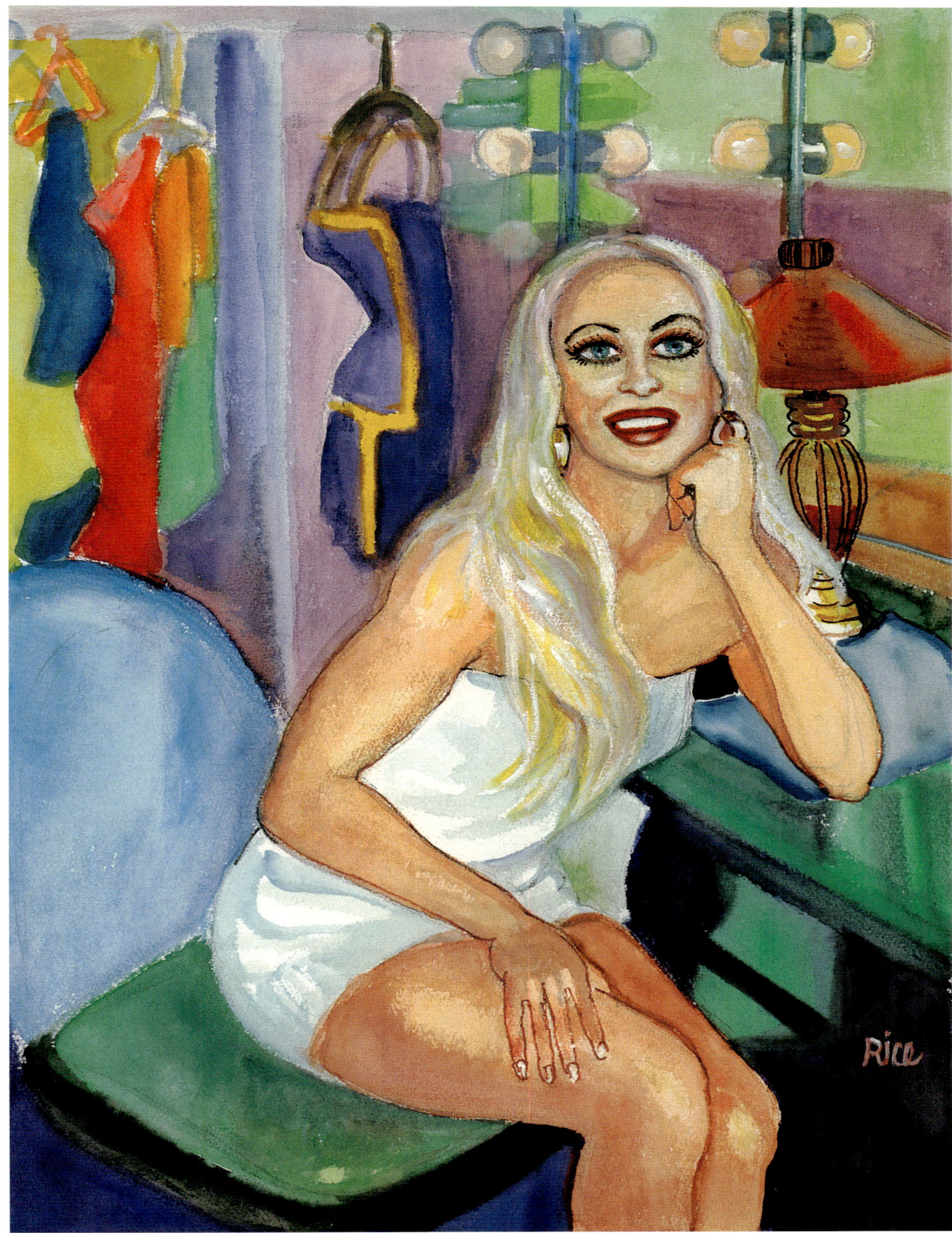

< THE STRATOSPHERE

Up, up and away—the Stratosphere Tower, Hotel & Casino rises to the heavens above Las Vegas. At 1,149 feet, it's the tallest observation tower in the U.S. and the ninth tallest structure in the world. In the time since its grand opening in 1996, (on the former site of Vegas World) the Stratosphere has established itself as one of the city's premiere landmarks. My unique perspective of the Tower came from painting it at the lowest levels, which feature an enormous casino (with some of the best odds in town), a showroom, a lounge, restaurants, a shopping mall and 1,500 rooms. High speed double-decker elevators whisk you to the lofty heights of the Observation Tower, where you'll find a stunning 360-degree view of the region, the rotating Top of the World restaurant, and the two highest thrill rides on the planet: the hair-raising roller coaster and the Big Shot. Recently, cast members from MTV's "Road Rules" and "Real World" series set a Guiness World Record by bungee-jumping from the Tower.

THE COMPLETE PACKAGE

Those long legs, that perfect shape, those gorgeous lips—that law degree? That's right, I learned "Showgirl of the 21st Century" Aki Alma isn't just beautiful—she's smart, too. As a showgirl in the Stardust's popular "Enter the Night" show, Aki's curvaceous, pouty image—complete with gigantic wigs, elaborate costumes and massive headdresses—is plastered all over town, on billboards and even an airplane. She also speaks five languages and is completing her legal studies in Nevada. The native of Eindhoven, Holland, got her first job performing at the Crazy Horse Saloon de Paris—the most prestigious (and sexy) show in France—before coming to the Stardust. I found Aki to be endearingly wistful, reflective and vulnerable, not to mention strong and brave—she was a real trouper when we met backstage after she performed through a painful injury. I was touched by her quality and impressed by her ambition.

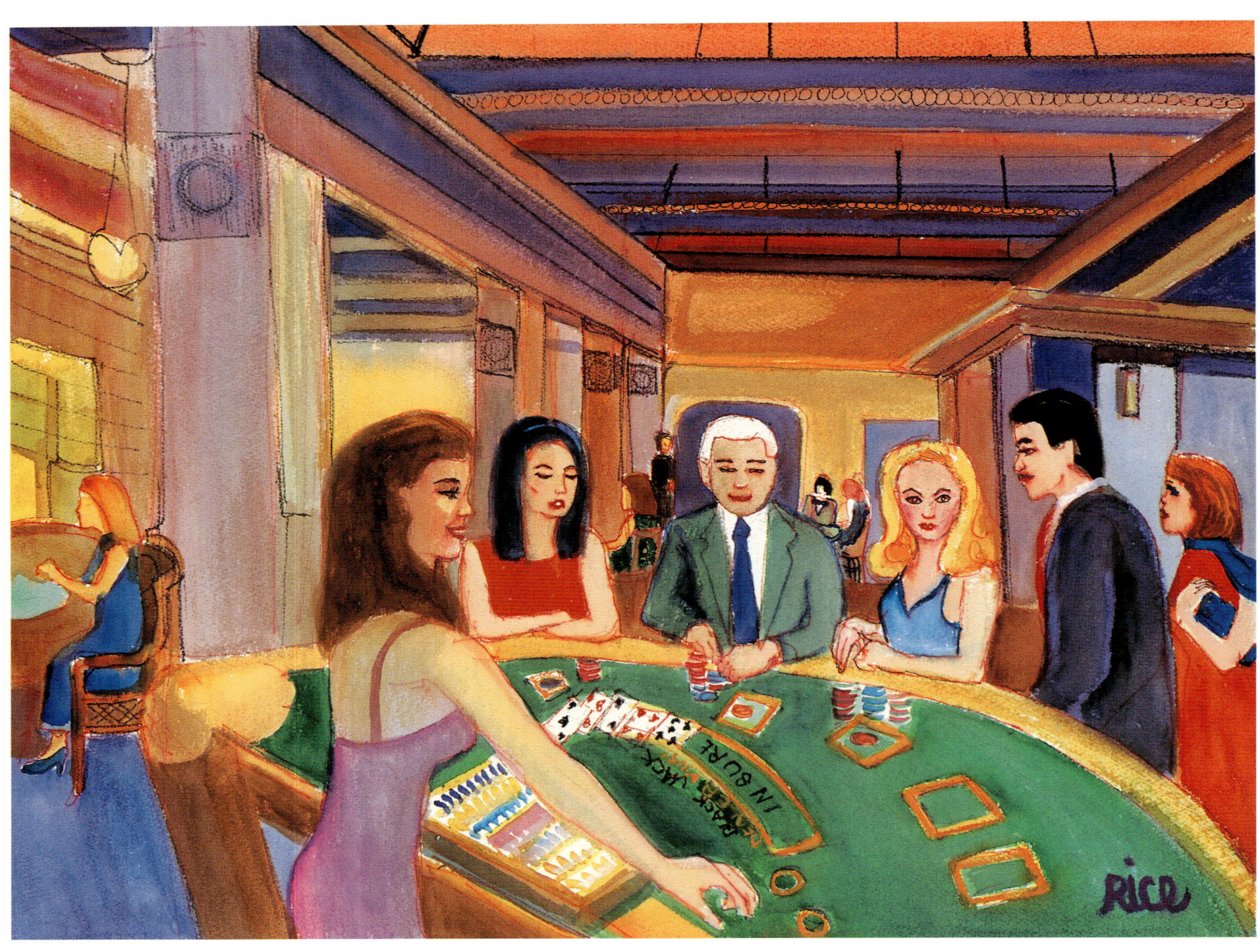

THE LONDON CLUB

The London Club, Las Vegas' first European-style high-roller luxury gaming salon, is the jewel in the crown of the refurbished Aladdin. A self-contained casino with a separate entrance and private lobby, it features 30 high-limit tables—including baccarat, roulette, poker and blackjack—and 100 high-denomination slots, as well as posh amenities like a private reception room, lounge and a five-star multi-ethnic restaurant with al fresco dining and a scenic view of the Strip.

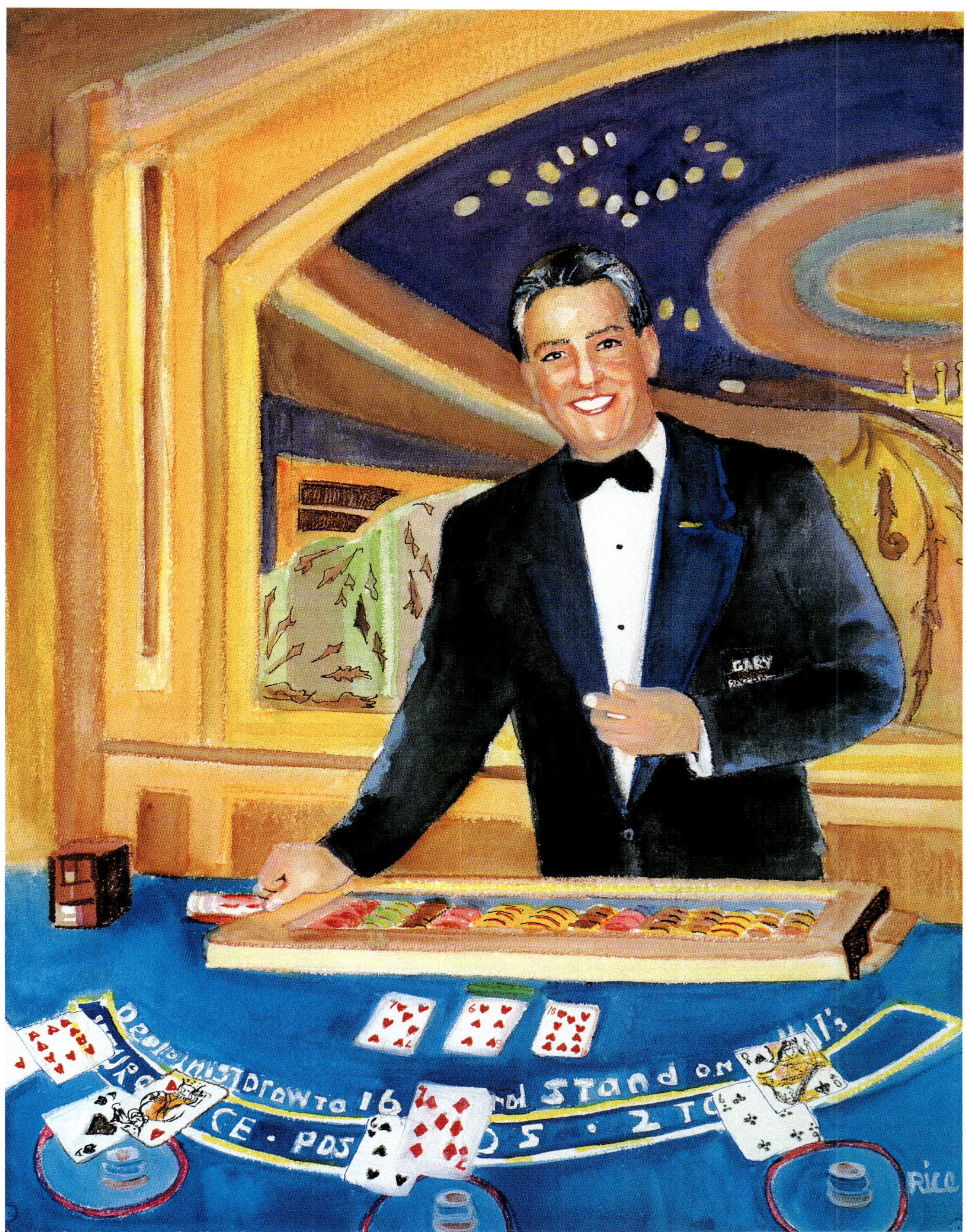

THE DASHING DEALER

I enjoyed my time at the blackjack table with Gary Van, the charming and dapper baccarat and blackjack dealer in the London Club Casino at the Aladdin Hotel. He has dealt to just about every prominent high-roller in the world. Gary is also a very good pianist—another role in which one can look great in a tuxedo. A true local boy, his father Garwood Van was the well-known orchestra leader who conducted at the opening of the El Rancho Hotel in 1942 and established the town's first music store and rock and roll nightclub, the Pussy Cat A Go Go. His mother is the lovely Joan Van, a former showroom dancer and model.

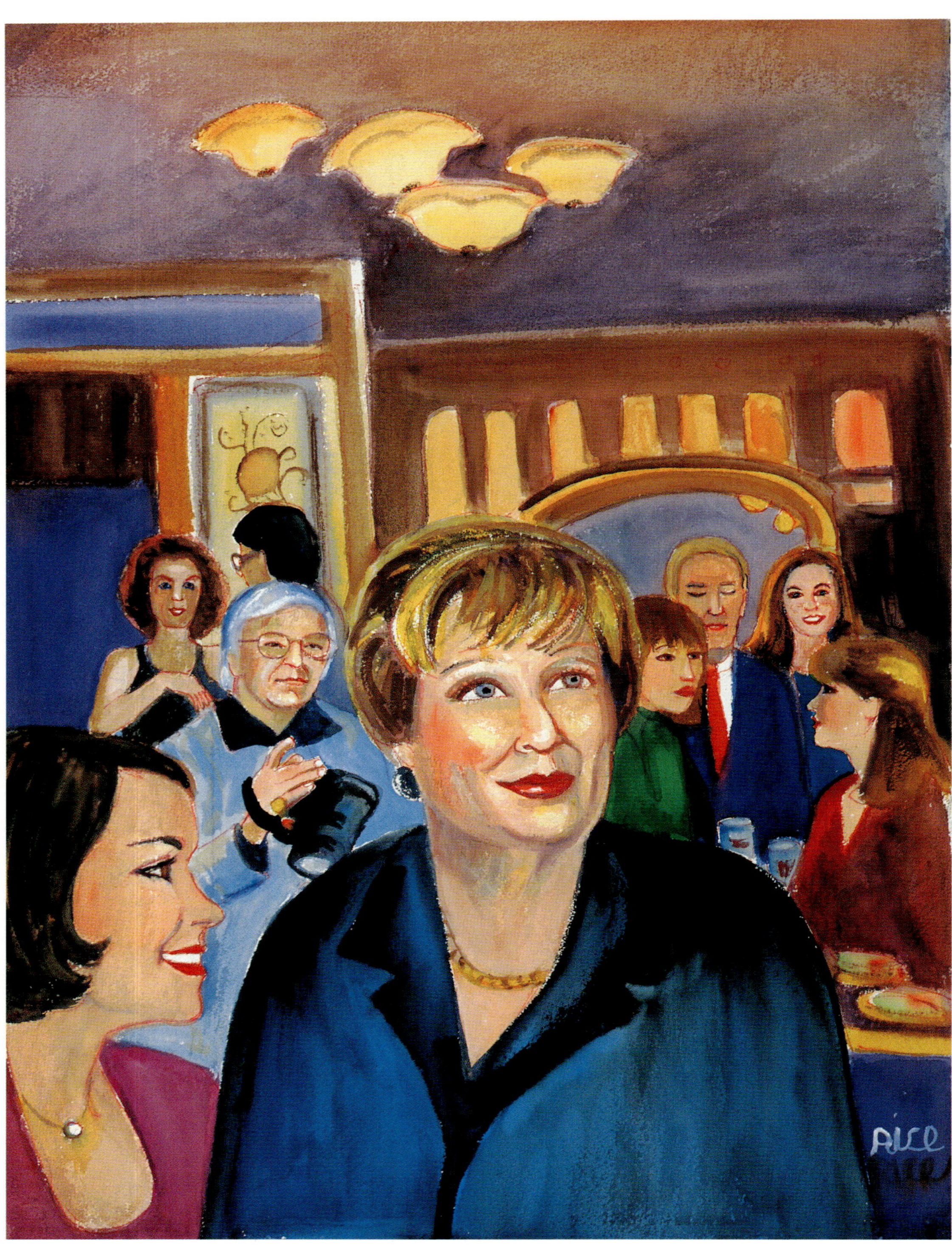

DOROTHY HUFFEY HOLDS COURT

Las Vegas' leading society columnist Dorothy Huffey was holding court during a party at Josef's, the chic French brasserie in the Aladdin's Desert Passage. For 20 years, Dorothy has written about where and when the city's elite meet and greet in the pages of the Las Vegas Review-Journal.

Dorothy's history is as interesting as her newspaper columns. Her great-grandfather James W. Haines was a Nevada senator who signed the State Constitution and hammered the famed silver spike at the meeting of the Transcontinental Railroads in Utah. Born in Reno, Dorothy met her husband, native Las Vegan Paul Huffey, at the University of Nevada, Reno—an institution to which she remains closely connected as the school's Director of Advancement. Once a Las Vegas school teacher, Dorothy has since become deeply involved in political, civic and charitable endeavors on the state and local level. Stephanie Boixo, Steve Crespi, Sharon Christal and Tara Orme were among those present. Well-connected and well-versed in the social graces, Dorothy's finger is always on the pulse of the Las Vegas social scene.

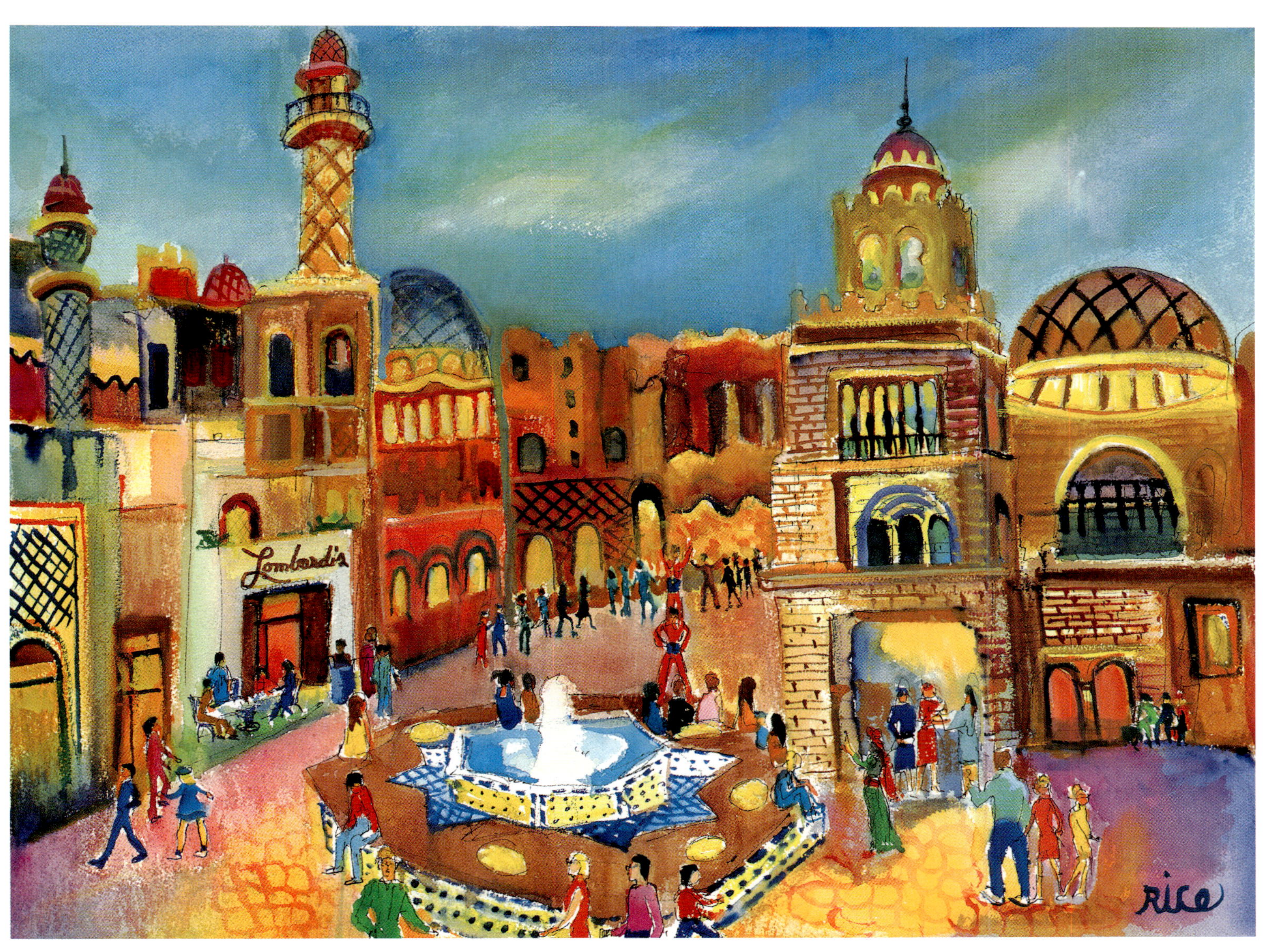

THE DESERT PASSAGE AT THE ALADDIN

From a wonderful vantage point on the bar balcony at Fat Anthony's restaurant, I spent an afternoon painting above the Aladdin's colorful Desert Passage. With more than 130 shops, 14 restaurants and the Prana nightclub, the Desert Passage captures the spirit of a Middle Eastern bazaar with acrobats, musicians, dancers and other exotic street performers cavorting around. "Rainstorms" occur in Merchants' Harbour every 30 minutes and there's a new surprise around every maze-like corner.

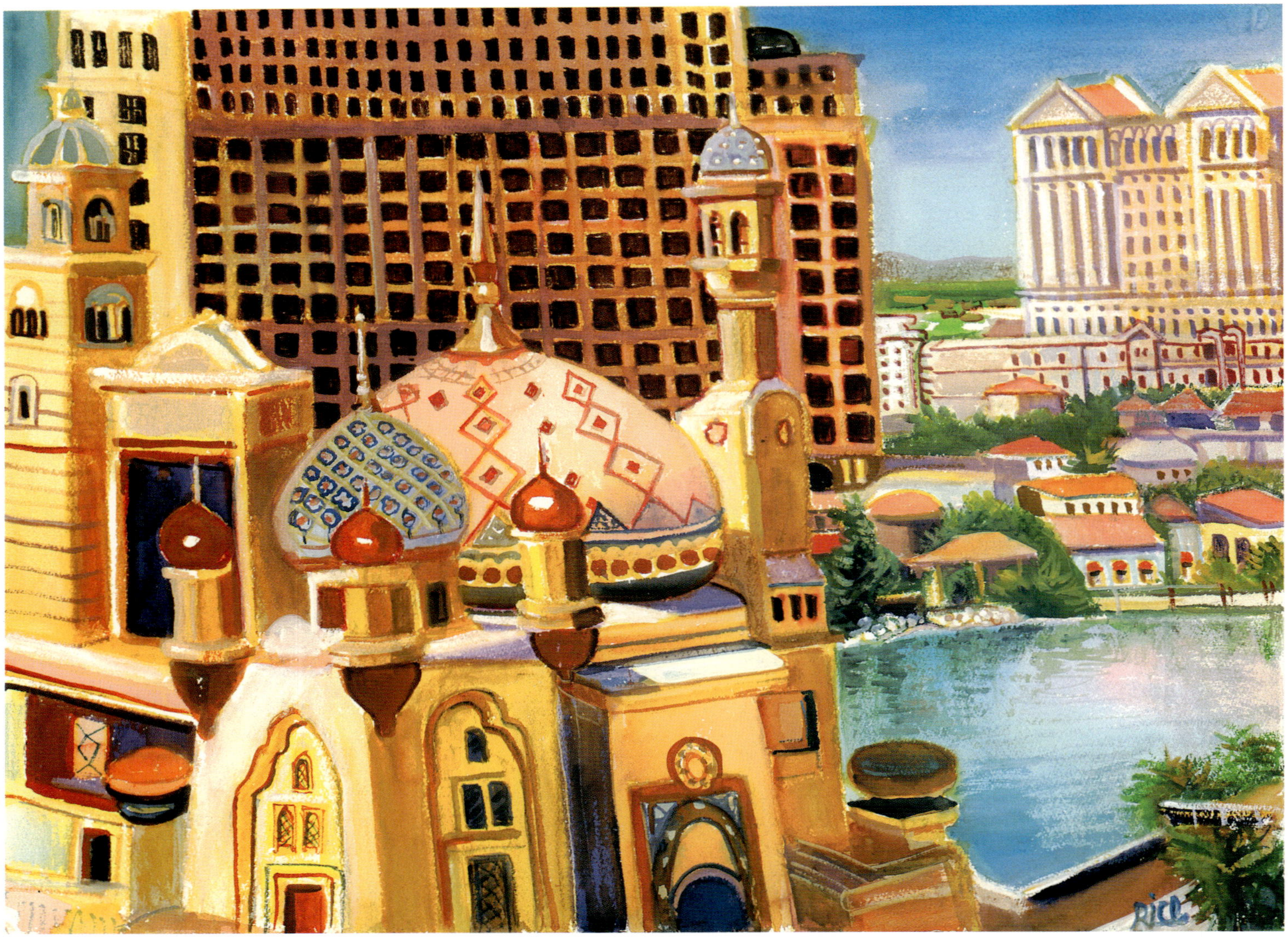

THE ALADDIN FROM MY WINDOW

For two weeks I enjoyed this "Eastern" view of the mosque-like domes of the Aladdin Hotel and Casino from my suite—plus I could see the Bellagio, Caesars Palace, Paris Las Vegas and the Rio in the background. Las Vegas is becoming a varied collection of architecture from every era and every land.

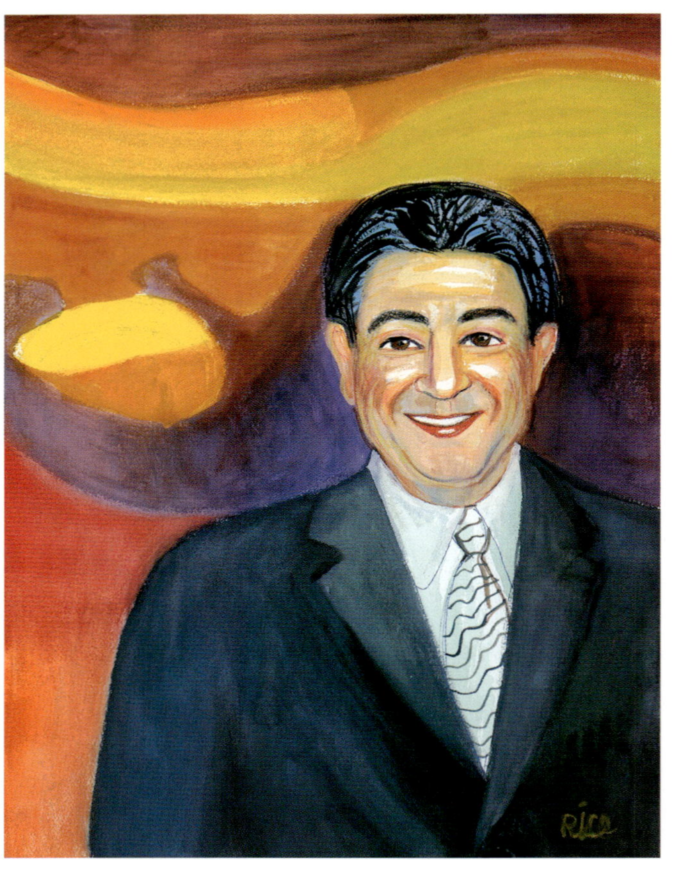

PRANA

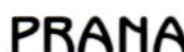

Sia Amiri tended to my every need when I visited Prana, a dynamic nightspot in the Aladdin's Desert Passage on Harmon Avenue. Prana is a hip operation, that alternates live music with a DJ, and has an elaborate sound system, a large dance floor, lighting effects and fish tanks encased in the walls. The exclusive mezzanine level has private luxury rooms, a cigar and bottle lounge and an opulent bar. It's a great place to dine on the finest Euro-Asian cuisine and dance the night away in the lap of luxury.

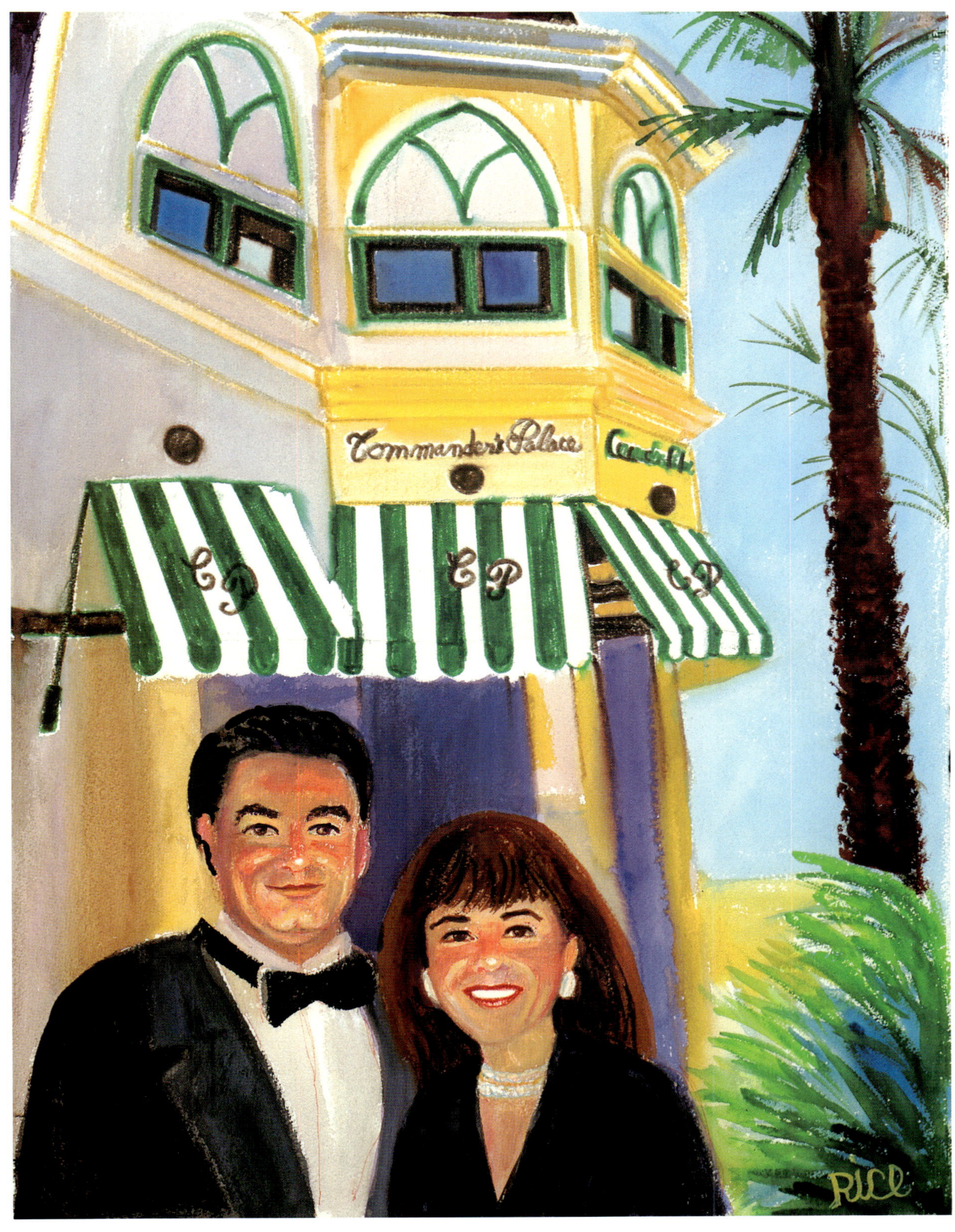

THE BRENNANS AT COMMANDER'S PALACE

Elizabeth and Brad Brennan, of the world-famous, award-winning Commander's Palace restaurant in New Orleans—a fixture since 1880 and one of my favorite restaurants in America—were my hosts at their Las Vegas outpost at the Aladdin's Desert Passage. Delicious Creole cuisine and other Louisiana favorites fill the menu. The Brennans said they treat all the diners as if they were guests in their own home. Brad—who began working in the kitchen of his family's eatery under Emeril Lagasse—has studied and worked in prestigious restaurants around the world, and today Elizabeth and he are already making their family's five-star legacy an institution in Las Vegas.

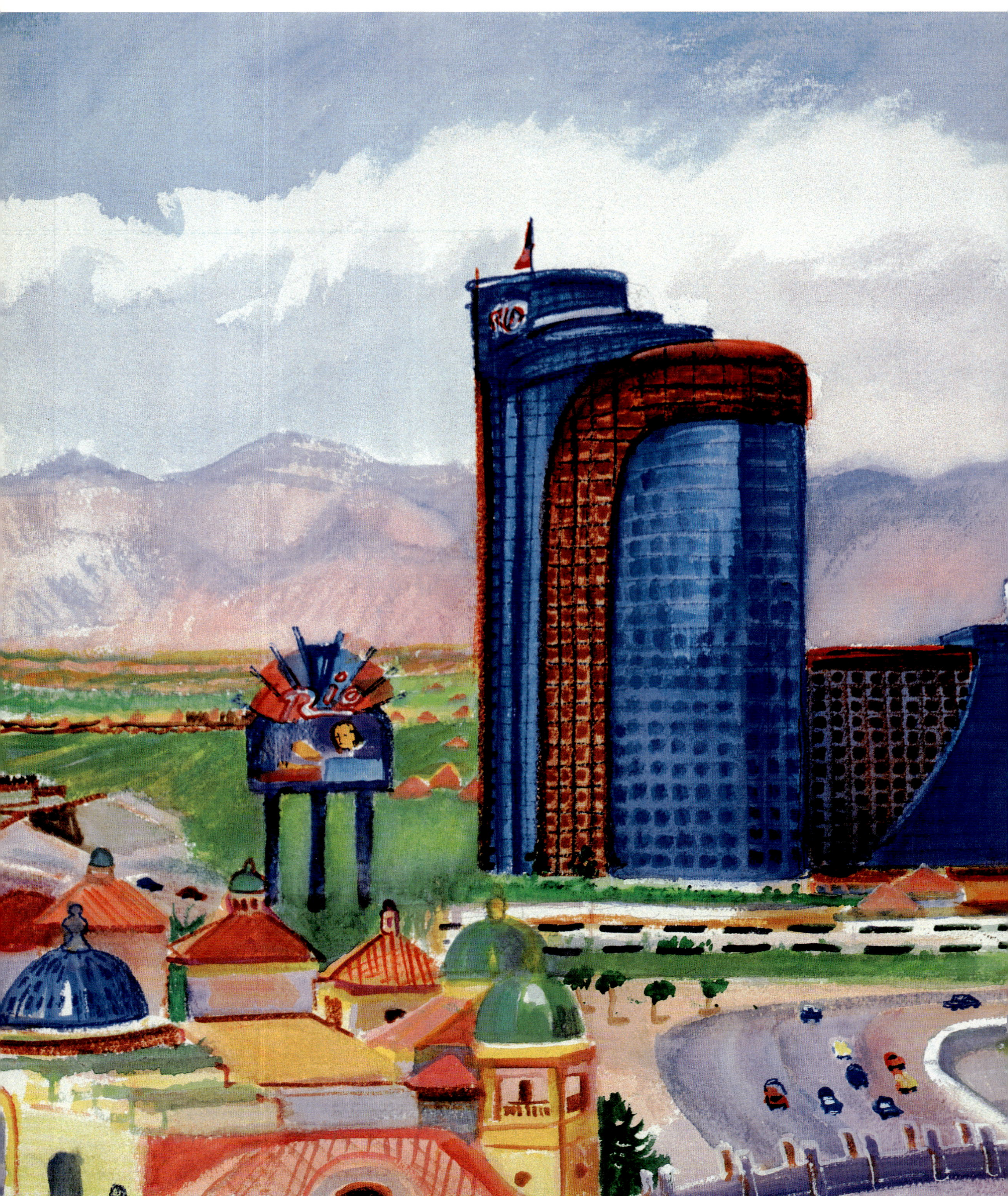
Rio
RIO

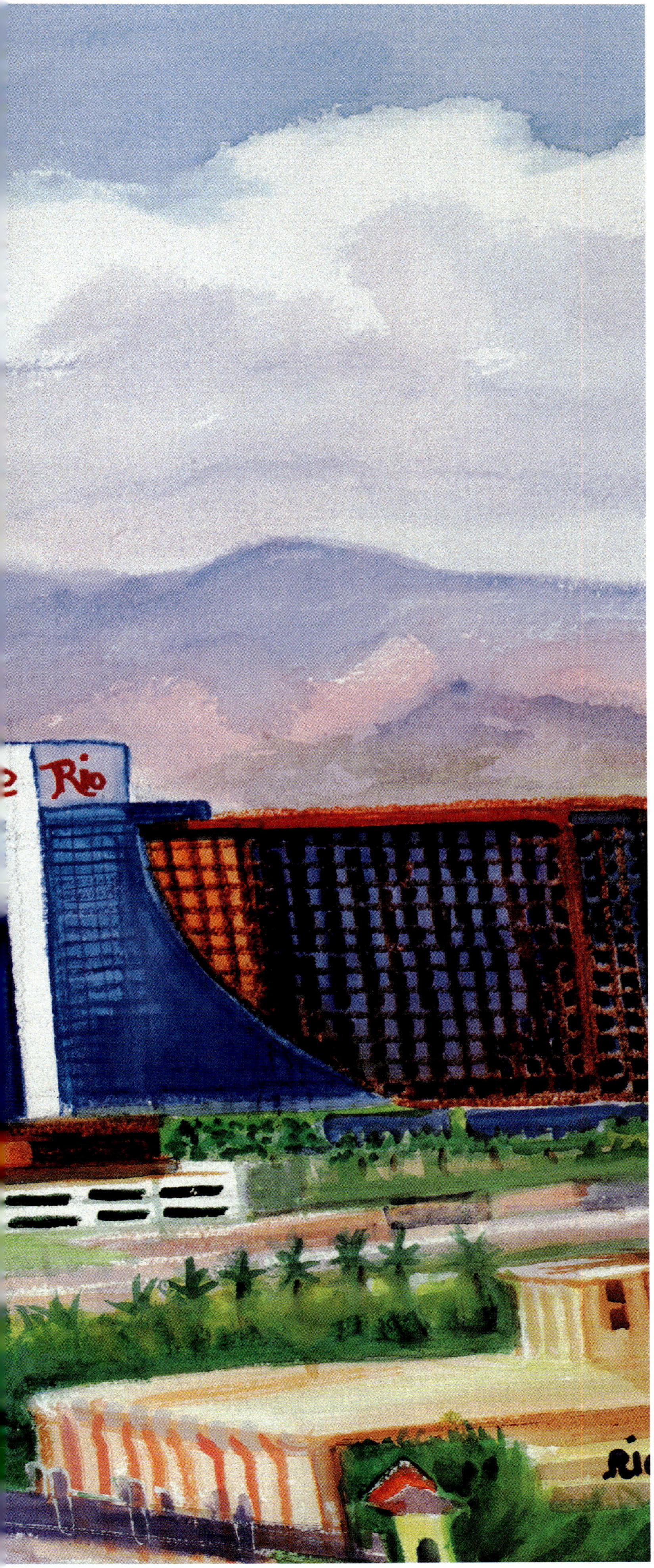

OFF THE STRIP

IF YOU THINK ALL THE ACTION IN LAS VEGAS IS either on the Strip or Downtown, think again! The areas surrounding the city's focal points have become bustling centers of excitement and activity of their own in recent years. For hotel-casino gaming, accommodations, attractions and entertainment, look no further than the Hard Rock, Sam's Town, the Rio, Orleans, Palace Station or the Las Vegas Hilton. There's also a variety of dining options, from the fine cuisine of upscale eateries like Piero's to the family-friendly fun of Joe's Crab Shack. Culture can be found in traditional forms—like the Las Vegas Art Museum—and the not-so-traditional—like the Elvis-A-Rama or Liberace museums. The Las Vegas Convention Center is a mecca for visitors from around the globe. There are institutions that keep Las Vegas moving on a civic level (the Clark County Government Center), a spiritual level (the Mormon Temple) and an educational level (UNLV). In fact, there's so much to do you just might not make it to the Strip!

THE RIO, RISING

The Rio on Flamingo Avenue was Las Vegas' first major hotel of the 1990s and made an instant big splash, bringing a Mardi Gras ambiance to town and snagging the coveted title of the best neon sign in Las Vegas. The bustling hotel is constantly expanding and adding to its party-hearty atmosphere with attractions like the rollicking Voodoo Room, which features fabulous high-angle views of the Strip.

MASQUERADE AT THE RIO

The Rio's "Masquerade in the Sky," a float-filled Mardi Gras-style parade, moves along a 950-foot track suspended from the ceiling over the casino, and is one of the best free shows I've seen in Las Vegas.

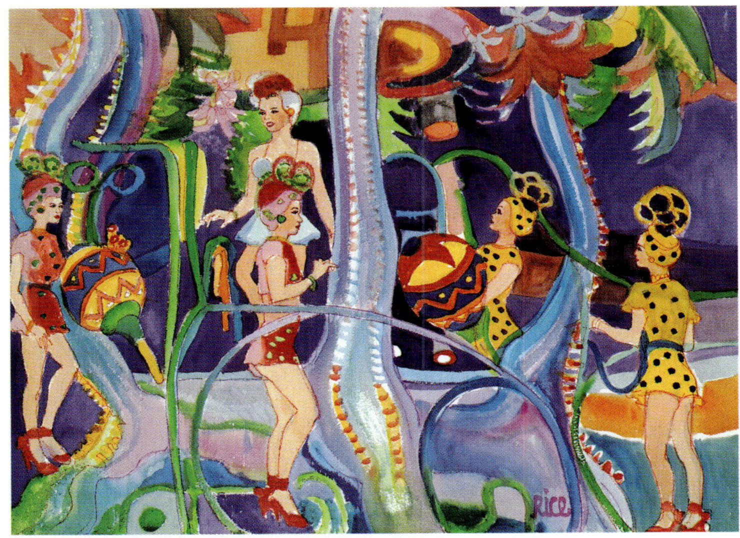

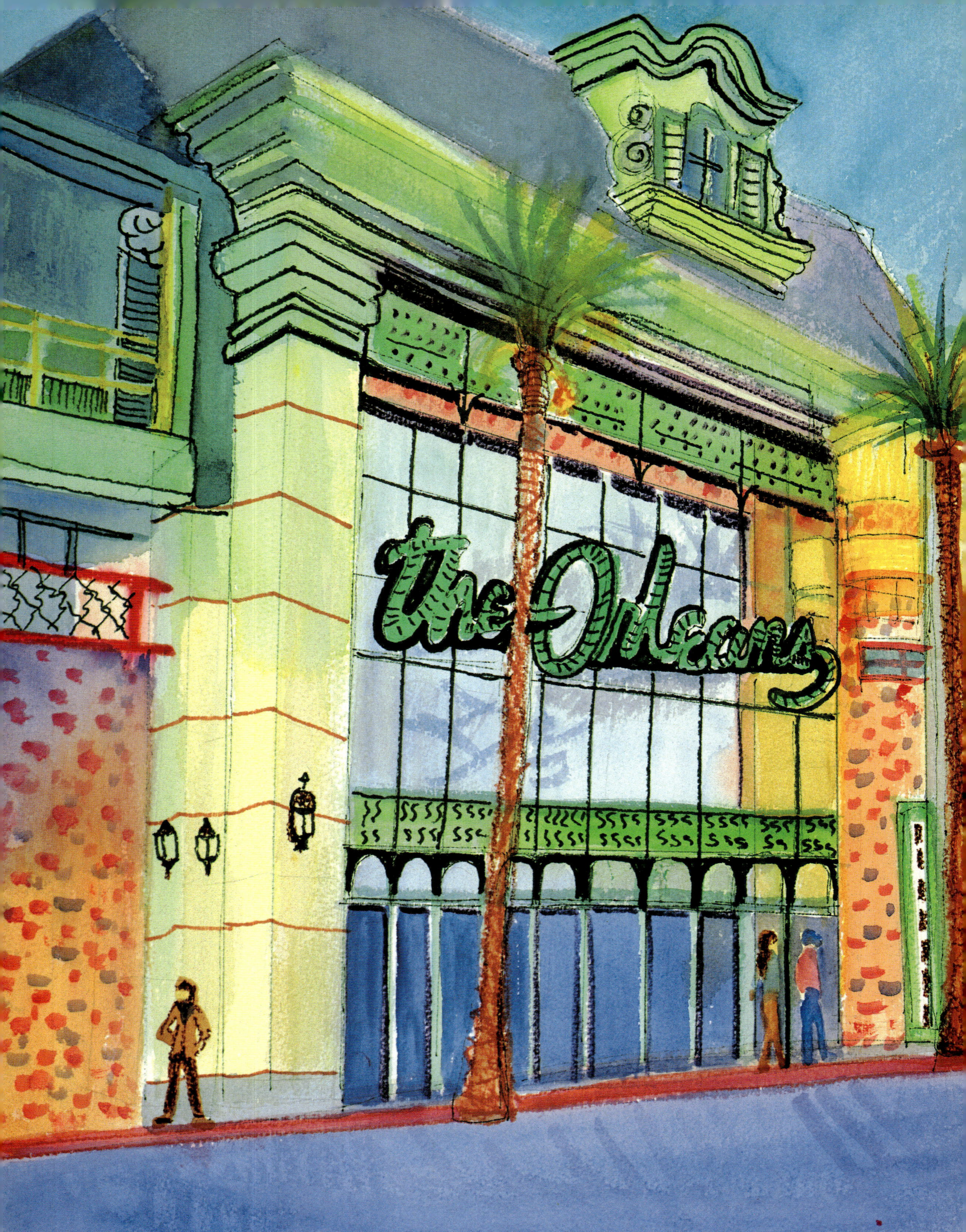
the Orleans
RICE

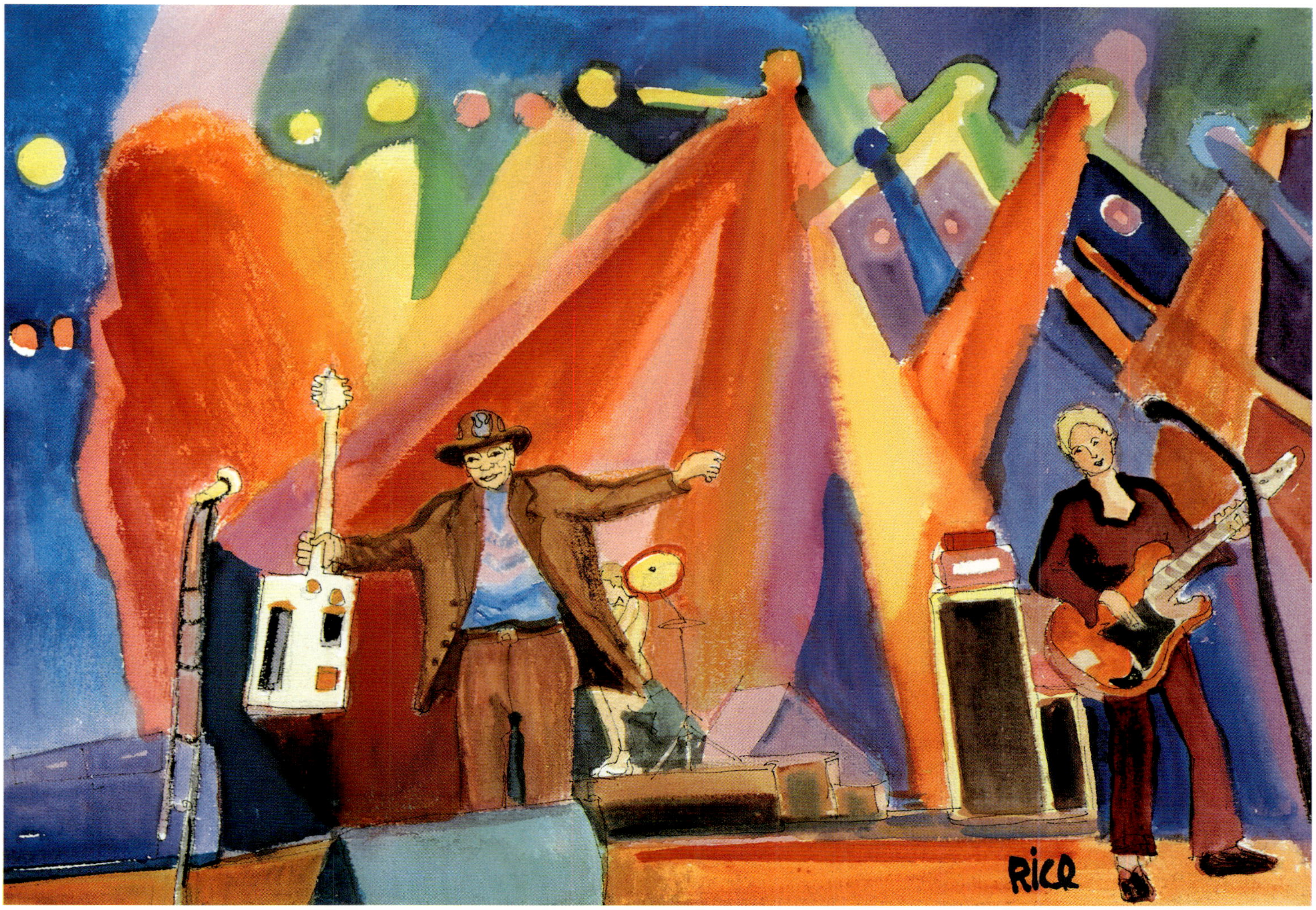

ROCKIN' BLUES WITH BO DIDDLEY AT ORLEANS

One of the few living musical artists to have a song named after him (okay, it's one of his songs), Bo Diddley has been wowing concerts audiences—like the one that gathered to watch him play at the Orleans Showroom—for nearly 50 years. "I've entertained your grandparents, your parents and now I'm entertaining you," he told us. Bo started out trying to sound like Blues legend Muddy Waters and eventually carved out his signature hard-driving beat which makes people want to jump up and dance. He has his own trademark instrument, the distinctive square-shaped guitar he first built in 1951 (a guitar company crafts them for him now). Bo has been performing in Las Vegas since his first local gig at the Showboat in 1959, part of a long career that proves sometimes it's hip to be square.

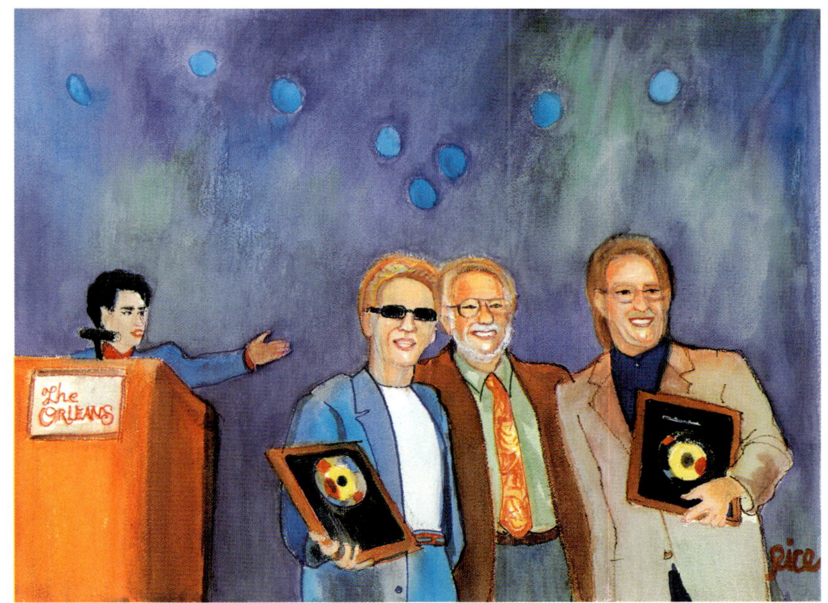

THE RIGHTEOUS BROTHERS MEET THE MAYOR

After a lively introduction from KSUL radio's Duke Morgan, Las Vegas Mayor Oscar B. Goodman presented the Righteous Brothers—Bobby Hatfield and Bill Medley—with plaques commemorating their enduring hit "You've Lost That Lovin' Feeling," part of a music awards ceremony at the Orleans Hotel and Casino. The singers autographed fans' memorabilia afterward at a fun cocktail and cake reception.

< THE ORLEANS

Since opening two miles from the Strip in 1996, up-and-coming Orleans has become popular with locals and visitors looking for something different. The hotel features a spacious casino, a bowling alley, an assortment of restaurants, movie theaters, a very "in" lounge scene featuring New Orleans jazz and big band swing, and a showroom that welcomes entertainers ranging from comedy legend Jerry Lewis to old-school crooner Al Martino to folk icons Peter, Paul and Mary.

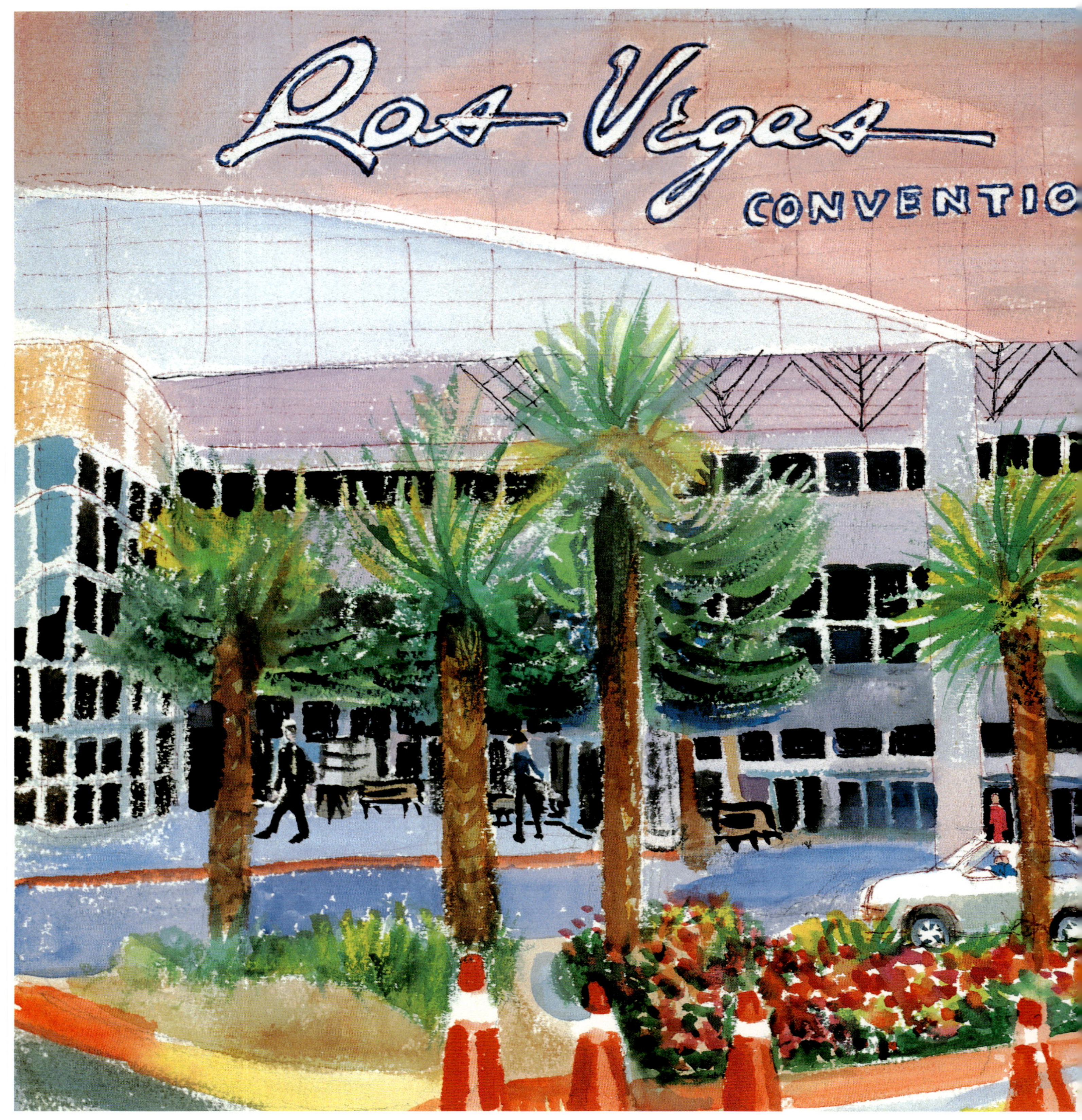

THE LAS VEGAS CONVENTION CENTER

Las Vegas' consistent climate and myriad attractions have made it a year-round destination for groups and organizations since five thousand Los Angeles-area Shriners gathered here for the first local convention in 1935. With over 2 million square feet of display space, the Las Vegas Convention Center has emerged as the city's premiere venue for conventions, meetings and trade shows. The attractively-designed Convention Center first opened in 1959 and has undergone tremendous expansions over the years, and today, its guests pump billions of dollars into the city.

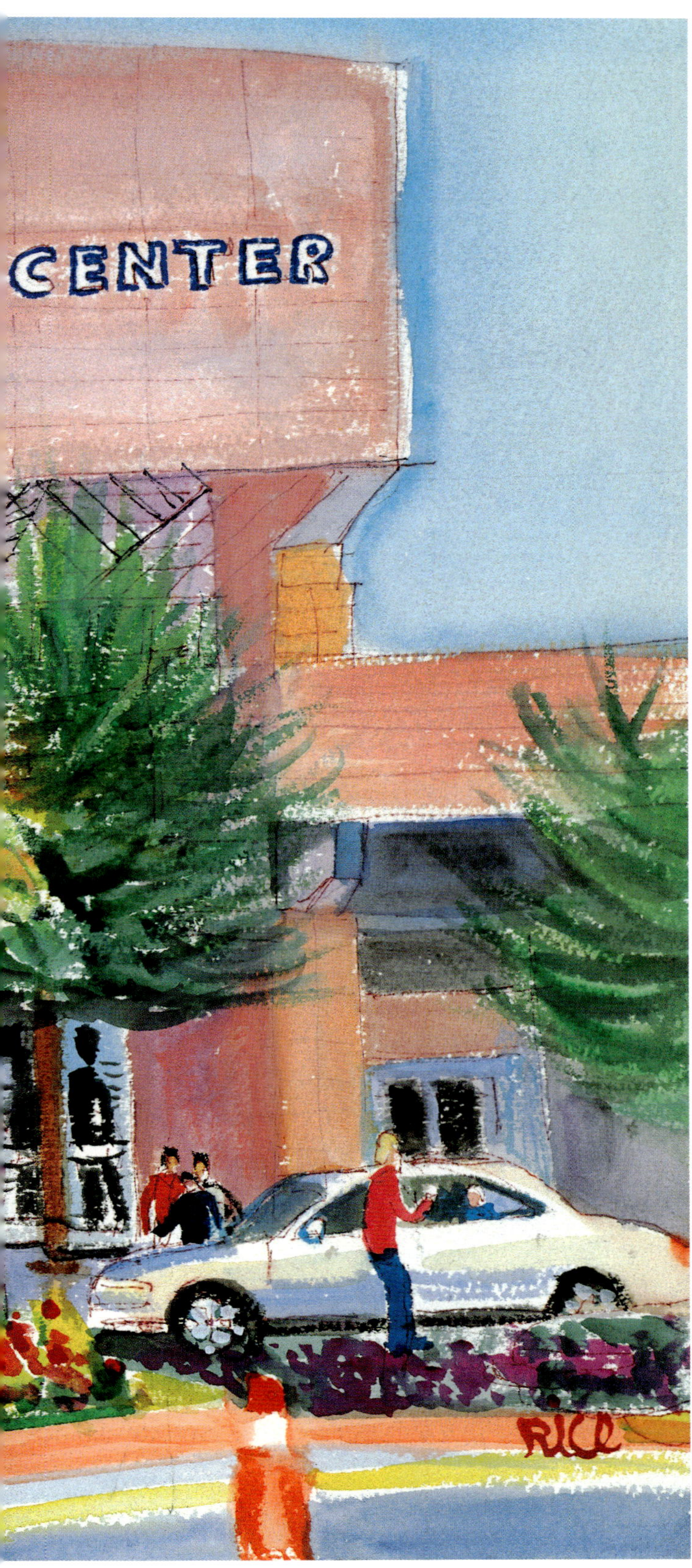

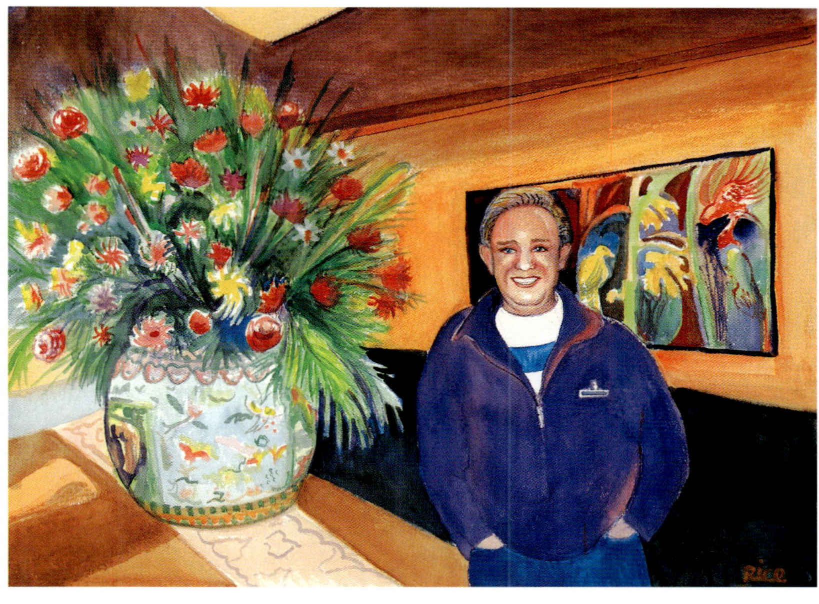

PIERO'S

Meet Freddie Glusman, the creator of one of Las Vegas' five-star restaurants, Piero's. A free-standing location with casual atmosphere and a fine menu created by chef Gilbert Fetaz, Piero's has become a singular sensation without being part of a huge hotel/casino, drawing the Las Vegas A-list as well as top celebrities from entertainment, sports and politics. A scene from "Casino" was even filmed here. Italian food is the specialty, of course, but the kitchen also authentically replicates other cuisines, including German, French and kosher dishes. Part of Piero's charm comes from Freddie himself, a real character who knows the secrets of good service and attitude.

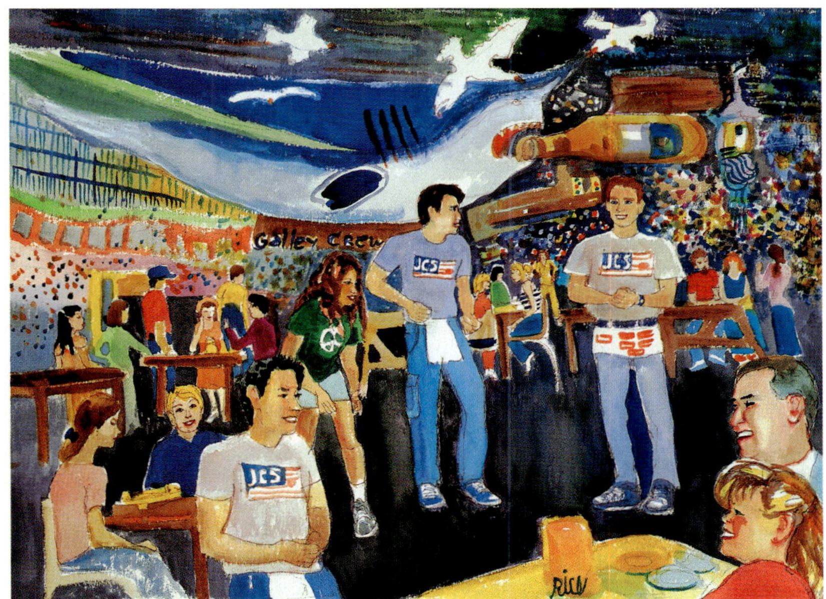

JOE'S CRAB SHACK

I had a terrific time over a tasty crustacean dinner at Joe's Crab Shack. The atmosphere was fun and informal, the food was just right, the enthusiastic clientele of all ages and the service—provided by waiters and waitresses as skilled as entertainers as they were as food servers—was thoroughly enjoyable.

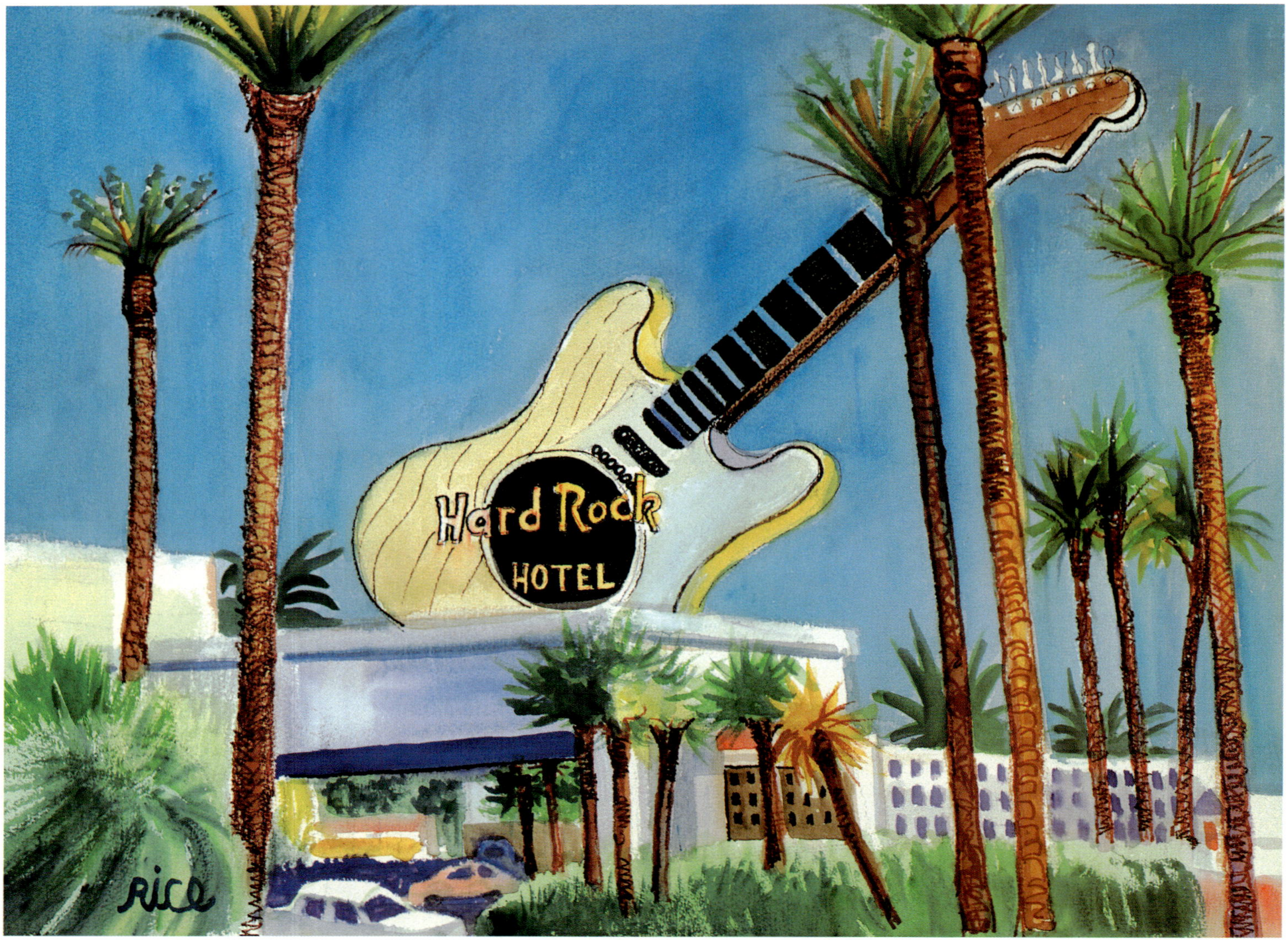

HARD ROCK HOTEL AND CASINO

The giant signature guitar that has graced so many of the popular Hard Rock Cafes around the world beckons those whose love of rock and roll extends beyond Elvis to the Hard Rock Hotel and Casino, off the Strip at Harmon Avenue and Paradise Road. The casino is packed with a wide variety of music memorabilia commemorating more than four decades of shaking, rattling and rolling. The spacious rooms are often hard to come by since the hippest visitors to Las Vegas flock to the Hard Rock to see concerts by everyone from cutting edge acts like Macy Gray to legends like the Rolling Stones.

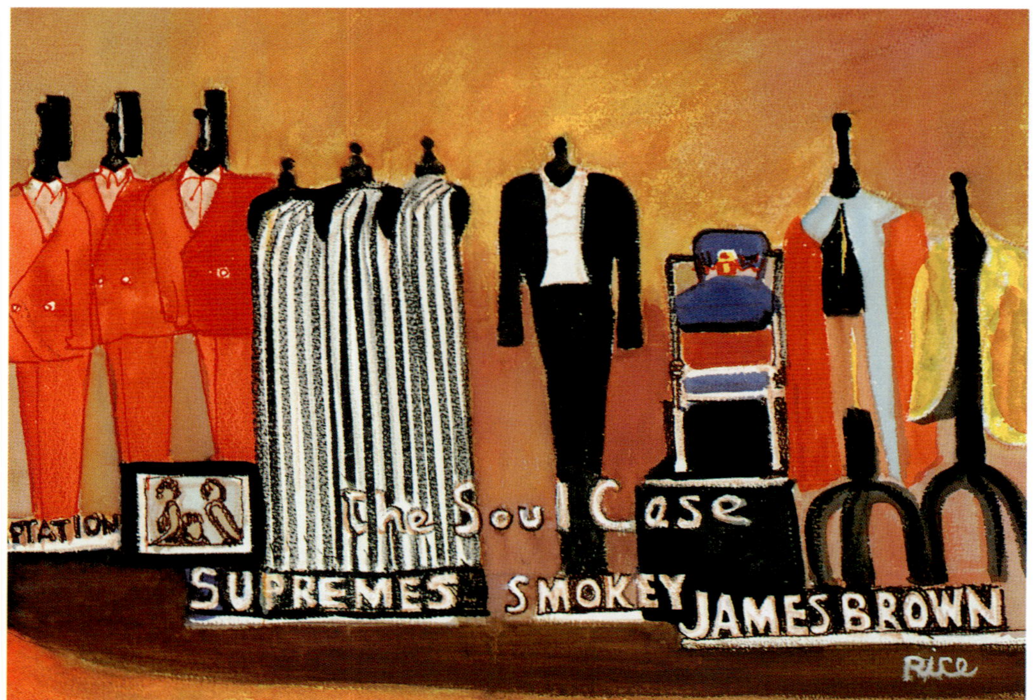

A LITTLE BIT OF SOUL

"The Soul Case," featuring wardrobe and other memorabilia belonging to such soul music acts as Diana Ross and the Supremes, Smokey Robinson, the Temptations and James Brown, is just one of the many pop music-themed displays at the Hard Rock Hotel and Casino.

BET WHILE YOU GET WET >

Admirers of the human form will want to check out the hardbodies trying to hit twenty-one at blackjack at the lushly-appointed pool of the Hard Rock Hotel and Casino, which features swim-up gambling and bar service right in the pool and a real sand beach. You can admire the bikinied beauties and jam-wearing hunks catching rays poolside or frolicking in the water. You can also check out the poolside action from anywhere in the world, any time of day thanks to its live webcam.

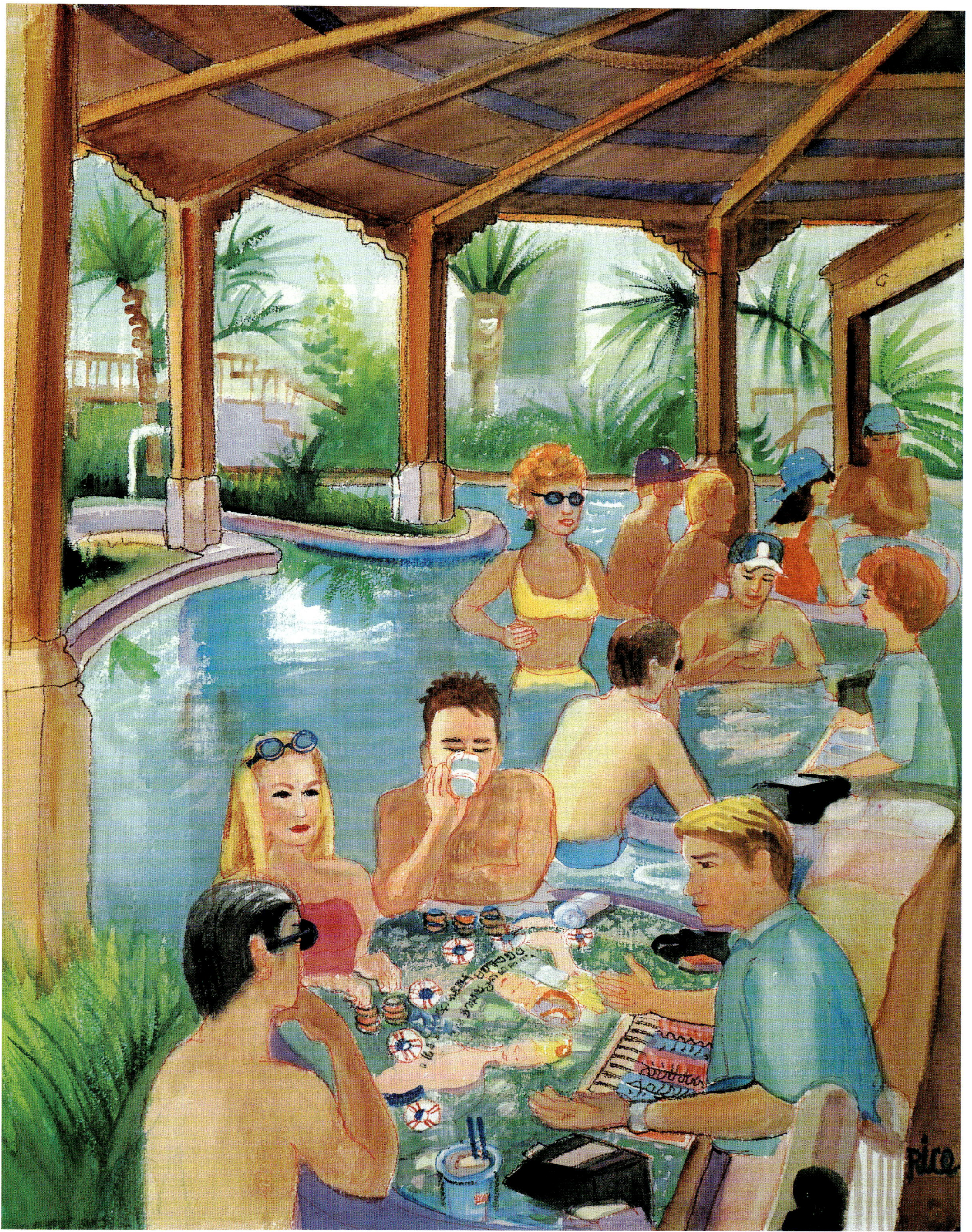
Rice

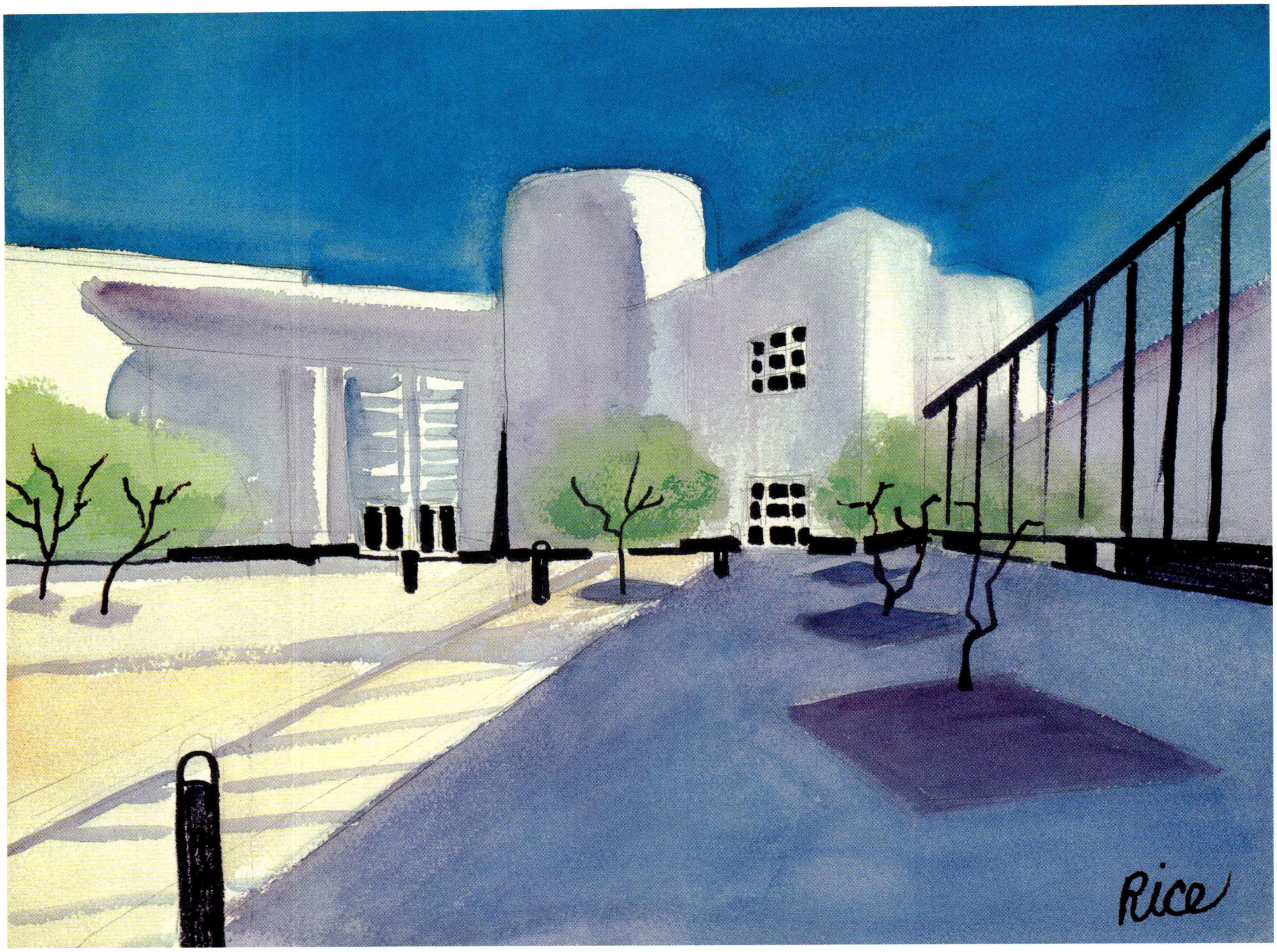

A WORK OF ART ITSELF

I liked the exterior design of the Las Vegas Art Museum, a $20 million state-of-the-art facility and the first fine arts museum in the city's history. Built to Smithsonian specifications, the museum features six major shows and three traveling exhibits each year, with an emphasis on art after Post-Modernism.

THE LAS VEGAS ART MUSEUM

The uniquely designed Las Vegas Art Museum by Tate & Snyder Architects, in conjunction with Meyer Scherer, Rock Castle, Ltd., is one of the latest cultural oases to debut in the desert. Works by artists Salvador Dali and Marc Chagall are among the wonderful exhibits that have been displayed here.

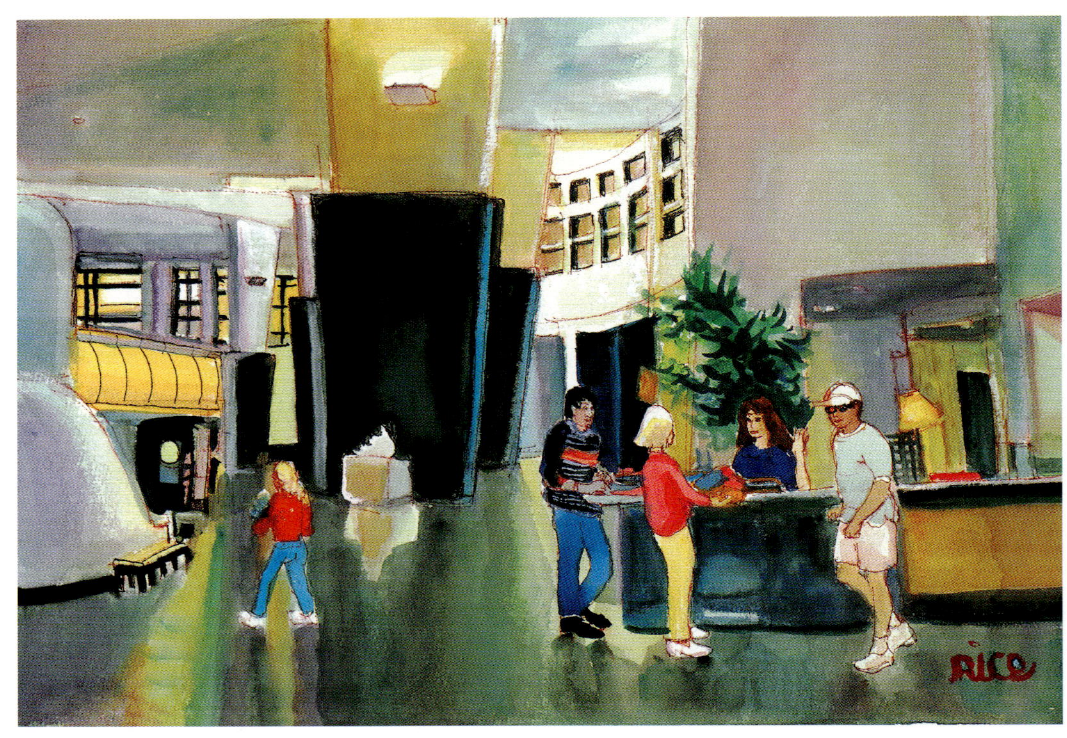

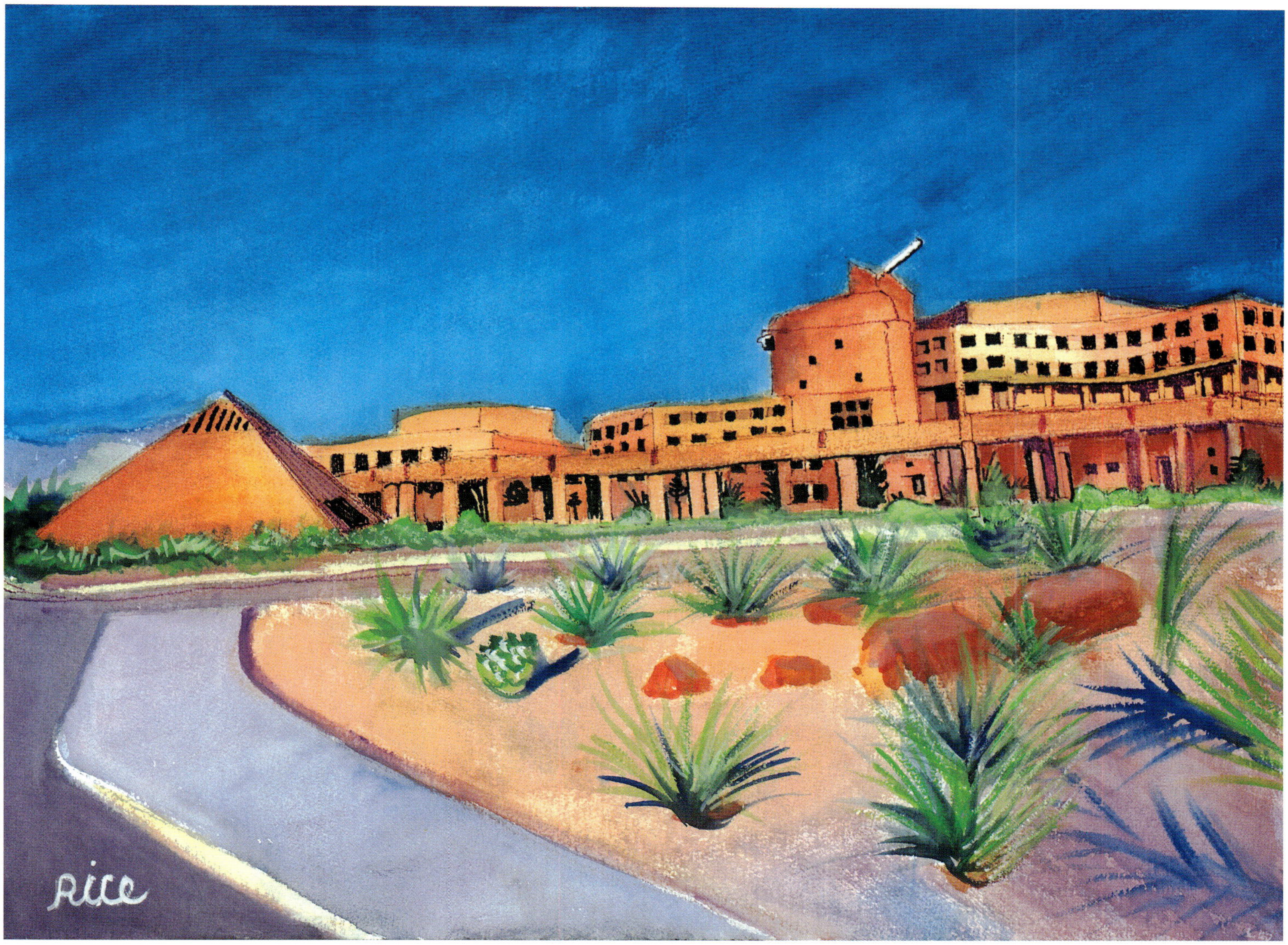

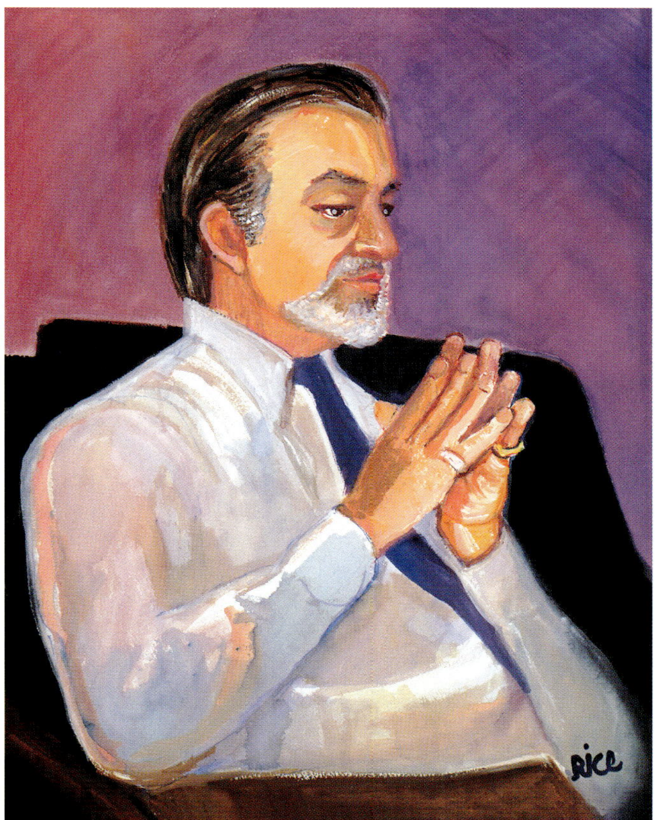

CLARK COUNTY GOVERNMENT CENTER

The unique 385,000-square-foot Clark County Government Center building—which has won numerous local and national awards as the best-designed building in Las Vegas—houses not only the seat of the county government and all its services but also as a civic events center and for emergency operations during crises.

DOMINGO CAMBEIRO

The new landmark Clark County Government Center was designed by the award-winning local architect Domingo Cambeiro in association with C.W. Fentress J.H. Bradburn & Associates, P.C. No one has built more government and educational institutions in Las Vegas than Cambeiro. Born in Havana, Cuba, Cambeiro opened his Las Vegas firm in 1962, and over four decades, he has designed nearly 100 educational projects for the Clark County School District, UNLV and the Community College of Southern Nevada. He's also worked on McCarran International Airport, the Latin Chamber of Commerce Building and the Showcase Retail/Entertainment Complex on the Strip. Domingo has proven he knows all about building strong foundations—both in buildings and in communities.

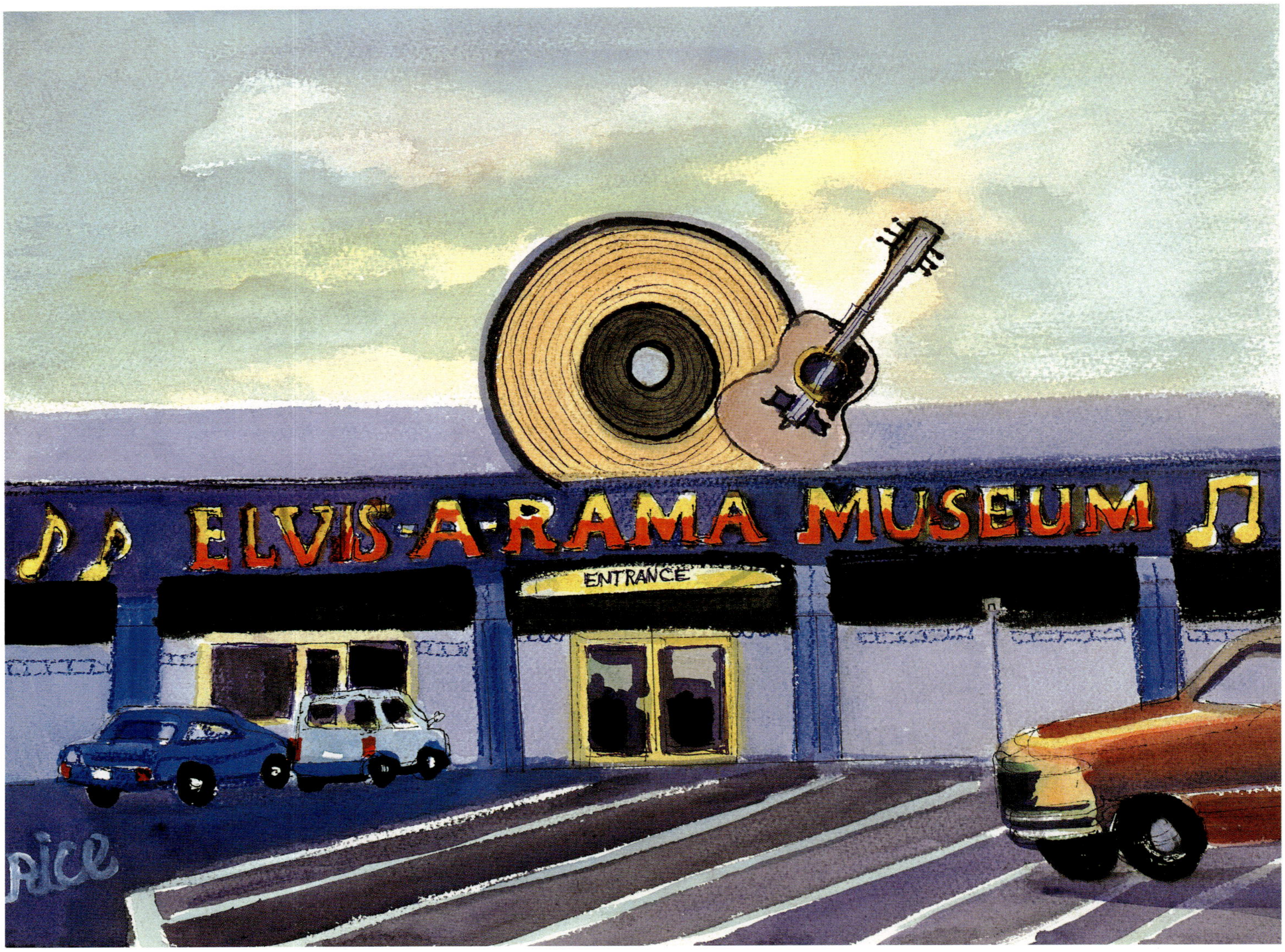

THE ELVIS-A-RAMA MUSEUM

Graceland may have been the place Elvis Presley called home, but Las Vegas was his element. No place remembers the King as fondly as the Elvis-A-Rama Museum, just a block off the Strip, where you can view such treasures as Elvis' 1955 Cadillac and his customized purple Lincoln, his Army-issue winter dress fatigues, his "peacock" jumpsuit and various movie wardrobe items and tons of other Memphis Mafia miscellany—even his Social Security card!

STAR TREK: THE EXPERIENCE

Many great nods to the past fill Las Vegas, but they haven't left out the future—the popular 24th Century of the many incarnations of Gene Roddenberry's TV sci-fi phenomenon, "Star Trek." Have you dreamed of boldly going where no one has gone before? In the words of Captain Jean-Luc Picard, you can "make it so" at the Las Vegas Hilton's "Star Trek: The Experience." Beam aboard the Starship Enterprise and experience a warp-speed adventure, or shuttle over to the Promenade of Deep Space Nine, and trade space stories in Quark's Bar. There are also dozens of props, costumes and other futuristic items from the various "Trek" incarnations on display. Just don't irritate any imposing Klingons, and watch your wallet around the greedy Ferengis!

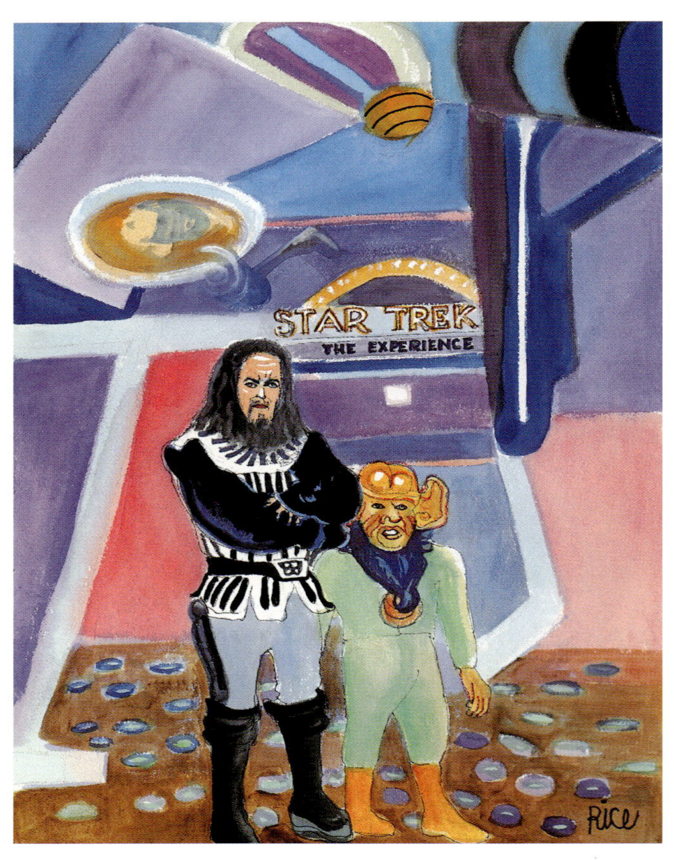

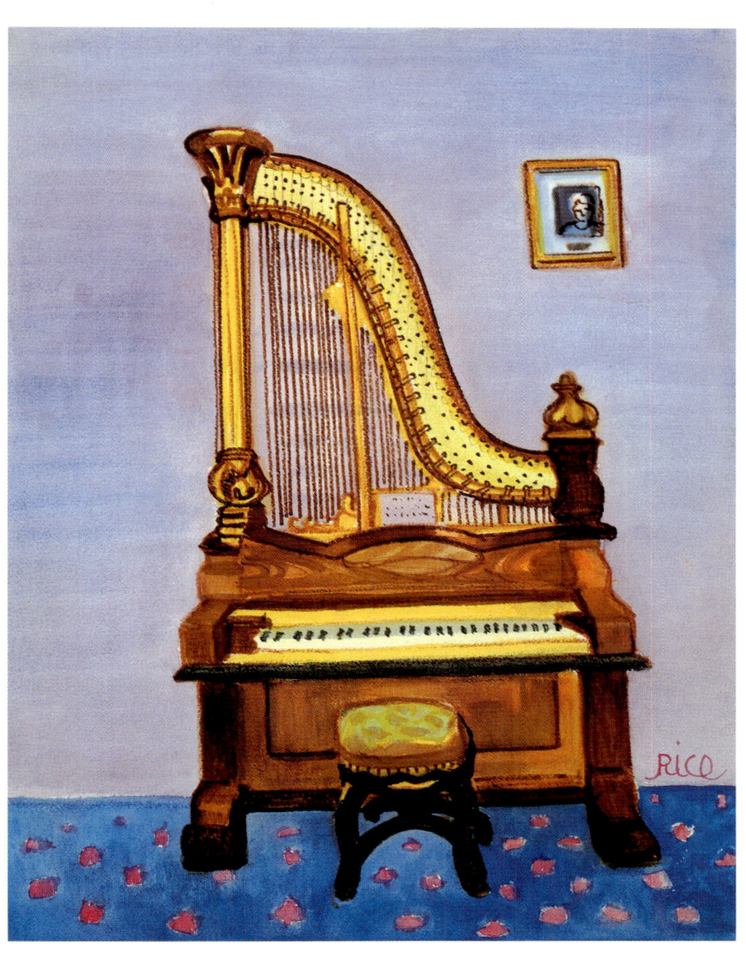

LIBERACE'S LEGACY

From the time the famed pianist Liberace made his debut at the Last Frontier in 1944, he became Las Vegas' undisputed "Mr. Showmanship." Liberace's musical talents were rivaled only by his flamboyance, adding elaborate apparel, ornate candelabras and baroque touches to his act. To display many of the sensational, one-of-a-kind treasures he accumulated over the years—including unbelievable custom pianos and cars and incredible art, jewels, memorabilia and antiques—he opened the Liberace Museum on Tropicana Avenue in 1979. It quickly became one of the most popular attractions in town. I found this elaborate piano/harp combo to be symbolic—Liberace's probably been dazzling the angels in Heaven—and outdoing all celestial grandeur—since his death in 1987.

LIED DISCOVERY CHILDREN'S MUSEUM

This interactive museum (pronounced "leed") on Las Vegas Boulevard is a great place for young kids to learn by doing, with more than 100 hands-on exhibits focusing on problem-solving and experimentation. Reach out and touch a tornado or peer at the world from inside a giant bubble. The popular Everyday Living exhibit offers a child-sized environment where kids earn a paycheck, shop for groceries and use an ATM. There's also an in-house radio station called K-KID and an eight-story Science Tower with plenty of high-tech tools.

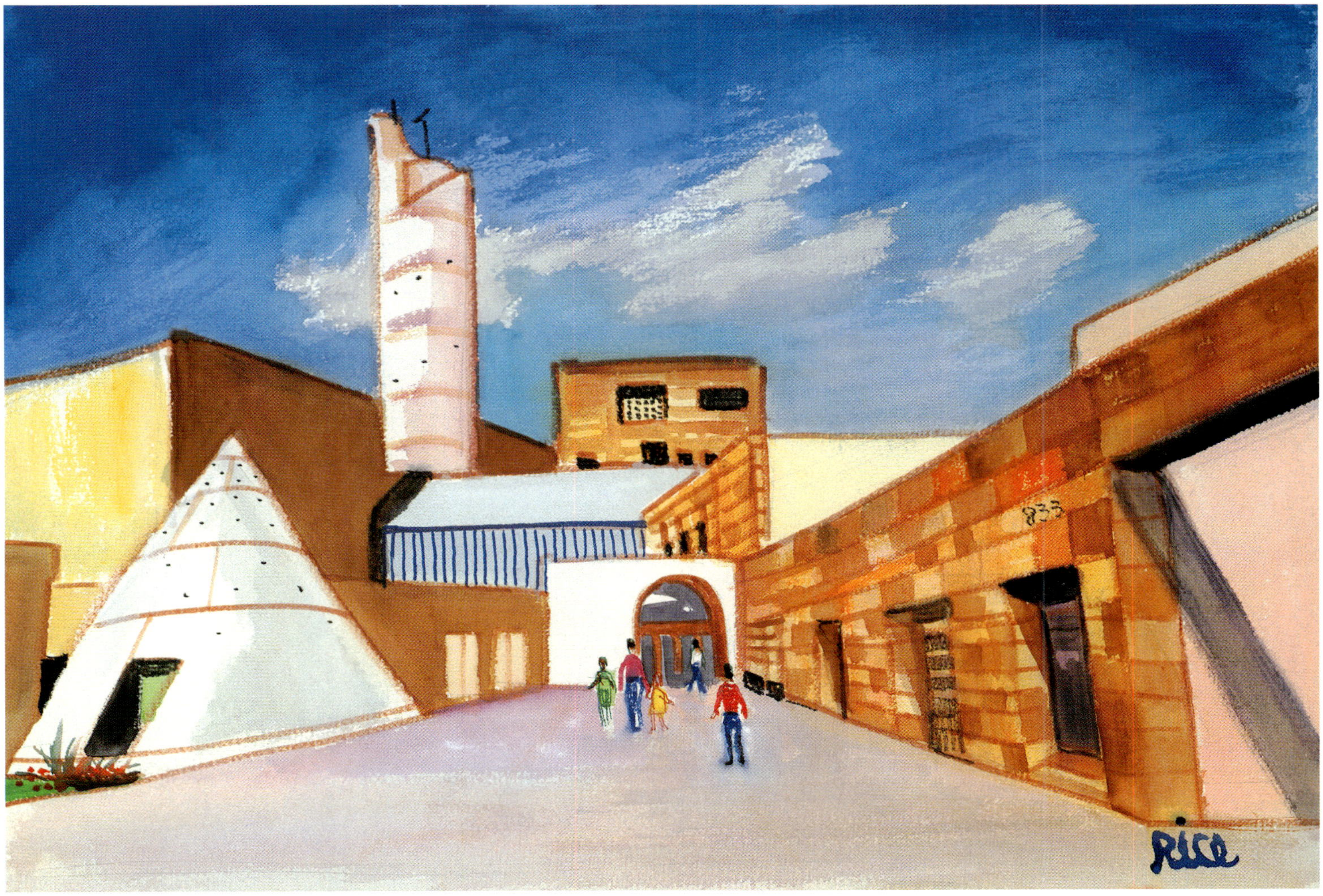

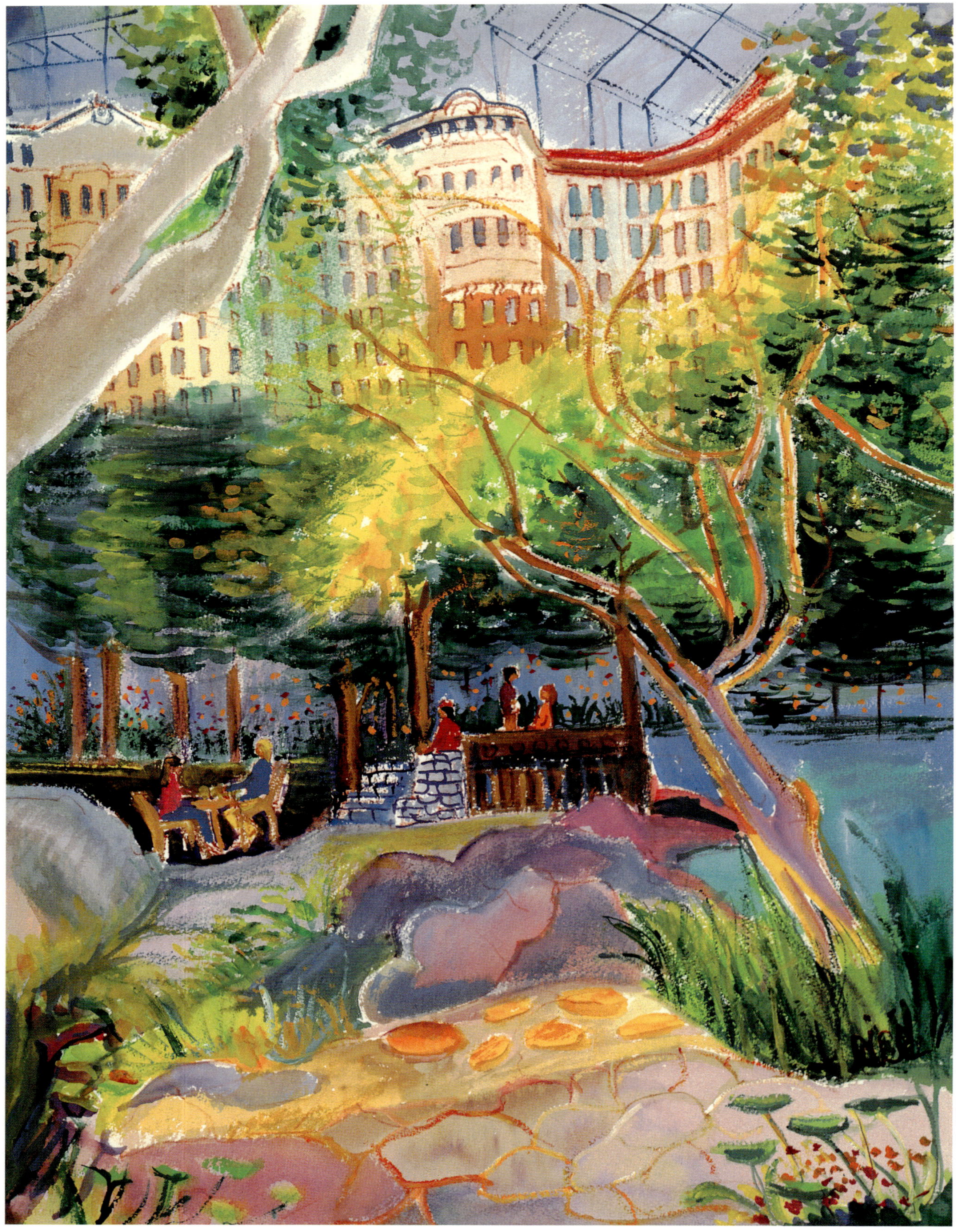

MYSTIC FALLS PARK AT SAM'S TOWN

I was amazed by the lushness of the Mystic Falls Park inside Sam's Town on Boulder Highway, a 25,000-square-foot atrium filled with trees, plants, flowers, waterfalls, meandering brooks, cobblestone paths and lifelike forest creatures (with realistic digital sound effects). The highlight is Sunset Stampede, a dancing water and laser light show choreographed to symphonic music. Opened in 1979, Sam's Town is an Old West-style hotel-casino known for its sophisticated gambling operation which includes an 18-screen Century Theater multiplex and a 1,200-seat entertainment complex.

Sam's Town was named for its founder, the late Sam Boyd. A former casino dealer who opened his first bingo palace in Las Vegas in the 1940s, Boyd ultimately owned several casinos in town. In 1985, UNLV re-named its sports center after Boyd.

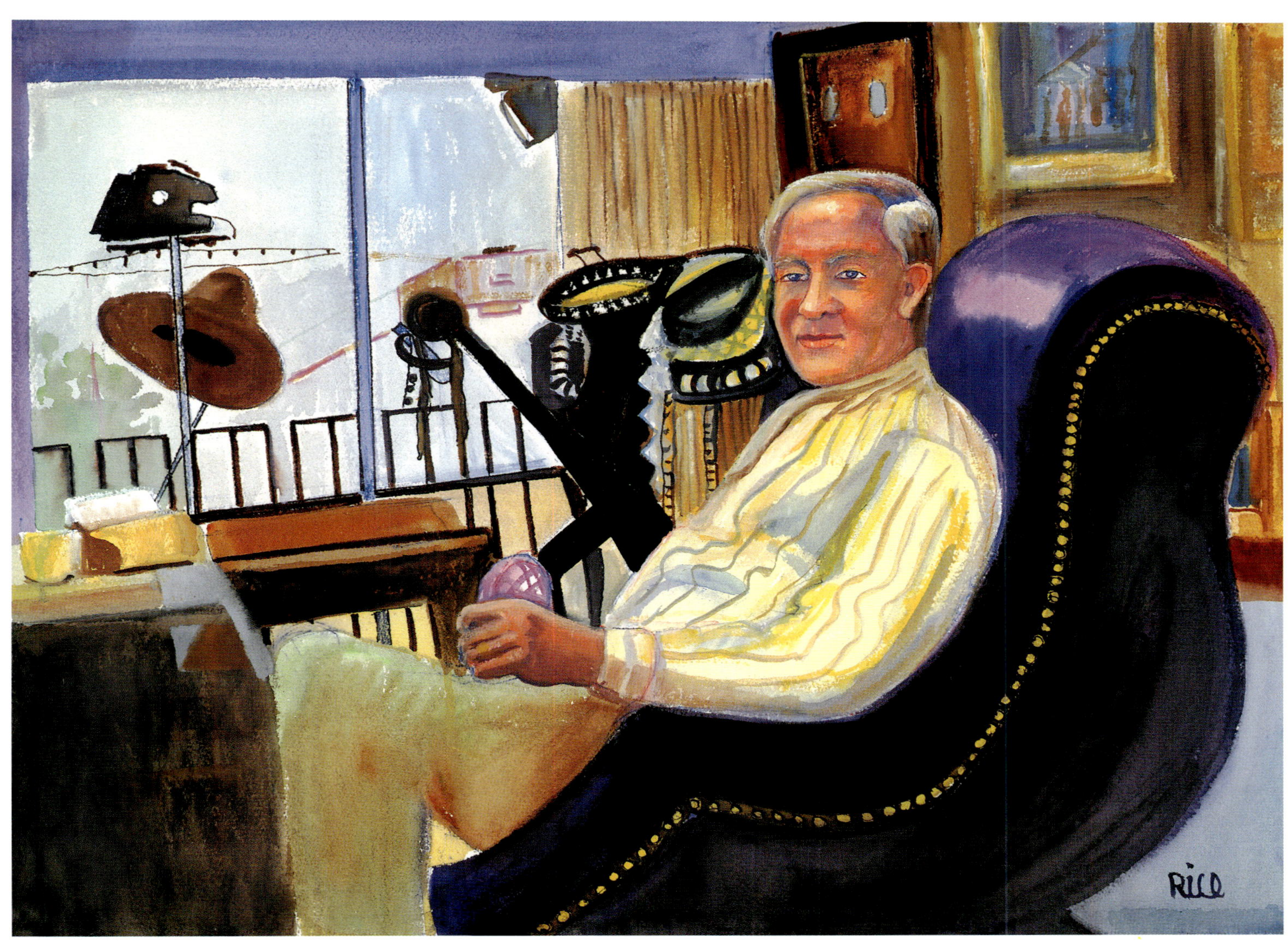

JAMES ROGERS

Getting acquainted with James Rogers and the collection of art and artifacts that fill his office—including an original Remington sculpture—was an artistic pleasure. A graduate of Las Vegas High School, James became a lawyer with a very successful local practice. He's best known for launching KVBC-TV, the local NBC affiliate, in 1979, and has since gone on to head the Sunbelt Communications Company, an empire of television and radio stations across the West. James has been ranked by TIME magazine as one of the top twelve philanthropists in the nation, donating multiple millions of dollars to educational and other worthy causes, including law, communications and music education.

James and his wife Beverly share a love of classic cars (with 100 in their impressive collection) and western folklore. They've teamed with the family of Roy Rogers to develop the Lone Pine Film Museum in the film festival town of Lone Pine, California.

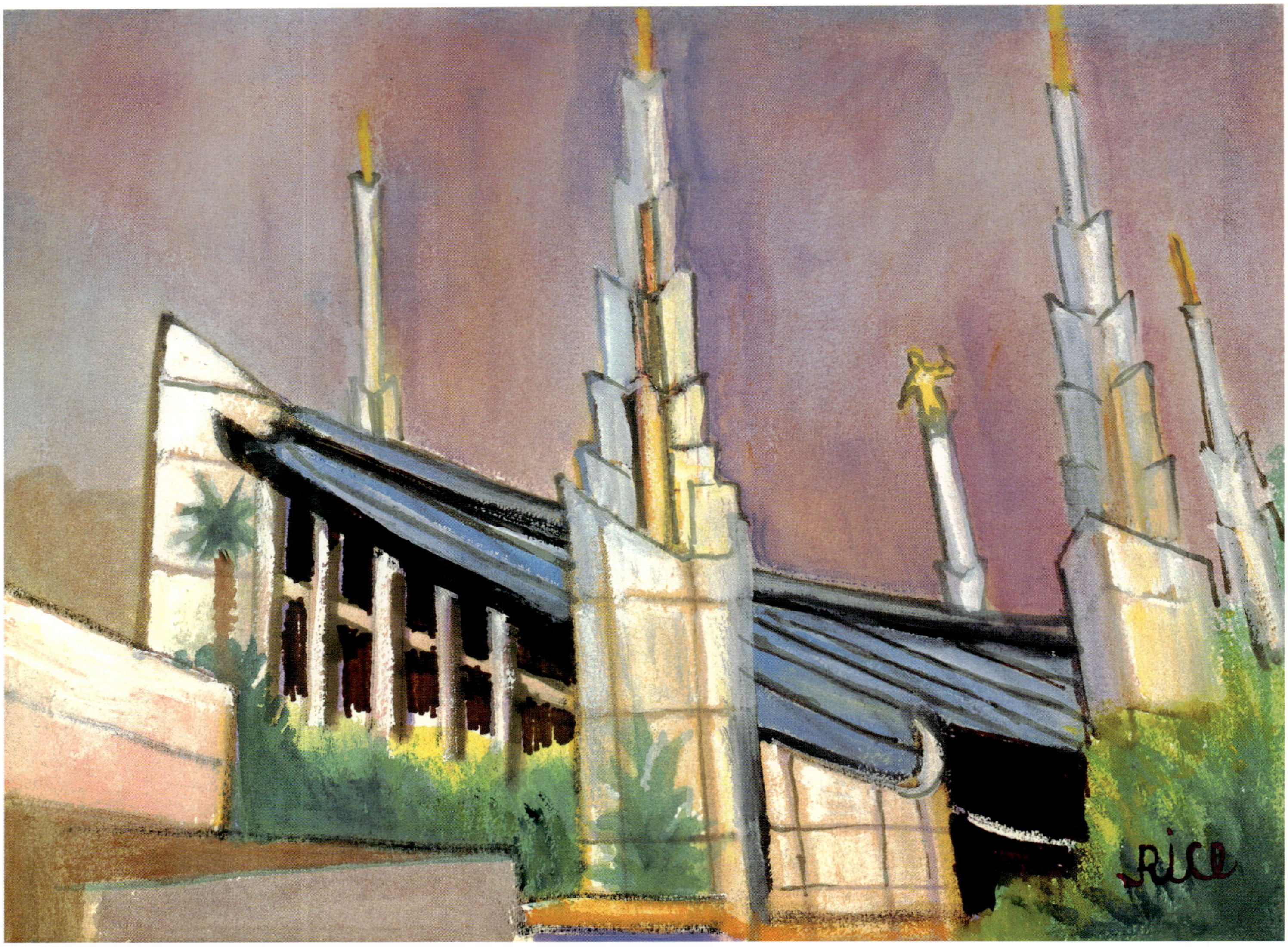

THE MORMON TEMPLE

From my vantage point in a Ford Expedition on a mountainside during a rainstorm, the modern Mormon Temple at the foot of Sunrise Mountain was a striking, inspiring sight to behold. Built in 1989, the Temple is one of only 100 in the world open only to invited members of their own churches. Ceremonies are conducted six days a week, but it is closed on Sundays, when its members worship at their neighborhood church. Illuminated at night, it can be seen throughout the Las Vegas valley.

LAS VEGAS HIGH SCHOOL

Students take a break on the stately steps of the original Las Vegas High School downtown, at Seventh and Bridger Streets near the Latino section of the city. This venerable public school opened its doors to 300 students in November 1930 and has since been listed in the National Registry for its historic architecture. It recently changed its name to The Las Vegas Academy. There are almost 200,000 students in the Clark County School District, the 10th largest in the nation.

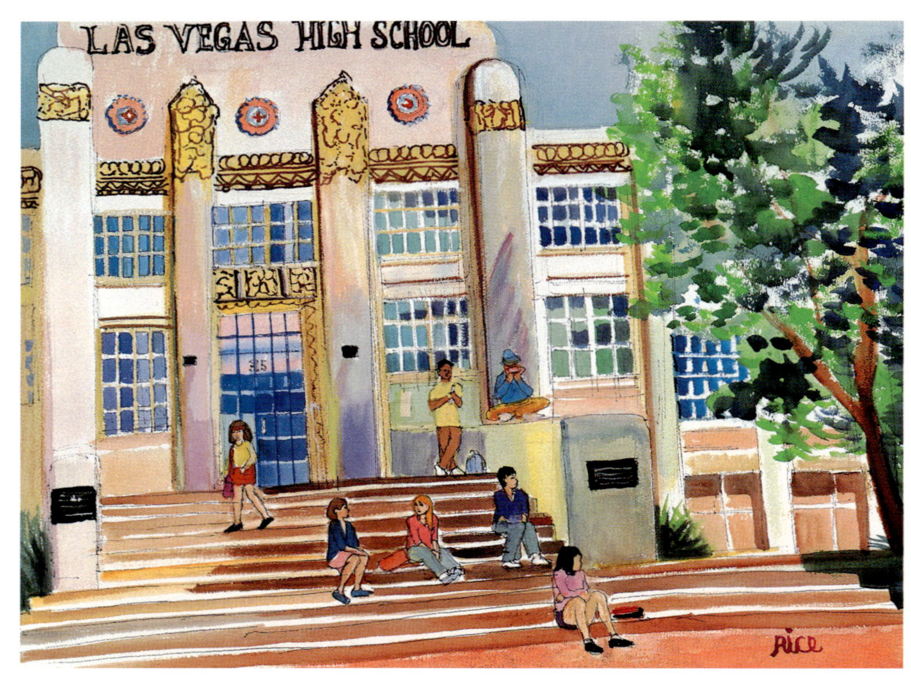

Chinatown

Off the Strip, on Spring Mountain Road, the area surrounding Chinatown Plaza is a great place to discover some of the best Chinese food in Las Vegas, as well as a variety of distinctly Asian shops and markets. Adding unusual character to the plaza are the full-sized dinosaur skeletons on display at the Jurassic Chinasaur Exhibit.

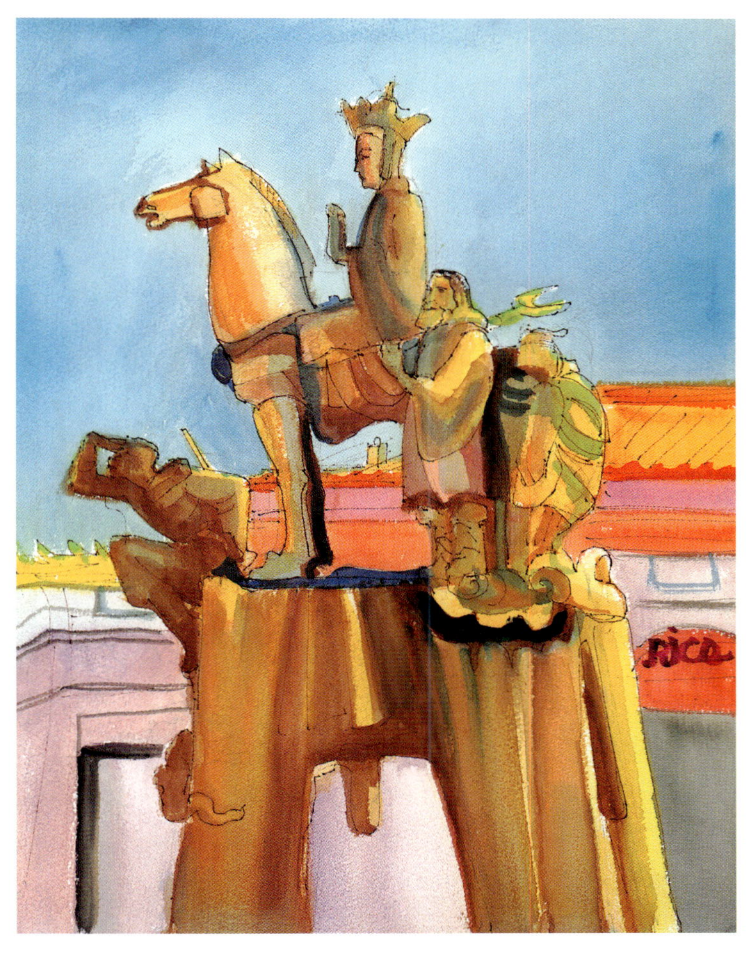

A TOUCH OF CHINATOWN

This stunning statue in Chinatown is a tribute to "Journey to the West," which tells the mythological adventures of Priest Xuanzang and his three disciples—the goblin, the pig, and the monkey—as they travel in search of Buddhist sutras, eventually ascending to Buddha's palace to live there as gods.

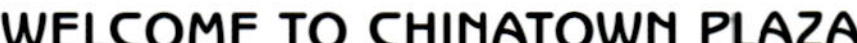

WELCOME TO CHINATOWN PLAZA

This family enjoys the sights of the Chinatown Plaza, the central hub of Las Vegas' Asian-owned business community and the heart of the Asian Pacific Cultural Center. The plaza's design is based on the Chinese Tang Dynasty Palace. You enter though the Gate of the Heavens (named from Chinese mythology) and can admire the 28-foot-tall "Journey to the West" statue and a mural depicting the legendary "Silk Road" traveled by Marco Polo.

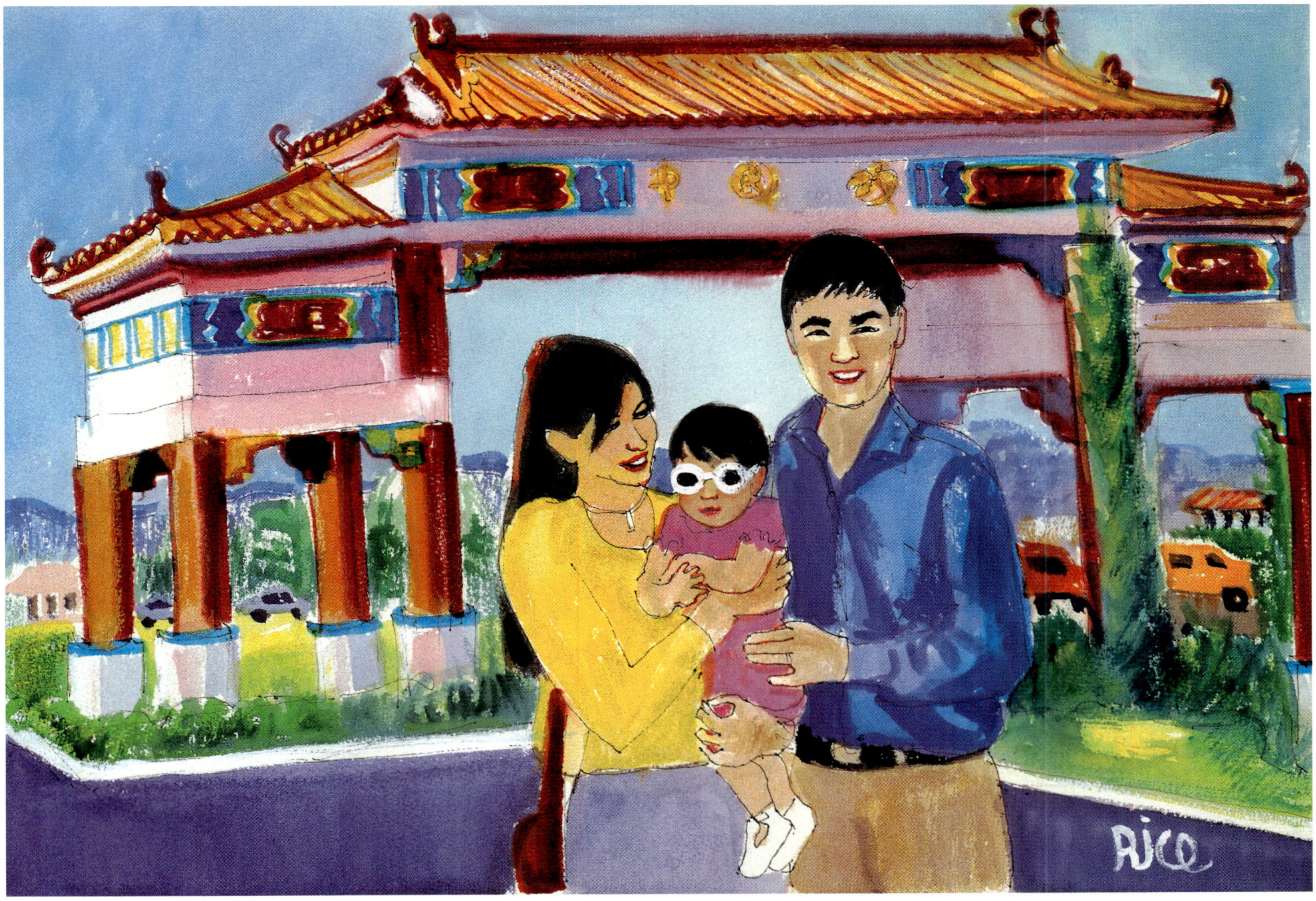

UNLV

The University of Nevada, Las Vegas is becoming a premier urban university providing students an excellent education at reasonable cost. Since its founding in 1957, the university has seen dramatic growth in both its academic programs and its facilities. There are more than 148 undergraduate, master's and doctoral programs offered to more than 20,000 students.

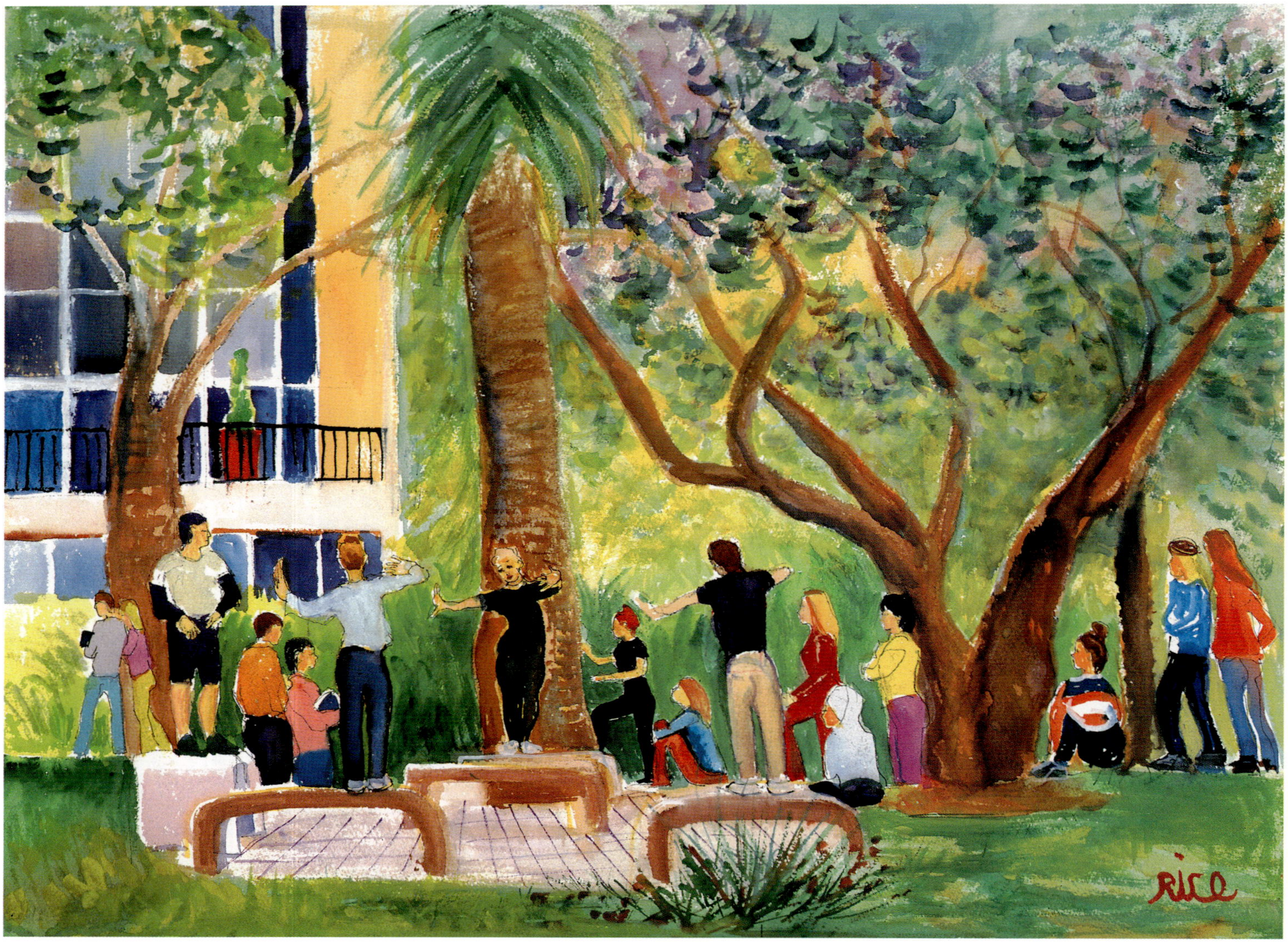

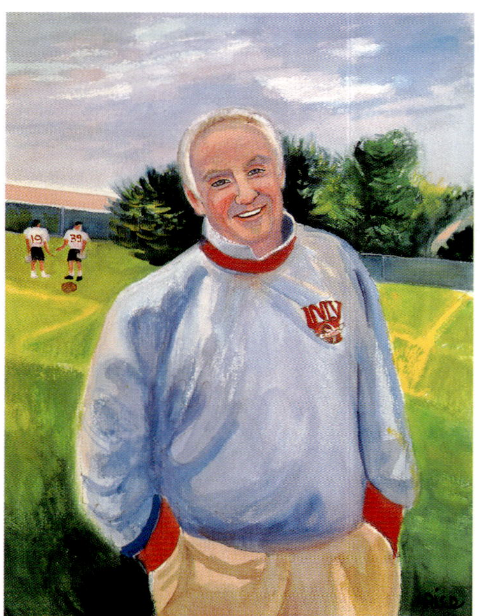

HEAD COACH JOHN ROBINSON

Among the ten winningest active head coaches in college football, John Robinson is only the eighth man to hold that title at the University of Nevada, Las Vegas. His arrival in 1998 brought interest in Runnin' Rebels football to an all-time high. A veteran leader of programs at UCLA, USC and the Los Angeles Rams, Coach Robinson has more than 100 career victories and the highest winning bowl game percentage of any coach—including an amazing 4-0 record at the prestigious Rose Bowl. I met him on the UNLV gridiron field and found him as winning off the gridiron as he is on it.

UNLV CAMPUS

The lush landscaping and Professor Margo Colbert's site-specific improvisational choreograhy class make for a relaxed afternoon atmosphere on campus.

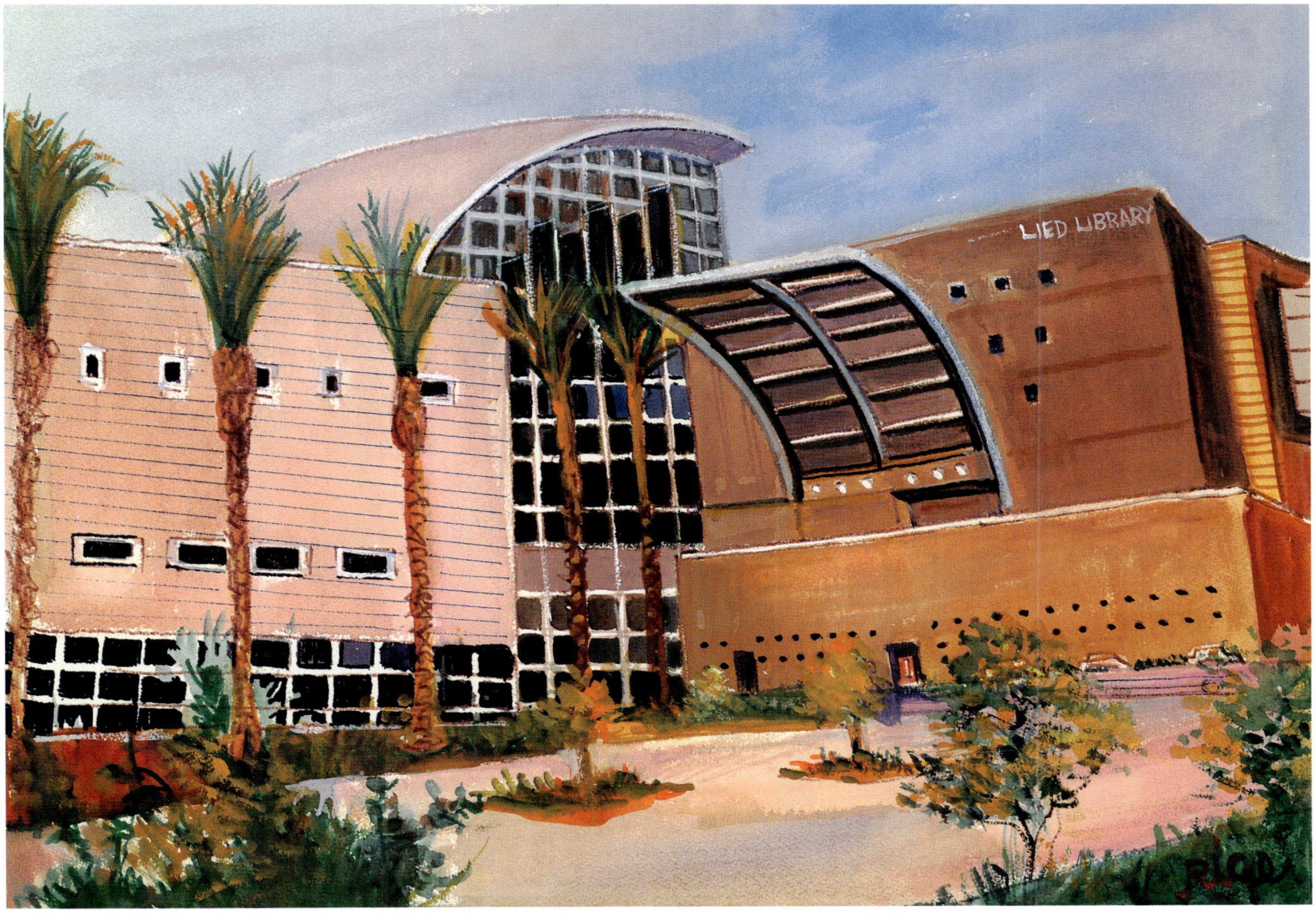

LIED LIBRARY

Opened in 2001, the uniquely-designed five-story Lied Library at UNLV is poised to become the city's major center of research and study. The $55 million complex is a state-of-the-art facility with an extensive electronic infrastructure and other reference materials.

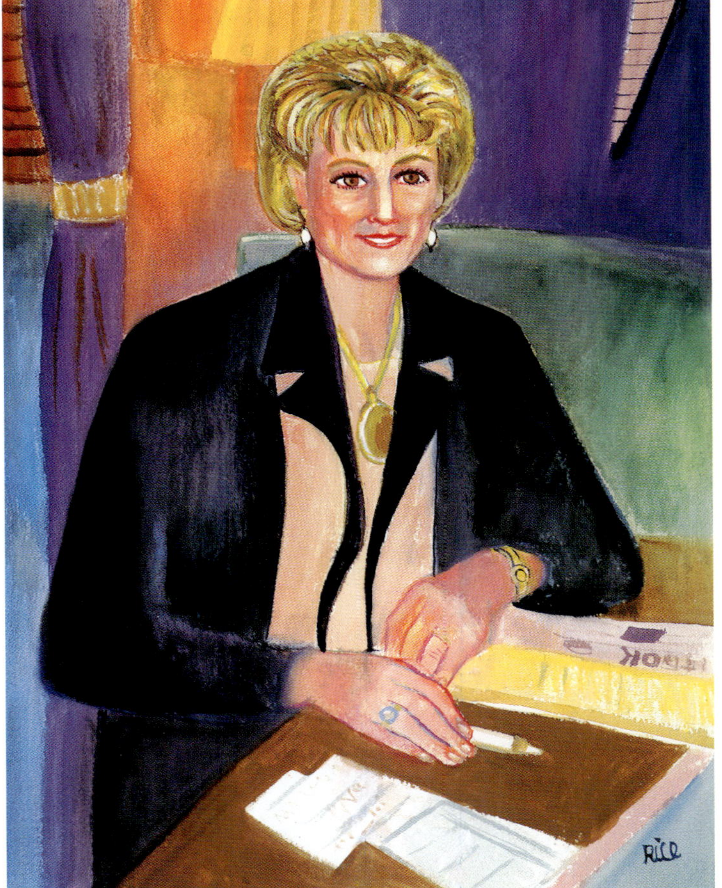

UNLV PRESIDENT CAROL HARTER

As the seventh president of the University of Nevada, Las Vegas, Dr. Carol Harter oversees a 23,000 student body on the 335-acre campus in the heart of Las Vegas. Upon her appointment in 1995, Harter initiated an ambitious strategic plan for the university that included new schools and degree programs, improved teacher training, expanded research activity and vastly increased fundraising efforts. Heading the $250 million school, she is recognized as one of the top female executives in Nevada. Impressive accomplishments for a girl from Brooklyn, New York.

Latino Las Vegas

Today, more than 250,000 Latinos live in Las Vegas—almost 20% of the population —and some 2 million Hispanic visitors pass through Las Vegas each year. With the fastest growing Latino population in America, civic organizations like the Latin Chamber of Commerce enjoy increasing influence.

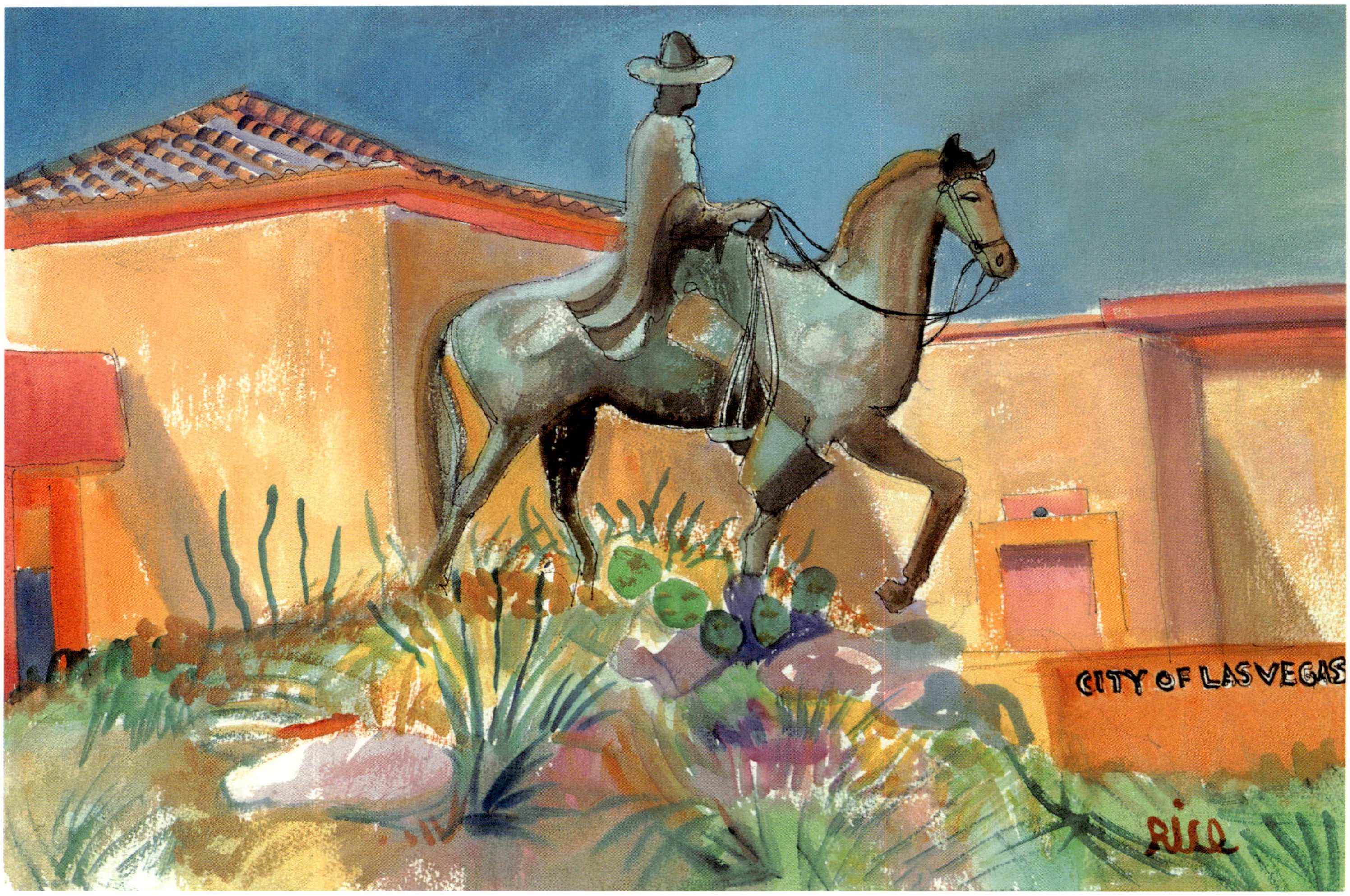

COMMEMORATING LATIN LAS VEGAS

Many have contributed to the success of Las Vegas, but most believe it all began with Rafael Rivera, a teenage Mexican trailblazer who became the first non-Native American to enter the Las Vegas Valley in December of 1829. Rivera departed from a caravan scouting a new route between New Mexico and California (later dubbed "the Old Spanish Trail"), and traveled a route through what is now Henderson into the lush Las Vegas Valley. He realized the snow-capped Spring Mountain range would provide abundant water and game. He found the bubbling waters of modern-day Cottonwood Springs, explored the region and then finally reunited with the caravan and shared the news of his discovery.

In the Eastern corridor of the valley, where many Latinos live, the original pioneer is remembered with a statue in front of the Rafael Rivera Community Center.

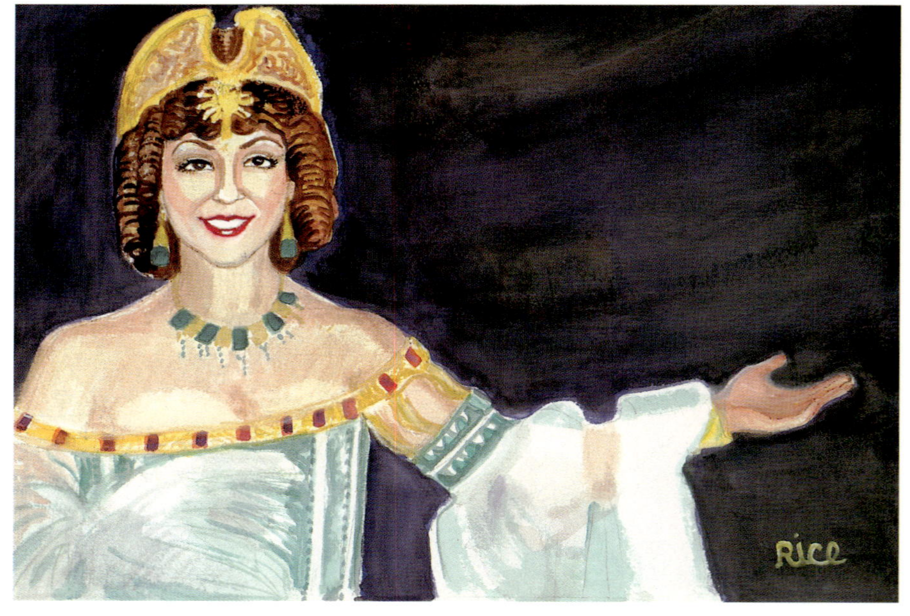

THE REAL SOPRANO

Las Vegas has its own "Soprano" and is singing her praises: Emily Herrera, a resident of nearby Henderson, wowed admirers at the opening of the Venetian. She has thrilled local opera fans with her performance as Musetta in "La Bohéme" at the Nevada Opera Theater. Known for her interpretive expression and consummate musicality, Emily's a rising diva in the most operatic sense of the word.

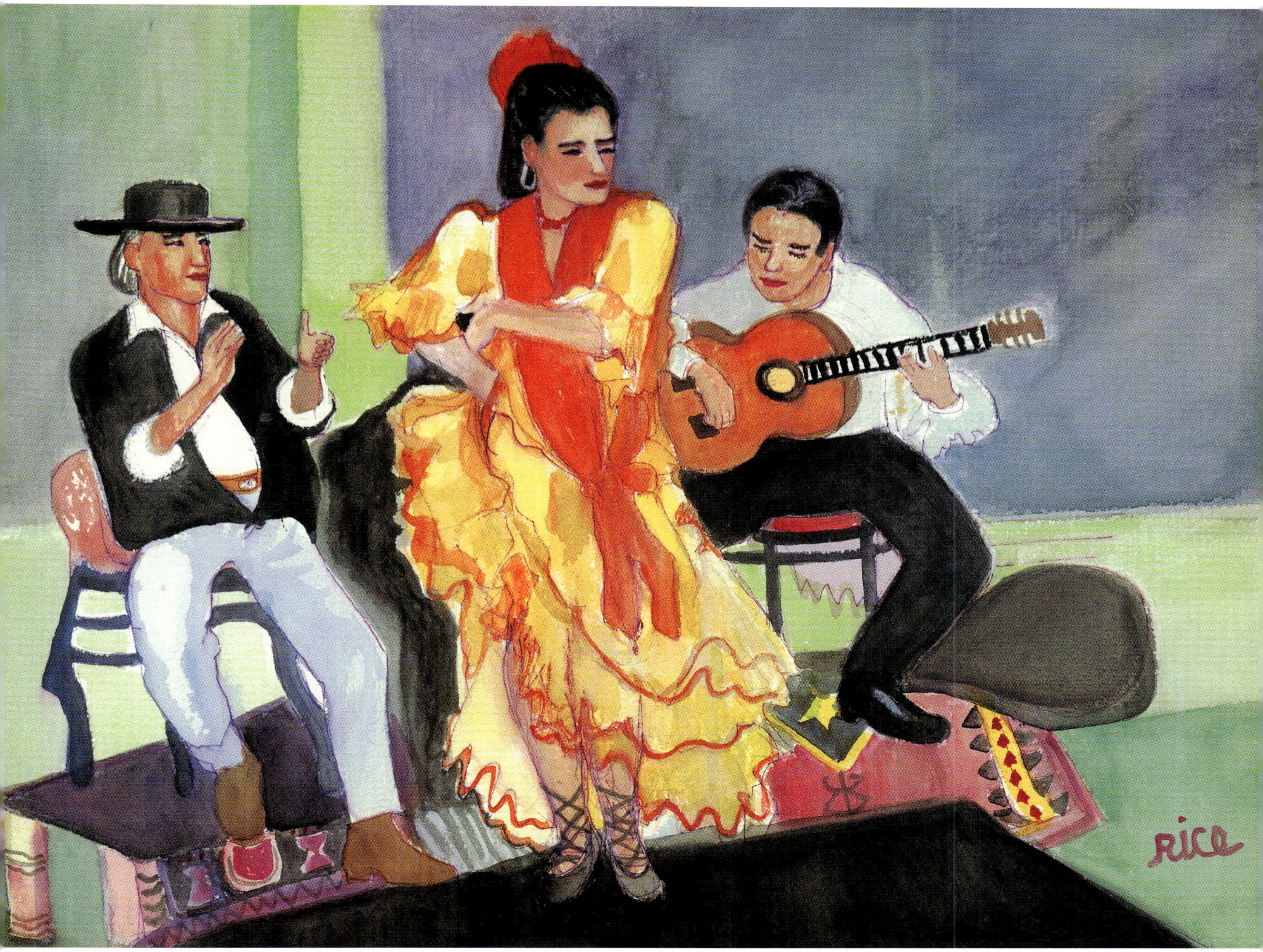

FLAMENCO LAS VEGAS AT NEYLA

No, it's not the city's famous Flamingo—It's flamenco, the popular and exuberant Spanish dance. I discovered this group, featuring father-and-son musicians Pepe and Jose Maria Roldan and nimble dancer Vannesa Alvarado, playing to a packed house at the MGM Grand's Neyla Restaurant.

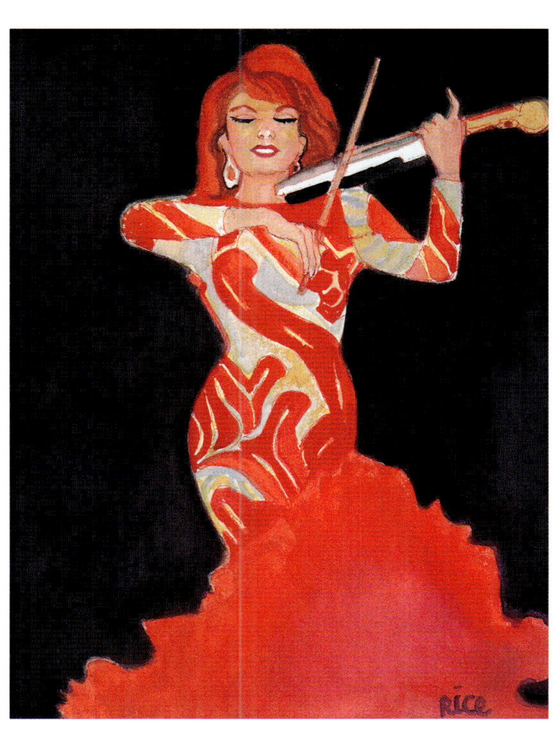

OLGA BREESKIN

The lovely violin virtuoso Olga Breeskin has taken Latin America by storm and is now winning over a U.S. audience, as well, with appearances in Las Vegas in her elaborately costumed and choreographed nightclub show, where she is known as "Super Olga." She's also been an actress since age eight, starring in several popular Latin films, soap operas and TV shows. There seems to be nothing she can't do, and do fabulously. As Placido Domingo put it, "When Olga plays, she takes you to paradise."

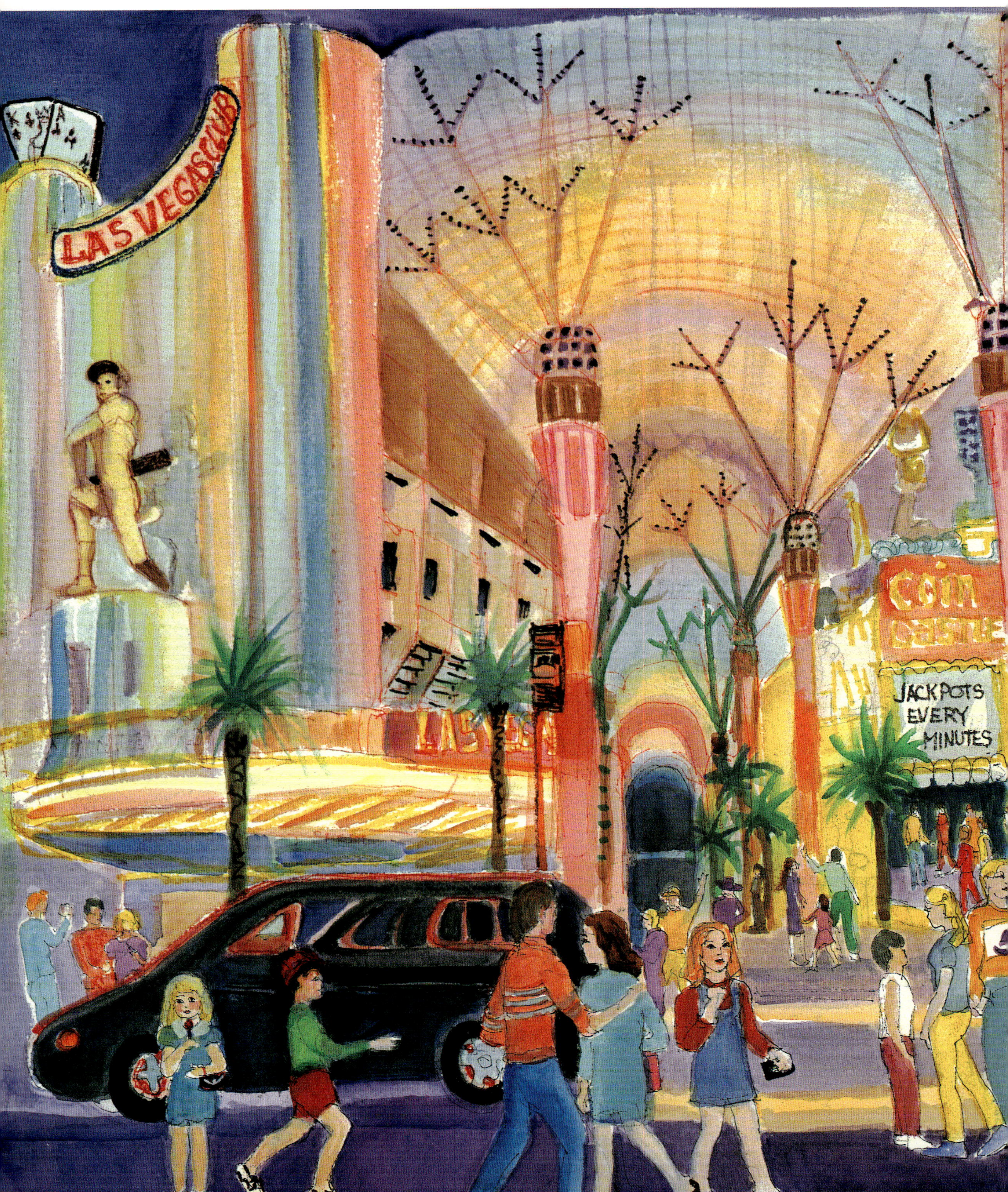
LAS VEGAS CLUB
Coin Castle
JACKPOTS
EVERY
MINUTES

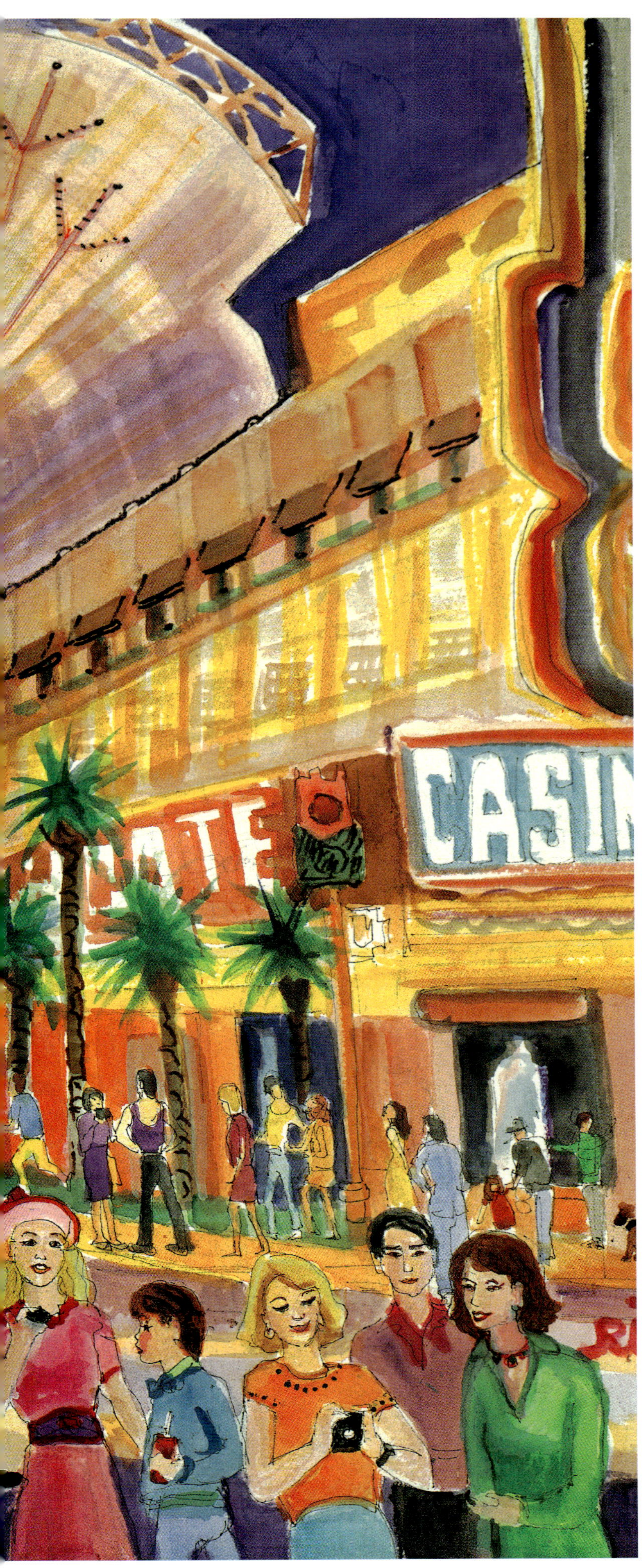

DOWNTOWN

THE AREA KNOWN TODAY AS DOWNtown, or "Old Town" Las Vegas, first sprouted out of the desert in the 1920s because of convenience: it was the main focal point for various railways and, thus, a logical place to start up a town. Vegas' more enduring industry—gambling—took hold in the 1930s when saloons, hotels and casinos like the Northern Club, the Silver Club and the Tango Club got the town's first gambling licenses and made Fremont Street the place to visit.

Fremont Street quickly became a colorful electric vista watched over by the famous neon cowboy "Vegas Vic" and it competed with the Strip for gamblers' attention, anchoring such legendary establishments as the Golden Nugget (the largest casino of its day), the El Cortez (the oldest original casino still in operation), Binion's Horseshoe and the Pioneer Club ("Vegas Vic's" home). Today, with hot spots such as Binion's, Four Queens, Lady Luck, the Fremont, Sassy Sally's, Main Street Station, Fitzgeralds, and the Plaza, the Downtown district has its own quirky character, distinct from the massive theme attractions that rule the Strip. "Vegas Vic" still stands watch (joined by the saucier "Vegas Vickie" across the street at Glitter Gulch, an exotic dance emporium) underneath the dazzling Fremont Street Experience, a spectacular series of electric light-and-sound shows displayed on a colossal awning encompassing Las Vegas' oldest—and still vital—gathering place.

THE FREMONT STREET EXPERIENCE

The night sky is illuminated by 2.1 million lights and the air is filled with over half a million watts of concert-quality sound that dazzles spectators along Fremont Street's four-block pedestrian promenade. The free display 90 feet above the street begins at dusk and continues with various theme presentations until midnight.

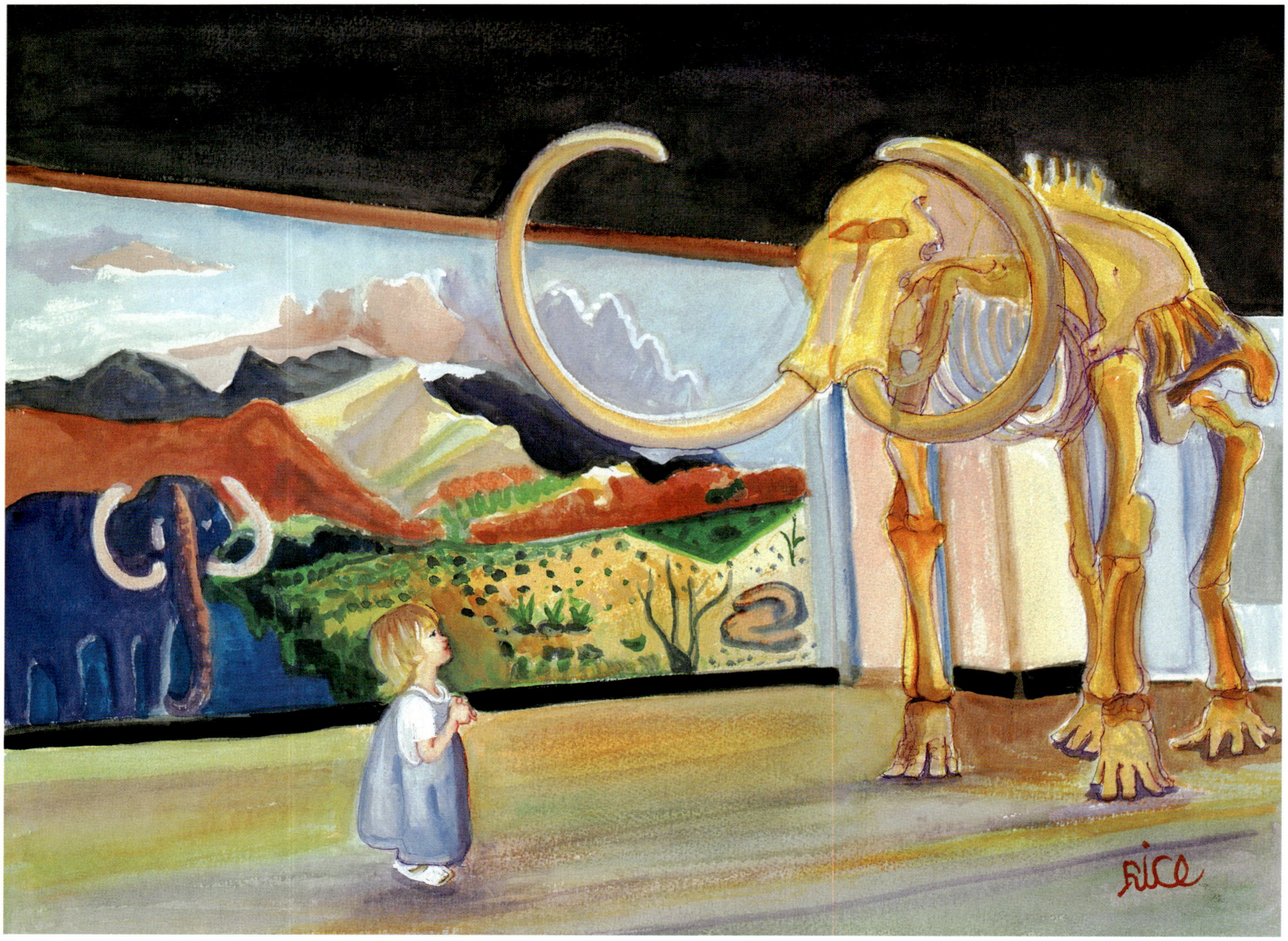

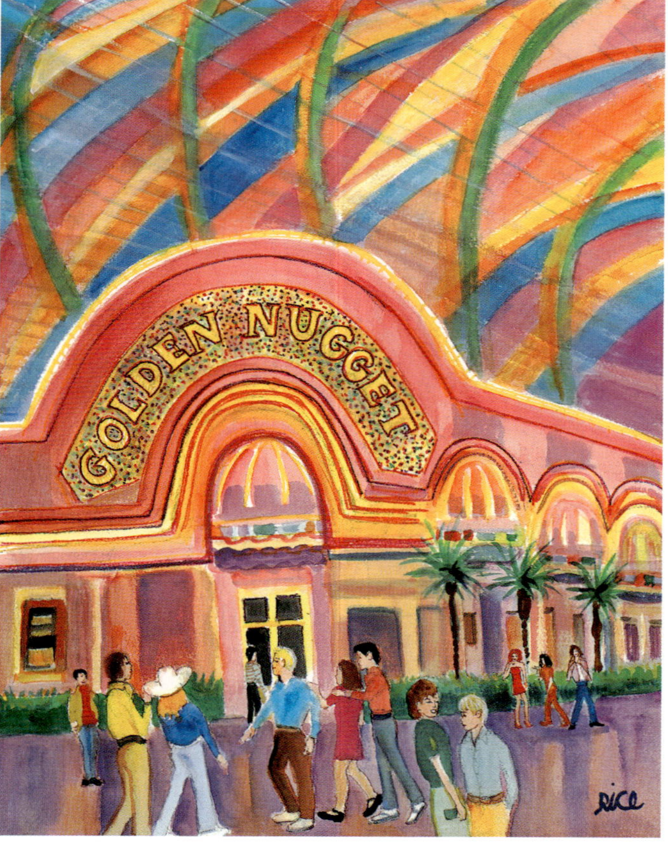

MAMMOTH APPEAL

Along with the gambling palaces downtown, you can also sample some culture at the slightly off-the-beaten-track Nevada State Museum & Historical Society in Lorenzi Park. Curator Frank Wright took me on a trip through time, from Las Vegas' Ice Age (complete with this life-sized skeleton of a Colombian Mammoth) to the indigenous wildlife to the early Native American settlers to a reproduction of Bugsy Siegel's 1940s hotel suite. It's a great place for research, to rent out for a party or to get a glimpse of the region's history.

THE GOLDEN NUGGET

When the Golden Nugget opened on Fremont Street in 1946, its frontier-style name belied the glamour inside: it was the classiest casino in pre-Flamingo Las Vegas. In the 1950s it boosted the biggest, brightest sign in town, a 100-foot neon number that proclaimed the casino's prominence. Steve Wynn came to Las Vegas in 1967 and by 1978, at age 31, he had controlling interest of the Golden Nugget, restoring its elegance, opening a 578-room tower and making the gambling den a hotel for the first time in its history. Since then, the Nugget, like Wynn's reputation as one of the sharpest businessmen in town, has just gotten bigger and better.

"VEGAS VIC" >

Say "Howdy, Pardner" to "Vegas Vic," an authentic local institution since the Young Electric Sign Company (better known as YESCO) installed him above the Pioneer Club in 1951. Vic has become one of the definitive symbols of Las Vegas, and YESCO has been the place to go to put your name up in lights since 1920, creating such glimmering icons as the famed Stardust casino sign (then the largest in the world), the Circus Circus clown, the Fremont Street Experience and virtually every other major neon achievement in town. As for Vic, one (probably apocryphal) legend claims that John Wayne once took a shot at him—but was it because he found Vic's trademark recorded greeting annoying or because he was the only cowpoke in town bigger than the Duke?

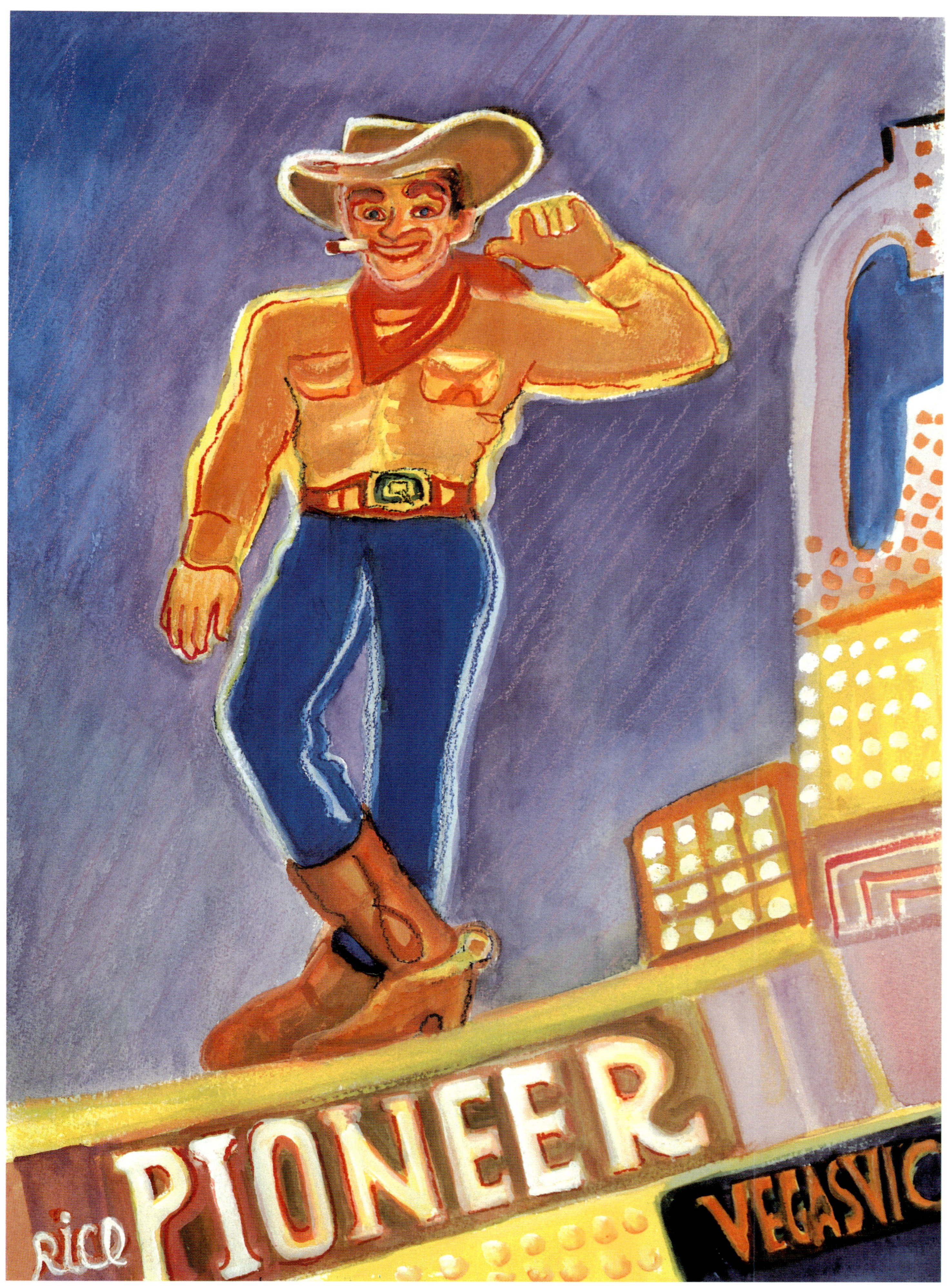
PIONEER
VEGASVIC
Rice

TONI JAMES

It was fascinating to catch talented Toni James transforming himself in the middle of his makeup session, halfway to becoming a very convincing Diana Ross.

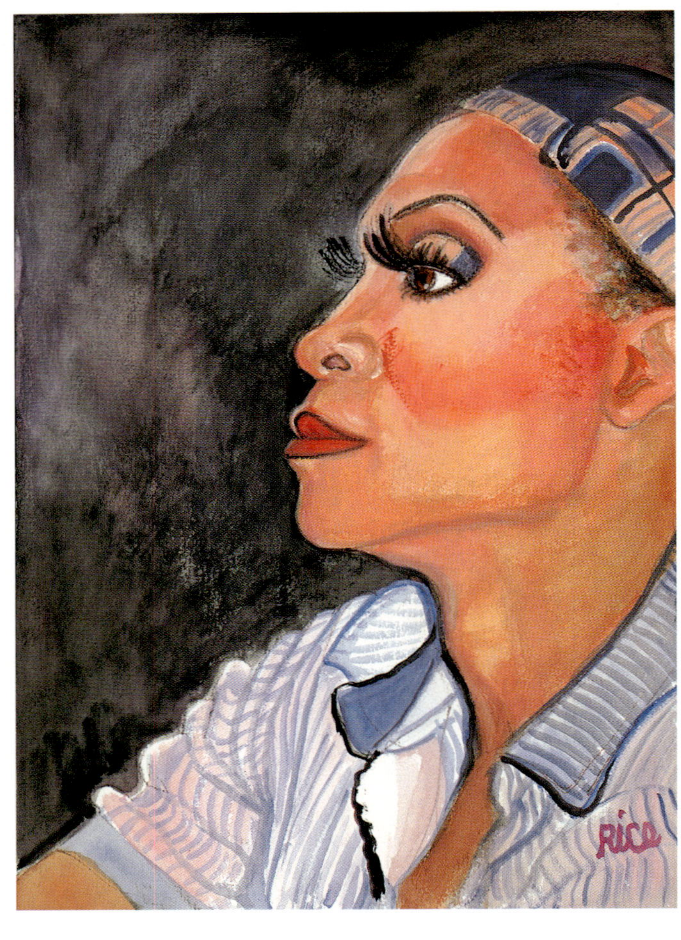

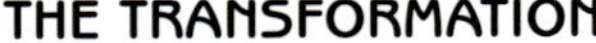

THE TRANSFORMATION

I discovered that the term "female impersonator" doesn't begin to encompass the many talents of Toni James, in his unmistakable guise as Diana Ross. Toni's career began as a champion twirler and bodybuilder and he later became the producer and manager of the Seattle Gay Men's Chorus, which led to a celebrated appearance at Carnegie Hall. While on vacation in Las Vegas, he was recruited by Kenny Kerr and wowed audiences with his full-diva interpretation of "Miss Ross." I found Toni to be warm, gregarious and very bright, and he quickly became one of my favorite people in the city.

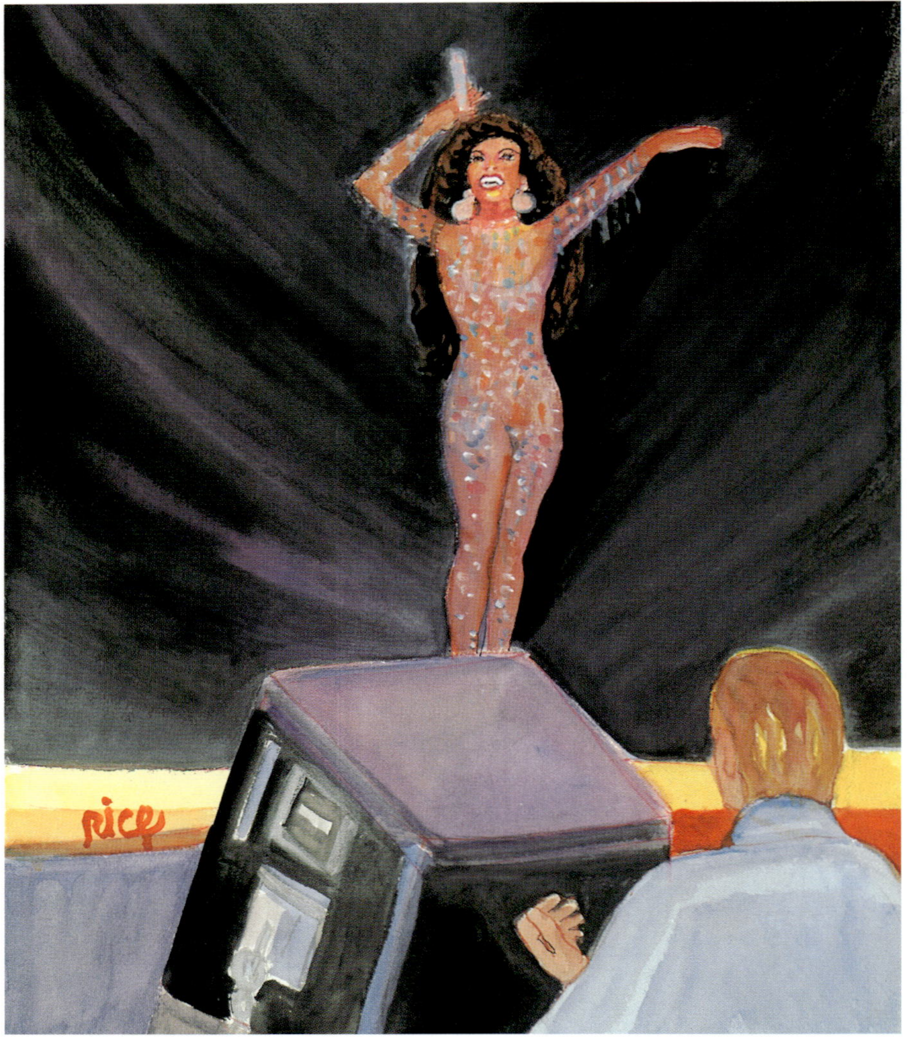

THE PLAZA HOTEL >

For the best view of the Fremont Street Experience, dine at the restaurant in the impressive, 1,000-room Plaza Hotel. Originally built in 1970 as the Union Plaza at Fremont and Main, the birthplace of Las Vegas overlooks the old Union Pacific yards. The hotel and casino, which opened the first race and sports book in town, was purchased by Las Vegas mainstay Jackie Gaughan in 1990 and re-christened, simply, as the Plaza Hotel.

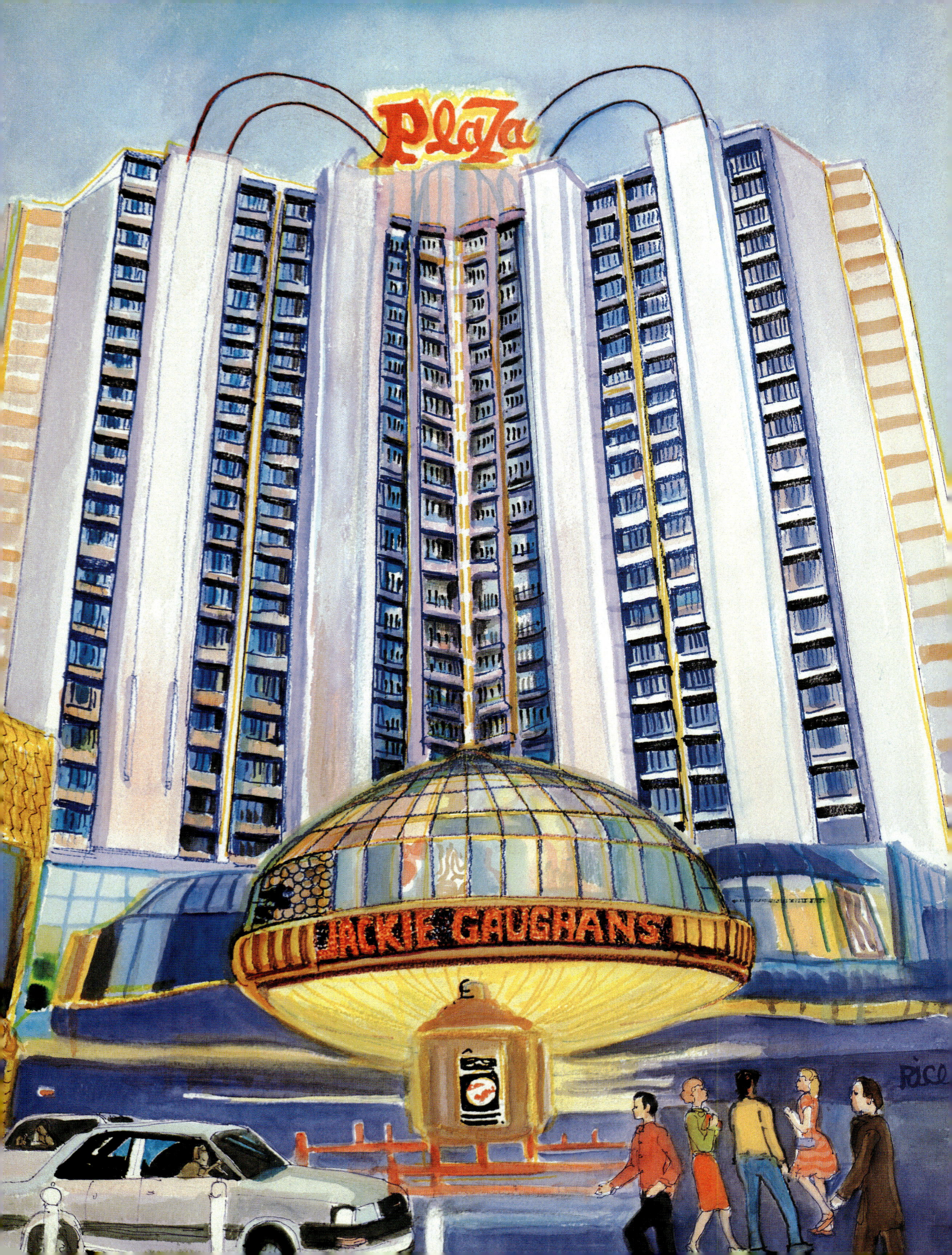
PlaZa
JACKIE GAUGHANS
Rice

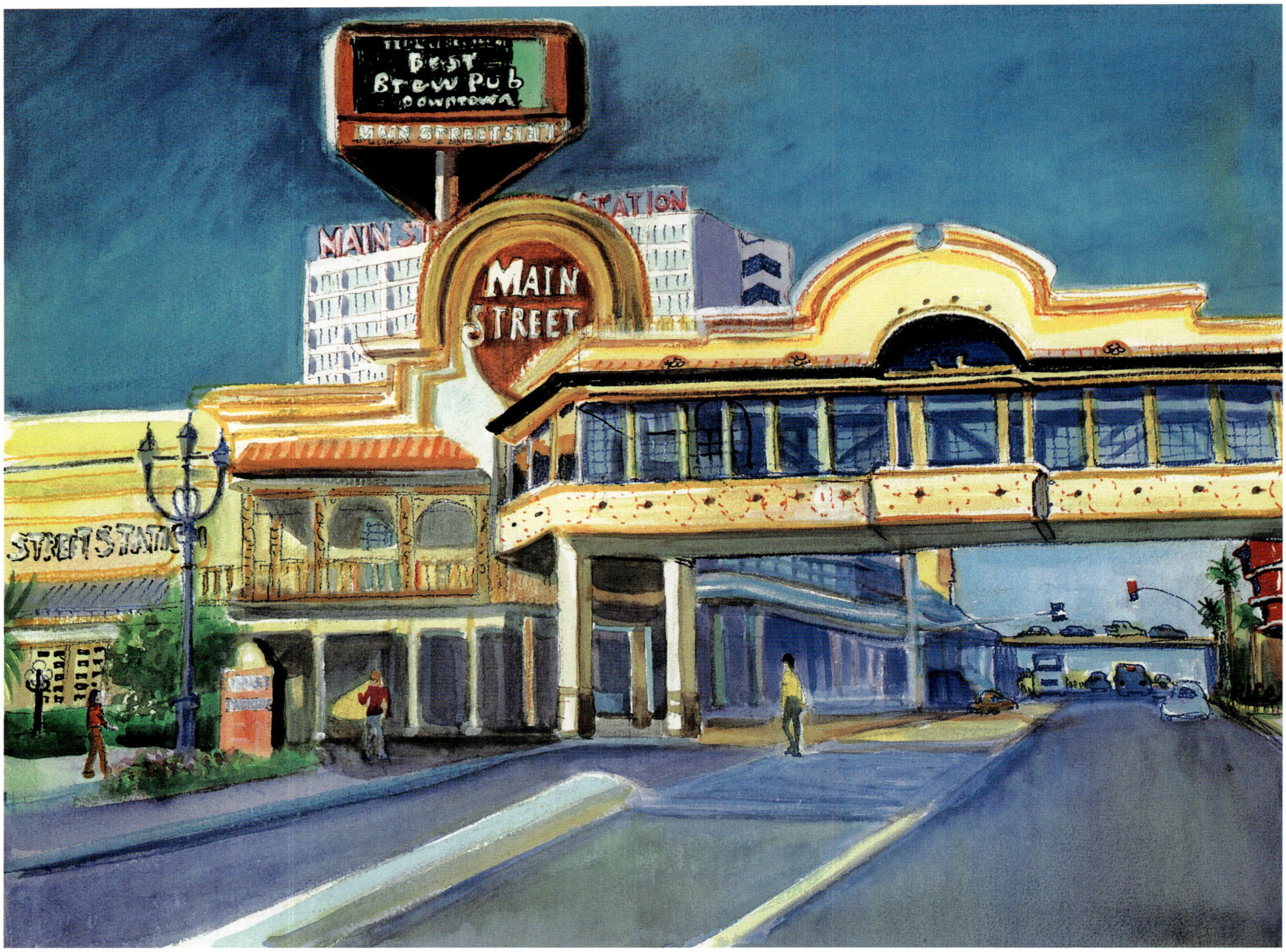

MAIN STREET STATION

With a decor of classic antiques, stained glass, marble, bronze and luxuriant wood details, I found the Main Street Station casino to have a lot of character. It has a microbrewery and one of the largest buffets I've ever seen. A mainstay that once had to shutter its doors, Main Street Station was reopened in 1996 by the Boyd Corporation. Its former head, the late Sam Boyd, was a local pioneer who rose from a carny and card dealer to a casino executive and founder of Union Plaza and The California Hotel and Casino.

GAMBLING AT MAIN STREET STATION

As this group of laid-back blackjack aficionados can attest, Main Street Station has become the casino of choice for local gamblers looking to double down without the distraction of throngs of tourists.

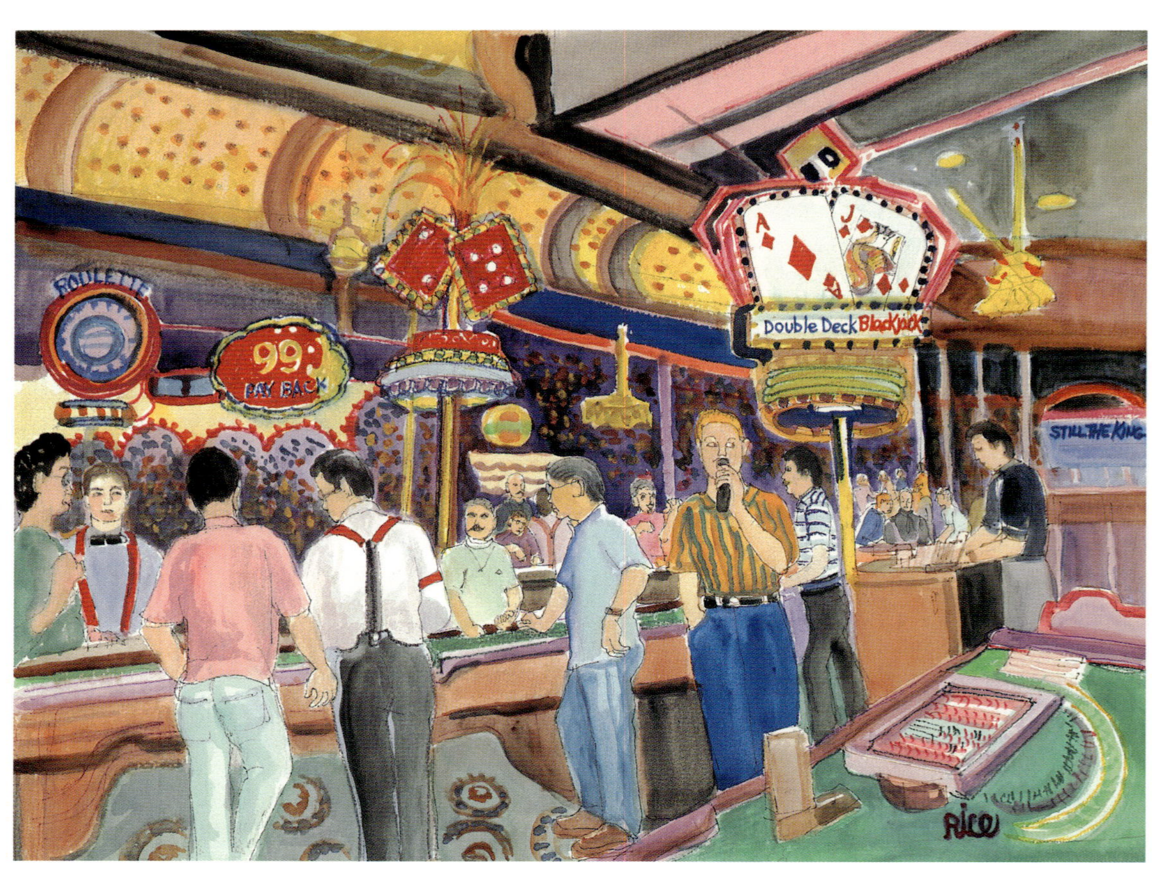

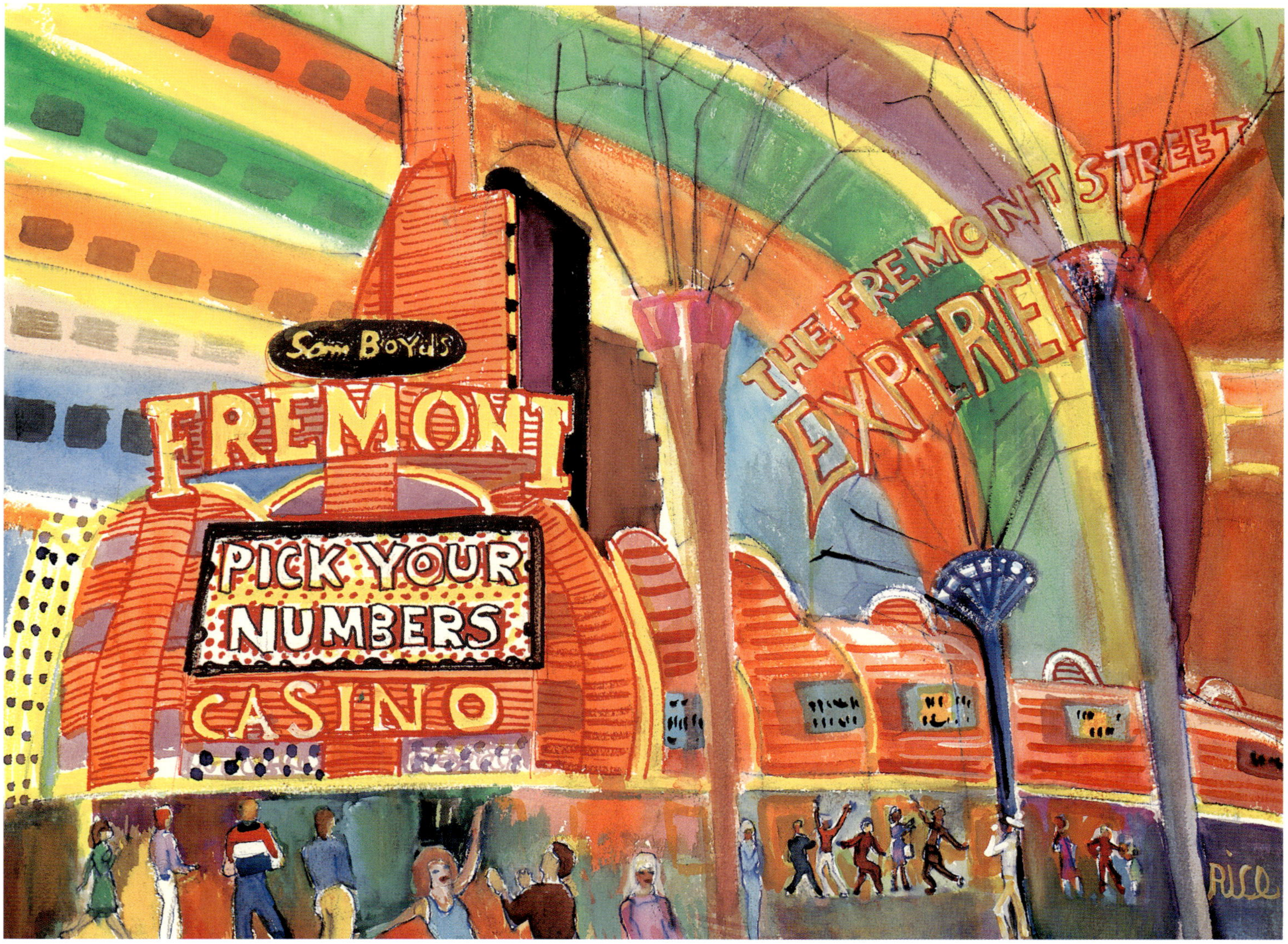

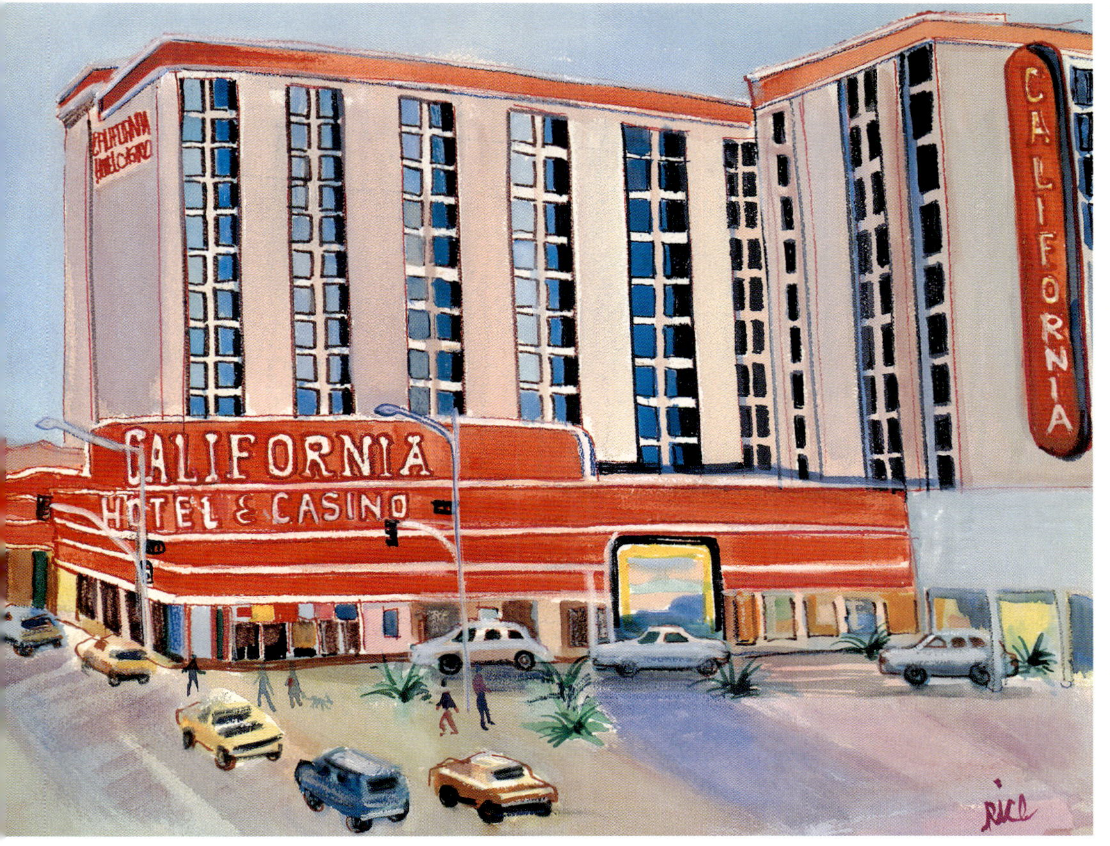

THE FREMONT

Opened in 1956 as Downtown's first Strip-style enterprise, the Fremont, founded by Bill Boyd, is best known as the place where Wayne Newton made his Las Vegas debut and for its block-long neon sign. Today it features a tropical theme like the California, its sister hotel-casino across the street.

Bill Boyd was a native Los Angeleno who moved to Las Vegas in 1941 with his father Sam. After a 15-year career as an attorney, Bill founded the Boyd Gaming Company with his father and opened the first of the company's properties, the California, in 1975, followed by Sam's Town in 1979. In the 1980s, the Stardust, the Fremont and other enterprises joined the Boyd Gaming empire, and today Boyd Gaming operates 11 casino properties around the country. Bill carries the torch of his father's legacy through his extensive contributions to the community—particularly at UNLV, where a dormitory bears the Boyd name and the William S. Boyd Law School became the first such institution in the state of Nevada.

THE CALIFORNIA

Actually more Polynesian in spirit than its name implies, the California Hotel & Casino has been saying aloha to guests since 1975—particularly tourists from Hawaii who like Las Vegas' interpretation of their tropical paradise.

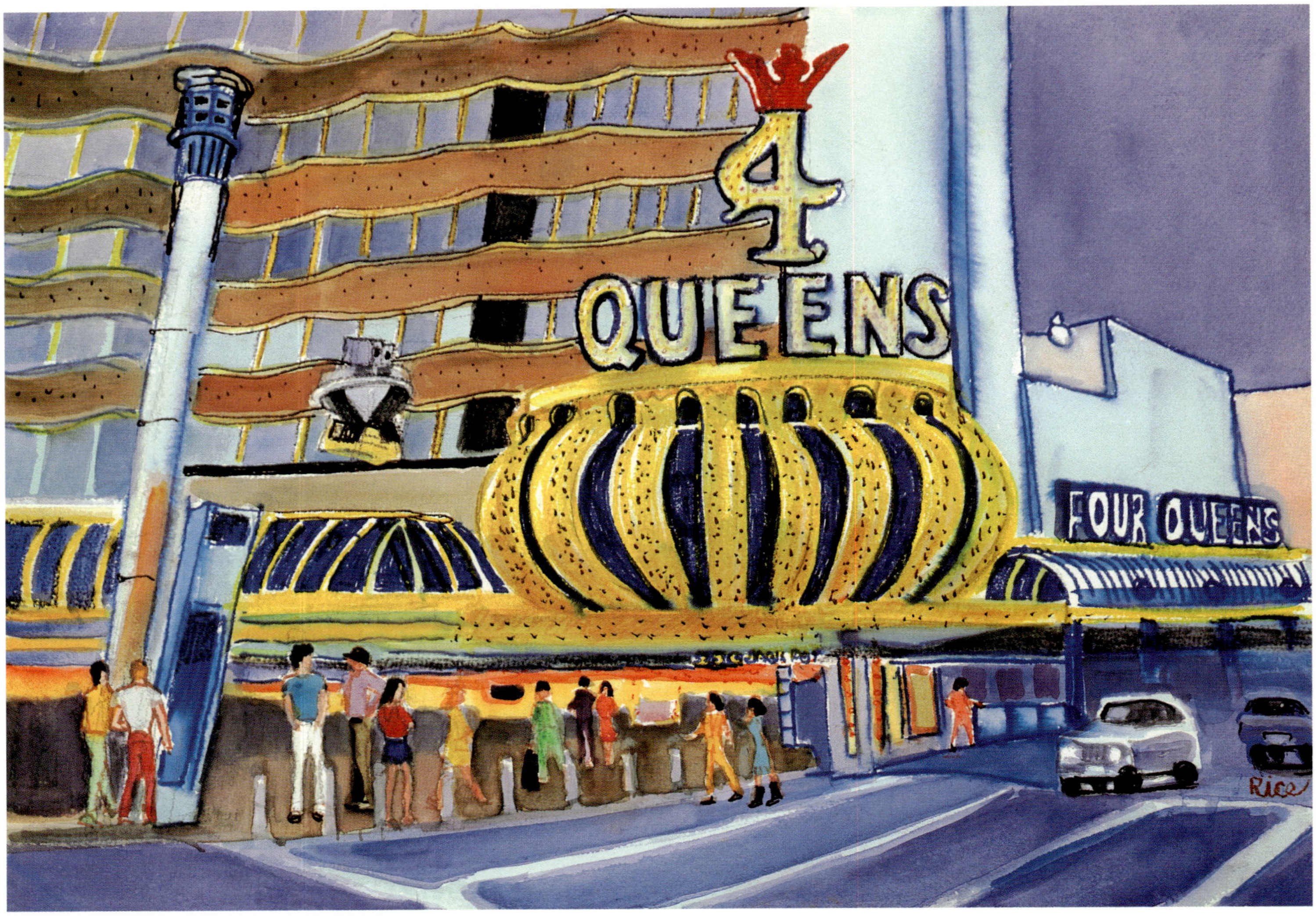

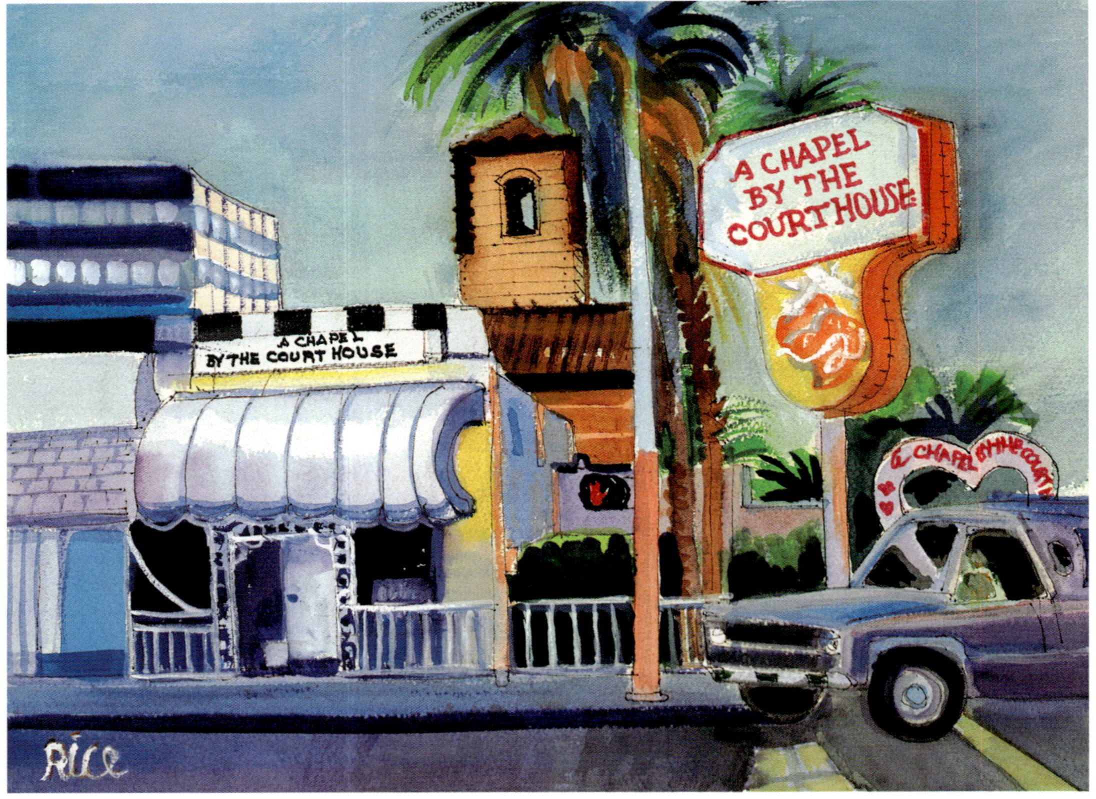

THE FOUR QUEENS HOTEL

Opened in 1965, the Four Queens Hotel brings a late 19th-century New Orleans ambiance to Downtown with vintage decor and live jazz playing in the French Quarter Lounge. In 1983, the 18-story, 400-room hotel tower was added. I learned that the hotel's name has a double meaning: besides the obvious playing card reference, the original owner also had a quartet of daughters.

A CHAPEL BY THE COURTHOUSE

Hey, you've got to stop by the Downtown courthouse to pick up your marriage license, anyway—why not walk across the street to walk down the aisle? Charolette Richards' A Chapel By the Courthouse makes it easy to get hitched in a hurry.

"VEGAS VICKI" >

"Vegas Vicki"—"Vegas Vic's" saucy female counterpart—beckons enticingly above the Girls of Glitter Gulch on Fremont Street, probably the most visible (yet fairly tame) exotic dance emporium in town and a reminder of the city's steamier side. Inside—I'm told—lovely topless dancers perform on high-tech catwalks to the delight of many a male patron.

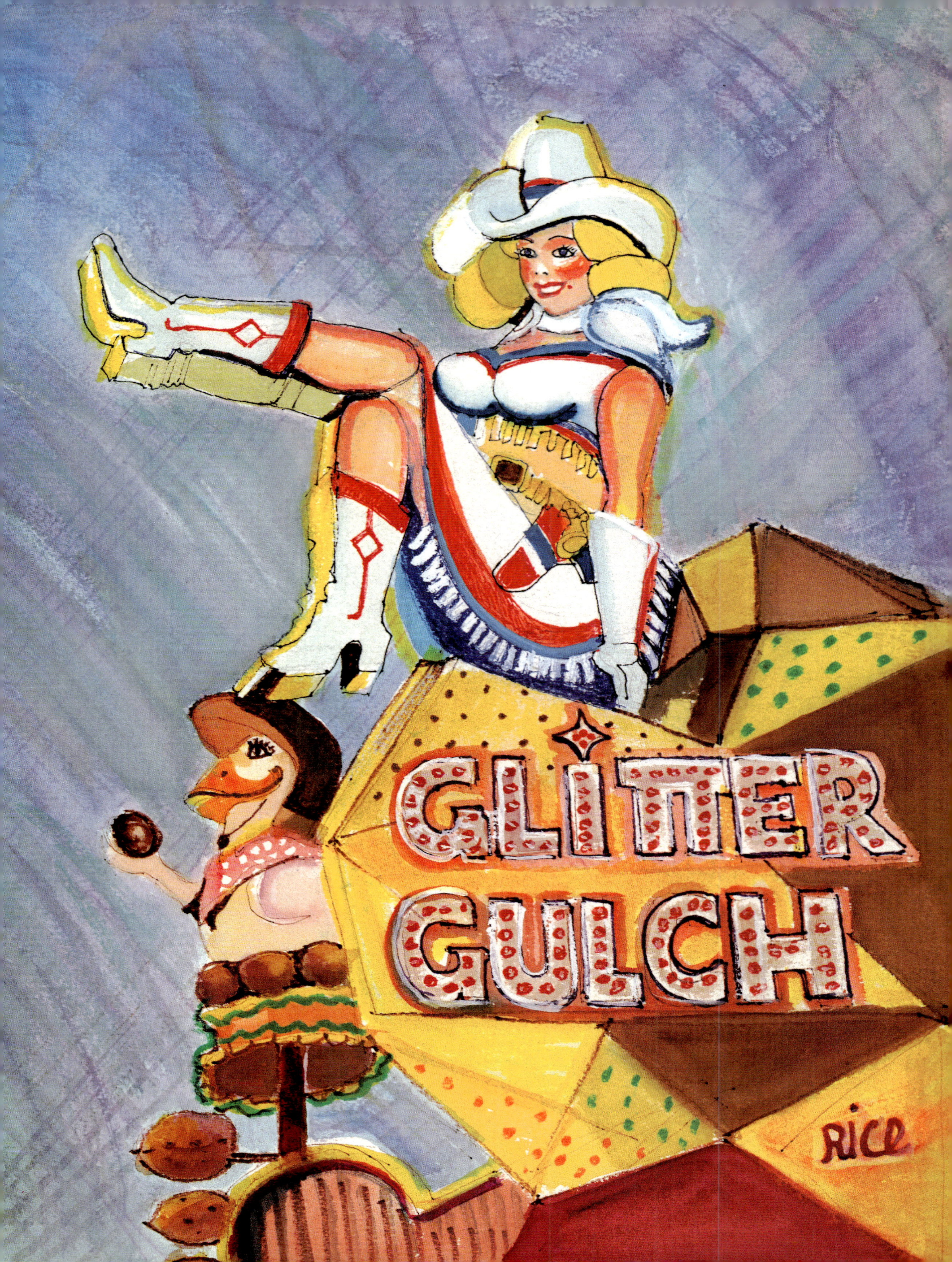
GLITER
GULCH
RICE

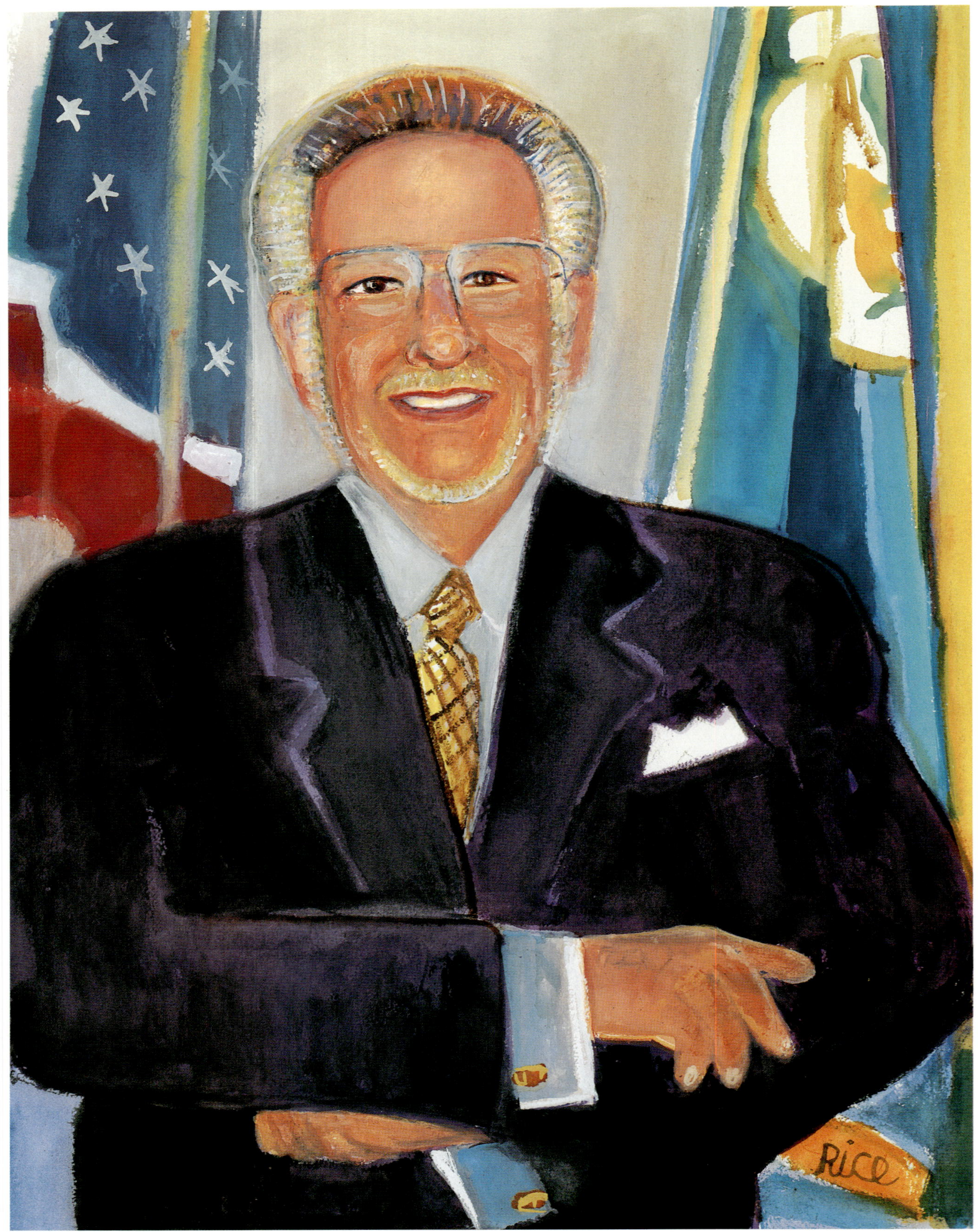

OSCAR B. GOODMAN, MAYOR OF THE CITY OF LAS VEGAS

Mayor Oscar B. Goodman is one of the hardest-working public officials around, known for beating the city staff to work in the morning. Early in his life, Mayor Goodman flirted with several career choices—sociology professor, football coach and rabbi—before becoming an assistant district attorney in Philadelphia. A case involving Las Vegas introduced him to Nevada's "land of milk and honey," and he and wife Carolyn made the move there with just $87. Establishing himself as a defense attorney, his love for his new hometown inspired him to make a successful bid for mayor. Now at the helm of a diverse city that's growing by leaps and bounds, he can tap all of his interests: the law, games, faith and, of course, people. Mayor Goodman's love for Las Vegas was apparent in the time we spent together. "I've never had a bad day since I got here," he said.

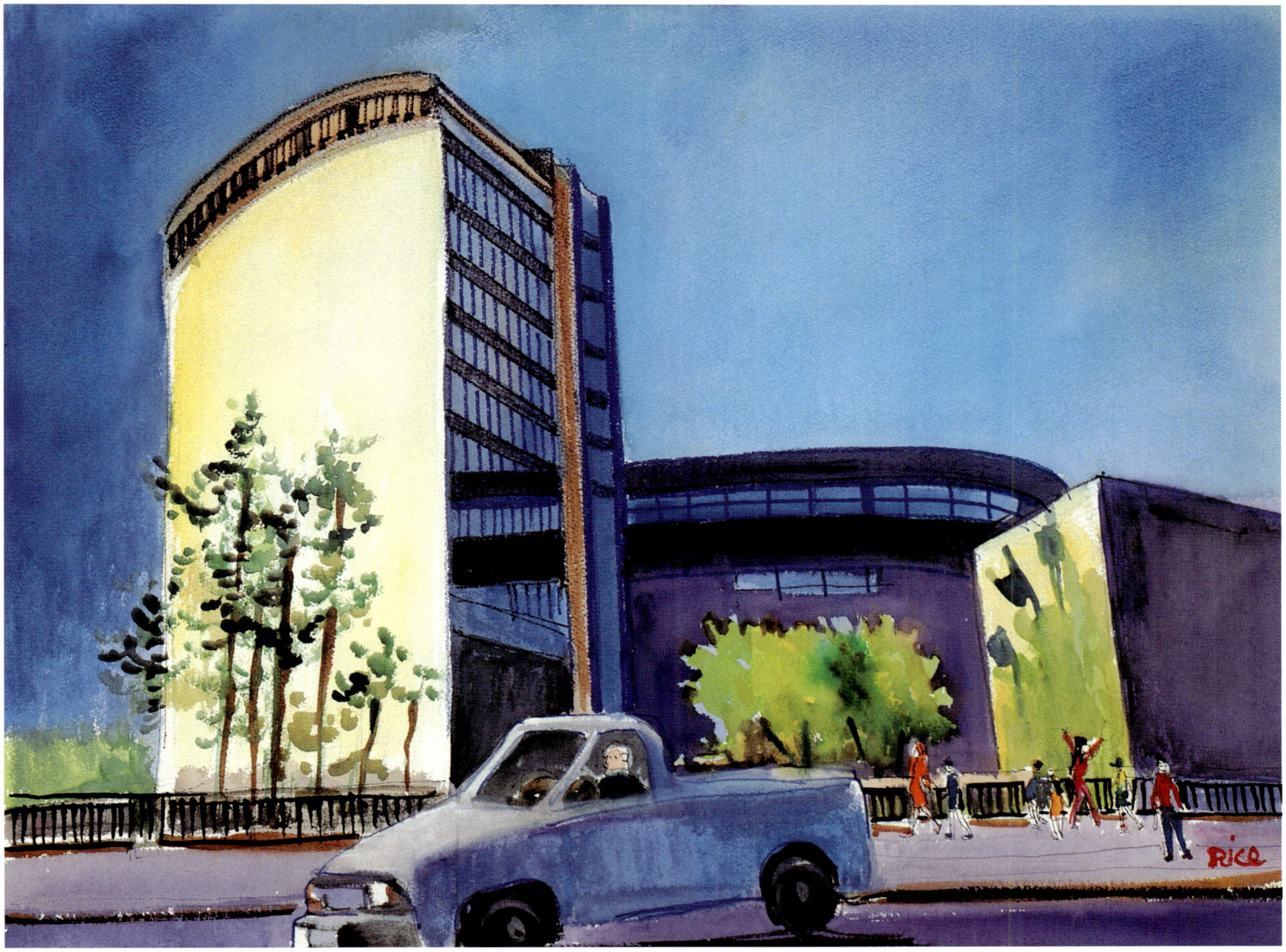

CITY HALL

The City Hall Building on Stewart Avenue is the seat of local government, with plenty of politicians, commissioners and civil servants working to ensure the quality of life for local residents. Something's being done right: Las Vegas is considered among the top five cities in the U.S. in which to live.

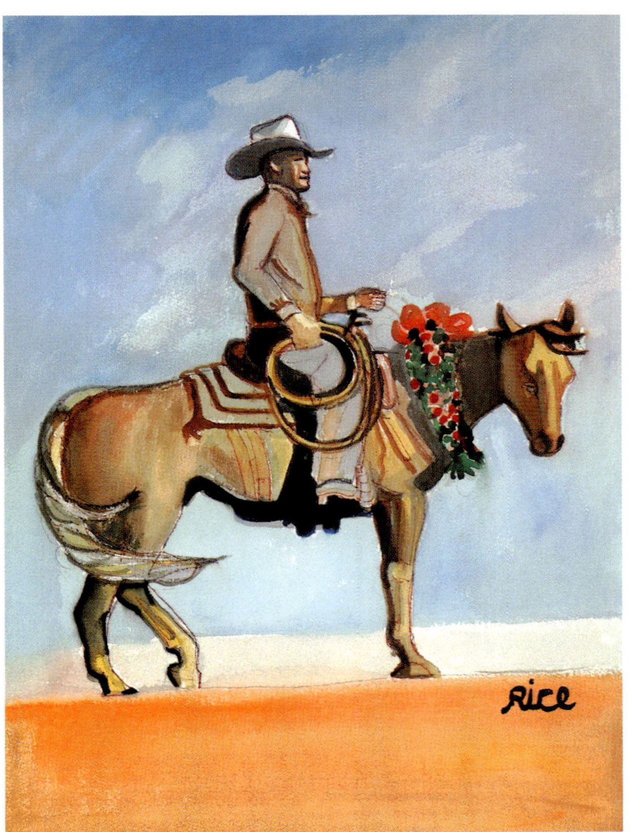

BENNY BINION REMEMBERED

Binion's Horseshoe founder Lester "Benny" Binion was a gambling boss and bootlegger who fled Texas for the more tolerant and lucrative Vegas scene, where he founded the Horseshoe in the early 1950s. Before his death in 1990, Binion attained a certain kind of respectability only Las Vegas can impart, and a statue of him astride a horse was erected Downtown. Binion's Golden Rule was, "He who has the gold makes the rules."

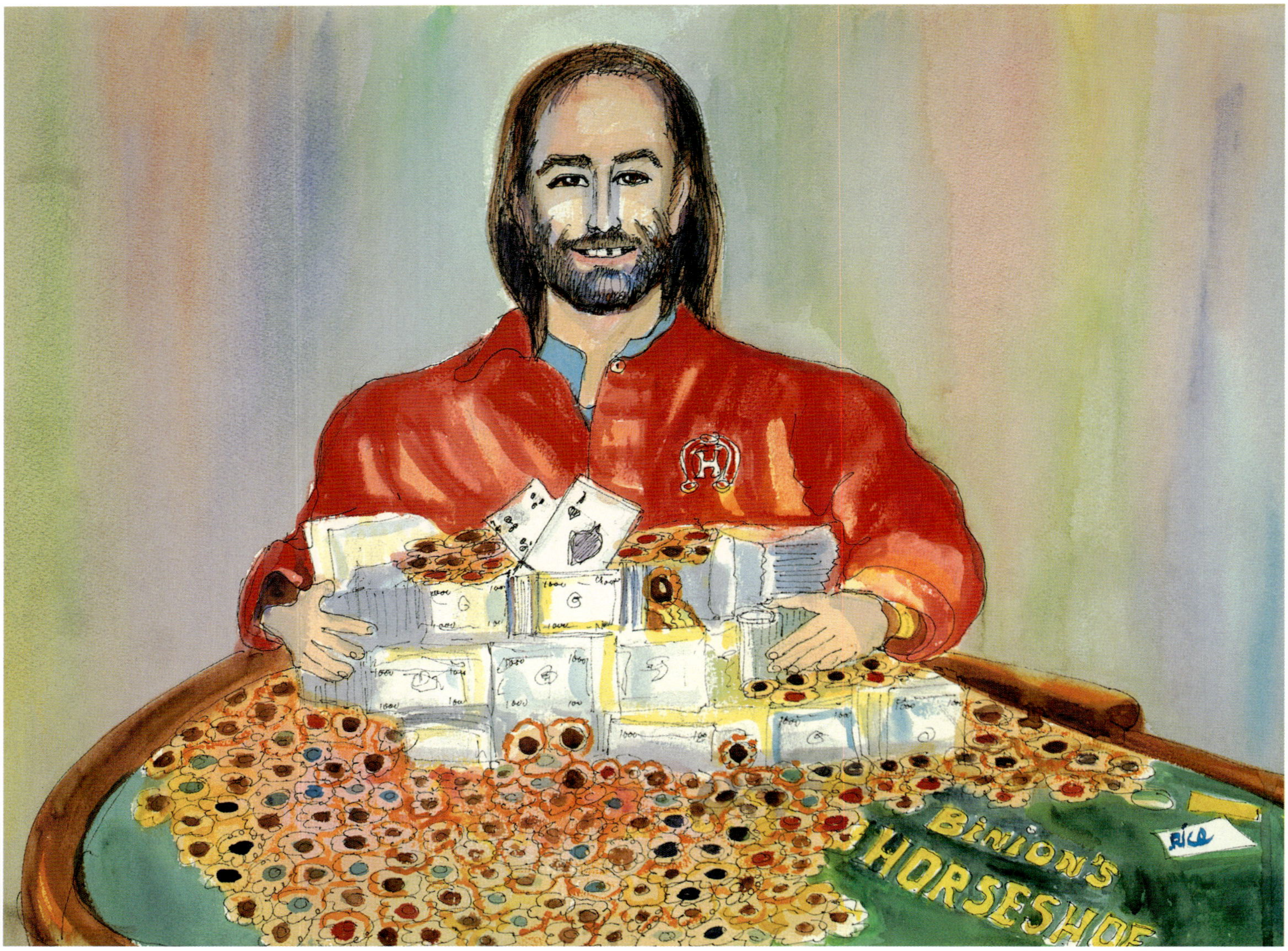

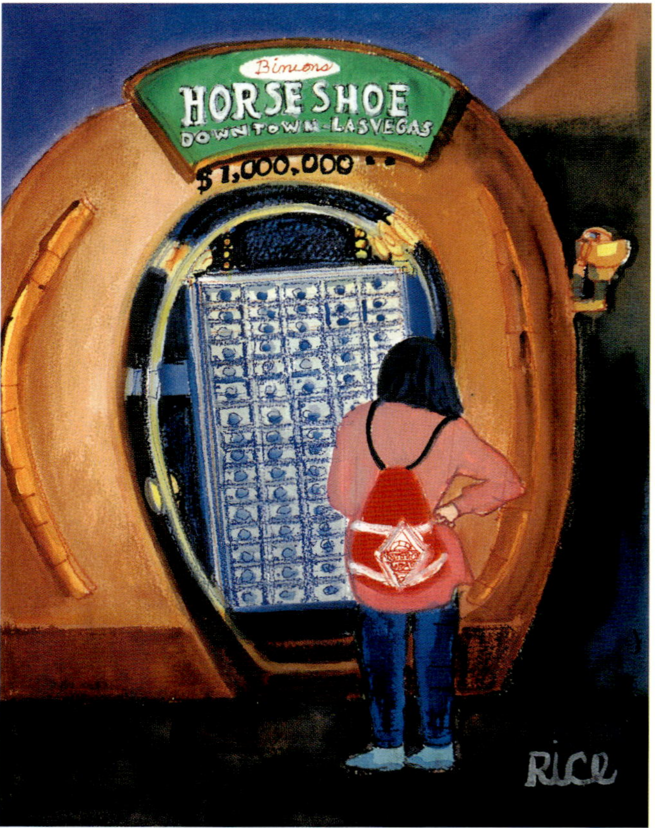

A BIG POKER PAYOFF

A professional poker player from Pacific Palisades, California, champion Chris Ferguson's ride to victory at Binion's Horseshoe began as one of nearly 5,000 players in the 31st annual World Series of Poker. Chris entered the four-day World Championship event with more than 500 other entrants and his last hand in the Texas hold-'em tourney pitted him against top competitor T.J. Cloutier in a dramatic finale. Although it looked like he needed a miracle to win, the man who likes to be called "Jesus" pulled it off and took home $1.5 million in prize money. He credits his father, a professor of game theory at UCLA, for teaching him about the profitability of poker.

Launched in 1970, the World Series of Poker's origin goes back to 1949 when the legendary gambler Nick "The Greek" Dandolos asked Benny Binion to start a high-stakes poker marathon. Binion arranged what became a five-month marathon in which Johnny Moss and Nick "The Greek" played until Moss—who later became the first World Series poker champ—walked away with the $2 million pot.

WHO WANTS TO BE A MILLIONAIRE?

If you get lucky at Binion's Horseshoe, you might walk away with a jackpot the size of the cool $1 million the casino once had on display (in rare, out-of-circulation $10,000 bills)—a shrewd way to put dollar signs in gamblers' eyes, literally. The long-controversial Binion family name was the talk of the town (and in national headlines) in 1998 when Horseshoe founder Benny's son Ted died of a heroin overdose. Two years later, his young, sexy, ex-exotic dancer girlfriend (and heir) and her handsome lover, a contractor who built an underground vault to hide Ted's secret stash of silver, were convicted of murdering Ted Binion for his money. Although Las Vegas is no longer the "Sin City" it once was, the seamy scandal was a reminder that the bad old days weren't all that long ago.

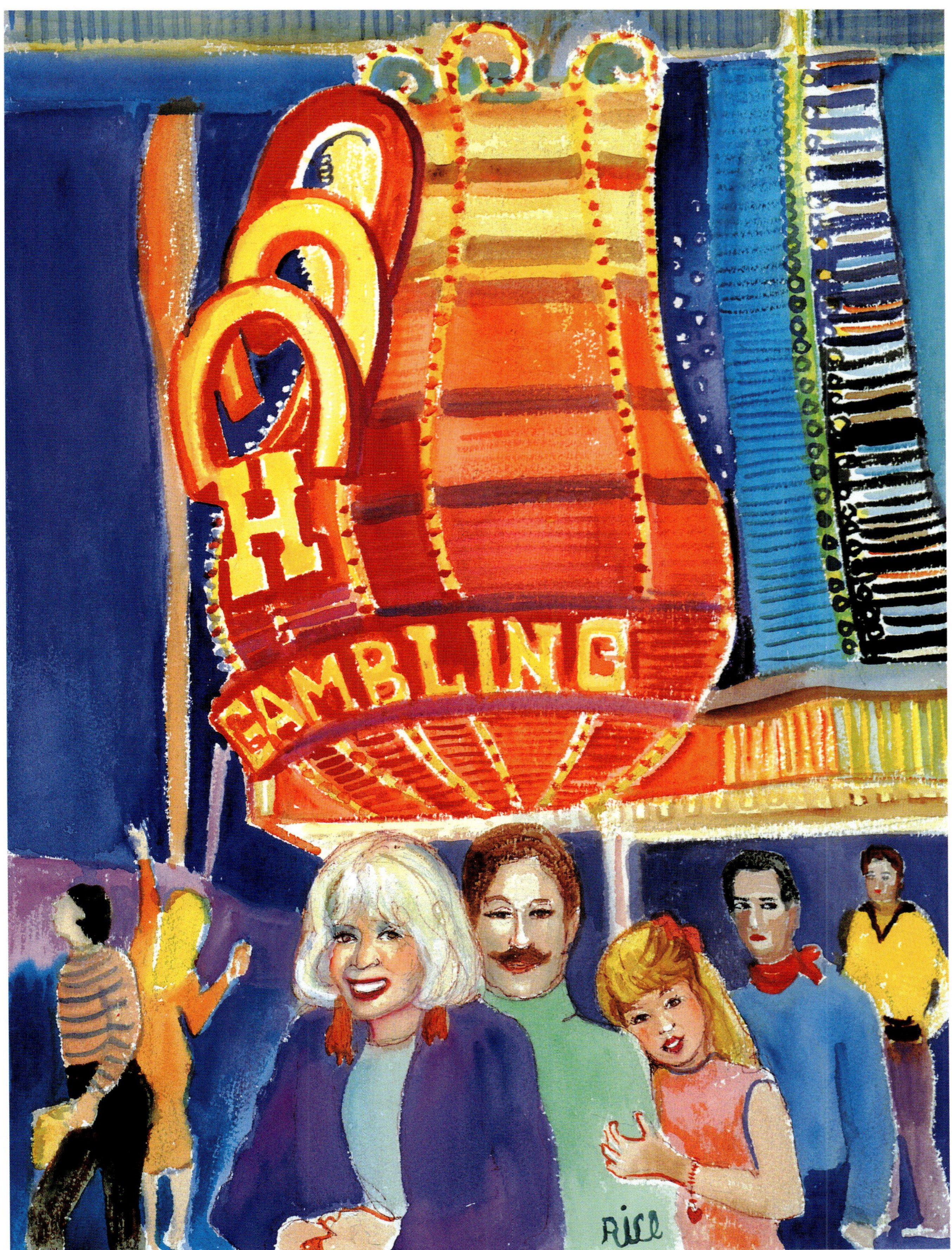

BINION'S HORSESHOE

My friend Lorna Greene, poet, artist and Las Vegas local, showed me around Downtown, her favorite part of the city. We ended up at Binion's Horseshoe, the town's quintessential gambling hall, which has a long history pioneering super-high stakes gambling and events like the World Series of Poker.

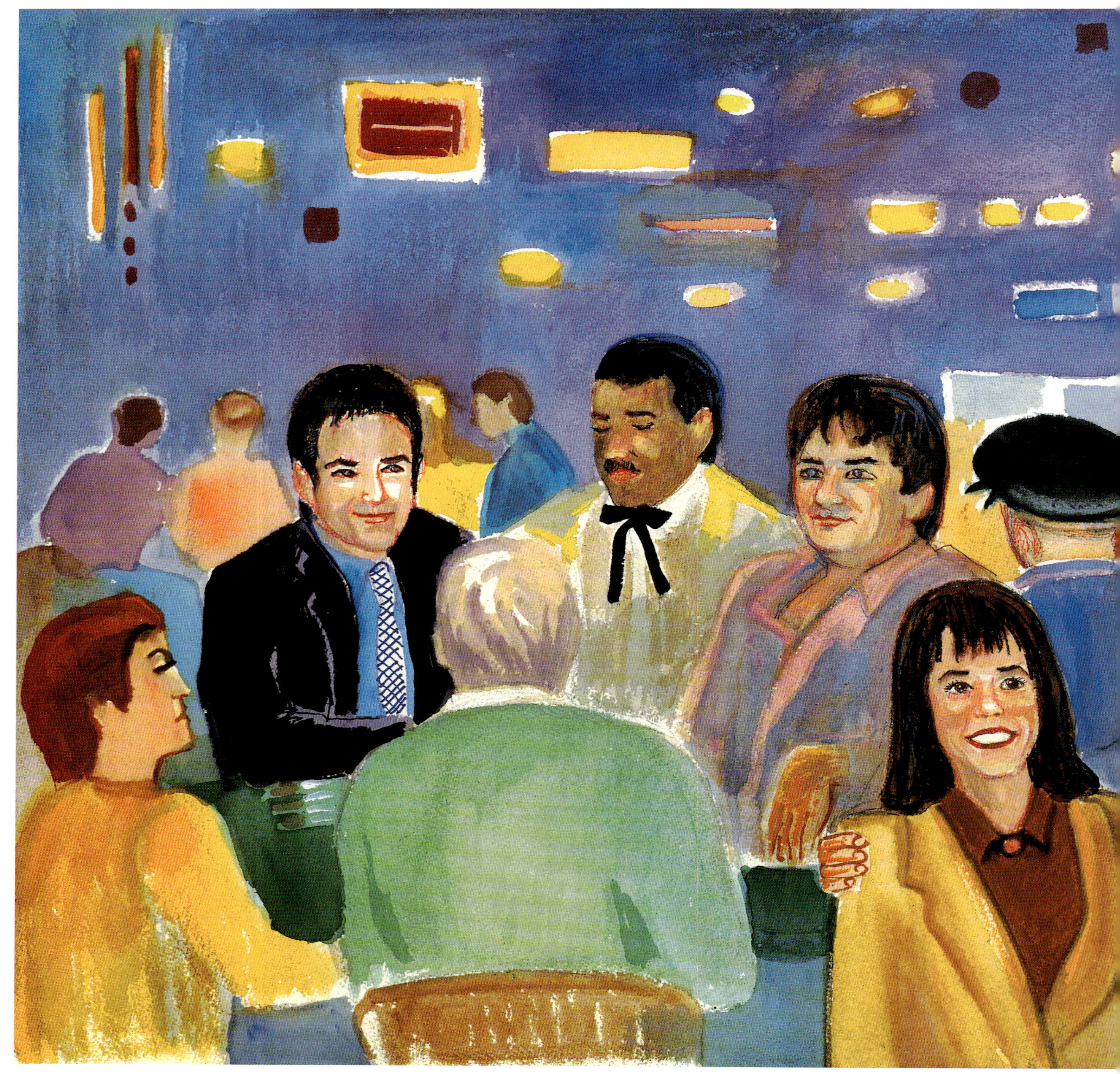

ANTE UP WITH CATHI WOOD

Cathi Wood, the poker room manager at Binion's Horseshoe, greets "player" Andy Anderson as Corey Steele and Larry Grossman contend with dealer Cris Simon. I learned about high-stakes poker from Cathi, a Las Vegas native who has dealt at the Horseshoe since 1991. As many as 200 players from around the world come to Binion's each day to ante up in the same room that hosts the World Series of Poker. Cathi oversees 70-plus regular staff members and coordinates the annual event. If Cathi knows when to hold 'em and knows when to fold 'em, it may be in her blood: her father Bob Thompson managed the Stardust poker room for years and serves as host of the World Series.

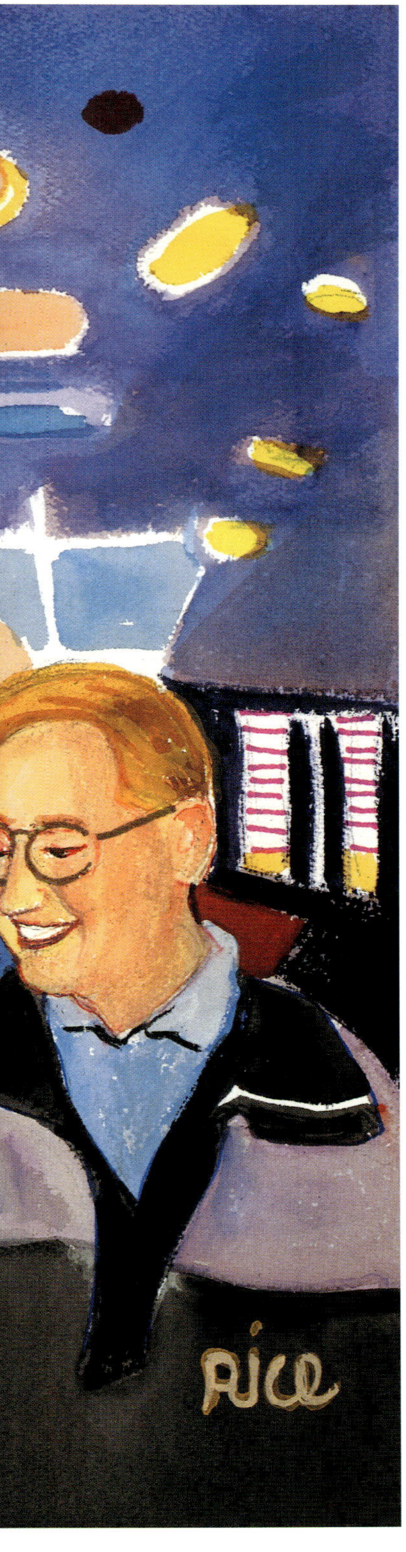

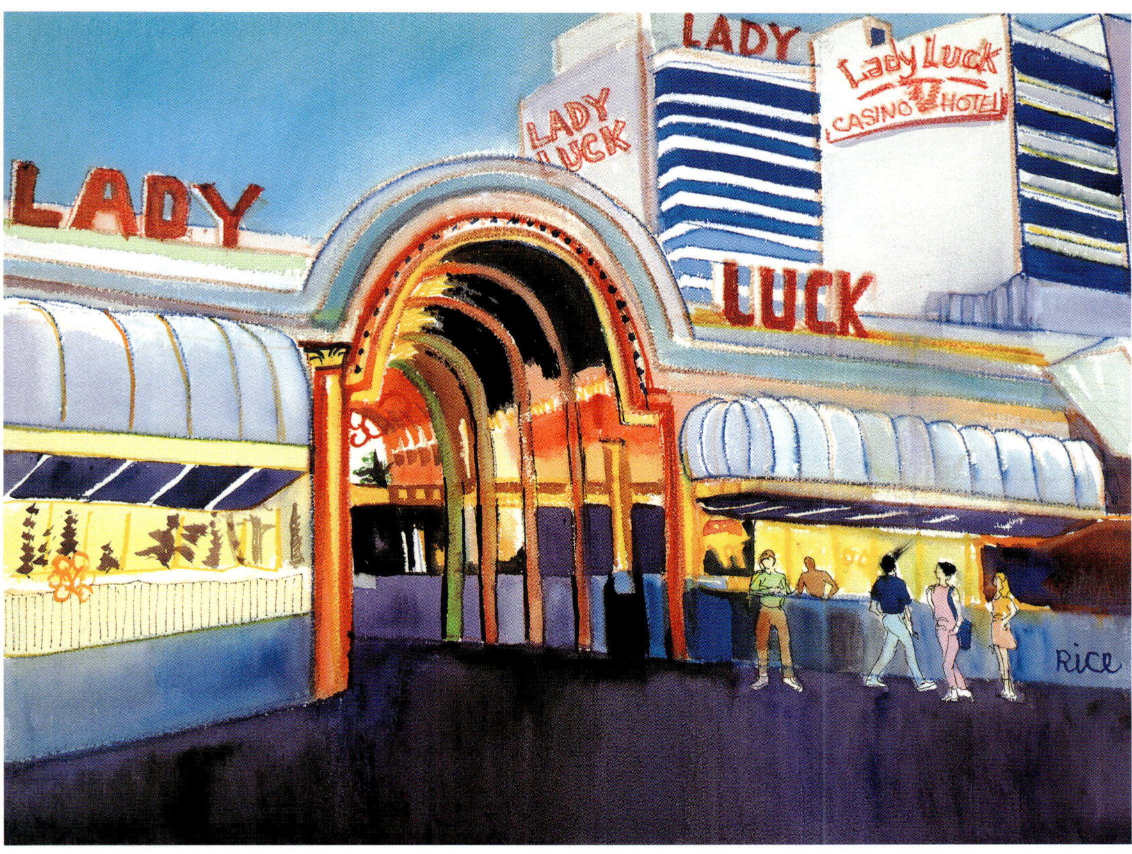

LADY LUCK

This hotel has certainly seen its share of Lady Luck, surviving and thriving since its beginnings in 1964 as a combination slot machine parlor and hot dog stand. Now it's a full-fledged hotel and today the famous foot-long hot dogs are free!

THE GOLDEN GATE

The site of the Golden Gate Hotel and Casino has a long history. The Hotel Nevada was the first to occupy it back in 1906, and some of its original rooms are still in use. It later became the famous Sal Sagev (that's "Las Vegas" spelled backward) in 1931 and was later converted by Bay Area gamers into the Golden Gate in 1955. It pioneered the practice of offering shrimp cocktails at rock-bottom prices.

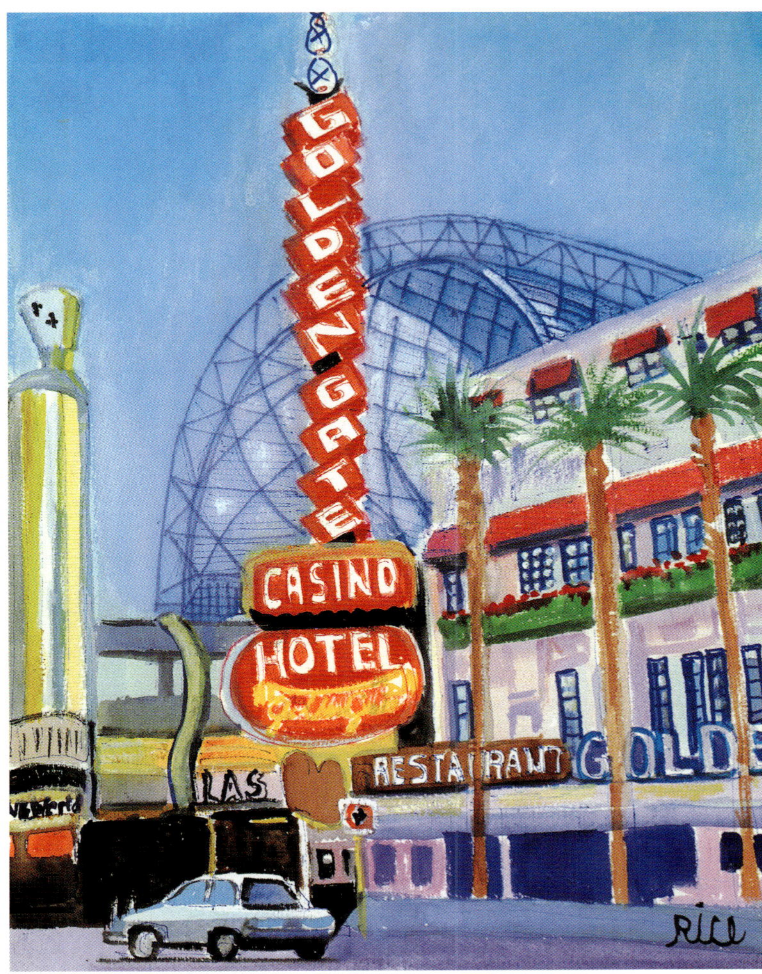

The Westside

Dubbed, "the Westside" by the early African-American Las Vegans who worked and settled here in the 40s, 50s and 60s, the western side of town was the place where fabled entertainers like Sammy Davis, Jr., Dorothy Dandridge, Nat "King" Cole, Lena Horne and Ella Fitzgerald stayed while they played at showrooms elsewhere in the city. That changed when the Moulin Rouge opened here and brought black and white patrons and performers together under one roof. Proudly African-American in heritage, today the area is a revitalized multicultural community, with blacks, whites, Latinos and Asians settling and building businesses here.

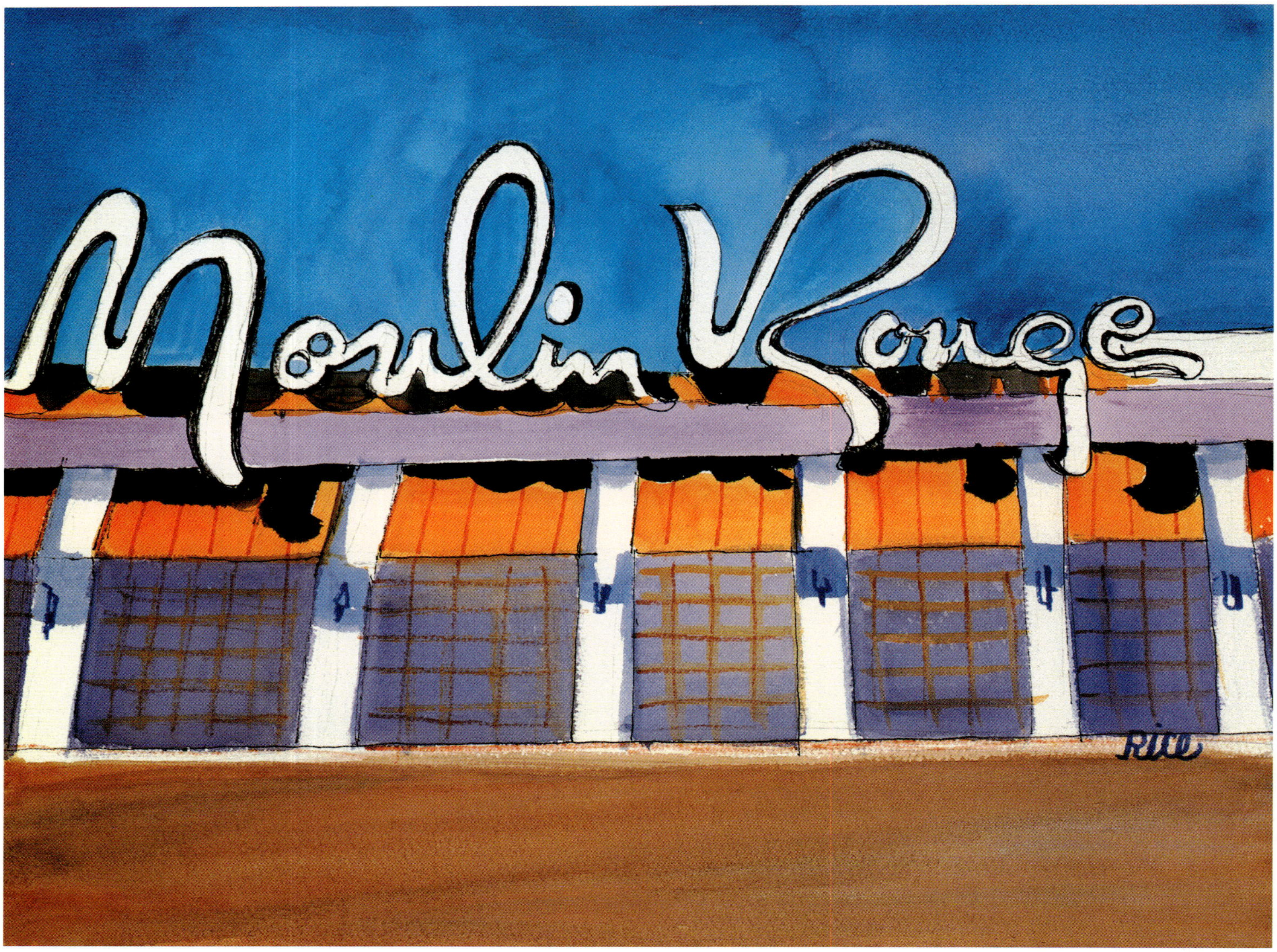

WAITING FOR THE MOULIN ROUGE TO RETURN

They wowed 'em on the Strip, but they couldn't stay in the hotels in which they performed. In 1955, the opening of the Moulin Rouge changed all that. The hotel recruited the best black singers, dancers, staff and managers—the only whites were the casino dealers, because no casino had ever trained blacks to deal. Soon the Moulin Rouge was the hottest, hippest place in town, where whites and blacks alike—including stars like Frank Sinatra, Louis Armstrong, Bob Hope and Lena Horne—crowded in to enjoy the happening scene. Despite (or perhaps because of) its integrated cachet, the Moulin Rouge mysteriously closed just six months after it opened. Today—decades later—a revival is underway, with the new, refurbished Moulin Rouge opening for business—as a casino for all people.

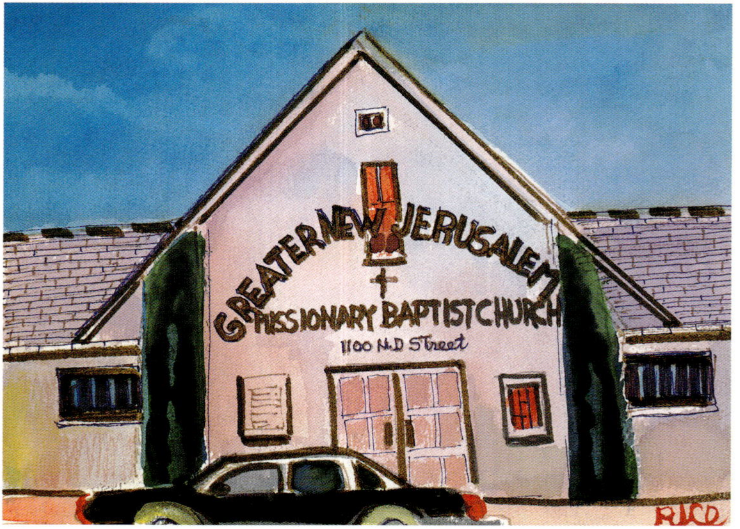

THE GREATER JERUSALEM MISSIONARY BAPTIST CHURCH

Walking the Westside, I strolled by the Greater Jerusalem Missionary Baptist Church, one of many Baptist congregations serving the area's African-American community.

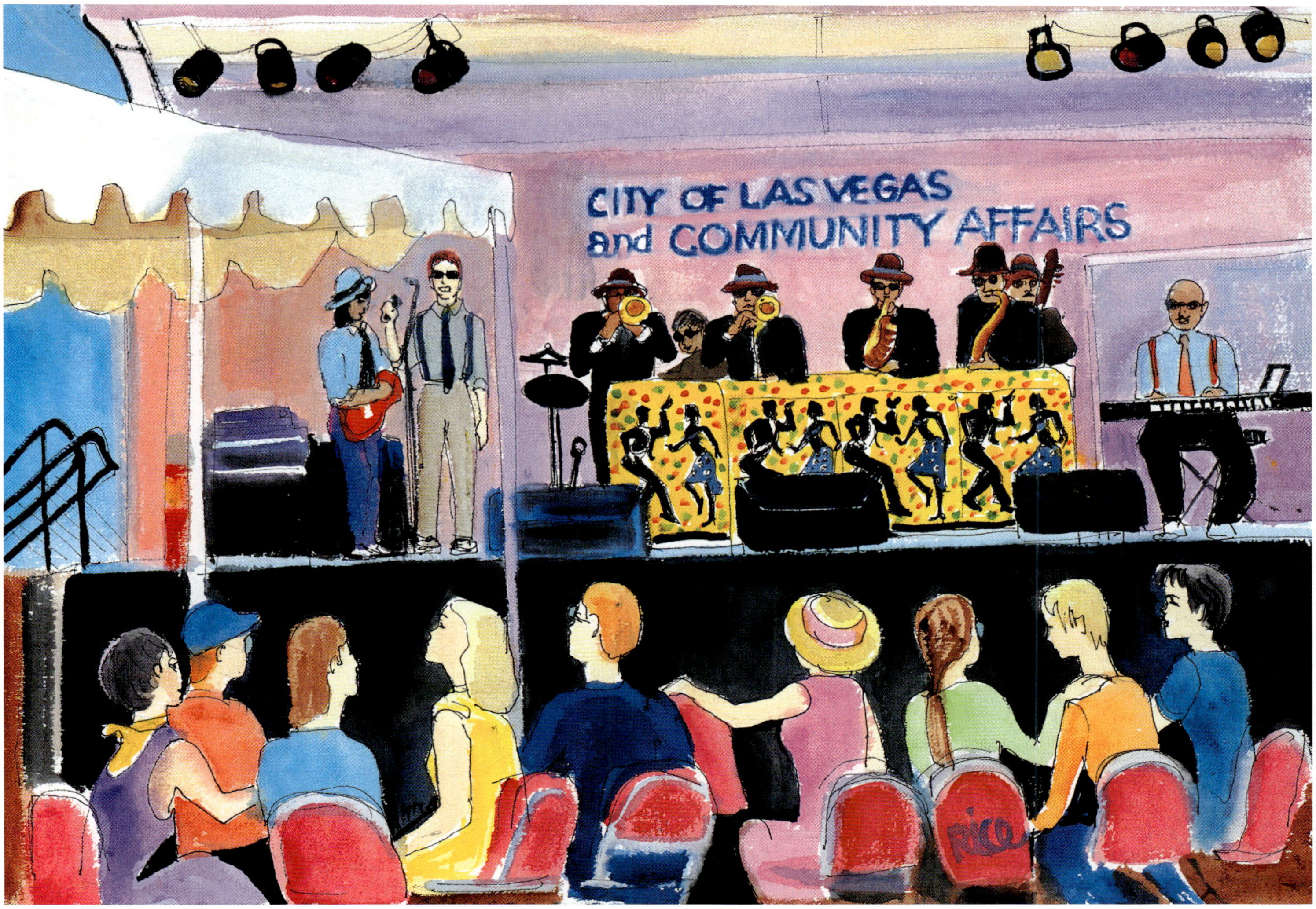

JAZZED UP ON MAIN STREET

Attracted by the music in the air, I caught this outdoor jazz concert on Main Street, part of an art fair sponsored by Las Vegas Community Affairs.

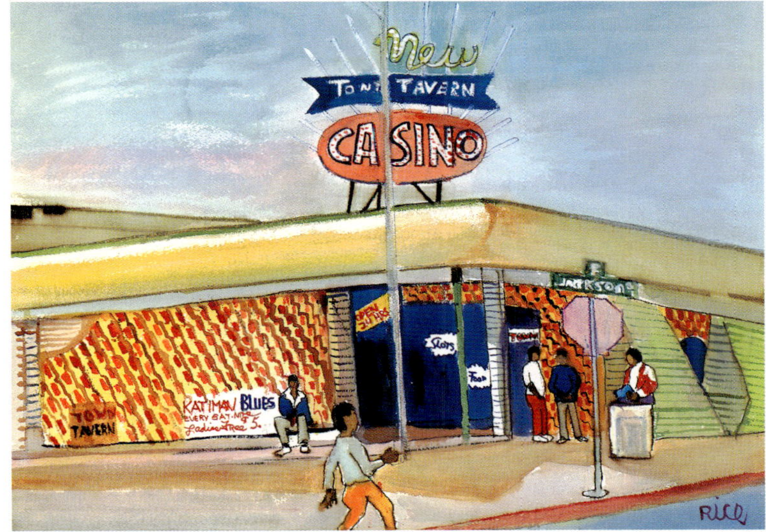

ON THE WESTSIDE

The New Town Tavern Casino serves as a major meeting place on the Westside.

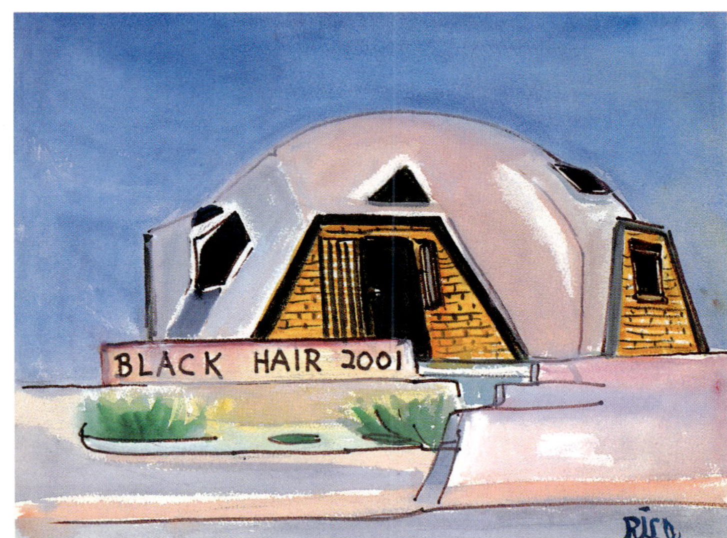

BLACK HAIR 2001

I found this adorable adobe and the hair salon within, très chic.

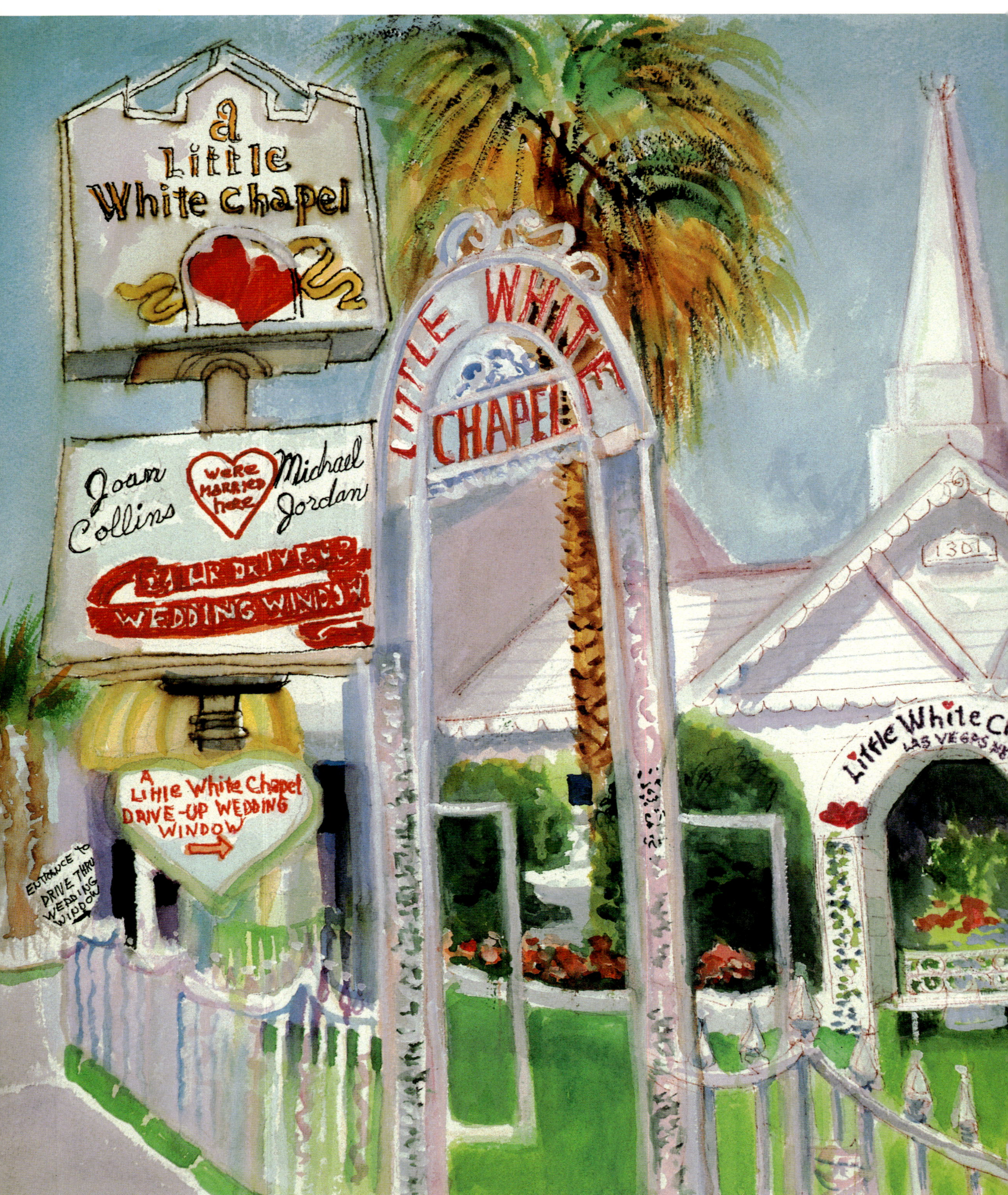
a Little White chapel
Joan Collins
were married here
Michael Jordan
LITTLE WHITE CHAPEL
1301
Little White
A Little White Chapel DRIVE-UP WEDDING WINDOW
ENTRANCE TO DRIVE THRU WEDDING WINDOW

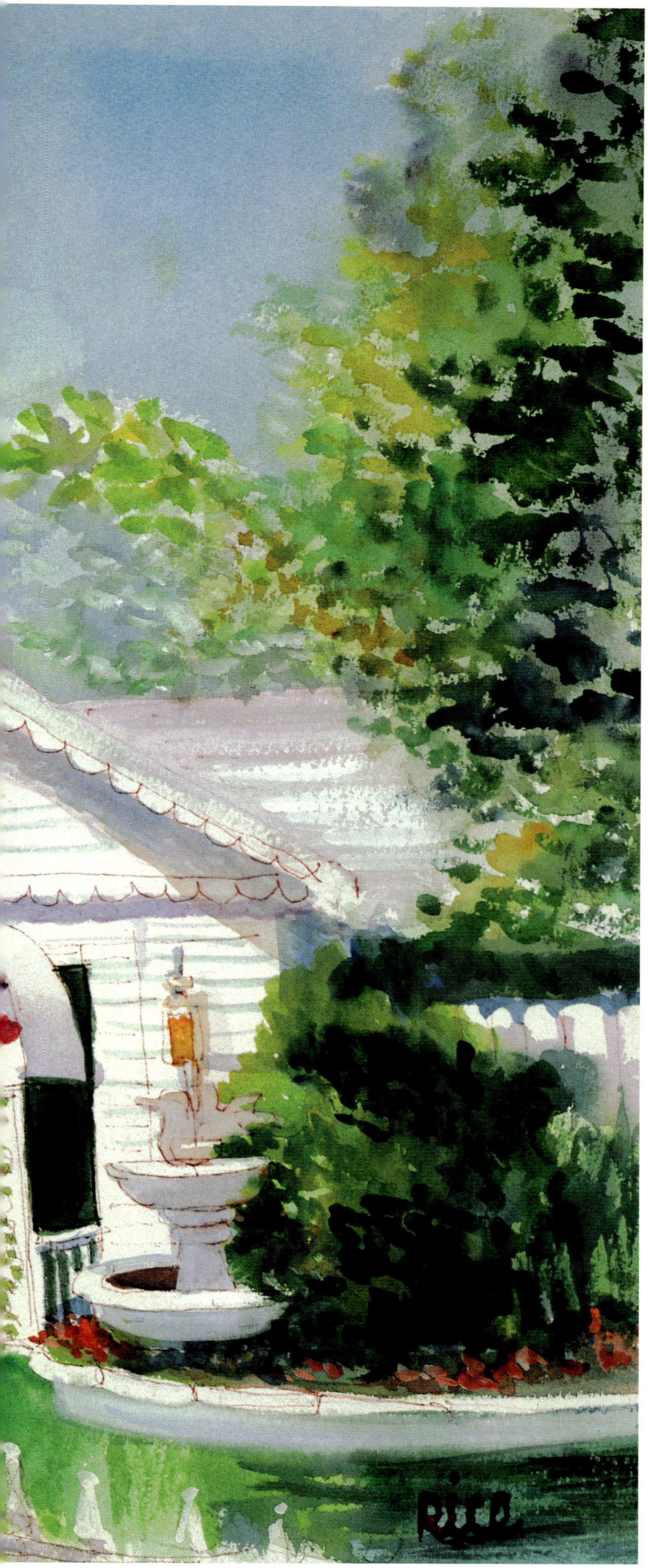

TYING THE KNOT

HOW MANY TIMES HAVE YOU HEARD of a couple foregoing an elaborate wedding ceremony and high-tailing it to Vegas for a quickie service? Over 100,000 couples do it at nearly 30 chapels each year, 3,000-plus on Valentine's Day alone. Some of my friends have done it, a few more than once. There's just something about the place that makes people believe they can hit the jackpot, be it at the slots or at the altar. There are a variety of ways to exchange "I Dos": you can be married by a conventional minister, an Elvis impersonator, or a futuristic Starfleet Admiral; you can trade vows in costume as Anthony and Cleopatra or in a traditional white gown provided by the chapel; you can make it legal under the disco lights of Studio 54; hurtling down the MGM SkyScreamer; aboard an 18th Century pirate frigate or in your car at a drive-up window. Hey, a no-frills Vegas wedding was good enough for couples like Richard Gere and Cindy Crawford and Bruce Willis and Demi Moore, right? Besides—in the interest of full service for all those who impulse-wed—Nevada's fairly liberal divorce laws make it almost as easy to untie the knot as it is to tie it.

A LITTLE WHITE WEDDING CHAPEL

When you absolutely have to be married overnight! The Strip's A Little White Wedding Chapel makes it easy with inside ceremonies and a drive-up wedding window that beats out any fast food restaurant you can think of. Famed multi-matrimonial celebs like Joan Collins, Judy Garland and Mickey Rooney have been hitched here at least once, while veterans of more enduring unions like Dan Aykroyd and Donna Dixon, and Michael and Juanita Jordan also got their start here.

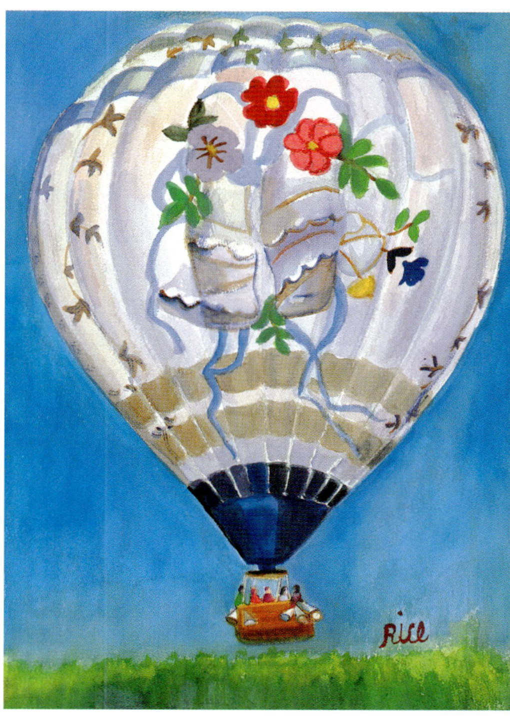

NEWLYWEDS ALOFT OVER LAS VEGAS

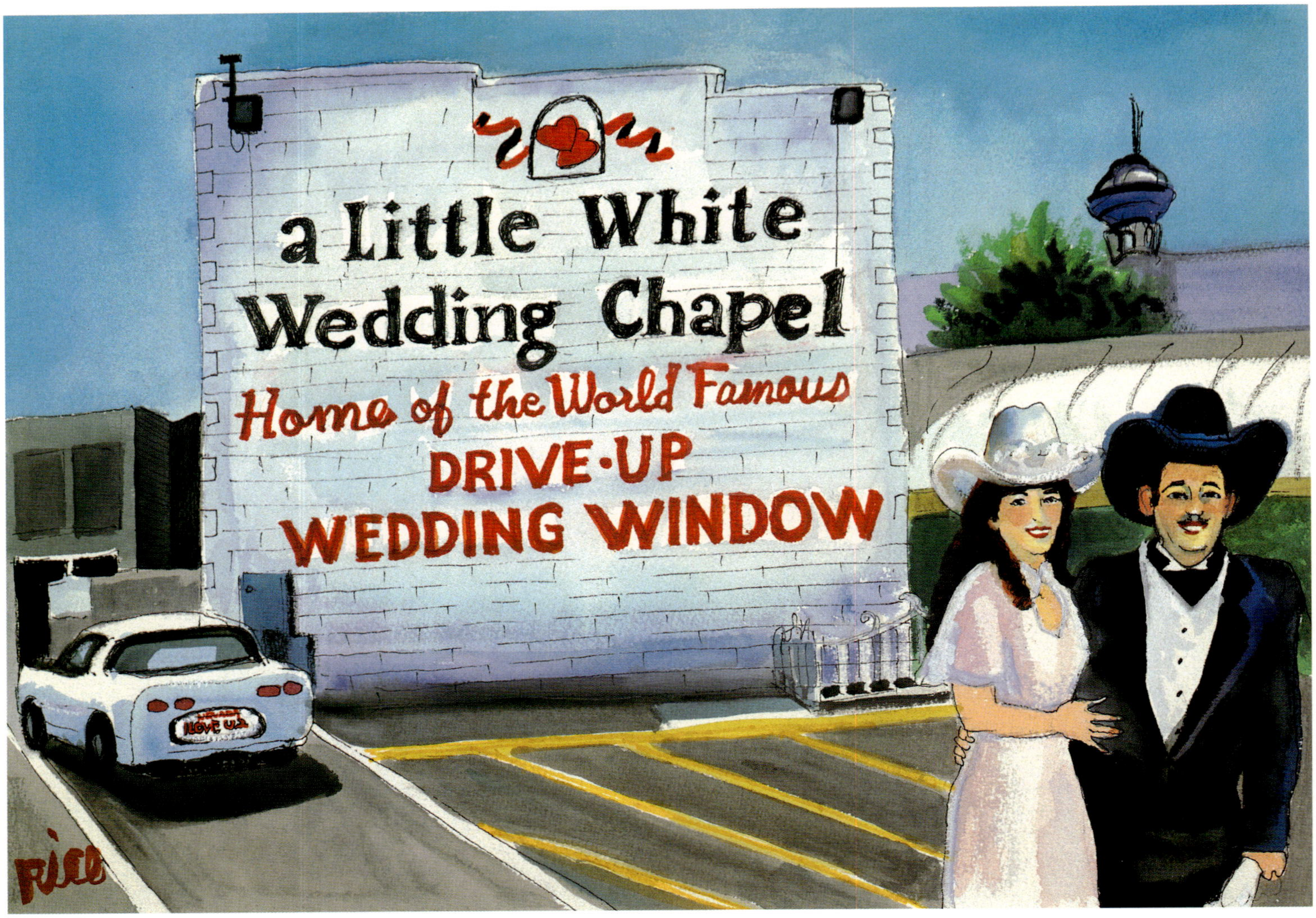

MAKING IT LEGAL AT A LITTLE WHITE CHAPEL

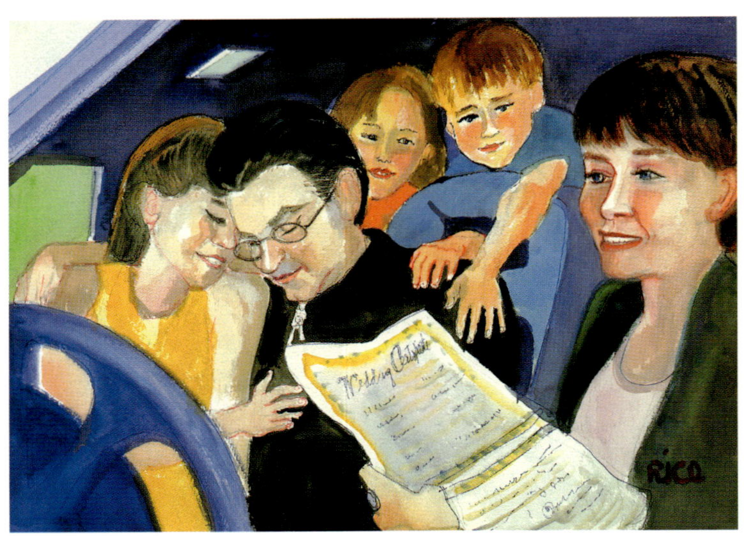

IDLING AT THE ALTAR

Charolette Richards—the Wedding Queen of the West renowned for quick, innovative and always memorable ceremonies—performs a drive-by wedding at her A Little White Chapel. Romance and bucket seats—what else could you ask for? The owner of three chapels and a matrimonial hot air balloon, Charolette's winning personality is infectious and she has the ability to quickly relate with anyone. She's helped countless couples—like Frank Sinatra and Mia Farrow—get hitched just about anywhere: atop mountains, hovering in helicopters, screaming down roller coasters, revving motorcycles, on roller skates, down water slides, on horseback, underwater, over the Internet and across the finish line of the Las Vegas Motor Speedway. Accelerated romance is her specialty.

THE LITTLE CHURCH OF THE WEST >

The Little Church of the West Wedding Chapel is the city's oldest "hitching post." The exact, half-size replica of a famed 1849 California church was added alongside the Last Frontier by the casino's owner, William Moore, in 1942. A National Historic Landmark, it was moved to its present location in the 1980s. About 6,000 fast-paced weddings a year are performed within the redwood chapel or amid its lovely gardens. The most eyebrow-raising ceremony in recent years was the quickie marriage of eclectic Oscar-winners Billy Bob Thornton and Angelina Jolie in 2000. The luscious-lipped, jeans-clad bride walked down the aisle sporting a new tattoo featuring the name of the groom, who wore a dark baseball cap. Twenty minutes and $189 later, the couple were pronounced man and wife. Actress Betty Grable and bandleader Harry James made it legal here in 1943, as did actor Richard Gere and supermodel Cindy Crawford in 1991. Judy Garland, Dudley Moore, Redd Foxx, Telly Savalas, Robert Goulet and marriage pros Mickey Rooney and Zsa Zsa Gabor have each tied the knot here at least once. Even Elvis did, sort of—his character married Ann-Margret's at The Little Church in the film "Viva Las Vegas."

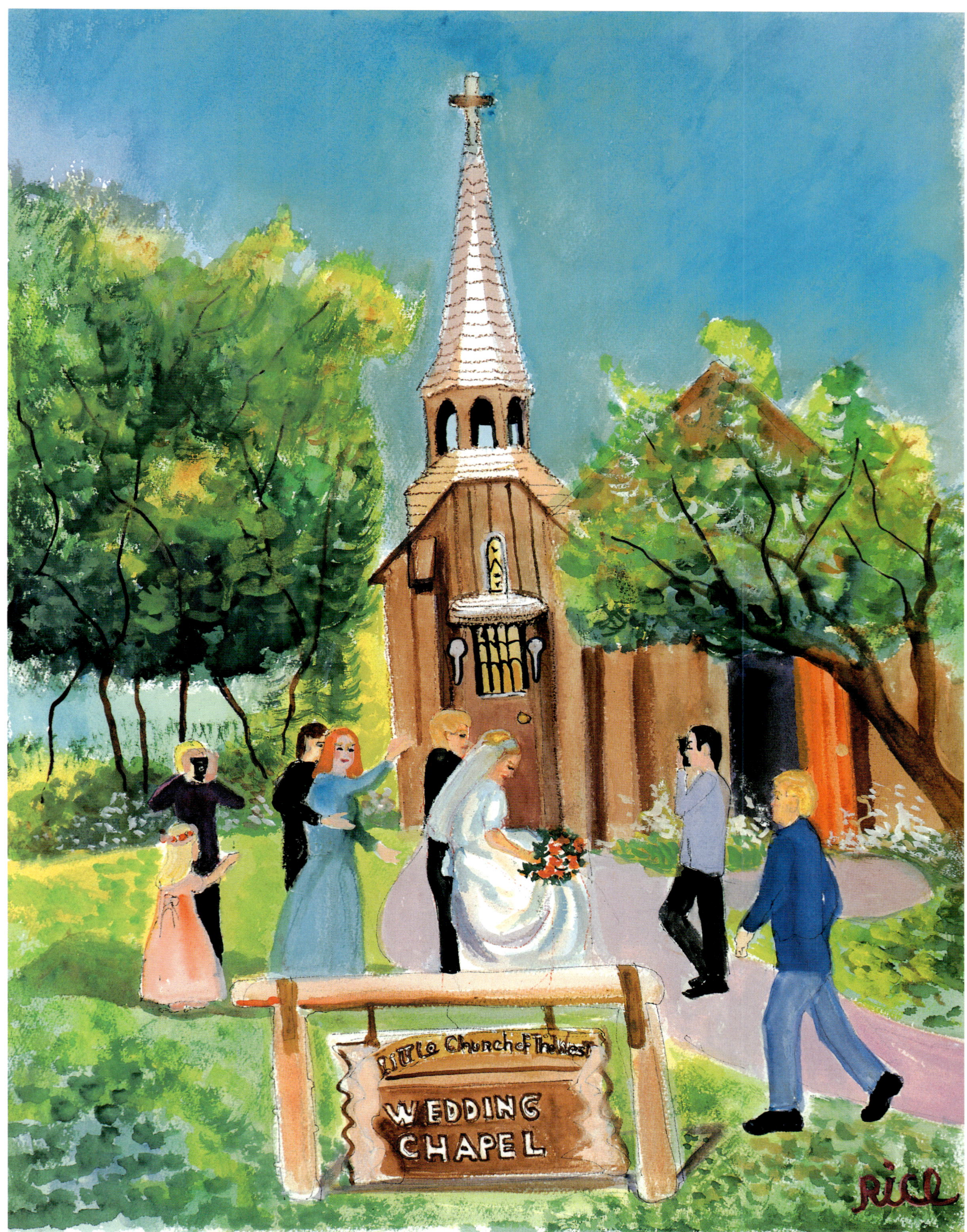
Little Church of The West
WEDDING
CHAPEL
Rice

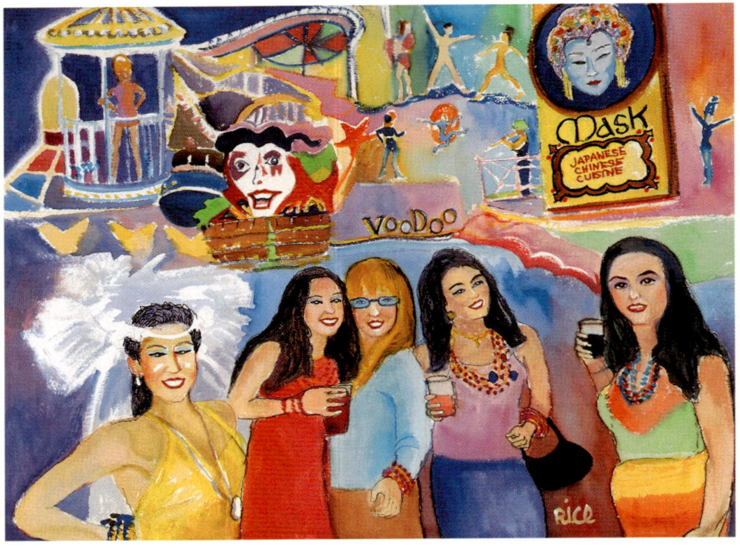

THE BRIDE-TO-BE'S BIG NIGHT OUT AT THE RIO

The only thing more festive than the Rio Hotel and Casino was this wild bachelorette's bash I spotted going on inside. The appropriately-veiled Erika Ybánez had come all the way from San Diego with a gaggle of girlfriends to celebrate one last crazy night on the town before her upcoming wedding.

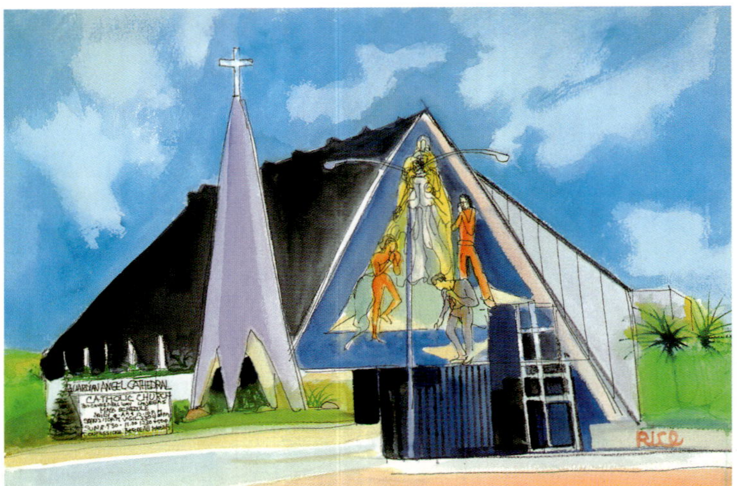

GUARDIAN ANGEL CATHEDRAL

The Guardian Angel Cathedral has been the city's most prominent Catholic house of worship since 1963, and—since it's located on the Strip—it features a few clever touches designed to appeal not only to locals but also to tourists whose casino experiences may have brought on a crisis of faith: 75% of Sunday Mass attendees are out-of-towners. The stained glass windows feature a harlequin above a hotel and a pair of tumbling dice at the base of a cross. Entertainer Danny Thomas was a regular here, and his contributions provided the church's stunning marble floors. Speaking of the collection plate, I'm told casino chips are gladly accepted along with more conventional offerings.

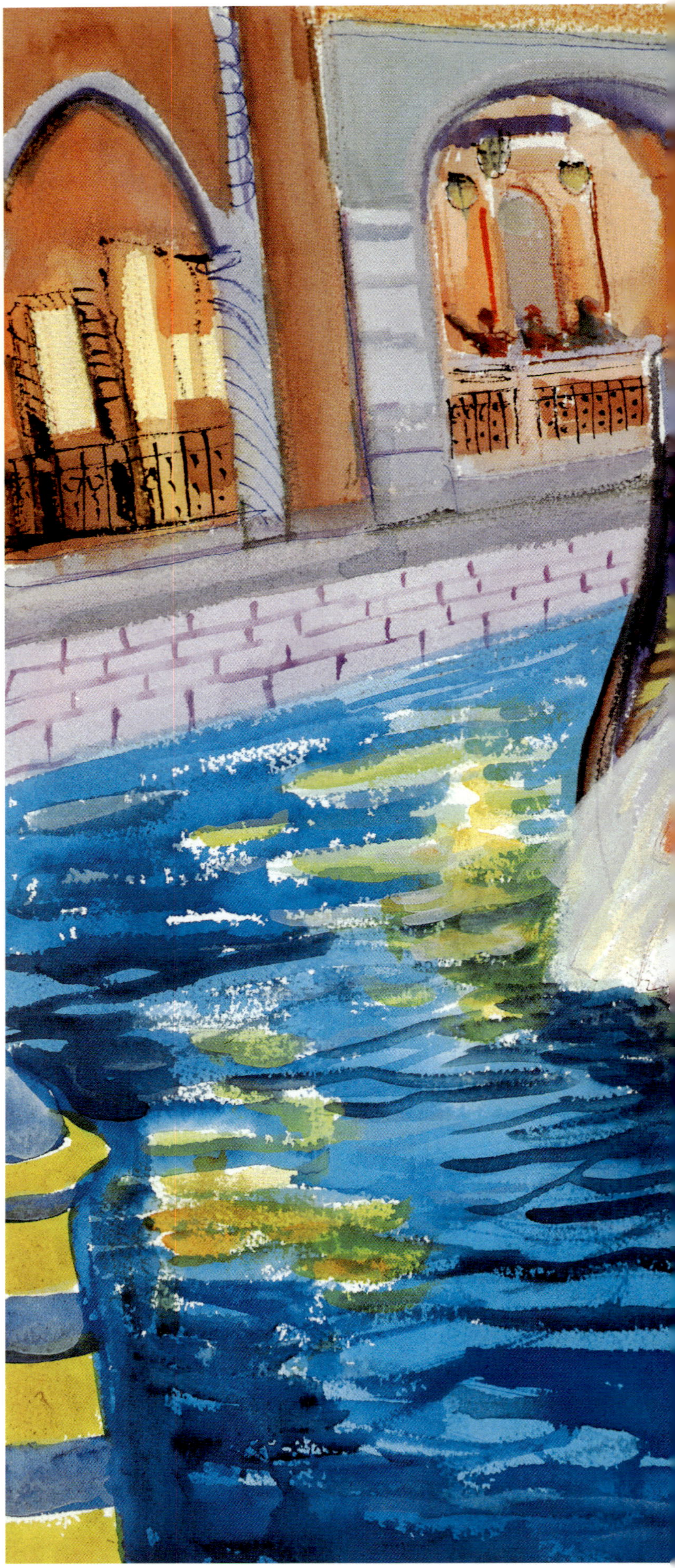

SAYING "SI" IN THE CANALS

What could be more romantic that a storybook gondola trip along the Grand Canals of Venice after your nuptials—especially when you don't have to pay for a trip to Italy? The Venetian Hotel offers a dreamy, floating alternative to an Italian honeymoon.

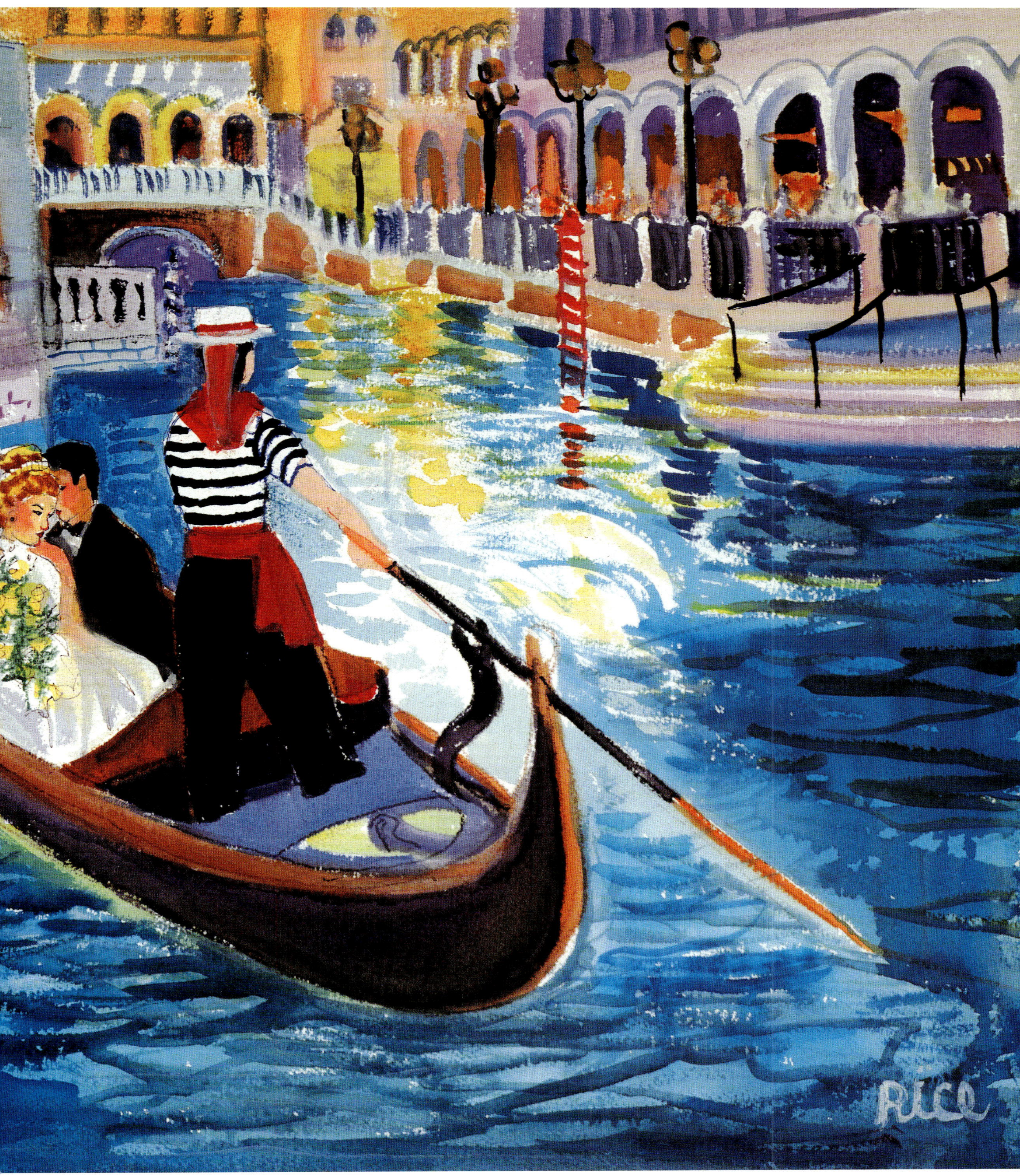
Rice

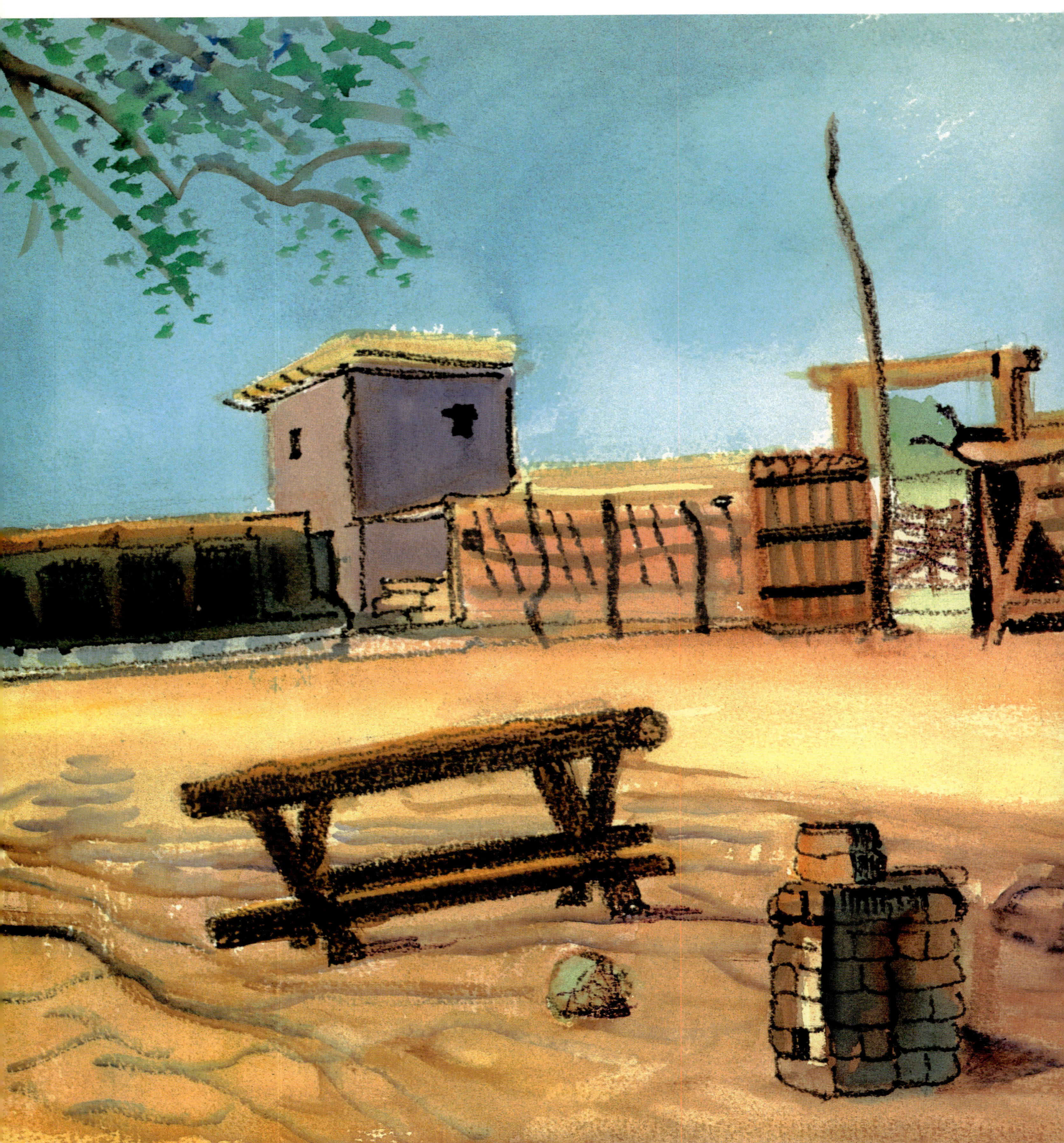

A TOUCH OF OLD LAS VEGAS

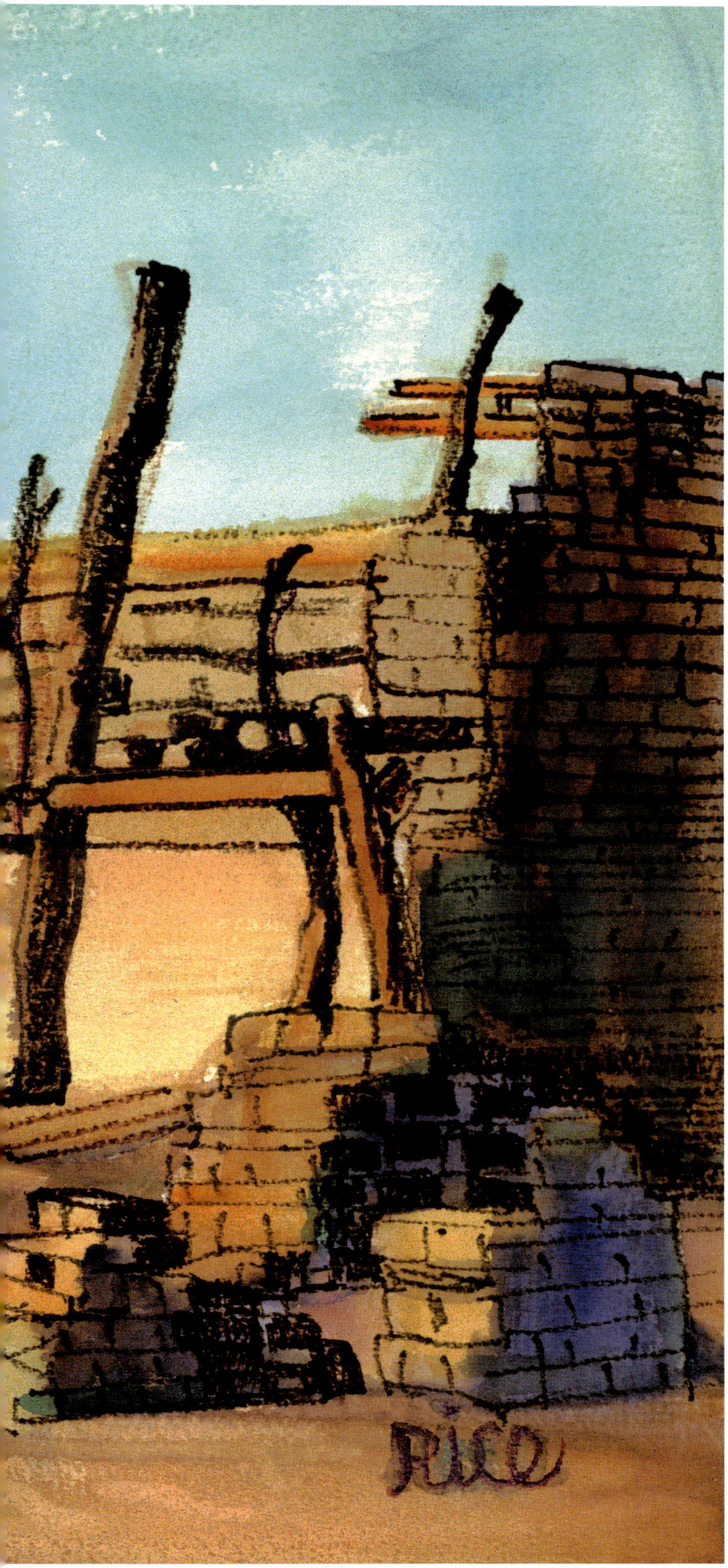

A TOUCH OF OLD LAS VEGAS CAN BE found all around, from rustic Bonnie Springs Ranch in Red Rock to the Old Mormon Fort to the hot springs that first drew settlers to the region. Wedding chapels and motels serve as touchstones to bygone eras, while venerable hotels are being refurbished.

For an alternative to the bombastic style of the Strip and the revamped glamour of Downtown, the area in-between is filled with out-of-the-way businesses and other reminders of the city's roots. There are several wonderful museums that preserve the city's heritage. It seems that no matter how large and exciting Las Vegas becomes, it will always remember its fascinating past.

THE OLD LAS VEGAS MORMON FORT

In 1855, a group of Mormon settlers—following the edict of their faith's leader, Brigham Young—arrived in Las Vegas to set up a mission and immediately set to work on an adobe fort to house their settlement. By 1858, however, unable to grow sufficient food and plagued by internal discord, they abandoned the outpost. It was sold and converted into a ranch but gradually fell into disarray, passing through the hands of various owners, including the U.S. Bureau of Reclamation (which built the Hoover Dam) and the local Elks Lodge. The property was finally acquired in 1991 by the Nevada State Parks Department, which preserves and protects the historic site for future generations.

THE DONALD W. REYNOLDS PRINT SHOP

Built on the grounds of the Clark County Museum, the Donald W. Reynolds Print Shop is an imagined historic structure, donated by the prominent Donald W. Reynolds Foundation.

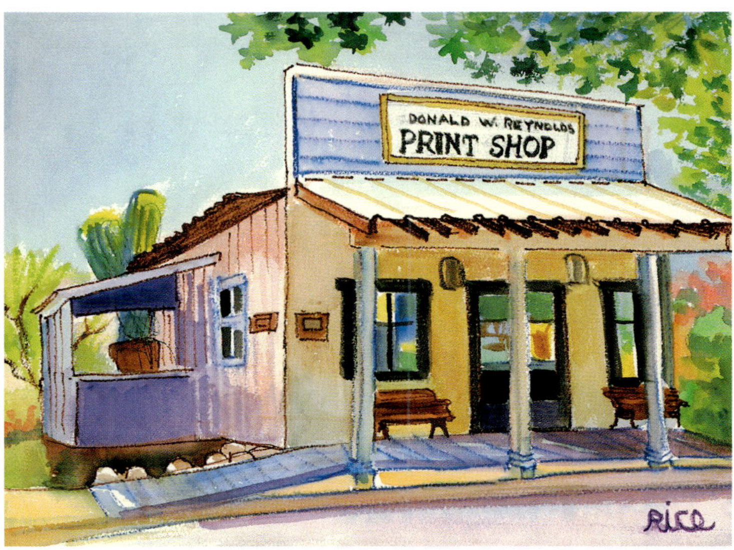

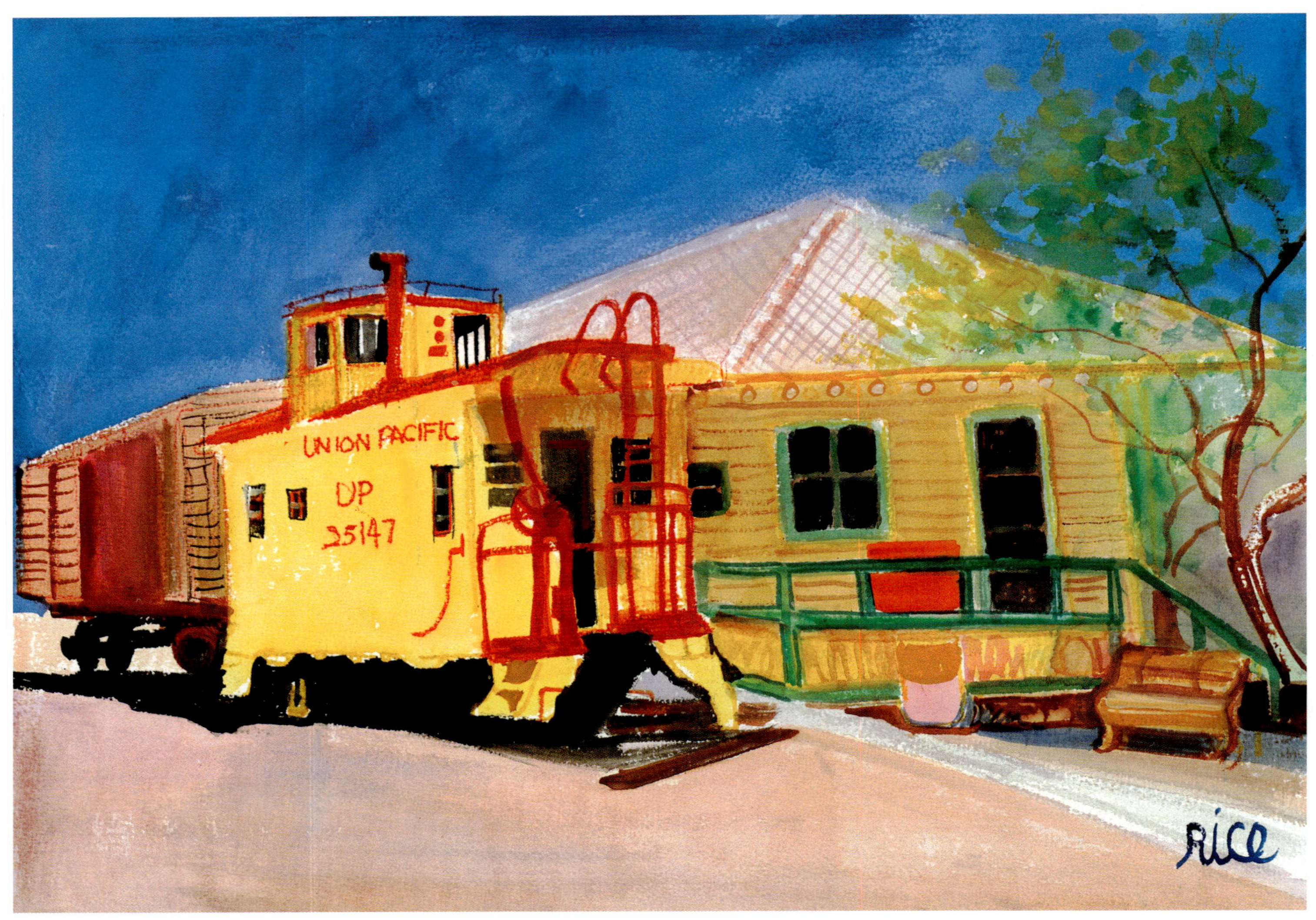

THE UNION PACIFIC CABOOSE

Without the railroads there would never have been a Las Vegas, so the Clark County Museum has preserved this original car from the Union Pacific line to remember the importance of trains to the region.

DONN BLAKE AT THE CLARK COUNTY MUSEUM >

When I met Donn Blake in front of the old railroad at the Clark County Museum in Henderson, it struck me that he looked so authentically "Western" he could have stepped out of the pages of a Louis L'Amour cowboy novel. Donn came to Las Vegas in 1955 from San Francisco and spent several years in the mining industry. Now retired and an avid Nevada historian, Donn served as chairman of the Las Vegas region's Bicentennial Committee and the city's Diamond Jubilee Committee, and he loves collecting antique maps, books and postcards about Nevada. At the Clark County Museum, much has been done to preserve the area's heritage, including relocating, restoring or replicating several significant buildings to create the effect of a Western town right out of the history books.

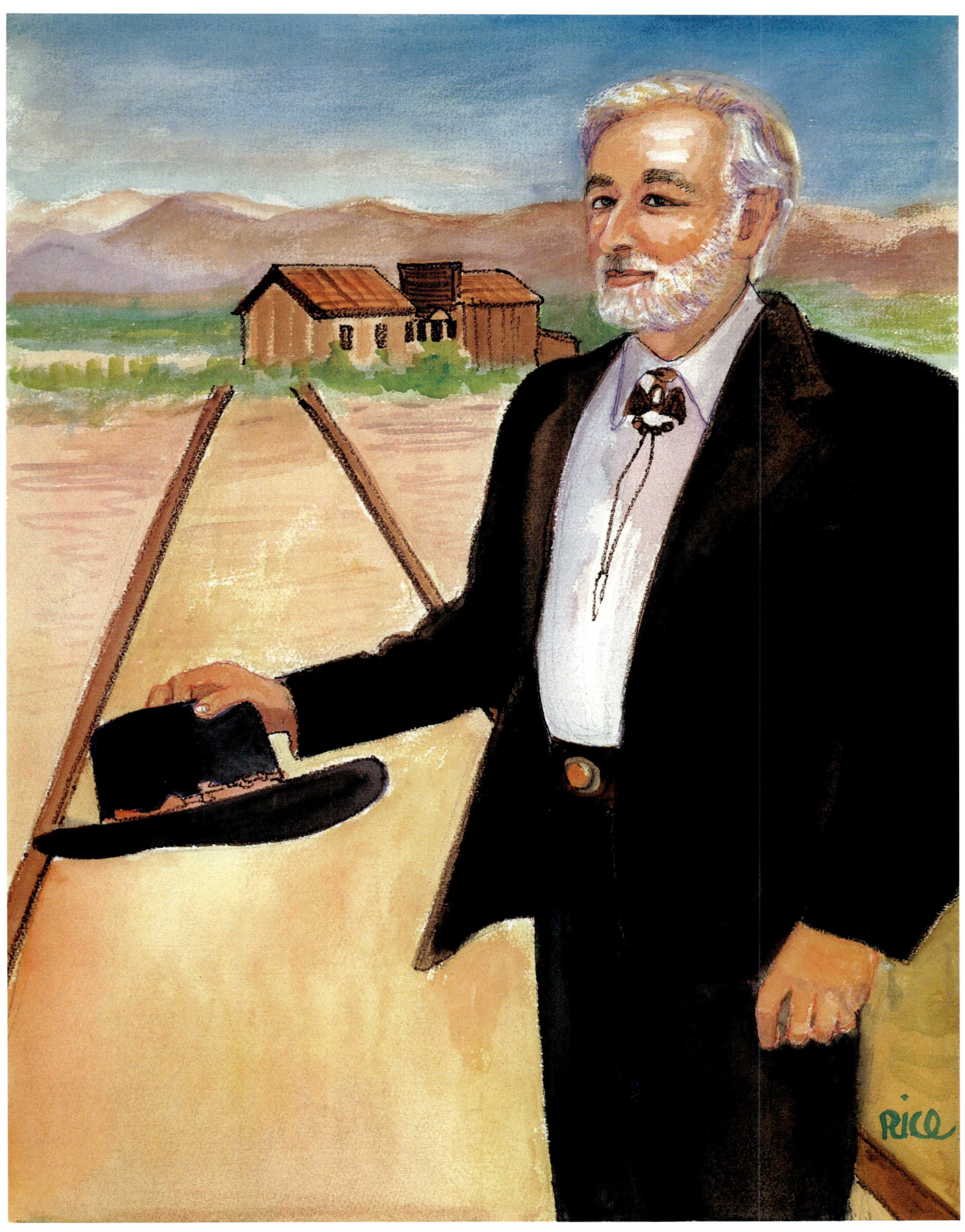
Rice

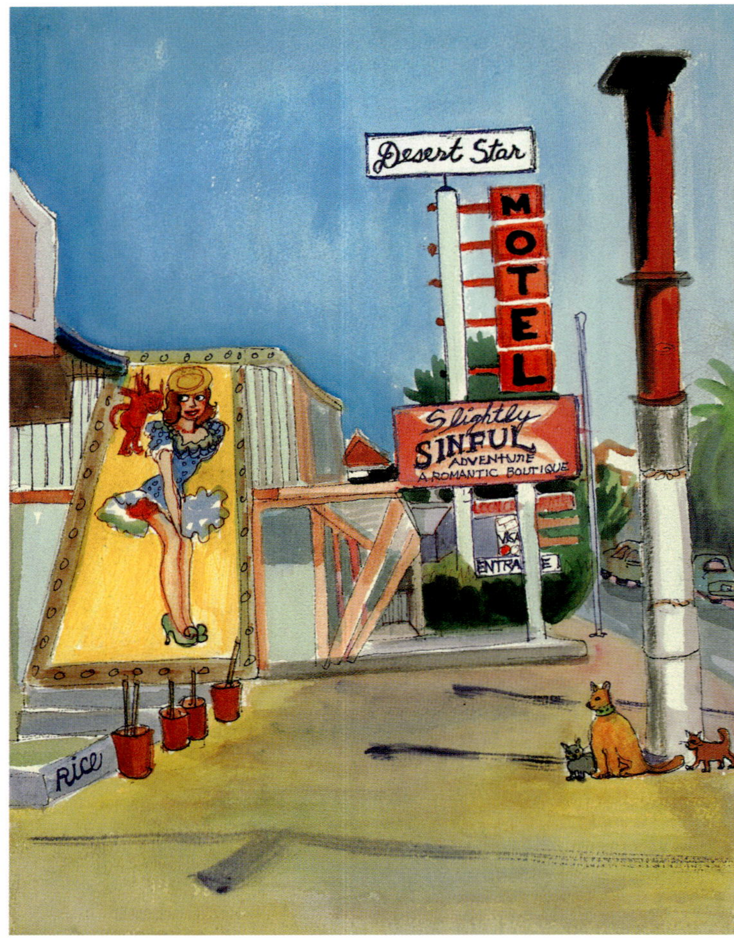

THE SLIGHTLY SINFUL MOTEL

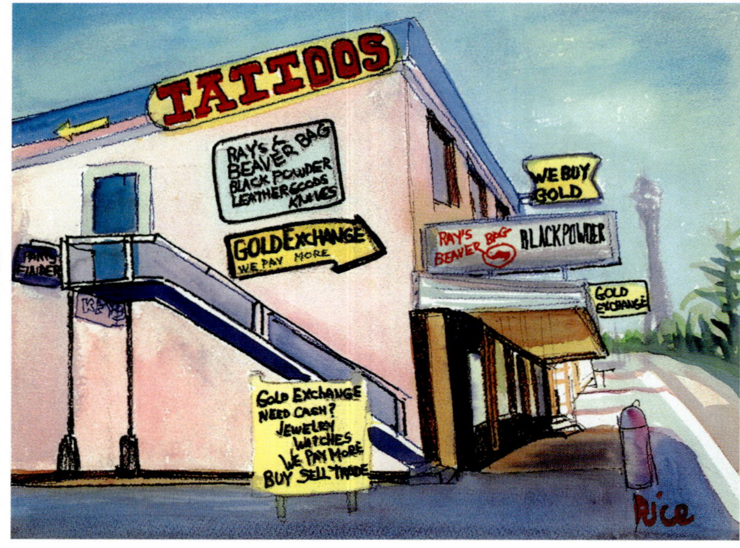

THE TATTOO PARLOUR

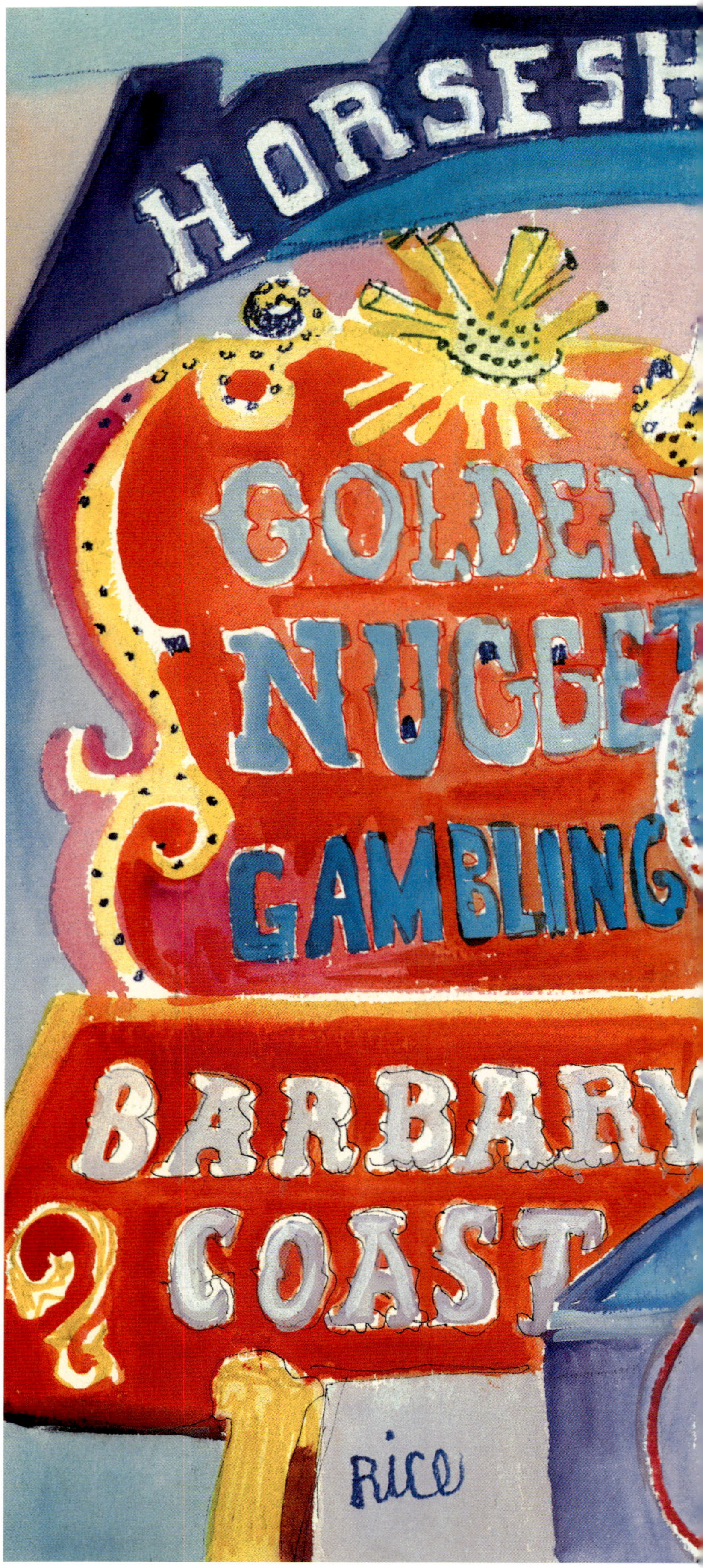

A HISTORY LESSON IN LIGHTS

I visited the YESCO sign yard where the early generations of the town's most famous neon signs have been retired. Although the yard is not open to the public, these brilliant relics will one day be on display Downtown at a planned museum called the Neonopolis.

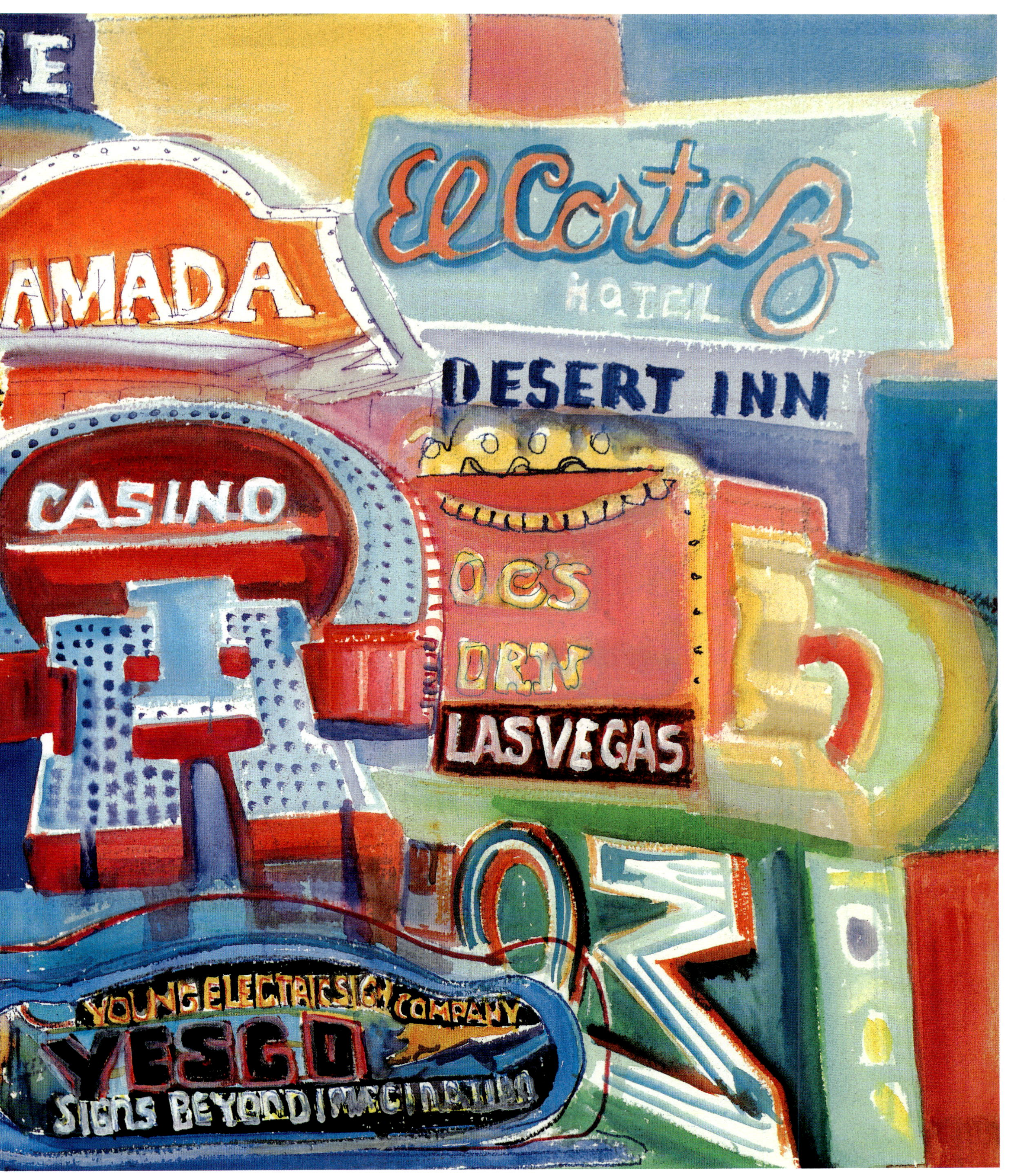
AMADA
El Cortez
HOTEL
DESERT INN
CASINO
LAS VEGAS
YOUNG ELECTRIC SIGN COMPANY
YESCO
SIGNS BEYOND

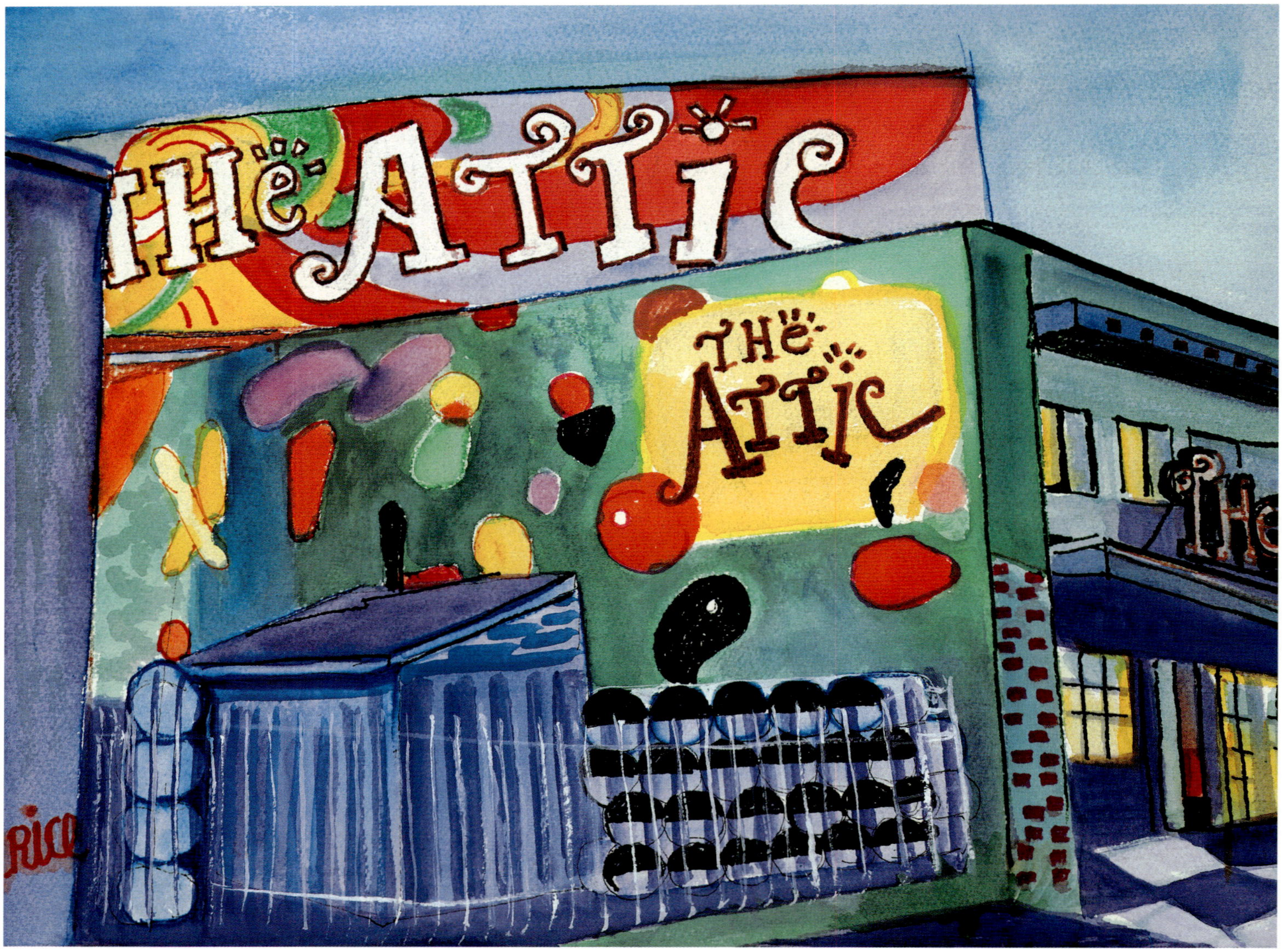

THE ATTIC

The Attic is a hip, funky second-hand shop that stands in the eclectic "limbo" between the Strip and Downtown. You may have seen it on TV when it was featured in a long-running American Express credit card commercial.

THE PAIUTE TRIBAL SMOKE SHOP >

The landmark Smoke Shop, which is packed to the rafters with all sorts of pipes, cigars, cigarettes and tobaccos, is owned and operated by the Southern Paiute Tribe, which inhabited the Las Vegas Valley long before whites set foot there. The Paiutes were a resourceful people who resisted the occupation of their land by explorers and settlers, leading to a long, hard struggle to preserve their traditional way of life. Today, the Paiutes live on a ten-acre plot of land that was once part of the historic Las Vegas Ranch, where the tribe operates the Smoke Shop. Fifteen miles north of Downtown, they operate a golf course in a developing master-planned community called Snow Mountain, which will include residential units, schools, parks, a tribal museum, ceremonial grounds, a factory outlet mall and a hotel-casino.

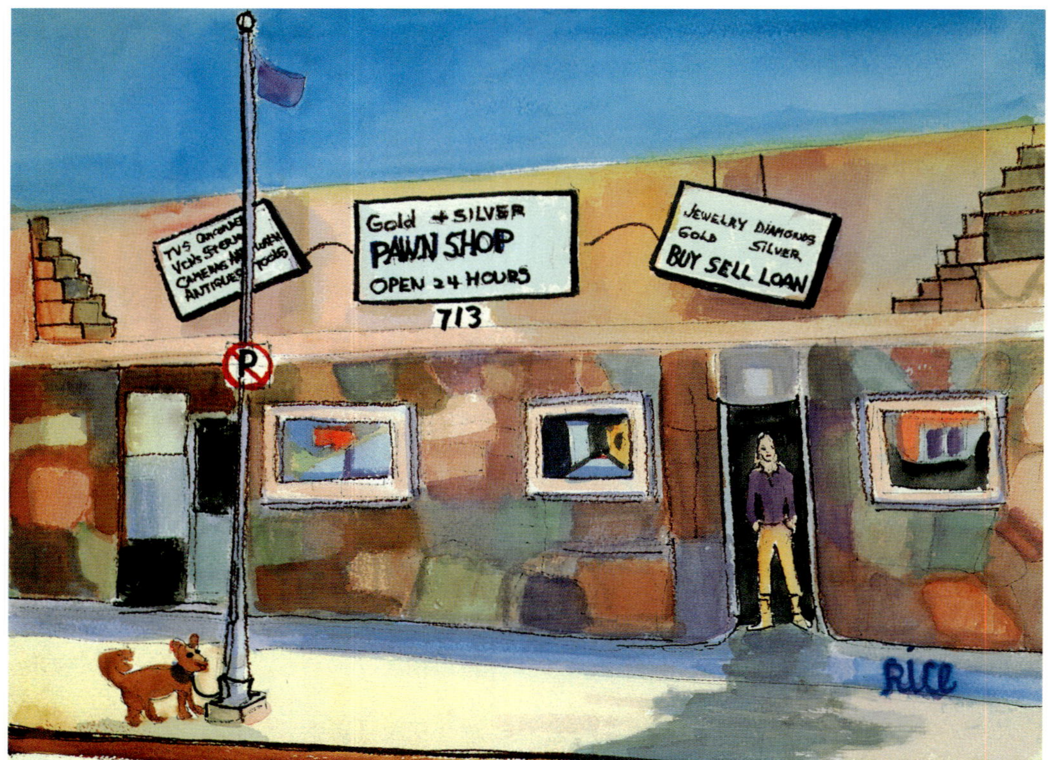

THE PAWN SHOP

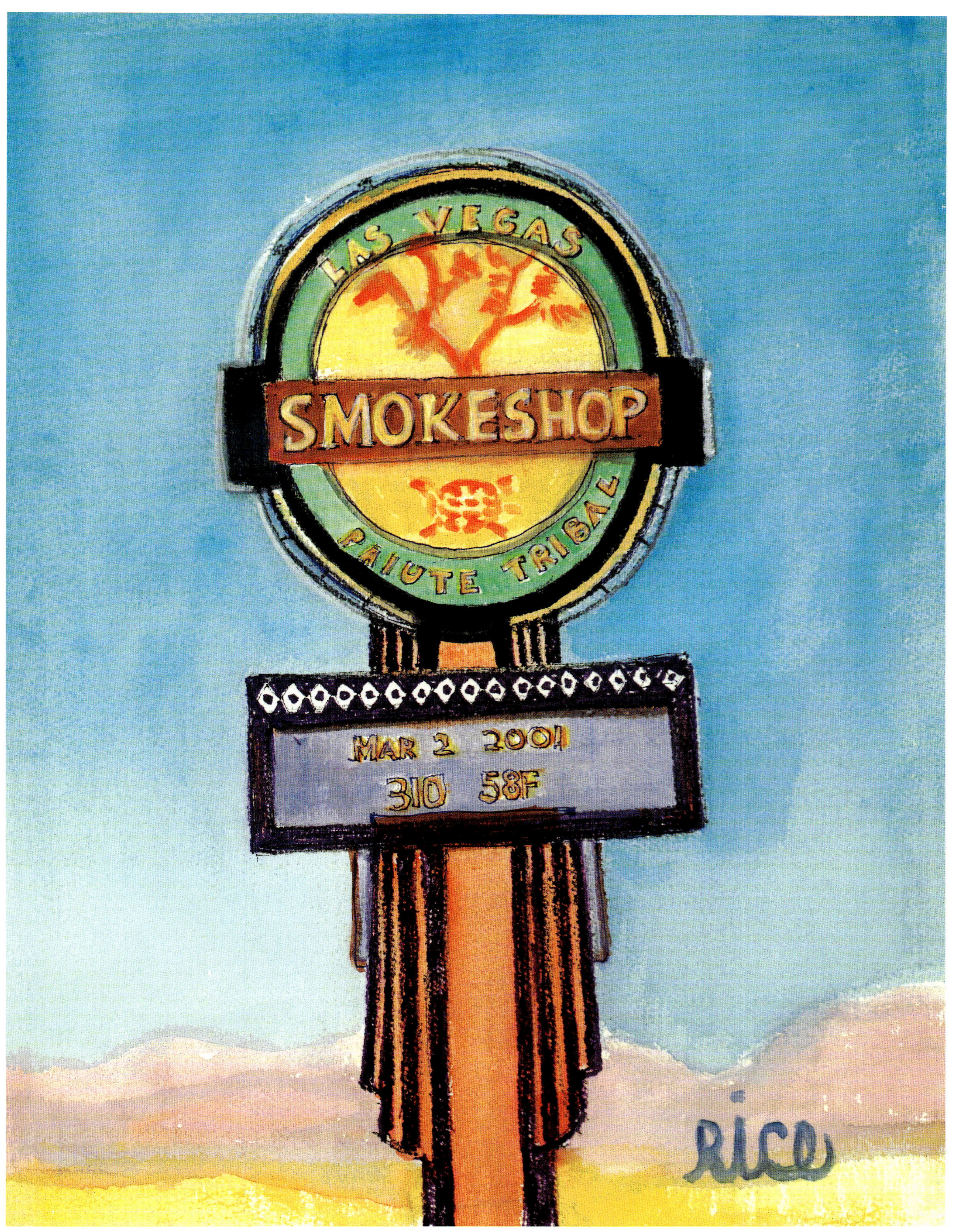
LAS VEGAS
SMOKESHOP
PAIUTE TRIBAL
MAR 2 2001
310 58F
Rice

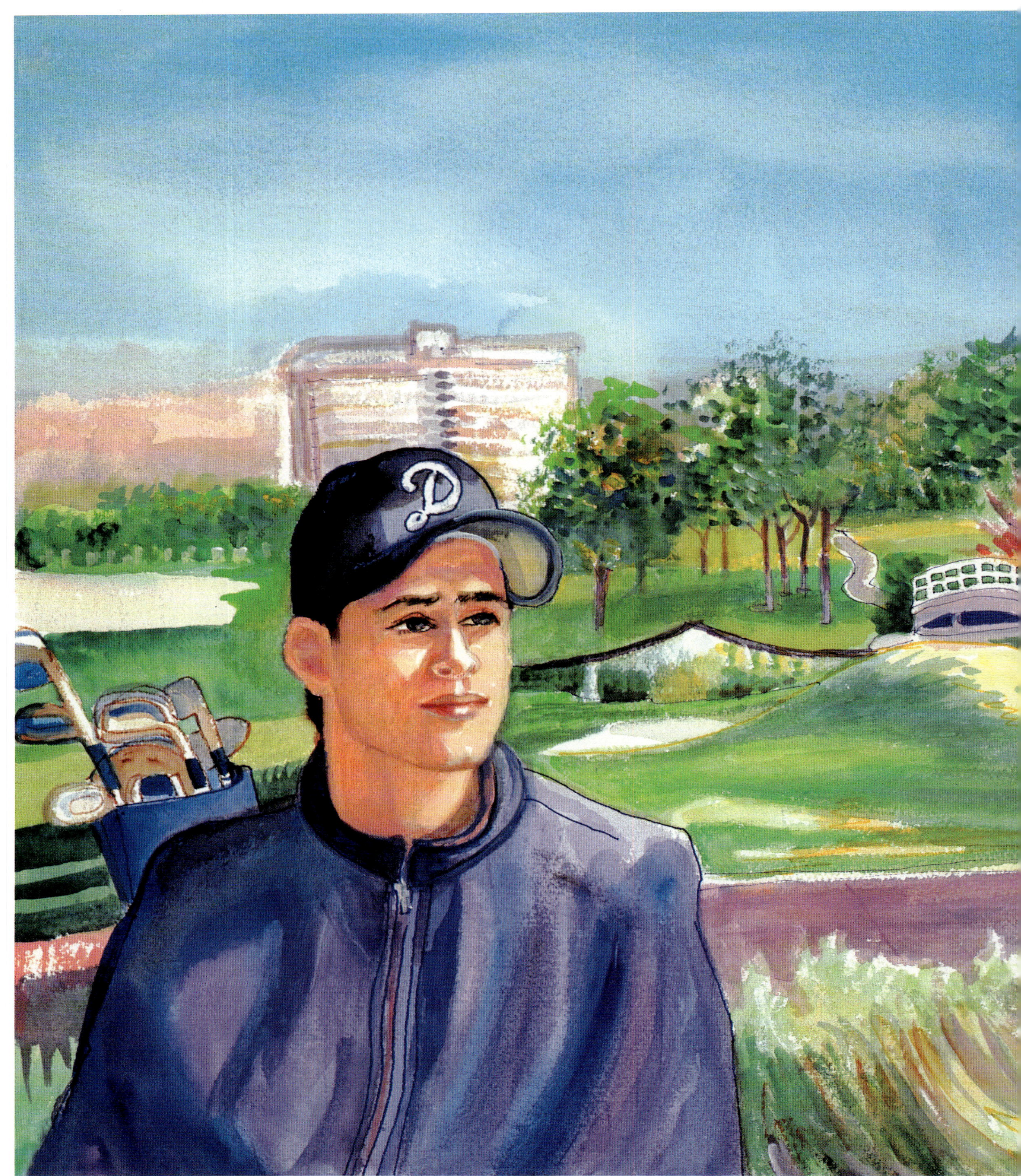

FORE!
Benjie Jack Sidney perfects his golf game on the magnificently maintained 18-hole greens of the Las Vegas Country Club. Determined to be the next Tiger Woods, Benjie counts the science of golf (the top recreational draw in town) as one of his primary fields of study at UNLV.

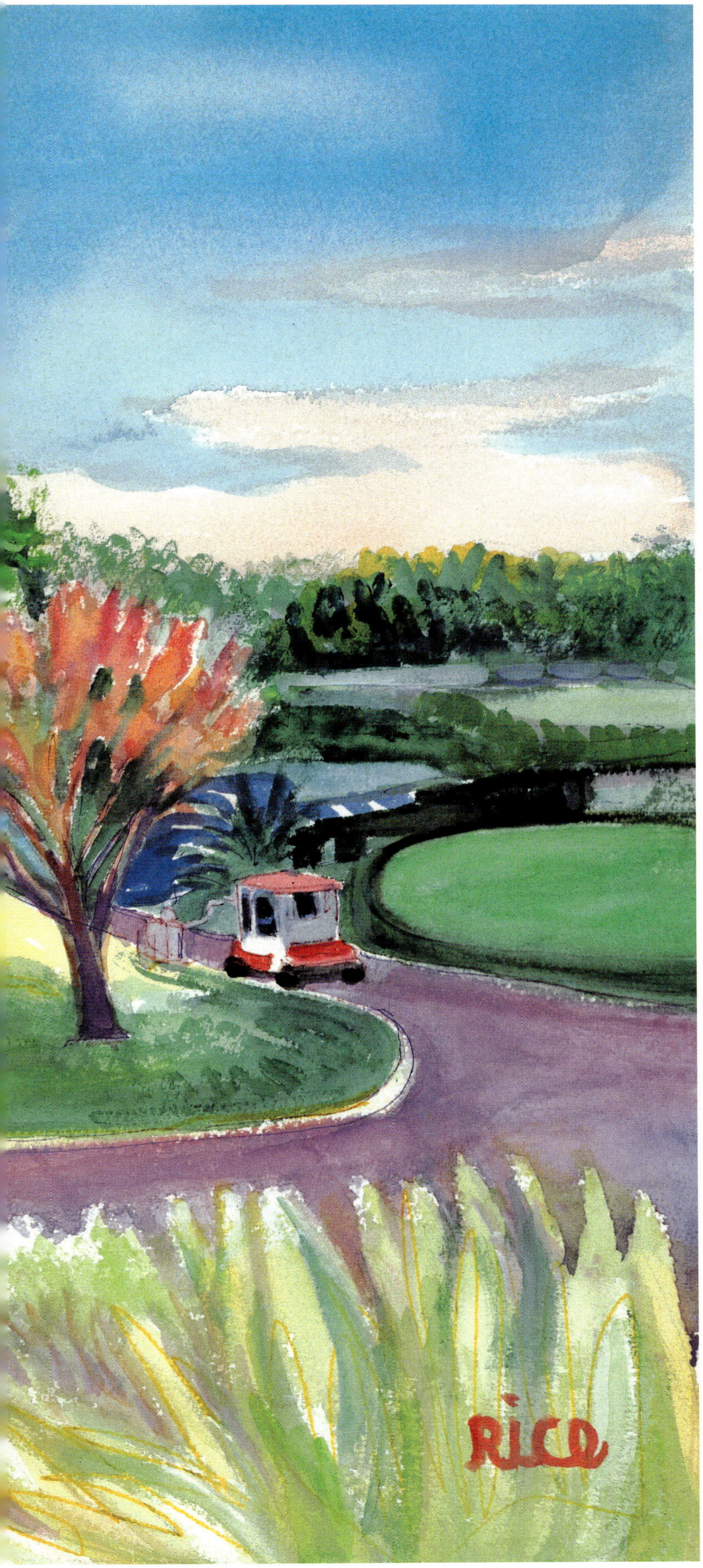

LAS VEGAS LIFESTYLES

LAS VEGAS ONLY SEEMS LIKE A CITY of tourists—1.4 million people call the region home. A steady tide of new residents puts down roots each year, making it the fastest-growing city in America. To my delight, I discovered an increasing number of fantastic residential communities throughout Las Vegas, each with its own individual flavor and character. Not only do people really live in Las Vegas, many of them live very, very well.

THE CLUBHOUSE AT THE LAS VEGAS COUNTRY CLUB
The gated Country Club is one of the poshest and most exclusive residential areas around—the "Beverly Hills" of Las Vegas. In the 1950s, the Country Club grounds were part of the Las Vegas Downs, a thoroughbred racetrack. The golf course was installed in 1967 and a year later, architect Julian Gabrielle designed the circular Clubhouse, where many upscale weddings and special events are held. The Country Club became private in 1971 and has more than 700 members, with tennis courts (including the only indoor facility in the state) and a fitness center in addition to golf. Many magnificent residences have emerged within the gated Country Club, par for the course as it is one of the most luxurious and leisurely areas in Las Vegas.

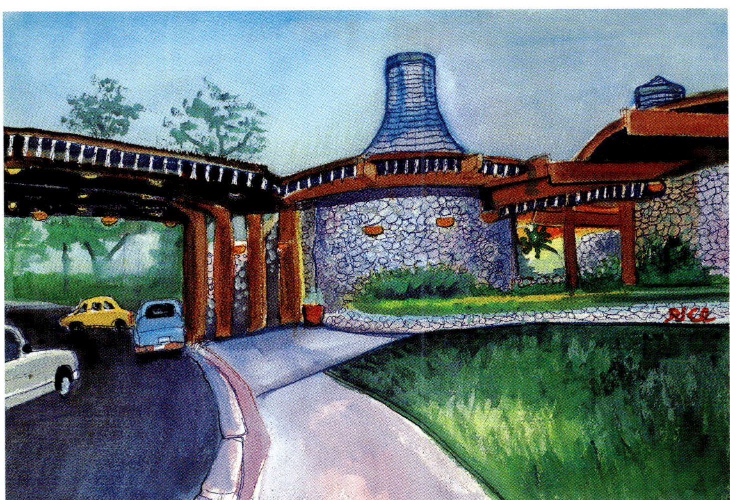

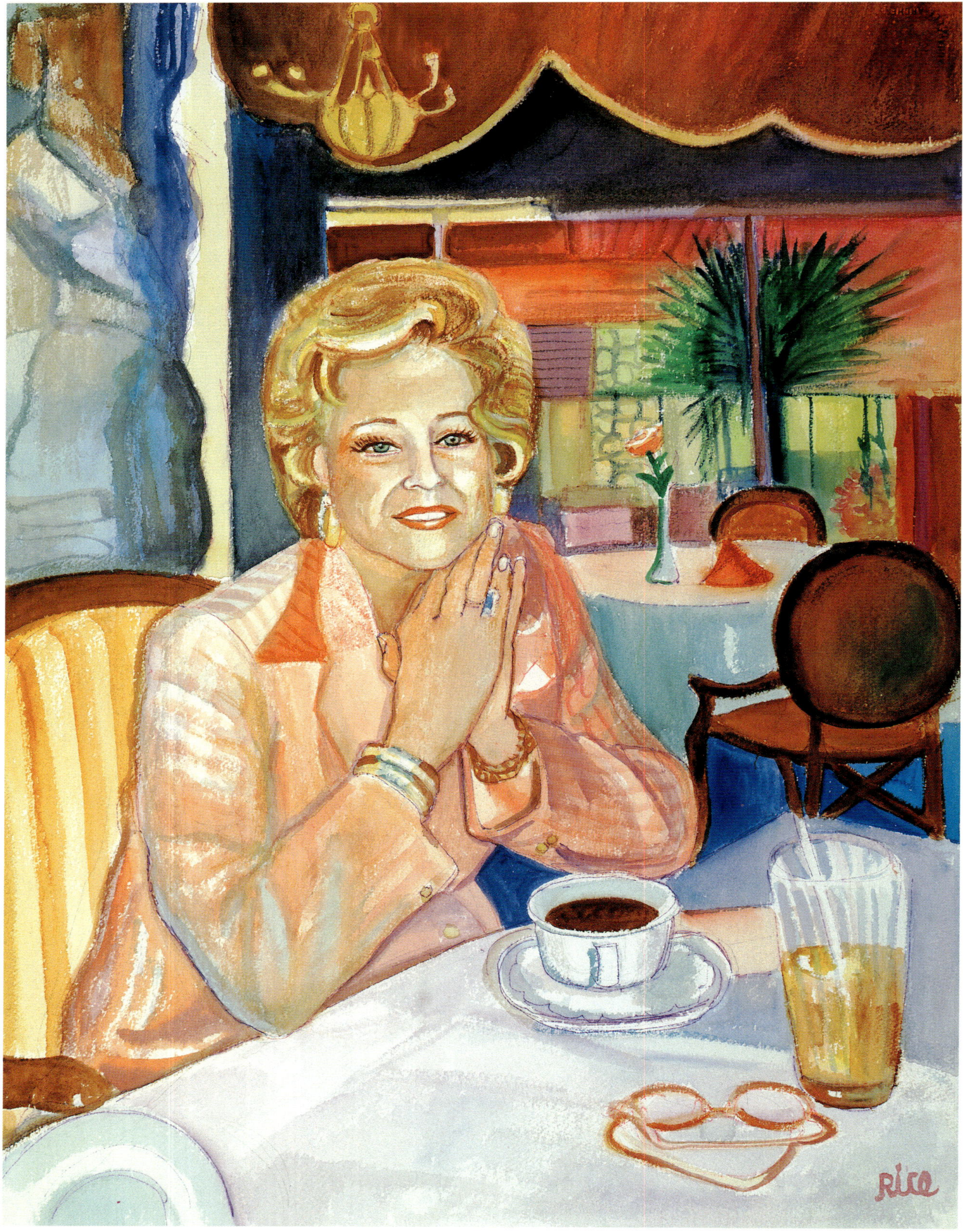

LUNCHING WITH CLAUDINE WILLIAMS

Taking a respite from her duties as Chairman of the Board of Harrah's Las Vegas, Claudine Williams met me for lunch at the Las Vegas Country Club. One of the most respected and honored women in Nevada's business community, the elegant and beautifully outfitted Claudine was one of the first females to achieve an executive position in the gaming industry, becoming a majority shareholder (along with her late husband Shelby) in the Silver Slipper from 1965 to 1969.

Claudine first became involved with Harrah's in 1972 when the property—then known as the Holiday Casino—was first built: she was the president, general manager and a major shareholder. When Harrah's bought the Holiday in 1983, Claudine became the chairman of the board, a post she's held ever since. She's also chariman of the board of the Nevada Commerce Bank, a founding member of St. Jude's Ranch for Children and a generous supporter of UNLV. Meeting her, I was struck—but not surprised, given her reputation and accomplishments—by her poise and charm.

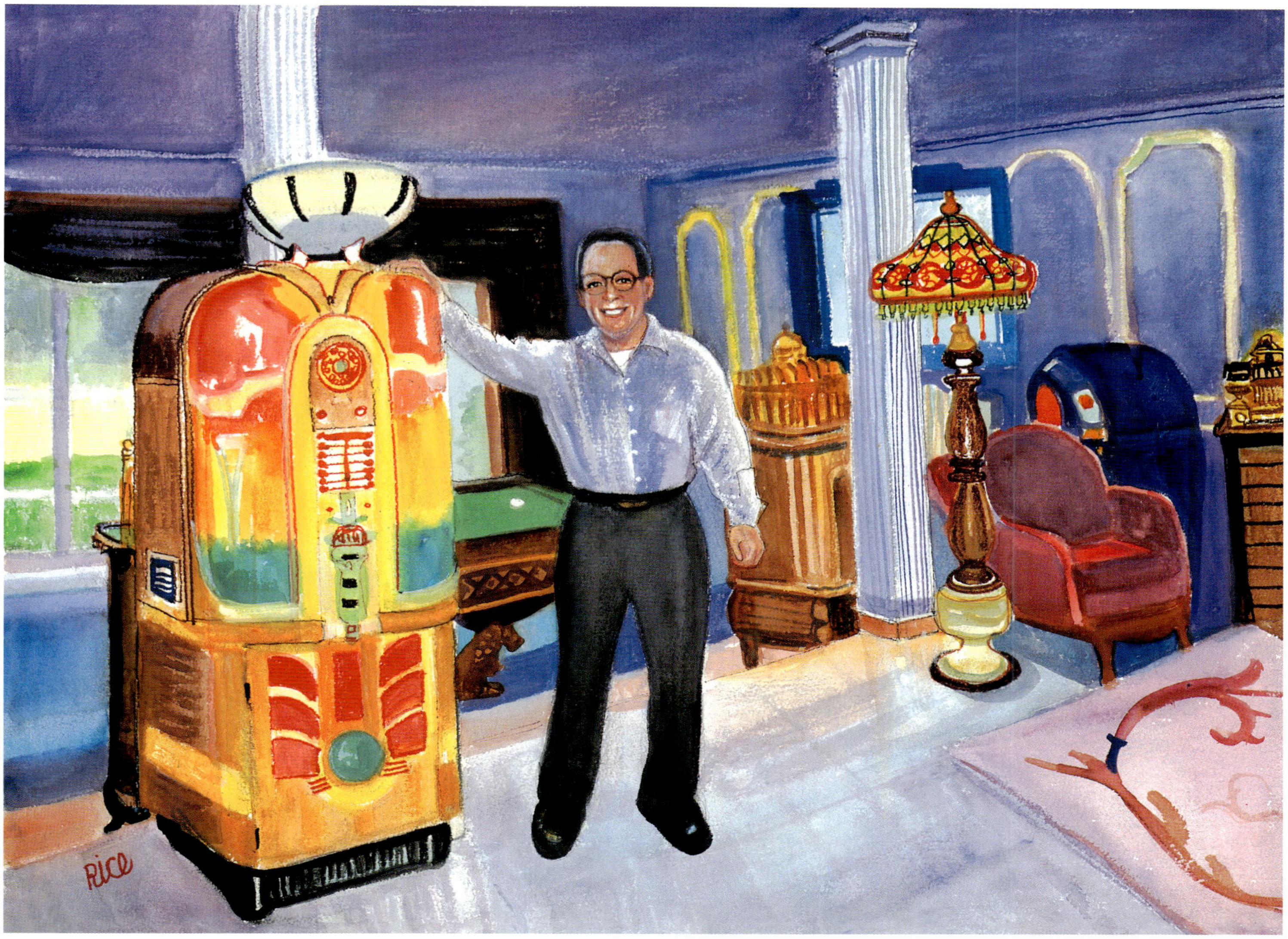

ARTEMUS W. HAM III

Artemus W. Ham III, a successful Las Vegas commercial real estate broker who once owned and operated the Friendly Club Casino before selling the property to the Golden Nugget in 1983, showed me his vintage Rockola Premier jukebox—one of the many beautifully-crafted items in his extensive antique collection, which also includes cash registers (like the 1880s model in the background, decorated with a nude lady), lamps (a Bigelow & Kennard seen here) and pool tables (that's an 1880s Brunswick behind him).

Art designed his home to showcase his fabulous collection, and I discovered that every room is put together with thought, care and creativity. As successful as he is today, he clearly has a great fondness for the past: he told me that in the early 1900s, his grandparents Artemus Sr. and Alta eloped and left Los Angeles to see the World's Fair in San Francisco. Eventually settling in Las Vegas, Artemus Sr. made his fortune as the only lawyer in town with a genuine legal education. Alta and he are remembered with buildings named in their honor at UNLV.

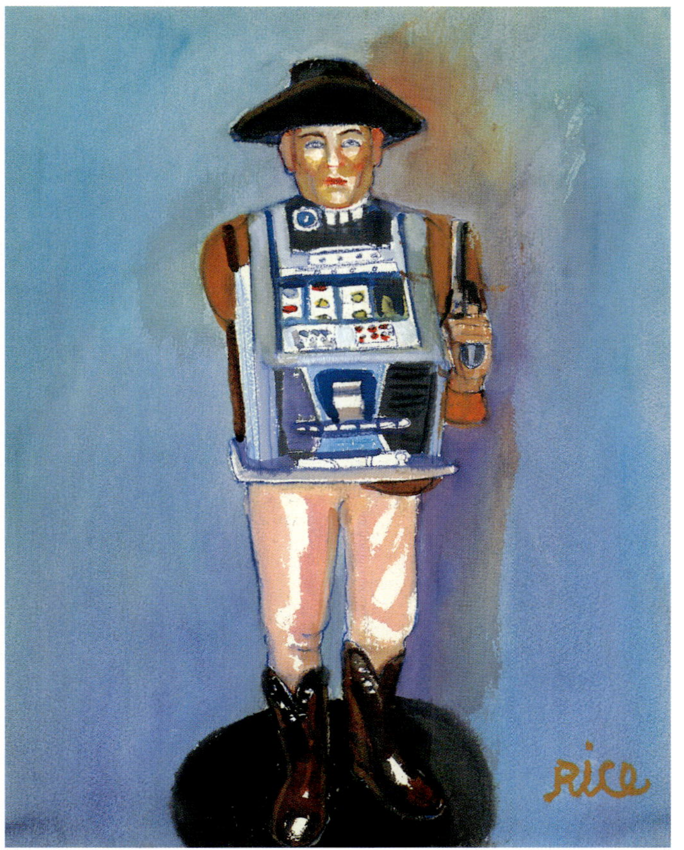

THE ORIGINAL ONE-ARMED BANDIT

I found this novel slot machine—a genuine one-armed bandit—in the collection of Artemus Ham.

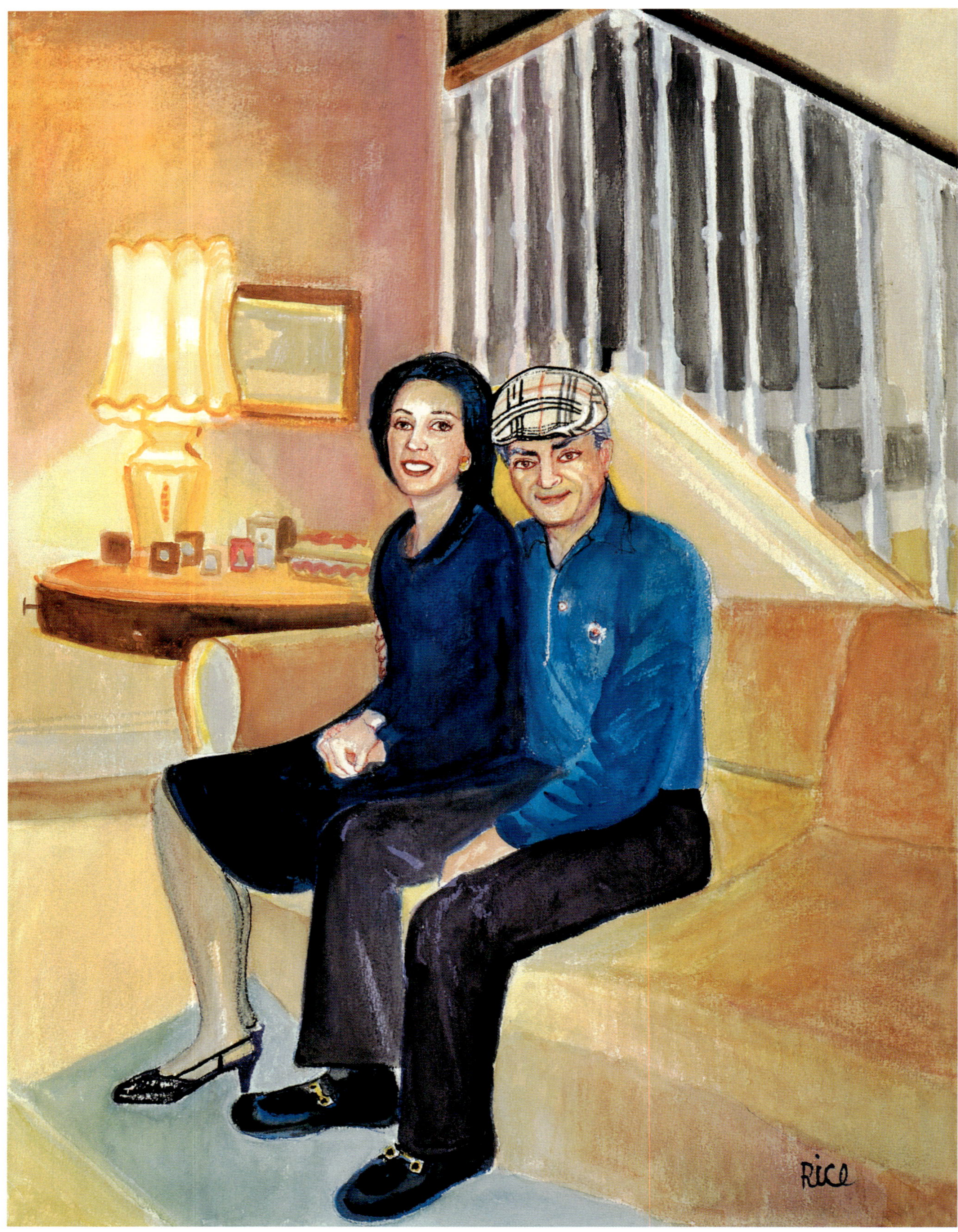

THE MALLINS

Avid golfers Stanley and Sandy Mallin told me that they first met at the Las Vegas Country Club, where Cupid quickly scored a hole in one. Stanley helped usher in the era of the Las Vegas theme hotel as one of the principal developers behind Caesars Palace and Circus Circus. Sandy spends most of her time fundraising and volunteering. In addition to serving on the board of Nevada First Bank, she is president of Temple Beth Sholom. Together they founded the Temple's highly-regarded Sandra and Stanley Mallin Early Childhood Center, where pre-school children are exposed to activities, the arts and Jewish tradition and values.

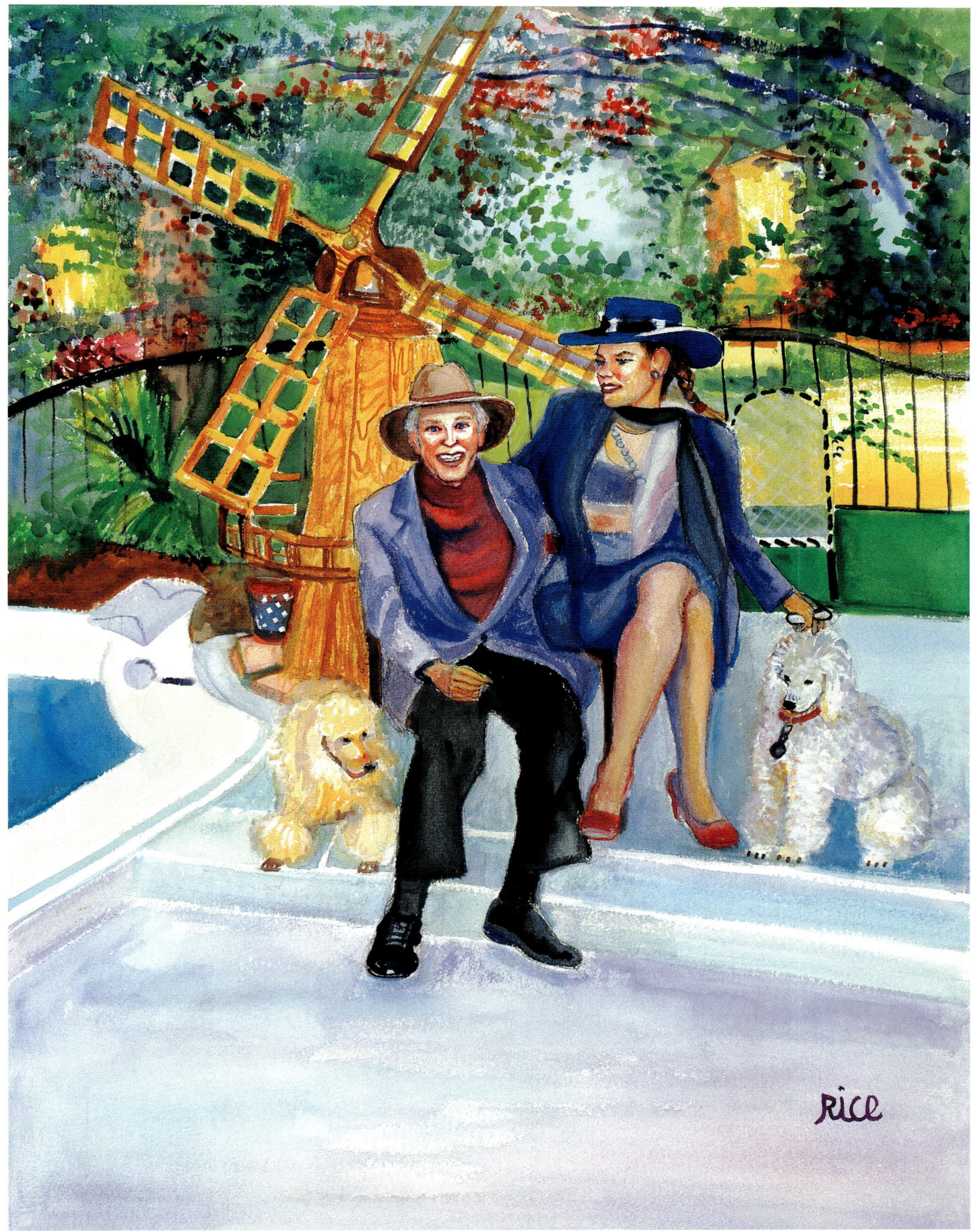

CORINNE AND GEORGE SIDNEY

Meet a couple with an infectious zest for life and enviable Las Vegas legacies. George Sidney was born into a showbiz family and starred in Hollywood films as a child with the likes of Tom Mix. Behind the camera, he became a top director-producer, beginning with the "Our Gang" comedies and moving on to dozens of splashy MGM musicals and period adventures. He redefined Vegas cool for the post-Rat Pack generation with 1964's "Viva Las Vegas" starring Elvis Presley and Ann-Margret. Corinne Sidney, a former showgirl, actress, Hollywood society columnist and Beverly Hills political candidate was also the wife (twice!) of Jack Entratter, the famed head of the Sands in Vegas' first heyday. George and Corinne met and married in Hollywood but recently moved to town and live on the grounds of the Las Vegas Country Club with their two poodles, Snob and Sir Henry Higgins, who have their own room. The devotion they share is admirable. George and Corinne are two people with so many laurels to rest on, yet who continue to dive headfirst into life.

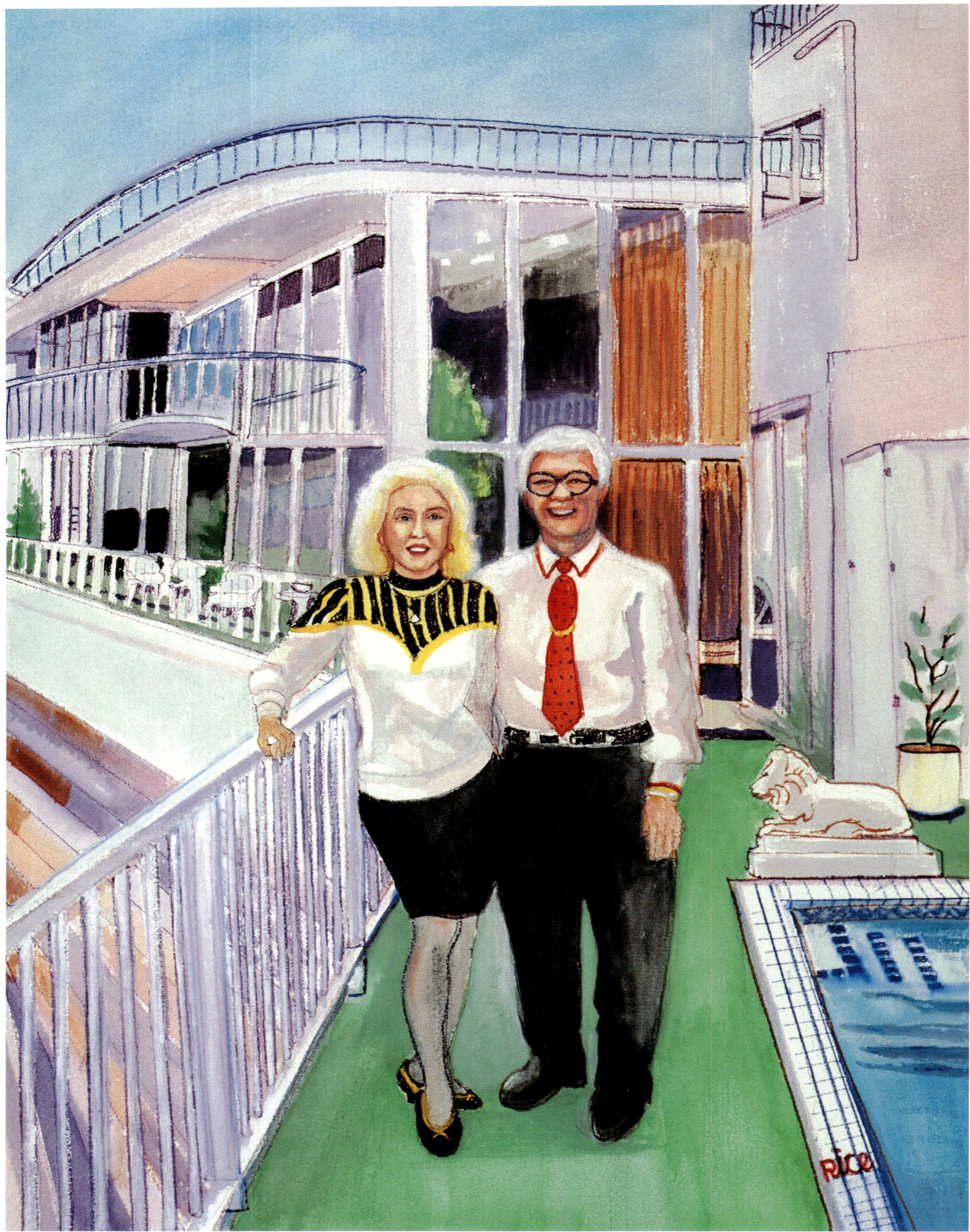

THE MACDONALDS AT HOME

I got to know Richard and Frances MacDonald, a couple at the top of the Las Vegas social scene. Originally from Philadelphia, their family arrived in town in 1959. They stayed for five years, with Richard working in real estate and Frances heading the dining room at the Sahara. After a lengthy sojourn in Hawaii, where Richard's realty business, MacDonald & Associates, boomed, the couple returned full-time in 1983 to tend to their Las Vegas properties in what is now called MacDonald Ranch. Sunset Ridge Professional Plaza, the MacDonald Ranch Country Club, Sunridge and the Green Valley Parkway Center are just some of their latest developments. Meeting them on the balcony of their gorgeous Regency Towers residence—comprised of two connected penthouse suites—I found them to be charming and down-to-earth.

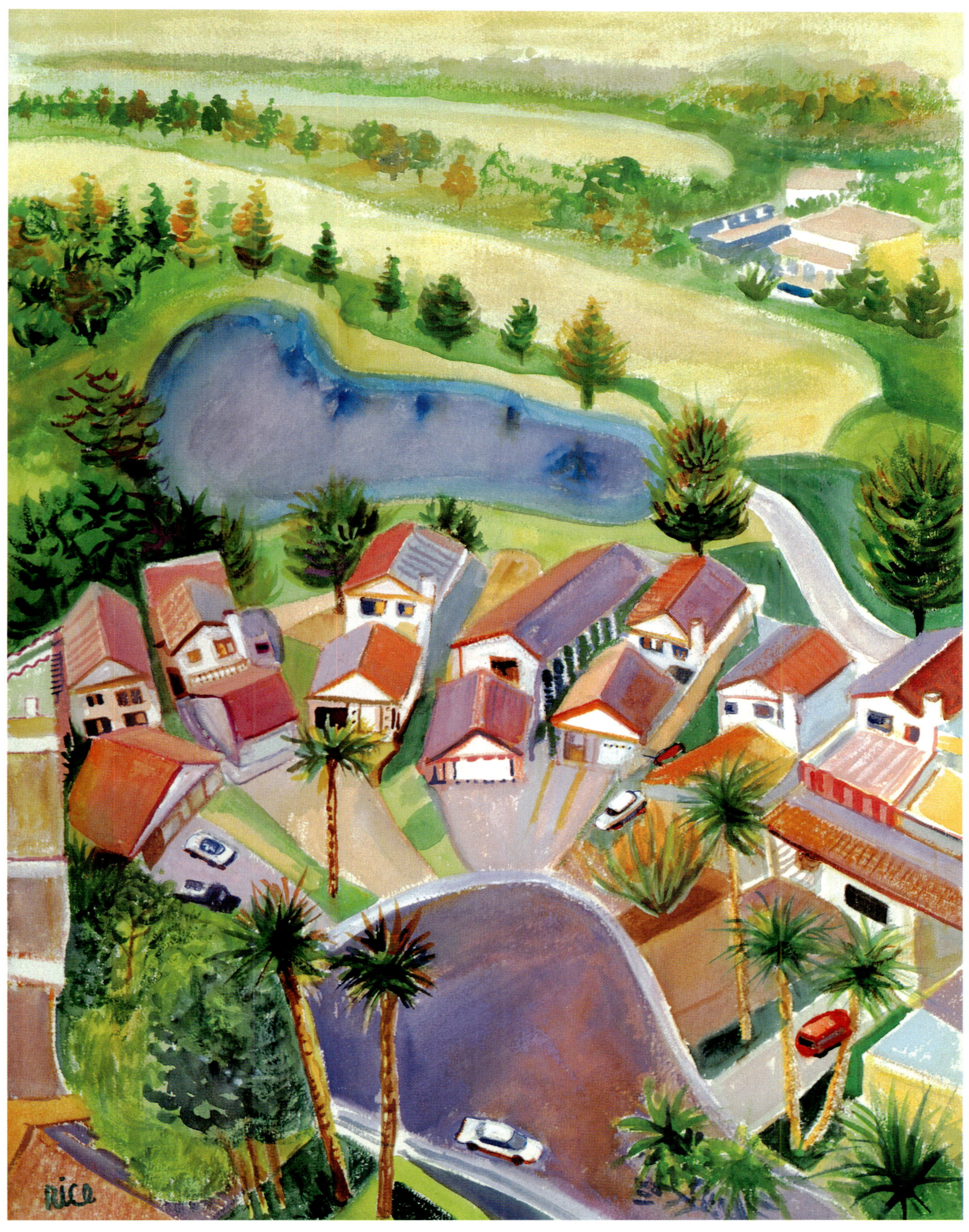

THE VIEW FROM THE REGENCY TOWERS PENTHOUSE

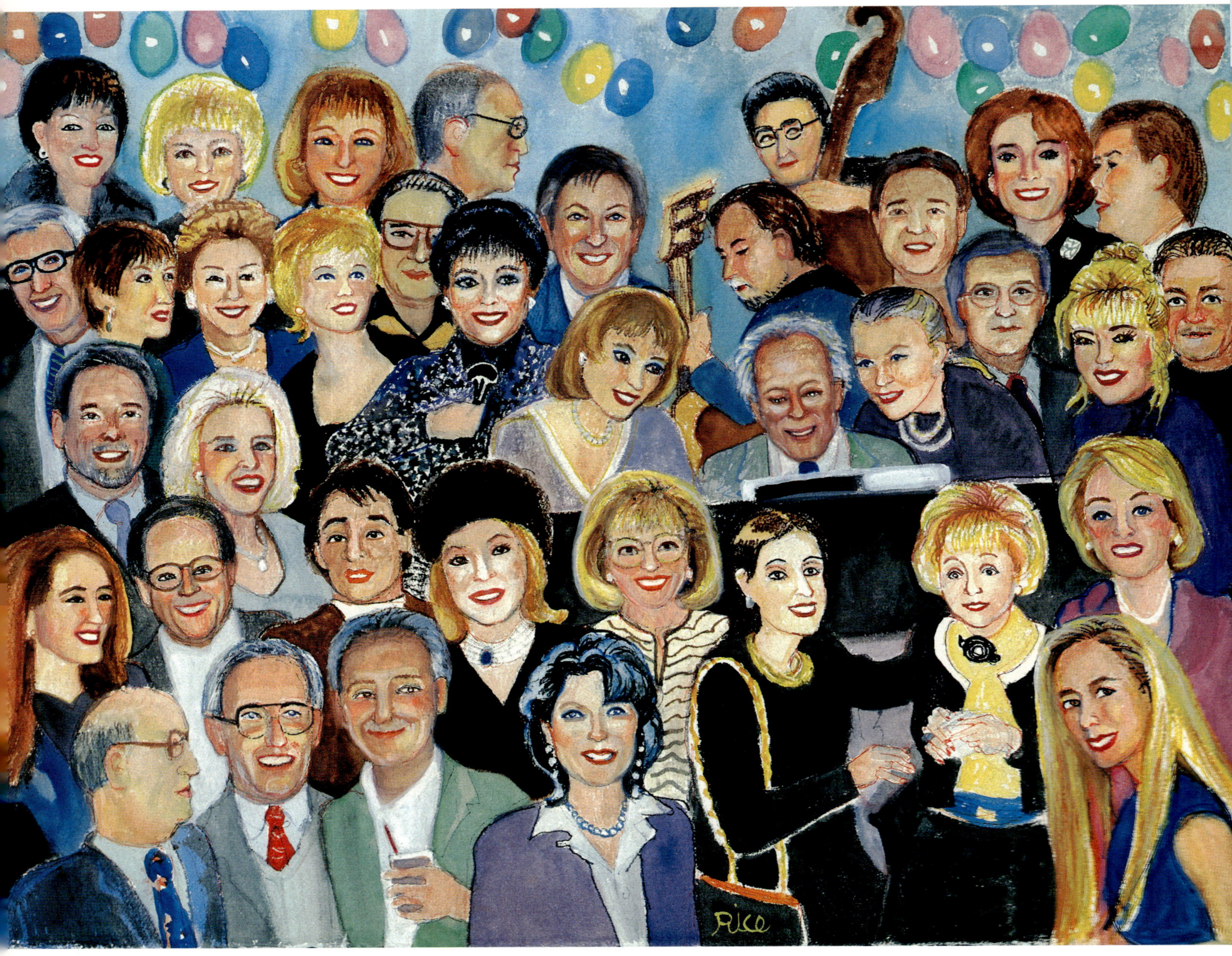

SEEN ON THE SCENE

I couldn't have asked for a better introduction to the creme of the local social whirl than the fantastic welcome party thrown in my honor by Corinne and George Sidney at their Las Vegas Country Club home. The reception included impromptu entertainment by three of the guests: songs from Phyllis McGuire (of the famed McGuire Sisters), Nevada Lt. Gov. Lorraine Hunt (a former professional singer) and the slightly notorious Gennifer Flowers (who sang "My Bill" and "The Lady Is a Tramp").

Among the other Las Vegans in attendance: Nancy and Kell Houssels, Carol Cling, David Atwell, Leslie and Roger Simon, Frances and Mac MacDonald, Bob Stupak, Joan and Gary Van, Loida Estrada, Renate Schiff, Gay and Don Sayre, Dr. Lisa Henderson, Michale Zane, Artemus Ham III, Heidi Hoffmann, Toni Clark, Larry Pinuf, Alan Miller, Peggy and Sonny King, Steve Crespi, Jackie Gaughan, Tony Gurvosky, Blackie Hunt, Gladys and Bill Freeman, Dr. George Semel, Steve Rossi, Finis S. Shelnutt, Jayne and Art Marshall, Claire and Michael Zito, Sandy and Stanley Mallin, Claire and Rich MacDonald, Maynard Sloate, Jan Gleiner, Arlene and Jerry Blut, Gail and Ed Miller, Candi Cazau, Seth Man, George Fumel, Omar Gutierrez, Benet Hudson, Tena Howser, Sandra and Dom Cambeiro, Carol and Phil Maloof, Duke Morgan, Don Suttle, Jan Glover, Arthur Man, Peggy Brown, Jorge Sucee, Jeff Anderson, Ruth Roy and the Doug MacDonald Trio. They all made me feel right at home!

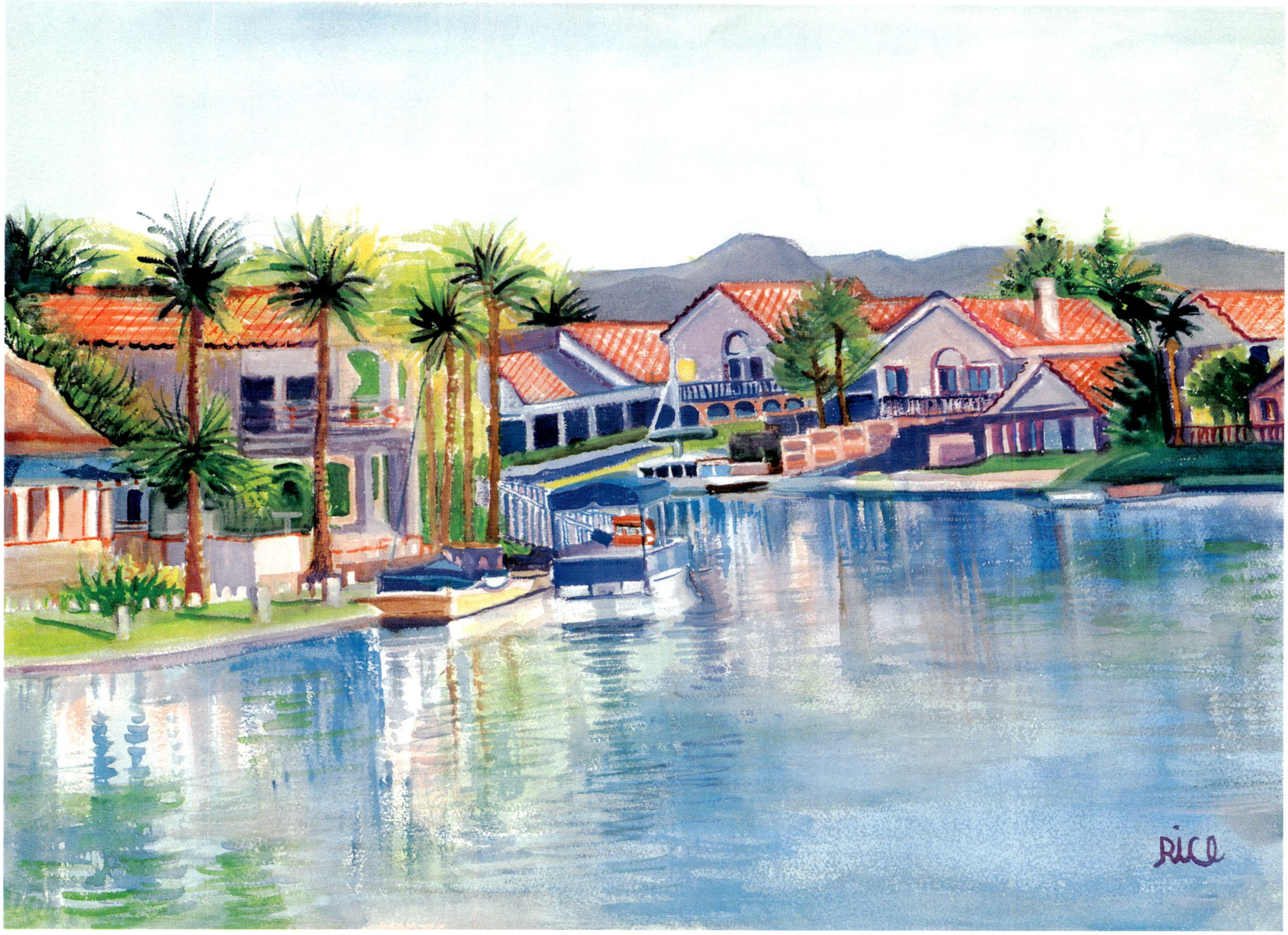

LIVING AT THE LAKES

The Lakes is a community that you might not expect to find in the Las Vegas desert. Thanks to modern technology, these dwellers can live on the shores of an artificial lake and enjoy the water throughout the year.

Hundreds of residences have sprouted up in the area called the Lakes since its establishment in the mid-1980s. A series of man-made lakes provide a picturesque setting for the homes, many of which are unified by a neutral tone, tile-and-stucco style, with boats docked alongside some residences.

PECCOLE CASTLE

Built for the Peccole children by their father and since sold, I was delighted to come across this "castle" beside a man-made lake, a real oasis in the desert.

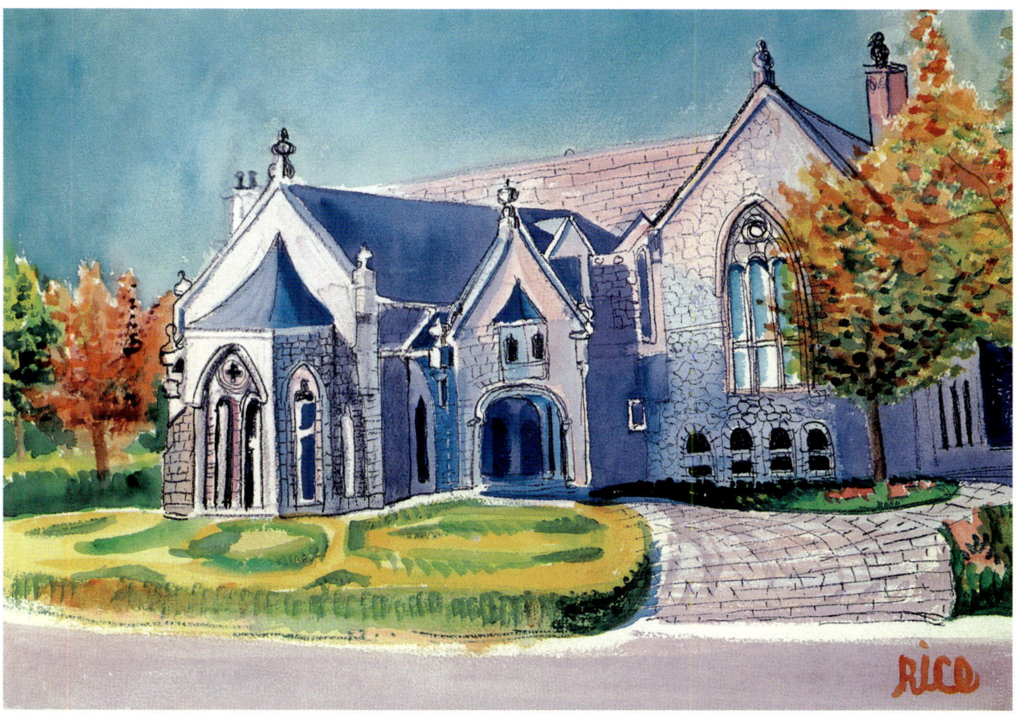

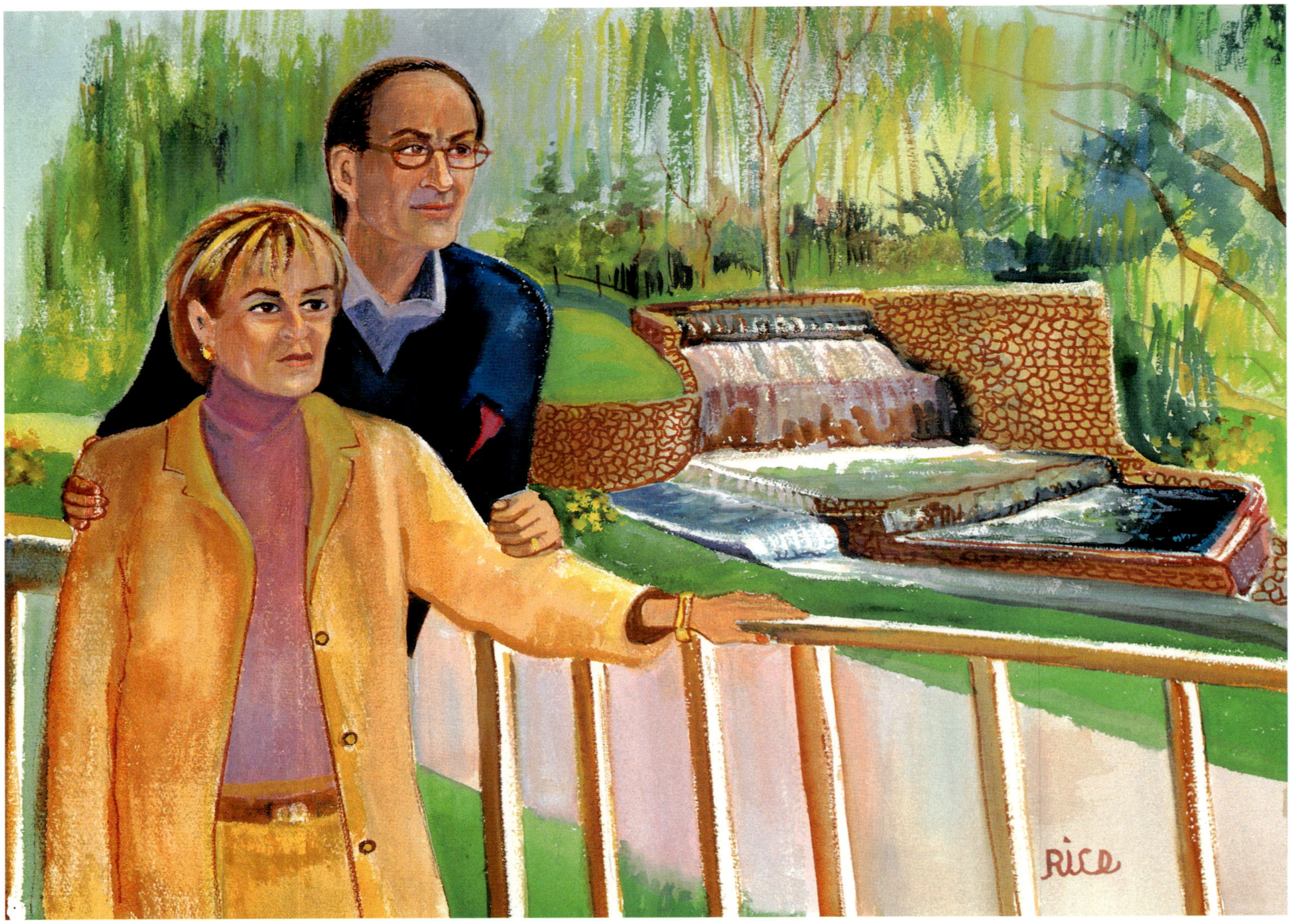

MONA AND CHARLES SILVERMAN

A vacation four decades ago led a former Chicago schoolteacher to Miami's Fountainebleu Hotel where she met a young man on a business trip. Mona and Charles Silverman subsequently married and eventually settled in yet another well-known city: Las Vegas. Charles is president of Yates-Silverman, Inc., a commercial interior design firm well-known for leading attractions like Paris Las Vegas, New York-New York, the Excalibur and the Luxor, as well as numerous other luxury theme projects across the country. Business has kept the Silvermans involved in Las Vegas for 30-plus years and they've recently settled in the Spanish Trail Country Club, an upscale West Valley development built around a golf course.

ENTERING TURNBERRY PLACE

The exotic-looking Turnberry Place is a new complex just off the Strip on Paradise Road. It features four 38-story luxury condominium towers centered around a 75,000-square-foot private club with fine and casual dining, card rooms and state-of-the-art spa and health club facilities. The ornate residential dwellings are loaded with deluxe amenities, including valet and concierge services.

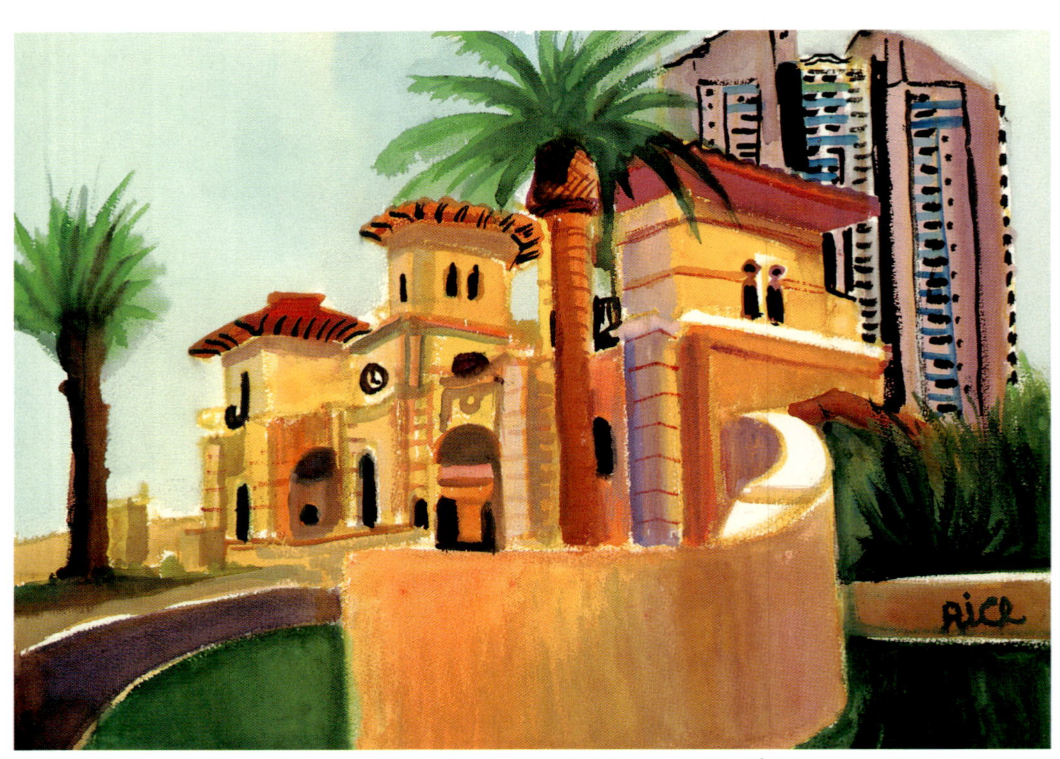

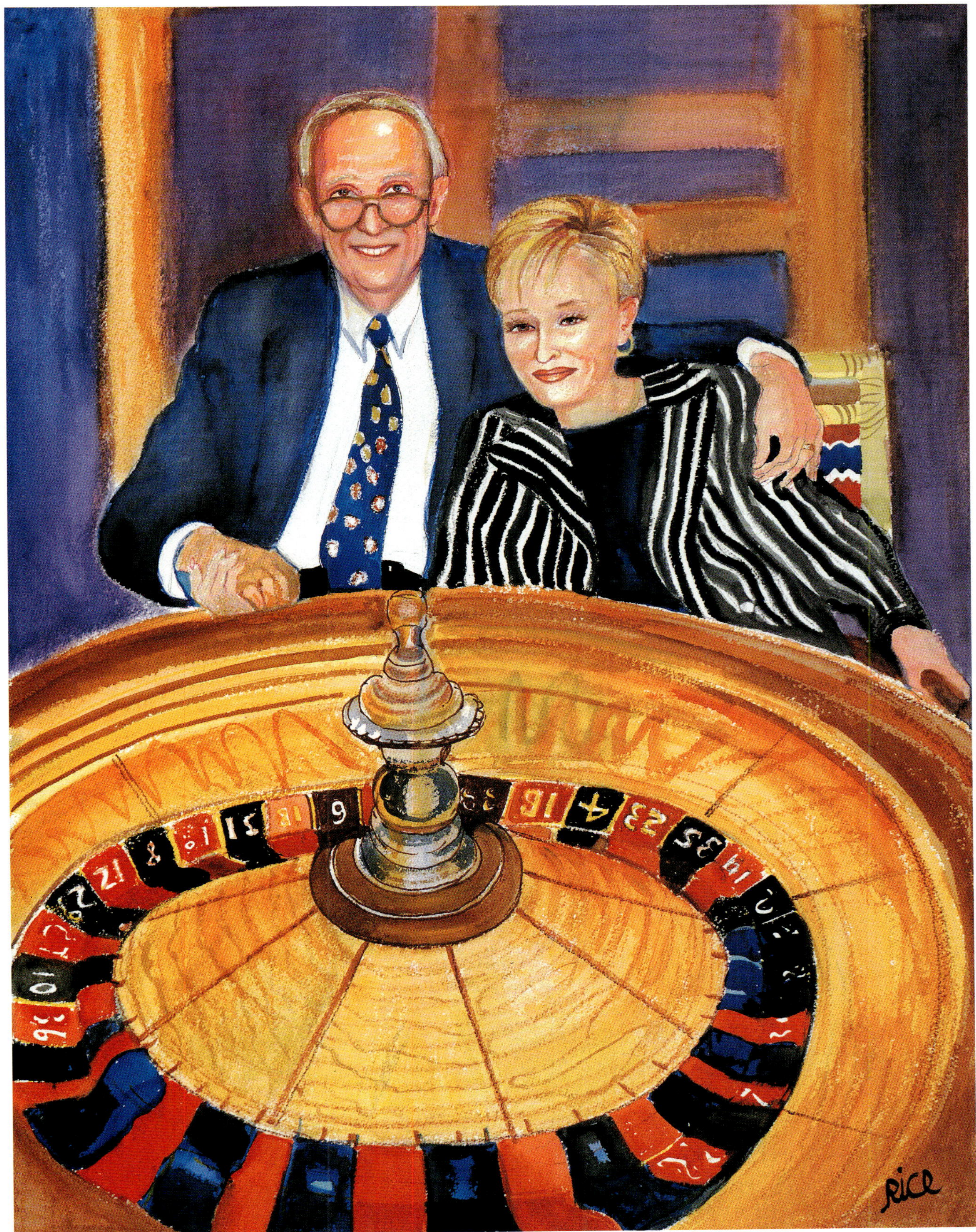

A SPIN WITH THE HOUSSELS

I went to a gorgeous 1964 home in Rancho Circle, one of the most prestigious addresses in the area, to meet J. Kell and Nancy Houssels, one of Las Vegas' most distinguished "power couples."

Kell has lived in Las Vegas since he was eight. His father founded the Las Vegas Club in 1931—that's the casino's roulette wheel the Houssels are proudly displaying! He worked in the gaming industry in top executive spots at the El Cortez, the Showboat and the Tropicana—where he closed the deal to bring in the Folies Bergère and helped elevate the hotel into the "Tiffany of the Strip." Today, Kell remains prominent in the community and active in gaming through breeding and racing of thoroughbred horses. The Houssels also raise Great Danes.

Nancy started dancing at age three and never stopped. She toured all over the world in the famous dance act Szony & Claire. She finally put down roots in Las Vegas as the closing feature act of the Folies Bergère. Retiring her dance shoes in 1969, Nancy married and started a family with Kell, turning her energies toward philanthropic efforts. This led to her involvement with the Nevada Ballet Theatre, which she co-founded with dancer-choreographer Vassili Sulich.

The Houssels are clearly a very lucky couple in the games of life and love.

Green Valley

Green Valley ranks as one of the largest master-planned communities in the nation. Although inside Henderson's city limits, Green Valley seems a world away, an independent-feeling community of deluxe condominiums and exclusive estates, as well as an increasing amount of commercial enterprises and casinos. Green Valley was developed by the Greenspun family's American Nevada Corporation, which sponsors family-style activities and art shows. Both its public schools and private schools are considered exceptional, and there are several parks catering to kid-friendly sports like soccer.

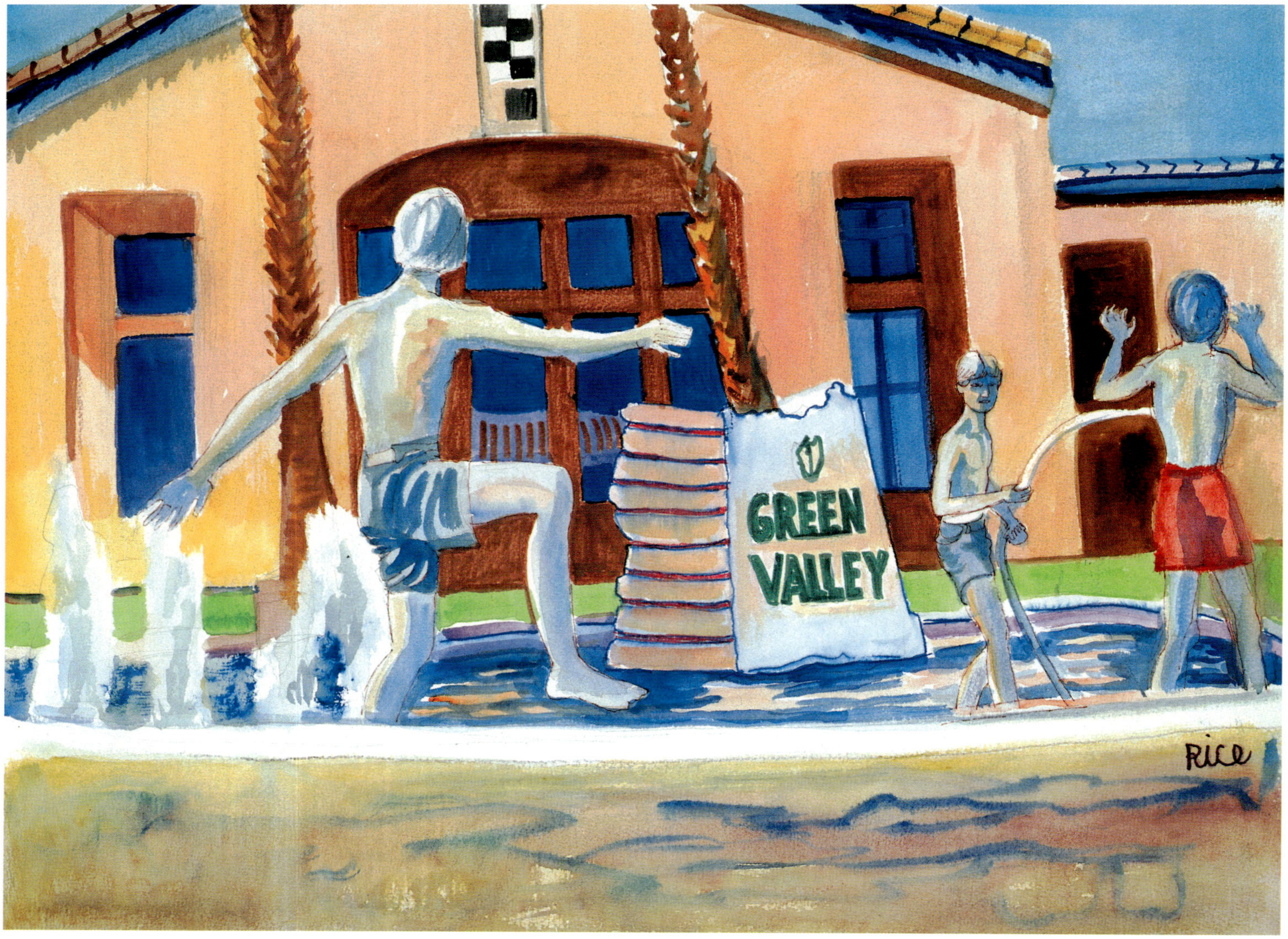

WELCOME TO GREEN VALLEY

The sprightly statues invite you to enjoy your visit to up-and-coming Green Valley. Begun in 1974 as an offshoot of the city of Henderson and developed by the American Nevada Corp., Green Valley extends over 8,400 acres and will have more than 21,000 homes. The area has a very upscale, suburban, non-Vegas feeling, with tree-lined streets, affluent shopping centers and a prominent mall.

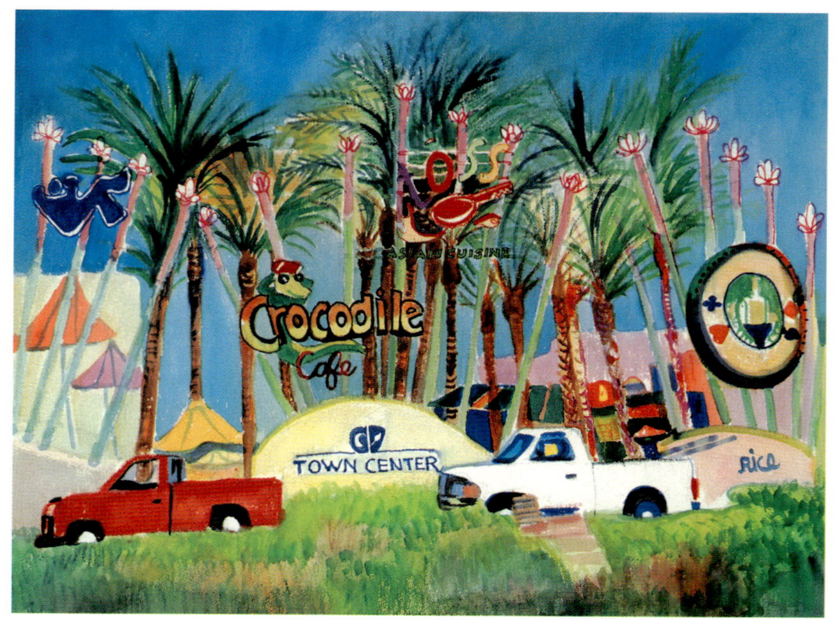

THE GREEN VALLEY TOWN CENTER

The Crocodile Cafe is just one of the many attractions of Green Valley's Town Center, a busy, active area in the heart of the Green Valley community where locals gather for family activities, picnics and barbeques.

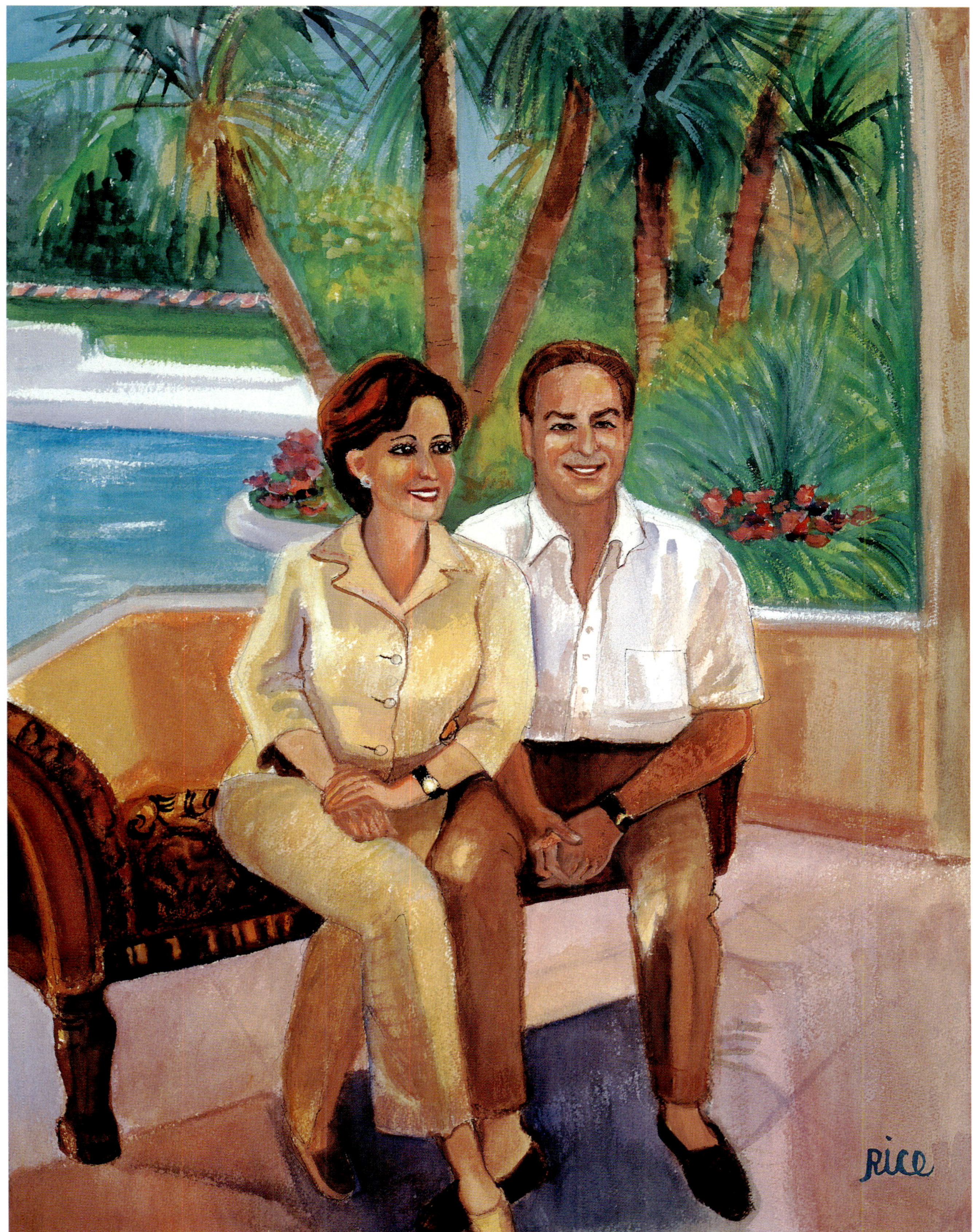

THE GREENSPUNS IN GREEN VALLEY

Myra and Brian Greenspun invited me into their lovely home in Green Valley, Nevada's first master-planned community developed by Brian's family. Brian's parents, Barbara and the late Hank Greenspun, founded the independent-minded Las Vegas SUN newspaper in 1950. The paper thrived and the family ventured into other businesses, most notably Prime Cable (now Cox Communications, one of the largest cable sytems in the country), the American Nevada Corporation (the developer of Green Valley) and the Hospitality Network. Today, Barbara is the publisher of the SUN and remains an active leader in all facets of Las Vegas life.

Son Brian guides the influential SUN—as president, editor and a writer of the "Where I Stand" column—as well as all of the Greenspun family interests, including cutting edge media ventures like Vegas.Com. Myra, a former fashion writer and travel consultant who married Brian in 1970, is active in many civic, charitable and political organizations and fundraising projects. I found them to be a lively couple, brimming with charm and good humor. Together with Brian's siblings Daniel, Susan and Jane, the family proudly continues the legendary Greenspun legacy of community involvement in Las Vegas.

Henderson

Henderson began in 1944 as an industrial city 15 miles southeast of Las Vegas, and its oldest sections still retain much of its early character and charm. Street names include Titanium and Magnesium; the downtown center has a 1950s flavor and there are several perfectly maintained period homes. Now the third largest city in Nevada, Henderson has evolved into a suburban retreat of comfortable residences, office buildings and attractions like the Clark County Heritage Museum and its own convention center.

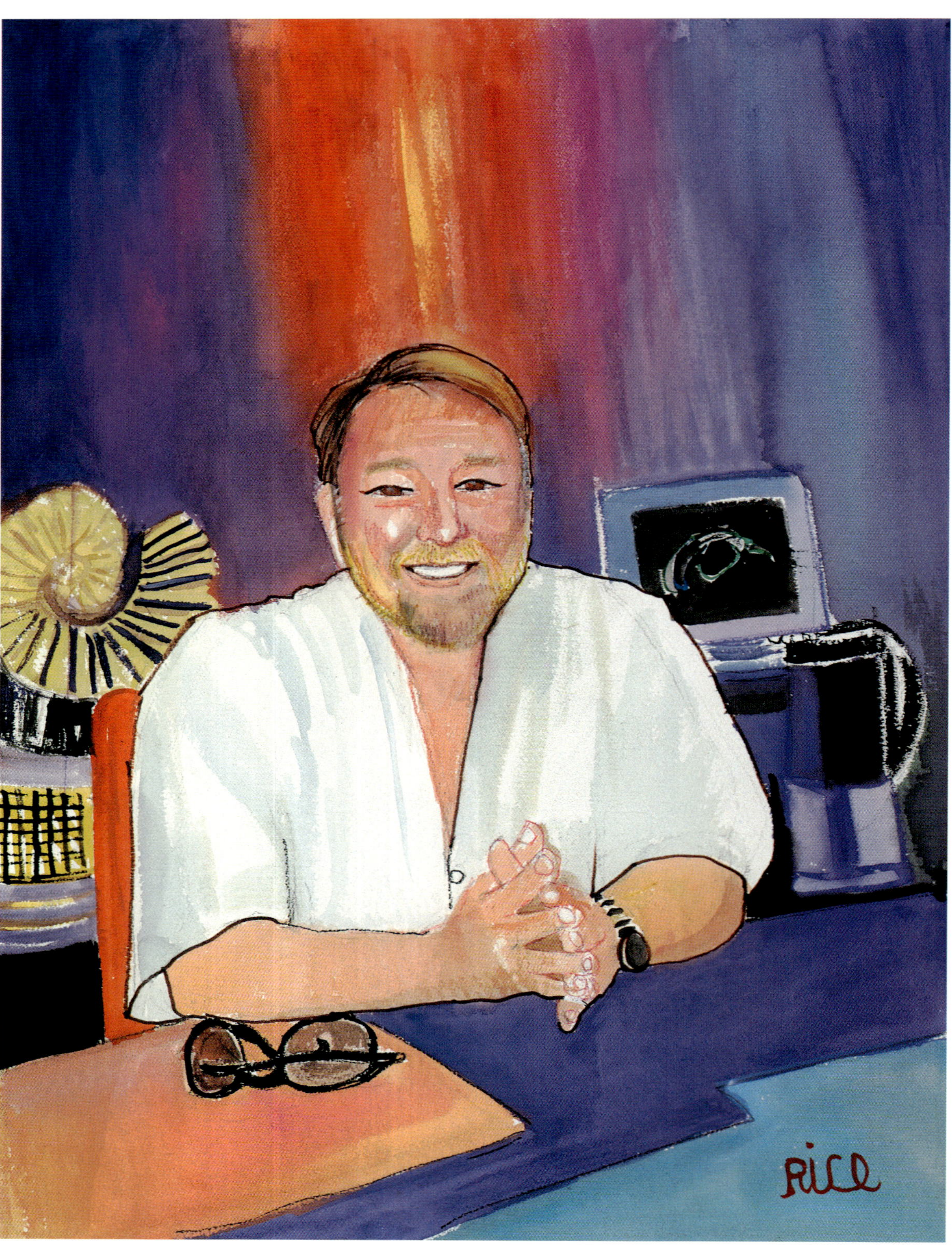

RICH MACDONALD

In 1970, Rich, along with his parents and an investment group, shrewdly purchased two sections of land in Henderson for $500 an acre. Today, land in the area (now known as MacDonald Highlands) is selling for $150,000 to $3 million per acre—not a bad investment! His projects include DragonRidge Country Club, MacDonald Ranch and the 600-acre Sunridge community. Rich has a passion for what he does and even after his tremendous success, remains on the lookout for fun and challenging projects—like a museum for ancient artifacts he has planned for MacDonald Highlands.

THE ETHEL M CHOCOLATES BOTANICAL CACTUS GARDENS >

Located on a 2.5 acre expanse in Henderson, the Ethel M Botanical Cactus Garden features more than 350 varieties of cacti, succulents and other desert plant life, beautifully displayed for the public. Opened in 1981, the Gardens have gone international with plant species from exotic locales like South America, South Africa, Japan and the Red Sea. The Ethel M Chocolates factory is located on the grounds, and delicious complimentary chocolates accompany the free tour.

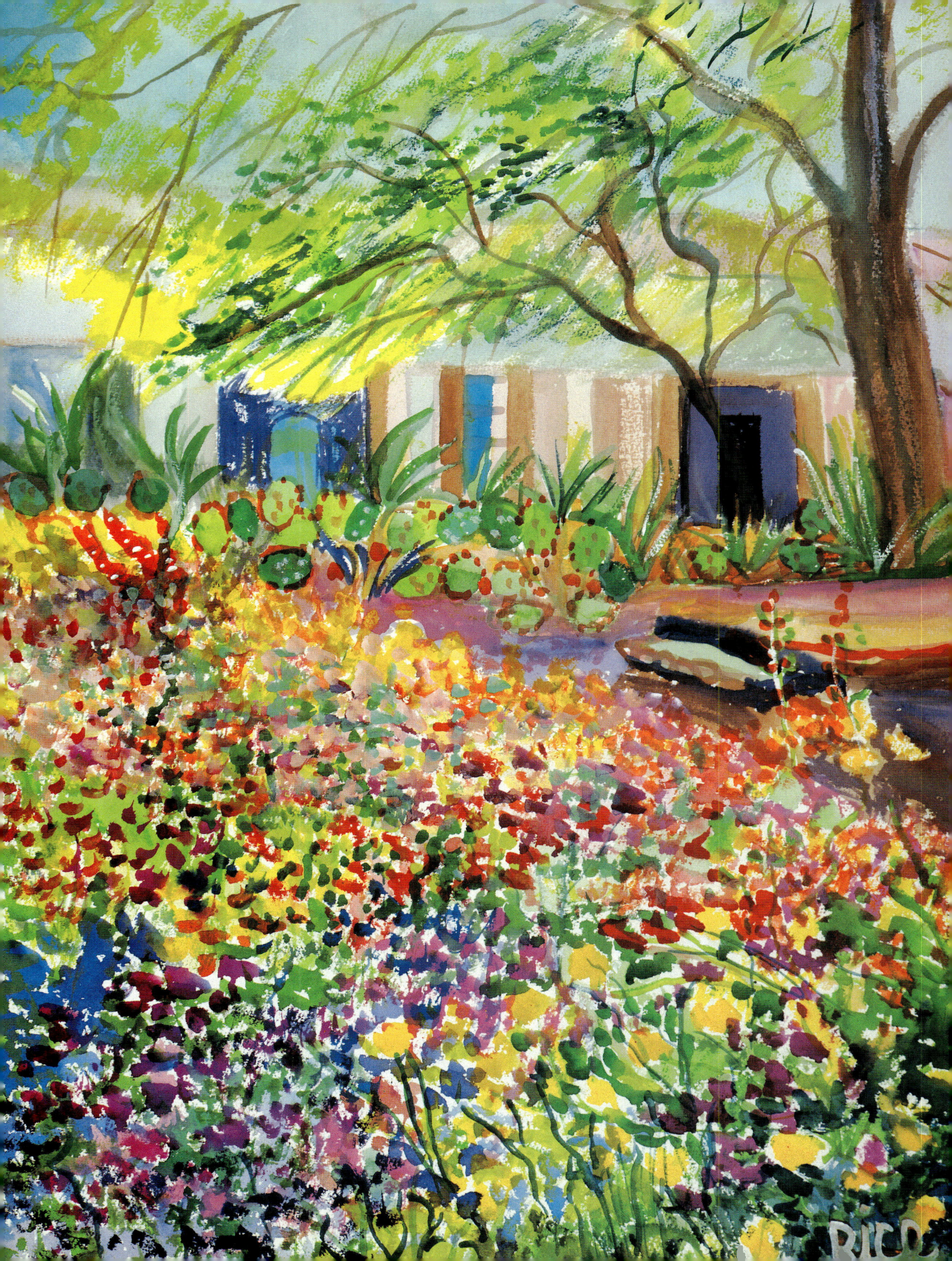

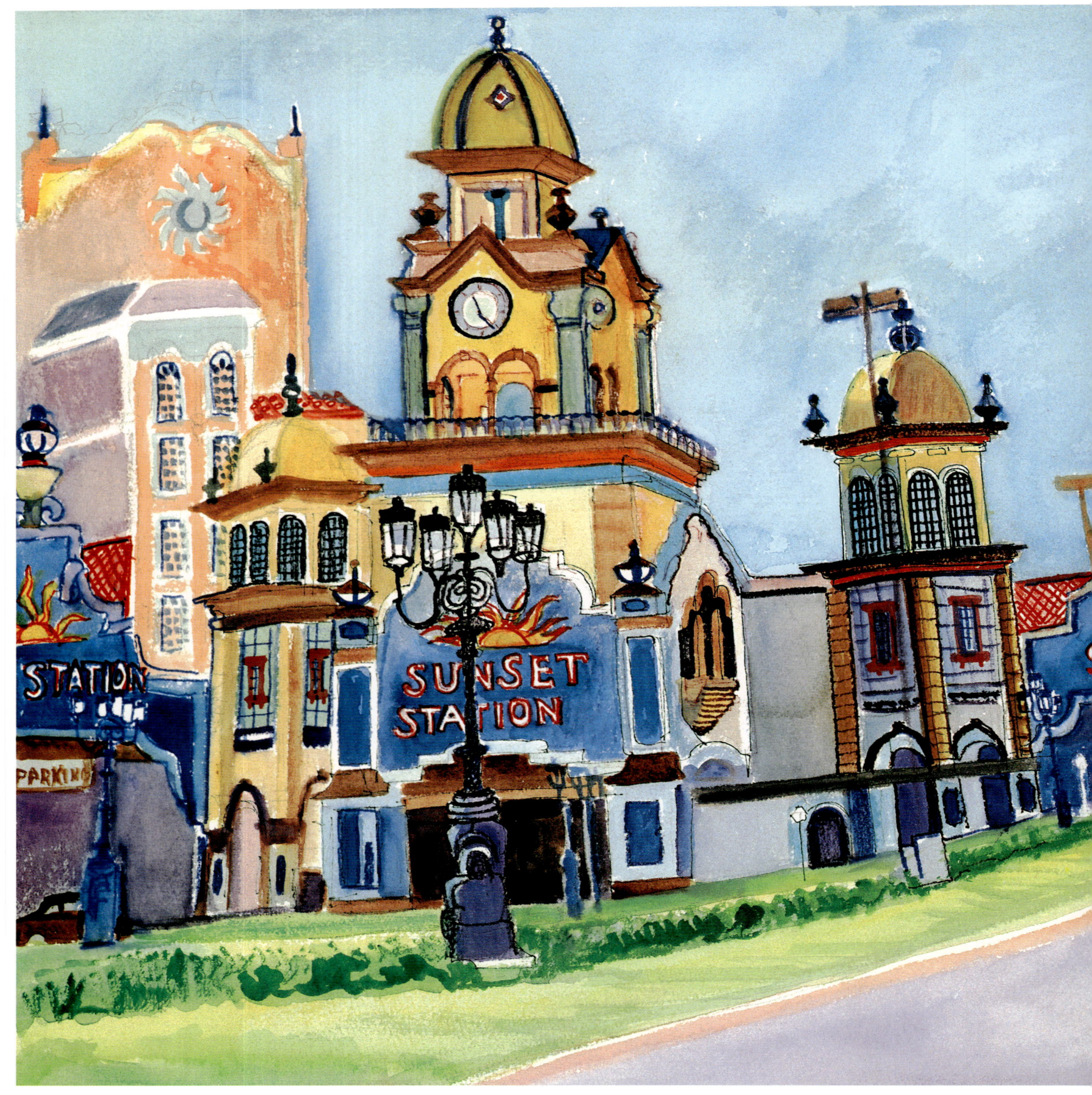

SUNSET STATION

Set on 100 acres in Henderson and featuring retro architecture in an innovative configuration, Sunset Station is the largest resort casino establishment operated by the Station Casinos company. Sunset Station has an 80,000-square-foot casino featuring a wide variety of games and a large number of popular nickel machines. The complex also has numerous full-service and fast-food-style eateries, a celebrity showroom, a lounge, a gaming arcade and a 10-screen movie theater complex.

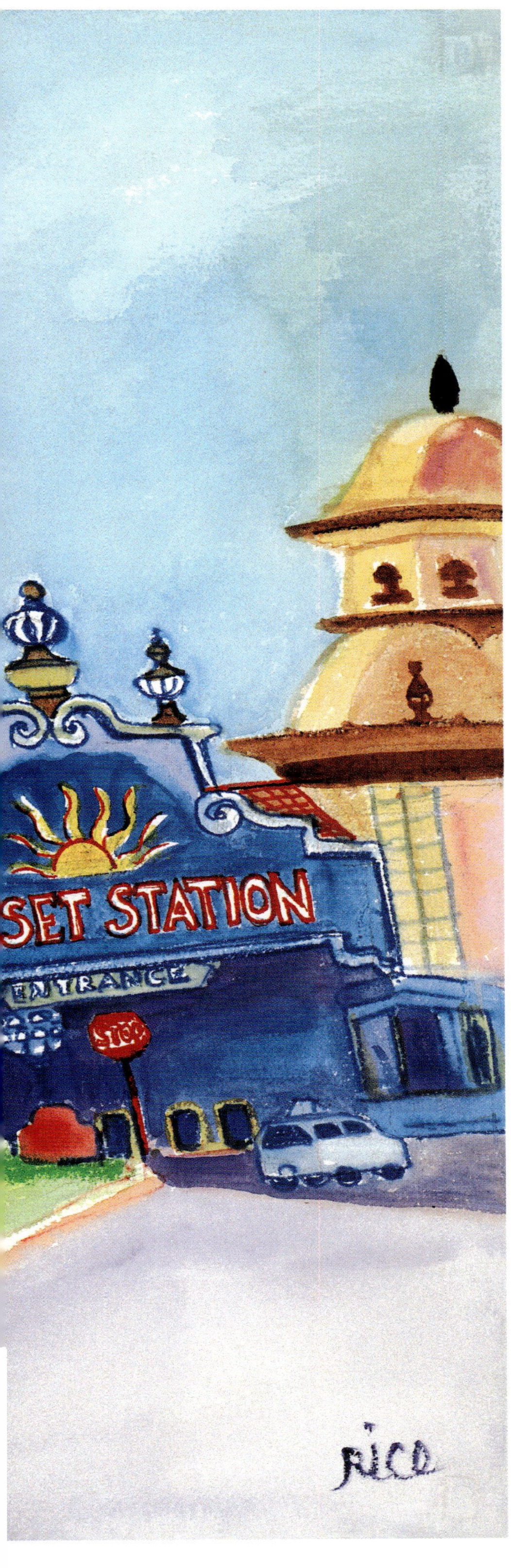

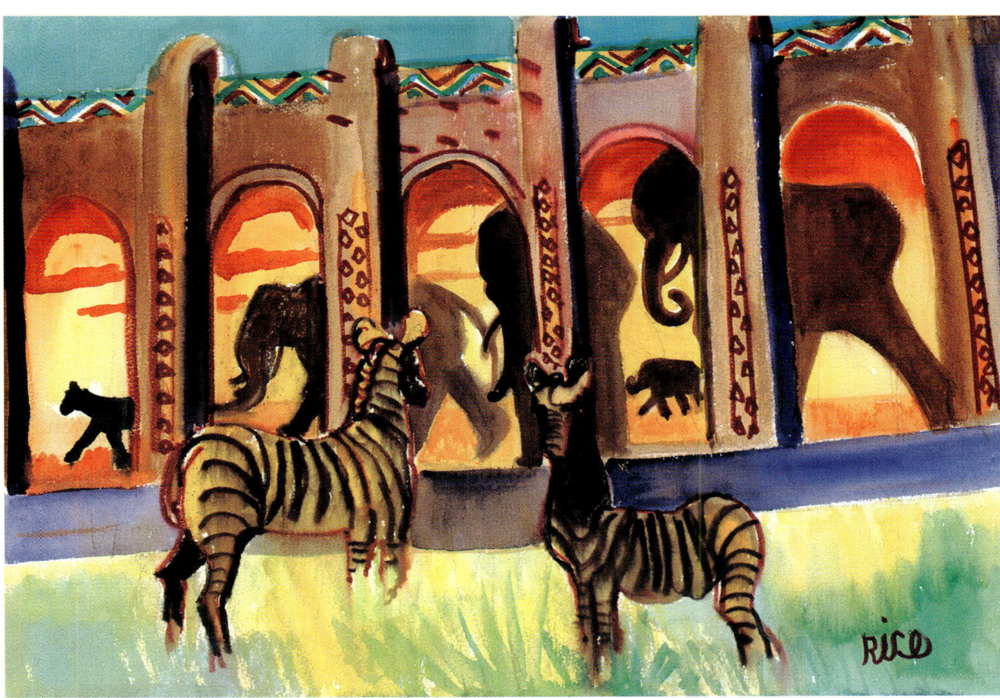

ROAMING AT THE RESERVE HOTEL CASINO

I was enchanted by the colorful design of The Reserve, an exotic, safari-themed Stations hotel-casino I visited in Henderson. Tall grass surrounds the parking lot, lifelike animals from the African veldt appear to roam outside the casino and gold monkeys adorn the rooftops.

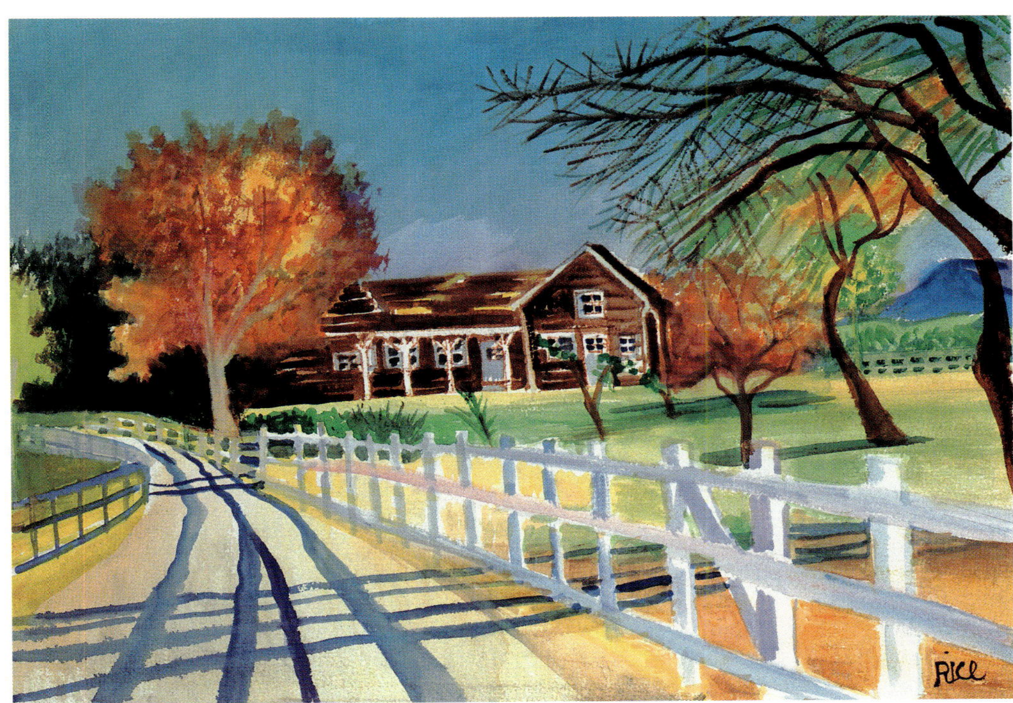

SPRING MOUNTAIN RANCH

You can take a walking tour of this picturesque ranch at the foot of the sandstone Wilson Cliffs. The quaint red ranch house and long green lawns make it a perfect place to spend the day enjoying a concert, a community event or an old-fashioned picnic. In the summertime, Spring Mountain's Supper Theatre hosts productions by local theater groups in the Spring Mountain State Park Amphitheater.

A combination working ranch and luxury retreat, Spring Mountain Ranch began its colorful history as a campsite in the mid-1830s. For years, the region was called Bill Williams Ranch after a mountaineer who raided horses from Mexican rancheros in California and traveled the dangerous, outlaw-plagued area. After the Civil War, Army Sgt. James B. Wilson and his partner George Anderson claimed the property and named it Sand Stone Ranch. By the 1920s, prominent Hollywood furrier Willard George took over, raising chinchillas along with cattle. Radio performer Chester Lauck ("Lum" of "Lum 'N' Abner") acquired it in the 1940s for his "Bar Nothing Ranch" and a German munitions industrialist finally dubbed it Spring Mountain Ranch in 1967. It passed through various hands before finally coming under the care of the Nevada State Parks Division in 1974.

Summerlin

A master-planned community developed by The Howard Hughes Corporation and divided into several "villages" connected by the scenic Summerlin Trail, Summerlin (named for Hughes' maternal grandmother) continues to push outward into the foothills along the western rim of Las Vegas. Summerlin ranks as America's best-selling master-planned community—a position it has held since 1992. This standard setting community is known for its parks, public facilities and full calendar of social and cultural events. Along with a luxurious resort, Summerlin offers a range of living options, from affordable apartments to upscale condos to multi-million-dollar mansions.

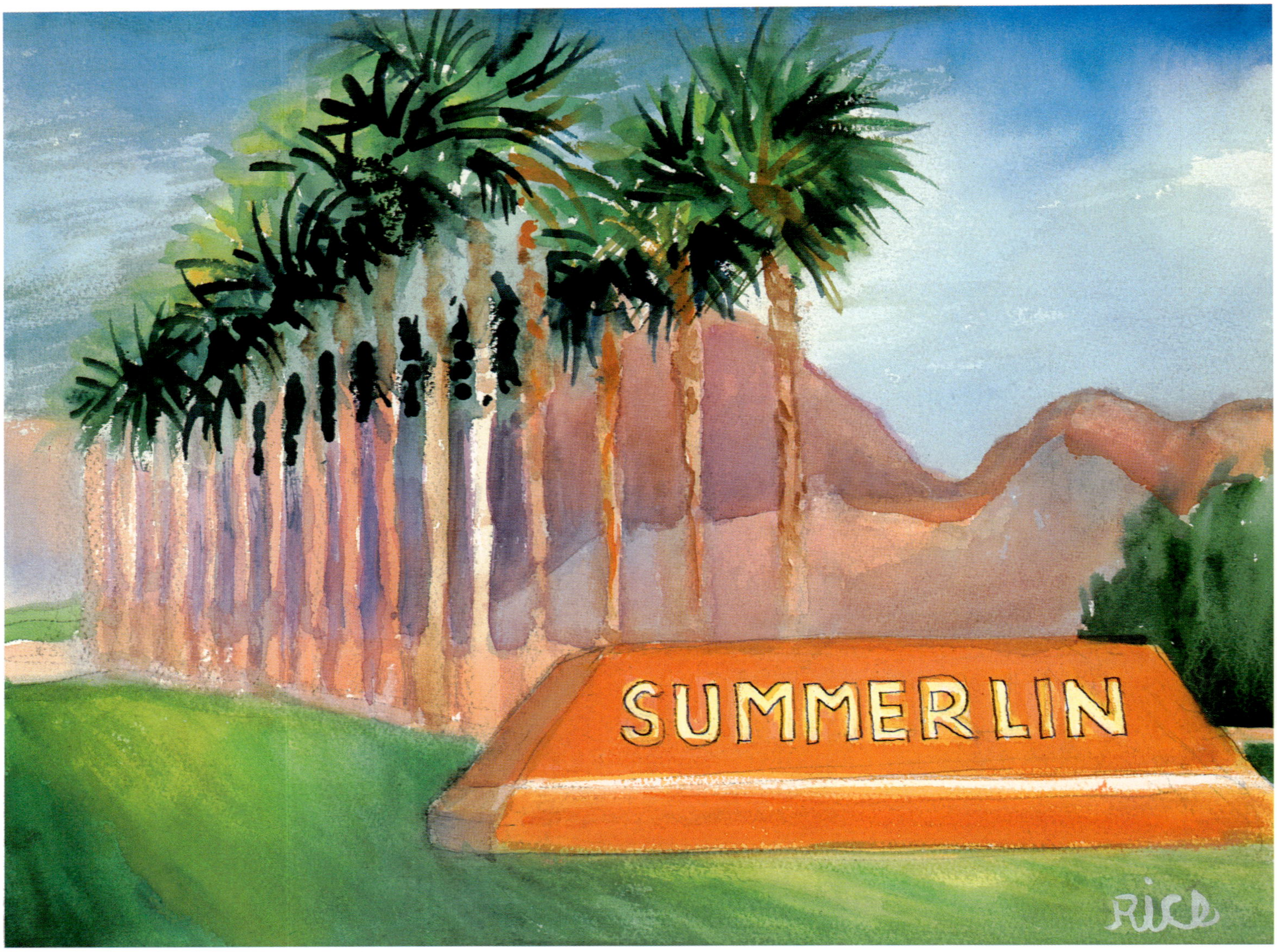

Howard Hughes

Industrialist and movie mogul Howard Hughes, one of the most prominent Americans of the last century and a billionaire in the days when billionaires were few and far between, also played a crucial role in the history of Las Vegas. He was a frequent visitor and a guest of the Desert Inn, the Flamingo and other hotels in the early 1950s.

By 1966, he took up residence in the Desert Inn's ninth floor, where he began building the greatest Las Vegas kingdom yet assembled, purchasing the Desert Inn, the Sands, the Frontier, the Castaways, the Silver Slipper, the Landmark, KLAS (the local CBS TV affiliate) and other properties on the Strip, around the airport and in Red Rock and Reno.

When Hughes died in 1976, he left Las Vegas a considerable legacy—the cleaning up of the casino system and the introduction of corporate ownership. Hughes' acquisition of 25,000 acres along the western rim of Las Vegas is today the site of Summerlin, one of the country's largest and most successful master-planned communities.

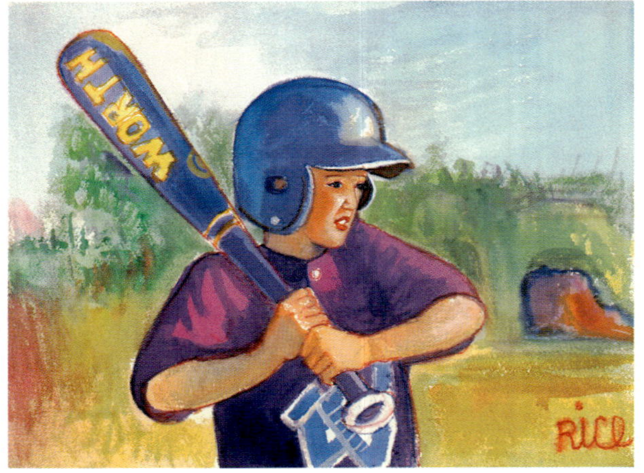

BATTER UP!
With a plethora of parks and fields, Summerlin is a great place for kids, like this aspiring power hitter at The Trails Park.

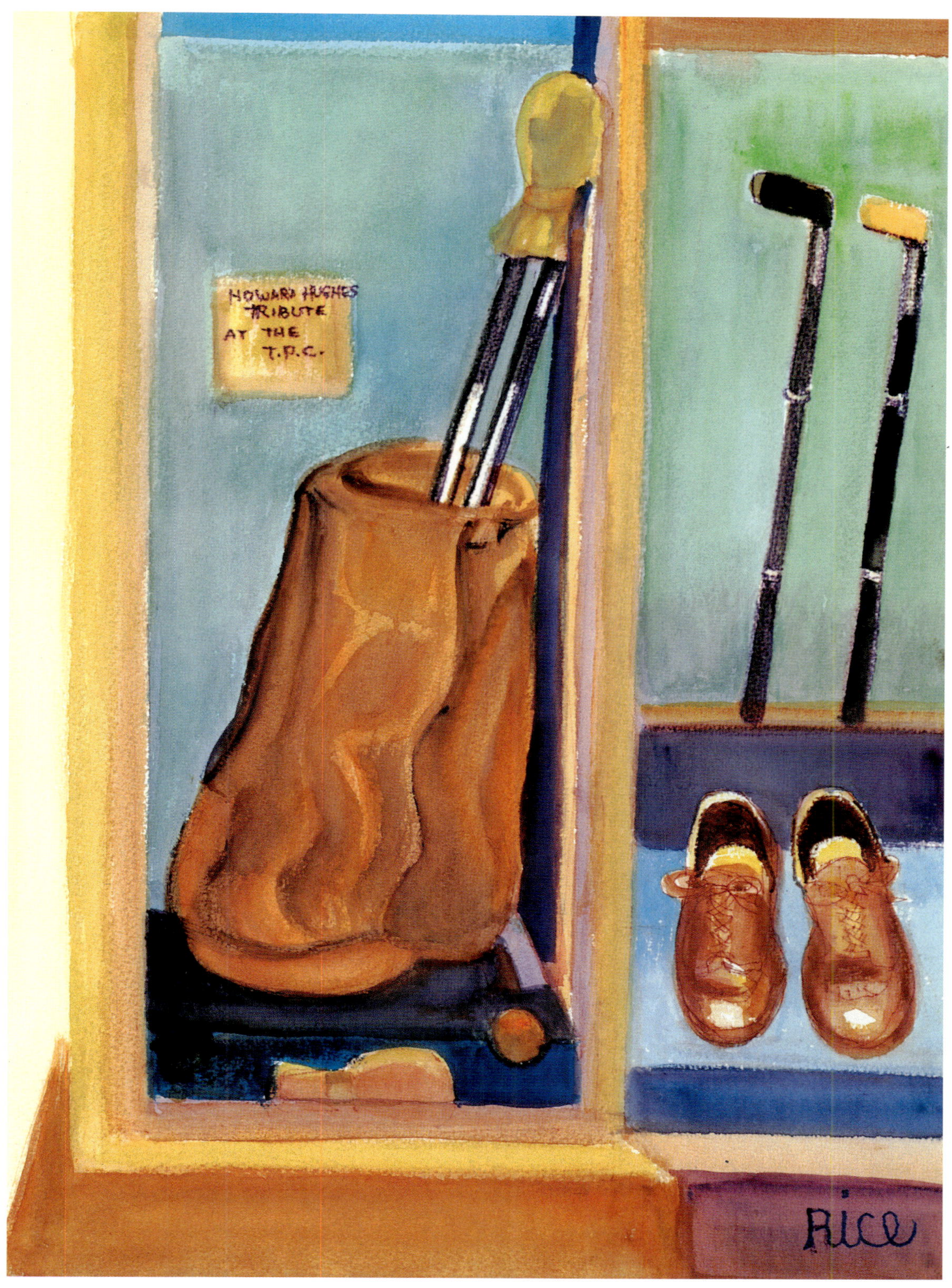

HOWARD HUGHES' GOLF CLUBS AT TPC

High finance, industry, aviation, show biz, a glamorous playboy lifestyle—Howard Hughes mastered almost everything he attempted, including golf. A two-handicap player, Hughes won his first amateur tournament at age 22 but, strangely, abandoned the sport forever just ten years later. Still, his early love of the game is remembered today with this display of his old equipment—shoes, clubs, bags and trophies—in a room full of Hughes memorabilia at TPC (Tournament Players Club) Summerlin. A par 72 course, TPC Summerlin, hosts two PGA events each year, luring top players like Bob May and Las Vegas local Robert Gamez. Tiger Woods won his first PGA Tour championship at TPC Summerlin at the prestigious five-day, 90-hole Las Vegas Invitational, now known as the Invensys Classic at Las Vegas, one of the richest plums of the PGA Tour.

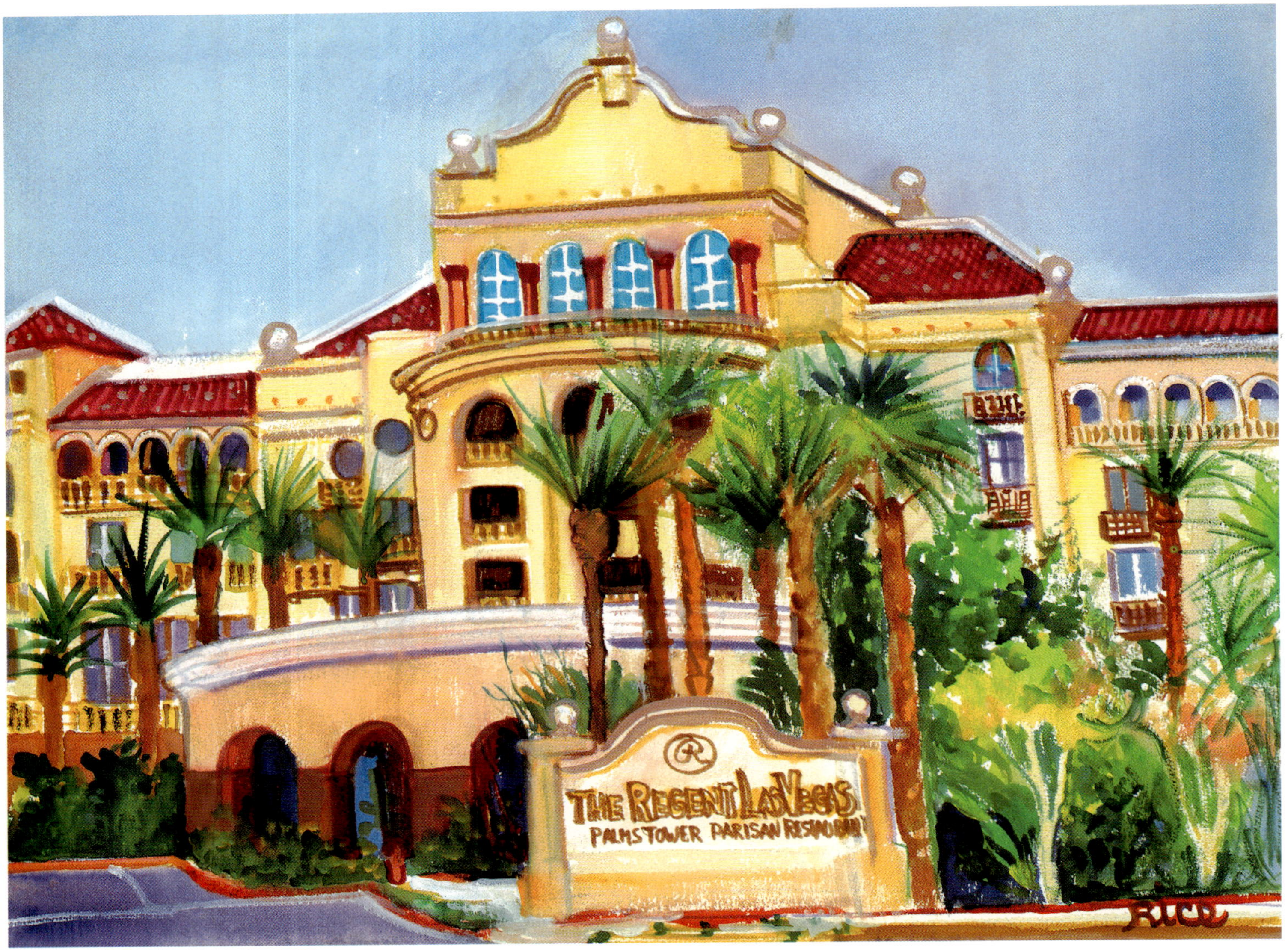

THE REGENT LAS VEGAS

The Regent Las Vegas is a sumptuous resort in Summerlin featuring a luxurious 40,000-square-foot health spa, a huge stand-alone casino with buffet, a state-of-the-art conference and banquet center, elegant restaurants and specialty shops of Paseo de Vida. The Regent is surrounded by three major golf courses—including the Tournament Players Club (TPC) at The Canyons. Its tavern, the Putting Green, overlooks two scenic bentgrass putting greens designed by Bobby Weed. The resort has become a natural gathering place for vacationing golfers.

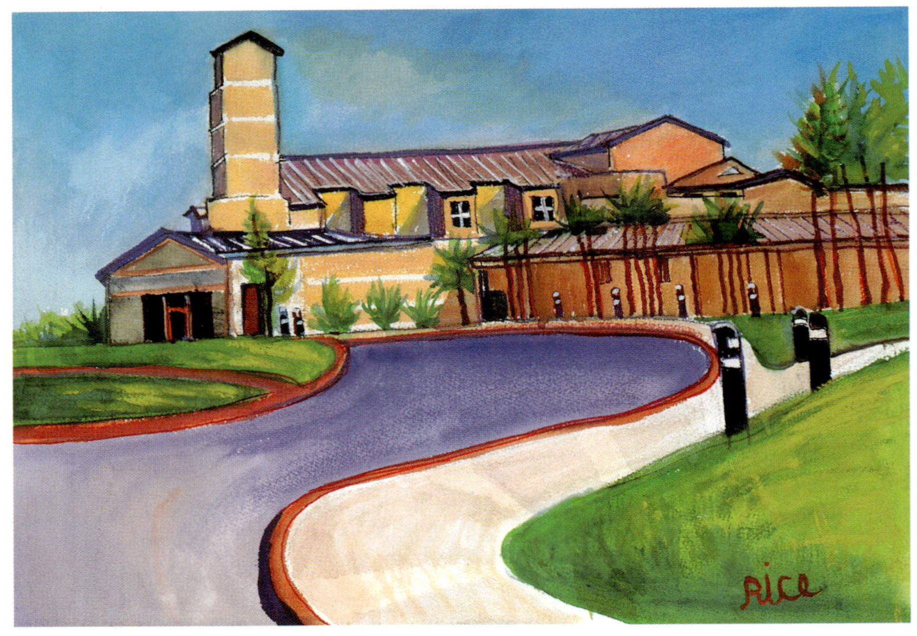

THE MEADOWS SCHOOL

The Meadows School opened in 1984 as the state's first non-profit, nonsectarian, co-educational prep school, and moved to its current 40-acre campus in Summerlin (donated by The Howard Hughes Corporation) in 1988. Today, the exclusive school, founded and guided by Carolyn Goodman, serves nearly 800 uniformed students—preschool through grade 12—and in addition to its highly regarded educational programs, it also features extensive athletic facilities and playing fields.

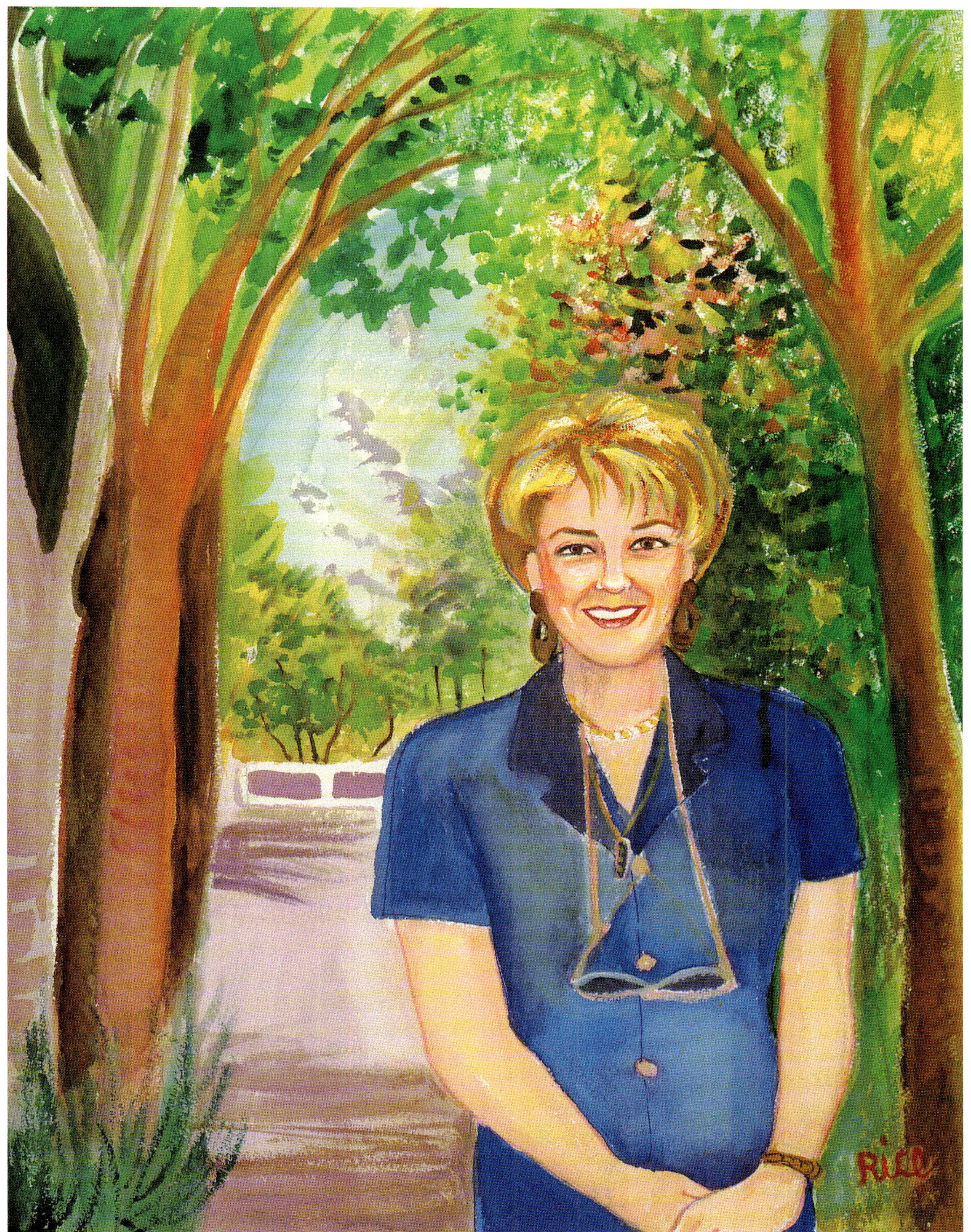

CAROLYN GOODMAN

Carolyn Goodman, the charming wife of Mayor Oscar B. Goodman, is more than just the "First Lady" of Las Vegas. A graduate of Bryn Mawr, Carolyn learned the value of a top-flight education and has put those lessons to use as the founder and president of the Board of Trustees at the prestigious Meadows School. She's also been involved with other academic institutions—such as UNLV, the Hebrew Academy, the Clark County School District and the University of Southern California—and is president and CEO of College Bound Counseling, which offers consultation on college selection, application, admissions and financial aid. She's an accomplished, warm woman.

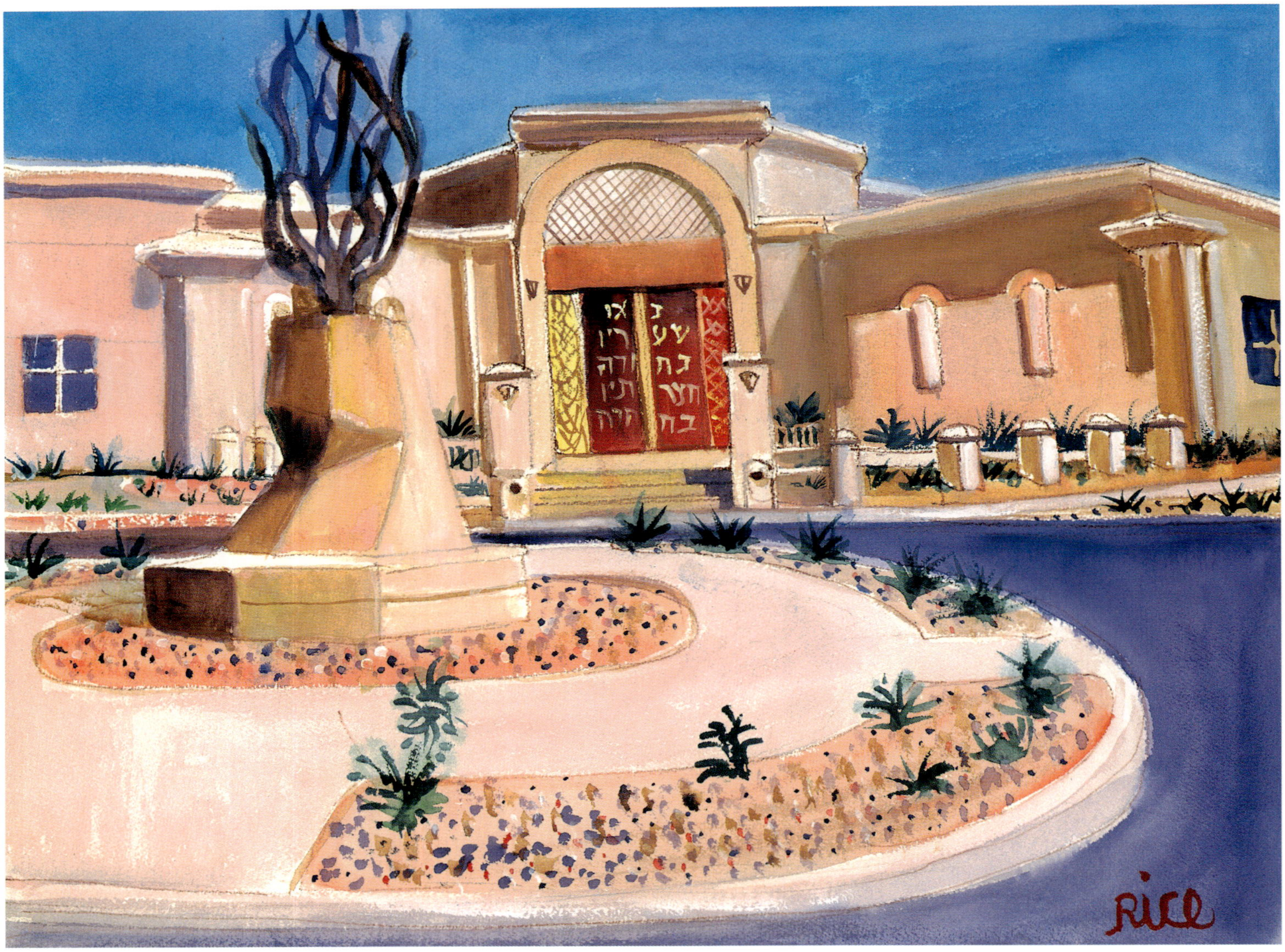

TEMPLE BETH SHOLOM

Founded in 1946 as the first synagogue in the state of Nevada, Temple Beth Sholom is where Sammy Davis, Jr., converted to Judaism and Elizabeth Taylor married Eddie Fisher (A second Temple Beth Sholom was opened in Summerlin in 2000.) Made of stucco and Jerusalem stone, this new Temple—designed by architect Brad Friedmutter—took three years to plan and construct.

WITHIN TEMPLE BETH SHOLOM, SUMMERLIN

With its beautifully designed interior and gorgeous stained glass windows, it's no surprise so many people find inspiration inside the new Temple Beth Sholom.

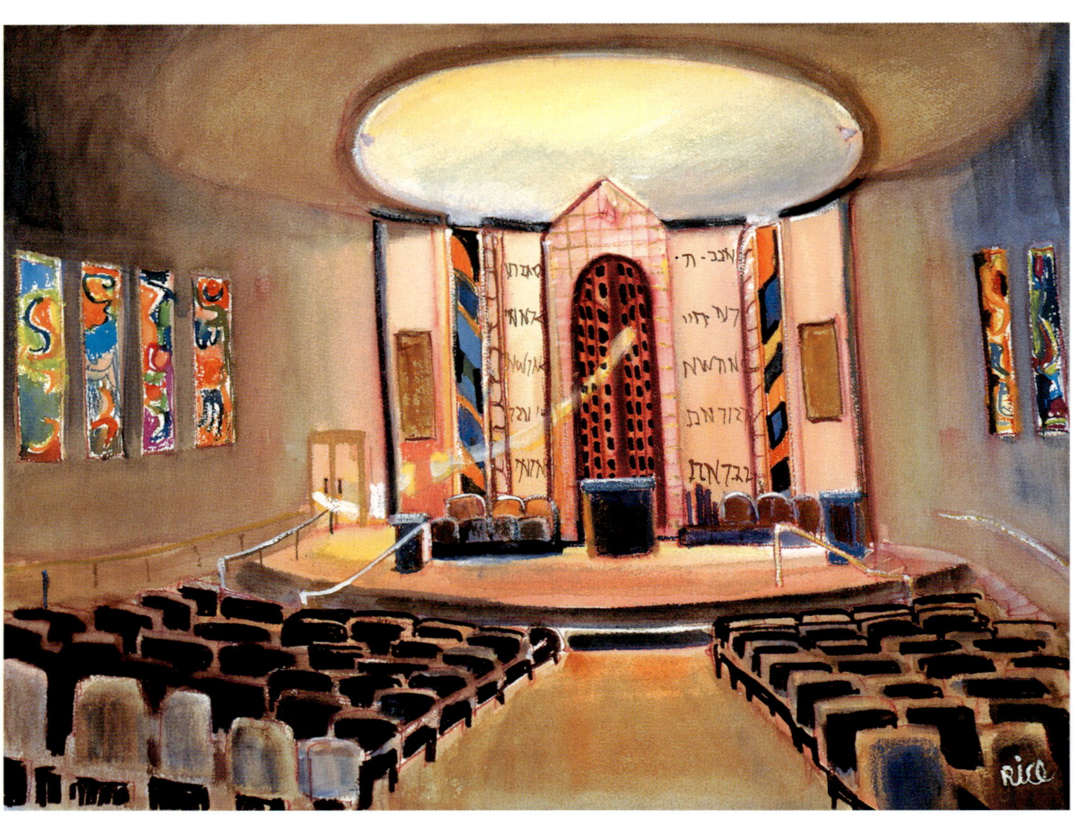

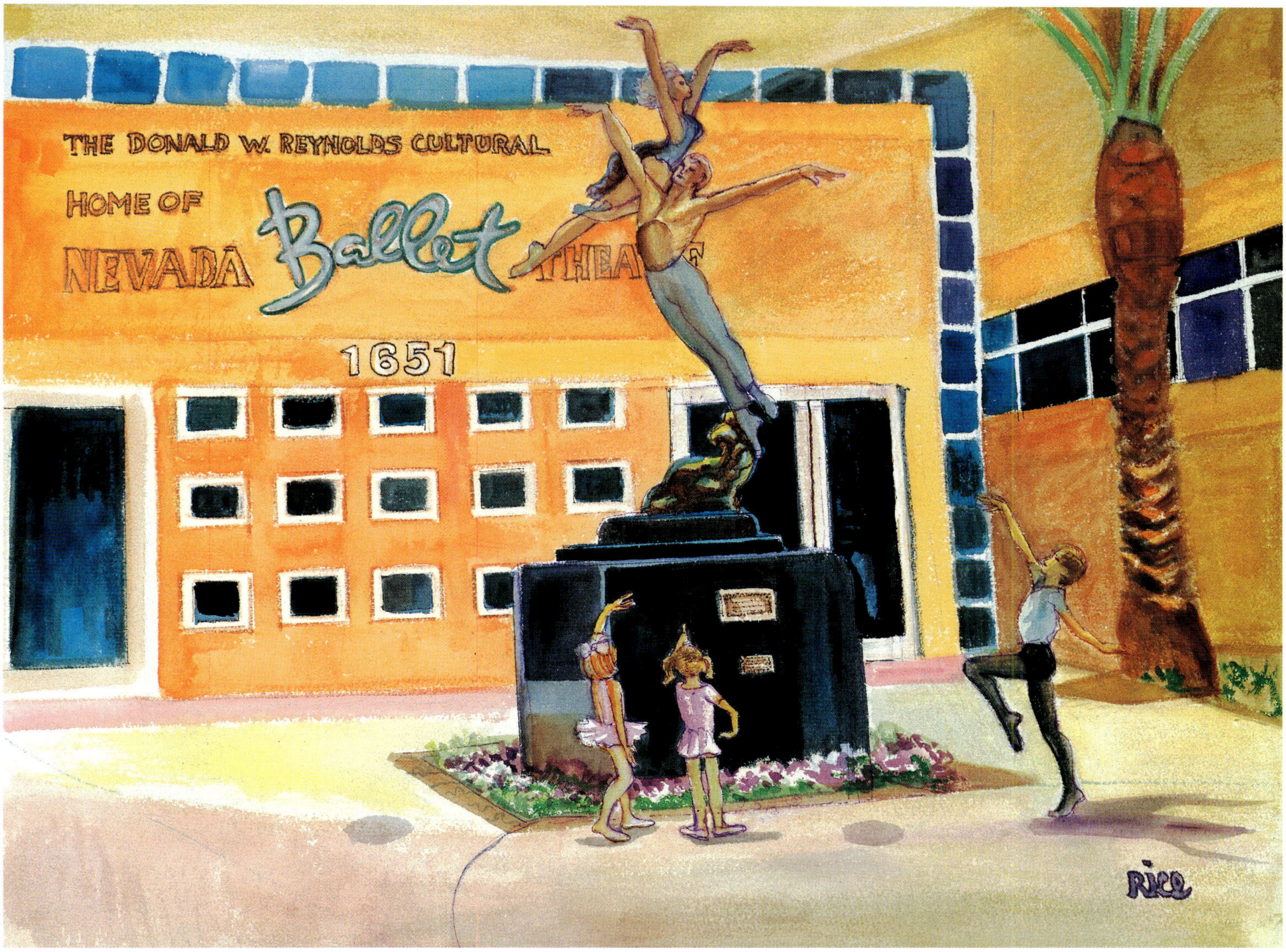

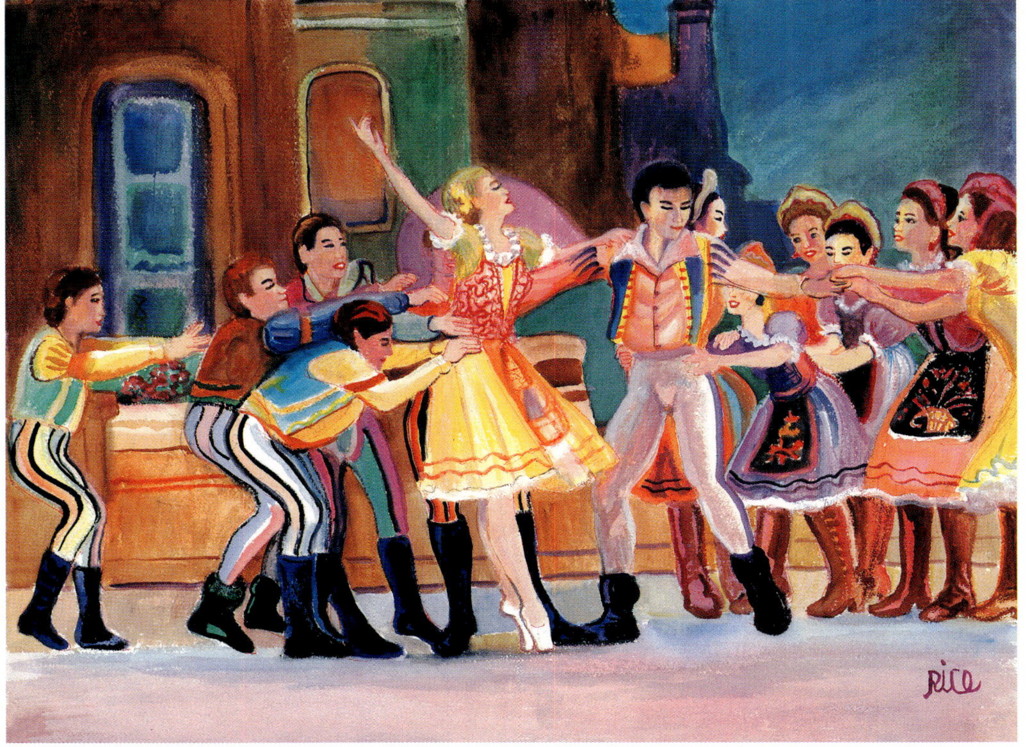

THE NEVADA BALLET THEATRE

This bronze sculpture of graceful dancers by Mario Jason (the children below were sculpted by his son Howard) embodies the artistic spirit of the Nevada Ballet Theatre, a keystone in the Las Vegas arts community. NBT was founded in 1972 by Yugoslavian dancer Vassili Sulich and Nancy Houssels. Nancy, also managing director of the resident ballet company, gave me a personally guided tour of this beautifully designed dance theatre, which has evolved into a company of 25 dancers that play to packed houses featuring some of ballet's most challenging and beloved programs. Located in the state-of-the-art Donald W. Reynolds Cultural Center in Summerlin, NBT is poised to leap into the role of a world-class ballet company.

THE MAGIC OF DANCE

Summerlin's Nevada Ballet Theater offers a culturally-enriching slate of entertainment, such as this vibrant performance of "Coppelia." The local community has rallied around such artistic endeavors, with ballet and other special programs growing in popularity.

Red Rock

The majestic rocky vistas of Red Rock Canyon provide a getaway spot and even a home for rugged individualists looking for gorgeous panoramas without any neon. Life among the spectacular rock formations moves at a different pace, but it is perfect for those who appreciate its cooler climate, lush vegetation and scenic sandstone canyons. Just a 20-minute drive from the Strip, Red Rock feels a million miles away.

DAWN AT RED ROCK

Few things are as breathtakingly vibrant as the early morning hues of the Red Rock Canyon National Conservation Area outside of the city, where genuine lizards lounge. Limestone, sandstone, cliffs, ravines, canyons, boulders, slopes, peaks, cacti, flowers, brush and wildlife—the shapes and colors of Red Rock are even more dazzling than those back in town. But after all, they were 600 million years in the making.

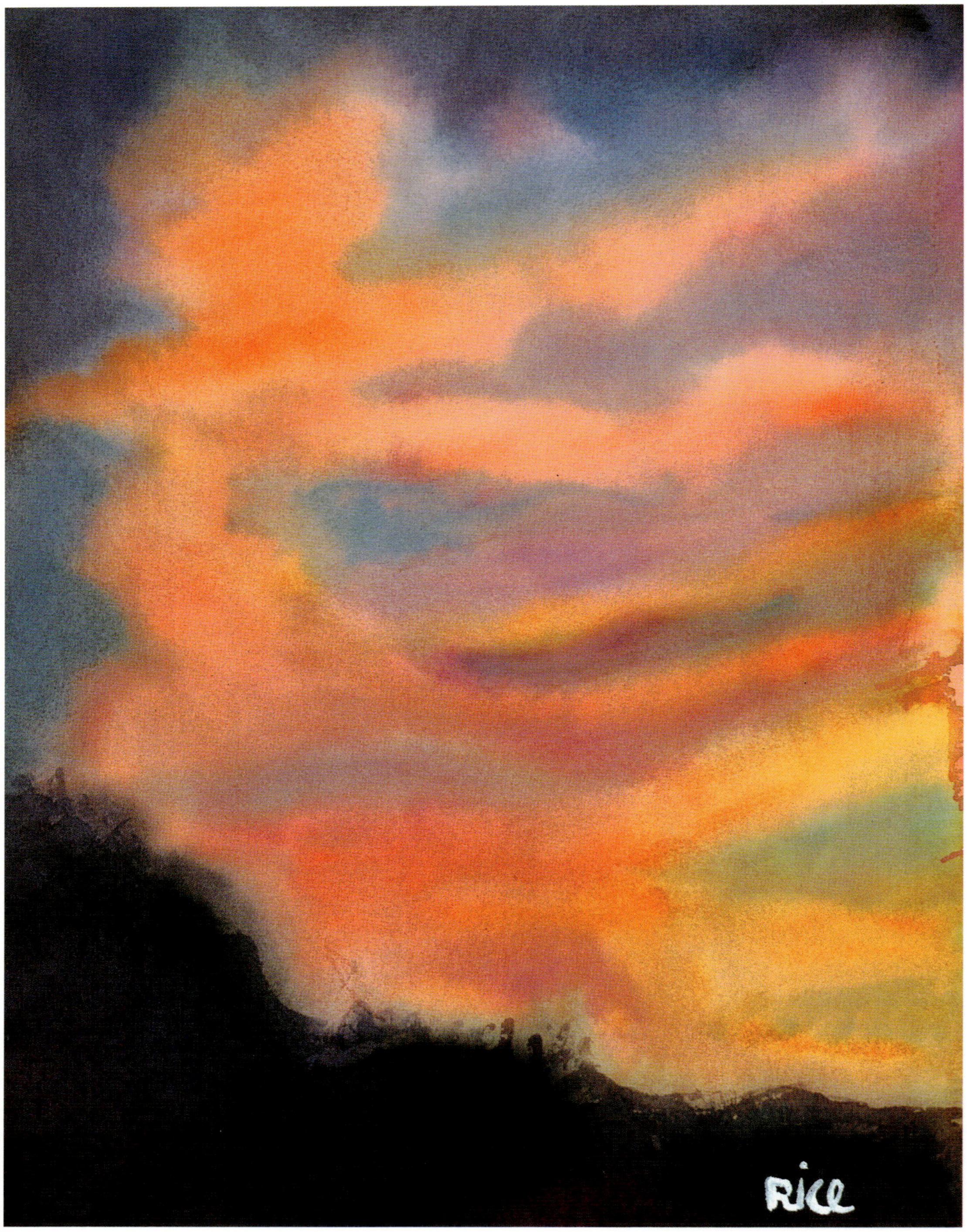

BURROS CROSSING THE ROAD

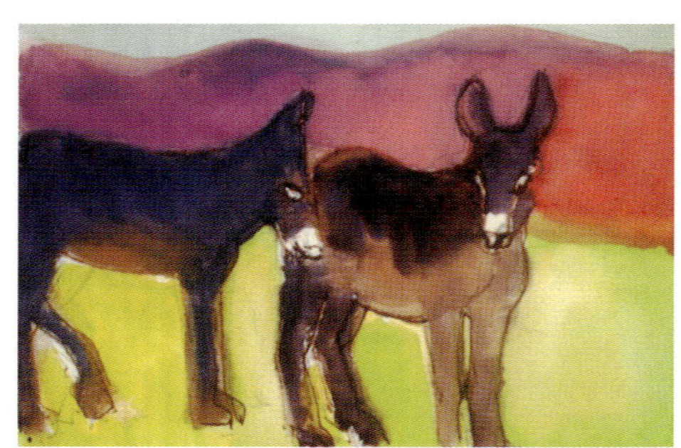

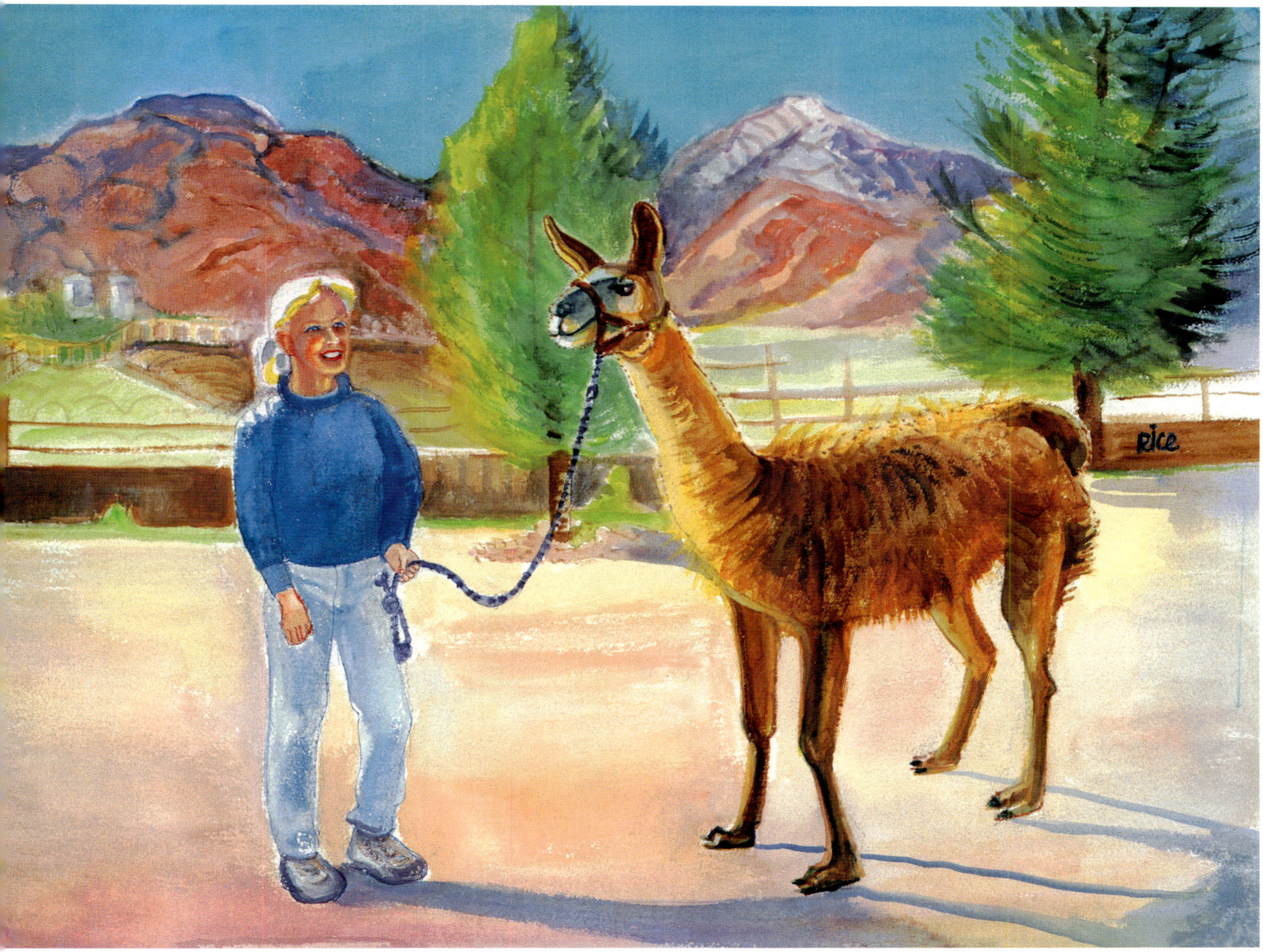

SUSIE AND SWEETIE THE LLAMA

Sculptress and poet Susie Pinjuv introduced me to her friends Beamer, Jimmer and Sweetie when I visited her in the majestic Calico Basin in Red Rock. The llamas are just part of a friendly menagerie—including horses, dogs, peacocks, chickens, white doves and a goat—which keeps Susie company at her home in the peaceful, unspoiled mountain region. Susie was born in Las Vegas and has watched the city evolve throughout her lifetime. Her father Lambert VanDerMeer arrived from Chicago in the late 1920s and started the Oppedyk Jersey Dairy and later, he launched the Polar Ice Company, supplying ice to all the city's major hotels before the advent of ice machines. Her mother Malena left a troubled marriage in Maine with two boys in a Model T Ford, started a gas station and later met Lambert at the Lorenzi Dance Hall. As a teenager, Susie played tennis at the Flamingo and cruised Fremont Street with her mom's gas and some of her dad's ice to keep cool. Today, she enjoys her family and animal companions, has reunited with her high school sweetheart and, while she keeps up with the ever-changing city scene, prefers to spend her days crafting wood art for Desert Sculptures Art Society and exploring the natural beauty of the Calico Basin.

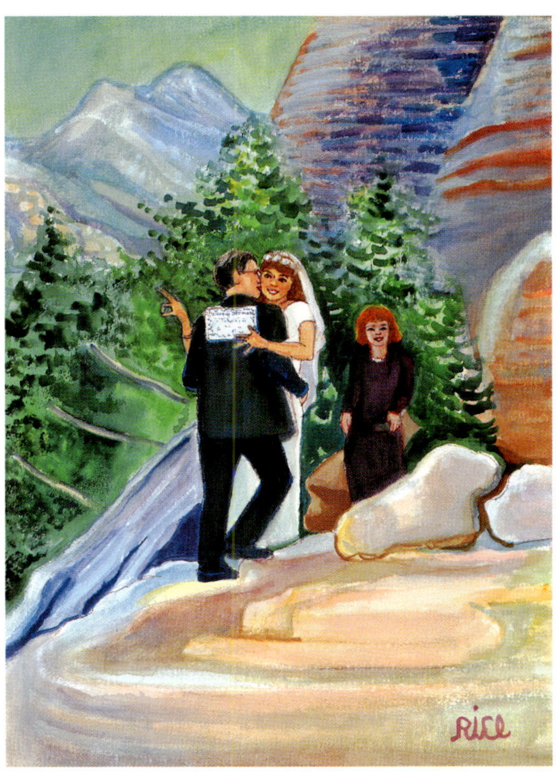

WEDDING AT RED ROCK

Sometimes when couples marry in Las Vegas, it's not always to tie the knot under flashy neon lights or at theme hotels. These newlyweds took a back-to-nature approach to their ceremony, uniting amid the natural splendor of Red Rock in a romantic ceremony conducted by Charolette Richards.

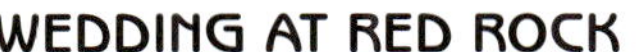

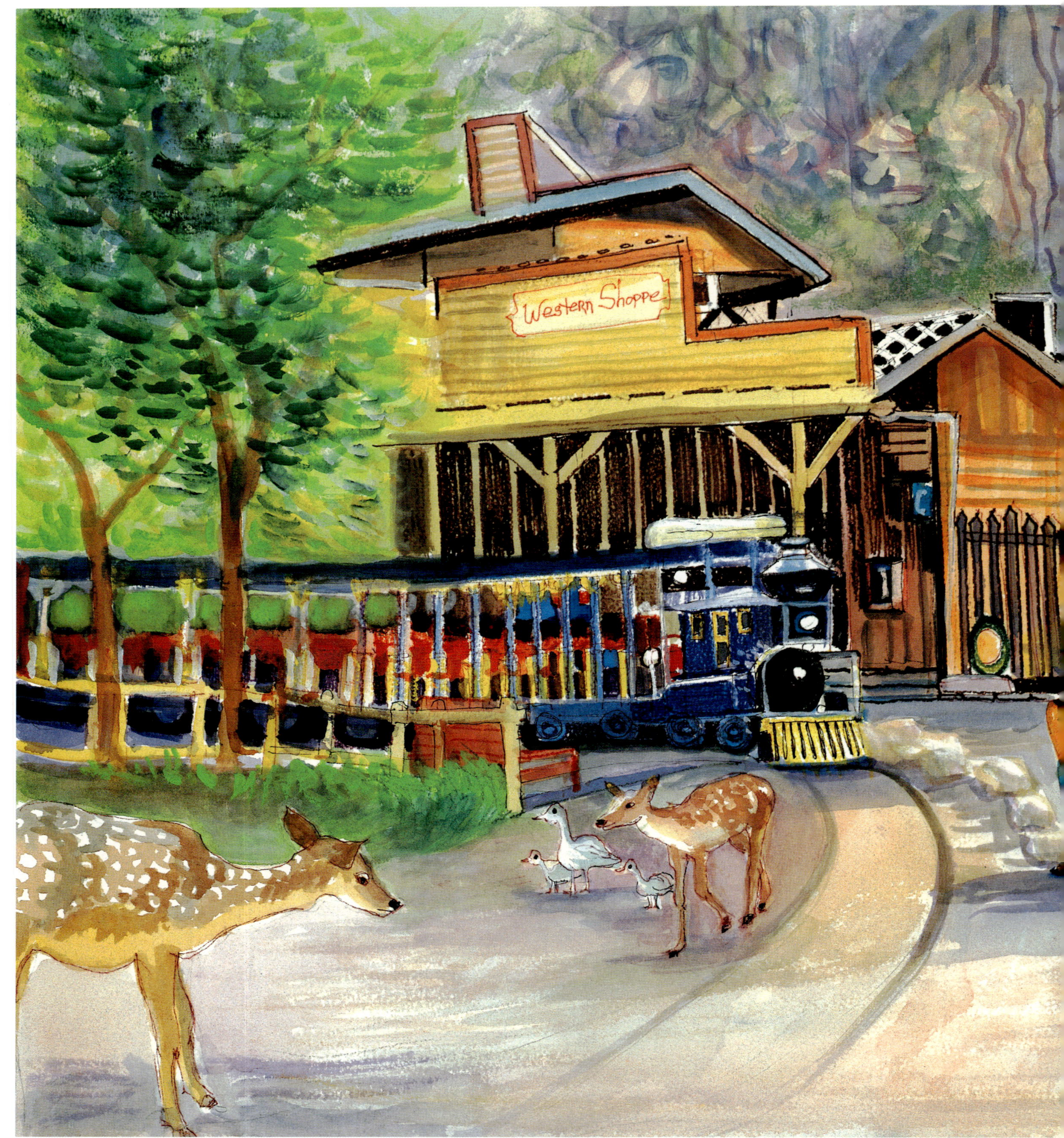

BONNIE SPRINGS AND OLD NEVADA

If you head west about 15 minutes from Las Vegas, you'll discover rustic Red Rock Canyon in the Spring Mountain range. Nearby lies Bonnie Springs and Old Nevada, a former cattle ranch that has been converted into a rugged reproduction of an 1880s mining town. A terrific haven for families (complete with lodging and dining), Bonnie Springs and Old Nevada feature Old West shoot-outs, a petting zoo, horseback riding and a fabulous mini-railroad that recalls Las Vegas' earliest days.

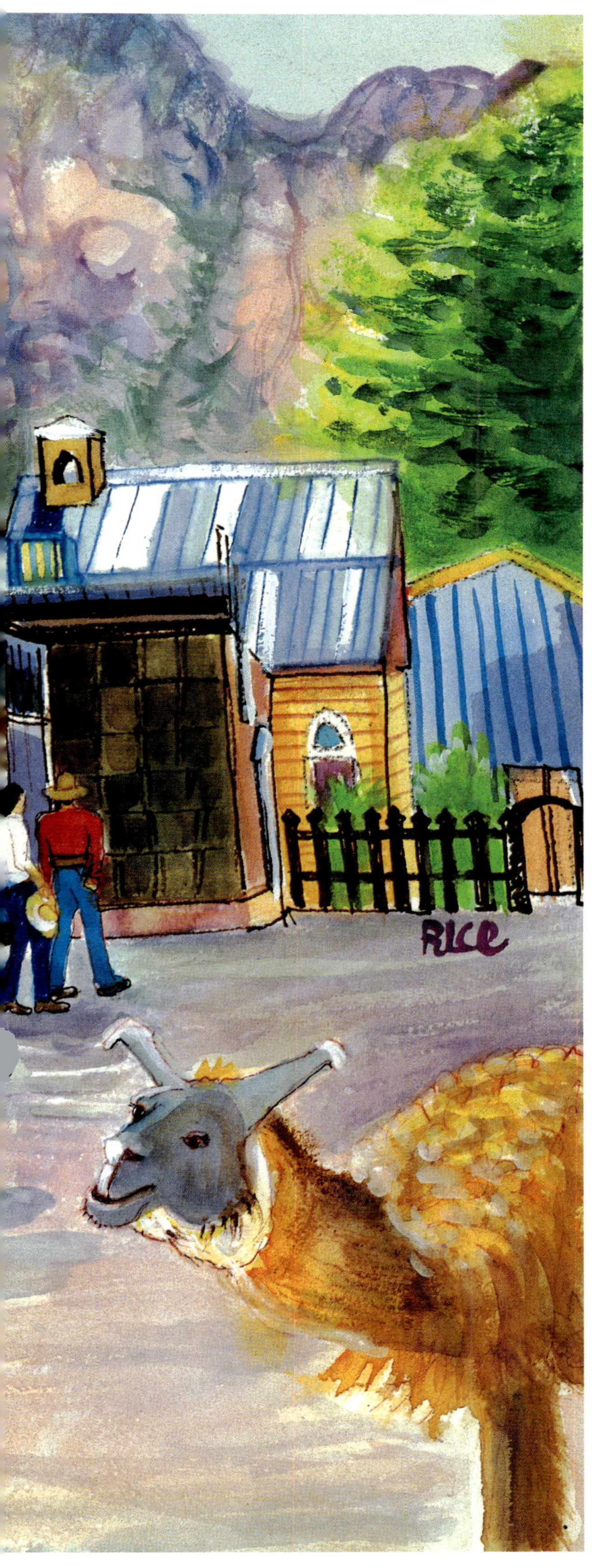

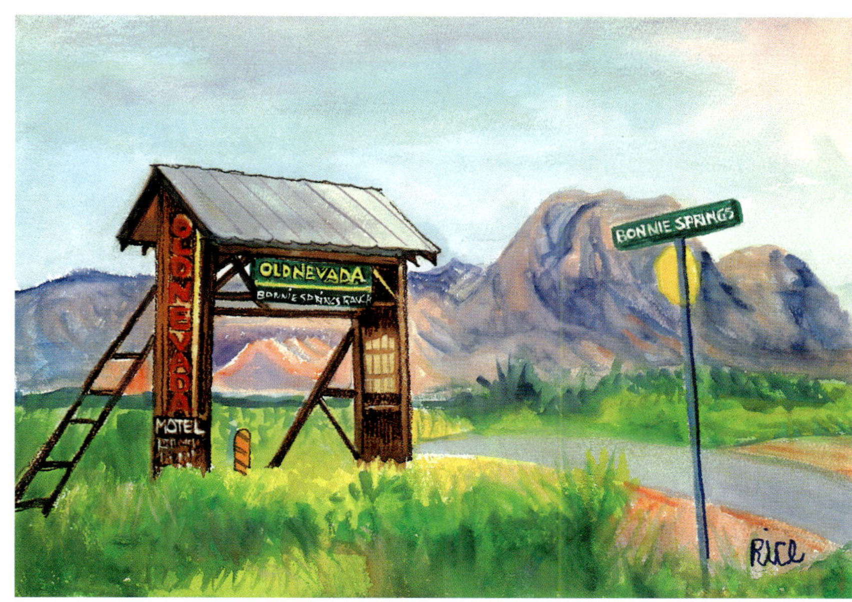

WELCOME TO BONNIE SPRINGS

TELL YOUR FORTUNE?

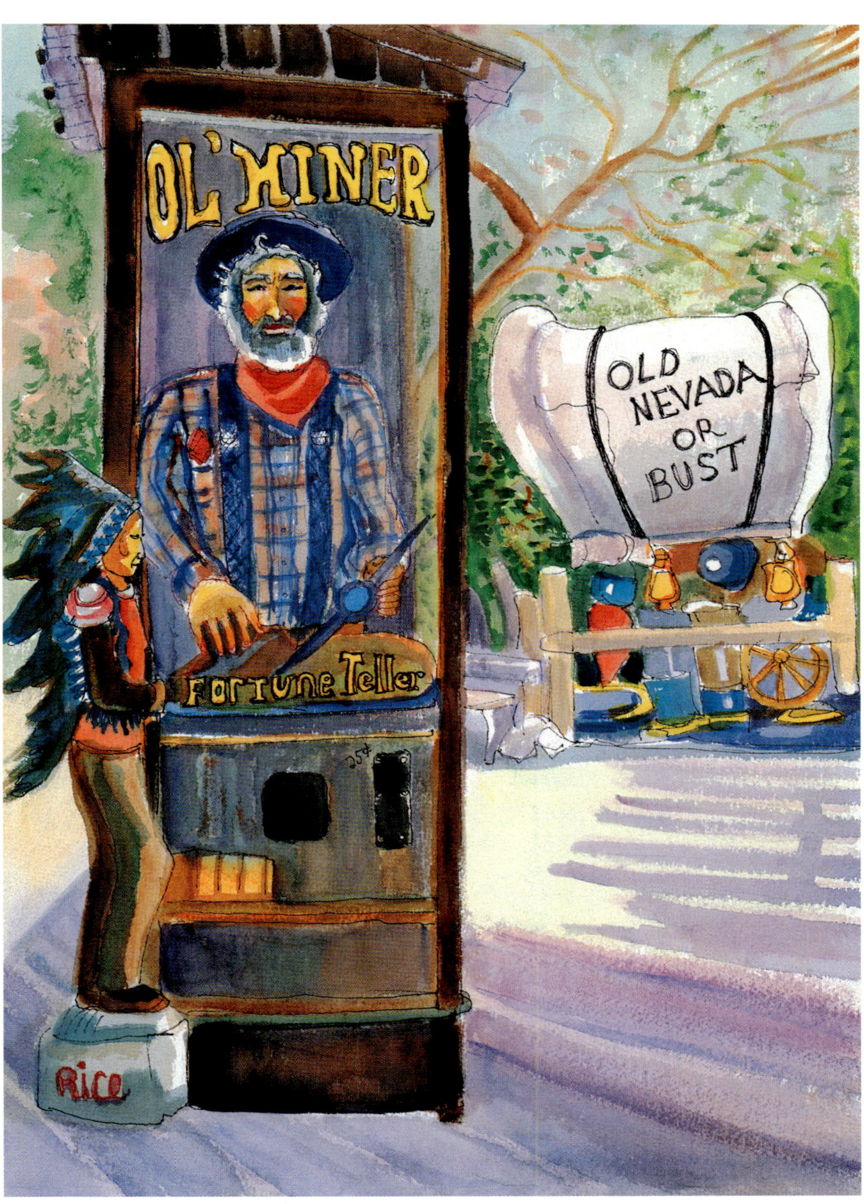

Hoover Dam and Lake Mead

Best known as a vacation spot, the Lake Mead/Hoover Dam region—with 550 miles of shoreline—has eight campgrounds with nearly 1,500 campsites for year-round use, and the 1.3 million acre National Recreation Area, which also includes Lake Mohave. That's in addition to resorts, motels, RV parks and marinas that offer a more pampered, less outdoors-y Great Outdoors feel. You can even rent a houseboat for the full aquatic experience.

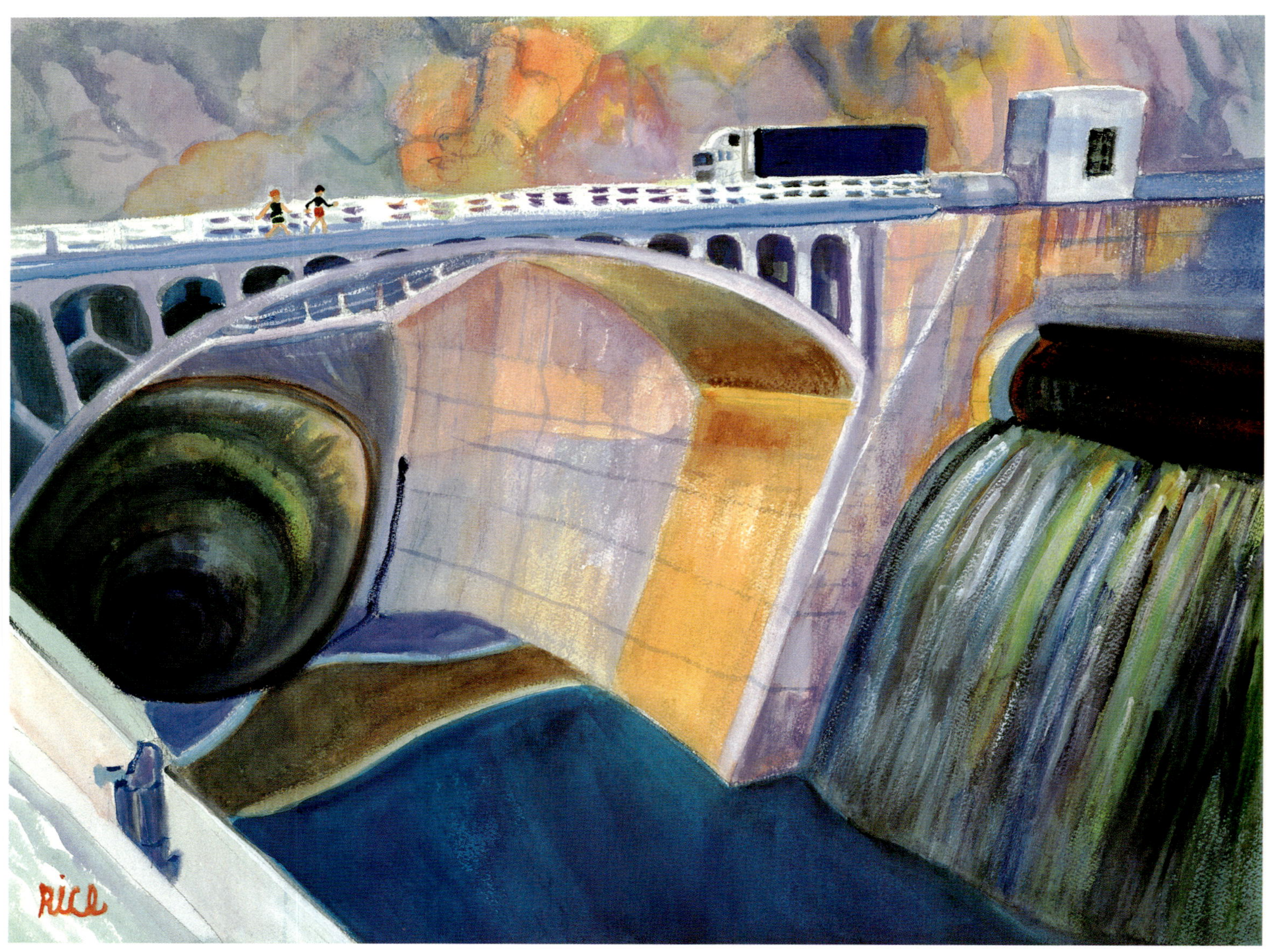

HOOVER DAM

Drive southeast of Las Vegas on U.S. 93 for about 45 minutes and, at the border between Arizona and Nevada, you'll discover the majestic, hydroelectric Hoover Dam. The massive concrete structure supplies the power to light all those neon lights back in town—and that's only 4% of its total output!

HOOVER DAM—AN EPIC ACCOMPLISHMENT >

Hoover Dam remains one of the most awesome and unparalleled engineering feats in history, harnessing the power of the mighty 1,400-mile Colorado River to provide power to homes across the Western U.S. Initially dubbed Boulder Dam—modeled on Indian and Art Deco designs—took years to conceive, approve and prepare to build (including diverting the river), with workers finally tackling the dam itself beginning in 1932. Their arrival, of course, signalled a new period of growth for Las Vegas, just 30 miles away. Lake Mead began to fill by 1935. Boulder Dam was rechristened Hoover Dam in honor of Herbert Hoover, then the Secretary of Commerce, who initiated it in 1929.

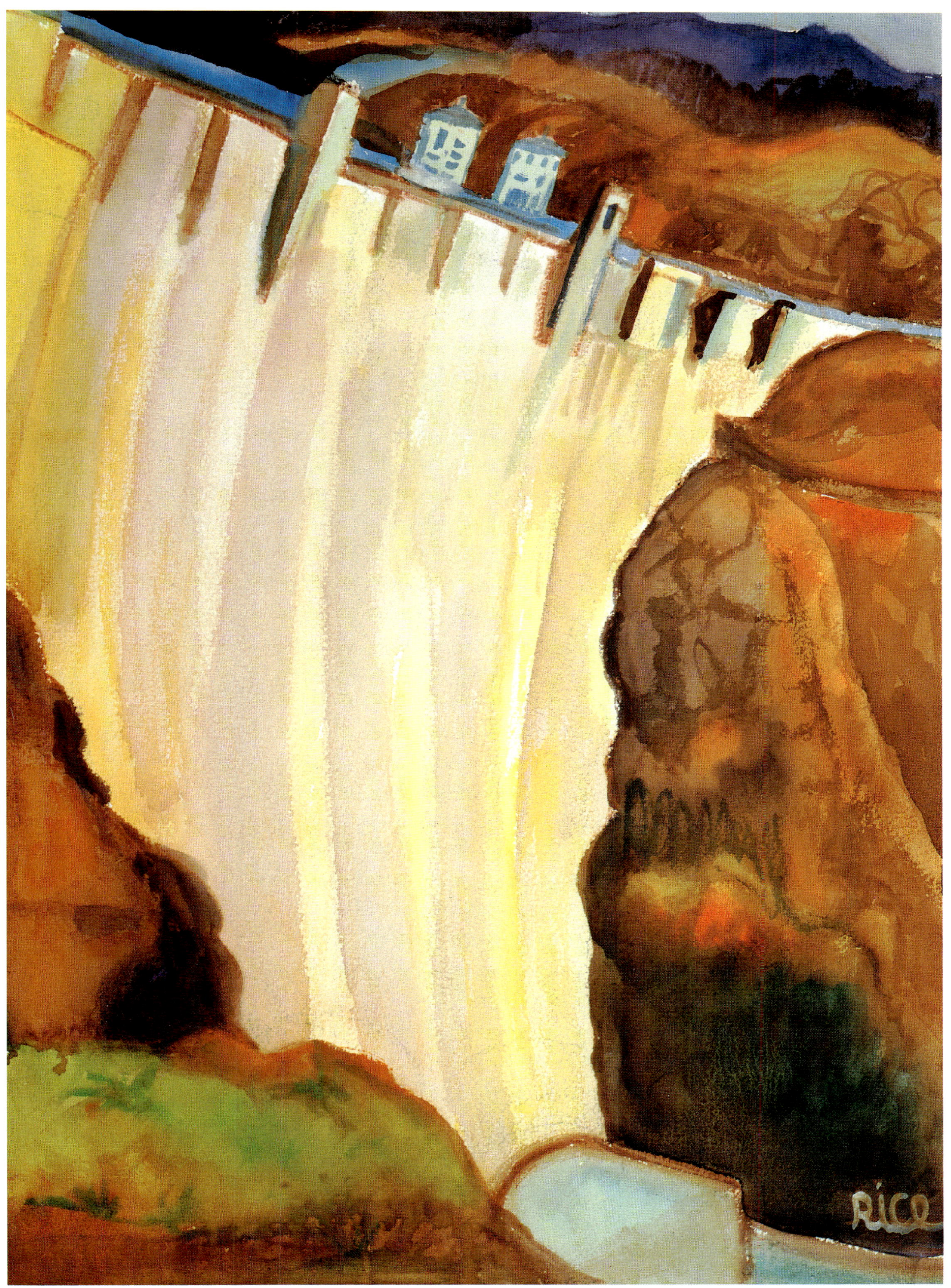
Rice

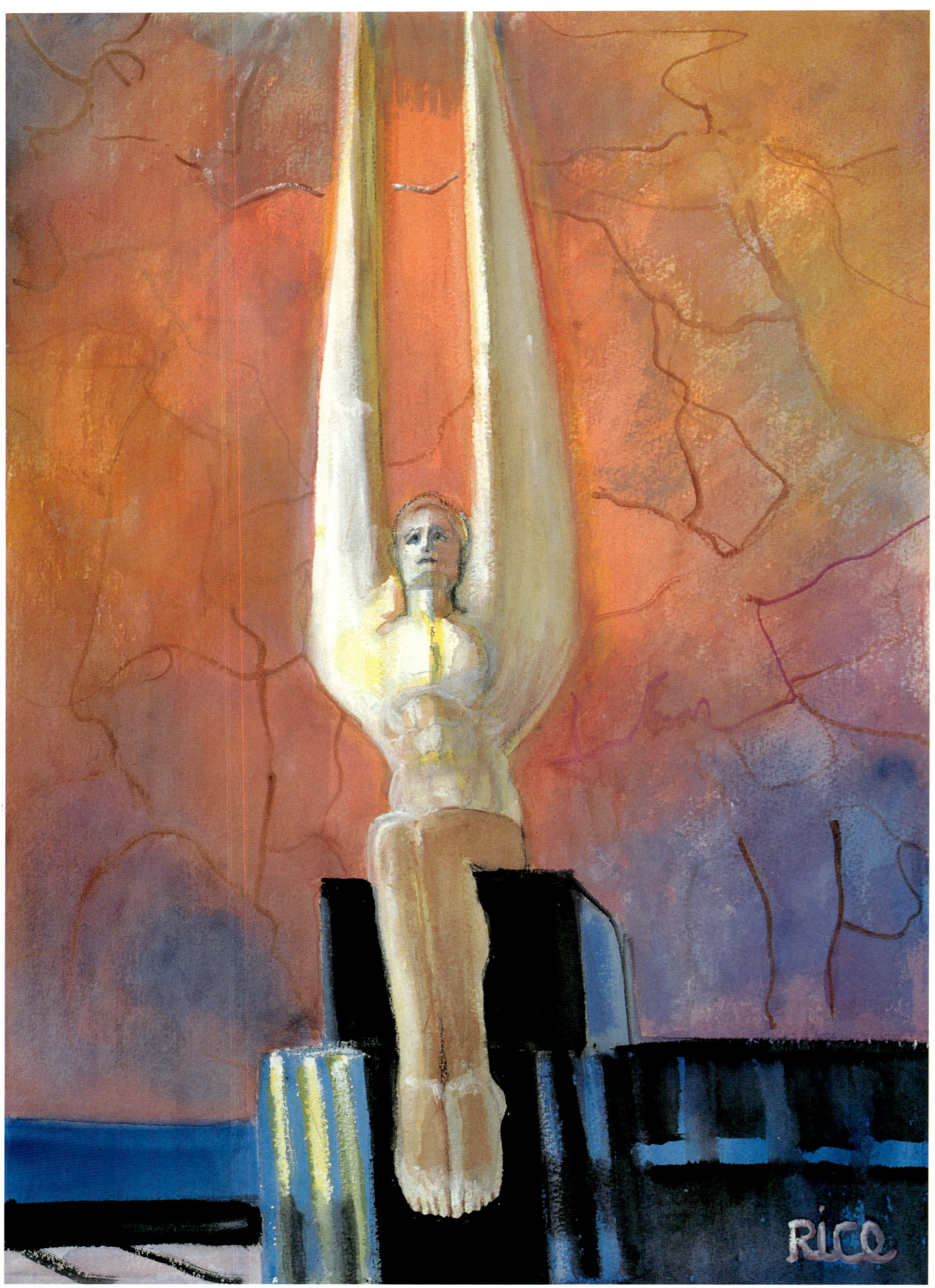
RICO

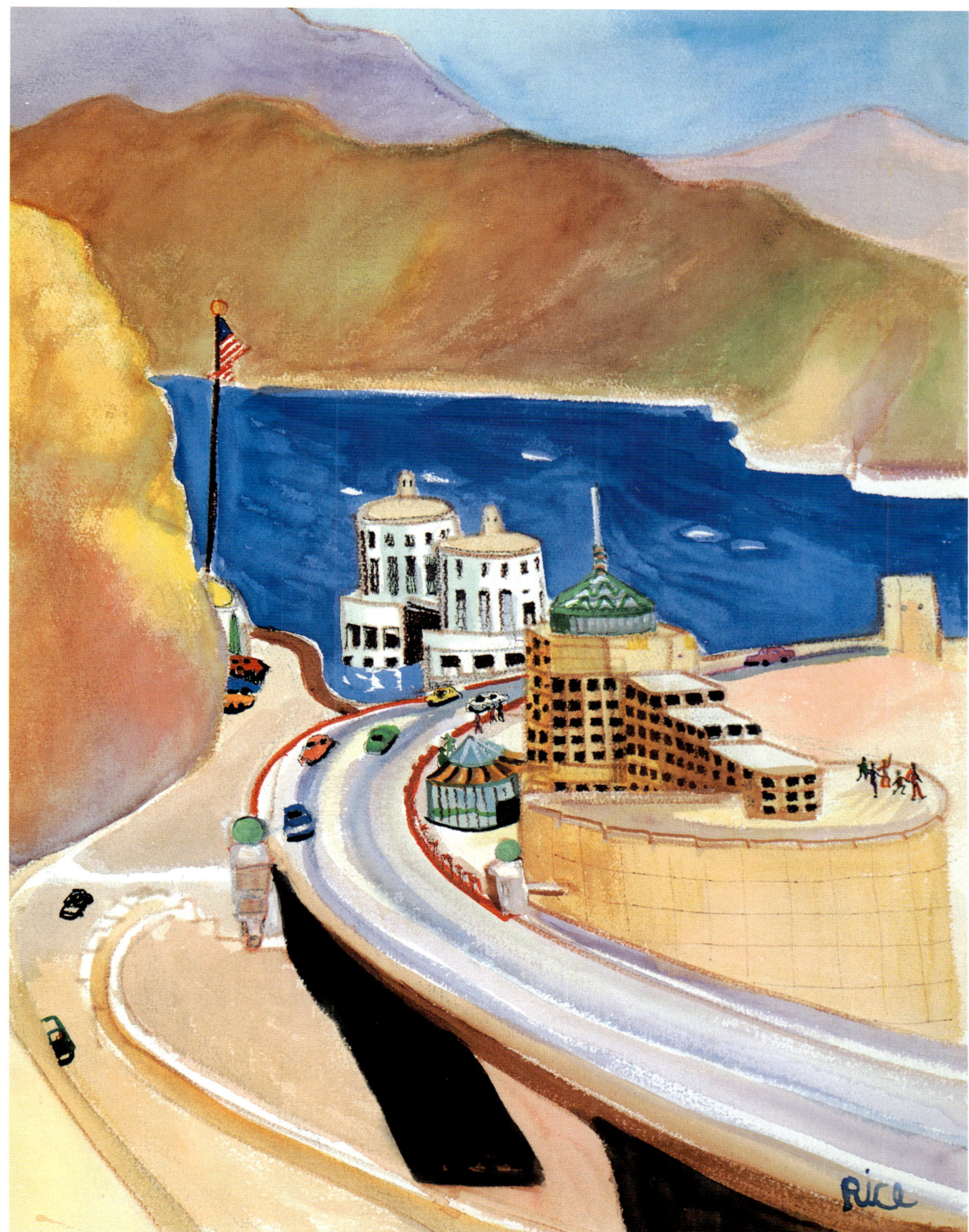

< THE ANGELS OF HOOVER DAM

This is one of a pair of magnificent Art Deco angels which stands permanent guard over Hoover Dam, placed in honor of the daring workers who tragically lost their lives during the construction of this unequaled undertaking, the first of its kind. There were an average of 50 injuries per day, and about 100 of the 5,000 workers over 46 months of construction were killed. The angels, sculpted by Oskar J.W. Hansen, are each 30 feet tall and are made out of four tons of statuary bronze, with bases of diorite. Visitors to the dam are encouraged to rub the feet of the angels for good luck. I did!

THE HOOVER DAM VISITORS CENTER

A dozen years and $120 million in the making, the Hoover Dam Visitors Center opened its doors to tourists in 1995. After you park and don a hardhat, an elevator drops you the equivalent of 53 stories in just over a minute to the bottom of the dam, where you can view its mammoth turbines while a guide fills you in on the dam's vital facts, figures and lore. The Center also has a rotating theater with three 145-seat sections. The towers of the Center provide an excellent opportunity to appreciate this extraordinary structure—and cool down in the hot desert heat!

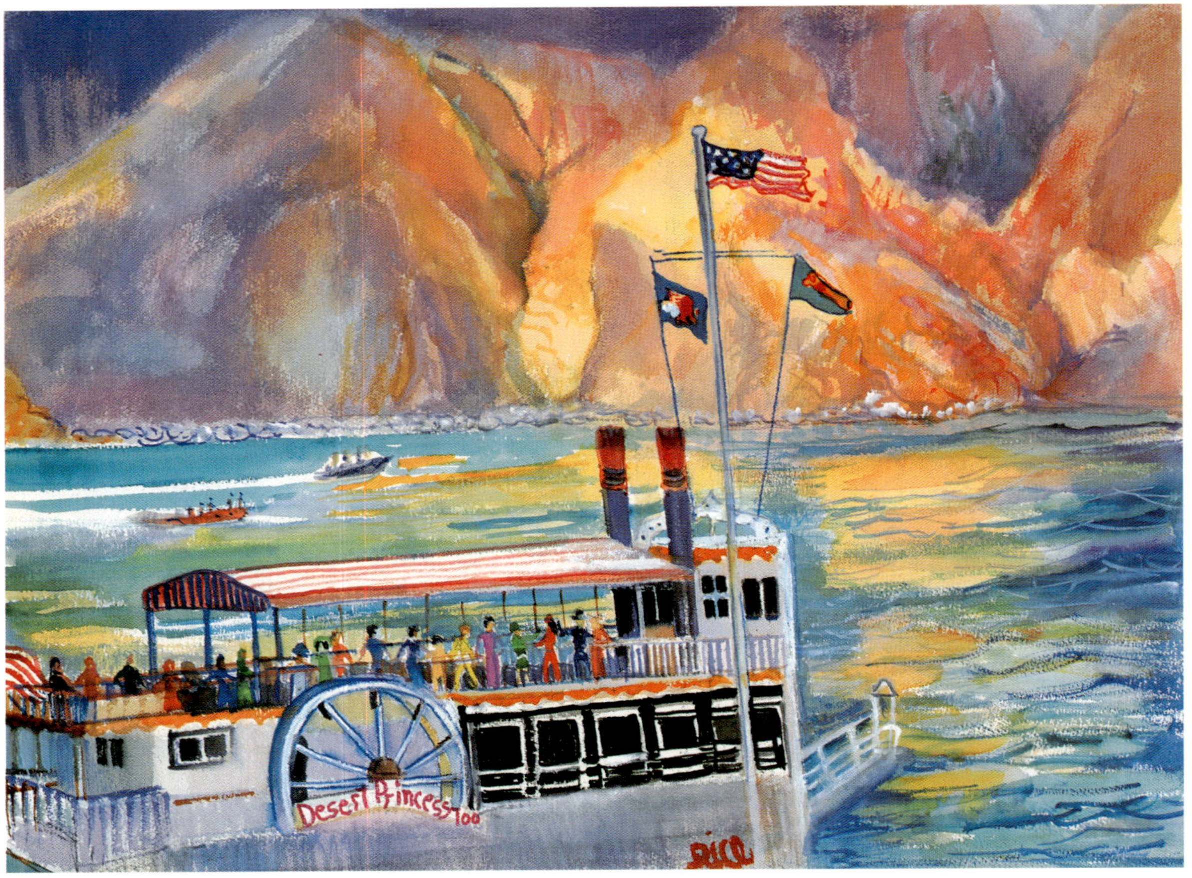

THE DESERT PRINCESS

Come aboard the Desert Princess, a 300-seat paddlewheel boat which offers regular tours of man-made Lake Mead. You can enjoy the trip from inside in perfect comfort (including dining, buffet and even dancing), or venture to the promenade deck for the full wind-and-spray experience.

FISHING ON LAKE MEAD

Several anglers try their luck away from the casinos, casting for the catch of the day on Lake Mead. The lake has an abundance of fish, including catfish, bluegill, trout, crappie and striped bass—some of which have tipped the scales at over 30 pounds.

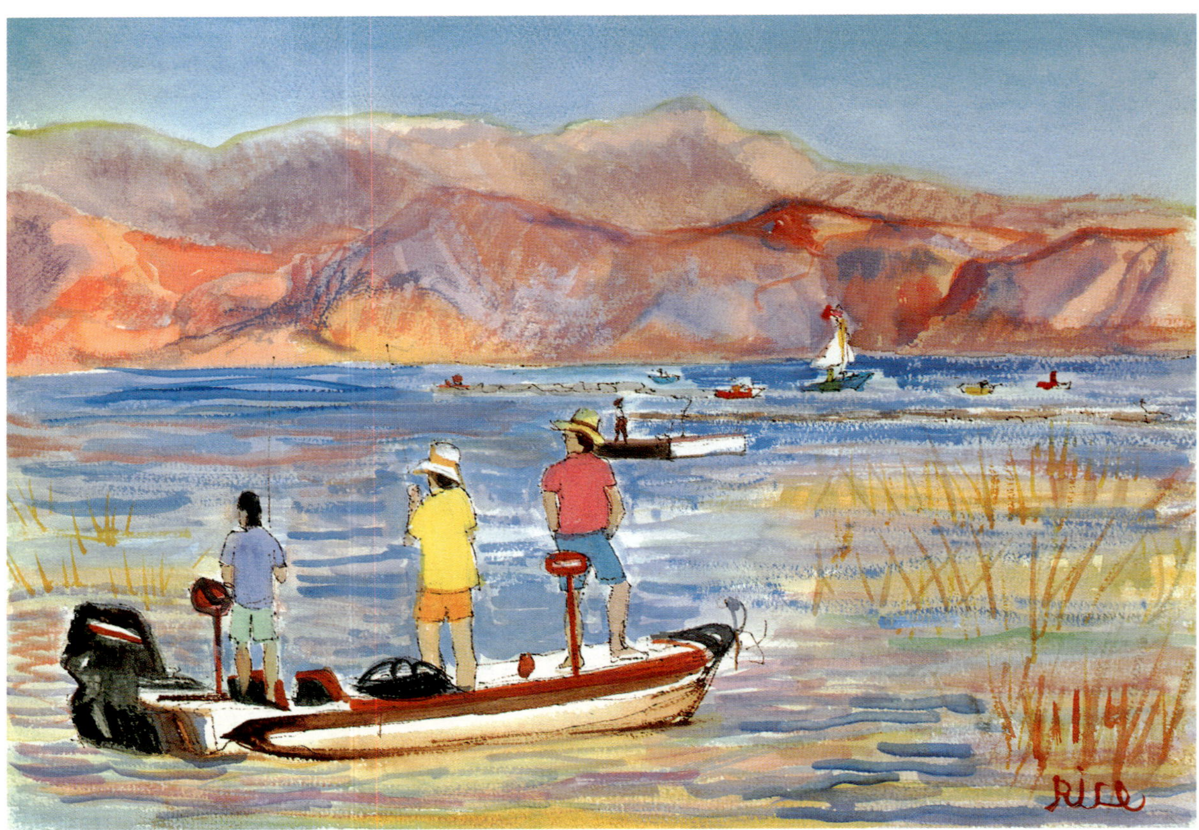

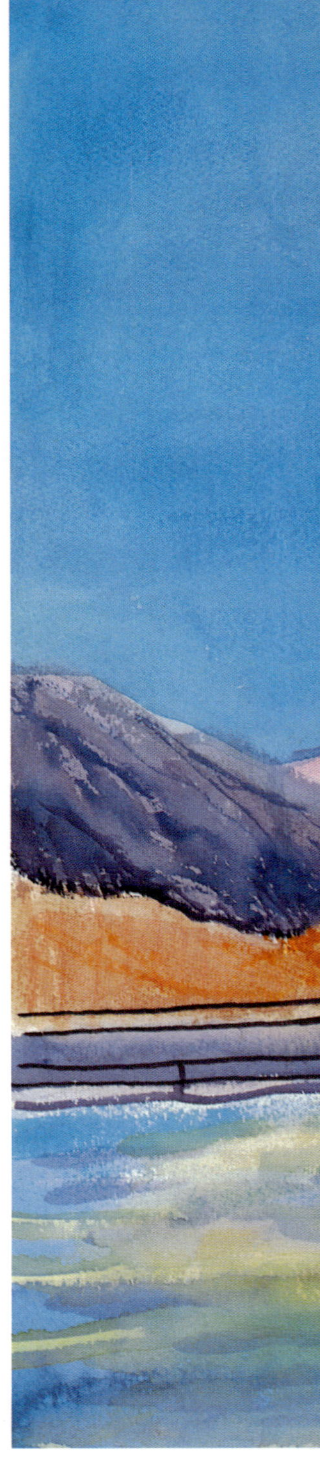

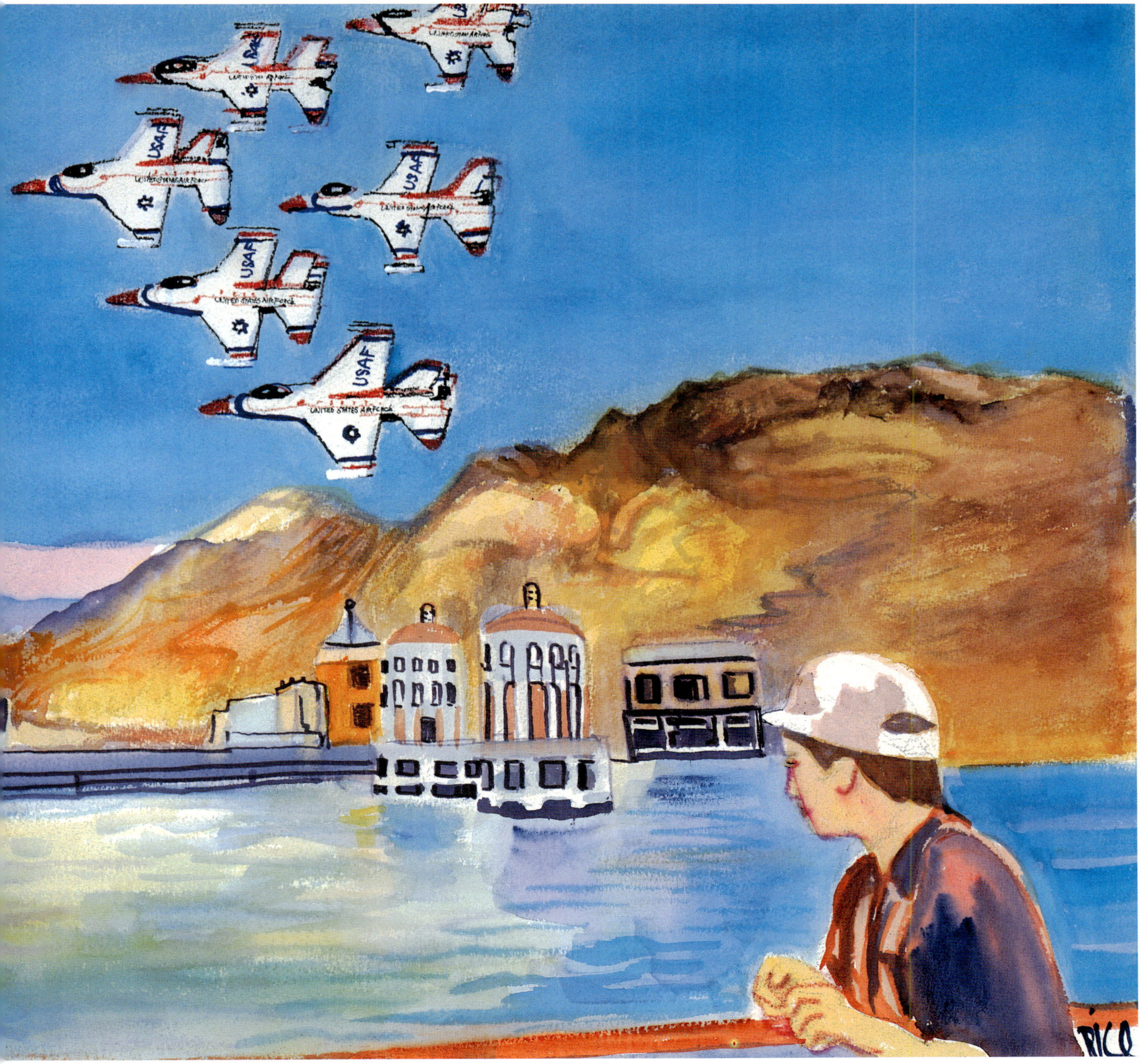

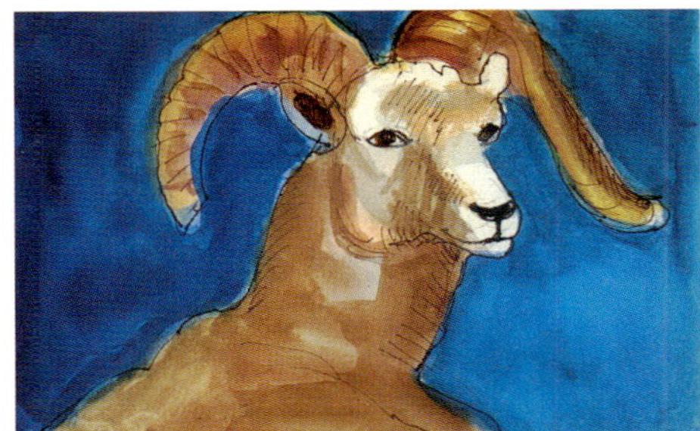

SPOTTING THE BIG HORN SHEEP

FLYING IN FORMATION

Six fighter jets from Nellis Air Force Base fly in precision formation above the Lake Mead side of Hoover Dam. In 1941, the mayor of Las Vegas signed over a dirt runway, a small operations shack and a water well eight miles north of town to the Army Quartermaster. Because flight weather here was near-perfect year-round, the Las Vegas Army Air Field was established as a combat school for aerial gunners. At the height of World War II, 600 gunnery students and 215 co-pilots graduated every five weeks. The influx of military personnel and their families caused a major boom in the local population.

In 1950, the base was rechristened in memory of William Harrell Nellis, a decorated fighter pilot shot down over Belgium in WW II. After the War, the base was reopened under the command of the newly-formed U.S. Air Force, and the training program shifted to jet fighters. Nellis AFB was also involved in nuclear testing, during which locals watched atomic mushroom clouds rise from what they thought was a safe distance, 70 miles away. Today, Nellis is the biggest Air Force base in the nation, home to the most demanding, advanced air combat training in the world. Virtually every type of combat aircraft from every branch of the military (as well as aircraft from allied nations) is flown here and the top aviators hone their skills to perfection.

Boulder City

Boulder City—which overlooks Lake Mead—was originally established for the workers who built Hoover Dam in the 1930s. The largest city in Nevada with approximately 200 square miles of territory, it's an unconventional residential community—gambling is illegal!—with strict growth controls.

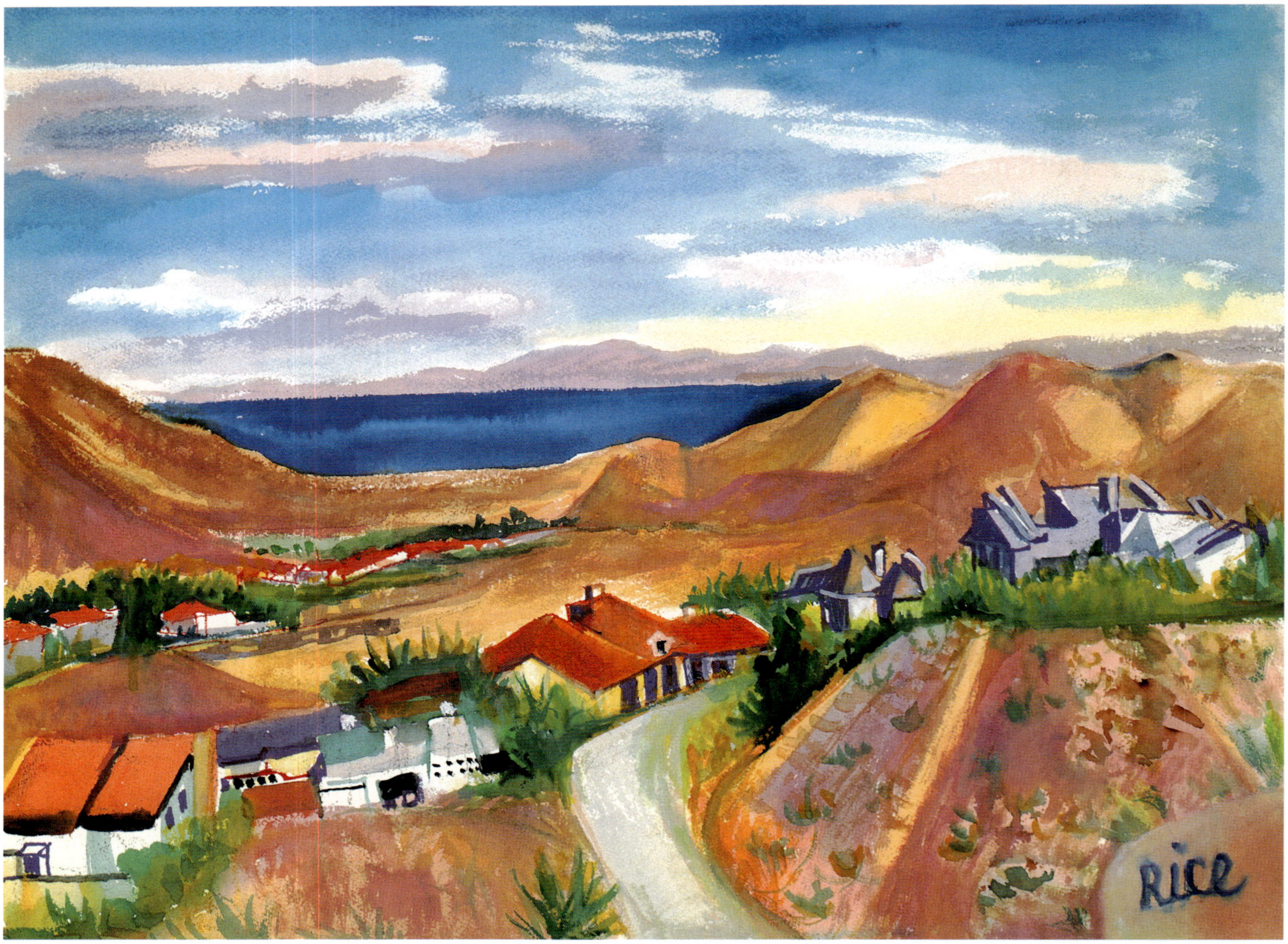

BOULDER CITY VIEW WITH LAKE MEAD

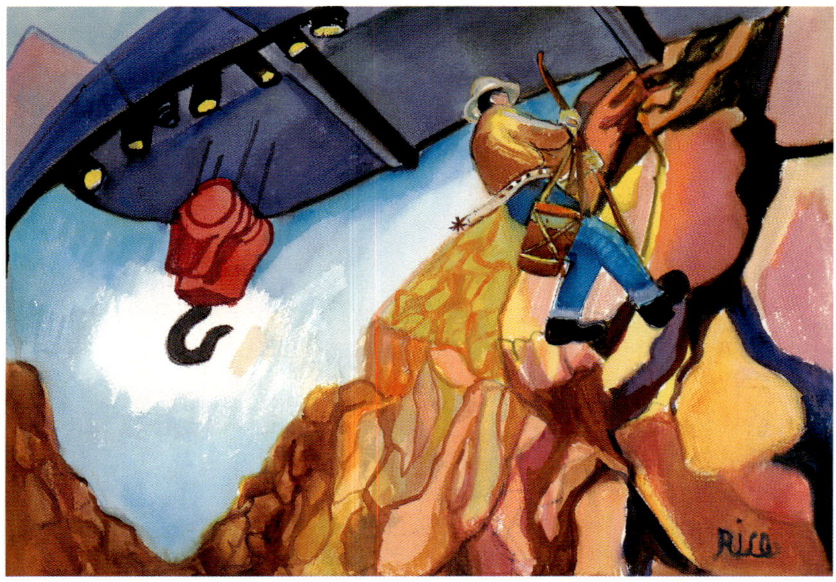

THE BOULDER CITY/ HOOVER DAM MUSEUM

The remarkable 3-D exhibit at the Boulder City/Hoover Dam Museum depicts the efforts of the workers who not only built the mighty dam, but also forged a community alongside it. The museum features interactive displays, an extensive archival library, a movie about the dam's construction and a gift shop featuring items like the "Dam Wear" line of clothing. It opened in 1998 inside the city's most famous historic landmark, the Boulder Dam Hotel on Arizona Street—a Colonial Revival-style building built in 1933. Once a popular hideaway for the elite, the hotel's former guests include Henry Fonda, Bette Davis, James Cagney, Cornelius Vanderbilt, the Shah of Iran and Margaret Bourke-White.

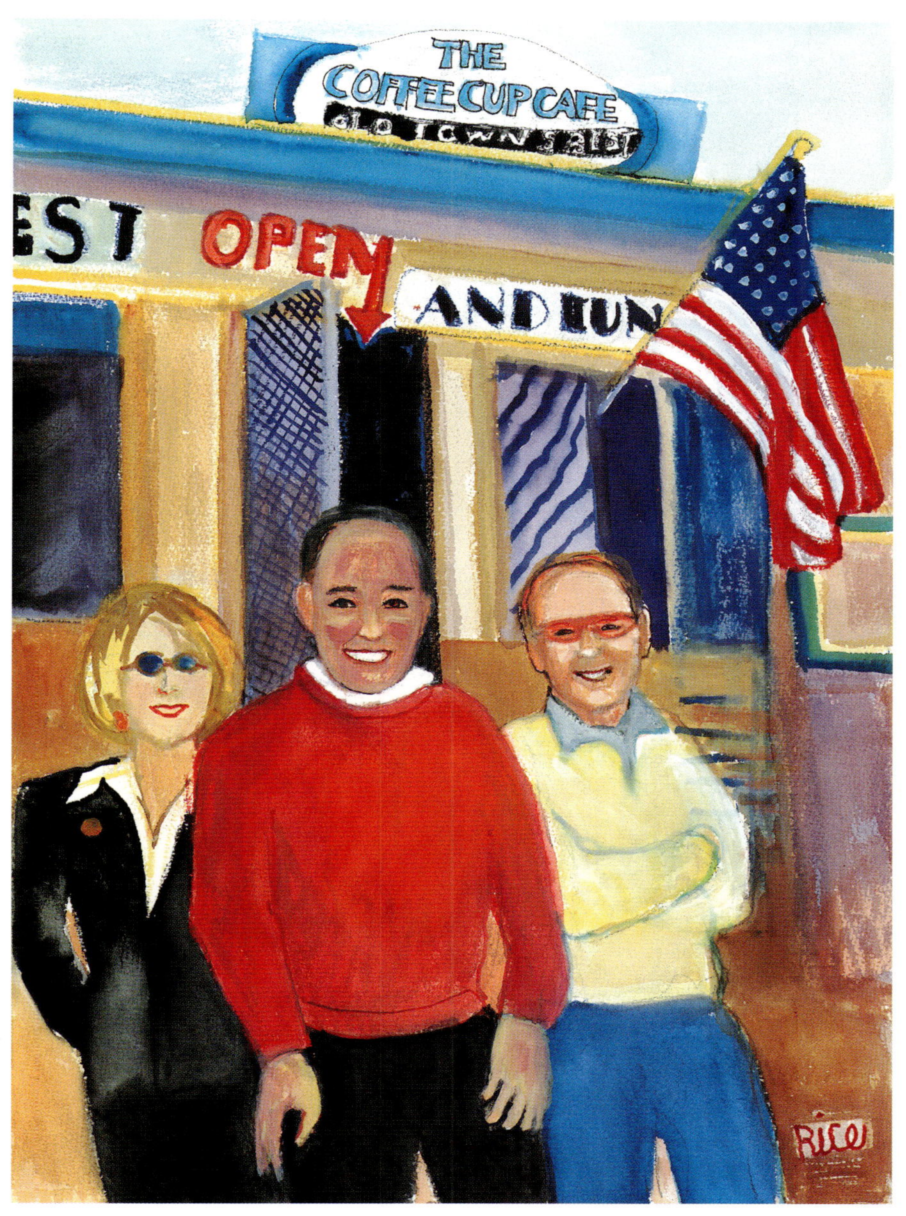

MAYOR BOB FERRARO OUTSIDE THE COFFEE CUP CAFE

Boulder City is a charming place, and its mayor, Bob Ferraro, has an equally charming personality. A familiar force on the local political scene since 1976, the three-time mayor has frequently been honored around the state (as president of the Nevada League of Cities and Nevada Public Official of the Year, among others). Bob is also an author and expert on antique and historic bottles. I met him and his constituents, Linda Faiss and Skogie Lenon, at the '50s style Coffee Cup Cafe.

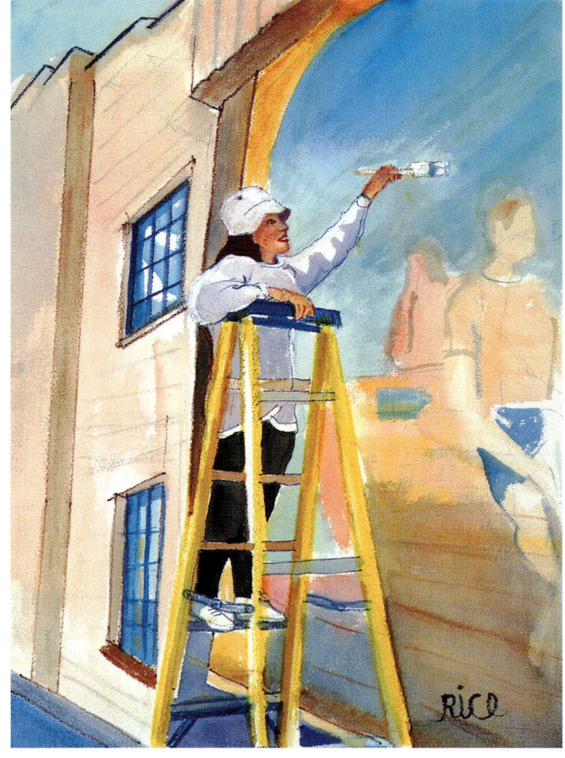

CONNIE BURNETT-FERRARO PAINTS THE TOWN

I don't know if it's due to her role as the "First Lady" of Boulder City (she's the Mayor's wife) or her natural artistic talents, but Connie Burnett-Ferraro takes beautifying Boulder City seriously. I caught her creating one of her murals depicting the city's early days, which appear on walls all over town. I discovered we have a lot in common: she also hails from New York City; her father was an artist; she performed on Broadway and in television (as a dancer); and, she studied art at NYC's Art Students League. She's found happiness in Boulder City and given it back with the gift of her art.

Lake Las Vegas

Nestled outside Henderson on the largest artificial lake in Nevada (320 acres, with ten miles of shoreline), Lake Las Vegas is a burgeoning resort development. Already home to world-class hotels, casinos, health spas and golf courses, Lake Las Vegas will soon have more high-end retail, luxury office space and gaming operations. The South Shore is being developed for residential use, while the North Shore will be a public playland.

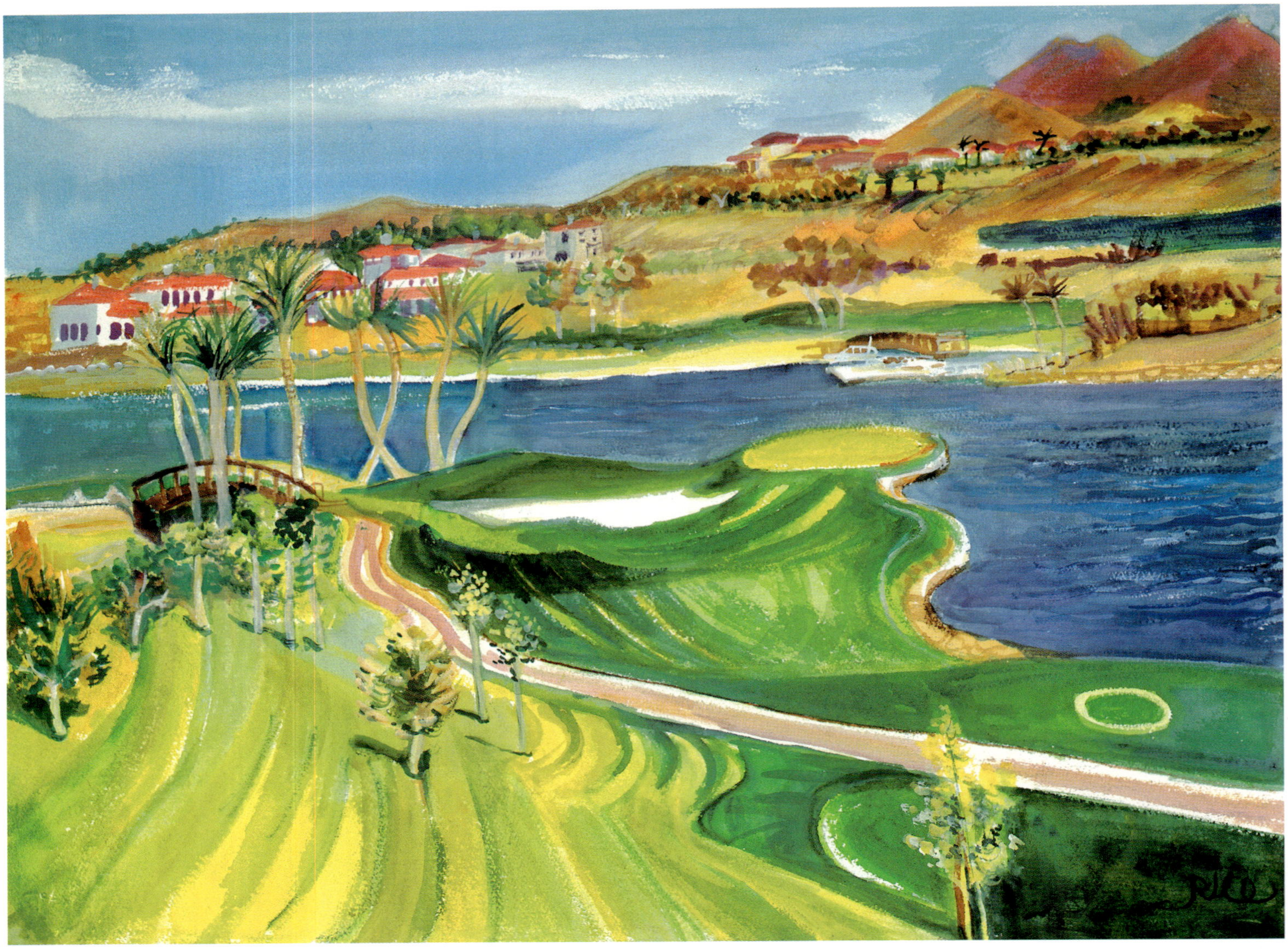

REFLECTION BAY GOLF CLUB

I was enchanted by this 7,261-yard, championship golf course at Lake Las Vegas Resort, designed by legendary PGA champion Jack Nicklaus. The par 72 course features dramatic vistas, with the last five holes spread on a mile and a half of scenic shoreline along the lake. Reflection Bay has served as home to the Wendy's Three Tour Challenge.

THE HYATT REGENCY LAKE LAS VEGAS RESORT

The Moroccan-themed Hyatt Regency resort brings Strip-style extravagance to scenic Lake Las Vegas. Among its upscale features are the 18-hole Jack Nicklaus-designed golf course, a European-style casino, fine dining, the full-service Spa Moulay and lake activities. The shoreline features an ever-increasing assortment of condominiums.

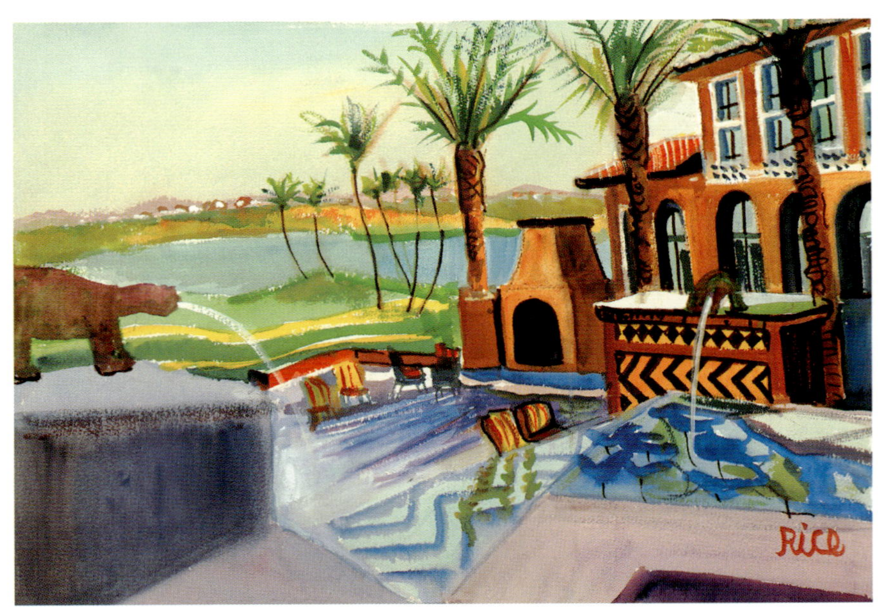

Mount Charleston

The Alpine beauty and cooler climate of Mount Charleston 40 minutes north of Las Vegas has lured many new residents enticed by its rustic lifestyle. While a dramatic change of pace from the city, Mount Charleston is home to resorts with all kinds of luxurious amenities, and is a haven for hikers, campers and horseback riders, as well as for snow lovers in the winter.

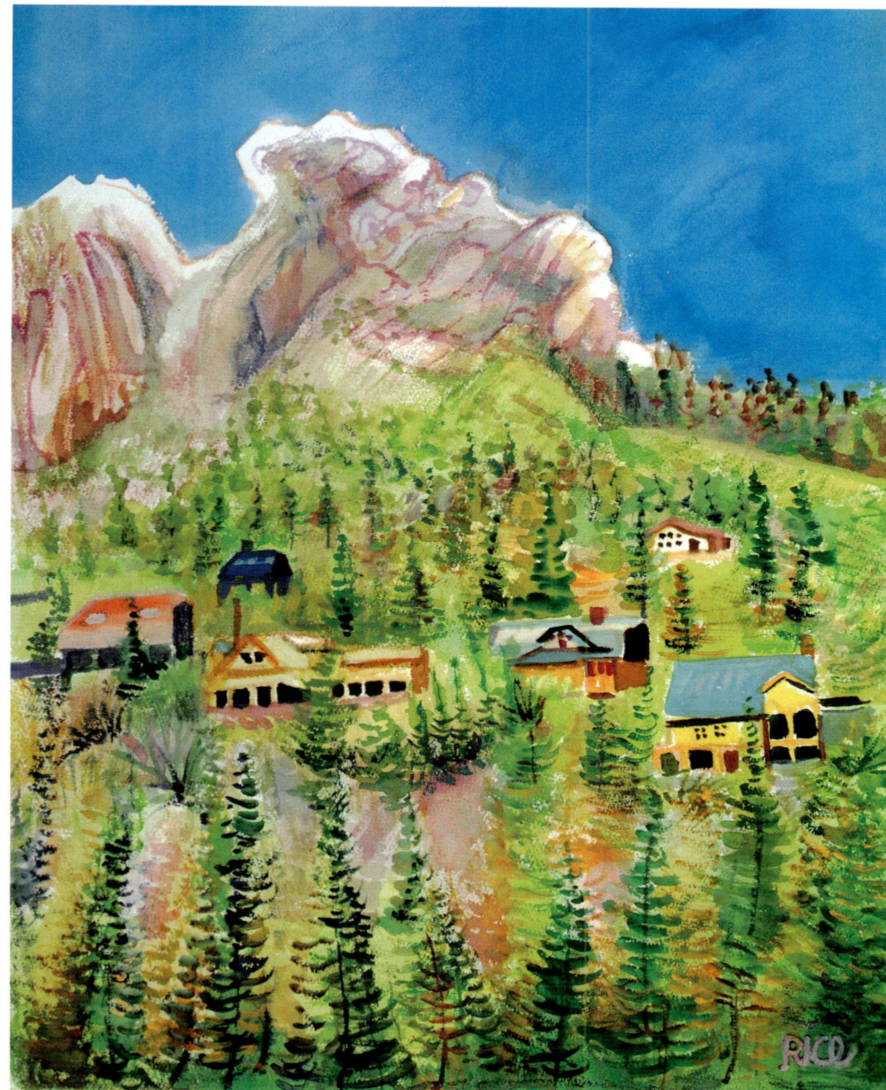

MT. CHARLESTON IN THE SPRING

The scenic peaks of Mt. Charleston offer a picturesque getaway, with six campgrounds open from May to mid-September. It's also a popular place for hiking, with a multitude of trails through the ponderosa pine and white fir forest. Best of all, you can escape the desert heat: temperatures rarely rise above 80 degrees and drops sharply after sunset.

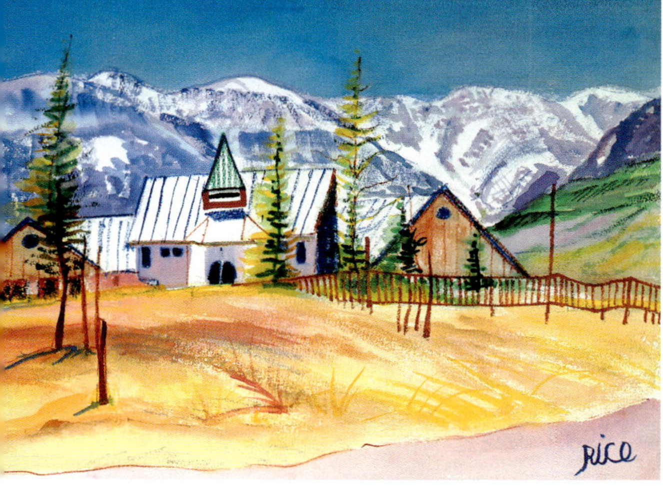

THE THAW

This Nevada scene looks almost Alpine as the snow slowly recedes from Mt. Charleston.

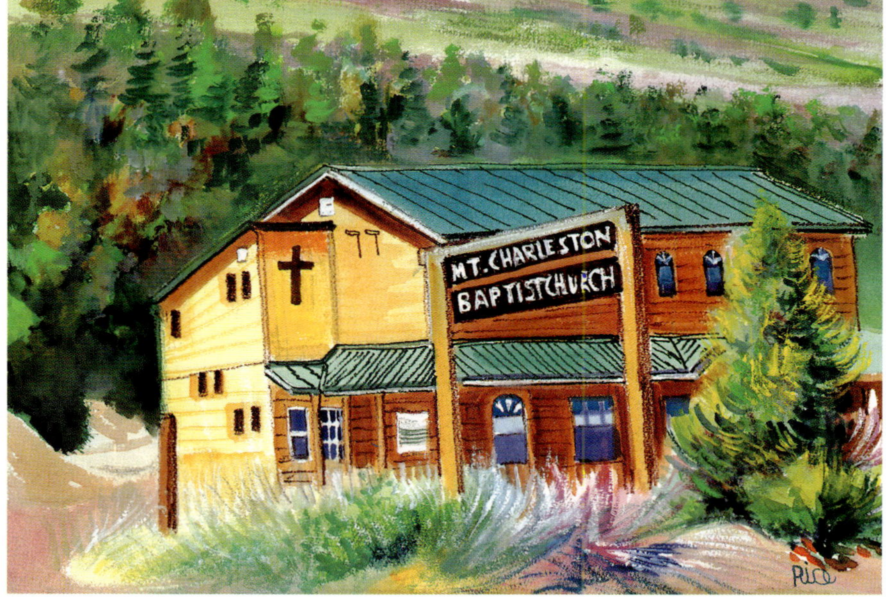

MT. CHARLESTON BAPTIST CHURCH

Where better to commune with a higher spiritual power than amid the natural splendor of Mt. Charleston?

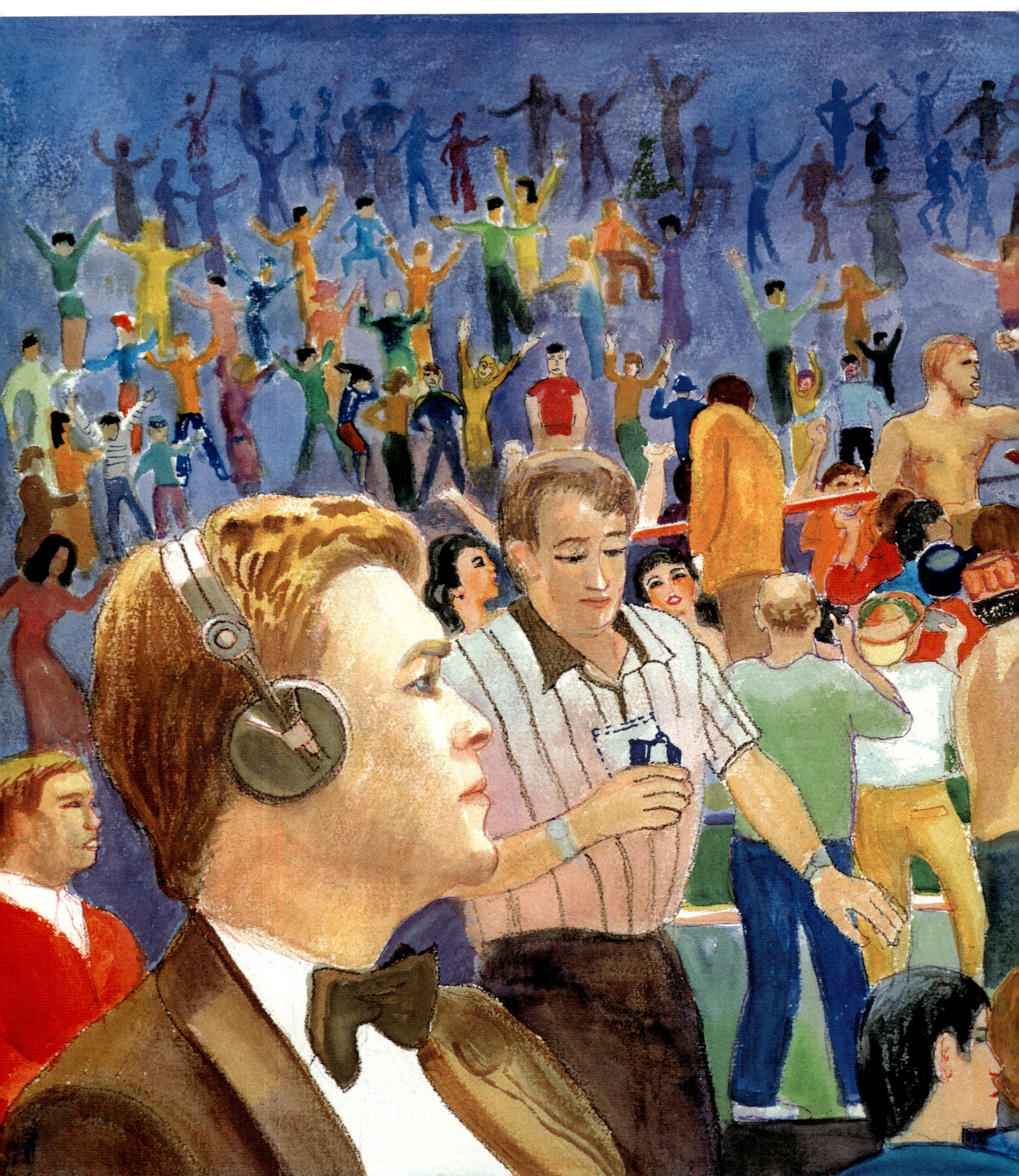

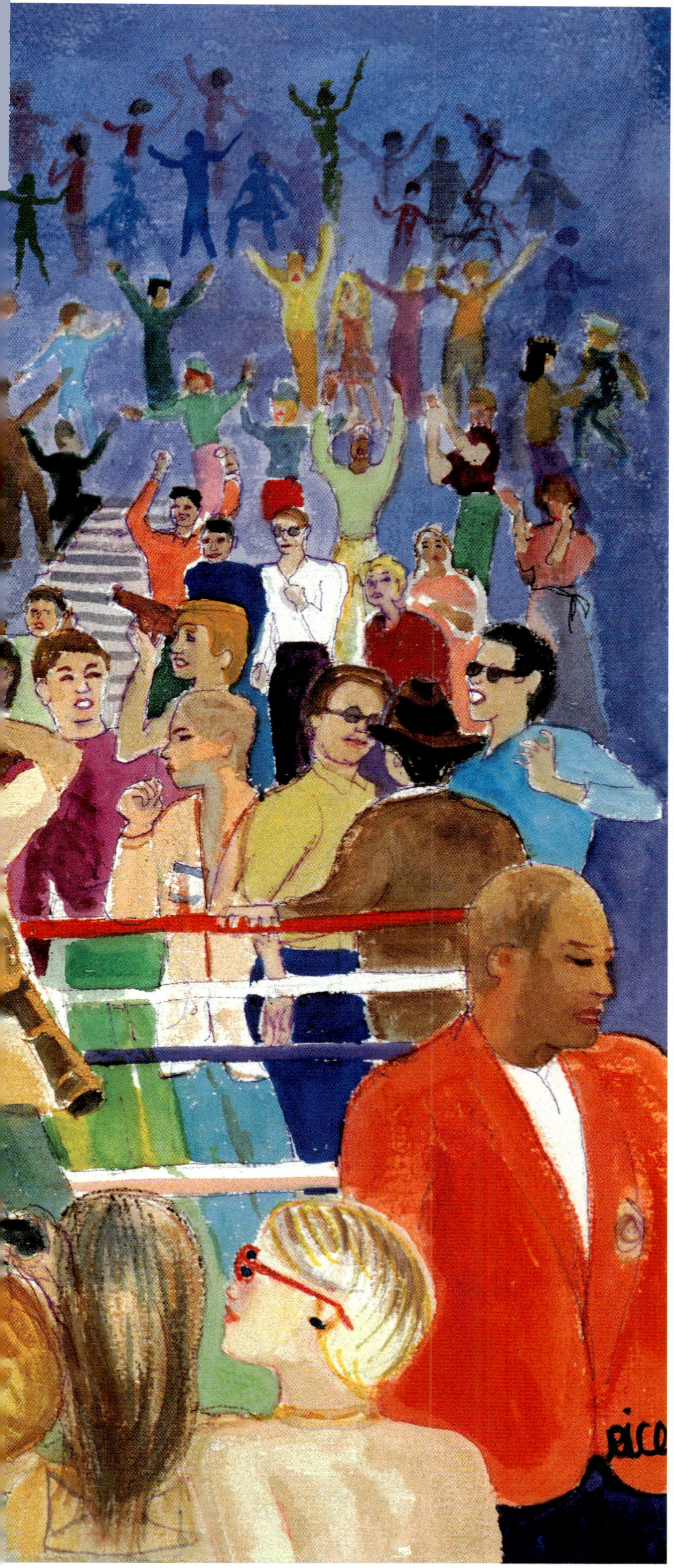

SPORTS & GAMES

GAMING HAS ALWAYS BEEN synonymous with Las Vegas and, today, inside the casinos, you can find action there beyond traditional games of chance. More and more people are visiting not just to play poker or gawk at the neon, but to watch or play in virtually every kind of professional, amateur and just-for-fun competition you can imagine. From championship boxing bouts to PGA golf tournaments; auto racing; UNLV teams; professional bodybuilding; country club tennis; family ice skating; outdoors adventures; bowling inside a hotel-casino, and more—Las Vegas has it all. Even some of the exciting hotel-casino attractions and shows require incredible athletic skill—and with the booming population, I imagine professional sports franchises can't be too far in the future. Forget "Sin City." Today's Las Vegas is truly "Fun City."

JIM LAMPLEY CALLS THE FIGHT

In a crowd full of fans of "the sweet science," as boxing is known, few people can claim to have heard or seen more about the sport than broadcaster Jim Lampley, master commentator for both HBO and TVKO. In 13 years, he's announced more than 300 championship bouts. Jim began his national television career in 1974 with ABC Sports, covering a wide variety of athletic competitions. At NBC Sports, he hosted golf, NFL and Olympic coverage—and covered more Olympic Games than anyone else. Since coming to HBO and its "Realsports" series, Jim's taken home a trio of Emmys and his production company has produced feature essays for the cable network's boxing telecasts. His wife Bree and he are Californians, but Las Vegas has become their second home. Whenever a major bout is on, you can bet Jim will be there—like this one I watched ringside at Mandalay Bay, in which the aggressive, determined 22-year-old fighter Fernando Vargas successfully defended his IFB Junior Middleweight title against Ike "Bazooka" Quartey.

HBO'S KNOCKOUT TRIO

Nobody calls a boxing match better than the ringmasters of HBO: former heavyweight champ George Foreman, Jim Lampley and Larry Merchant. Together to cover a championship bout at the Mandalay Bay, these three know the fight game inside and out.

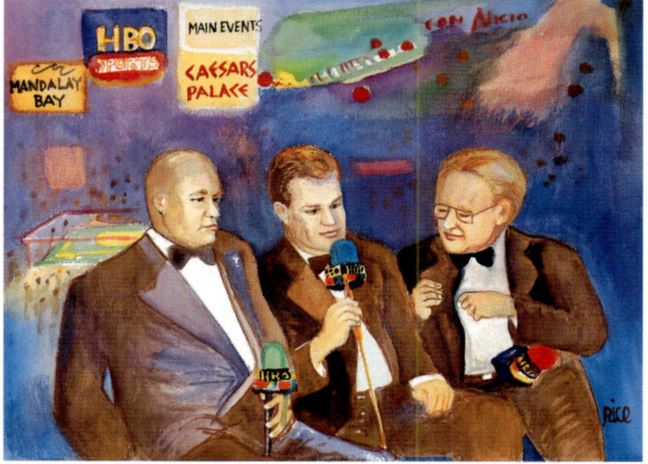

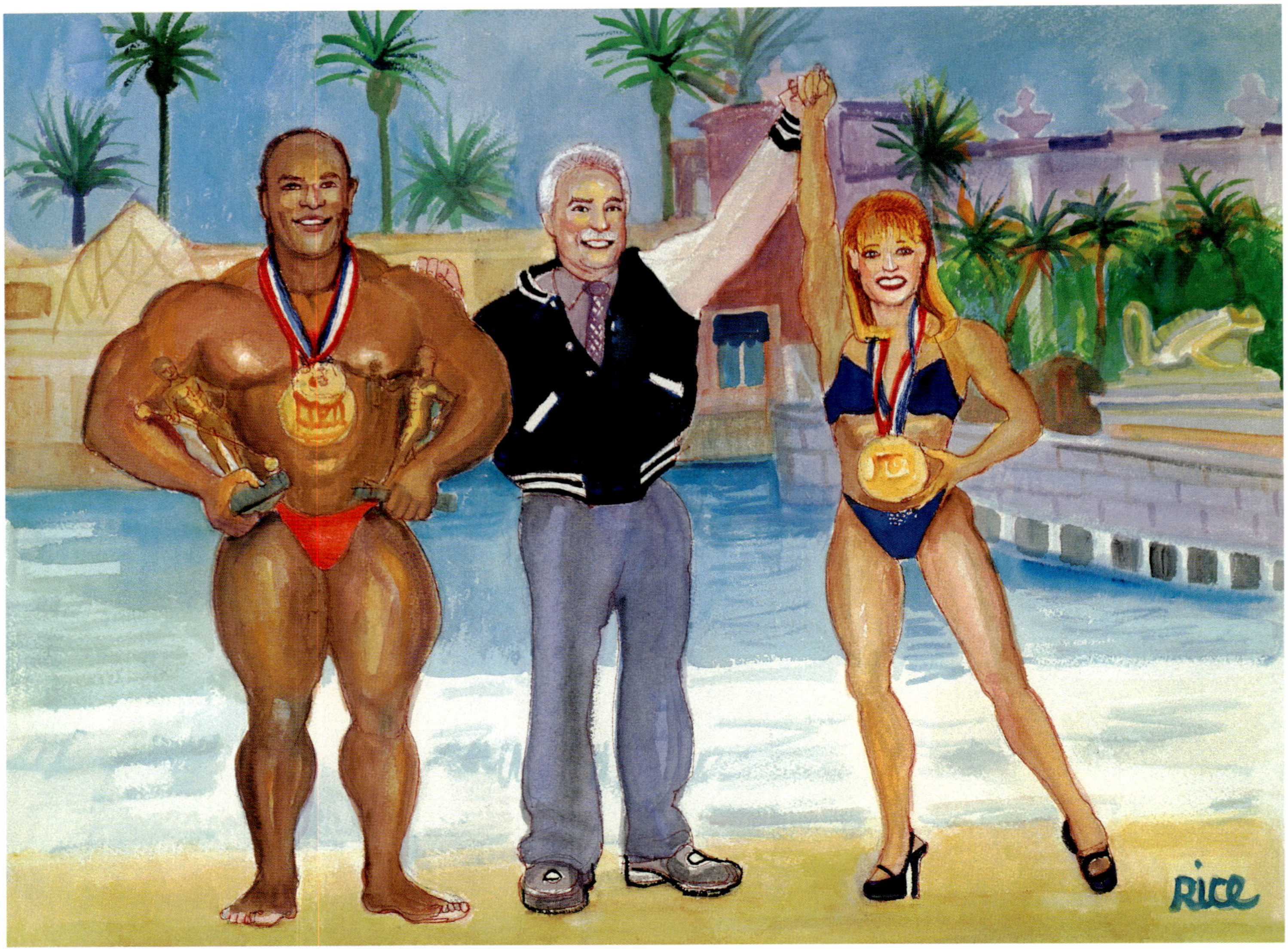

BODIES BEAUTIFUL

Three-time (1998-2000) Mr. Olympia, Ronnie Coleman, and 1999 Fitness Olympia champion, Mary Yockey, joined famed fitness publisher, Joe Weider, for the annual Olympia Weekend at Mandalay Bay's "Muscle Beach." The hotel used its famous sand beach equipment and displays for the International Federation of Body Builders' top professional competition—the "Superbowl" of fitness enthusiasts—which drew almost 5,000 spectators. Ronnie is a full-time police officer in Texas and Mary is a former real estate agent from Colorado. As the creator of the Mr. Olympia contest (Arnold Schwarzenegger is a former title holder), Joe is an award-winning pioneer in promoting professional bodybuilding for a mass audience. He's a strong advocate of alternative health care, and he oversees a publishing empire which includes Flex, Muscle & Fitness, Men's Fitness, Shape, Fit Pregnancy, Natural Health and Jump.

VROOM!

I trekked to the Las Vegas Motor Speedway to watch the city's All-Harley-Davidson Drag Race, where motorcycle enthusiasts from all over, like Lee and Mac Perry of All-American Motorcycle Co., convened for the premiere event in Harley racing. The goal, simply put, is to win the quarter mile race by being the fastest on the track, with speeds exceeding 200 mph.

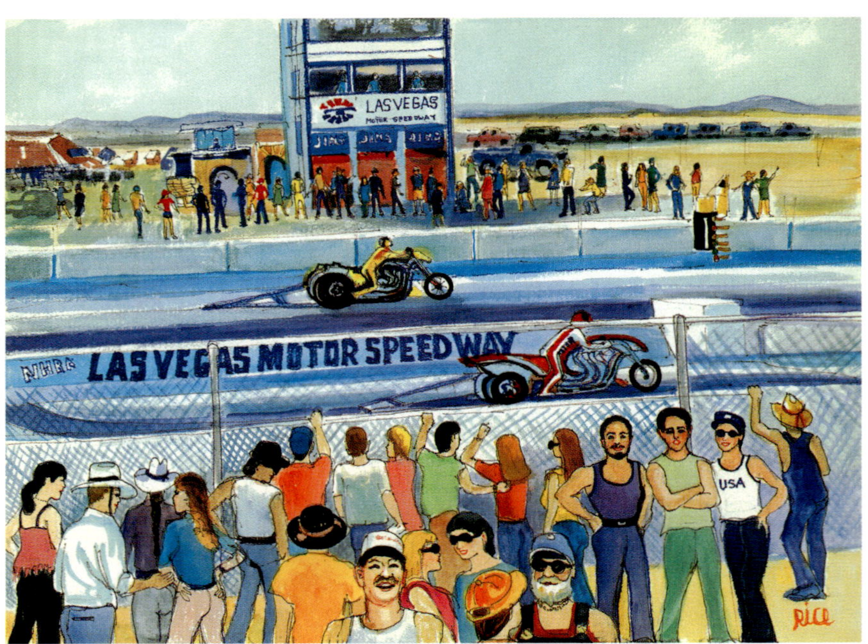

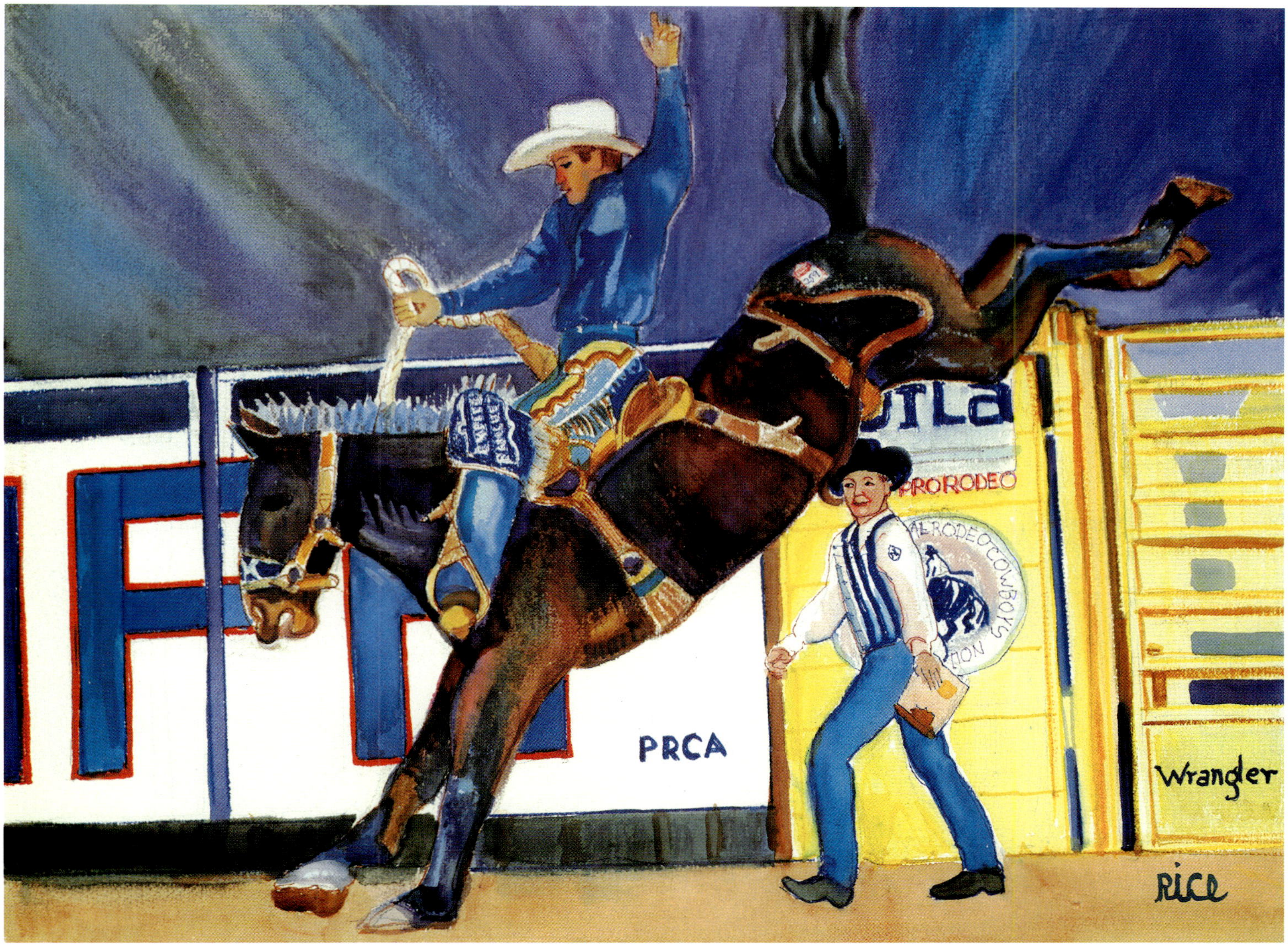

RIDIN' AT THE RODEO

Champion rodeo cowboy Billy Etbauer holds on tight as he takes a wild ride on a bucking bronco at the National Rodeo Finals at the Thomas & Mack Center. Members of the Professional Rodeo Cowboys Association compete each year, testing their roping and riding skills. Billy, who hails from Edmond, Oklahoma, won the world saddle bronco riding title in 1992, 1996 and again after this ride in 1999, taking home a championship belt buckle and a sizable cash prize.

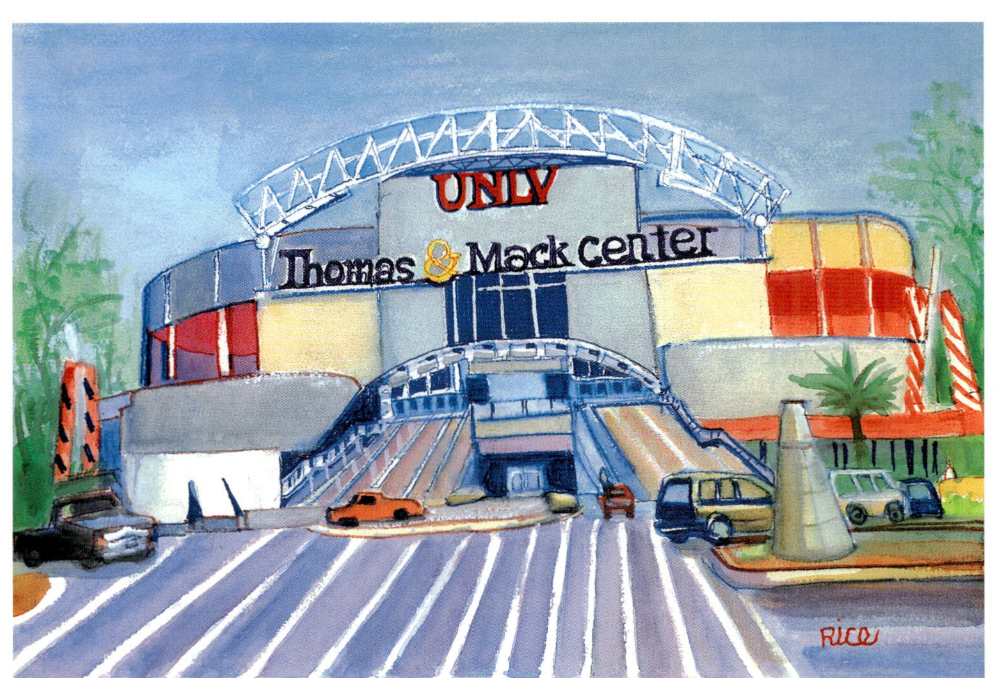

THE THOMAS & MACK CENTER

Originally opened in 1983 on the campus of the University of Nevada, Las Vegas, the Thomas & Mack Center has for years served as the home for the Runnin' Rebels basketball team, as well as the site of the National Rodeo Finals and sell-out concerts featuring the likes of Garth Brooks, Celine Dion and the Spice Girls. A recent renovation added more ticket booths, increased the comfort of the seating, upgraded the amenities like fun zones and food courts, and made room for the UNLV Sports Hall of Fame.

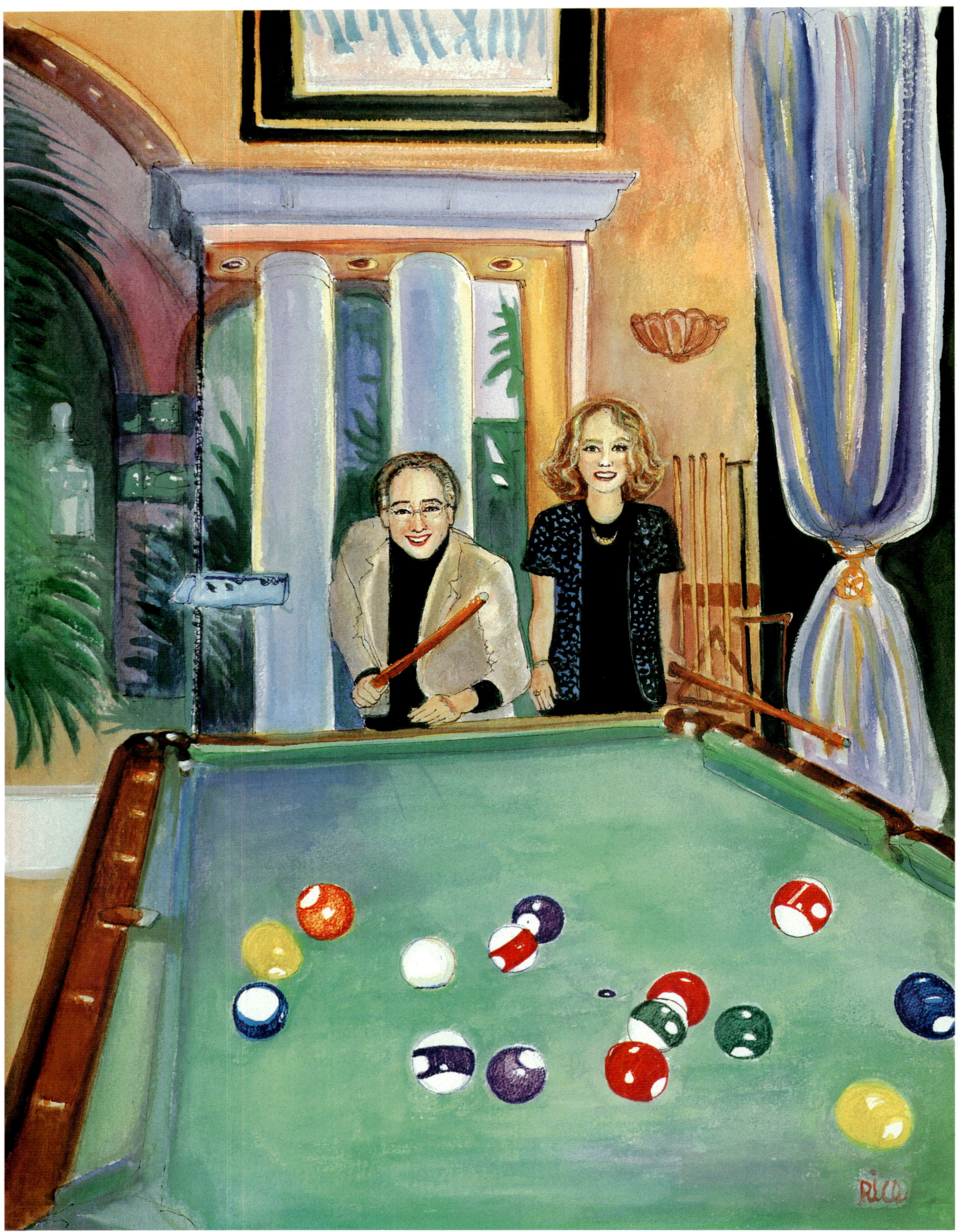

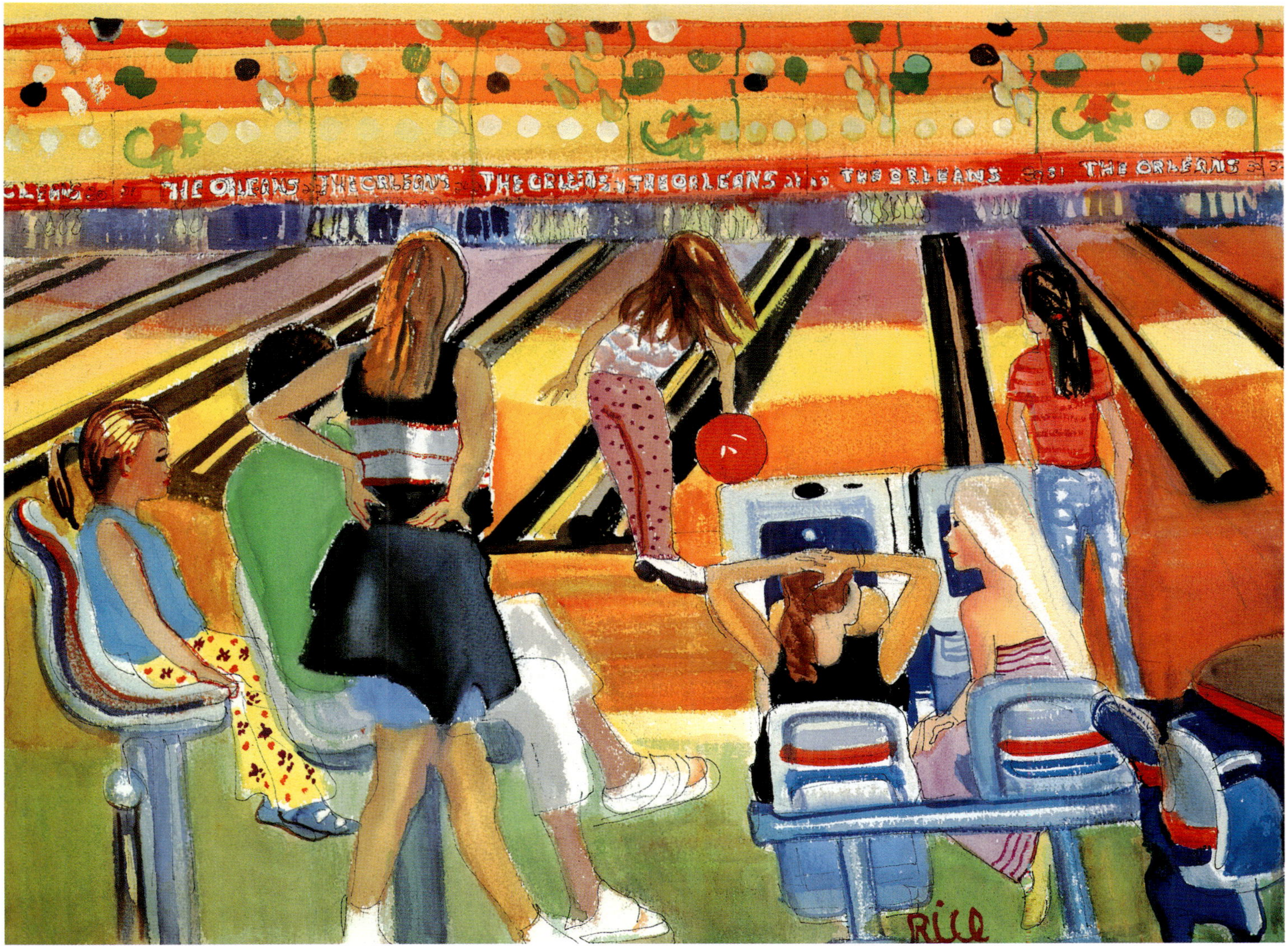

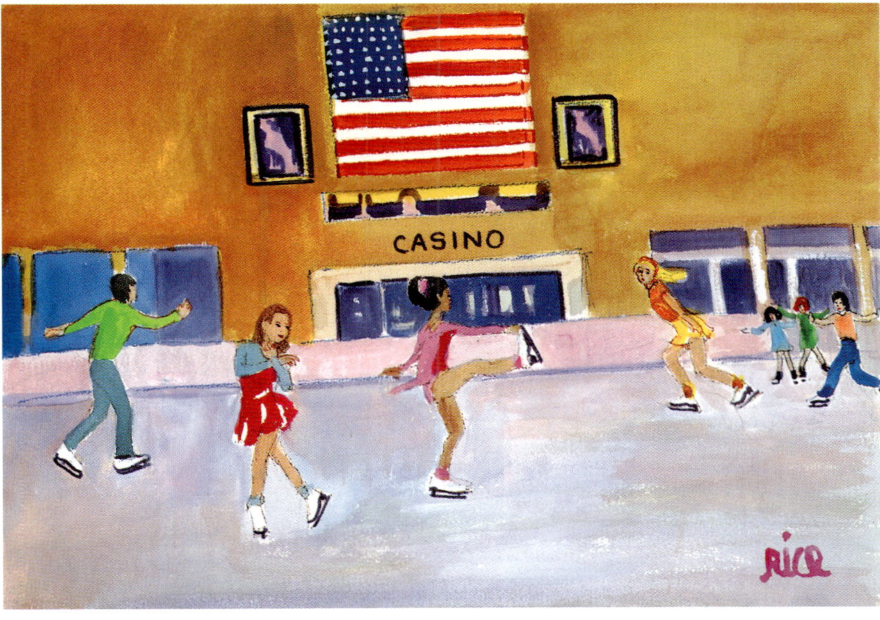

BOWLED OVER AT ORLEANS

There truly is something for everyone in Las Vegas: The Orleans Hotel is the proud home of a 24-hour, 70-lane bowling center.

SKATE'S GREAT AT THE SANTA FE

If the Las Vegas weather gets too hot, but you don't want the action to cool down, you can go to the Santa Fe Hotel Ice Arena, a 17,000-square-foot rink where you can rent figure skates or join a hockey league. The laid-back, Southwestern-themed Santa Fe, a Stations property, is surrounded by gorgeous desert and mountains, a perfect fit for those who need a break from the typical Las Vegas bustle.

< THE GAMES PEOPLE PLAY AT HOME

I attended a party at the chic home of pool players Jerome and Diane Snyder, who have lived in Las Vegas since 1964. Jerome was the visionary behind the Bingo Palace (predecessor to Palace Station) and has a hand in various ventures ranging from banking and real estate to health care and travel. Diane, who enjoys painting, impressed me with her savvy interior design sense. Her touch adorns their stylish home in the upscale Canyon Gate section of Las Vegas.

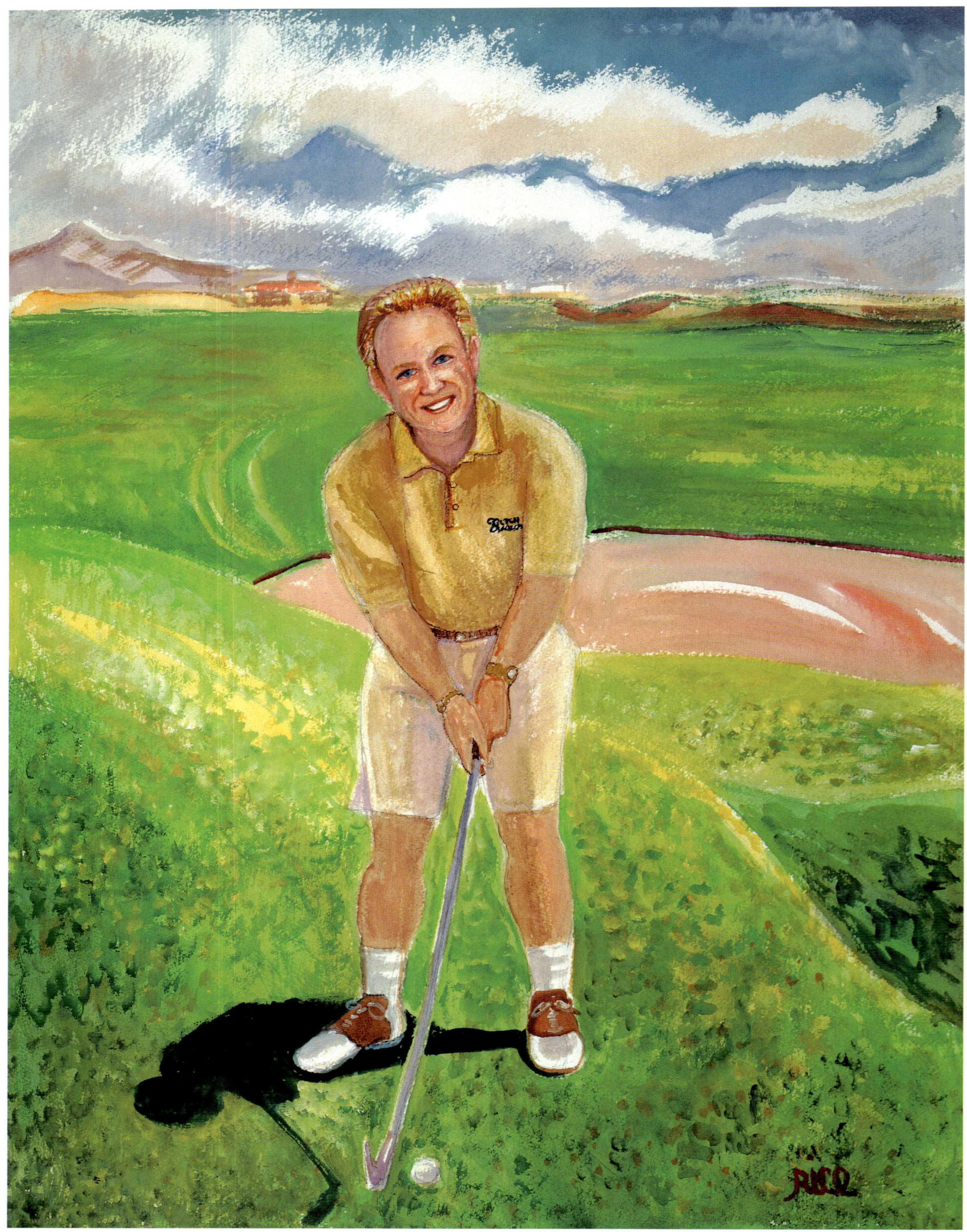

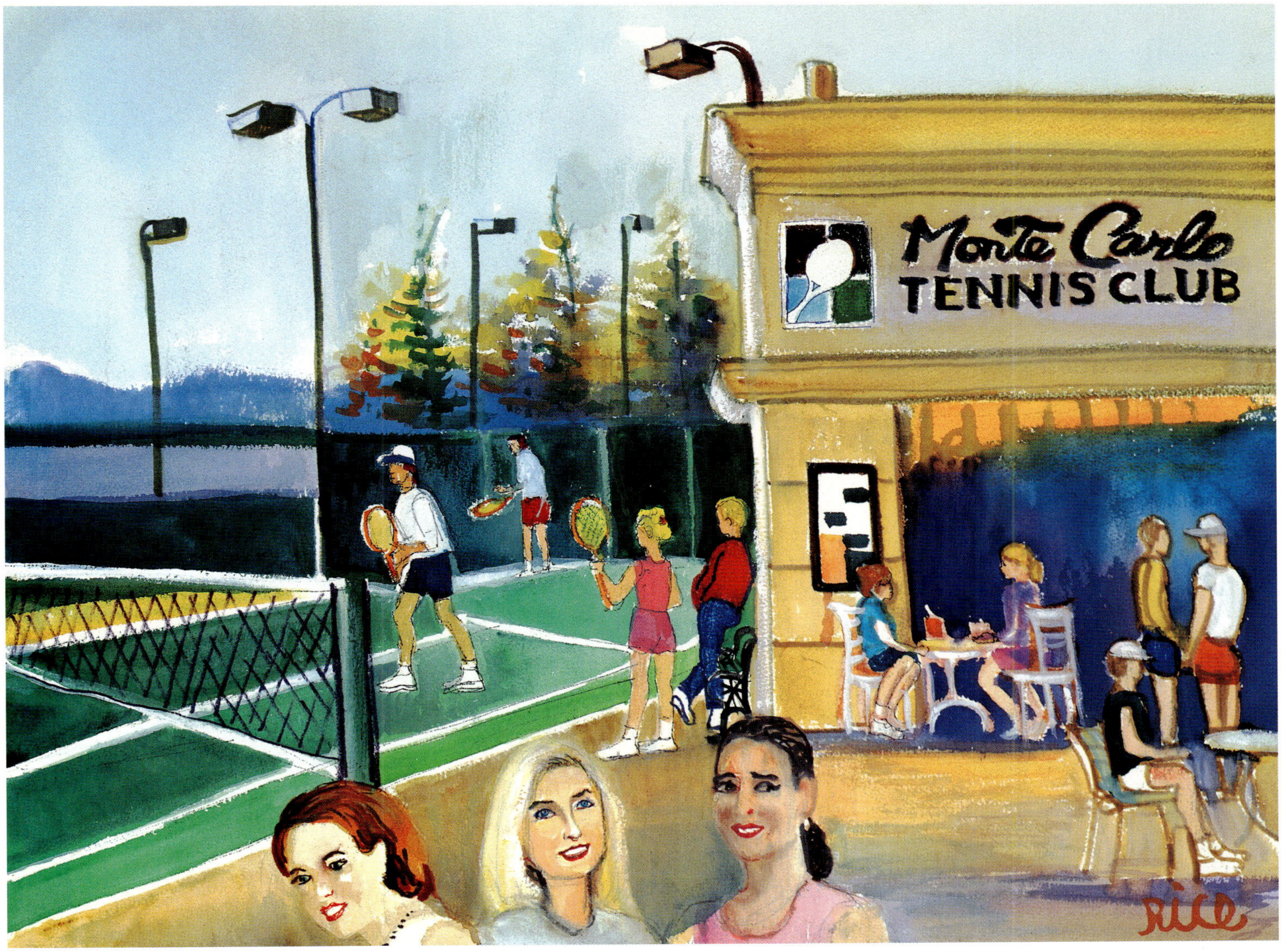

MONTE CARLO TENNIS CLUB

The Monte Carlo Tennis Club, with its lighted, professionally designed courts, doubles as a place to perfect your love match both on and off the court: it's also a popular luncheon and meeting place.

TIGER WOODS SWINGS AT DRAGONRIDGE

The incredibly popular professional golfer, Tiger Woods visited the exclusive DragonRidge Golf and Country Club within the luxurious MacDonald Highlands community to conduct a golf clinic benefiting the Tiger Woods Foundation, which helps disadvantaged children. Woods, the youngest player ever to win all four major golf championships, delighted the DragonRidge members with 300-yard drives—he even juggled the ball on the end of his club before knocking it into the distance, just like on his famous TV commercial. Along with its prestigious course, DragonRidge features a 30,000-square-foot clubhouse including a golf shop, exercise facility, swimming pool, tennis courts and dining rooms.

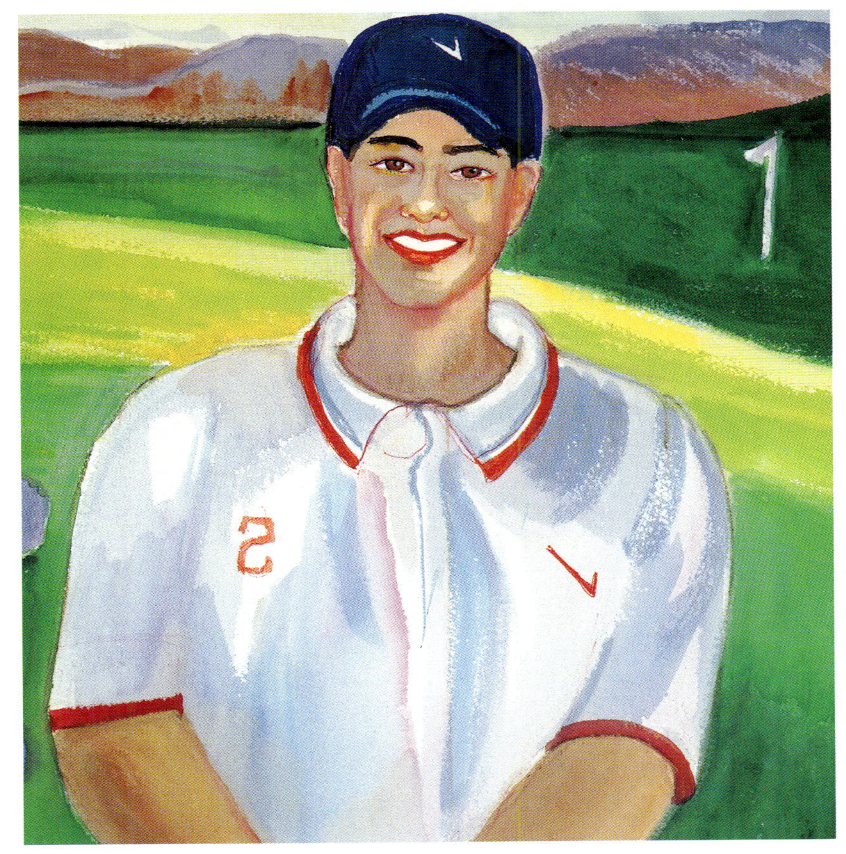

< BUTCH HARMON AT RIO SECCO

The very personable Claude "Butch" Harmon took me out on the links of the Reese Jones-designed Rio Secco Golf Club, a world-class par 72 golf course for guests of the Rio Hotel. Butch, the son of 1948 Masters champ Claude Harmon Sr., teaches at his own School of Golf at Rio Secco. As a swing coach to pros like Tiger Woods and Greg Norman and dignitaries like Morocco's King Hassan II, you can bet he's always in high demand among golfers of all levels of talent. A three-day instruction package with Butch (including accommodations, nine holes of play, video and computer analysis of play) goes for $4,500. If you end up swinging anything like Tiger, it's well worth it!

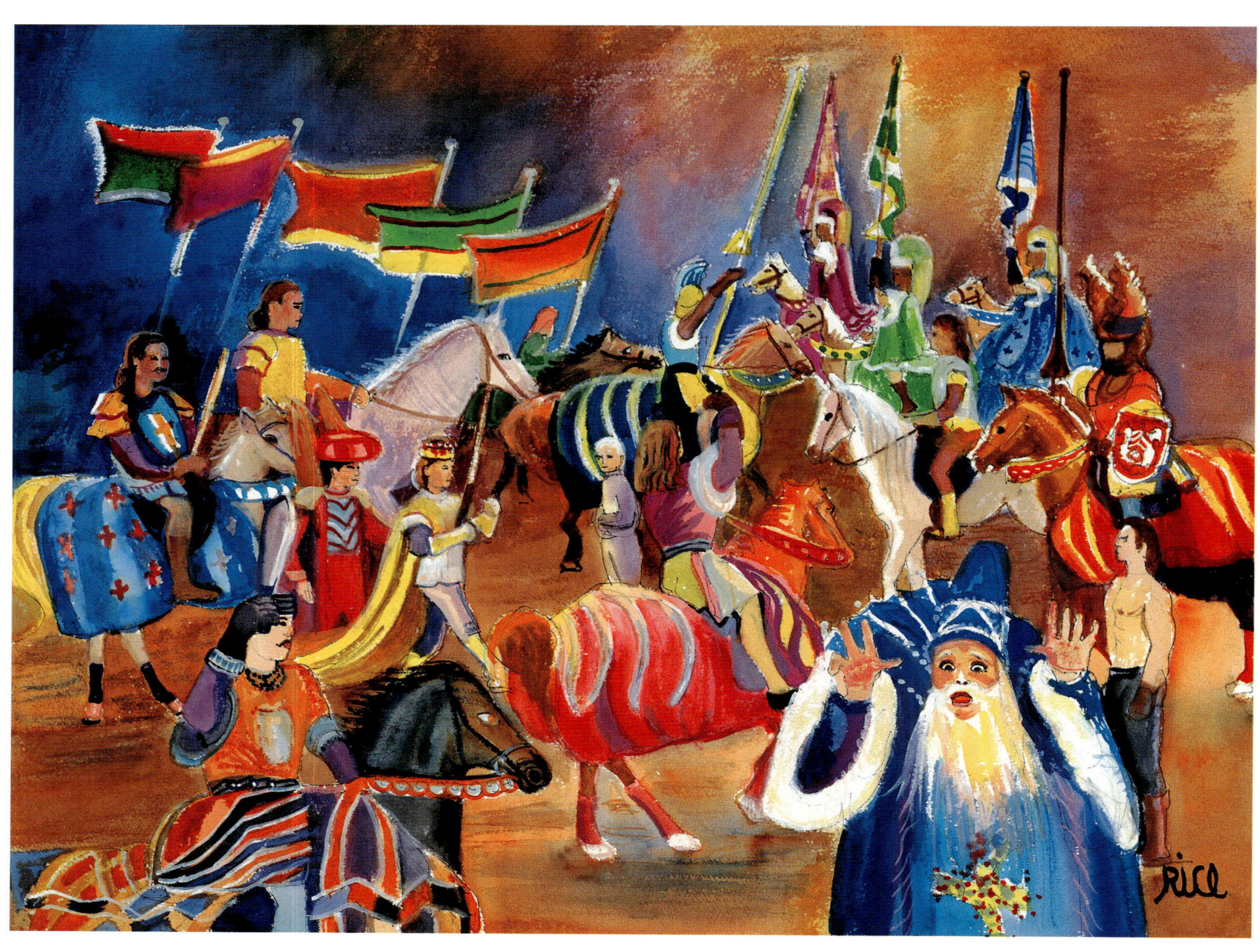

"TOURNAMENT OF KINGS" AT EXCALIBUR

Chivalrous knights jousting in shining armor, thundering steeds, dramatic sword-play, wizards who dabble in laser light shows, fair maidens dancing and a king who fights for his throne. It's all part of the Excalibur's nightly "Tournament of Kings" dinner show, in which you can feast on Cornish game hen with your fingers while enjoying Camelot-style entertainment. The audience cheers on the champions and hisses the villains.

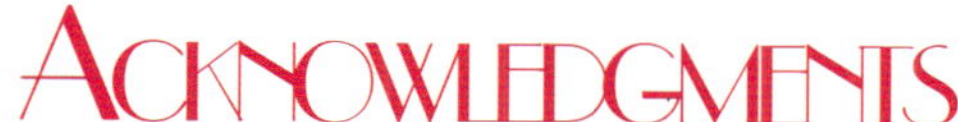

Acknowledgments

My thanks to:

Stanley Chase for his encouragement and dedication to making this book a reality;

Scott Huver, editor and researcher;

Dana Levy for the book and jacket design;

Donn Blake, Steve Crespi, and **Florie Brizel**, editorial consultants;

Rickie Barlow, Stephanie Boixo, Slim Brandy, Lexy Capp, Henry Colman, Mike Coperman, Steve Cutler, Bob Dowd, Sophia Djalimand, Deboragh Gabler, Jesse Garon, Lorna Greene, Larry Grossman, Teresa Gutierres, Art Ham, Joe Ham, William Hellinger, Toni James, Jenna and Blake Lefkoff, Connie Martinson, Oscar Merida, Renee Miller, Marvin Paige, Polly Peluso, Lori Rupp, Monica and **Morgan Tushitchi, Irving Weinberger;**

Charolette Richards for her faith and her limousines that took me where I had to go;

Corinne and **George Sidney** for their wonderful welcoming party;

The City of Las Vegas and, of course, the many people, communities, places, stars, shows, sights and sounds of this extraordinary city, as well as the fun-loving visitors from all over the world who make Las Vegas the number one destination on the planet for excitement.

In memory of

Bernice Friedes, New York City; Ruth Conn, New York City; Jacqueline Abitol, Morocco; Robert Littman, Beverly Hills; Jenny Jenner, London; Shirley Collier, Los Angeles; Beth Shaw, Vero Beach, Florida

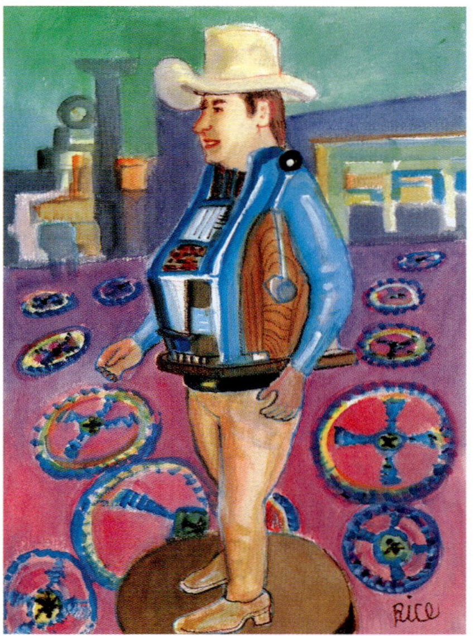

THE COWPOKE SLOT

"Vegas Vic" isn't the only cowpoke in town—this is just one of several charming, popular slot machines in the Western-flavored New Frontier, which has also imported country singer Mickey Gilley's famed Gilley's Saloon, Dancehall and BBQ.

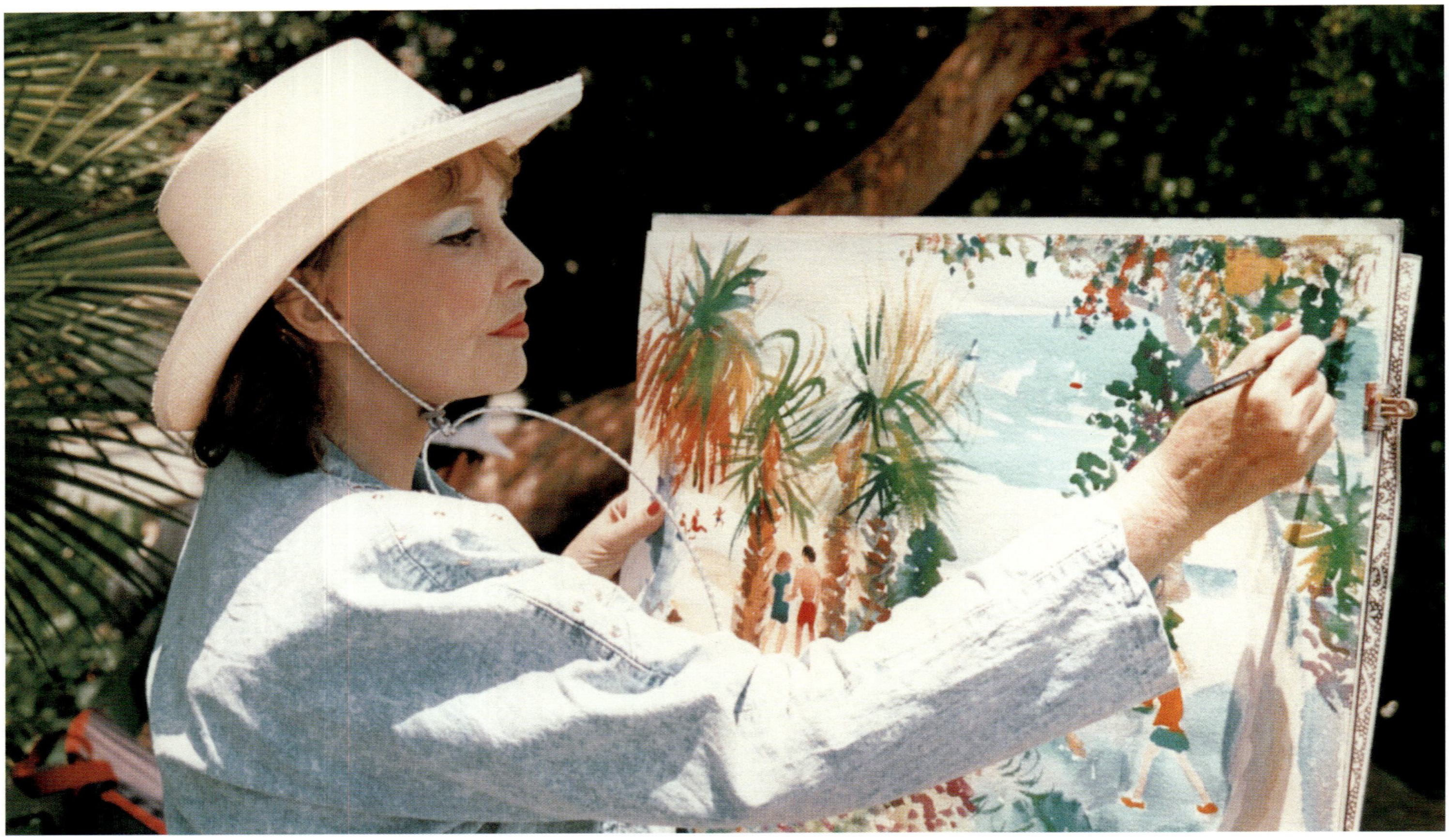

All photographs by Stanley Chase

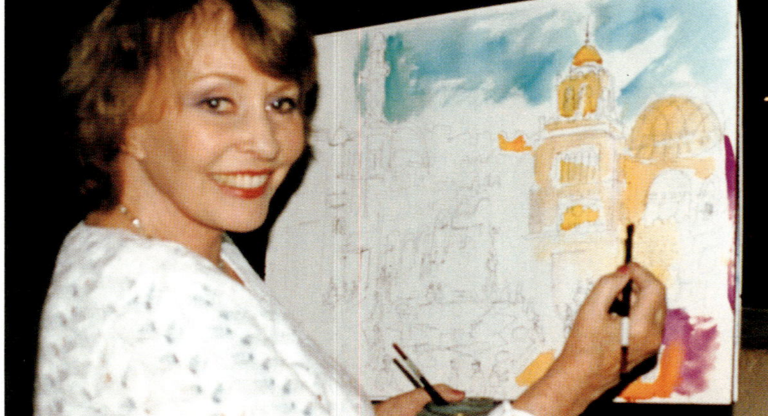

Painting at the Desert Passage

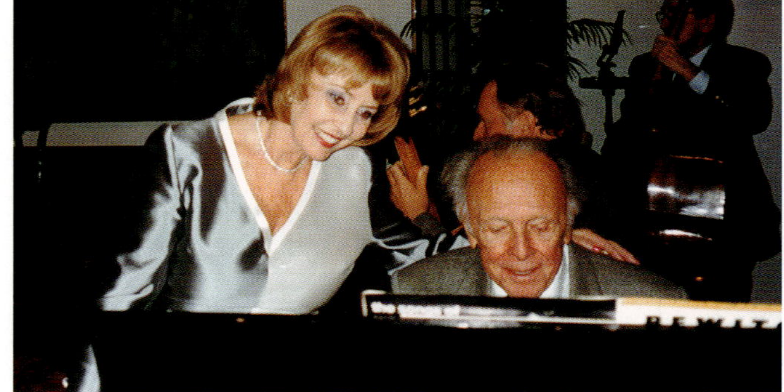

George Sidney at home

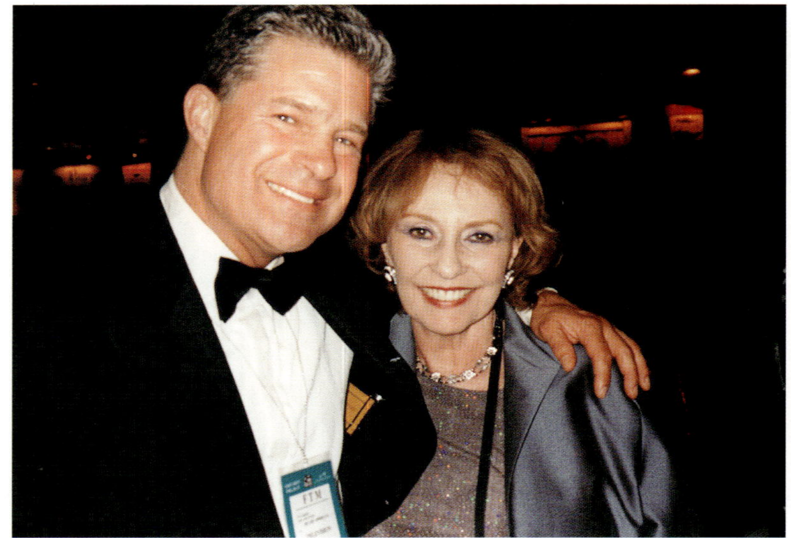

Jim Lampley at a Championship Title fight at the Mandalay Bay

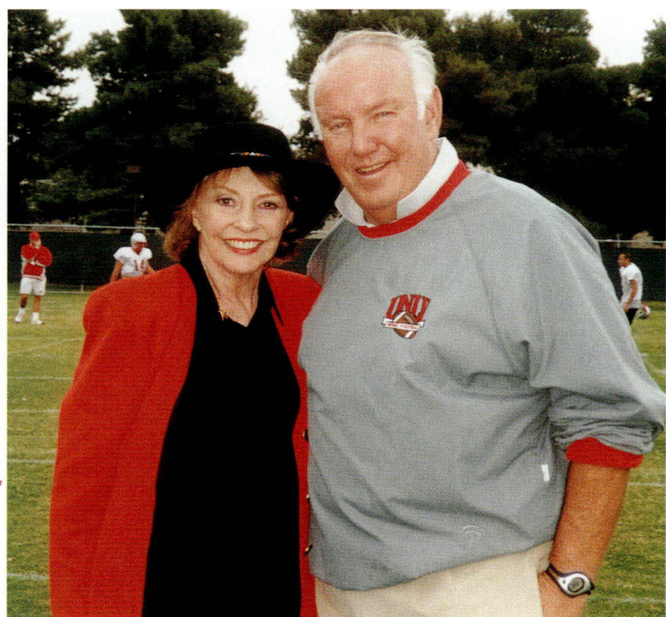

Coach John Robinson at UNLV practice field

ABOUT DOROTHY RICE

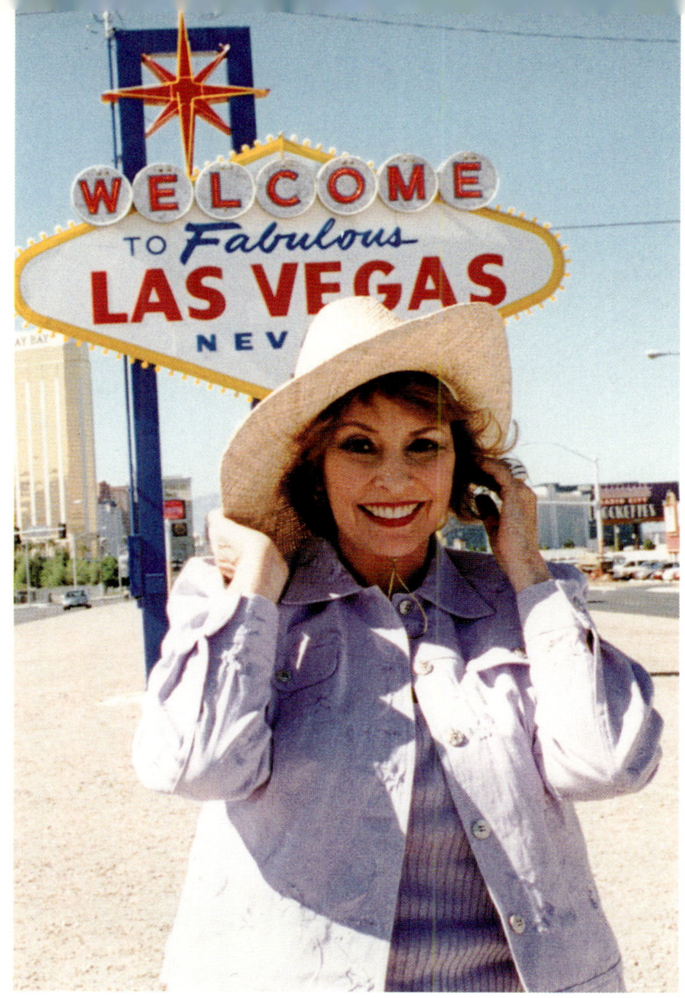

LAS VEGAS WITH LOVE IS ARTIST/author Dorothy Rice's fifth art book, an appreciation of one of the world's premier tourist destinations and a place which has defined showmanship and thrills for generations. She masterfully crafts her stunning watercolors to capture a diverse assortment of people, places, architecture and lifestyles, and provides vital background information and engaging personal observations that blend to create a joyous and vivid picture of life in extraordinary Las Vegas.

Growing up in New York City, Dorothy Rice's childhood was enlivened by the procession of illustrators and photographers who worked at her father's commercial art studio. Her art training began with night classes at the Art Students League in Manhattan while attending high school.

John Rawlings, the renowned fashion photographer for *Vogue*, "discovered" Dorothy at age 14, and *Vogue* selected her to travel to Paris, where she soon became the world's top photographic model, posing for legendary couturiers including Dior and Balenciaga. The resulting international acclaim led her to a career as an actress, performing on Broadway, off-Broadway and on television.

She moved from New York to Beverly Hills to continue her successful acting career. Inspired by her new surroundings, she was drawn back to her first love: painting. She has frequently been seen setting up an easel on sidewalks, streets and other byways to create on-the-spot watercolors—images that were published in her first book of paintings, Los Angeles With Love, an artist's-eye-view of the City of Angels.

Ms. Rice studied at the Otis/Parsons Art Institute, the Art Center College of Design in Los Angeles and Santa Monica College, as well as the University of Guadalajara in Mexico. She adroitly works in a variety of media—including oil, palette knife, watercolor and pastel—and is one of the few Americans ever to be honored with an invitation to paint a mural in Mexico, known for its tradition of spectacular muralists.

Her successful one-woman show of lush Mexican oils, Serenata Mexicana, at the prestigious Southwest Museum in Los Angeles was so popular it was extended for two months. Private collectors and corporations have purchased paintings, and her work has been exhibited in the Palm Springs Museum, the National Arts Club in New York City, Madison Avenue art galleries and other venues across the United States and abroad.

Each of her art books has met with critical praise and public acclaim. Israel With Love depicts her sojourn through Israel, a project so well-received that the Israeli Ambassador in Washington, D.C., honored her with a gala reception at the Embassy of Israel. Artwork from Israel With Love is on a sponsored tour of the United States. In her third book, Manhattan With Love, Ms. Rice embarked on a journey of the heart back to the city of her youth, creating an exceptional homage to an unparalleled city. Her fourth opus, Beverly Hills With Love, brought the artist full circle to her adopted stomping grounds with an affectionate tribute to the glamorous state of mind known as Beverly Hills. Saks Fifth Avenue honored Ms. Rice by exhibiting her work in all its window displays.

Many publications and critics have spotlighted Dorothy Rice and her signature style, including Architectural Digest, which devoted a major article to her work, illustrated with many of her paintings. Her paintings also can be spotted on the permanent set of the hit ABC morning show "The View." As Ray Bradbury has written, "Dorothy Rice has fresh eyes and her own palette. Which means a talent for making the familiar unfamiliar, younger than when you last saw it."

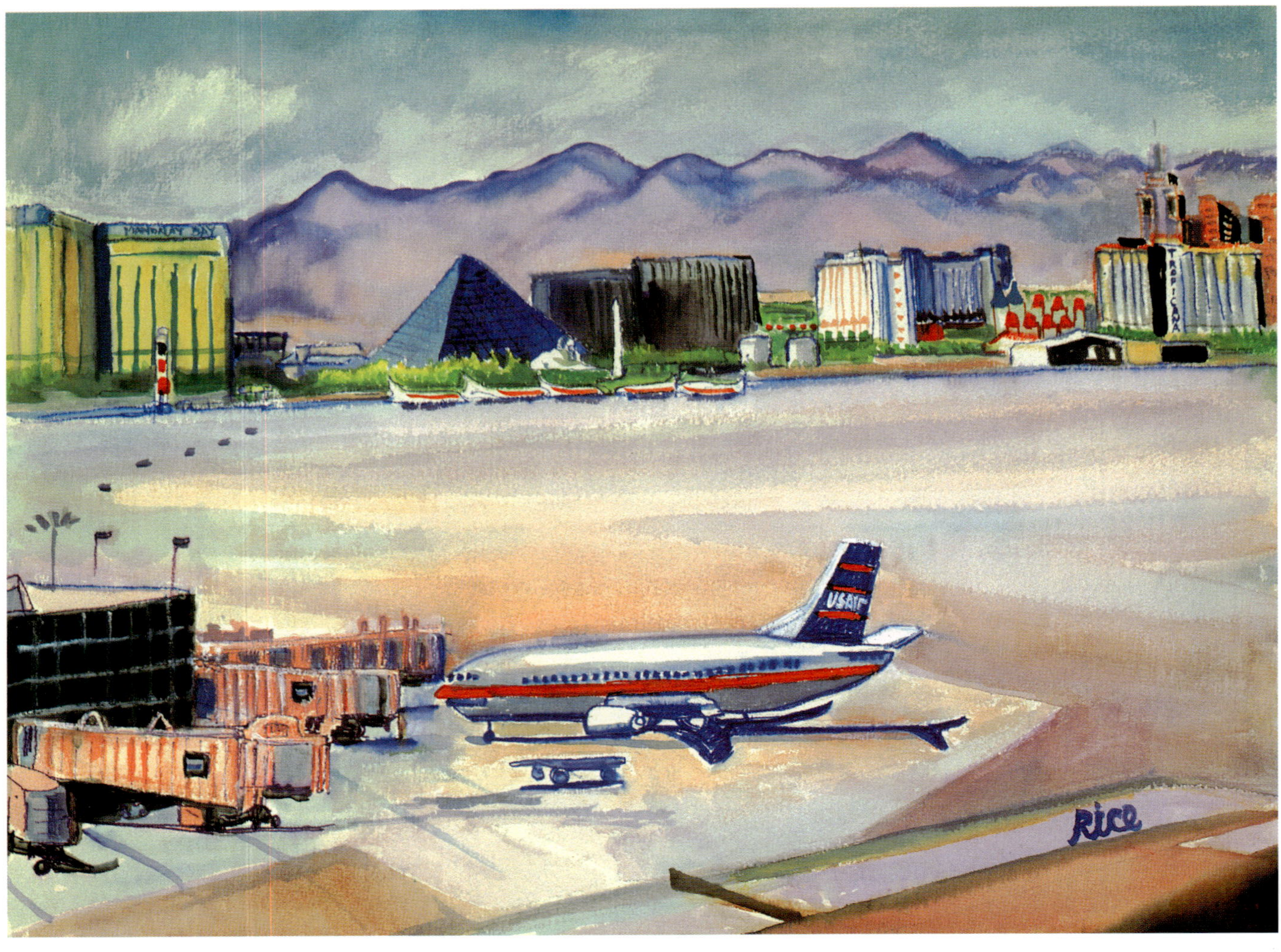

McCARRAN INTERNATIONAL AIRPORT

More than three million people on 850 flights a day, pass through the gates of McCarran International Airport every month, making it the eighth busiest airport in the world. McCarran was named for Nevada Senator Pat McCarran, who was instrumental in developing U.S. commercial aviation policy. The airport became an international airfield in 1968. Along with many amenities like restaurants and shops, the airport has a unique art program that displays school children's interpretations of various city skylines from all over the world.

ISBN 0-918269-04-0
First Edition
Printed in Hong Kong

Library of Congress Cataloging-in-Publication Data
Rice, Dorothy.
Las Vegas with love : painting and text / by Dorothy Rice—1st ed.
p. cm.
ISBN 0-918269-04-0
1. Rice, Dorothy—Themes, motives. 2. Las Vegas (Nev.)—In art. I. Title
ND 1839.R48 A4 2001
759.13--dc21 2001023582

GLEN HOUSE COMMUNICATIONS

P.O. BOX 3663, BEVERLY HILLS, CA 90210-0666

(310) 475-4236; FAX (310) 474-5720

e-mail: chaseprods@aol.com